MADRAS IN THE OLDEN TIME

MADRAS IN THE OLDEN TIME:

BEING A

HISTORY OF THE PRESIDENCY

FROM

THE FIRST FOUNDATION TO THE GOVERNORSHIP
OF THOMAS PITT, GRANDFATHER OF
THE EARL OF CHATHAM.
1639-1702.

J. TALBOYS WHEELER

IN THREE VOLUMES
VOL. I

GYAN

Published by

Gyan Publishing House
5, Ansari Road
Daryaganj, New Delhi-110002
Phone: 011-47034999, 9811692060
E-mail: books@gyanbooks.com

Distribution Network
gyanbooks.com
India, USA, Canada, UK, Australia, France

ISBN: 978-81-212-8395-3 (Set)
978-81-212-8394-6 (PB)
First Published, 1861

2nd Impression 2023

Printed at: Gyan Press, Delhi.

MADRAS IN THE OLDEN TIME (VOL. I)
Author: J. TALBOYS WHEELER

MADRAS IN THE OLDEN TIME.

MADRAS IN THE OLDEN TIME:

BEING A

HISTORY OF THE PRESIDENCY

FROM

THE FIRST FOUNDATION TO THE GOVERNORSHIP
OF THOMAS PITT, GRANDFATHER OF
THE EARL OF CHATHAM.
1639–1702.

COMPILED FROM OFFICIAL RECORDS.

BY

J. TALBOYS WHEELER,
Author of the "Geography of Herodotus," &c. &c. and Professor of Moral Philosophy and Logic at the Madras Presidency College.

MADRAS:
PRINTED FOR J. HIGGINBOTHAM, MOUNT ROAD,
BY GRAVES AND CO., SCOTTISH PRESS.
1861.

PREFACE.

The present volume of sketches and illustrations of Madras in the Olden Time, is a republication of a series of papers which have already appeared from week to week in the columns of the "Indian Statesman." The compiler has long been anxious to obtain some information respecting the early history of the English settlements on the Coast of Coromandel. Hitherto the century commencing with the first establishment of Fort St. George, and closing with the war between the French and English in which the intriguing of Dupleix was defeated by the genius of Clive, has been emphatically a blank in the history of India. The Government Office was known to be crowded with documents illustrative of the period; but no one appears to have had sufficient leisure to commence the task of historical research. Some two years ago however Mr. Hudleston, the present Sub-Treasurer of the Board of Revenue, made a few extracts from the earliest volumes of the Madras Records, and read them before the Committee of the Madras Literary Society. The extracts disclosed a state of society so curious and interesting, that all who heard them were anxious that they should be continued ; but the pressure of official duties, appears to have compelled Mr. Hudleston to abandon his task just as he had discovered the true value of the mine.

The Compiler of the present work confesses that his curiosity was powerfully excited by the extracts selected by Mr. Hudleston ; and shortly afterwards circumstances enabled him to gratify it. In the course of last year he was appointed by the Madras Government to report upon the character and relative value of all the Records in the Government Office, with the view to the destruction of those which should prove on examination to be not worth preserving. In the progress of his task he necessarily became familiar more or less with the whole of the Records ; and subsequently by the kind permission of the Madras Government, he was enabled to make use of the earlier Records for historical and antiquarian purposes.

The present volume, though only to be regarded as a first instalment, is in reality complete in itself.

The period over which it extends corresponds almost exactly with the period of Lord Macaulay's history. It opens with the foundation of Fort St. George, just on the eve of the great civil war between Charles the First and his Parliament; and it closes with the blockade of the Fort by Nabob Dawood Khan in the Governorship of Thomas Pitt; an event which took place in 1702, the year in which William the Third was carried to the grave, and Queen Anne ascended the throne of England.

The design of the compiler has been to convey to the reader all the pleasure and interest to be derived from a perusal of the original records, without the painful labour of wading through a mass of commercial detail. Moreover, in order to render the work more generally entertaining, he has freely used all facts in independent histories which served to illustrate or explain any allusions in the Records. Thus the histories of Mill, Elphinstone, Grant Duff, Bruce, Briggs, Dow, and others, have been generally consulted; and indeed no fact has been stated, which does not appear in the Records, or does not have the sanction of one or other of the established Indian authorities. The reader however will readily perceive that the bulk of the book is taken from the Records; and that other historians have only been consulted for purposes of illustration or explanation.

As regards the pictures of society here represented, the English portion will be found to correspond generally with the old fashioned pictures which appear in the novels of De Foe. Few perhaps in this decorous age will confess to having read not only Robinson Crusoe and Captain Singleton, but Colonel Jack, Moll Flanders, Roxana, History of the Devil, and others which need not be named. Those however who have revelled in the quaint simplicity of the " True Born Englishman," will find ample evidence in the following pages of the truthfulness of his delineations of English life and character at the close of the seventeenth and opening of the eighteenth century.

In conclusion the writer must acknowledge with thanks the facilities afforded him by the Madras Government in the prosecution of his task, and the interest which has been displayed in the undertaking. The autographs of six Madras Governors, and of Sir John Goldsborough, Governor General, at the commencement of the volume, were carefully traced from the originals in the Government Office, and transferred to stone by one of the students in Dr. Hunter's School of Arts.

MADRAS,
23rd February, 1861.

CONTENTS.

CHAPTER I.

EARLY SETTLEMENT IN INDIA. ANTE 1640.

CHAPTER II.

EARLY YEARS OF FORT ST. GEORGE.

CHAPTER III.

MADRAS IN THE REIGN OF MERRY KING CHARLES—A PICTURE.

CHAPTER IV.

GOVERNORSHIP OF SIR WILLIAM LANGHORN, 1670—1677.

CHAPTER V.

GOVERNORSHIP OF MR. STREYNSHAM MASTER, 1677—1681.

CHAPTER VI.

GOVERNORSHIP OF MR. WILLIAM GYFFORD, 1681—1687.

CHAPTER VII.

GOVERNORSHIP OF MR. WILLIAM GYFFORD, (*continued*) 1681—1687.

CHAPTER VIII.

GOVERNORSHIP OF MR. ELIHU YALE, 1687—1692.

CHAPTER IX.

GOVERNORSHIP OF MR. ELIHU YALE—(*continued*) 1687—1692.

Page.

CHAPTER X.

GOVERNORSHIP OF MR. ELIHU YALE, (*continued*) 1687—1692.

CHAPTER XI.

GOVERNORSHIP OF MR. ELIHU YALE, (*continued*) 1687—1692.

Page.

CHAPTER XII.

GOVERNORSHIP OF MR. NATHANIEL HIGGINSON, 1692—1698.

Page.

CHAPTER XIII.

GOVERNORSHIP OF MR. NATHANIEL HIGGINSON, (*continued*)—1692—1698.

CHAPTER XIV.

GOVERNORSHIP OF MR. NATHANIEL HIGGINSON, (*continued*)—1692—1698.

CHAPTER XV.

GOVERNORSHIP OF MR. THOMAS PITT, 1698—1702.

CHAPTER XVI.

GOVERNORSHIP OF MR. THOMAS PITT, AND DOINGS OF NABOB DAWOOD KHAN, 1701.

HISTORY OF THE MADRAS PRESIDENCY.

CHAPTER I.

EARLY SETTLEMENT IN INDIA.

Old Madras! What a multitude of associations are called up by the simple words; what curious pictures of the past flash before our eyes. Those who are old themselves will recall the days of their youth; the good old times of Elliot, of Munro, or of Lushington, when Hotels and Clubs were not, but when boundless hospitality, aristocratic exclusiveness, choice scandal, and occasional duels were the order of the day. But our present object would rather be to recall Madras in an age long antecedent to these comparatively tranquil times. We would endeavour to picture Madras as it was some two centuries ago; when Members of Council rode about in bullock bandies, and the guards of the President were armed with bows and arrows, swords and shields; when gentlemen wore large hose, "peasecod bellied" doublets, preposterous breeches, and hats with conical crowns and bunches of feathers; when the ladies, very few in number, wore long waisted stomachers and powerfully starched ruffs; when the Fort was nothing more than a fortified Factory, in which the Factors and Merchants bought and sold, gave their orders, and made their payments, just like any merchant firms of modern date; when all took their meals together, attended daily prayers, and lived like a little brotherhood, who were all kept under by a strict discipline, and who, but for the attractions of burnt wine, punch, native beauty, and occasional quarrels, may be said to have lived as sober and God fearing lives in this Presideney, as were led by their brethren in Leadenhall Street or Cheapside. Whether we shall continue our task in future issues, and bring our familiar sketehes of Madras down to the days of our grandfathers, will depend very much upon the degree of sueeess which may attend our early efforts. For the present we shall content ourselves with endeavouring to paint a picture of the little Presidency, with all its hopes, joys, and fears, as it was about the time of Charles II. and his immediate sueeessors. In a word, to furnish a few gossipping chapters upon our early Colonial life, during the first eentury of our settlement in Madras; a period which is full of interest, but whieh at present is almost a blank page in the annals of India.

Before however we begin to depiet the little world within, we must endeavour to deseribe the great world without. Our readers need not be alarmed. Our history shall not be very formidable. We shall follow the true Macaulay method of only dwelling on what is interesting, and then striding with the speed of seven leagued boots over all that is dry and dull.

From time immemorial the rich productions of India had been eagerly desired by the civilised world. Her cottons, spiecs, jewels, and perfumes had been carried up the Red Sea to the Courts of Solomon, of Ahasuerus, and of the Cæsars; and during the Middle Ages, many of her choicest productions were conveyed by the Venetian merchants from the ports of Egypt to the Courts of the European kings. But the fifteenth and sixteenth centuries saw a vast revolution in commercial enterprise. Spain had discovered and conquered Mexico and Peru. Portugal had discovered the route round the Cape, and opened the trade with India. For nearly a century, that is from about 1500 to 1600, the Portuguese enjoyed the monopoly of the Indian seas, and possessed rich and extensive settlements on both sides of the Indian peninsula. Indeed, not content with being merchants, they claimed to be kings; but instead of conciliating the natives, they rendered themselves hated by their haughtiness, their arrogance, their religious intolerance, and their dissolute lives. But still they continued to monopolize the trade, and all merchants from other European countries, and even shipwrecked mariners, were treated with the utmost severity, if not with cruel barbarity.

In Europe the great merchants were the Dutch. In other words they had become the great carriers of Europe, and their country had become the emporium of trade. In a former century they had obtained the products of India from the Italians; but now the rich traders of Amsterdam, proceeded every year to Lisbon to purchase spices from the Portuguese. In 1580 the Dutch threw off the yoke of Spain and formed themselves into the United

Provinces. That very year the famous Don Sebastian, King of Portugal, either fell or disappeared during an expedition against the Moors. He vanished without leaving any children, and Philip II of Spain obtained the Portuguese crown. Philip was a spiteful man. He thought to punish the Dutch for their revolt, by excluding them from his dominions. This policy proved most suicidal. The Dutch, instead of being good customers, became formidable rivals; instead of purchasing Indian commodities in the Lisbon market, they pushed on bravely to the Indian seas, and soon became ruinous competitors with Philip's Portuguese subjects for the Indian trade. They commenced with caution. They did not attempt to interfere with the Portuguese trade on the coasts of the Indian continent, but they directed their attention to that portion of the Malay Archipelago, which is known by the name of Spice Islands. In 1600 they had already erected a factory at Bantam in Java, and commenced a trade with the large island of Sumatra and the small Spice Islands. Subsequently, the factory in Java, swelled out into the great but unhealthy city of Batavia; which henceforth became the seat of the Dutch Government in the East, and the centre of their trade. Meantime the power of the Portuguese declined. The annexation to Spain proved their ruin. They received no further reinforcements from Europe, and their more enterprising rivals soon began to establish factories on the continent. In 1610 the Dutch erected the fort at Pulicat, about twenty three miles to the northward of the place where Madras now stands. In 1660, they took Negapatam from the Portuguese. In 1663, they took Cochin in like manner. Thus they became the great merchant princes of the East, possessing important settlements both on the coast of Coromandel and the coast of Malabar. The seventeenth century was indeed the golden period of Dutch commerce. Without any native produce to export, and without even a piece of timber fit for ship building, the foreign trade of Holland was at this period greater than that of all Europe besides.

Meantime the merchants of London had been equally yearning for a share in the riches of the Indian trade. Throughout the reign of the great Elizabeth, their longing for the gold of Ophir had been stimulated to the highest pitch by the successes of Spain and Portugal. They tried in vain to cut out new routes by the north-west and the north-east, and even attempted to open an overland trade; the successive circumnavigations of the world by Drake and Cavendish still giving additional stimulus to the spirit of enterprise. They next sent some ships round the Cape, but the experiment failed in consequence of disease and shipwreck. But soon all London was ringing with the successes of the Dutch, and the British merchant was almost mad with exasperation. At last in 1599 an association was formed under the title of "Merchant Adventurers." A fund was subscribed, and the subscribers petitioned the Virgin Queen to allow them to fit out three ships, to export bullion, and to be exempted from payment of customs for six voyages. At that very moment a peace was pending between England and Spain. The Spanish Armada had been utterly destroyed ; Cadiz had been taken by Effingham and Essex ; but still the English Government was anxious not to imperil the peace, by giving countenance to an expedition, which might be supposed to threaten the Indian possessions of Portugal. In vain the Merchant Adventurers petitioned for an immediate warrant. The Privy Council maintained that a peace with Spain would prove more beneficial to England than even the Indian trade. But the ardour of the Merchant Adventurers could not brook delay. They presented another Memorial in which they enumerated first all the Indian settlements belonging to Spain and Portugal ; and secondly, all the kingdoms and islands which were wholly out of their dominions ; and they concluded by challenging the Spanish Commissioners to show any just and lawful reasons why Her Majesty, and all other Christian princes and states, should be barred from the Indian seas, and from the dominions of so many free potentates in which neither Spain nor Portugal possessed the shadow of authority. The memorial was referred to the celebrated Sir Foulkes Greville, who returned another long and curious report on the limits of the Portuguese jurisdiction in the East Indies. The royal consent to the project of the Adventurers was then freely granted. The Association entrusted the management of the business to twenty-four Directors ; and on the 23rd September 1600, the first Court of Directors of the East India Association was held at "Founder's Hall."

The geographical information furnished by the Merchant Adventurers and Sir Foulkes Greville, is very interesting. It was derived from various authors,—Portuguese, Spanish, Italians, Dutch, and English,—whose names are now only known to the antiquarian; and it contains a flood of information which shows how rapidly geographical science had progressed in that age of enterprise. Of course most of the marvellous stories of Sir John Mandeville were popularly believed; but still a large amount of faithful description had reached Europe, and every day the torch of truth was carried further and further into the regions of fable. As regards India, much geographical information respecting the coast of Malabar had already been published; and the maids of honour in the Court of Elizabeth, had long been giggling over the stories of a country where the ladies had as many husbands as they pleased; or else were denouncing the cruel law which compelled a beloved wife to burn herself with the body of her deceased husband. Even the Coast of Coromandel was known. The Portuguese had already penetrated to Bengal; whilst a century before the country had been a terra incognita, and the country now called Orissa was believed by many intelligent Englishmen to be peopled by men who had horses heads and fed on human flesh.

We are not reviewing the history of the late Company, and therefore shall content ourselves with saying, that in 1601 the first fleet set sail, not for the Indian continent, but, like the Dutch, for the Indian Archipelago. At that time the English and Dutch nations were on the best of terms, for Elizabeth had nobly supported the Dutch against Spain. Again the English did not want to come into collision with the Portuguese. Above all, the cloves, nutmegs, and mace of the Molucca and Banda isles, the pepper and camphor of Sumatra, and the endless productions of Java, would furnish as valuable a cargo as any which could be carried to Europe. One little incident may be mentioned as strikingly illustrative of the character of the Adventurers that went on the voyage. The Lord Treasurer requested the Directors to employ Sir Edward Michelbourne on the expedition. But it seems that the business qualifications of gentlemen of the court are rarely appreciated by the commercial community; and the dashing gallants of the Elizabethan era, adventurous and brave as they doubtless were, appear to have enjoyed but little favour in the eyes of the trading citizens of London. Accordingly the Directors resolved on consultation, "not to employ any gentleman in any place of charge;" and they requested "that they might be allowed to sort their business with men of their own qualitye, lest the suspicion of the employment of gentlemen being taken hold uppon by the generalitie, do dryve a greate number of the Adventurers to withdraw their contributions."

We need scarcely say that the early voyages of the East India Company were very successful, realising from a hundred to two hundred per cent. on the capital expended. For the first few years, the English merchants and factors apparently lived on friendly terms with the Dutch; and this continued so long as the English were satisfied with the goods they could obtain in Sumatra and Java, and refrained from trading at the small Spice Islands, now known as the Moluccas and Bandas. These Islands, as we shall presently see, were regarded by the Dutch as their peculiar property; and they alone produced the finer spices, such as nutmegs, for which fabulous prices could be obtained in the markets at home.

Thus the English established two principal factories; one at Acheen in the Island of Sumatra, and the other at Bantam in the Island of Java. The goods they brought out consisted partly of British staples, such as cloth, lead, and tin; partly of British manufactures, such as cutlery and glass; and partly of foreign merchandize, such as quicksilver and Russian hides. In return they obtained cargoes of raw silk, indigo, pepper, cloves, and mace; articles which, together with even the more precious nutmegs, are now to be found in every cottager's cupboard in Great Britain, but which in the days of the Stuarts and early Georges, fetched prices which would strike terror into the hearts of modern housekeepers. But a great event was at hand, no less than the establishment of an English Factory on the Indian continent. As early as 1608, the Factors in Java reported home that there was a great demand in the Islands for the cloths and calicoes manufactured on the Indian peninsula. About the same time, as we have already seen, the heavy but enterprising Dutchmen had begun to entertain the same notions. They however directed their attention more to the Coast of Coromandel, whilst the English were more attracted by the Coast of Malabar. As early as 1610 the Dutch began to build a square fort on the Pulicat lake. The English found more difficulty in establishing themselves. The Portuguese were as yet the lords of the continental trade; but whilst they possessed settlements at St. Thomé and other spots on the Coromandel Coast as far as the mouths of the Ganges and Straits of Malacca, yet their chief trade was on the Coast of Malabar. For nearly a century, the town and fort of Goa, about half way down the Malabar side, had been the centre of their commerce and the seat of their power. There they had led a life of intolerance and luxury, of piety and oppression. They also possessed another important settlement at the ancient town of Surat; near the top of the same coast, and about 400 miles northward of Goa. Surat, which is mentioned in the Ramayana, has been famous for its commercial wealth from time immemorial. Swarthy traders from Jerusalem and Sidon, from Memphis and Aden, from the Ægean Sea and the Persian Gulf,—had anchored in the river Taptee and crowded the narrow streets of Surat,—had sunned themselves in the smiles of Surat beauty, and laid their offerings upon her idol shrines,—when Priam yet reigned in Troy, when Solomon held the sceptre of Judah from his golden throne and golden footstool, and long ere the stern old Romans had built their rocky nest on the Palatine hill. For countless ages the coasting trade had been carried on over the Erythræan; and now when the adventurous Portuguese had opened the route round the Cape, the "white faces" were bearing away the gold, the pearls, the diamonds, and the ambergris, the silks, the cottons, the fragrant woods, and the brilliant dyes,—just as had been done by the Phœnicians of olden time. The gems which would have sparkled on the necks of Solomon's queens, were now lighting up every court in Europe; the incense which would have been offered on the altar of Jehovah, or on the shrines of Zeus or Apollo, was now being burnt in the censers of Christendom, and stimulating the devotions of every people who acknowledged the authority of the Holy See.

In 1612 the English first obtained a settlement in Surat; but they only succeeded after some desperate conflicts with the Portuguese; just as the Portuguese themselves had fought their way against the Arab merchants, who had previously monopolised the Red Sea trade, and carried Indian goods to Alexandria for the Venetians to bear away to the west. The successes of the English over the Portuguese, excited the admiration, the respect, and even the gratitude of the Native authorities; and an imperial firmaun was actually obtained from the Great Mogul, authorising the English to establish a factory on payment of a duty on all goods of 3½ per cent.

Thus the "English House," as it was called, was opened at Surat. The native Surat merchants readily bought our broadcloths, kersies, quicksilver, lead, vermillion, sword blades, knives, and looking glasses; whilst the English Factors obtained calico, cotton yarn, indigo, and drugs. The latter articles were sent home, but the calicoes and cottons were carried to Java, and exchanged with the utmost advantage for pepper and spices. At Surat the object of the English Agent was to extend the trade to the inland markets as well as to the adjoining sea ports. At Java the object was to open a trade with China, Japan, and Siam; and above all to put a foot into the little but precious Spice Islands. In both directions the English had to contend against formidable rivals. In Western India they had to encounter the hostilities and intrigues of the Portuguese. In the Islands they had to encounter the growing animosity of the Dutch. The principles of Free Trade were totally unknown. The object of one and all of the three nations of English, Dutch, and Portuguese, was to obtain and secure a monopoly of the trade in the Indian seas. But the immediate cause of the deadly quarrel between the English and Dutch was the nutmegs!

Having thus fairly landed our countrymen on the shores of India, it will be necessary to glance at the state of Hindustan at the time of our story. From time immemorial India has been a conquered country. Wave after wave of the great Tartar or Turanian races of Central Asia, have poured in from the North, bringing with them noble languages, but rites so utterly barbarous as to be almost beyond belief;—horrible institutions in which human sacrifices were offered to appease the wrath of ghosts and demons, and in which men and women herded together like cattle. The Brahmins next appeared upon the scene; a people altogether different, and belonging, not to the Tartar, or Turanian race, but to the same great Arian race, as the Greeks, the Romans, and our noble selves. These Brahmins gradually civilised the Tartar inhabitants, divided them into castes, taught them the worship of Vishnoo and Siva, and made themselves the priestly sovereigns of the country. Subsequently the priest was compelled to give way to the soldier,—the Brahmin to the Kshetrya,—and India fell under the dominion of Rajahs. Such was the state of things when the Mussulmans,—Turks and Mongols,—poured in successive eruptions over the valley of the Punjab, and at last established a throne at Delhi.

The history of the Mahommedan Empire in India is about the driest in the world. Even in the hands of a writer like Mountstuart Elphinstone, it is as heavy as lead; and until some historical romancer can be found with sufficient boldness to leave out all the wars, all the geography, and all the proper names, and confine himself to "Arabian Nights"-like stories of love adventures and court scandal, combined with a few operatic plots of murder, suicide, royal peasants, and peasant kings,—the history of Delhi will be a blank to the general reader.

Our narrative therefore shall be very brief. The first Mahommedan conqueror who invaded India was Mahmoud the Ghaznavide. Every one who has read "Lalla Rookh" knows the story of Mahmoud, who flourished about the time of William the Conqueror :—

"Land of the Sun ! what foot invades
  Thy Pagods and thy pillar'd shades—

Thy cavern shrines, and Idol stones,
  Thy Monarchs and their thousand Thrones ?

'Tis He of GAZNA—fierce in wrath
  He comes, and INDIA's diadems

Lie scatter'd in his ruinous path.—
  His bloodhounds he adorns with gems,

Torn from the violated necks
  Of many a young and lov'd Sultana ;

Maidens, within their pure Zenana,
  Priests in the very fane he slaughters,

And choaks up with the glittering wrecks
  Of golden shrines the sacred waters !"

Mahmoud of Ghazna was thus the tyrant, who slew the youthful patriot, whose last drop of blood the Peri carried to the angel at heaven's gate, but which, alas, proved not to be "the gift that is most dear to heaven," and therefore would not open the crystal gates of Paradise to the wandering Peri. Mahmoud was also, like a true follower of the Prophet, a great destroyer of idols. He piously plundered the great temple of Somnaut, a feat which has been since immortalized by the proclamation of Lord Ellenborough. The story goes that he found a tremendous idol at Somnaut, which he prepared to break in pieces. The Brahmins vainly offered immense sums for the ransom of their god ; he declared that he was a breaker and not a seller of idols. The deity was smashed forthwith, and an immense store of diamonds and pearls were found concealed in the belly of the idol.

But to our story of India. Successive dynasties reigned first at Ghiznee, and afterwards at Delhi; and gradually extended their conquests over Hindustan and a large part of the Dekkan. The Ghaznavide dynasty was succeeded by an Afghan dynasty; and then followed the Slave kings, the house of Khilji, and the house of Toghlak. The history of their reigns is nothing more than the annals of conquest, of disputed successions, of assassinations, of massacres, and of rebellions and their suppression. It extends over the usual period of four centuries, namely from A. D. 1000 to A. D. 1400; a period which commences with the invasions of Mahmoud, and closes with the still more terrible invasion of Timour the Tartar, and the sack, the conflagration, and massacre at Delhi. During the anarchy which attended this last event, many of the Hindoo powers in Southern India recovered their independence; but subsequently, after the lapse of a century or so, they were again overthrown by Mahommedan adventurers, and their territories formed into Mahommedan kingdoms. Two of these kingdoms are worthy of especial mention from their connection with the subsequent history of Madras; namely, the two great kingdoms of the Dekkan,—Bijapoor and Golconda. Both were established about A. D. 1500; and neither were overthrown until the reign of Aurungzebe, and about half a century after the first foundation of Fort St. George.

But we must now return to Delhi; for notwithstanding the anarchy which prevailed, and the retirement of Timour from India, the descendants of the famous Tartar were destined to hold the sceptre of India, and reign at Delhi under the title of "Great Moguls." The first monarch of this new dynasty was Baber, the son of a great-grandson of Timour; who, after a series of adventures which have stamped him the knight-errant of Asia, obtained the throne of Delhi about 1525. The last of the "Great Moguls" was the miserable wretch, who, after reaching an advanced old age in the enjoyment of the splendid bounty of the great Company, treacherously gave his countenance to the great mutiny of 1857, and now expiates his offence in imprisonment at Rangoon.

The reigns of Baber, of Humayoon, and of Akbar, extended over the whole of the sixteenth century. They thus corresponded to the period of Portuguese dominion in India,—to the period of the Reformation,—and to the reigns of Henry VIII, Edward VI, Mary, and Elizabeth. The name of Akbar occupies a considerable place in Oriental history; but in the present article we only care to review such portions of Oriental history as will illustrate our own. He died whilst the English and Dutch were just beginning to quarrel over the pepper and nutmegs in Java and the Spice Islands; and he was succeeded in 1605 by his son Jehangir.

Jehangir is celebrated for his passionate attachment to the beautiful Nourmahal, the "Light of the Haram;" and the story of his loves has been duly sung by that love making Irish bard, Tom Moore :—

"If woman can make the worst wilderness dear,
Think, think what a Heav'n she must make of
CASHMERE !

So felt the magnificent Son of AKBAR,
When from power and pomp and the trophies of war
He flew to that Valley, forgetting them all
With the Light of the HARAM, his young NOURMAHAL.

When free and uncrown'd as the Conqueror rov'd
By the banks of that Lake, with his only belov'd,
He saw, in the wreaths she would playfully snatch
From the hedges, a glory his crown could not match,
And preferr'd in his heart the least ringlet that curl'd
Down her exquisite neck to the throne of the world."

Sir Thomas Roe was sent as an ambassador from James I to the great Jehangir; and presented his Imperial Majesty with some English bulldogs, some famous red wine, and above all with some English pictures. Our story strips off much of the sentiment which attaches to the name of the lover of Nourmahal. Jehangir was much such a hero as our own George IV. He approved mightily of the bulldogs. He drank so much of the red wine, that in the warmth of his heart he vowed that he would make no distinctions between Christians, Moors, and Jews, but that he would love them all; but then alas! it was discovered that his Majesty was crying drunk, and "sighs stole out and tears began to flow." The pictures proved less successful in pleasing his taste. He drew out a painting of a beautiful Venus leading a dark coloured Satyr by the nose; and not being familiar with classical story, he unfortunately supposed it to be a representation of himself being led by the nose by the beautiful Nourmahal. That unhappy interpretation had well nigh ruined the success of Roe's embassy; but we believe that another beaker of red wine washed away the angry suspicions of the tipsy Mogul. Moreover, the bard of Erin did not tell the whole truth of Nourmahal. Jehangir had put her husband to death in order to marry her; and this was the cause of their early estrangement, and not, as Moore represents it,—

> "A something, light as air—a look,
> A word unkind or wrongly taken."

Shah Jehan was the son and successor of the sentimental and convivial Jehangir. He constructed the famous peacock's throne, and the splendid mausoleum of white marble decorated with mosaics, known as the Taj Mahal. His reign, which almost exactly corresponded to the reigns of Charles I and Oliver Cromwell, is chiefly remarkable for the rebellion of his sons. It terminated in the accession of the crafty Aurungzebe in 1658, the very year that Cromwell died.

Our story of the events which led to the first foundation of Madras is now drawing to a close. The settlement took place in the reign of Shah Jehan. There had been a tremendous quarrel between the Dutch and English about the nutmegs. Attempts were vainly made to arrange matters by a treaty, in which the trade and expenses in Java, and even in Pulicat, were to be alike shared. The Dutch were far the stronger, and the English were like lambs endeavouring to live in terms of amity with wolves. As early as 1620, the English had been compelled to leave Pulicat, but had managed to effect a settlement at Masulipatam. At last the quarrel reached a climax in the massacre of the English in one of the Spice Islands; an event which is still remembered with horror as the "massacre of Amboyna."

For many a generation afterwards the English and Dutch continued to be at deadly enmity in the East; but meantime the English managed to effect a permanent settlement on the Coromandel Coast. In 1625 the English obtained a piece of ground at Armaghaum, about forty miles to the north of Pulicat, and made it a subordinate station to Masulipatam. It was well for them that they did so; for three years afterwards they were all compelled to retire from Masulipatam to Armaghaum in consequence of the oppressions of the Native Governor. Subsequently some of them returned to Masulipatam, but still the oppressions and embarrassments went on; and it was apparent, both to the Factors out here and to the Court of Directors at home, that if a trade was to be carried on in these seas, some spot must be obtained more favourable to trade, and offering more security to the Company's servants and property. Accordingly Mr. Francis Day, member of the Council at Masulipatam, was dispatched to examine the country in the neighbourhood of the Portuguese settlement at St. Thomé.

Mr. Day met with unexpected success. He found that though the surf was heavy and dangerous, yet that the locality was favourably situated for obtaining coast goods. Moreover he received great encouragement both from the native powers and the Portuguese. The Naick of the district promoted his views to the utmost, and procured for him a grant of land, with permission to built a fort, from the Rajah of Chandragheri; whilst the Portuguese at St. Thomé behaved to him in the most friendly manner, and offered to give him every assistance in formiug the new establishment. The territory granted extended five miles along shore and one inland.

Thus was formed the first establishment in Madraspatnam in 1639, in the reign of his Majesty Charles I, and just before the breaking out of the great civil war. Iu the present number we have confined ourselves to sketching the circumstances which led to our first settlement in Madras, and describing the previous condition of India. In a future issue we hope to resume our story, and furnish our readers with a sketch of the early history and condition of the infant Presidency, and the nature and character of its relations with the native powers.

CHAPTER II.

EARLY YEARS OF FORT ST. GEORGE.

At last then we have alighted at old Madras. In our previous issue we carried our readers from London to the Spice Islands, and from the Spice Islands to Surat and Fort Saint George; lingering however upon our way to gossip anent the Great Moguls who reigned at Delhi. But now that we have fairly crossed the surf, we will take the opportunity,– whilst Mr. Day is building up his Fort for the protection of the Agency,—to take a rapid glance at the world around us; and above all, to tell the story of that Rajah of Chandragheri, from whom the grant of territory was originally obtained.

The present generation will not submit to much geographical detail. Otherwise we might descant lovingly on the Tamul country which extended from Comorin to Pulicat; on the Canarese country to the west; on the Telugu country to the north; and on the strange old land of Orissa, or Urya country, still further away. The history however may not be thus scurvily treated*; and

* We are afraid that some of our readers will consider the present article to be rather too historical. But in the first place the sketch of Native history will be found absolutely necessary to enable us to understand the early relations of Madras with the Native powers. Secondly, no Records of any description appear to have been preserved in this Presidency to throw light upon the internal manners and mode of life during the Governments of Sir Edward Winter and Mr. Foxcroft. After the year 1670 we tread upon new ground.

indeed some knowledge of it is absolutely necessary, before we can understand the peculiar position in which the little colony of our countrymen found themselves two hundred years ago.

In times primeval, when the gods danced on alternate legs and gave milk to little pigs,* and when the curses of Brahmins and the prayers of sages were sufficient to overthrow the deities and convulse the spheres,—in those days a large portion of Southern India was occupied by the two old Hindoo kingdoms of Chola and Pandya, whose relative positions may be indicated by the position of their respective capitals. The capital of the Chola kingdom was Conjeveram; the capital of the Pandya kingdom was Madura. Both cities are still celebrated for their magnificent pagodas, in which sculptures and architecture alike exhibit the struggle of the old material religion of the Tartar races, with the more spiritual and philosophic tenets taught by the fair complexioned Brahmin. In olden time the sovereign of Pandya had sent ambassadors to the Court of Augustus Cæsar; whilst the kings of Chola had ruled Tamuls and Telugus as far as the banks of the Godaveri. But when Mr. Day first landed on these shores, these two kingdoms only existed as relics of the past. Their power and dignity had been battered down by the conquering Mussulman. They had shrunk,

* Some of our readers may require to be informed that these are allusions to genuine Tamul legends, and that the circumstances are gravely related as amongst the sacred amusements of the gods!

like withered beauty, almost into nothingness; and their last hour was fast drawing nigh.

The early wars in the Dekkan between Mussulmans and Hindoos, resembled the conflict of an advancing flood against a strong head wind. Sometimes the wave of Mahomedan invasion dashed on to Cape Comorin; sometimes, as its force subsided, the weakened tide was flung back to the Nerbudda river. Early in the fourteenth century,—whilst the Mussulman power at Delhi was torn to pieces by internal dissensions, and the invasion of Timour was already looming in the distance,—the famous old Hindoo family, afterwards known as the Sree Rung Rayeel, established a throne at Bijanagur in the Canarese country. Bijanagur, or "city of victory" was seated on one of the tributaries of the Kistna, and about thirty miles from Bellary. In a few years the new Hindoo kingdom became the most powerful state in Southern India. Its conquests extended over the greater part of Chola and Pandya, and thus included the country in which Madras now stands; and it was one of its later Kings, named Narsing Rajah, who erected the forts of Chandragheri and Vellore. Whilst this Kingdom of Bijanagur was extending its dominions, a successful revolt against the imperial power at Delhi led to the establishment of an independent Mussulman dynasty in the country now called Hyderabad, known to historians as the Bahminee kings of the Dekkan. For a century and a half, the Hindoo house of Bijanagur, and the Bahminee kings of the Dekkan, were at constant war. About the end of the fifteenth century, and about the time of the first appearance of the Portuguese on the Coast of Malabar, the power of the Bahminee kings was broken up, and five independent Mussulman monarchies were erected upon the ruins. Terrible wars still continued to desolate the Dekkan; sometimes between the Mussulman kings themselves, and sometimes between the Mussulmans and the Hindoos. At last, in 1564 the Mussulman kings combined to overthrow the Hindoo dynasty at Bijanagur. A great battle took place on the Kistna. The Hindoos were utterly defeated. Their brave old Rajah was taken prisoner and put to death in cold blood; and until very lately his head was still kept as a trophy at Bijapoor.

But notwithstanding this decisive overthrow, the family of the Sree Rung Rayeel was not extinct. The next heir still retained the name of Rajah; and he and his descendants were allowed to retain several districts in jaghire for some generations. The brother of the deceased Rajah removed to the Fort of Chandragheri, about seventy miles south west of Madras; and there seems to have become Rajah of the country, and to have maintained a rule more or less nominal over the Naiks of the surrounding districts, and amongst others over the Naik of Chingleput. It was either this very brother, or else one of his descendants, that gave the grant of land to Mr. Francis Day, with permission to erect the Fort, which, in honour of the guardian Saint of England, was named Fort St. George.

A melancholy incident, illustrative of that anxious desire possessed by every Hindoo, of having his family name handed down to future ages, is connected with this grant. The old Rajah of Chandragheri, who still retained the name of Sree Rung Rayeel, had expressly stipulated that the new town, which was expected to spring up in the neighbourhood of the Fort, should be called by his name "Sreerungaraja-patanam." But before the grant had been fairly executed, another name had been given to the town, which has continued down to our own time. The Naik of Chingleput had previously intimated that the new settlement would be founded in the name of his own father, Chennapa; and the name of "Chenna-patanam," or "city of Chennapa" having been once applied to the confused assemblage of bamboo huts which sprang up near the Fort, was never afterwards superseded, and still continues to be the name by which Madras is known amongst the Natives. Meantime the poor old Rajah was fast losing his power. The petty Naiks and Poligars refused to pay him any allegiance, and even invited the advance of the Mussulman. At last, in 1646 he fled away to Mysore, and his name seems to have died gradually out of the land.

We must now return to the proceedings of Mr. Day. The grant obtained from the Rajah of Chandragheri was dated 1st March 1639; and the station was considered to be so important by the Agency at Masulipatam, that they directed Mr. Day to begin building the Fort at the Company's expense, without waiting for the orders of the Court of Directors. This proceeding however was not approved at home. The first General

Letter sent by the little Agency at Fort St. George to the Court of Directors, is dated 5th November 1642, and contains many arguments to show that a fort for the protection of the Carnatic trade was as necessary on the Coast of Coromandel as at Surat or Bantam; and that the Dutch had acquired a large share of the Coromandel trade entirely through the fortifications which they had erected at Pulicat. In 1644, the sum expended on the Fort amounted to £2,300; and it was computed that the expenditure of £2000 more, and a garrison of a hundred soldiers, would render the place impregnable. But all this sort of thing was much objected to by the Court of Directors. In 1652 the garrison only consisted of twenty-six soldiers. In 1653 the Agency was raised to the rank of a Presidency, and henceforth maintained a supremacy over the Factories on the Coast of Coromandel and in Bengal. But in 1654 the new Presidency was ordered to reduce its civil establishment to two Factors, and its garrison to ten soldiers only. We know very little of the internal history of the settlement at this early time. No records have been preserved in this Presidency of an earlier date than 1670; and our information concerning Madras at this period, has been obtained from "Bruce's Annals" and other antiquated volumes. The first President whose name is preserved and whose acts are celebrated, was Sir Edward Winter, who was appointed in February, 1661.

The Factory at Fort St. George had now been established more than twenty years. But the times were bad. Trade had been very bad at home, as well as on the Coast of Coromandel. England had been distracted by the great Civil War, between Charles and his Parliament, and business was almost at a stand still. The Company had also suffered in another way. When king Charles returned from his war against the Scots, he was in such pressing want of money, that he was compelled to resort to the most extraordinary means for obtaining it. Amongst other things he bought from the Company six hundred thousand lbs. of pepper, on credit, at two shillings and a penny per lb. amounting in all to £63,000. For this sum four bonds were given by the farmers of the customs, of which only one appears to have been ultimately paid. The pepper was sold for ready money at one shilling and eight pence per lb.; and thus the king realised a sum of £50,000. During the Civil War, and especially during the reign of the Puritans, no articles would command a sale, excepting those of intrinsic value. Silks and pearls were an abomination in the eyes of Presbyterians and Independents; who for generations had been denouncing the luxuries of the age, with all the energy with which the Hebrew prophets of old time denounced the chains, the bracelets, the earrings, the nose jewels, and the changeable suits of apparel of the mincing beauties of Palestine.

At Fort Saint George, the Factors had as many difficulties as the Directors at home. The Native wars were frequent and threatening. Sometimes it was the Mussulmans fighting with the Hindoos, osmetimes there were terrible struggles for supremacy between the two great Mahomedan kingdoms of the Dekkan—Bijapoor and Golconda. Madras, after the flight of the Rajah of Chandragheri had become dependent upon the king of Golconda, and had obtained from him a cowle for the fort and town of Chennapatanam. Meantime Aurungzebe had been appointed by his father Shah Jehan to the command of the Mogul army in the Dekkan. Another terrible war ensued, which filled the country with bloodshed up to the very walls of Fort St. George. All this time the Dutch were opposing the English in every possible way. They endcavourcd to drive the latter out of the market by selling cheaper and buying dearer than there was any occasion. This however would be considered fair play in these days of free trade. But the Dutch went much farther. The English having obtained possession of one of the precious little Spice Islands, the Dutch sent a number of people every year to cut down the nutmeg trees. The English coasting trade was almost stopped by the Dutch cruisers, who swarmed in the Indian seas, and who were as ready to commit acts of piracy, as to purchase native merchandize. Sad tales might be told of that time. Besides the horrible massacres at Amboyna, in which Englishmen were subjected by the Dutch to tortures rivalling those of the inquisition, stores and houses had been burnt down in Java, and it would almost seem that murders as well as robberies were committed, during that terrible period of commercial rivalry. The Dutch were even said to have committed piracies under the English flag against ships belonging to the native powers, and for which the English Company had themselves to pay a hundred thousand rials of eight. But in 1652, matters became even more threatening. Cromwell declared war against Holland, and the Factors in the Fort were now in imminent peril. They prayed to the Directors to increase their little garrison, and permit them to complete their fortifications; and above all to be allowed to construct a curtain towards the sea. But all to no purpose. The little Agency in Fort St. George thus felt that they were in constant danger, not only from some plundering native chief on land, but from a cannonading from the Dutch on the side facing the sea.

Meantime the English at Fort St. George and the Portuguese at St. Thomé, seem to have lived together on the best of terms; but the Portuguese had not unfrequently embroiled themselves with the natives, in consequence of their improvident zeal to make converts to the Roman Catholic faith. In 1650 the Portuguese nearly endangered the permanency of their establishments at St. Thomé. A Padre had refused to allow a Hindoo religious procession to pass his church, and a terrible uproar was the result. The English at the Fort wisely avoided interfering in the dispute; but they reported the matter to the Court of Directors at home, and expressed the following opinion upon the impracticability of overcoming the religious prejudices of the Natives:—"By this you may judge of the lyon by his paw, and plainly discerne, what small hopes, and how much danger we have of converting these people, that are not lyke the naket and brut Americans, but a most subtle and pollitique nation, who are so zealous in their religions, or rather superstitions, that even amongst their owne differing casts, is grounded an irreconcilable hatred, which often produceth very bloodie effects." At the same time there was no lack of religious zeal on the part of the English, as we shall presently see; but still there was a larger amount of religious toleration than we should have expected in that age, and certainly far more than was approved by the Directors at home.

The friendship between the Portuguese and English was probably cemented by their common enmity towards the Dutch. Indeed the Dutch possessed so powerful a force in the Indian seas, that it seemed as though no nation could stand against them. They took Ceylon and excluded the Portuguese from the Island. They blockaded the Portuguese capital of Goa; they blockaded the English settlement at Bantam; and it was fully expected that if Goa fell, the Dutch would blockade the Surat river, and thus put themselves in possession of the whole of the trade on the Coast of Malabar.

In 1654, a treaty was at length concluded between the English and Dutch, known as the treaty of Westminster. Four Commissioners from each nation were appointed to adjust the rival claims for injuries received during the previous forty years. The English Company brought in a little bill of

£2,700,000. But the Dutch Company was fully prepared for such a contingency, and brought in a bill of nearly £3,000,000! The award of the Commissioners proved that they considered that most of the transactions upon which the accounts were based were purely mythical, or at any rate that they belonged to a mythical period. It was decided that the Dutch Company should pay to the English Company £85,000; that they should also pay £3,600 to the heirs or executors of the sufferers at Amboyna; and that all past injuries and losses should be buried in oblivion by both parties.

But whilst peaceful relations were thus concluded between the English and Dutch, the infant settlement at Madras continued to suffer from the badness of trade, the interference of interlopers, the appearance of the Mahrattas, and the bloody Civil war between the four sons of Shah Jehan for the throne of the Great Mogul. The two latter events, and their bearings upon the condition of the Colony we shall discuss in a future number. For the present we will simply follow the history of Fort St. George.

We have already noticed the appointment of Sir Edward Winter to the Presidency of Madras in 1661. At home the whole kingdom was mad with joy and excitement at the downfall of the Commonwealth and restoration of Charles II. The reign of the Puritans,—of sad coloured gentlemen, and pinched up sombre ladies,—was gone at a bound. Silks and taffeties, brilliant jewels and gay apparel, once more sparkled at Whitehall;

whilst French licentiousness, worse than the most Puritanical tyranny, spread from the Court to all parts of the kingdom, and even to the colonies abroad. But meantime trade revived. Fresh consignments of bullion were dispatched to Fort St. George, and coined into Pagodas in the Fort mint; and whilst part of the money was sent to Java and Sumatra for the purchase of pepper and spices, a large proportion was sent to Bengal for the purchase of silks and muslins to set off the exuberant charms of the gay young ladies of the Court of merry king Charles.

The appointment of Sir Edward Winter marks a new period in the history of Madras. Hitherto the Factors had been plain business men, trying to keep on good terms with every one, and especially with the Native Powers. Their principal vice appears to have been a strong tendency to trade on their own account, rather than on account of the Company. This itching for private trade Sir Edward Winter was especially called upon to put down by all the means in his power. The Factories in Bengal and on the Coast of Coromandel* were all placed under his immediate superintendence, and were ordered to transmit to him regular accounts of their proceedings. He was empowered to dismiss from the service any of

* A Factory had been established at Balasore in Orissa, by the same Mr. Day who had founded the Factory at Fort St. George. This was in 1642, but another Factory had been previously founded at Piply as early as 1635. The Factories at Masulipatam and Armaghaum have already been noticed.

the Company's servants who should be found to have engaged in private trade, and to send them back to England. Moreover, a warrant under the Privy Seal was obtained from king Charles, authorising the new President to seize and send to England, all other persons not in the Company's service, who had engaged in the private trade of the country, or in navigating the vessels of the country powers.

Sir Edward Winter held the government from 1661 to 1665 by right, and from 1665 to 1668 by usurpation. His name is barely mentioned by the historians of India; and the opinion which the Directors had been first led to adopt, in consequence of the representations made to them by the other members of council at Fort St. George, is also adopted without question by Mill and others, namely, that he was recalled in consequence of his being implicated in private trade. We must confess that we have arrived at a very different opinion. To us Sir Edward Winter appears to have been a brave and loyal subject of his Majesty; who had excited the enmity of his subordinates by his vigorous correction of abuses, and aroused their fears by his manly efforts to teach the Natives that Englishmen were their equals and not their slaves; but who at last fell a victim to a hot headed zeal which we may sincerely deplore, but which we must not too hastily condemn.

The whole story of Sir Edward's administration is so illustrative of the times, as well as intrinsically interesting, that we must tell it at full length.

On his first arrival at Fort St. George, he found that the country trade was still much depressed by the constant wars in the Carnatic. On one occasion the Fort itself seems to have been beseiged, though unsuccessfully, by Neknam Khan, nabob of Golconda, or rather Commander-in-Chief of the army of Abou Hassan, king of Golconda or Hyderabad. Accordingly the new President directed his attention to improving the sea trade with Bengal, and Bantam; and at the same time proposed to retaliate on Native vessels at sea for the depredations committed by the Native powers on land. It was plain indeed that without some such strong measures the trade never could be expected to revive; and it was by such measures alone that the Dutch had been able to keep the Native powers in awe as regarded themselves. Mere remonstrances were utterly useless. Sir Edward Winter had himself represented to a Naik, that goods passing from the up-country towns to Madras were plundered by his followers; and that duties were levied by mere arbitrary will, without any regular scale. The Naik significantly replied that "when the English horns and teeth grew, then he would free them from the duties."

But the little trading body in Fort St. George refused to support the spirited policy of their President. Such open hostilities might indeed have protected the public trade of the Company, but would have sadly interfered with the nice little private speculations, without which the Coast of Coromandel was no more profitable than Tower Street or the Cheap. Accordingly they thwarted him in every way; until at last he sent home his resignation; in the expectation that his public services would have been so highly valued by the Directors, that they would have requested him to continue in the Government, and at the same time would have increased his powers. But meanwhile the other members of council had contrived to set the Court of Directors against him. They secretly charged him with private trade, and with exciting the hostility of the Native Chiefs. The latter complaint tallied with the recommendations which Sir Edward Winter had already sent home, respecting the necessity of assuming a bold front at sea. Accordingly, the resignation of the Governor was accepted, and Mr George Foxcroft was appointed to reign in his stead.

We have now to record a very curious incident in the early annals of the Presidency; but before doing so it will be necessary to glance at what seems to have been the difference between the character of the old President and the new. Sir Edward Winter appears to have been a loyal Cavalier, in those days when loyalty to Church and King was ranked as the highest virtue under heaven. Nor are we inclined to depreciate the sentiment. The single minded and generous fidelty of the gentlemen of England two centuries ago, were the salvation of the Church, and, but for the utter faithlessness of the reigning sovereign, might have been the salvation of their king. But during the wearisome period which succeeded the struggle, the high chivalric devotion of the old Cavalier degenerated into a bitter hatred and contempt for the opposite party, and had led to a readiness to draw the sword upon hearing the slightest depreciation of the Lord's anointed. Mr. Foxcroft, on the other hand, was evidently a plain business citizen from Leadenhall Street; and, like most of the commercial community of that day, was probably a sober God fearing man, who may have been a regular attendant at his parish Church, but who would not shut his eyes to the vulgar debaucheries that disgraced the Court of the Second Charles. It might easily have been foreseen that matters would not pass pleasantly between such a trader from the city, and such a cavalier from Whitehall; even supposing that there had been no such subject for secret exasperation as the supercession of the latter in the command.

Mr. Foxcroft arrived at Fort St. George in June 1665. He presented his Commission, and was received by his predecessor with respect; and Sir Edward Winter was allowed to act as second in council, until he should take his departure for England. Three months passed away, when on one memorable day, Sir Edward Winter, assisted by a few others, suddenly made an attack on Mr. Foxcroft and his son, and a Mr. Sambroke; and after a desperate conflict, in which one man was killed and several were wounded, Mr. Foxcroft, his son, and Mr. Sambroke were put into confinement, under an accusation of having uttered seditious and treasonable expressions against His Majesty's Government. Sir Edward Winter then assumed the administration, assisted by one of the Merchants, and the Lieutenant of the troops in garrison; and, in reporting the matter home to the Court of Directors, he explained that he could bring living proofs of the disloyalty of Mr. Foxcroft, on the affidavits of the Chaplain and one of the Factors.

We have not the slightest doubt but that Mr. Foxcroft uttered some imprudent expressions, which Sir Edward Winter, carried away by his hot zeal, interpreted to signify sedition and treason of the blackest dye. But at home suspicions were excited that the accusations were not true. Sir Edward Winter was not content with merely reporting the matter to the Court of Directors, but he actually addressed letters both to the king himself, and to the Archbishop of Canterbury; declaring that loyalty to his most gracious sovereign had been his only motive for arresting and imprisoning his successor in the Presidency of Fort St. George. Moreover, he dispatched the letters direct, without allowing them to pass through the hands of his honourable masters; and without reflecting that such letters were calculated to awaken suspicions at Whitehall, that a spirit of disloyalty prevailed amongst the servants in the Company's Factories in India.

Meantime Mr. Foxcroft applied for assistance to the Agent at the subordinate Factory at Masulipatam, and through him to the President at Surat. Both expressed themselves satisfied that he had been excluded from the Presidency of

Fort St. George on a frivolous pretext; and both remonstrated with the persons who had assisted Sir Edward Winter, and assured them that the matter could only end in the Fort falling into the hands of the Mussulmans, the Dutch, or the Portuguese.

It was only natural that under these circumstances, the fears, as well as the suspicions of the Directors should be powerfully excited. The King was persuaded to interpose his authority; but still a considerable time necessarily elapsed before anything could be done. The year 1666 passed away, and Sir Edward Winter still maintained his authority, and kept Mr. Foxcroft in confinement. It was reported that he intended to deliver up the Fort to the Dutch Governor of Ceylon, and that the latter had prepared a vessel for him to make his escape. But such a report was wholly untrue; or certainly so far untrue that no thought of such disloyalty seems ever to have crossed the mind of Sir Edward Winter. Another year passed away. In 1667 the treaty of Breda was concluded with the Dutch, on the principle of the "Uti Possidetis," which was to take place on the 10th May 1668. Warlike preparations were now made at home for the recovery of the Fort of Saint George. Five ships were consigned to the Fort, equipped for war as well as for trade. The Directors seem to have made up their minds that the place had been delivered up to the Dutch, and sent general orders accordingly. If Madras had been given up before the 10th May, then the Agent at Masulipatam was to apply to the nabob of Golconda to order the place to be restored to the English; if it had been delivered up after the 10th May, then a protest was to be entered that the Dutch had refused to give it up in aeeordance with the treaty of Breda. If however Sir Edward Winter still eontinued in possession of the Fort, one or more of the Company's ships was to stand off in the Roads, and bloekade Madras so as to prevent the entrance or departure of any vessels whatever. If the blockade failed, then the Agent at Masulipatam, and the Commanders of the Company's ships were to hold a eonsultation, and offer five thousand pagodas to the nabob of Goleonda for the cession of St. Thomé to the Company. Supposing St. Thomé were thus obtained, thcy were to land ordnanee and military stores, and fortify themselves in it until further instructions should arrive from England. If however all these plans proved ineffectual, and St. Thomé could not be obtained, then Fort St. George was to be abandoned altogether; and the Agent at Masulipatam, in eonsultation with the Commanders of the ships, was to endeavour to form a new establishment on some other part of the Coromandel Coast, at whieh goods suited to the Bantam and Europe markets eould be obtained.

In addition to these general orders, a commission from the king was directed to the Captains of the ships, empowering them to form the soldiers and seamen into five Companies, and to train them in the use of ordnanec and small arms, in order that on arriving at the Coast thcy might make an attack upon the Fort by sea and land. Scerct instruetions were also sent to promise an cstablishmcnt for those soldiers and seamen who should be active in recovering the place, and a provision for the wives and families of those who might suffer in the action. Pardon and reward was also to be promised to any of the adherents of Sir Edward Winter, who would return to their duty and assist in the recovery of Fort St. George.

Meantime Sir Edward Winter continued in possession of the Fort, fully convinced that by so doing he was manifesting his loyalty towards the king. The Agent at Masulipatam sent him certain propositions founded on the King's commission, but he treated the commission as a forgery intended to seduce him from his duty. At last on the 21st May 1668 two of the Company's ships arrived in the Madras Roads. Mr. Proby and Mr. Locke, members of council, went on board, but were at once detained as prisoners. Mr. Proby was directed to write a letter informing Sir Edward Winter that he had seen the king's Commission and the Company's orders to the Commissioners; and that the Commissioners would come on shore and take possession of the Fort in His Majesty's name. Sir Edward Winter in reply, demanded that Mr. Proby should be first set at liberty, and that personal safety and protection of property should be guaranteed. The Commissioners were only too glad to accede to these terms; and on the 22nd August they took possession of the Fort, and released Mr. Foxcroft from his three years imprisonment, and reinstated him in the Presidency.

Such was the end for the time of this extraordinary proceeding, and the expensive armament which it entailed. Imprudent language on the part of Mr. Foxcroft, and intemperate zeal on the part of Sir Edward Winter, had thus led to a train of circumstances which are not the least interesting in the old annals of Madras. Subsequently the opinion of the Court of Directors as regarded the two men underwent a material change. Sir William Langhorne and six other Commissioners were appointed to investigate the whole of the transaction; and Mr. Foxcroft was to be allowed to continue as Agent for only one year, and then was to be succeeded by Sir William Langhorne. Mr. Foxcroft the younger was sent home; Sir Edward Winter was allowed to remain at Madras to dispose of his property and recover his debts; and the Court expressly ordered that he should be treated with every respect and allowed a passage to England. The inquiry ended in the recall of both Winter and Foxcroft, and the return of both to England about the year 1670.

CHAPTER III.

MADRAS IN THE REIGN OF MERRY KING CHARLES—A PICTURE.

Brightly before the imagination rises up the Fort of St. George and the straggling town of Madraspatanam, under the presidency of the Honorable Sir William Langhorne, Baronet, in the middle of the reign of merry king Charles. The same surf is rolling heavily upon the beach, and almost the same naked boatmen are labouring at the oar, amidst the deafening cling-clang of some old Tamul refrain; but only two, or perhaps three old fashioned ships, are lying in the roads, with old fashioned cannon peeping from their decks, and a still stranger old fashioned crew dropping the anchor or taking in the sails. We wil suppose them to be new arrivals from England, and that all is bustle and excitement. The sun is just rising over the bay of Bengal, and flashing its early rays over the dark blue billows. Two or three sedate members of council have just taken their morning draught, according to the fashion of the time, and are being pushed off from the beach. They are arrayed in their best Sunday attire of gay doublets and enormous hose, and are endeavouring to assume courtly airs, which sit but ungainly on those rough and unpolished traders. Beside them is seated the Captain of the little garrison, in his best uniform, somewhat the worse for wear, and stained may be with spots that might have been blood, but are far some likely to have been the droppings from a flask of red wine. He too is brushed and buckled as if for parade, and carries as swaggering an air as a man may do who is being tossed and rolled about by a stiff Coromandel surf. All seems to betoken the arrival of some extraordinary person or personages, who must be welcomed with unusual pomp to the Factory in Fort St. George.

Such indeed we may assume to be the case on that early morning. Not only had more gold and silver ingots, woollen cloths, looking glasses, cutlery, and various other sorts of home manufactures arrived for the Factory; not only had some reckless recruits and unwieldy fire arms arrived for the Fort; not only had the second part of the works of the learned Dr. Hammond, and the fourth volume of Mr. Pool's famous Synopsis, been sent by the honorable Directors for the use of the Chaplain and of all readers of the ponderous theological literature of that period;—but due advices had been received that certain ladies had been allowed to go out from England to Fort St. George; and such an incident in those days was well calculated to excite the liveliest emotions in the breasts of every unmarried European in the Factory, from the Apprentices who helped to sort the goods, up to the Senior Merchants who sat in the Council and determined what to buy and what to sell.

The relations of the colonists as regards the fair sex, were certainly peculiar in those odd old times. Shut out from the world of Europeans, and of course shut out from the companionship of their own fair countrywomen, excepting perhaps that of one or two hardy sun-burnt matrons, who had bravely followed their husbands to the Indies; we cannot feel surprised that our predecessors in this burning settlement should have been often seduced, like the Israelites of old, who yielded their hearts to the women of Moab and Midian. As for the dusky beauties of the country, they seem to have been ever willing to smile on those who courted their charms. In some cases such connections were looked upon as real marriages. When Captain Hawkins carried a letter from James I. to the Great Mogul in 1609, Jehangir, who at that time reigned at Delhi, was anxious to engage his services and keep him in the country, and accordingly offered him a pension and a wife. Hawkins yielded to both temptations. Though an English ambassador he did not scruple to accept a salary; and as the imperial harem contained a large assortment of ladies, he was provided with a maiden bride, who not only took his fancy, but who succeeded in gaining his affections.* Subsequently he retired from court and fairly carried away his wife to Europe, though not without a desperate conflict with her brothers. Stories illustrative of less moral connections crowd the pages of the old travellers, who frequently tell us how, at the courts of native princes, and even at the houses of European Factors, dancers of surpassing loveliness were pressed upon their attention and

* She is said to have been an Armenian Christian.

invariably refused! Such stories may be partly true and partly false; but if we may only believe the tales which such travellers tell of each other rather than of themselves, we can only come to the conclusion that there were more Don Juans than Josephs in those free and easy times.

The early English settlements were peculiarly situated in this respect. The Dutch Company encouraged the matrimonial desires of their servants, and invested husbands and fathers with peculiar privileges; and to this day the effigies of many a rare old Dutch vrow may still be seen in the strange antiquated burying ground at Pulicat. The Portuguese were even more fortunate, for their king had been long in the habit of sending out small cargoes of orphan girls, well born and indifferently well portioned, to become wives to his subjects of India; and a good story is told how a Portuguese ship, with three of these maidens on board, was captured by the Dutch and carried in triumph to Surat, where the young ladies were promptly married to three of the most eminent Dutch merchants in the settlement, to the everlasting despair and desolation of the amorous Portuguese. For a long time, however, scarcely a single English lady was to be found at the English Factories; the thing was altogether discouraged by the Directors, and the result may be easily inferred:—

"The heart, like a tendril, accustomed to cling,
  Let it grow where it will, cannot flourish alone,
But will lean to the nearest, and loveliest thing,
  It can twine with itself, and make closely its own."

Within the Fort all was outwardly fair enough, and the morals of the Apprentices and Writers were tolerably well seen after, for Sir William Langhorne was somewhat of a martinet in that direction. But still if walls had ears and tongues they might tell strange tales; and there were very many goings on in Black town which we care not to record. In the outstations, such as Masulipatam and Armaghaum, there would seem to have been no restraint whatever. Sometimes, as we have already indicated, connections were formed which were as sacred in the eyes of the parties themselves as the marriage tie could have made them. Sometimes, and there is no denying it, the household of a Factor bore a stronger resemblance to the harem of some Mussulman voluptuary than to the household of a Christian trader.

As for the soldiers of the garrison, they lived much as soldiers might be expected to do. Many of them actually married the women of the country; not indeed the poor heathen girls, but the Native Portuguese women, who were Roman Catholics. Accordingly such marriages were celebrated by the Portuguese padres; and in process of time, marriages, baptisms and buryings were conducted by the same priesthood, and the children were educated in the Roman Catholic religion. Those who are familiar with the history of the seventeenth century, are well aware of the suspicious enmity which was then felt by every Protestant communion towards the Roman Catholic body. The discovery of the gunpowder plot in the reign of James, the terrible "Thirty Years War," the knowledge that the mother of Charles II was a Roman Catholic, and that the next heir to the throne was himself a Roman Catholic, had culminated about this time in the pretended discovery of a Popish plot, and the English nation was literally driven mad with the vile perjuries of Oates and Bedloe. It is not therefore surprising that the wrath of good Master Patrick Warner, the chaplain at Fort St. George, should have been powerfully kindled. He wrote a long letter home to the Directors, complaining of the backslidings of the soldiers, the drinking and dicing of Writers and Factors, and the sinful toleration of Sir William Langhorne, who had actually fired a salute in honour of the foundation of a Roman Catholic Church within the walls of White town. We reprint the letter at full length, at the end of the present article. We have corrected the spelling, but have left the reverend gentleman's language untouched. There may be a word or two which modern decorum would prompt us to cut out, but not one which may not be found in the authorised version of the Bible; and therefore we do not see any necessity for adapting the plain speaking of a divine of the seventeenth century, to the tastes of our more polite times.

The honest merchants in Leadenhall Street seem to have been powerfully affected by the letter from their God-fearing Chaplain; and they adopted extraordinary means for preserving the orthodoxy of Fort St. George. They sent out strict orders that if any man was married by a Roman Catholic priest, or allowed his children to be baptised by a Roman Catholic priest, or did not have his children educated in the Protestant religion, he was to be sent home without delay. Moreover they sent out both to Bombay and Fort St. George, a few Protestant women for the soldiers to marry, and even permitted certain ladies to come out under restrictions, but on something very like matrimonial speculation.

Thus it was that three or four English ladies first arrived in Madras; plain honest women enough, and no doubt tolerably educated for those times, when the Protestant Manual and the Housekeeper's receipt book were the principal subjects of study. Seven or eight months had probably passed away since they had been wished "God speed" by the worthy gentlemen of the Court of Directors, and had fairly set sail down the silver Thames, for the hot country of Indians and idolaters. Poor souls! they must have had strange thoughts as they gazed out from the anchorage, and pondered upon the curious world they were soon to enter. But stranger still they must have felt, when the two members of Council, and the Captain of the garrison, climbed up the sides of the ship and welcomed them to Madraspatanam. But upon this part of the picture we need not dwell, but will simply imagine them to have been carried over the surf with many displays of gallantry, and finally landed in safety upon the beach in front of Fort St. George.

A strange old fort it was even to the English gentlewomen of that time; but it would seem more strange to us; whilst our extensive buildings would have seemed stranger still to that simple minded generation. There was the Warehouse piled high with goods of all descriptions ; some which seemed fresh from Aldersgate Street or the Cheap ; others,—silks, muslins, coloured calicoes, and other choice articles,—which had been brought from mysterious towns far inland. Then there was the little Chapel, where every man in the Agency, from the youngest Apprentice up to the Honorable Governor himself, was compelled to attend the daily reading of Morning and Evening Prayers, besides two sermons on Sundays, and something extra on Wednesdays. There was the Refection Room, where all the members of the Agency took their dinners and supper at times which very nearly corresponded to our tiffins and dinners ; and where on certain afternoons in the week the younger men were taught some one or other of the languages of the country, being stimulated thereunto by the promise of large rewards for proficiency,—twenty pounds being given for the knowledge of an Indian language, and ten pounds for a knowledge of Persian. There was the School room where all the children of the soldiers, and others were taught to read and cypher, and above all were imbued with the principles of the Protestant religion ; and be it told to the credit of the merchants of London in the godless reign of king Charles, that they constantly sent over supplies of Bibles and Catechisms for the use of this school, and directed that " when any shall be able to repeat the Catechisms by heart, you may give to each of them two rupees for their encouragement."

Other rooms there were, adorned with the heavy old fashioned furniture of the time, but still looking mighty bare and plain and rough. Last of all we must mention the Council Chamber, where all the members of council were summoned to attend on every Monday and Thursday morning, at eight o'clock, either by the Secretary himself, or by one of the Writers and Factors under him. It was also the Secretary's duty to enter all their Consultations in the book appointed for that purpose, together with all other occurrences and observations after the manner of a Diary; and to take care that a duplicate copy was fairly written out by the Factors and Writers appointed to that duty, so that one copy might be retained by the Secretary, and the other be sent home to the Directors. And from that day to the present, from the Governorship of the Honorable Sir William Langhorne in 1670 to the Governorship of the Honorable William Morehead in 1860, all these "Consultations" have been preserved in thousands of volumes; and it is from these original Records that we are now writing the history of the Madras Presidency.*

* The editor takes this opportunity of acknowledging the liberality of the Madras Government in granting him access to those volumes of the earlier Records, which may be expected to throw light on the ancient history of this Presidency. The labour of examining the old Records is very like that of a gold digger in Australia. Sometimes days of weary reading will pass away, without obtaining a single fact available for the purposes of history. Sometimes, however four or five lines of crabbed writing will prove as valu-

Our readers however may possibly be getting anxious for the welfare of the ladies to whom we introduced them at the commencement of this article. But alas, having brought them prominently forward on their first appearance in Madras, we have but little further to say respecting them; though that little may as well be said at once. There is nothing further about them in the Records, saving that some years afterwards, two of them still remained unmarried, and were living in the Fort on a small allowance granted by the Company. Thus we can only infer that the connubial speculation had failed, as we know that it failed at this very time in the new settlement at Bombay. We shall no doubt have to return to this subject in a future chapter.

But though we are thus compelled, from want of a better acquaintance, to turn our backs upon the ladies, we have much pleasure in introducing our readers to the other members of the society of Fort St. George. The English servants of the Company, exclusive of Apprentices and Soldiers, seem to have only been about twenty-four in number. First of all there was the Honorable Agent and

---

able as a nugget, and enrich a whole column. We hope to leave all the dross in happy obscurity, and present our readers with nothing but the gold. Fortunately our labours during the first ten years have been much lightened by the previous labours of a gentleman who wishes to remain unnamed, but who has laboriously collected a number of extracts from the oldest records, which have proved to be of the highest possible value as historical material.

Governor, Sir William Langhorne, who was first member of council, but who only received the modest salary of three hundred pounds a year. Next came the "Book-keeper," who kept all the establishment accounts, such as salaries and contingencies, as well as the general commercial accounts; and who, in virtue of his financial powers, was second member of council, and received a salary of a hundred a year. After him came the "Warehouse-keeper," whose duties are tolerably well indicated by his name, and who occupied the third seat in council, with a salary of seventy a year. The fourth member of council was called the "Customer," and a curious customer he was. He seems to have been the chief buyer of native merchandize, and the receiver of the rents and customs for the Company's town of Madras; and above all he practised in the Choultry as a sort of justice of the peace. For these duties he was paid the magnificent sum of fifty pounds per annum. In all there generally appears to have been five or six members of council, each receiving a salary rarely exceeding a hundred a year, though with occasional gratuities as rewards for good service. One and all however, appear to have engaged more or less in some private trade; from which far better profits were to be reaped than from the gratitude of the Directors. In vain were these proceedings denounced in the strongest terms by the honest gentlemen of Leadenhall Street; private trade continued to be carried on to a considerable extent until a much later period in the history of the Presidency.

Commissioners of inquiry and sentences of dismissal were of no avail. Occasionally a "black sheep" was sent home on the charge; but we are led to believe that, whatever might have been the ostensible accusation, other circumstances must have excited the enmity of his brethren beyond a little private dabbling in the trade.

The members of council were denominated "Merchants" and "Senior Merchants," a rank to which all the servants of the Company might aspire. Sometimes the young men came out as "Writers"; sometimes as "Apprentices" only. Every "Apprentice" seems to have served the customary period of seven years before he was promoted to a higher rank; a rule which was rigidly adhered to in all trades throughout Europe until a very recent period, and which seems to have had its origin in the mystic period during which Jacob served an enthusiastic apprenticeship to Laban, in order to gain the hand of the fair Rachel. During the first five years, the aspiring youths in the Company's service seem to have been allowed five pounds a year for the purchase of clothes. During the last two years of that time, whilst panting for the termination of apprenticeship, they were allowed Writer's salary of ten pounds a year. At the end of that period they were raised to the rank of "Writers," and after one year more, or eight years service in all, they became "Factors;" after which they rose in due time to the rank of "Merchants" and members of Council.

Besides these servants of the Company, there

were others whose duties may be easily inferred from their names. There was the "Chaplain" who had a hundred a year, and who must have had a hard time of it with daily prayers, and Sunday's preaching and expounding. There was the "Schoolmaster," at a salary of fifty pounds a year, who had been sent out to teach all the children of English parents to read, write, cypher, and hate the Roman Catholics. Any parents whatever, —Portuguese, Hindoo, or Mussulman,—might likewise send their children to be similarly taught; but only on the condition that they should also be instructed in the principles of the Protestant religion.

Some of our readers will probably ask how many of these gentlemen were married. In January 1678-9 it appears that out of the whole twenty-four gentlemen, only six were married, and only five had their wives with them; whilst five unmarried ladies were also dwelling in the Fort, two of whom were our lady friends still unwedded, and the remaining three were widows. Besides the civilians mentioned, there were sixteen other Europeans dwelling either in White Town or in Black Town, and who got a living by keeping houses of entertainment or other similar means. Of these only six were married, namely, two to English women, one to a Dutch woman, one to an English half-caste, and two to Portuguese half-castes.

The military portion of the population was more numerous. The number of European soldiers varied with the times, or with the fears of the Directors at home. Sometimes, as we have seen, they were reduced to a very small number; but during the reign of Charles II trade was rapidly increasing, and the garrison of Fort St. George increased to two companies of eighty or a hundred men each. In addition to these were a number of native peons, armed with swords and bucklers, bows and arrows, and other primitive weapons of the country.

Our readers will now find but little difficulty in realising the inside of Fort St. George, as it was some two centuries ago. They will hear the gun fired at early morning, and they will see the gradual stir of the inhabitants,—the measured tramp of the European soldier,—the little stately peon with his sword and buckler,—the rush of noisy naked coolies,—the appearance of Apprentices, Writers, Factors, and Merchants in half Hindoo costume,—the assembly for morning prayers in the little chapel, with good Master Patrick Warner officiating in his gown and bands, and indignant at the smallness of his congregation,—the opening of the Factory and jabbering crowd of Native traders,—the grand displays of European goods for sale, and the packing up of Native merchandize for export home,—the little school room and long array of different shades of little boys and girls,—the orderly dinner shortly after noon, where all are assembled at the general table from the Apprentices to the Honorable Governor himself,—the return to the labours of the desk and warehouse, until the joyous hour of closing has arrived, and the jaded Europeans recruit their exhausted spirits with the pleasures of punch, tobacco, and other pursuits which we need not and cannot name. If it is Sunday, all would be changed; for in old times English Sundays were rigidly observed as little festivals. Then the Europeans, civilians as well as soldiers, dropped their half native attire, and were apparelled in the European fashion of the time. Then for a brief hour or too the Chaplain would be a greater man than the Governor. Then he could denounce vice and popery to his heart's content, and expound the Scriptures by the light of a theological learning, which was almost general in those days when the Church was a living reality, but which is fast passing away now. Then the Church could boast of literary giants, such as Walton, Lightfoot, Selden, Stillingfleet, Beveridge, Pearson, Bull, and a thousand time honoured names. She has few men to boast about now.

Perchance however our readers would like to step out of the Fort, and see a little of the country around. They must not go far, for the Company's dominion only extends about a mile inland, and no man is allowed to go more than three miles from the Fort without permission of the Governor. Possibly however they may merely wish to go and peep into the gardens, where Writers and Factors occasionally assembled to drink down the sun, and sing such jolly ballads as "Ho Cavaliers," "Brandy nosed Noll," "Cherry Ripe," or "Chevy Chase" according to the humour of the times. But even then we should advise them not to go too far. What they are likely to see will not do them much good. They had better stay with us, and look out upon the country around from the old ramparts of Fort St. George.

We wish we could present an exact picture of that scene to modern eyes. Unfortunately no plan appears to have been preserved of an earlier date than 1737, or more than sixty years after the period we have been describing. But still by comparing this plan with certain topographical notices in the earliest records, we think we may convey a general idea of the Fort and the neighbourhood.

The district which the Company had obtained, first from the Rajah of Chandragheri, and afterwards from Golconda, stretched five miles along the sea, but only one inland. On the south it extended along the road to St. Thomé some little distance beyond the Triplicane river. On the north it extended a similar distance along the road to Trivatore. Inland it was bounded by the river, which still runs parallel with the sea, and which in former times used to run right through the part now occupied by the centre of the present Fort, but was diverted from that course when the Fort was enlarged in the succeeding century. The old Fort being thus bounded by the river on the inland side, was only half the size of the modern Fort, but still it included the European houses known for many generations afterwards as White-town.

Fort St. George and White town were thus synonymous terms. In Europe the quarter was known as Fort St. George; but in India it was called

White town, from its being occupied by Europeans. It extended about 400 yards in length from north to south, and about 100 yards in breadth from the sea to the old channel of the river already mentioned. The fortified Factory which had been constructed in the first instance by Mr. Day, was a very different thing from the Fort which existed in the time of the Honorable Sir William Langhorne. The Fort in the first instance must have somewhat resembled some of those old Forts which were knocked about during the Civil War. The first thing that was required was a population; and accordingly Mr. Day, and the Agents who immediately preceded him, invited the Portuguese and Indo-Portuguese to settle in the neighbourhood; and even lent them money to build upon the open sand under the protection of the Fort guns. Subsequently these foreigners had become naturalized Madrasees. As the fortifications progressed, their houses were walled in, and thus formed a part of White town; whilst they themselves did the duty of trained bands in watching and warding upon the outworks in time of trouble. Of course under these circumstances they neither paid nor were expected to pay any rent or acknowledgment for the land they occupied, and they never took out any leases. But during the Governorship of Sir William Langhorne, the White town was found to be too much crowded; and, many of the married servants of the Company were obliged to take houses in Black town, receiving an allowance for the extra expenses of board and lodging which they thereby incurred. Of this arrangement the Directors frequently complained, but still such were the existing difficulties in the way of expelling the Portuguese, that no alteration could be made. But even with the addition of the Portuguese, White town for nearly a century afterwards, never contained more than fifty houses, in addition to the Factory and other buildings of the Company. It was surrounded with a slender wall, defended with four bastions and as many batteries; but these were slight and defective, and undefended by outworks.

To the north of White town was the much larger quarter which was occupied by the Natives, and which for the sake of distinction was called Black town. Here the houses and population had rapidly increased in numbers; and the streets bore a very different appearance from the collection of bamboo huts which rose up during the earlier days of the colony. In the Choultry Plain to the southward of the Fort, the weavers and painters in the employment of the Factory, appear to have erected a little village for themselves; whilst the fishermen at the mouth of the Triplicane river were living, marrying, and dying,—catching fish, making nets, and celebrating their own peculiar festivals,—just as they had done in the old days of the kings of Chola and Pandya, and in all probability just as they will still be doing some thousand years hence, when Lord Macaulay's New Zealander comes poking about our tombs, and wondering what manner of people we have been. Two or three miles off were the little Native villages of Nungumbaukum, Egmore, Persewaukum, and Perambore, which were too far off to be often visited by the Europeans of that day.

Such then were the White town and Black town of Madraspatanam in the reign of merry king Charles, when trade was flourishing, and when the nation in general was increasing in wealth, and but for the Gallic tendencies of the Stuarts might have taken a high place amongst the European powers. The period was one in which there was much loyalty, much religion, but much loose living and debauchery. The times were rough, and the distance from Europe, and the absence of such female society as would have polished manners, rendered the little settlement rather tumultuous. Drunkenness, duelling, gaming, and licentiousness were, as we have already indicated, only too common, although the strictest rules were laid down. Sir William Langhorne had issued express orders,—and certainly his views were liberal,—that no one person was to be allowed to drink above half a pint of arrack or brandy and one quart of wine at one time, under a penalty of one pagoda upon the housekeeper that supplied it, and twelve fanams upon every guest that had exceeded that modest allowance. Drunkenness was to be punished by a fine and the stocks. All persons addicted in any way to the social evil were to be imprisoned at the discretion of the Governor, and if not reclaimed were to be sent back to England. All persons telling a lie, or absenting themselves from morning or evening prayers, were to be fined four fanams for each offence. Persons being out of the Fort after eight o'clock, would be punished;

and any one committing the heinous offence of getting over the walls of the Fort upon any pretence whatever, was to be kept in irons until the arrival of the ships, and then to be sent to England to receive further condign punishment on his arrival. It was also ordained that all persons swearing, cursing, banning, or blaspheming the sacred name of Almighty God should pay a fine of four fanams for each offence; that any two persons who should go out into the fields to decide a quarrel between them by the sword or fire arms should be imprisoned for two months on nothing but rice and water; that any soldier giving another the lie should be made fast to a gun, and there receive ten small blows with a rattan, well laid on by the man to whom he had given the lie; and that any Officer who should in any way connive at the offence, or at any mitigation of the punishment, should forfeit a month's wages. But notwithstanding these and other similar rules, public decorum was frequently outraged, as the letter of the Chaplain recorded below abundantly proves. Brawlings were not unfrequent, and were by no means confined to the Barracks, the Punch shops, or the Warehouse, but even were to be occasionally heard in the Council Chamber itself. One little circumstance which took place during the meeting of council on 6th June 1676, is singularly illustrative of the disturbances which occasionally arose. Nathaniel Keeble, buyer of jewels, uttered some provocative words concerning the wife of Mr. Herries, a member of council. Herries was of course present, and a fight took place in the Council Chamber. The combatants were soon parted by the Governor and Council; but Keeble had received a bloody nose from the clenched fist of the indignant husband, and swore to be revenged upon him though he were hanged for it. Herries then swore the peace against Keeble, and the Governor ordered the latter to be confined to his chamber until he had furnished security that he would keep the peace for the future. The same day however Keeble broke from his arrest, leaped down the Fort walls, and sprained his leg; and was accordingly ordered to be confined in the "Lock house" until the arrival of the ships, when he could be dispatched to England. The next day however the whole matter was arranged. Nathaniel Keeble sent in his humble submission and promised amendment, and the Government mercifully forgave him. Incidents such as these are sufficient to prove that however strict rules might be laid down, yet the times were as lawless in Fort St. George as they were in Covent Garden or the Strand. That they were not worse is abundantly proved by the character of the literature and condition of the people of England during the reign of the second Charles.

Here then we close our picture of the Fort and Factory of St. George, about the middle of the reign of king Charles. In a future issue we shall return to the history, which we trust will be found of deeper interest, now that we have given to the reader a glimpse of the society in which the events transpired.

APPENDIX TO CHAPTER III.

Letter of the Reverend Patrick Warner, Company's Chaplain at Fort St. George, addressed to the Court of Directors on the 31st January, 1676, bringing to their notice the vicious lives of the Soldiers and some of the Writers in the Fort.

Right Worshipfuls,

It is my trouble that I have so little acquaintance with your Worships, because of this I could not take the confidence of writing to you, nor had I anything worth the writing, having then remained so short a while in this place; but now having been a servant under you in the ministry of the Gospel some considerable time, I have to my grief met with that which maketh me, contrary to my inclination, break of my silence, and give you the trouble of these lines.

I have the charity to believe that most of you have so much zeal for God, and for the credit of religion, that your heads would be fountains of waters, and eyes rivers of tears, did you really know how much God is dishonoured, his name blasphemed, religion reproached amongst the Gentiles, by the vicious lives of many of your servants. Did I not therefore complain of them, I should not be faithful either to God or you, or to their own souls. And if it be not a desire to approve myself in some measure faithful unto all those, God the searcher of hearts and tryer of reins will one day discover, if it be not, I say, such a desire that moves me to the present undertaking.

It may be for a lamentation to hear and see the horrid swearing and profanation of the name of God, the woful and abominable drunkenness and uncleanness that so much reign and rage among the soldiery; and these not secretly or covertly, but as it were in the sight of the sun, and men refuse therein to be ashamed, neither can they blush. Some, after they have lived a long time in uncleanness, their whores persuade them to marry them, and several such have been married, who within a little time have found them treacherous and adulterous, and thereupon have either run away from them, or carried them along with them and sold them to the Infidels and Moores. Some unmarried persons keep whores in their houses, and some married whose wives are in England do the same. Most of those whores are popish christians; and if those that marry them do not fall into the former inconveniences, they hardly escape being seduced by their wives and wives' families into popery. There have not been wanting instances of this also. Since I entered into this place, I have constantly refused to celebrate any such marriages except one that I was urged into, and this not before she had solemnly and before several witnesses renounced popery, and promised to attend upon ordinances with us; but she had not been many weeks married when at the instigation of some popish priests here she perfidiously fell from those promises.

I wish your Worships may consider it be not requisite to inhibit such marriages, for the children turn either infidels or popish. I do also earnestly wish there may be more inspection taken what persons you send over into these places; for there come hither some thousand murderers, some men stealers, some popish, some come over under the notion of single persons and unmarried, who yet have their wives in England, and here have been married to others, with whom they have lived in adultery; and some on the other hand have come over as married persons, of whom there are strange suspicions they were never married. These and other abuses there are among the soldiery. There are also some of the Writers who by their lives are not a little scandalous to the Christian religion, so sinful in their drunkenness that some of them play at cards and dice for wine that they may drink, and afterwards throwing the dice which shall pay all, and sometimes who shall drink all, by which some are forced to drink until they be worse than beasts. Others pride themselves in making others drink till they be insensible, and then strip them naked and in that posture (horresco referens) cause them to be carried through the streets to their dwelling place. Some of them, with other persons whom they invited, once went abroad to a garden not far off, and there continued a whole day and night drinking most excessively, and in so much that one of the number died within a very few days after, and confessed he had contracted his sickness by that excess. A person worthy of credit having occasion to go the next day into the same garden could number by the heads 36 bottles, and the best of his judgment they were all pottles, for it is their frequent custom to break bottles as soon as they have drunk the wine, and this they have done sometimes within the walls of the Fort, and withal, sing and carouse at very unseasonable hours. And this their drunkenness is not alone, but in some attended with its ordinary concomitant uncleanness, for some have been found breaking open in the night time doors where they suspected whores to be, others have been whole nights in the room with another man's wife alone. They can find time and leisure for these things, but cannot find any time or leisure for the worship of God, which is exceedingly neglected by all, notwithstanding your orders to the contrary. I have sometimes, having waited long enough, been forced at length to begin duty with only three or four persons present, and when we have done there hath not been above twelve or thirteen in all; but who amongst the writers are most guilty in this, your Worships may know by the enclosed list of their absence taken by me indifferently, some appointed thereunto by the Governors; of others no account is taken.

But because it is no less a sin to condemn the just than to justify the wicked, I must bear witness for most of the young men, that they cannot, to the best of my knowledge, be accused of the former enormities. There are but a few of them that are guilty in the manner before described; whose names I would have inserted, that so I might clear the others, but that they have been lately sick, and some small hopes there are that they may amend; they have given some ground to expect it. But if they shall return with the dog to the vomit, I will, if it please God to spare me so long, give your Worships a more full account thereof by word of mouth, upon my arrival with the next ships; for as you have already been informed, I intend to return with them, and I hope with your good leave so to do. Therefore what I have written may in charity be supposed, not to proceed from expectation of any advantage to myself, but from respect to the glory of God, and their good and the encouragement of succeeding ministers.

I did write, what the last year's ships give an account, in a letter to Captain Broockman, upon the civil usage I met with from the Governor and others of Council, and indeed generally from all as to mine own person, which I do not now retract, only I could wish they were more zealous. When I have complained of those former abuses, I have been told by several that persons here are a good deal more civilised than formerly they have been. If it be so, there is great cause to admire the patience and long suffering of God, but withal cause to fear that if those things be not reformed he will not always keep silence. The Governor I understand hath refused to listen to any that would prevent his firing of great guns, and then vollies of small shot by all the soldiers in garrison, at the consecration of a popish church within the walls; if he be therein acquitted by you I have no more to say, but pray that God himself would discountenance that idolatry and superstition so much countenanced by others, and prevent the hurt that may redound to the place and to your interests thereby.

One Mr. Mallory, formerly Surgeon's mate in the

President, and now Surgeon's mate in this place, and another, Barnes, who formerly went to sea as master of some small vessel, but having wasted the money entrusted to him, lives now idly and out of any employment. These two are constant companions with any of the young men in whatever debaucheries they were guilty of, and it gives ground for suspicion that they may be guilty of enticing them thereunto.

There are some other things that I would humbly have remonstrated to your worships, but because I intend, if it shall so please God, to see you with the next ships, at which time if it be acceptable it may more conveniently be done. I do therefore at present forbear, only praying that God would continue to prosper your undertaking, and enable you faithfully to design his glory therein, and lead you to the reasonable means that may conduce to his glory, in the encouragement of godliness, and restraint of sin in these places where your power reacheth. I am or desire to be

Right worshipfuls,
Your faithful servant,
According to my station,
PATRICK WARNER.

MADDRASS,
Jany. 31*st* 1676.

CHAPTER IV.

GOVERNORSHIP OF SIR WILLIAM LANGHORNE.

1670—1677.

Before proceeding with the domestic history of Madras, we will leave the little Fort and Factory of St. George for a brief interval, and fly twelve hundred miles to the northward to the great city of Delhi. In 1670, Aurungzebe, the Great Mogul, reigned over Hindustan. Two centuries have since passed away, but still we may take a glance at the imperial city, as it was in olden time. The mosques, domes, and minarets of Delhi, are gleaming in the morning sun. The wide straight streets are filled with pomp and grandeur. We see the airy houses, with courts and gardens, trees and fountains; and we may even peep into the interiors, and gaze on the hangings of rich embroidery, the carpets of thick silk radiant with flowers of every hue, the ceilings brilliant with gilding and colour, the quilted cushions of brocade interspersed with gold and silver. Without, the streets are enlivened with magnificent processions,—prancing horses, stately elephants, noble riders, dashing soldiery, and magnificent palanquins,—all glittering with variegated housings, and set off with sparkling jewels, and never ending displays of precious metal. A thousand instruments of music sound discordantly on the ear, whilst ever and anon the metallic strains are drowned in the booming of heavy artillery. Perchance it is the birth day of the Great Mogul; and the crowd of Omrahs, whose honours, riches, and very lives depend upon the breath of his favour, are crowding to the great hall, to lay their choicest gifts before the "peacock's throne" of gold and gems. Perchance it is some great pageant, some combat of elephants or show of wild animals, at which the Tartar Emperor, and all his lords, and all the endless beauties of the seraglio, are to sit in state and grace the scene. But soon the eye palls. The air is reeking with perfumes.

—"The gorgeous East with richest hand,
Showers on her kings barbaric pearls and gold;"

but all is barbarism still; and we gladly permit the pageant to disappear, like a dream that is dreamed.

We wonder whether the court of merry king Charles was more civilized than the contemporary court at Delhi; whether the gaming, the drinking, and the licentiousness at Whitehall were more refined than the elephant fights, the pageants, and the banquets of Aurungzebe; whether the Nell Gwyns, the Palmers, the Querouailes, or the Davis's were more polished and enlightened than yon array of dusky beauties; or whether the Rochesters, the Buckinghams, or the Killegrews were more high minded and chivalrous than the Omrahs of the Great Mogul. But all men know the history of the reign of king Charles; let us glance for a moment at the character of the reign of Aurungzebe.

At the period of our story the power of the

Great Moguls had reached its zenith. The intrigues, the hypocrisies, and above all the remorseless murders by which Aurungzebe had obtained possession of the empire, were whispered amongst the trembling Omrahs of the court; but still these nobles ostentatiously sounded the praises of their sovereign in every quarter where it might reach his ears. Unlike the feudal nobility of Europe, their rank and pay depended wholly upon the imperial will. No son could inherit their titles or their estates; for the title was but a mark of personal favour, created by a smile, and fading away before a frown; and when they died, all the riches they left behind were claimed by the Emperor as sole heir. Thus, whilst every man in Delhi,—from the highest Omrah admitted to the presence, down to the fruitsellers, the confectioners, the porters, or even the sweepers of streets,—were all alike conscious that the Great Mogul was deeply concerned in the death of his brethren, if not implicated in the death of his father; yet all were declaring him to be the greatest, the wisest, and most pious emperor that ever adorned the peacock's throne,—king of kings, and sovereign lord of all the nations of the earth. Every enthusiastic moullah applauded his religious bigotry; and every astrologer in the empire,—from those who sat on the cushions with princes, to those who arranged their books and instruments on rusty carpets in the crowded bazaars,—all declared that he would live for ever, and that his power would be for everlasting.

In 1670 nothing could be more imposing and resplendent than the outward aspects of the imperial rule. East and west the empire extended from Cashmere to Chittagong. In the south, the two great Mussulman Kingdoms of the Dekkan,—Bijapore, and Golconda,—were still in existence; but preparations were already being made to overwhelm them, and to extend the sway of the Mogul over Mussulman and Hindoo to the southern extremity of Comorin. A little cloud, as yet scarcely bigger than a man's hand, was appearing on the western ghats in the shape of the Mahrattas; and their daring leader Sevajee had already rendered himself formidable in the Dekkan against the decaying Mussulman powers—Bijapore and Golconda. As for the white faced traders at Surat or on the Hooghly, they were only known in the court of the Great Mogul by the presents they gave and the firmauns they desired; and it is more than doubtful whether the name of Fort St. George had at this time been ever heard at Agra or at Delhi.

The little district of Madraspatanam, could not, had its existence been known, have excited much interest at Delhi. It was separated from the dominions of the Great Mogul, by the large kingdom of Golconda or Hyderabad; a kingdom which had been recently compelled to pay tribute to Sevajee, but which yet apparently extended over Hyderabad and the Carnatic. For more than a century and a half, Golconda had been ruled by a dynasty of Mussulman kings, known as the Kuttub Shahs; but the commander in chief in the Carnatic appears to have been a man bearing the title of Neiknam Khan. To this commander-in-chief, the Presidency at Fort St. George gave the title of Nabob; and it was from him that they obtained the cowle for the district of Madraspatanam after the flight of the Rajah of Chandragheri.

In preceding chapters we sketched the history of Madras from the foundation of Fort St. George to the dispatch of Sir Edward Winter and Mr. Foxcroft to England about the year 1670. We also drew up from the records a picture of Fort St. George, as it existed in that early time. In our present issue we propose to resume the history from 1670 when Sir William Langhorne became Governor; and to pursue it until the year 1677, when he was recalled from the administration of affairs and Mr. Streynsham Master, was appointed in his room.

The history of the Governorship of Sir William Langhorne opens another curious series of events, which find little or no place in published history. As early as 1665, the Directors at home had heard that a French East India Company was being formed, and that a French expedition would shortly be sent out to compete with the Dutch and English in the profits of the Coromandel trade; and it was this circumstance which led to the enlarging and strengthening of the fortifications of Fort St. George, and to the great increase in the garrison. The intelligence proved to be perfectly correct. Colbert, the greatest financial and commercial statesman of the age, was Comptroller General under Louis XIV. His genius had been largely devoted to the extension of the foreign trade of the French nation; and at this period he was in the receipt of some very able communications from Bernier,—

the celebrated French physician who was then residing in the Court of Aurungzebe,—respecting the government of India, its pecuniary resources, its military strength, and its immense expenditure. Accordingly he had procured from his royal master an arrêt for the establishment of a French East India Company, under the patronage of Louis, and under the management of twelve Directors of which he himself was the President. Large subscriptions poured in, and an armament was prepared, but three or four years appeared to have elapsed before the expedition appeared in the Bay of Bengal.

Some of the causes of this delay may be gathered from the political history of the period. The foreign policy of the Stuarts generally, had lowered England to the condition of a third or fourth rate power; but the foreign policy of Charles II was a deep disgrace to the whole nation. Whilst Louis was rapidly becoming the arbiter of Europe and threatening to become master of Spain and the Netherlands, England had submitted to his insults, and madly engaged in a war with the Dutch. At last the old national spirit of Englishmen was aroused. Sir William Temple was sent to Holland, and concluded the celebrated Triple Alliance, by which the three Protestant powers,—Great Britain, Holland, and Sweden,—were united to resist the encroachments of France. For a moment Louis was checkmated. But the love of the Protestant religion found no echo in the breast of Charles. In heart he was a Roman Catholic; in heart he was anxious to fling off the constitutional restraint of a British Parliament. Louis plied him with money, and Charles accepted the bribes. Louis endeavoured still further to bind him through his pleasures. An artful beauty was sent over, named Louise Querouaille; and Charles eagerly caught at the bait, and not only made her his mistress, but created her Dutchess of Portsmouth. These intrigues resulted in a secret treaty in 1670, by which Charles sacrificed the Dutch and entered into an alliance, thus selling himself and his crown to the designs of Louis. In 1672, the deception came to light; and the people of England, who had hailed the Triple Alliance with enthusiasm, found that their treacherous sovereign had allied himself to Roman Catholic France, and that the two powers had combined to make war upon Protestant Holland.

The East India Directors at home, and their agencies abroad, hated alike the French and the Dutch as commercial rivals; but still they never forgot that the Dutch were Protestants like themselves; and their commercial hatred towards the French was aggravated by the old national hatred, which was at this time further stimulated to the highest pitch by the antagonism of religion. Both before and after this unnatural war against Holland, if a member of the Dutch Agency at Pulicat visited Fort St. George during a time of festivity, he was warmly entertained at the Factory; and a notice is still preserved in the records, that at one Christmas time, the third member of the council at Pulicat, having come that morning to Madraspatanam, with his wife and other friends, they were all invited and entertained at the general feast, which the Presideney was accustomed to give at that joyous season to all English men and English ladies of the town. In what light our French allies were regarded, we shall have occasion to tell hereafter. For the present we must go on with our narrative.

In 1671, the French armament of twelve ships under the command of Admiral De la Haye, appeared off the coast of Malabar, and commenced their trading by the old Dutch system of giving extravagant prices for Indian products, and selling European goods at rates ruinously low. The next year the same fleet appeared off Ceylon, and established themselves at Trincomalee, notwithstanding the opposition of the Dutch. From Trincomalee it sailed up the Coromandel Coast, an event which is remarkable as the first appearance of the French in the Bay of Bengal. In 1672, the French admiral unexpectedly landed three hundred men and some guns at St. Thomé. At that time St. Thomé, like all the neighbourhood, was in the occupation of the Mussulmans, inasmuch as it was included in the dominions of the Kuttub Shahs of Golconda. The Mussulman forces in the district assembled in considerable force, but their resistance was of no avail. In July the French took the place by storm, and all efforts made by the Golconda authorities to expel them were equally vain.

We need not dwell upon the excitement which this event created at Fort St George. Sir William Langhorne was in a position requiring the utmost prudence and foresight. The French were allies of King Charles, and as such he dared not attempt to expel them from St. Thomé. At the same time he felt that their vicinity to Madraspatanam was dangerous in the extreme. If the French alliance continued,—an alliance at that time so hateful to the bulk of the British nation,—the vicinity of the French to the English Factory, would embarrass the trade in every possible way. If on the other hand the alliance should be broken, and another war break out with France, then the conflict between Madraspatanam and St. Thomé would be a war to the knife, which could only be terminated by the destruction of one settlement or the other. In this dilemma Sir William Langhorne seems to have determined not to interfere. England was at war with the Dutch and in alliance with France. He would not assist the French because, irrespective of any national dislike, such a step would subject him to the fierce hostility of the Golconda authorities; at the same time, he could not assist the Dutch because Holland was regarded as an enemy, nor attack the French because France was regarded as an ally.

Meantime the Dutch fleet, under Rickloff Van Goens, the Dutch Governor General of India, was cruising along the coast of Coromandel. Van Goens laid seige to St. Thomé, and endeavoured to wrest it from the French, but this attempt failed, and throughout 1672 St. Thomé continued in the hands of the Gallic invaders; a circumstance which is said to have had a damaging effect upon the influence of the Dutch with the Golconda authorities. The Dutch were unfortunately more successful against the English, who ought to have been regarded as their friends. The Dutch fleet of fourteen vessels encountered the English Company's homeward fleet of ten ships on its passage from Bengal. A running engagement took place on the 22nd August 1673, of which no details appear to have been preserved, but in which one ship was sunk by the enemy and two fell into his hands. The remainder escaped to Madras, and after being repaired, were enabled to proceed on their way to Europe.

The position of Sir William Langhorne all this time was difficult in the extreme. The French at St. Thomé were exasperated with him for not assisting them against the Dutch. They also tried to borrow money of him, which being civilly refused, rendered them more inveterate than ever. At the same time he found that the officers of the Mussulman army,—who, like the Dutch, were vainly endeavouring to reduce St. Thomé,—were equally enraged at his declining to help them to drive out the French; and it was determined in consultation to send presents of scarlet broad cloth, looking glasses, sandals, and other similar articles, at a cost of some three hundred and sixty Pagodas in order to appease the Commanders, Havildars, and Chief Brahmins in the Mussulman camp, and put an end to the lying complaints which were said to have been reported to His Excellency the Nabob, or, as we should call him, the Commander-in-Chief of the army of Golconda. It may here be remarked that the General of the Mussulman force encamped against the French, was a certain Bobba Sahib; and that the above mentioned presents failed to remove his hatred to the English

Agency at Fort St. George. In after years Bobba Sahib had cause to regret this exhibition of hostility, as will be seen by the following extract from the consultations of the Agency, dated 6th May, 1678 :—" Bobba Sahib, formerly general of the king of Golconda's force against the French at St. Thomé, and in those days a bitter enemy to the English, but now in disgrace and debt, has been some days here trying all ways to borrow money, and to have an interview with the Governor, which is refused him by reason of his former unkindnesses when he was in power, and he in despair quits the place for Pullimalee, intending to go to his own country.

But to return to our story. A year and a half passed away, and the French still remained in possession of St. Thomé. Within that time they had established a camp at Triplicane, and fortified it far more strongly than the English were fortified at Fort St. George. Sir William Langhorne and his Council were even contemplating the advisability of abandoning Madraspatanam altogether; but afterwards decided on more energetic measures. At a consultation held on the 2nd February 1674, it was recorded that the interests of the Honorable Company, as well as the lives of the members of the Presidency, were staked upon the issue of the seige. That their enemies at sea and land were within musket shot; that their walls were slight and tottering; that they were pestered with the great native town close to them; and that the Dutch Governor General was daily expected with a large fleet. Under these circumstances they resolved, after mature consideration, to enlarge and strengthen their fortifications as much as possible; but their efforts in this direction do not seem to have much increased their strength, or to have rendered them more independent of the belligerent powers. Four Frenchmen from Java were staying in Fort St. George; and in May, we find the Dutch and Mussulmans peremptorily requiring their removal. For a long time Sir William Langhorne refused to comply, as the Frenchmen were allies; but at last the Mussulman army fairly laid seige to Fort St. George, and would hear of no further delay. The Frenchmen, on their part, refused to leave the place unless they were permitted to go to St. Thomé, and there the Dutch and Mussulmans would not allow them to proceed. At last, the President in Council resolved to send them under passports and an escort to Bijapore; and there they seem to have gone, loudly protesting however against the proceeding, inasmuch as they were subjects of the king of France, a friend and ally of the crown of England.

For two years the French thus held possession of St. Thomé. At length, on the 26th August 1774, they surrendered to the Dutch, on the condition that the garrison should be transported to Europe. The Dutch in their turn agreed to cede St. Thomé to the Nabob; and the President and Council at Fort St. George hoped that the place would be demolished altogether, so that it might never again be occupied by an European power. Fortunately for the Agency, at that moment the news arrived from Europe, that in the preceding January peace had been concluded between England and Holland. But for that happy peace, the Dutch would have followed up the capture of St. Thomé, with the seige of Fort St. George; and there can be but little doubt but that the fall of the place would have followed, for the fortifications were still but weak, and there were only two hundred and fifty men in garrison.

Such was the famous French occupation of St. Thomé from July 1672 to August 1674; an event which for many a long year afterwards was a household tale in the little settlement, but which has now faded away from the memory of men. The incidents connected with it, which are recorded in the consultations, are but few in number. The garrison was often kept in a state of alarm by the Dutch and Mussulmans. One night the Captain of the auxiliary forces, whilst on guard, was shot dead by the sentinel at the Choultry gate, who seems to have suspected him of being an enemy. At intervals however, the trade of the Agency went on after a fashion, through a merchant named Cassa Verona, who figures largely in the early annals. This Cassa Verona seems to have taken off large quantities of the goods from Europe; to have supplied such Native goods as were required by the Agency for shipment to England; to have distributed such presents as were sent by the Agency to the Mussulman Chiefs; and to have assisted in the transmission of money from one station to another. The Directors at home appear to have been very suspicious of Cassa Verona; and believed, not without show of reason, that he was the channel through which the members of the Agency carried on their private trade, and other doubtful but very profitable undertakings. In a general letter to the Presidency, they expressed their decided objection to the trade being limited to one firm; and they requested that all merchants might be encouraged to supply goods, and that thus a healthy competition might be introduced into the Native markets. This laudable attempt to plant free trade in India, whilst violently fighting for their monopoly at home, does not seem to have met with the success which it deserved. Cassa Verona continued to be the confidential adviser of the members of the Agency for many a year afterwards; ostensibly on the plea that by so doing the Company was preserved from bad debts, but in reality on private grounds which we shall presently have occasion to disclose.

The subserviency of the merchants at Fort St. George to the chief officers of state in the Court at Golconda or Hyderabad, was very striking throughout the whole of the present period. They likened these ministers of state to the Lieutenant General, the Lord Chancellor, and the Comptroller General of European Courts; and treated them with far more respect than they would have treated the English officers of state at home. The Fort of St. George and Town of Madraspatanam had been held by a cowle, originally granted by Neiknam Khan, who, as we have already stated, is styled Nabob of Golconda, but who in all probability was Commander-in-Chief of the army of the Carnatic.* By this cowle it was stipulated that the Agency at Fort St. George, on paying 1200 pagodas per annum rent, was to hold the Fort and Town free of any other imposition whatever. In 1672 Neiknam Khan died and his successor Mirza Ibrahim Khan is said to have confirmed the firmaun of his predecessor. Accordingly the usual presents were made to Mirza Ibrahim Khan; and subsequently, during the French occupation of St. Thomé, the favour of the Court was still further sought by means of presents to the principal officers of state. Amongst the latter is specially mentioned "Maddana the great Bramany who is the great Mogumdar and the chiefest person in power next to the king himself;" an individual whom we have not the slightest hesitation in identifying with Madna Pant, who conducted the government and financies of Abul Hassan, king of Golconda, and who pos-

---

* No traces of this Neiknam Khan can be discovered in the history of Golconda; and indeed the name is an ordinary title, and another Neiknam Khan is mentioned by Bernier as an Omrah residing in the Court of Shah Jehan. His successor, whose name is variously spelt in the records as Moussa Khan and Mirza Ibrahim Khan, and who is also styled Nabob, is to be identified with the Ibrahim Khan, who, according to Elphinstone, was the commander-in-chief of the forces of Abul Hassan, the last king of Golconda. As Neiknam Khan is stated in the rocords to be the predecessor of Ibrahim Khan, we have assumed that, as like him he is called "Nabob," so like him he was Commander-in-Chief· No English history of the period appears to be in existence sufficiently full to clear up the matter.

sessed the full confidence of his royal master, but who was subsequently murdered during a tumult in the city. The Naiks in the immediate neighbourhood of Madraspatanam were also conciliated in a similar manner. In 1674, shortly before the retirement of the French, the Agency resolved to make a present to the Naik of Chingleput and the Naik of Palavarum, who were said to be old friends of the Company, and who were about to go to Golconda to celebrate the marriage of the first Naik with the daughter of the king's "Mufti," who was reported to have great influence with his Highness the king. On that occasion the Agency received in return more valuable presents than those they had given, so that the Company were gainers by the transaction; and accordingly, as it is naively recorded in the consultations, it was determined that the difference should be made up on some future occasion.

Another story, dug out of the records of the same year, is worth relating, as fully illustrating, not only the relation of the Agency at Fort St. George to the Court of Golconda, but the necessity which existed for those constant presents to the officers of the state and to the Naiks in the neighbourhood. Lingapa, the Naik of the Poonamalee district, appears to have been remarkably fond of peiscush, and very angry when he could not get it. His course of proceeding appears to have been to procure firmauns from His Highness, the king of Golconda, and then to extort presents in return for the firmauns. By these means he succeeded in obtaining peiscush from the Dutch at Pulicat, and accordingly tried it on with the English at Fort St. George. Sir William Langhorne however resisted the demand. By the cowle and firmaun already obtained from Neiknam Khan, the Company was exempted from transacting any business excepting with the Divan; and accordingly the Agency sent Cassa Verona to Poonamalee to inform Lingapa, that they declined to take the firmaun and refused to pay the peiscush. Lingapa however appears to have had his revenge. Having paid a visit to the court at Golconda, he had a long conversation with the Chief Brahmin concerning the English and their town; the substance of which subsequently reached the ears of the English Agency through Cassa Verona, and was placed upon record. It appears to have been as follows. Lingapa informed the Chief Brahmin, that when he first entered upon the government of the Poonamalee district, he paid a visit to the Dutch at Pulicat, and was warmly welcomed and presented with a horse and other gifts; and that he then paid a visit to the Dutch at Sadraspatam, who received him with the same kindness, and gave him a gold chain, with many other presents. Here Lingapa paused. The Chief Brahmin took up the conversation by asking him, what the English at Chinnapatanam had given him on the same occasion. Then Lingapa grew eloquent and pathetic. He had, he said, carried a tasheriff to the English, and they had refused to take it; and they had further showed their contempt for him by neglecting to invite him to come to their town. That

Cassa Verona had experienced similar unkindness from the English, and had accordingly put a stop to a good part of his trade with them, and had come to him, Lingapa, and had spoken good words, and given him a gold chain valued at four hundred Pagodas. That he, Lingapa, having no encouragement to go to the English, had sent them a firmaun by his own people, which he had otherwise intended to have carried himself; and in return the English had only given his people some broadcloth and looking glasses, and nothing more.

The Chief Brahmin seems to have been much impressed by Lingapa's story. He remarked that the English were a scornful people, and that they had the government of a town which produced great sums of money. In former times, he said, Neiknam Khan had unadvisedly and foolishly let them have a town, which yielded several thousand Pagodas per annum, for the small rent of twelve hundred Pagodas per annum; and he even wondered that Lingapa, as Naik of Poonamalee, should suffer the English to retain the town on that score, and not keep an Havildar there. Lingapa replied that the English would not regard his authority; and that when he sent any of the Divan's corn to Chinnapatanam they actually made it pay custom. The Chief Brahmin then said that the cowle which had been given by Neiknam Khan had certainly been confirmed by the late king, Abdalla Kuttub Shah; but now that both were dead, the cowle must be considered to have died with them; and that on the next day he would go to the reigning king Abul Hassan, and prevail upon him to send a Persian to be set over Chinnapatanam.

The Chief Brahmin was as good as his word; and thus by neglecting to conciliate the new Naik of Poonamalee with invitations and presents, the Agency at Fort St. George imperilled the existence of their settlement. The Chief Brahmin laid all the circumstances before the king Abul Hassan; and the king, as is usual in such cases, said that he would think about it. But other great persons of the court, who were present at the time, took upon themselves to remark that since St. Thomé was bereft of its inhabitants, Chinnapatanam had been very much enlarged both in population and trade, so that it had become a far more important place than even Pulicat, and that His Highness would do well to take some course respecting it. The subsequent advance of the Mahrattas appears to have distracted the attention of the Court of Golconda from the little district of Madraspatanam; but still many evil consequences fell upon the Agency. The trade in corn and paddy was forbidden. A request was made by the king of Golconda for a thousand yards of broad cloth; and the Agency felt obliged to send him six hundred yards, lest the trade in calicoes should be forbidden in like manner. Again, Mirza Ibrahim requested payment of the rent of the town six months in advance; and the Agency, considering such requests as equivalent to commands, sent the money to Golconda at once. Nor was this the worst. The power of Lingapa increased so greatly throughout the country from Armaghaum to Bijapore, that the Agency felt themselves constrained to raise an additional force of a hundred soldiers and a hundred and fifty peons, and to collect provisions, and to order a thousand Pagodas worth of paddy, corn, and fuel from Masulipatam. Subsequently, by means of presents Lingapa became somewhat mollified; but we shall have occasion to tell other stories of this gentleman in a future chapter.

Such were some of the principal events which belong to the history of the Madras Presidency during the Government of Sir William Langhorne, which lasted from about 1670 to the end of 1677. Concerning the character of Sir William Langhorne himself we can say but little. He seems to have been a shrewd business like man, and far more tolerant of the religious opinions of others, than could have been expected in that intolerant age. He it was that fired a salute on the consecration of a Roman Catholic church within the walls; a piece of courtesy which very much offended, the Protestant Chaplain, Patrick Warner, and also brought down upon his head a severe rebuke from the Directors. "We note," said they in a General Letter of this period, "what, you say of firing your guns upon the naming of a church by the papists; we cannot approve thereof, and desire to give as little countenance and encouragement to that religion, as they do to ours; and we would have you discountenance, and discourage all of our nation that any ways incline to that profession."

Sir William Langhorne fell a victim to those charges of private trade, which seem to have been brought against almost every servant of the Company at every one of the Indian stations. The sums acquired by these, and other doubtful transactions, were indisputably large. When considerable and certain profits were to be made, they preferred trading on their account, rather than on the account of the Company. Then again, the European goods of the Company were sold to merchants like Cassa Verona at low prices; and Indian goods were purchased from those merchants on behalf of the Company at high prices; and of course for such favours large presents were made to the several members of council. During the governorship of Sir Edward Winter, Cassa Verona and his partner were said to have thus defrauded the Company to an extent of something like 200,000 Pagodas; and with such small salaries as were paid by the Directors, there can be no doubt but that these underhand dealings were carried on to a degree which we must leave to the imagination of the reader.

In 1676 the Directors sent out a Major Puckle to inquire into existing abuses; just as some six or seven years previously they had sent out Sir William Langhorne to inquire into the quarrel which had broken out between Sir Edward Winter and Mr. Foxcroft. Sir William Langhorne was charged with receiving annually the sum of 20,000 Pagodas from Cassa Verona, in consideration of undue advantages said to have been afforded to the latter in reference to the Company's trade. The accusation was indignantly denied by both parties; but its truth or falsity must be left to the judgment of our readers. If true, it must be confessed that the sum in question, amounting to something like £7000 sterling per annum, must have made a pretty addition to the £300 per annum allowed to the President by the honorable Company. At any rate the charge was believed by the Directors; and Sir William Langhorne was recalled, and Mr. Streynsham Masters reigned in his stead.

There is one other incident belonging to the administration of Sir William Langhorne, which may be narrated here. During the French occupation of St. Thomé, and whilst Dutch and Mussulmans were exciting general apprehension by their vicinity to the Fort, it became necessary to clear away a number of houses which clogged up the opening to a part of the fortifications called Caldera point, upon which at that moment an attack was expected from the Dutch. Amongst these houses was one which had been built at the very foundation of Madras; and accordingly the owner petitioned for compensation, on the ground that his ancestors had been invited to settle there by Mr. Francis Day, the first Agent; and that they could not possibly have known that the house they were building would ever prove offensive to the garrison. The petition is sufficiently quaint and curious to warrant our inserting it at length; though we fear it will somewhat confuse and weary the reader, from the fact that it does not contain a single full stop, until the petitioner fairly pulls up at the last word.

Petition of Mr. Thos. Clarke.

To ye Hon'ble Sir Wm. Langhorn, Barronett, Agent and Governour in Councell, for Affairs of ye Hon'ble English East India Company in Fort St. George.

The humble Petition of Thos. Clarke,

SHEWETH,—That since ye late unhappy warr with ye arrivall of ye French to St. Thomè, occasioned both ye Dutch our enemies and Mores (not over-friendly, but for their own ends) to settle so near this place, thereby filling ye whole Town with reasonable apprehensions of danger, if not prevented by your wisdomes, and seeing your Wordship so well applyed ye remedy, by clearing ye passage surrounding ye Caldera point, clogged up with ye too neare approach of houses, among which was one belonging to your Petitioner, built thirty-foure yeares since, when either bulwarks nor scarce a house of noate appeared, becoming ye first Inhabitant through ye invitation of ye then Agent, who removed about that time from Armogon, do presume to hope being strongly led thereto by a promise from your Worship that I should be ye first person satisfied, since I have so sedulously and willingly obeyed your Worship's command in putting it downe without consulting what a great loss and inconvenience I must unavoidably suffer by such a deprivation, being reduced to very slender accommodation, since I need not mention to your Worship how impossible it was for my ancestors to imagine when first 'twas built, that it could be any waies offensive to ye Garrison, having allready declared no workes were then begun nor that they had the Agent's permission, he having invited my said ancestors to ye place, but leave all to your wise consideration, which, as I with confidence trust, will be sensible of my great suffering; so shall patiently wayt the effects of your goodness and justice, which I doubt not but will oblige your petitioner ever to pray for your prosperity, and be ever ready to express himself.

Hon'ble Sir, &c., Councell,
Your most obliged and humble servant.

This petition was apparently forwarded about September 1675, as on the 28th of that month, it was resolved in council to order the Justices of the Choultry to levy from the inhabitants of Madraspatanam,– or rather the inhabitants of Black town, and other localities outside the wall of Fort St. George,—the sum of one hundred Pagodas towards the compensation of Mr. Clarke; and a further sum of a hundred and thirty Pagodas in return for a payment made by Cassa Verona in behalf of the Agency, for the removal of the sand from the sea side of the Fort. The levy scarcely amounted to two fanams per house, and yet it was found impossible to raise it. All the inhabitants of the place, and even all the merchants of the Agency excepting Cassa Verona, shut up all their shops and assembled in the pagoda; and at the same time they sent instructions to their castes up country to stop all supplies of provisions coming to Madraspatanam. They were even prepared to leave the place rather than submit to the levy; not, it is said, because they grudged payment of the money, but because they dreaded the precedent. Under such circumstances the Agency were compelled to abandon the proposed assessment.

In future issues we shall have frequent occasion to refer to the steps taken at various times to raise similar assessments from the inhabitants of this district, and which subsequently led to the institution of a Mayor and Corporation. But the above attempt is worthy of record as the first that was made in this Presidency, and with it we close our history of the Governorship of the Honorable Sir William Langhorne in 1677, being the seventeenth year of the actual reign of King Charles, the second of that name.

CHAPTER V.

GOVERNORSHIP OF MR. STREYNSHAM MASTER.

1677—1681.

The Governorship of Sir William Langhorne had been marked by the French occupation of St. Thomé. The Governorship of his successor, Mr. Streynsham Master, is distinguished by events of still greater significance, amongst which may be especially mentioned the first appearance in Southern India, of Sevajee, the great Mahratta. Before therefore proceeding with our history of Madras, it may be as well to glance at the strange circumstances and remarkable adventures, which are connected with the early life of the founder of the Mahratta empire.

Few events in Indian history are more deeply interesting than the rise of the Mahrattas. These short and sturdy mountaineers occupied the northern part of the chain of Ghats, which lines the western coast from Surat to Canara; and their appearance on the stage of history, about the commencement of the seventeenth century, is as refreshing as iced water. Wearied with the intrigues, the sensualities, and the barbaric splendour of Delhi, it is truly delightful to enter upon the stories of hairbreadth escapes and adventurous deeds, which enliven the annals of the Mahrattas.

The name of this famous people scarcely appears in the previous history of India. They first emerge into notice in connexion with the Mussulman kingdom of Ahmednuggur, which lay between the Ghats and the kingdom of Golconda. There many of the Mahratta chiefs distinguished themselves in the wars between the Nizam Shahs who reigned at Ahmednuggur, and the Great Mogul who reigned at Delhi. Amongst others was Mallojee, a member of the family of Bhonslay; a family which was then merely respectable, but which afterwards attained the highest eminence. This Mallojee was the grandfather of that great Mahratta chieftain, who, under the name of Sevajee, became terrible, not only to the Mussulman kings of the Dekkan, but even to the Great Mogul.

The story of the rise of the Bhonslay family is so romantic, that we shall inflict it upon our readers. Mallojee's patron was Jadow Row, a commander of 10,000 men in the army of Ahmednuggur. One day a festival was celebrated at the house of Jadow Row; and Mallojee attended with his little boy Shahjee, who was then only five years old. Presently the little boy began to play with the little daughter of Jadow Row, who was only three years old. Jadow, looking on, said that they were a fine pair, and ought to be man and wife. To his great surprise Mallojee instantly started up, and called on the company to witness that the daughter of Jadow had been contracted to his son. Jadow was thunderstruck at what he believed to be the presumption of his inferior, and a rupture ensued between the two. But meantime Mallojee was on the road to fortune; and he was subsequently raised to the command of 5,000 horse, with the title of Mallojee Raja Bhonslay. The objection on the score of rank was thus removed. Shahjee was actually married to the daughter of Jadow, and became the father of Sevajee, the founder of the Mahratta empire.

Sevajee was born in 1627. He was brought up at Poona, where his father possessed a jaghire; and there he received a regular Mahratta education. Like William of Deloraine, he never could write his name; but he became a good archer and marksman, and could use the sword and spear right well. Above all he was an admirable horseman. His early associates were the cavalry soldiers under his father's command, and not unfrequently, the plundering highlanders of the neighbouring Ghats. But still his intellectual culture was not wholly neglected. He delighted in the fabulous stories told in the Maha-Bharata and Ramayana; and especially in those tales of the gods, intermixed with music and song, which are known as Kuthas. He thus imbibed an early love of adventure. At the age of sixteen his hunting excursions had familiarized him with every path and defile throughout the Ghats; and he was even suspected of sharing in several extensive gang robberies committed in the Concan. Amongst his own countrymen, however, and especially amongst the wild inhabitants to the west of Poona, he was extremely popular; and he had already been imbued with a rooted hatred to the Mussulmans, and indulged in the idea of rendering himself an independent prince in the country.

Meantime the circumstances of the family had undergone a great change. The kingdom of Ahmednuggur had been extinguished by the Great Mogul, and Shahjee, the father of Sevajee, had entered the service of the king of Bijapore. The attention of the government at Bijapore was soon attracted by the proceedings of the young Mahratta hero. At the age of nineteen, Sevajee took possession of a hill fort, and then sent Vakeels to the court of Bijapore to represent the advantages which would result from such an operation. Subsequently, he was fortunate enough to discover a large quantity of gold in the fort, and accordingly set to work to build another. The suspicions of the court were aroused, and letters were sent to Shahjee, who was in the Carnatic, calling his attention to the conduct of his son. Meantime, however, Sevajee had usurped his father's jaghire, and evaded paying up any revenue. Shortly after this, partly by bribery and partly by force, he took possession of other forts; and at length, at the age of twenty-one, he fairly revolted against the government of Bijapore. He seized a convoy of royal treasure, and attacked the Mussulman Governor of the northern Concan; and not only did he take the latter prisoner, but he also took possession of the country.

The court of Bijapore suspected Shahjee of being implicated in the proceedings of his son, and accordingly imprisoned him as a hostage for four years. Meantime Sevajee continued to maintain his independence, and on the release of his father recommenced his aggressions. He even ventured to plunder some provinces belonging to the Great Mogul; but afterwards found it necessary to tender his submission, and profess his devotion to Aurungzebe.

We cannot follow the career of Sevajee in detail. In 1659, when about thirty-two years of age, he renewed his attacks upon Bijapore. A general was sent against him with a large army, but Sevajee pretended submission and prayed for a personal interview. The request was granted. The Mussulman general, proud of his success, advanced with only a single attendant. Sevajee was seen approaching with a timid and hesitating air, and apparently unarmed; but under his cotton tunic he wore a shirt of chain armour, and moreover had provided himself with a concealed dagger, and a terrible weapon known as "tiger's claws." This last weapon consists of sharp hooks of steel, which are fastened on the fingers, and lie concealed in the closed hand; but by opening the hand, the steel hooks spread out like claws, and enable the wearer to inflict a treacherous tiger-like blow, too horrible to be imagined. The wily Mahratta couched in obeisance before the Mussulman; and then struck him down with his claws, and despatched him with the dagger. Meantime the Mussulman army had been secretly surrounded by the Mahrattas; and at a given signal the whole were suddenly attacked and vast numbers were slaughtered. Subsequently, the king of Bijapore marched against Sevajee in person. Hostilities lasted for two years, but at last terminated in a peace, which left Sevajee in possession of his territories, and of an army of 7000 cavalry and 50,000 infantry.

An adventure which occurred about this time is still a theme of exultation to the Mahratta. Some of Sevajee's horse had been again ravaging the Mogul territory; and a Mogul general, named Shaista Khan, was sent against him. Shaista Khan advanced to Poona, and Sevajee felt himself compelled to retire to Singhar, a hill fort about twelve miles distant. At Poona, Shaista Khan had taken every precaution to prevent the admission of Mahrattas into the town, either individually or in large bodies. Singularly enough he occupied the very house in which Sevajee had passed his boyhood; and the latter determined at all hazards to revenge himself on the intruder. One evening after sun set, he proceeded to Poona with twenty-five men. He posted small bodies of infantry at intervals along the road, but only approached the town with the twenty-five. An arrangement had been previously made with the leader of a marriage procession, that Sevajee and his companions should join the wedding party. This arrangement was now carried out. Sevajee and his companions joined the noisy crowd, and paraded the town. When all was quiet, he proceeded straight to his old house, and suddenly gained admission through a back window. The women raised an alarm, but only just in time. Shaista Khan rushed to his own window, and lowered himself into the court; but in the very act of doing so, he received a blow which cut off two of his fingers. His son and most of his attendants were killed on the spot. Sevajee retreated before the town was alarmed, and as he retired was joined by the parties posted along the road. Presently the whole body lit their torches, and the Mogul forces at Poona had the satisfaction of seeing their enemy ascend the hill fort at Singhar amidst a triumphant blaze of illuminations.

It was shortly after this event, namely, in the year 1664, that Sevajee first came into contact with the English at Surat. He had proceeded to the northward under the pretence of a religious pilgrimage; but had suddenly turned off with four thousand horse, and fallen upon the rich and defenceless city of Surat. The Native Governor of the place at once shut himself up in his castle. Most of the inhabitants took to the boats, or fled away up country. The English Factory contained property valued at eighty thousand pounds; but the Factors were brave men, and made such an obstinate resistance, that they not only saved their own property, but much that belonged to the Natives. Sevajee however plundered the town for six days, and finally carried off an immense booty.

The Great Mogul now sent a large army against Sevajee, and the latter again tendered his submission, and assisted the Moguls in their war against Bijapore. He even received a letter of compliments and thanks from Aurungzebe, and was invited to Delhi; but there the narrow minded bigotry of Aurungzebe was displayed in such an offensive manner, that Sevajee was mortally offended. Subsequently an apparent reconciliation was effected, and Sevajee was acknowledged as an independent Rajah. His successes at this time were almost dazzling. He compelled the two kingdoms of the Dekkan,—Bijapore and Golconda,—to pay him a yearly tribute. He reduced his military and civil government to a regular system; and he managed to identify his own cause, with the cause of the national religion of the Hindoos as opposed to the bigoted measures of Aurungzebe.*

In 1670 Sevajee again plundered Surat, an event which is worthy of special mention, inasmuch as the English Factory was saved by the gallantry of Mr. Streynsham Master, at that time member of council at Surat, but afterwards Governor of Fort St. George. Meantime, the attention of Aurungzebe was drawn away from the Dekkan, by revolts in his more immediate neighbourhood. Sevajee rapidly increased in power and reputation; and even proposed to extend his conquests to the south of India. Towards the close of Sir William Langhorne's government, he marched for Hyderabad with 40,000 infantry and 30,000 horse, and made a definite treaty with Abul Hassan, king of Golconda. Shortly afterwards he passed close to Madras, on his way to the capture of Gingee and Vellore; but after conquering a large territory in Mysore, he was recalled by the intelligence that Golconda had been invaded by the Moguls.

We now return to the history of the Madras Presidency. Mr. Streynsham Master seems to have been in one way a different character from his im-

* The authorities for all facts obtained from published histories, independent of the public records, will be acknowledged at the conclusion of the present work.

mediate predecessors. He had not been sent direct from home to take up the government of Fort St. George, but he had already enjoyed considerable experience in the Company's trade. Originally he appears to have belonged to the Surat establishment, and there he was appointed acting President during the absence of President Aungier on a visit to the new colony at Bombay. Subsequently, after the return of Aungier, Mr. Master distinguished himself, as we have already indicated, by a gallant defence of the Company's house at Surat. About this time the Directors at home were much harassed by continual disputes regarding the succession to the Governorship of their Agencies in India. Accordingly, two years before the recall of Sir William Langhorne, Mr. Streynsham Master was appointed to succeed him, in the event of any contingency taking place, which would deprive the Agency of the services of Langhorne. In order to qualify Mr. Master for this high rank, he was sent first, to act as Agent at Masulipatam; then he was ordered to proceed to Bengal, and introduce a new system of administration in the Factories on the Hooghly; and lastly, he was directed to act as second member of council at Fort St. George, until the term of Sir William Langhorne's government should expire.

It is difficult to ascertain the exact month when Mr. Streynsham Master became Governor. We only know that it occurred in 1677. His administration lasted for only four years. Like his predecessor, he soon lost the confidence of the directors; but the causes of his recal will be sufficiently manifest from the history of his Government. With the exception of the approach of Sevajee and his quarrel with Lingapa, the events of his Government are chiefly of a domestic character. It is evident from the records that the little Agency was somewhat alarmed at the tidings which reached it from time to time of the doings of Sevajee; and its alarm was in no way lessened by the stories, which Mr. Master could himself tell, of the previous plunder of Surat. On 9th May 1677 we find recorded a resolution to prepare for defence in consequence of the approach of Sevajee. Five days afterwards a messenger was received from Sevajee, and it would seem that Mr. Master's experience had enabled him to propitiate the great Mahratta. But we extract the official narrative from the consultation:—

"14th May 1677. Having this day received a message and a letter from Sevajee Rajah by a Brahmin and two others of his people, requesting some cordial stones and counter poisons, we resolved to send him some, together with a civil letter, by a messenger of our own, as a small present, together with some such fruit as these gardens afford, and to bestow upon his Brahmin three yards of broad cloth and some sandalwood, not thinking it good to require the money for so small trifles, although offered in his letter; considering how great a person he is, and how much his friendship does already and may import the Honorable Company as he grows more and more powerful and obvious to them." The value of the present thus sent to Sevajee is carefully stated in detail; from which it appears that the cost of the whole was something like sixty pagodas.

A few days afterwards Sevajee sent for more cordials and medicines, and again the orders of this dangerous Mofussil customer were promptly attended to; the bill being ignored a second time, in a fashion which is but rarely followed by the modern mercantile community of this Presidency. Subsequently, Sevajee asked for some English engineers; but that application was politely declined. In August 1678, news reached the Agency from Conjeveram, forty miles from Madras, to the effect that some fifteen hundred of Sevajee's horse were at that place under the command of his brother, and that the latter intended to advance and take the Fort at Poonamallee. Sevajee, as it was there recorded, was in full possession of all the countries round the strong forts of Gingee and Vellore, worth yearly about eleven lakhs of pagodas, or about half a million sterling. Subsequently the Brahmin engaged to look after the interests of the Agency at Golconda, sent the comfortable intelligence to Fort St. George that Sevajee had given orders for the plunder of Sadraspatanam, Madraspatanam, and Pulicat. Fortunately, the return of Sevajee to his own territories dissipated most of these fears; and the Agency was gladdened by the intelligence that the Mahrattas had retired after having had some terrible engagements with the Naik of Mysore. The following extract entered in the Consultation book in January 1679, respecting the army of Mysore, will be sufficient to indicate the savage character of Native warfare :—

"Their custom is not to kill, but to cut off the noses with the upper lips of their enemies; for which they carry an iron instrument with which they do it very dexterously, and carry away all the noses and lips they despoyle their enemys of, for which they are rewarded by the Naik of Mysore according to the number, and the reward is the greater, if the beard appear upon the upper lip. This way of warfare is very terrible to all that those people engage with, so that none care to meddle with them; they being also a resolute people, and have destroyed many that have attempted them, for though they kill them not outright, yet they dye by lingering deaths, if they make not themselves away sooner, as for the most part they do that are so wounded, the shame and dishonor of it being esteemed greater than the pain and difficulty of subsisting."

The principal domestic events in the administration of Mr. Master appear to be the erection of a high Court of judicature, the building of St. Mary's church in the Fort, the introduction of stringent laws respecting the Roman Catholics, and the extraordinary disasters which befel the Agency in consequence of the continued intrigues of Lingapa. The history of these curious circumstances we shall now proceed to record in detail.

The new Court of judicature originated in March 1678. The inhabitants of Madraspatanam had greatly increased, and many complaints had been made of the want of an administration in justice in cases which could not be decided by the Justices of the Choultry. Accordingly the Agent and

Council resolved that, under the royal charter, they had power to judge all persons living under them, in all cases, whether criminal or civil, according to the English laws, and to execute judgment accordingly; and therefore it was determined that the Governor and Council should sit in the Chapel in the Fort on every Wednesday and Saturday, to hear and judge all causes; and that the Justices of the Choultry, and constables under them, should execute all orders of the Court, such as writs, summonses for Jurymen, executions after judgment, and apprehensions of criminals. This high court of judicature was by no means intended to supersede the court of the Justices of the Choultry. All small misdemeanors, breaches of the peace, actions for debt not exceeding fifty pagodas, were still to be decided by these Justices.

The establishment of this Court had indeed become a great public necessity. In cases of murder or manslaughter, the delinquent was frequently kept in prison for a year or more, and then sent home to be tried by the English courts. Only two or three months previously, two soldiers had been sent home after long confinement, to be tried for a crime committed during the administration of Sir William Langhorne. The case is sufficiently interesting to be narrated at length, and we accordingly print the official memorandum:—

"Memorandum, that in or about three of the clock in the afternoon, one Thomas Savage, soldier of Fort St. George, being in drink, did abuse with bad words his Officer, by name John Waterhouse, Serjeant, who at that time had the command of the

Choultry Guard, under his Ensign John Trimbrell, who was then absent. Upon being thus abused the said Serjeant Waterhouse commanded the Corporal, Edward Short, to tie Savage down upon his cot; but Savage continuing to be abusive, the Serjeant commanded the said Corporal to bind him neck and heels, the which was forthwith performed, but it seems that the Corporal not doing it as he ought, the prisoner Thomas Savage complained, saying 'do not hang me.' The Corporal replied, 'No Thomas, I won't hang thee, but I will tie thee fast.' So after he had been bound the time of three or four inches of match were burnt out, which was by command of the Serjeant lighted, he was unbound, and being loosed, was found dead, and not seen to stir. Whereupon, notice being brought to the Governor Sir William Langhorne, Baronet, by Captain Lieutenant James Bett, the Governor ordered the said Lieutenant Bett to go to Timothy Wilkes one of the Justices of the Town, to desire him to send some sufficient gentlemen of the English nation, to go along with him, the said Wilkes, and to see the dead body, and then to make inquiry how his death happened, before its burial, which accordingly was immediately performed." As we have already mentioned, the Serjeant and Corporal were sent to England for trial during the Government of Mr. Streynsham Master.

Within a few days of the establishment of the new Court of judicature, the first foundations were laid of St. Mary's Church in the Fort, one of the most interesting structures which are still existing in this Presidency. The ground was first broken up on Lady day, in the year 1678; and in consequence of this circumstance it was resolved to give to the Church the name of St. Mary. On the following Easter Monday, the laying of the foundations of the new Church was fairly commenced. The expenses of the building were to be entirely defrayed by the voluntary subscriptions of the English in those parts. According to the records it was to be eighty feet long, and fifty-six feet broad, within the walls; and it was to be built with three aisles, arched with brick and stone. The building of the church was completed in two years and a half from the date of laying the foundations; and we extract the following account of the consecration from the consultations, in which however many of our readers will perceive with regret that the worthy Chaplain, Patrick Warner, had really returned to Europe, and that his pulpit was occupied by a successor, the Rev. Richard Portman:—

"Thursday, 28th October, 1680. The new Church was dedicated by virtue of commissions directed to the Government, and to Mr. Richard Portman the minister, from his Lordship the Bishop of London. The solemnity was performed in very good order, and concluded with vollies of small shot fired by the whole garrison drawn out, and the cannon round the Fort. The church named St. Mary's as at first intended, and from this day forward all public service to be there performed.

"It is observable that at the dedication of a new Church by the French Padres and Portuguese in 1675, Sir William Langhorne then Agent, had fired guns from the Fort; and yet at this time neither Padre nor Portuguese appeared at the dedication of our Church, nor so much as gave the Governor a visit afterwards to wish him joy of it."

Poor Sir William Langhorne! Five years had passed away, and yet the memory of that Protestant saltpetre, which he had burned in honour of a Roman Catholic Church, had not yet passed away from the nostrils of Fort St. George. Mr. Master was a better Protestant in one sense than his predecessor. His great difficulty was the intermarriage of the soldiers with the Roman Catholic women of the country. The same year that the Church was dedicated, the whole matter was discussed in Council; and the resolutions arrived at, and the order issued in consequence, are all so illustrative of the age, that we give the extracts at length.

"Monday, 22nd March, 1680. It fell under consideration whether it consisteth with our religion and interest to admit of marriages between Protestants and Roman Catholics in this place, and upon the debate resolved:—

"1st, That it is not against the law of God in Holy Scripture, nor the laws of England, and hath frequently been practised in England for Protestants to marry Roman Catholics.

"2nd, That the Roman Catholics of this place, being the offspring of foreign nations, chiefly Portuguese, and born out of England, and not liable to the laws of England provided against Roman Catholics, they always owning themselves vassals to the king of Portugal.

"3rd, That it is our interest to allow of marriages with them, especially our men with their women, to prevent wickedness, and in regard there is not English women enough for the men, and the common soldiers cannot maintain English women and children with their pay, as well as they can the women of the country, who are not so expensive and not less modest than our ordinary or common people are, and in matter of marriages we have already gained by them many hopeful children brought up in the Protestant religion.

"It is also further to be remembered that these Roman Catholics of the Portuguese nation were invited hitherto upon our first settlement; ground was given them to build upon; a Church and French Priests were allowed, to encourage them to come in and inhabit here; and they have been loyal and serviceable in the defence of the place in time of war, and are a great security to us on that account. Moreover our greatest income arises from the customs upon their commerce."

Bravo Streynsham Master! a true type of the merchant. Whatever is profitable must be virtuous, and in this case toleration was profitable. Unfortunately, at that time, there were two Protestant Chaplains at Fort St. George, viz. the Rev. Richard Portman, and the gentleman sent out to succeed him, a Rev. Richard Elliot. Accordingly on the following Thursday these two Chaplains were taken into Council. The result may be easily imagined, but we give the incident in full:—

"Thursday, 25th March, 1680. The marriages

of Protestants with Roman Catholics being again taken into consideration, the Honorable Company's two Chaplains, Mr. Richard Portman and Mr. Richard Elliot, were sent for into the Council, and upon the debate it is concluded, resolved, and ordered.

"That upon the marriage of a Protestant with a Roman Catholic, both the parties to be married shall solemnly promise before one of the Chaplains of the place by themselves, or some for them, before the Banns shall be published, and also in the Chapel or Church by themselves in person, upon the day of marriage and before the parties shall be married, that ALL the children by them begotten and born, shall be brought up in the Protestant religion, and herein due care shall always be taken by the overseers of the orphans and the poor."

How happy is the interference of the State in matters of religion. It was profitable to the Government to suffer their soldiers to marry Roman Catholics, but the happiness of the mother was to be sacrificed. How pleasant to the feelings of a mother to remember that she had bound herself by oath to give up every pledge of conjugal affection to be educated in what she believed to be a heresy.

Before leaving this subject it may be as well to remark that at this period the Agency was far more inclined to favour the French priests, who were Capuchins, rather than the Portuguese who appear to have made themselves very disagreeable. As the subject is interesting, we extract the following resolution from the consultations:—

"Thursday, 4th April, 1678. And in regard the Town is very much pestered with Portuguese Popish Priests more than in former times, it having always been the care of the first Agents in this place not to suffer those sorts of Priests to intermeddle, or to admit them to have anything to do in this Town, but wholly left the government of the Roman Church to the two French Capuchin Friars Ephraim and Zenon (for whom the Church was first licensed to be built)—men that have ever behaved themselves with all due respect to the government of the place and the English interest; it is therefore thought fit that convenient opportunity be taken by degrees, as they shall give occasion through ill behaviour, to remove some of the Portuguese Priests out of the Town, that there may not remain more than is necessary to content the inhabitants of that nation and religion, and not such a number as will be a charge and burden to them, and breed disturbance in the Town."

The attitude of the English towards the Natives is strikingly illustrated by the remarkable train of circumstances, which followed the resistance offered by Mr. Master to the intriguing demands of Lingapa. This gentleman, as we indicated in our last chapter, was Naik of Poonamallee, and collected the rents of all the surrounding neighbourhood for his royal master Abou Hassan, king of Golconda. During the present administration, he seems to have chiefly carried on his intrigues through Cassa Verona, the native merchant through whom Sir William Langhorne was said to have carried on some extremely profitable speculations. In August 1678, Lingapa was about to go to Golconda, to treat upon some offers he had made to the Divan for improving the king's revenue. Accordingly he wrote to Cassa Verona, threatening to do the town of Madraspatanam all the mischief at court that he possibly could do, unless Verona lent him a sum of money; if however the loan were granted him, then he promised to be very kind at court as regarded the affairs of the English Agency. Shortly after this he wrote another letter saying that he should return again with much greater authority than ever, and that it would be to the interest of the English Agency to part very friendly with him, in other words to give him a peiscush. To all this nice little intriguing, Vernoa replied that Mr. Governor Master was very busy at present with the dispatch of the ships to Bengal, so that he had no leisure to receive a visit from Lingapa; and that the English Agency acknowledged no other authority than that of the king Abou Hassan, and the Nabob Mirza Ibrahim Khan. Upon this Lingapa endeavoured to stop the coining of pagodas in the mint at Fort St. George. He wrote another letter to Verona, saying, that he had sent his men to bring away immediately all the shroffs and coiners in Madraspatanam, together with all the chops and stamps for coining pagodas. Verona of course communicated this intelligence to the Agency, and was directed to reply to the effect that the shroffs and coiners in the Fort mint were Company's servants; and that the chops and stamps were not in their custody but in the custody of their English masters; and that consequently the shroffs and coiners could not go, nor could they take the chops and stamps with them, without the permission of Mr. Governor Master. Verona also added, that Lingapa was ill advised to send for the men from Madraspatanam, inasmuch as they were entirely at the command of the English Agency; for both the late king Abdallah Kuttub Shah, and the reigning king Abou Hassan, had settled the command of the Town and Mint upon the English, in the same way that the latter had possessed it in the time of the Hindoo Rajah of Chandragheri, before the country fell under the dominion of the kings of Golconda.*

In the following month Lingapa came in person

* A singular accident which befel the Fort Mint at this time may be recorded in a note. "The Coiners in the Mint having melted down 170 ounces of alloy $\frac{4}{5}$ silver $\frac{1}{5}$ copper in an earthen pot to alloy the gold, and having taken it off the fire, going to pour it into water mixed with cow dung, the said pot or crucible of melted alloy flew all into the air, giving a report like a great gun, so that it hurt many people near it, and the sentinels at the doors. It flew up upon the curtains, and it stuck fast upon the walls like small sand or dust. The pot it was melted in, and that in which they were pouring it, flew quite away, so that neither of them could be found; and there was lost about 40 ounces of the alloy, the rest being gathered and swoop up as aforesaid. The reason of this accident is supposed to be caused by the water, into which they went to pour the melted alloy, not being of a sufficient heat to receive it."

from Trivalore to Madraspatanam. Verona had recently lost his wife, and Lingapa ostensibly came on a ceremonious visit to condole with him; and accordingly proceeded to Verona's garden house which was situated outside the town. The ceremony of condolence being over, Lingapa informed Verona that the King of Golconda, and his great minister Madana Pant, had revoked the orders for his going to court, and had appointed him to stay in the country and use all diligence in the collection and improvement of the king's rents; and that he had received a firmaun in Persian and Gentoo, which he showed to Verona, requiring all the commanders of the royal forces in those parts to obey his orders. At last after much similar discourse, having peiscush for its object, he asked Verona why Mr. Governor Master took no notice of him, and why he had not sent to compliment him. Verona replied that he ought to have sent and acquainted the Governor with his coming. "Why," cried Lingapa, "do you think he does not know that I am here." "Yes," answered Verona, "no doubt he knows it, for he has intelligence of the smallest matter; but he is not concerned to notice it, unless you had first communicated with him."

Lingapa now changed his tactics. Like a thorough bred Asiatic he began to extol himself, and to boast of his great honours and employments. He had, he said, been entrusted with the collection of two lakhs of pagodas per annum, and he wondered that the English Governor should think himself in any way equal to him. He was surprised that Mr. Governor Master, who had lived so long a time in Gujerat, and who understood the Mussulman language and customs, should not give him a peiscush. In this strain he went on talking until midnight, and then on taking leave he said that he had something still more important to impart. This was that for the future he would not accept Verona's own yearly present in broad cloths and looking glasses; but that he would have it all in gold chains; and that he must have two hundred pagodas this year more than usual, and also a Persian horse, because the English Governor had not made him any present. To this proposal, he said, he expected an answer in five days, and threatened if Verona did not punctually comply with it, then he would impede all his business and investments in the country. Having thus brought his discourse to an end, he departed before day break to return to Poonamallee, and thence on to Trivalore.

The above authentic relation furnishes a very correct illustration of the difficulties which the English had to contend with in dealing with the Native powers. Cassa Verona died in 1680, and then further difficulties arose, in which Lingapa exhibited his power and entailed immense loss on the Agency. On one occasion a native officer named Shiek Ahmed, came to Madraspatanam, attended with peons beating drums and carrying a flag as Havildar. This man declared that he had been appointed to take the command of the town for the king of Golconda. The Governor promptly sent three files of soldiers after him, and brought him into the Fort; and after examining him sent him out of the town. Subsequently the Brahmin who superintended the affairs of the English at the court of Golconda, advised the Agency that a Havildar had been sent, but recommended that he should not be admitted. Meantime, our old friend Lingapa, stopped the native goods going to Madraspatanam, because the Havildar had not been received. Remonstrance seemed to be in vain. Lingapa declared that now Verona was dead, he must have a rental of 2000 pagodas for the town, instead of the 1200 pagodas paid previously. The embargo continued for months and extended to provissions as well as goods. Sometimes an armed force was marched out of the Fort, and obtained the goods and provisions by force. In December 1680, Lieutenant Richardson set out for Poonamallee at the head of 400 peons and 12 files of garrison soldiers, and carried off a large quantity of property belonging to the Agency. For this service all concerned were rewarded in a way which will seem strange in the eyes of the present generation. A silk scarf was given to each of the four commissioned officers; a hogshead of arrack was given to the soldiers of the garrison; the chief peon got two and a quarter yards of broad cloth; and five pagodas were distributed amongst the main body of the peons to enable them to have a feast worthy of the occasion.

It is impossible to over-estimate the troubles that befel the Agency at this time. The Agency even contemplated removing to some settlement in the Gingee territory, which should be altogether out of the dominions of the king of Golconda. Neither food, nor fuel to cook it could be obtained; for the inhabitants of the neighbouring villages had been expressly ordered by Lingapa to sell nothing to the English. Madraspatanam was filled with complaints, and even the officers and soldiers of the garrison were reduced to great straits. At last, in April 1681, the brave Lieutenant Richardson already mentioned, obtained permission from the Governor and council to try their fortunes in the country. We cannot do better than extract the narrative of the affair from the public records :—

"Saturday, 9th April, 1681. There being a great complaint in the Town for want of rice amongst the poor, and for want of fuel amongst the better sort, the Governor ordered the drum to be beaten about Town, that such as were in want of food or fuel should go and buy it at the neighbouring villages, and if they refused to sell or give it they might take it by force, and should not be punished for it, excepting Triplicane our own village. Hereupon the officers and soldiers being in want, got a Company of men together; and Lieutenant Richardson desired the Governor to permit them to try their fortune in the country, which he granted. The orders were that whatsoever place they went to they should first summons the people to carry fuel and provisions to town as formerly, and at present to sell them something to satisfy their hunger, or if they would not sell to give it them. If they refused all, then the soldiers might take by force what the could lay their hands upon that was food or fuel; and if the people made any resistance they might fire or pull down their houses or otherwise offend them, as they should find necessary in the action. With these orders Lieutenant Richardson marched out about five o'clock with about fifty soldiers and fifty peons, and came to Condore about sunset, and summoned the people of the town, and declared to them his orders. To this the people answered that Lingapa had forbid them to carry anything to Chinnapatanam; and he could not persuade them to sell or give them anything, not so much as water to drink. Whereupon the Lieutenant told them that if they would observe Lingapa's order and be safe, he should have sent a force to defend them, for he was come with a force to compel them to break those orders. Thereupon after he had forborn them until after midnight, he set the men to take such things as they could find, which for the most part was geese in Verona's* house; and they pulled down the Poligar's house, who being conscious of his guilt, had fled and hid himself. That fellow is the watchman of St. Thomé, Triplicane, and Condore, and all that part of the country; and was very busy in setting his watches to stop the goods, and in abusing the poor people upon the first orders from Lingapa. With this enterprise and small booty, the Lieutenant returned with his men about five o'clock next morning.

"Sunday, 10th April, 1681. The Governor sent peons to Trivatore, Egmore, St. Thomé, and

---

* A relation of the Verona who was dead.

the other villages about us, declaring to the inhabitants that if they did not send in provisions and fuel as heretofore, they would suffer the same fate as Condore had done; but doing so, they might remain safe in their houses without danger. To which they all returned answer, that they would come to the Governor in a day or two, and send all sorts of things as formerly, except Lingapa sent a force to hinder them, and in such case they must not suffer from us."

It will occasion but little surprise to learn that the spirited defence offered by Mr. Streynsham Master to the intrigues of a deceitful native like Lingapa, should have excited a strong opposition to his measures in the breasts of the Directors at home. Indeed we are sorry to say that the latter exhibited a meanness of spirit, which strongly contrasts with the volunteer movement of our own times; and they were perfectly willing that their servants in this country should succumb to every petty native chief who chose to insult them, or who endeavoured to worry them into sending peiscush. Indeed the Directors continually urged upon the Agency that Fort St. George was only intended for the protection of the goods; and that the true safety of the Factory depended not upon the strength of their fortifications, but upon the firmauns and cowles they might obtain from the princes of the country. Men like Sir Edward Winter and Mr. Streynsham Master could see very plainly, what Clive and Dupleix saw sixty years later, that an exhibition of forcc was necessary in all dealings with natives. Master had already experienced the moral value of making a vigorous resistancc to the Mahrattas in the attack on Surat. He had felt how much the English had then gained upon the respeet of the Mogul authorities, by the display of Anglo-Saxon pluck in the hour of danger. He was anxious to carry out matters with the same strong hand on the coast of Coromandel, as had already bcen done on the coast of Malabar. But in this policy he was systematically opposed by the Court of Directors. They attributed all the troubles which befel the Presidency to his pride and presumption; and because it was morally impossible for him to send off the ships with the usual despatch, whilst Madras was almost in a statc of blockade, they had the meanness to ascribe the delay to his being so much engaged in private trade! In vain Master proudly referred to the incrcase in the population and revenues of the town during his administration; the Directors declared that the amount was more than counterbalanced by thc increased expenditure during the troublcs. In a word, just at the moment when Master seemcd to be on the eve of dcfeating Lingapa, and of finally placing the foreign relations of the scttlement upon a satisfactory footing, he was rccalled by the Court of Directors; and on the 3rd June 1681 we have thc announcement that thc mcrchant ship "Bengal" from England "arrived in this road, whereon eame the worshipful William Gifford to takc possession of the Agency immediately upon his coming ashore, which was accordingly delivered up to him upon reading his

Majesty's Letter and the Honorable Company's Commission."

The subsequent illtreatment of Mr. Master will be noticed in the next chapter. Here we would chiefly glance at an isolated event which occurred during his administration, which is worth noting, and which will be found fully described in the following extracts from the consultations :—

"Monday, 1st October, 1680. The painters and other disaffected persons who are withdrawn out of town to St. Thomé, gathering great numbers of people together, and giving out threatenings against many people in this town if they do not join with them, after the Gentoo manner,—it is resolved and ordered to entertain about 100 Topasses or Black Portuguese into pay, the better to guard the Washers, who do as yet stick close to their business, and are the more to be encouraged by reason of their usefulness in whitening the cloth at this time, being in the height of that business.

"And the better to prevent and frustrate the evil designs of the said mutineers, it is thought fit to encourage the Painters of the Malabar Coast, by appointing them to choose two chief persons amongst them, whom the Governor will confirm and tasheriff; and hereafter, as opportunity shall offer, two chief Painters of the Gentoos also, which may prevent any such evil consequences for the future."

"Saturday, 6th November, 1680. The Painters and others gathered at St. Thomé, having sent several letters to the several castes of Gentoos in town, and to several in the Company's service, as dubashes, merchants, washers, and others, and threatened several to murder them if they came not out to them; now they have stopped goods and provisions coming to town, throwing the cloth off of the oxen, and forbidden the people in all the towns about to carry any provisions or wood to Madraspatanam.

"Monday, 8th November. Resolved and ordered that the wives and children of the merchants, cattamaran men, and coolies, and all others that have left the town upon this mutiny of Painters, be taken out of their houses and driven into the Pagoda, as an expedient to bring the men back again.

"Resolved and ordered that a party of soldiers and peons be sent out to bring as many of the mutineers into town as they can lay hold upon, and to disperse them so that they may not make head again, or at least come not so near as St. Thomé, where they have several times abused our towns people."

These outrages continued for more than a month. At last on the 29th November, proclamation was made by beat of drum, that unless the mutineers delivered themselves up to the Governor, or to the Justices of the Choultry, within ten days,—all their houses, goods, and estate within the jurisdiction of Madraspatanam would be forfeited to the Company. Accordingly on the 7th December, we find this entry:—"Our peons brought in the chief men of the mutineers from St. Thomé, who were committed to prison; and immediately this evening all the rest of them came into town and submitted themselves."

The only other event which is worth noting is the appearance of the celebrated Comet of 1680, known as Newton's Comet, which duly attracted the notice of the Agency. The appearance is thus recorded in the consultation book :—

"Wednesday, 22nd December, 1680. The Blasing star which in the middle of the month of November appeared about 4 in the morning, in the middle of this month (December) appeared in the evening just at the setting of the sun, and does now appear 15 Degrees above the horizon, at half an hour after six at night, the tail pointing to the north-east 65 Degrees long."

This Comet is of peculiar interest, inasmuch as it first attracted the attention of Newton to cometary astronomy; and it was with reference to it that the law of gravitation was first applied in the calculation of a Comet's orbit.

CHAPTER VI.

GOVERNORSHIP OF MR. WILLIAM GYFFORD.

1681—1687.

The advent of a new Governor,—"our too easy Agent Gyfford," as the Directors subsequently called him,—naturally led to something very like a revolution in the Madras Presidency. Like Mr. Master, the new Governor had enjoyed a considerable amount of commercial experience. Ten years previously he had been appointed Deputy Governor of the settlement at Bombay, and had been subsequently sent across the Bay of Bengal to open a trade at Tonquin. But he seems to have been far more easy going and subservient than Master; and he was prepared to yield to the demands of native chiefs like Lingapa, rather than offer any amount of resistance. About the time of his appointment, however, a change had come over the Directory at Home. Mr. Josiah Child had been elected Chairman to the Board; the first man in England who appeared to have formed a just conception of what ought to be the relations between the English and the Natives in this country. The sharp, arbitrary, and decisive letters, sent at this time to the different Agencies sufficiently manifest his overbearing spirit; but bitter and insulting as they were, the trade of the Company flourished greatly under his regime, and the most distant

Agencies were kept in awe. His policy may be indicated in a few words. To put down all private trade on the part of the Company's servants in any of the articles which the Company chose to reserve to itself. To put down all Interloping and Interlopers of any kind whatever. To raise such a revenue from the Native inhabitants of the Company's town, as should defray the charges of the fortifications and garrison. Lastly, to establish a strict obedience to all orders, whatever, whether as regards the trade or as regards the private administration, which might be transmitted from home.

In carrying out all these objects, excepting one, Josiah Child could not have found a better Agent than Streynsham Master. But that one was in the eye of the celebrated Chairman, the most important of them all. Master was quite ready to put down Interlopers of every description, by any means within his power, foul as well as fair. He was also perfectly ready to levy a tax from the native inhabitants of Madraspatanam. He was indeed charged with bringing the town into trouble; but, as we shall presently see, his policy, in this direction was precisely the same as that of Child, though, as it was directly opposed to the general policy of the Directors, it was found convenient at the time to bring it forward as one of the articles of charge. Again, he was accused of being implicated in private dealings, but we think he might have been forgiven, if he had been only attentive to the temper of the man with whom he had to deal. But he was disobedient to orders; and especially he resented the insulting letters of Child. He stood too much upon his own dignity, and boasted too much of his own services. In an evil hour he engaged in an unequal combat with his superior, and he fell the victim of a pride which has ruined thousands.

But notwithstanding this error,—the error of many a high and noble heart which has subsequently been broken by the keen sense of wrong, —the conduct of the Company towards the fallen Governor was disgraceful in the extreme. The natives, thinking him a ruined man, poured in their charges in thousands. He was thrown into prison until the claims against him were settled. He was literally hunted to death in a spirit which has been but too often manifested in this Presidency. His health suffered and his memory failed him. He found resistance was useless, and at last gave in, and yielded to all demands. Eight months after his recall he returned to Europe, a disgraced and to all appearance a broken hearted man.

Meantime Mr. Gyfford was endeavouring to make peace with Lingapa, and to get a new Cowle from the king of Golconda. Lingapa, seeing that the Agency was at his mercy, now attempted to thwart the English in every possible way, so as to enhance the value of the peishcush, which would have to be given to him ultimately as the price of his friendship. He protected the Interlopers, who at this time were beginning to swarm along the coast. As this matter has already been sufficiently discussed, it will be sufficient to say that some 7000 pagodas were subsequently sent to Lingapa, on the condition that the Interlopers should be no longer protected; and that a new cowle for the district of Madraspatanam was finally obtained from the king of Golçonda, at the previous rate of 1200 pagodas per annum. This event, which we have somewhat anticipated, is thus recorded in the consultations:—

"Monday, 12th November, 1683. This afternoon at four o'clock, the Agent and Council (being attended with the Factors and Writers, the Company's merchants and two companies of soldiers) went to the Hon'ble Company's new Garden house to receive the king of Golconda's firmaun; after which, at the drinking of the king of Golconda's health, there was fired three vollies of small shot, and thirty-one great guns. When the ceremony was ended, the messenger that brought the firmaun attended upon the Agent to the Fort, where at drinking a health to Madana and Accana, the Chief Ministers of State, there was one volley more of small shot fired, and so the messenger was dismissed for the present."

The administration of Mr. Gyfford, though tolerably full of domestic interests, is somewhat wanting in connection with the general history of India. During his administration the last war broke out between the Great Mogul and the kingdoms of Bijapore and Golconda, which terminated in the final fall of these two powers; and we find some applications from Golconda for the assistance of the English against the Great Mogul. But these requests seem to have been declined or evaded, and the Agency was little disturbed by external events until the latter part of Mr. Gyfford's government, Under these circumstances we have arranged in chronological order, some of the most interesting extracts we could find in the consultation books of this period, illustrating them when necessary by extracts from the general letters received from home. The very abruptness of some of these extracts will convey to the reader a better idea of the original records than the most elaborate introductions in the world.

"Monday, 5th June, 1682. Thomas Burrett having most impiously in his cups drank a health to the Devil, the Agent and Council have thought fit (in regard to his crime is so notorious, and of so black a dye) to order him to run the Gantlope, and to remain in prison until an opportunity of ships presents to send him away from hence to be an example, and to deter others from committing crimes so hellishly wicked."

"Thursday, 29th June. Mr. James Wheeler coming (from Madapollam) to the Fort without leave from the Agent, and it being contrary to the orders made by Mr. Master in anno 1679, it was thought fit, inasmuch as he was very penitent and sorry for his contempt of said orders, and did promise never to be guilty of the same offence again, only to give him a severe check and reprehension."

"Tuesday, 11th July. The sea having for about 10 days past encroached upon this town, and we, hoping as it is usual, that it would retreat again of itself, forbore any remedies to keep it off; but now that instead of its losing it mightily gains ground upon us, and that without a speedy course be taken the town will run an apparent hazard of being swallowed up, for it has undermined even to the very walls, and so deep that it has eaten away below the very foundation of the town,—and the great bulwark next to the sea side, without a speedy and timely prevention, will certainly, in a day or two more, yield to its violence: it is therefore ordered forthwith that the drum be beat to call all coolies, carpenters, smiths, peons, and all other workmen, and that sufficient materials be provided, that they may work day and night to endeavour to put a stop to its fury: for without effectual means be used in such an eminent danger and exigency, the town, garrison, and our own lives, considering all the foregoing circumstances, must needs be very hazardous and insecure."

The foregoing curious account is further explained by the following extract from a General Letter from England, dated 31st May, 1683:—"We take notice of the great inundation that endangered our Town and Fort, and we would have you endeavour to prevent such future accidents by laying such a deep and strong foundation with chunam, as you mention, that may be sufficient in all human probability to prevent damage by any such accident hereafter. And in all other respects we would have you to strengthen and fortify our Fort and Town by degrees, that it may be terrible against the assault of any Indian Prince and the Dutch power of India, if we should happen to have any difference with them hereafter. But we must needs desire you so to contrive your business (but with all gentleness) that the inhabitants may pay the full charge of all repairs and fortifications, who do live easier under our Government than under any Government in Asia, or indeed under any Government in the known part of the world. Their saying they pay customs is a frivolous objection, and relates only to their security at sea under our Passes, and under the guns of our Fort in port; but the strong fortifying of the town, etc., and the raising new works is a security to their lives, houses, wives, and children, and all that belongs to them."

We return to the consultation book.

"Monday, 17th July, 1682. The ship "Resolution" having arrived in this road, Mr. John Littleton and Mr. Slaughter Lee came ashore and brought a letter from the Captain intimating that it was the Company's order that two of the Council should repair on board ship. In compliance thereto Mr. Timothy Wilkes and Mr. John Bigrig (third and fourth members of council) went, and a small time after returning again brought with them the Honorable Company's pacquet and other letters sealed up in a bag, which were immediately opened and the Honorable Company's letter to the Fort perused; and finding in the 2d paragraph the Company's positive order concerning Mr. Bridger (second member of council), he was acquainted with it and the charge against him. To the first he quietly submitted; to the last he confessed that he did send diamonds and pearls to England, but protested it was not for the lucre of saving the 2 per cent, but for some other material reasons. But as to the business of Interloping Alley, he avowed he was wholly innocent. The Agent and Council notwithstanding immediately ordered Mr. John Nicks and Mr. John Littleton, members of the Council, —John Willcox, Secretary,—Mr. John Stables and Mr. Henry Alford, Factors,—and the Captain of the Guard,—to go forthwith to Mr. Bridger's house, and to seal up his papers and other effects which they should find there. Which they immediately did put in execution, having put the Honorable Company's seal upon his counting house and chests, where any papers, accounts, or other valuable effects were found; which being performed they all returned to the Fort, and gave the Agent and Council an account of what they had done."

The order which led to the above arbitrary proceeding, was conveyed in a General letter, is dated London, 18th November, 1681, and bears the signature of Josiah Child. But even without the name it would be impossible to mistake the writer. The following extract will be found interesting from its reference to Mr. Master as well as to the sudden arrest of Mr. Bridger:—

"By the "Sampson" we received our late Agent Master and Council's letters of the 13th of September and 20th of December, in which he follows his old strain of errors, pride and offence, which we shall not further endeavour to confute or convince him of; but leave him now at his greater leisure, freed from the temptation and incumbrance of that greatness and immensity of gains, which our bounty had conferred upon him, to recollect himself, and consider, whether he did well or wisely for himself, or honestly by us.

'We have seldom observed such peremptoriness, in servants, but at length we find it accompanied with infidelity, as lately in Mr. John Bridger, whom we have discovered to hold correspondence with the late Interloper Alley, and also to send over great quantities of diamonds, pearls, etc. in the ship "Sampson," unregistered, contrary not only to his trust, but the oath he took of a freeman, before his going to India; and therefore we do hereby require you upon first sight of this our order forthwith to seize all his books, papers, money, and effects that you can meet with in India, and send him and all his books and papers home to us (leaving him copies of them) by this year's shipping, and to dispose of his money and effects in the country to his best advantage, but bring the proceed of them into our cash, which shall be duly accompted to him, upon clearing of his account with us here."

To return to the constitution book.

"Wednesday, 13th September, 1682. The Agent having notice of an Interloper lying in Tuticorin Bay, immediately sent for the Council to consult about it; the result of which was to send two persons thither forthwith to see who it might be, with orders if it should prove an Interloper to impede and obstruct him in all ways possible. In order to which there was a letter sent of this date to the Chief and Council of the Dutch there, cautioning them not to be assisting to them; and that it would be to their prejudice if they did. Likewise ordered them to go on board and read his Majesty's proclamation to them, and to entice his men away if he should prove refractory, and so disable him by that means. Upon which account it was ordered that pagodas 500 be sent with them, to be distributed amongst those that should comply, with farther promises of greater preferment if they would come to the Fort and serve there." From a subsequent entry we learn that before the arrival of the Company's officers, the Interloper had set sail for Bengal.

The following extracts from a letter written by Mr. Child to Mr. Gyfford, dated "London, 9th October, 1682," will throw some light upon the progress our ancestors were making in the matter of costume in the reign of Charles II :—

"You will find in a list of goods one article for shifts of all sorts, which I would have you look upon as a matter of great concernment to the company; being the only way I know to introduce the using of calico for that purpose in all these northern parts of the world; and therefore I most earnestly recommend to you to provide 200,000 shifts ready made of the strongest sorts of calicoes, some finer and some coarser, and be sending them as fast as you can.

"Let some of the coarser sort, for seamen's and ordinary people's use, be of strong blue cloth; and some white for the like ordinary use; others white middling, for citizens and middle sorts of people; and some fine enough for ladies and gentlewomen. If some be wrought on the breasts, and on the sleeves, and in the collar with needlework, the price here will suffieiently pay for the work and eost there, where labour and art are so cheap. Take special care that the sewing be very good, and all the cloth strong in its kind, as well fine as eoarse."

The following eurious incidents we shall extract from the consultation books. They refer in the first plaee to the establishment of the Madras Bank, an institution which was in reality started in the reign of Charles II, though it is popularly referred to the governorship of Lord William Bentinek in the first deeade of the present century. Next follows the proeeedings that were taken to prevent the exportation of slaves from this Presidency; and after that, we find an aeeount of the establishment of a Court of Admiralty, in the place of the High Court of Judieature established in the governorship of Mr. Streynsham Master. But we leave the extraets to tell their own story.

"Thursday, 21st June, 1683. The Honorable Company having sent us a Law with referenee to the Natives, as also an Order for the raising of a Bank of money to the value of one hundred thousand pounds sterling at six per cent, it is ordered that the first be translated into Portuguese, Gentoo, Malabar, and Moores, and proclaimed solemnly by beat of drum, and afterwards set upon the Gates; as also our declaration for the weighing of what monies shall be brought in upon the latter, to be likewise translated into the above languages, and also set upon the Gates, a eopy whereof is as followeth:—

"By the Honorable East India Company's

order, we, the Agent and Council of Fort Saint George, do hereby publicly declare unto all persons whatever, that we will at any time take up and receive what sums of money soever shall be brought to us, at six per cent per annum Interest, for six or twelve months time, or any other longer term of years, but not less than six months, nor to exceed the time we shall agree for; and we shall for the better security of such persons that shall so let out their money, give our receipt for the same under the Hon'ble Company's seal."

"Monday, 18th September, 1683. There being great number of slaves yearly exported from this place, to the great grievance of many persons whose children are very commonly privately stolen away from them, by those who are constant traders in this way, the Agent and Council considering the scandal that might accrue to the Government, and the great loss that many parents may undergo by such actions, have ordered that no more slaves be sent off the shore again."

"Monday, 13th November, 1683. An Order in English, Portuguese, Gentoo, and Malabar, for the preventing the transportation of this country people by sea and making them slaves in other countries, was read and past and ordered to be hung up in four public places of this town. The contents are as followeth:—

"Whereas formerly there hath been an ill custom in this place of shipping off this country people, and making them slaves in other strange countries. We, therefore, the present Governor and Council of Fort St. George, have taken the same into our serious consideration, and do hereby order that, for the future, no such thing be done by any person whatsoever, resident in this place. And we do hereby also strictly command all our officers by the water side, whether they be English, Portuguese, or Gentoos, to do their utmost endeavours to prevent the same; or else suffer such punishment, either in body or goods, as we shall think fit to inflict upon them. And if any person, being an inhabitant of this Town of Madraspatanam, shall hereafter presume clandestinely to do anything contrary to this our order, by shipping such slaves of this country, and it be proved against him,—he shall pay for every slave so shipped off or sent away, fifty pagodas, to be recovered of him in the Choultry of Madraspatanam; one-third for the use of the Honourable East India Company, one-third to the poor, and one-third to the informer."

"Thursday, 10th July, 1684. The Honorable Company having advised us in their General Letter, dated the 14th of August, 1683, that a Judge Advocate should soon be sent hither for the hearing and determining of all suits and causes under this Government, with the assistance of two merchants, and also sent us a copy of his Majesty's new charter ordering the said proceedings, which occasioned the silencing our former Court of Judicature, and has given great dissatisfaction to the creating many disturbances and complaints for justice, to the discredit and disgust of our Government; and though the Honorable Company have in that General appointed their President to supply the place of Judge Advocate till he shall arrive; yet having no directions for those proceedings, and being unacquainted with the methods thereof, it is thought and agreed to be of absolute necessity to the peace, justice, security, and honour of this Government, that the old Court of Judication be organized, and that causes be heard and decided there by Jurors as formerly, by the authority of the first charter, till the Judge Advocate shall arrive, or we prohibit further proceedings therein." Subsequently a Judge Advocate was sent out, and a Court of Admiralty was established. This new Court superseded the Court previously held in the Chapel, in which the Governor acted as Judge, and twelve jurymen were sworn in. The principal object of this new Court was the summary punishment of Interlopers.

The next important event in the history of the Presidency, was the attempt made to levy a house tax which should serve to defray the expences of the fortifications and charges of the garrison. Mr. Streynsham Master had actually succeeded in levying some such a tax; and this very circumstance formed the ground of one of the charges which the natives preferred against him on the arrival of Mr. Gyfford. The new Governor had accordingly remitted the tax; but was subsequently compelled, much against his inclination, to levy one in its place. As early as the 20th September, 1682, Mr. Josiah Child had written to the Agency as follows:—

"Our meaning as to the revenue of the town is that one way or another, by Dutch, Portuguese, or Indian methods, it should be brought to defray at least the whole constant charge of the place, which is essential to all governments in the world. People protected ought in all parts of the universe, in some way or other, to defray the charge of their protection, and preservation from wrong and violence. The manner of raising which revenue we shall leave to your discretion, as may be most agreeable to the humour of that people."

This order was frequently repeated, and the results will be found described in the following extracts from the consultation books:—

"Thursday, 14th August, 1684. We have also consulted several ways for the inproving the revenues of this town, and contributing to the charge of walls, etc,; necessary buildings for the conveniency and security of the inhabitants. Upon which we have agreed to propose levying of a small tax amongst them to be paid monthly, which if they so oppose, as formerly, that we cannot be successful therein, then to offer it as a voluntary contribution to all the inhabitants in this Town, both English, Portuguese, Moors, and Gentoos, which possibly may have a better effect upon their wilful tempers; but first to press and receive the 500 pagodas per annum, which was three years past promised by the several castes of the Gentoos towards the charges of the garrison."

"Thursday, 21st August, 1684. The several heads of the castes of the town inhabitants were sent for to mind them of their promised supply towards the charges of the garrison, who sent us word this not being a good day, they desired we would excuse their coming till to-morrow."

On the following Monday the promised interview took place. The heads of the castes pleaded that they had lived in Madraspatanam near forty years free from such impositions, and moreover that they had constantly paid customs. They were told however that if they could not obey the Company's law, they had liberty to sell their houses and remove where they pleased. At last after much persuasion they agreed to pay annually nine fanams for every great house, six fanams for every small house, and three fanams for every little round house." The degree of success which attended this arrangement will appear in our next chapter.

The following event is perhaps the most interesting which can be found in the records of this period. On the 6th February, 1685, Charles II had passed away to his fathers, and James II was proclaimed king. The news reached Madras in tolerable speed for those days ; for six months after the death of the king, we find the following graphic description of the proclamation of his successor in the consultation books of Fort St. George.

"Thursday, 13th August, 1685. No Consultation. This morning our dread sovereign king James the Second was proclaimed with this following solemnity.

"The whole Council, with the Commanders of Ships, and the rest of the Right Honorable Company's servants and English Gentlemen inhabitants of the city, came to attend the President at the Garden house, in a handsome equipage on horseback. After that came Peddy Naik with his peons, and the chief merchants, with great number of the inhabitants of the Gentoo town, all in arms, bringing with them also elephants, kettle drums, and all the country music. From thence we set forward with this numerous Company of people through the Gentoo town, the houses and streets being adorned all the way. Peddy Naik's peons, the chief merchants, and Gentoo inhabitants went first; elephants carrying our flags, the kettle drums and music playing before them. After that went 12 English trumpets with silk banners, and 6 hautboys, all in red coats, playing by turns all the way. Mr. Coventry (Clerk of our Court) on horseback, bare headed and with his sword drawn, carried the proclamation in his hand open. Then the President and Council, and the rest of the English gentlemen went in due order. The troop was commanded and led by the President, Mr. Thomas Lucas, Cornet; and the rear was brought up by Mr. Elihu Yale. And when we came to enter the garrison at the Choultry Gate, (one of the chief entrances into the city), there was in readiness three complete companies of soldiers, and all the principal Portuguese, to receive the President and Council, and other English gentlemen, who marched before them to the Fort Gate, Sea Gate, and back to the Choultry Gate, (three of the principal places of the city); at all which places the proclamation was read by Mr. Coventry, all persons being uncovered and their swords drawn. The proclamation ended with great shouts and joyful acclamations, crying "God bless king James Second", and at every place of reading there was a volley of small shot, the trumpets sounding, and hautboys playing. Which done, the President, etc. returned in the same order to the Garden house, the great guns both of the Fort and Town firing all the way; and after that all the Europe and country ships did the like. And soon after the President, etc., were returned, the Persian and Siam ambassadors, with great state and a numerous retinue, came to congratulate our solemnity, and to bring their good wishes for his Majesty's prosperous reign; who after some small stay, being handsomely saluted and treated according to their quality with a banquet, music, and dancing, they took leave and departed to their houses with great satisfaction. And then a general invitation being made, we drank his Majesty's health and long and happy reign; and at night there was bonfires and fireworks, wherewith this solemnity ended."

With this event we close the present article. It was our original intention to give a history of the administration of one Governor in a single issue; but as we proceed the matter grows upon us, and we now find it necessary to separate the accounts of Mr. Gyfford into two parts, of which we hope to present our readers with the second portion in our next chapter.

CHAPTER VII.

GOVERNORSHIP OF MR. WILLIAM GYFFORD.

(Concluded.)

1681—1687.

The concluding years of Mr. Gyfford's administration are marked, not only by events of domestic interest, but by incidents which find a place in the annals of India. Before however reviewing these last particulars, it will be advisable to complete the series of extracts commenced in our last issue, so far as they illustrate the internal history of the settlement in Madraspatanam.

Our first extract will exhibit the Government mode of treating those civil servants of the Agency, who chose to deviate from the paths of morality and good manners.

"Thursday, 2nd April, 1685. Whereas it hath been sufficiently testified to us, the President and Council of Fort St. George, that Thomas Child, Company's Factor, hath been guilty of most excessive drinking, swearing, cursing, and divers other disorders and contempt of government, so that we esteem him not fit for any Christian or civil society; and when also upon examination we find that himself and Charles Carr, another Factor, have impudently reflected very dishonorably and scandalously upon the President and others:—We do agree and think it very convenient, not only not to admit either of them to go of Council for Priaman (in Sumatra), as was intended them, but that both of them be confined to their chambers; and that they shall have nothing given them to eat or drink but boiled rice and water, according to the rules in such cases established; and that none shall be suffered to come near them, to supply them with other provision, or to be corrupted by the vile conversation of Thomas Child, or encouraged by either of them to the like contempt of their superiors; and this punishment we have thought fit to inflict upon them shall continue till we shall perceive a sensible repentance in them, and that they do make a public acknowledgment of their offences, and beg forgiveness of the persons they have so maliciously and wrongfully abused, with unfeigned engagements never to commit the like, that we may restore them to their former privileges and give them the employment we designed for them, or such other as we may find them capable of, or esteem them to deserve. And this our order is to be set up in the Hall or Dining Room in the Fort, and a copy thereof given to each of the said offending persons, to the intent that themselves and all others in the Right Honorable Company's service may know the cause and justness of their punishment."

"Saturday, 11th April. Received a Petition from Thomas Child and Charles Carr, the contents as followeth.

"*To the Honourable* WILLIAM GYFFORD, *Esq.*, *President and Governor of Fort St. George.*

May it please your Honour. Whereas your Petitioners whose names are underwritten, being sensible of the many enormities which have been committed against your Honour, etc., and out of a deep sense of our crimes, we humbly implore your goodness, that you would vouchsafe to pardon and pass by these heinous crimes, confessing and very well knowing your acts are very equitable and just in confining us to our chambers, nay merciful too, the least of which we do not in the least deserve; but having intelligence that your Honour intends a public paper, to be set up in the Hall, which will certainly tend to the utter destruction of your poor Petitioners; our humble request is, that your Honour will condescend so far, as not to expose your said poor Petitioners to public view, which paper (though justly) must inevitably do; wherefore we humbly beseech you that your Honour will recall your order for setting up the said paper, and permit us to come in your presence, and humbly acknowledge ourselves offenders as in the said paper is inserted against us.

Your humble Petitioners

THOMAS CHILD, CHARLES CARR."

We learn from a subsequent date that this Petition was favourably considered.

The following curious incident which occurred at Ennore, with reference to a sloop bound from Madras to Sumatra, will interest our local antiquarians.

"Sunday, 10th May, 1685. Received this morning a letter from William Dixon, Master of the sloop "James" from Ennore, dated this day, advising that he was forced to put in there, the sloop being so leaky, that they pumped every glass.

Upon which the President and Council ordered the Secretary to write him answer to his letter, and order him to ride as near Ennore Bar as he could, that they would send two Mussula's to unlade the coals, and that then he should carry her into that River, and when that was done he should receive further orders.

"Wednesday, 20th May, 1685. This morning William Dixon, Master of sloop "James," arrived here from Ennore, who gives an account that the sloop was got into with that River, that all her stores and coals were landed, and that upon firing of a gun, the powder that was under the cabin abaft, took fire, and blow up her deck. Two Englishmen were killed and several Lascars wounded, but how the accident happened is not known, the two men that are dead being the only persons about the powder."

Seven months afterwards, namely on the 4th January 1685-6, this sloop was still in Ennore River, as we learn from the following entry of that date:—"Notwithstanding we have so often endeavoured to get the sloop "James" out of the Ennore River, we have not been able to do it for want of water upon the Bar, occasioned by reason of dry weather."

The following Petition from Dr. Heathfield, dated 20th May, 1685, will throw some light on the prospects of the Company's Surgeons in the olden time.

"*To the Honble President &c., and Council.*

May it please your Honour and Council, it was

in the year 1673 that I was taken prisoner by the Dutch, with the ship President, at which time I underwent many hardships, besides the total loss of what it had pleased God to bestow upon me, by my endeavours in five years before in the Hon'ble Company's Service; and after my confinement I was then received into the Hon'ble Company's serviee again as Surgeon at Mechlepatam and Madapollam; and after seven year's service there, was called up to this place (Madras) where I have served as Surgeon upwards of four years: my experience in this time, and observations I have made upon the Honorable Company's affairs, I humbly coneeive have rendered me capable of serving them in another station, which I am desirous of, in hopes of future preferment, and knowing that it has been the eustom of your Honour, ete., and other nations to alter the employment of their servants. I therefore humbly beseeeh your Honour, etc, to receive me as a Factor, and to give me what employment you shall think suitable for me; wherein I will behave and deport myself with that fidelity, eare, and diligence, that my future serviees shall approve themselves not unworthy of this your great favour and kindness; and as I am in duty bound to be a faithful servant to my Honorable Masters, so I lie under no less obligation to yourselves as my benefactors, than of approving myself with all gratitude and thankfulness.

Hon'ble, etc.

Your most humble and obedient servant,

JOHN HEATHFIELD."

We cannot discover whether the prayer of this petition was granted or rejected.

Our next extract will serve to further illustrate the relations between the Agency at Fort St. George, and the Native chiefs. The story of Lingapa will enable the reader to form some conception of the position of the English in this country, under the sovereignty of Golconda; the following story of Gopall Pundit will throw a light upon the ordinary mode of proceeding, when a distinguished Native paid a personal visit to Fort St. George.

"Tuesday, 15th September, 1685. Gopall Pundit being come to St. Thomé, acquainted the President with it, and desired that he might give him a visit privately that night; so it was thought convenient that Mr. Lucas (third member of council) go to him to St. Thomé, and Mr. Yale (second member of council) to meet him at Triplicane, to bring him to the Garden house.

"Thursday, 17th September. Gopall Pundit having rested himself yesterday, sent a message this morning that he desired to see the Fort, and to be received publicly there this afternoon. Which was accordingly done with as much honour and respect to him as we could, according to his quality, where after some time being spent in viewing the city from the top of the fort house, firing great guns, and the like, he desired to have some discourse with the President and Council: so they retired for that purpose, the sum of which was chiefly his magnifying his great services done the Company, and how great a friend he was to them, to the intent, we believe, to cause us to make him some considerable gratuity, or to lend him money. But on the other hand, the President and Council endeavoured to lessen that value he set upon himself, in regard they endeavoured to make it appear that once it lay in his power to have done much more in reference to a better settlement at Cuddalore, and told him (he being now going to Court) if he could there use his interest, and procure liberty for the Right Honorable Company to build a fortification at Cuddalore or Porto Novo on the place that the President and Council should choose for the conveniency of their business, that they would consider him, but for lending him any money, they absolutely denied it, it being attended with so many inconveniences.

"Friday, 18th September. This morning Gopall Pundit sent Sanerogee (his chief confident) to the President to acquaint him that he would use his endeavours to obtain what was recommended to him yesterday; and desired the President to write a short letter to Haja Raja, referring him to what Gopall Pundit had to say to him from us.

"Monday, 21st September. Gopall Pundit having been at a great charge in coming hither with such a numerous retinue, and in consideration of our new settlement at Cuddalore, that we may engage him (in part at present) to continue his friendship, to obtain some more and better privileges there, than we have as yet,—It is ordered that he with his attendants be Tasherift as followeth.

To Gopall Pundit in private,—gold chains to the value of pagodas 150.

Do. in public,—6 yards scarlet, 1 telescope, 1 fowling piece, 1 pair of pistols, some flint ware and toys, 4 pair of spectacles, a chest of rosewater, and some sandal-wood.

To Gopall Pundit's brother Vittlepa in private,—pagodas 20 in gold chains.

Do. in public,—3 yards scarlet.

To Sanerogce in private,—pagodas 20 in gold chains.

Do. in public,—3 yards broad cloth ordinary.

To Gopall Pundit's kinsman,—2 yards scarlet.

To 3 captains, 3 havildars, 3 mussumdars,—each 3 yards broad cloth ordinary.

To the Maldars, etc.,—pagodas 14.

To servants,—3 pieces beteelaes."

The mode in which the agency acted in the case of any of its servants dying, and leaving widows and families behind them, may be gathered from the following entry.

"Monday, 21st December, 1685. Mr. Edward Fowle, late Engineer of this place, having been sent to the West Coast of Sumatra, to give directions about the building of a Fortification, and being very diligent therein, as per the advice we received from thence, and dying at Bencoolen, —It is agreed and ordered that what wages is due to him be paid to his widow, as also that a gratuity of twenty pagodas be given her, in consideration of the great loss she hath had in his death, and the poor condition he hath left her and her family in. Also Teggapa, the Right Honorable Company's Chief Dubash here, having been very serviceable in the new Settlement on the said West Coast, and dying in his return hither;—It is ordered that his son be allowed four pagodas per month for the maintenance of the family, and to be employed at the sea side, and that ten pagodas be given to the widow as a gratuity for her husband's good service."

The next event we have to record is one of peculiar interest. We have already referred to the attempt made in 1684 to levy such a tax from every house in Madraspatanam, as should defray the charges of the fortifications and garrison. The matter however was delayed from time to time; Mr. Gyfford shrinking from making the levy, whilst Mr. Josiah Child, the Chairman of the Court of Directors, became more and more angry at the delay, and more and more bitter and peremptory in his orders. At last the Agency felt compelled to act, and the event abundantly proved that firmness and decision were alone required to render the experiment successful. Indeed it is plain that Mr. Child understood the Native character far better than Mr. Gyfford. He saw that the inhabitants of Madraspatanam were flourishing under British protection, and that they were bound to pay for that protection. But the following extracts will tell the whole story.

"Sunday, 3rd January, 1686. In pursuance of the Right Honorable Company's positive orders to us of the 16th of March, 1684, for the raising a contribution upon the several houses in this Town, in consideration of the great charge of maintaining, repairing, and fortifying this garrison, for the defence and security of them, their families, and estates ;—Mr John Littleton was appointed to collect the same by all moderate ways and fair means possible, that they may not be discontented, or any disturbance arise thereby. Notwithstanding this, and the oft repeated reasons and arguments with them for the ready and quiet payment thereof, they did this morning, in contempt of the Government and our orders, tumultuously and mutinously combine together, commanding the several castes to desist from their labour, and service to us ; also forbidding and hindering the shops to be opened and grain to be brought into Town ; insolently declaring that they would continue their rebellion, till they were freed from the said present and all future taxes. Whereupon soldiers were drawn out to secure all the passes of the outer Town, and other places, to suppress the tumult ; and as great inconveniences and dangers may succeed from their violent proceedings, it is also agreed and ordered, that the Choultry Drum be beaten about the Town, with this Proclamation :—

"That if the heads or chiefs of the several castes of the inhabitants do not come in and submit themselves before this day's sunset to the President and Council, begging pardon for their great crime of insurrection against the Government, and disobedience to the late just orders for a small contribution towards the necessary fortifying, and bearing part of the great charge of maintaining this garrison, that their several dwelling houses be to-morrow pulled down and the ground sold at the Choultry, and them and their families for ever be banished the town.

"Also that all persons in the Right Honorable Company's service, or belonging thereto, do immediately repair to their several charges and business; otherwise to be put out of their employments, and never more to be entertained in the Right Honorable Company's service.

"And that if the Chetty Bazaar people do not immediately open their shops and sell their grain, etc. as usually, that the goods and commodities in their several shops be confiscated to the Right Hon'ble Company, and moreover be fined ten pagodas each for their mutinous crimes; and in case of any disobedience to this our merciful invitation and indemnity, it is then agreed that the President in Council do personally to-morrow see the aforesaid orders strictly executed."

This Sunday was remarkable in other respects. The proclamation of James II against Interlopers was read in St. Mary's Church, which coming so close after the Christmas sermon on peace and good will to all men, must have been highly edifying to the audience. In the evening we are told that "the heads of the several castes came in and acknowledged their great crime and desired to be heard to-morrow by the President and Council; so with a severe check were dismissed to their several houses, and advised and ordered to suppress the present tumult they had raised."

"Monday, 4th January. This morning the

heads of the several Castes appeared before the President and Council, to be heard according to their desire; and after begging pardon for the great crime they had committed in raising such a mutiny, delivered in their Petition, translate whereof is as follows.

"*To the Hon'ble Governor and Council.*

"The inhabitants of this town declare, that it is now forty years and upwards, from the foundation of this Fort, and that they were invited to people and increase the town upon the word and favour of the English, under whom they have till now lived, receiving many honours and favours without paying any tribute or rent. Only in the time of the past Governor Mr. Master, who imposed a tax upon arrack, and upon paddy, and causing us to pay for cleansing the streets;* also increasing the

---

* The following extract from the consultation books during the Governorship of Streynsham Master, will explain the nature of this municipal assessment. The entry is dated 13th July, 1678:—

"The Governor having proposed a way for keeping the Towne cleane after the manner in England, by taxing every house at a moderate rate and to appoint a Scavenger to collect said moneys and therewith to hire cooleys to carry away the dirt and filth, which in this as in all other townes in these countrys lyes in the streets very offensively, the principall persons with many others of the Gentu towne came this day to the Governor, requesting that there might not be taken a particular list or roll of all the houses in the Towne, they offering rather then soe, to make a collection among themselves upon each cast or sect, as they have used to doe for some other generall expences upon their festivalls. Whereupon the Governor asked them

Choultry customs of goods imported and exported; also the rents of the fields of paddy, and ordered that double custom should be received of tobacco which came from other places, and because the owners could not pay said custom, they carried their tobacco to St. Thomé, by which means the Choultry hath been hindered of the customs formerly paid. Also the close siege this Town suffered, which upon your Honour's arrival was taken off, whereby this Town was newly revived from death to life, hoping that your

---

why they approved not of the way he proposed; to which they answeared that the Devan or the Mogull and Braminy Governors of the country for the King, might come to know the great number of houses and familys, that is in this Towne, and thereupon might raise new impositions upon them and create trouble to the Towne; but the matter being more nearly enquired into, it seems they were afraid that if such a roll were taken, it would be a ready way to lay a tax upon the Towne for the building and repairing the outwalls or any other new imposition never yet imposed upon them; and thereupon 'twas urged to them, why all the Towne ought not to bear an equal share in repairing those slight mud walls as well as those poor people only that lived next to the walls; to which they could answear no further than that it has never yet been required of them for these 40 years, and the Company has thriven well and were better able to bear it themselves now than ever, therefore hoped 'twould not be imposed upon them now; and for clearing the streets they would take care to doe it among themselves without further trouble to us: Whereupon the Governor referred them to Verona to consider further of this affaire.

"By this it may be observed, how jealous this people are of being imposed upon by new customes."

Honour would have relieved us from all tributes and rents; but instead thereof we find you go about to impose and increase other new tributes upon our houses, which can in no wise be, nor ought your Honour to do it. Wherefore we beg your Honour for the sake of the most high God, and in the name of the most serene king of England and of the Hon'ble Company, that you will free this Town from so heavy a yoke, as is this tax laid upon our houses, seeing we are a poor people, and live upon our labour and trouble; this Town having the fame, and is called place of Charity, and we shall live confident in your favours and assistances, and the whole Town lightened by your goodness, as they hope from Honour.

"Signed by the heads of the several Castes underwritten, viz. chuliars, painters, tailors, husbandmen, coolies, washers, barbers, pariahs, comities, oilmakers, fruiterers, shepherds, potmakers, muckwas, patanava, tiaga, cavaree, nugabunds, pally, goldsmiths, chitties, weavers.

"Upon perusal of said Petition, the President and Council told them, that it did not lie in their power totally to excuse them from contributing towards the charges of this Garrison, in regard it was the Right Honorable Company's positive orders, they commanding to have the Black Town walled round at the charge of the Inhabitants; and there was no remedy but that they must be conformable thereunto, it being a very small matter, only three fanams a year for a small house, six fanams for a middle size house, and nine fanams for a great house, which could be no burthen to them. But they continued very obstinate, and declared themselves unwilling and unable to pay, for reasons given in their Petition; and further that it would breed a custom, and they feared it would be increased hereafter. But it was still replied it must be done, and they as positive on the other hand refused, offering two of their heads, if that would satisfy, to excuse them from this tribute and heavy yoke, as they call it. After which they were one by one asked whether they would leave the town, make war upon us, or submit to our orders and government; to which they every one answered they would submit, but on a sudden all at once denied what they had said, and that they would not pay do what we would to them; which forced us to cause the drum to beat, and declare our resolution to some of the chiefs that we had kept (others being run away), that we would execute our orders declared to them yesterday by beat of drum. Which when they perceived us so much in earnest, at last submitted, promising to be obedient to our government, and that they would take off the prohibition laid upon their people and our provisions, and that all things should be at peace and quiet. So they were dismissed, and after awhile, the shops were accordingly opened, provisions brought in, and the washermen, muckwas, catamaran-men, coolies, and servants returned to their several businesses; and now it only remains that they be obedient in paying their contributions."

Notwithstanding however these patriotic hopes

expressed in the consultation book, Mr. Gyfford's subsequent letters home could not have been very satisfactory to the Directors. Unfortunately no copies of the general letters to England have been preserved amongst the Madras records of an earlier date than 1692; but the following sharp orders, extracted from the general letters from England and evidently from the pen of Mr. Josiah Child, abundantly show that the great chairman was very much dissatisfied with Mr. Gyfford's conduct in the matter.

On the 9th June, 1686, he writes as follows:—"This pro and con between us and you, which was begun by Sir William Langhorne, ended with Mr. Master, is now revived on the subject, will never end well. Pray let us have no more of it... A revenue we will have aliquo modo for that infinite charge we have been at to raise that Town (which hereafter we shall call a city) from so despicable a condition as it was in when we settled there.... With your leave we will have a ground or quit rent yearly for every house within your precinct, and a small poll money for every head, as the Dutch have at Batavia."

Again on the 6th June, 1687, he writes as follows:—"We do hereby order and ordain as a law in our city of Madras (which we require you to publish with the usual solemnity) all persons, owners or occupiers of any houses or lands within our precinct, that shall neglect or refuse, for three months after publication, to bring in the arrear of their respective quit rent imposed upon them, such shall for ever hereafter stand charged, and pay to the Company, double the quit rent formerly imposed upon them."

We now turn to an event which is interesting as being one of the earliest recorded attempts at mutiny in this Presidency. A short time previously the company had established a settlement at Priaman on the west coast of Sumatra; a plaec that proved so fearfully unhcalthy, that most of the merchants and factors died, and the loeality was regardcd with horror. At this time however an expedition against Bengal, whieh we shall have oeeasion to deseribe hereafter, was in preparation, and the Portuguese soldiers in Fort Saint Gcorge were ordered on the service. But we leave the consultation book to tell its own story.

"Wednesday, 4th August, 1686. Thc several companies of this garrison being in their arms, the Portuguese soldiers appointed for the Bay of Bengal, being asked whether they were willing to serve the Hon'ble Company in that expedition, did one and all refuse to go, upon pretence that we would send them to the West Coast (of Sumatra), though the President assured them to the eontrary. So thcy had thcir arms taken from them, and being of such a dangerous consequence, a Gallows was caused to be ereeted before the Fort Gatc, resolving to hang two or three of thc ringleaders to terrify the rest to their duty, having now the power of martial law; and when they pcreeived our intentions, they submitted to proceed upon the voyage; so had their arms returncd to them, though we can expect no very hearty service from sueh backward pitiful fellows; and it is resolved, as soon as English soldiers can be provided sufficient for the garrison, that all Topasses be disbanded, and no more entertained, since there is so little dependence upon them."

The following little proceeding as regards our first possession of St Thomé, is very suggestive.

"Thursday, 19th August, 1686. Whereas the Right Honorable Company have ordered the renting of St. Thomé from the Divan, and we have thought it not convenient to rent it in the name of the Right Honorable Company because the Rent would thereby be enhanced,—we have desired Chinna Vencatadry and Allinga Pillay to rent the said Town of St. Thomé in their own names, and do promise to allow them all the charges which they may expend for procuring a firmaun for the said Town, and to save them harmless from whatever loss may accrue unto them by the rents of said Town; provided the said Chinna Vencatadry and Allinga Pillay, do from time to time give us an account of their charges, as the same is expended, and of the rents as the same are received, and that the profits accruing thereby be to the use of Right Honorable Company."

The following extracts are of very great value. They fully explain the police arrangements in the native town of Madraspatanam in the very earliest times. We have alre dy explained that whilst the settlement was first made about 1640, no records have been preserved in this Presidency prior to 1670. The intervening period we filled up as well as we could by means of the abstracts of general letters preser ed in Bruce's "Annals;"

but even they furnish no record of a governor earlier than Sir Edward Winter. From the following entries however we observe a reference to a Sir Thomas Chamber, who appears to have been governor about 1659, and thus to have immediately preceded Sir Edward Winter. Moreover we obtain from them a glimpse of Madraspatanam when it could have been little more than a rude assemblage of bamboo huts, and when twenty peons were sufficient to watch over the interests of the inhabitants. These entries originated in certain charges of neglect of duty which were brought against Padda Naik and his peons, in other words against the police establishment of Madraspatanam, in the year 1686, and which led to a reference to the original cowle granted for the maintenance of the force. But the extracts will tell the whole story.

"Monday, 3rd November, 1686. Whereas divers of the Inhabitants of this Town, have made their complaints to us, that they have been great sufferers by the many robberies that have been committed of late; and forasmuch as it hath been made appear to us that the Pedda Naik and his Talliars (who should take care, for the yearly revenue they receive for the same, that no such thing be done, or else make satisfaction) have concealed some of the stolen goods, and imprisoned one of the thieves for fear he should make a discovery of others among themselves, and that the said Talliars do make it their constant practice to receive half the stolen goods and let the thieves escape with the rest:—we the President and Council do therefore unanimously agree and resolve, that the said Pedda Naik shall make due satisfaction to every person for whatsoever losses they can justly make appear to have sustained by robbery, either in the inward on outward Town, now or hereafter; which is also agreeable to the contents of his Cowle given him by Sir Thomas Chamber the 22nd June 1659."

It appears from the Cowle, which is printed at full length on the page following the above entry, that in a very early period of the history of Madraspatanam, Pedda Naik had guarded the town with twenty peons. Subsequently, when the town had greatly increased in size Pedda Naik had given up the office on the ground that the number of peons was insufficient for the duty, and that the maintenance granted him was also insufficient. Accordingly eighteen paddy fields were granted to Pedda Naik duty free, together with a variety of petty customs on paddy, fish, oil, betel nut, pepper, and other similar articles; and he in return engaged to guard the town with fifty peons, under the following arrangement, which we shall describe in the words of the Cowle granted by Sir Thomas, Chamber.

"Also that the 50 peons aforesaid, shall be employed about the Town, as he that hath the charge of the Choultry shall think fitting. And if any man shall be delivered by us into your custody, and shall make his escape, that you shall pay the debt the person escaped owed. Also that if we (the President) should go abroad at any time to take our pleasure, you shall procure 150 or

200 peons to accompany us. And if occasion shall require 150 or 200 peons, your Timmapa with the said peons shall go upon what employment we shall send him, and also allow them 4 days catty; but if we should detain them longer then we are to give them catty.* Also if any house is robbed, that you shall make satisfaction for what is lost. And if any merchant or inhabitant of this Town shall run away, and any of your people having knowledge thereof shall conceal it, that then you are to bring that party run away again, and correct him that knew of his departure. This being the Cowle given you by us you being peaceably and quietly to take your duties aforesaid, and to do the Company what service you are able. Dated in Madraspatanam, the 22nd June 1659.

THOMAS CHAMBER."

The result of the present complaints appears to have been that the Pedda Naik agreed to make good all real losses.

Before proceeding farther with the extracts it will be necessary to glance at the general history of India. Aurungzebe, the Great Mogul reigning at Delhi, had been compelled by an Afghan war and a religious insurrection to suspend his military operations in the Dekkan. Meantime Sevajee, the great Mahratta, had pursued his conquests in Southern India, and, as we have already seen, passed within a few miles of Madras during the governor-

* Catty, or more literally "Kuttoo," is a Tamil word signifying "batta."

ship of Streynsham Master; but he was shortly afterwards cut off in the midst of his career in the fifty-third year of his age. Sevajee was succeeded by his son Sambajee; but the latter was idle and debauched, and possessed but little of the ambition of his great father.

It was under these circumstances, that in 1683, Aurungzebe moved the whole force of the Mogul army into the Dekhan, with the intent of subjugating Bijapore, Golconda, and the Mahrattas. The story of that long campaign would prove of little interest to the general reader. Sambajee woke up from his life of sensuality, and harassed the Moguls in every possible way. In 1686 the kingdom of Golconda was well nigh overthrown by Prince Moazzim, the eldest son of Aurungzebe. Moazzim drew near the capital and was joined by the greater part of the army of Golconda. The Brahmin minister Madna Pant was murdered in a tumult. The king Abul Hassan fled from his capital of Hyderabad to the neighbouring hill fort of Golconda, which had given its name to the whole kingdom. For three successive days Hyderabad was plundered by the troops of Moazzim. Aurungzebe however thought proper to grant a peace to Abul Hassan, upon payment of a large contribution.

Aurungzebe is supposed to have come to terms with Abul Hassan, simply to prevent his son Moazzim from being regarded as the conqueror of Golconda. In 1686 he took Bijapore in person, and destroyed that monarchy. In 1687 he again attacked Golconda, and in September, after an obstinate siege of seven months, he captured the fort and took Abul Hassan prisoner. In 1689 Sambajee was drinking in a favorite pleasure house, when he too was taken prisoner by an officer of Aurungzebe, and sent in triumph to the imperial head quarters. Some of the Omrahs suggested that the life of the Mahratta sovereign should be spared, in order to induce the Mahratta chiefs to surrender their forts. Aurungzebe was willing to save him on this condition; but Sambajee had now awakened to a sense of his degradation, and courted a death which would wipe away his shame. In this temper Sambajee employed every epithet of abuse to induce some rash soldier to kill him. Aurungzebe sent a message offering him his life on condition of his becoming a Mussulman. "Tell the emperor," cried Sambajee, "that if he will give me his daughter I will become a Mussulman;" and he then gave a keener edge to this insulting offer by pouring out a torrent of invectives upon the prophet of Islam. Aurungzebe was exasperated to the highest degree. He ordered a red hot iron to be drawn across the eyes of Sambajee, his tongue to be cut out, and his head to be severed from his body. The terrible sentence was carried out in the camp bazaar, in August, 1689.

The effect of these events upon the Agency at Fort St. George might be fully gathered from the general letters sent home by the Agency, which, as we have already said, are wanting amongst the Madras Records. Some idea however may be obtained from the notices which appear in the general letters from home, as well as in the Madras consultation books. In a general letter, dated 22nd March, 1687, and evidently penned by Josiah Child, we meet with the following remarks :—

"We know the King of Golconda is rich enough to pay for any assistance you give him, either in diamonds or pagodas ; and therefore we intend to be at no charge for his assistance against the Mogul, but what he shall pay us for beforehand, or put diamonds into your hands for the security of our payment, both principal and interest."

Again in another letter dated 6th June, 1687, we find the following :—

"For the King of Golconda's writing to you, you may acquaint him in a decent and friendly manner, that we are none of his subjects ; wherein we would have you be guided by the old Proverb, "suaviter in modo fortiter in re." But if nevertheless he pretend to any dominion over your city, you may, when you are in a good condition, tell him in plain terms that we own him for our good friend, ally, and confederate, and sovereign and lord paramount of all that country, excepting the small territory belonging to Madras, of which we claim the sovereignty, and will maintain and defend against all persons, and govern by our own laws, without any appeal to any prince or potentate whatsoever, except our Sovereign Lord the king, paying unto him the king of Golconda, our agreed tribute of 1200 pagodas per annum. And if ever he break with you upon these terms, we require you to defend yourselves by arms, and from that time renounce paying him any more tribute.

It being strange to us that while he is oppressed by the Mogul on one hand, and by a poor handful of Dutchmen on the other, you should make yourselves so timorous and fearful of asserting our own king's just right and prerogative to that important place."

The nature of the information previously furnished to the Court of Directors may be gathered from the following entry in the consultation book.

"Tuesday, 15th February, 1687. Upon advice from Mr. James Paiva at the Mines, that the Mogul was lately in a short time to take Golconda, and consequently be master of this king's dominions, and that the French and Dutch had made their applications to him with great presents to settle their affairs in this country:—it was taken into consideration what we should do in behalf of the Right Hon'ble Company, and agreed (in regard of our present hostility against his subjects in Bengal)* that we should only write him a plausible letter of complaint of government injuries to us in Bengal; and that, upon consideration of our difference there, we would not make our applications as the French and Dutch had done; otherwise

* The allusion in the foregoing extract to hostilities against the Mogul's subjects in Bengal, refers to an expedition which was ordered about this time against the Mogul governor of Bengal, in consequence of his tyrannical and oppressive conduct towards the English settlements on the Hooghly. This expedition was sent out during the government of Mr. Gyfford; but its results belong more properly to the annals of his successor Mr. Elihu Hale. We therefore reserve the story until our next chapter.

that our respects were as ready and great as theirs; but desire him to hear our Vakeel concerning our grievances (which have been the occasion of our differences), to redress the same, and to confirm the Right Honorable Company's ancient privileges in Bengal. It is likewise thought convenient to write to his Nabob, to desire his friendship, and to favour us with the delivery of our said letter to the Mogul; and to write to our Vakeel at the camp, sending him said letters to deliver, with copies for his perusal, and directing him to show the Nabob what we write to the Mogul, and that he be sure to represent our case to his Majesty, and make haste to procure a good and lasting firmann."

"Monday, 22nd February. Taking into our serious consideration the great danger we may be in, in case the Mogul should take Golconda, which in all appearance at present he is likely to do,—we think it absolutely necessary to make all manner of provision for our defence, in regard of our present hostility with him and his subjects, and therefore it is ordered that the persons in their several places do proceed and take care of the particulars here undermentioned:—

"*Mr. Warell's charge is viz.*

"To build up the Caldera Point with Battlements that the men may stand by the Guns.

"To make haste to finish the new Platforms formerly ordered to be built at the Sea side and River side, and for the present to get all materials ready.

"To take care that all the Sallyports at the River side between the round Point at Caldera Point, be secured with double Doors, Iron Bars, Bolts, and Locks; that all the inlets to the Town between said Point be made up with Brick, and all the void places built up; and that all Buildings, Rubbish, and what else may be prejudicial that lies round the wall of the Christian Town and in the River, be cleared away.

"That Stores of Brick, Iron Stone, and Chenam, be in a readiness to make up any breaches, and put in the Hog yard, or any other convenient place, within the Walled Town.

"That the Smiths, Bricklayers, Carpenters, Coolies, Muckwaes, and what other workmen or under workmen may be useful to this garrison upon a Siege, have notice given them at such time, as we shall think convenient, to be in readiness upon occasion, and that such persons shall have provisions provided for them.

"To order Pork, Beef, and Fish to be salted, and put up in Jars and Cask, as also Eggs or anything else that may be thought of to keep, as much as can be procured till further order, and to be put up with such care that they may be preserved.

"To be laying in of what wood can be got by degrees, as also Salt, and make Biscuit.

"To order Iron Stone or Red Wood to be laid upon the top of the Fort Walls, to fling down upon the Ladders if they should attempt to scale, and some forks to lie ready to thrust off the ladders.

Mr. Cheney's charge is viz.

"To remove the Powder from the Powder house to the Godowns under the curtain next St. Thomé (or some other convenient place) and brick them up for the more safety, and some powder to be put in the Round Point, in a place that's built for that purpose.

"To get what great Jars he can to put wheat in, and Chenam them up, and set them round the Fort Curtain.

"To make what Powder he can with all expedition.

"To give in an accompt of what stores of Powder, shot great and small, match, etc., ammunition or provision for war (in any kind) we have in readiness; and to fit up the Granado Shells and Mortar Peices, and to make a trial of them beforehand.

"To take care that all the Small Arms be fitted, and constantly looked after, and cleaned.

"To take care that what Stores of Grain we have, or shall be brought in upon this occasion, be put into fitting Granaries within the Walls, to preserve it; and that it be brought into the air and often shifted; and Mr. Fraser, or who else he, Mr. Cheney, shall choose, is appointed to assist him in this.

"To buy Provender for the Horses.

Doctor Wilmot and Doctor Plummer's charge is vizt.

"To provide and make salves for wounds, and to be as sparing of the small surgery box on the Rebecca as they can, that we may not want upon great occasion."

A week afterwards we find the following entry.

"Monday, 28th February. It being of so great concern to be continually mindful to provide for the defence of this Garrison against the Mogul's forces, which we have great reason to fear will come upon us, after he has taken Golconda, therefore we have thought convenient, and order that the persons hereunder named, have further in charge as followeth.

Mr. Wavell's charge is vizt.

"To build a small Point to command the Bridge, and that part of the Town, and the two blank sides of the Caldera Point, large enough to plant six Guns, or eight if there shall be occasion.

"To build a large Tank in some convenient place, within the walled Town, for a store of fresh water, which will be much wanted in case of a siege, all the wells in the Christian Town being brackish.

"*Mr. Cheney's charge is vizt.*

"To put so many great guns upon the Point at the Garden as convenient for ten or fifteen men, and lay in such provisions and ammunition in the lower room, as shall be hereafter upon occasion thought necessary.

"To put six or eight great guns into the new Point, that is to be built for the security of the Bridge, etc. with ammunition for them.

"To fill the new Tank that is ordered to be built, with the best fresh water, and besides to provide and fill what Cask and Jars he can get.

"To make ten Field carriages and fit guns to them.

"To put two or three great guns in the Powder house.'

"It is thought convenient for the safety of this Garrison, securing the Right Honorable Company's estate, and annoying of the enemy in case they should besiege this place, that two or three ships do from this time ride in this Road; and there being none of the Right Honorable Company's ships here, nor any expected (till some may arrive from England) that can be spared upon this design, in regard that they are to go down into the Bay, or already are upon other expeditions:—It is ordered to hire any good serviceable country vessels that may offer, to that number; and that Mr. Cheney do send Men, Guns, Ammunition, and Provisions, or what else may be thought convenient for service, aboard them, on the Right Honorable Company's account."

"Monday, 7th March. Taking into consideration the absolute necessity of having the letters from Bengal delivered to the Mogul (which were sent back by our peons from Mr. Paiva at the mines near Golconda, the 27th of last month, they not finding the Vakeel in the camp) that he, the Mogul, might rightly be informed of our grievances in the Bay, in particular the occasion of the last skirmish :—It is agreed to take advice of Senor Mannche, an Italian doctor inhabitant of this Town, who was formerly in the Mogul's service, which is as follows.

"That we send them (the letters) by a servant of his (the doctor's), that is well acquainted with the Mogul's camp, accompanied by four Rajpoots, to deliver them to two Englishmen there, viz. Thomas and Richard Goodlad ; to the intent that when they observe the Mogul's coming forth, they may hold up said letters, so as to be seen by him, which, he says, the Mogul will receive from the hands of strangers, which otherwise is delivered to some great men to peruse before they come to him, which might prevent the Mogul's having an account of the true contents thereof, which is usual when it is a complaint against any of their friends or great men : and that a small present of oil of cinnamon, oil of mace, and some other rarities be sent to the Englishmen, to give as they shall see occasion : and that the Mogul may have an account of the wrongs and dangers that the Right Hon'ble Company have sustained in the Bay."

The siege of Golconda by the Mogul army lasted seven months, and the place was not finally captured by Aurungzebe until the month of September. All this time great fears were entertained at Fort St. George, that the Mogul would revenge himself upon Madraspatanam for the hostilities which had taken place in Bengal. On the 16th June, we find the following entry in the consultation book :—"It being much to be feared that the King of Golconda cannot hold out long, and that when the Mogul comes to have the possession of the country we have great reason to believe that he will endeavour to revenge himself upon us, as he threatens, there being war declared in Bengal by us, and (as we hear) on their side also."

But before the termination of the siege the administration of Mr. Gyfford was closed, and Mr. Elihu Yale, the first Member of Council, was appointed governor in his room. The following extracts tell their own tale, and close our history of the governorship of Mr. Gyfford.

Saturday, 23rd July, 1687. This evening late the Box of Letters, etc., from the Right Honorable Company per the "Williamson" was brought on shore, and deferred till Monday to be perused.

"Monday, 25th July. The General Letters and Commission from the Right Hon'ble Company were perused, and the President finding by said Commission that Elihu Yale, Esq., was constituted President, and President Gyfford's Commission revoked, he delivered up his charge, which with President Gyfford's best wishes for all good success and prosperity to the Right Hon'ble Company's affairs, under the management of the new President concludes this Consultation Book."*

---

* The records of each Governor spread over several volumes of Consultation Books, but a new Book is always opened with the advent of a new Governor.

CHAPTER VIII.

GOVERNORSHIP OF MR. ELIHU YALE.

1687—1692.

The latter years of the Governorship of Mr. Gyfford, and the early years in Mr. Yale's administration, are marked by circumstances which belong more to the general history of India than to the domestic annals of the Madras Presidency. These circumstances may be indicated in the briefest possible manner. In 1686 Mr. Josiah Child sent out secret instructions, that the English should retaliate upon the Mogul for the injuries they had received in Bengal. The war was fully approved both by the Court of Directors and the reigning sovereign James II. An expedition was sent out with orders to seize Chittagong, and then to march upon Dacca; and further reinforcements were to be supplied by the Presidencies in India. Unfortunately hostilities were commenced before the whole of the forces reached Bengal. The Native troops were defeated, but the Subahdar seized the Factory at Patna; and the English retired to Chutanuttee, or Calcutta, until some arrangement could be made, and a firmaun be obtained from the Mogul. Subsequently the attempt was made to seize Chittagong, but failed. These hostilities, combined with the fact that the Mogul was personally engaged in the conquest of Golconda, rendered the position of the Agency at Fort St. George, one of extreme peril; of which abundant illustrations may be found in the records.

The first incident worthy of notice in the administration of Mr. Yale, is an attempt made by the Portuguese to re-settle at St. Thomé, contrary to the interest of the Agency. We subjoin the original entry.

"Tuesday, 26th July, 1687. The Right Honorable Company having in their former General letter to us of the 14th January, 1685, positively ordered the renting of St. Thomé town from the Divan, but being satisfied it would raise many scruples and difficulties in them, or at least enhance the rent, if we appeared in it, or treated about it ourselves, or in the Right Honorable Company's name:—It was therefore then thought most prudent and convenient, that Chinna Vencatadry undertook the business in his own name, as formerly he and Verona had done, which would make less discourse and noise; and accordingly the President and Council gave him an order under their hands for the same, which, as he tells us, he has ever since been treating about, but that the late and present wars and troubles in the country had thus long obstructed and delayed the conclusion. Meantime, some of our Portuguese inhabitants, since our demanding taxes and advance of customs, have privately negociated this matter by one of their Padres at Golconda, who procured them a firmaun for their re-settlement and trade in the country; and since that, and the news of the Mogul's success against Golconda, with the probability of his coming or sending thither, and our danger thereby,—they have privately, basely, and ungratefully sneaked away to St. Thomé, and there been treating with the Seer Lascar, etc. to take a Lease of St. Thomé Government, and there to fortify and hoist their Flag, which they thought themselves so secure of that they had advanced their standard. When the President, sending away to the Brahmin Governor of these parts about it, and so mind him of his promise thereof to Chinna Vencatadry, with a promise of a gratuity, their grandeur was immediately stopped, and their Flag Staff lowered and we hear since greatly discouraged, which we hope will continue to their return hither with shame and sorrow for their vain expense.

"It is therefore agreed and ordered that Chinna Vencatadry do so prosecute the business as to disappoint them, though we pay something more for it than they offer, which we doubt not in time to recover from them. Besides it is of such absolute necessity to rent that town, as well for preventing the diminishing our trade and customs, as also our force; five parts of our soldiers being Portuguese topasses, who if they should settle at St. Thomé would certainly run thither from us in our necessity."

"Thursday, 4th August, Chinna Vencatadry being returned from Conjeveram, brought the Brahmin Governor's final resolution about the renting of St. Thomé, which was, that he would let it to Chinna Vencatadry for three years, that is the Town, Customs, and adjacent Towns and

Paddy grounds belonging thereto, at the rate of Pagodas 4000 per annum, to be paid at three payments, each four months, one-third part of the rent as customary in this country; also to pay one thousand Pagodas upon receipt of the Cowle from the Seer Lascar, as a peiscush to the Brahmin Governor for his kindness therein. Nothing was to be abated thereof and if we did not presently comply therewith, that he would conclude with and let it to the Portuguese. In consideration whereof, and the many prejudices it may do this city, under those ill circumstances we are at present; and being informed by Chinna Vencatadry that the Town Customs, etc., were let last year at Pagodas 4,100, and that the crop and revenues this year rather promised profit than loss:—it is agreed and ordered that Chinna Vencatadry do rent the same according to the aforesaid terms, in his own name for the Right Honorable Company's account, and not to exceed anything if the Governor should play his usual tricks; as he has already done with the Portuguese, who already have given him Pagodas 500; and that no peiscush be given him, till the Seer Lascar's cowle be delivered to us."

From a subsequent entry, dated 23rd August, 1688, we learn that the Portuguese still held out, but that Mr. Yale had obtained a Cowle on agreeing to pay 3800 Pagodas yearly. "Notwithstanding," we are told, "the many difficulties we have had about the renting of St. Thomé, the President has by private correspondence procured a Cowle for renting the Town and Customs of. St. Thomé and the adjacent countries as far as St. Thomas's Mount; notwithstanding the Portuguese huffs and noise of the Mogul's firmaun for their free enjoyment of the town, which has cost them by their envoy priest at least 7000 Pagodas to the Mogul's officers; and it is now reported their mighty firmaun proves only a compliment referring them to former customs in the King of Golconda's time, and to agree with the Government of St. Thomé as well as they can." The Cowle however was obtained in the name of Chinna Vencatadry, both in consequence of the hostilities with the Mogul and his aversion for the English, and especially "that we might not too much exasperate the Portuguese in their loss and disappointment of a place they retain a most superstitious veneration for, which possibly might provoke them to mutiny or rebellion, or at least some disturbance or mischief; they being at present two-thirds of our soldiers, and at least six for one to the English inhabitants."

The next extract refers to the old practice amongst the members of the Agency, of all dining together in the dining room of the Fort. It would appear that the previous President Mr. Gyfford preferred living at the Government Garden House, which had been erected outside the old Fort, and not far from the site of Munro's statue. The Directors however complained of the expense of keeping two tables; but we give the original entry.

"Friday, 29th July, 1687. The Right Honorable Company in their General Letter, having complained of their great charge in keeping two tables, which was chiefly occasioned by President Gyfford's indisposition, the Fort being always unhealthful to him, necessitated his living at the Garden, which he found to agree with him much better. And though the Council do suppose and believe that the Right Honorable the Company do still retain a good esteem and respect for him and his services, yet in obedience to their Honour's orders we cannot presume to continue that charge; and President Gyfford desiring to excuse his coming to the Fort, and to continue at the Garden during his short stay in India,—it is thought fit and ordered to be allowed him Pagodas 25 per month for his diet while here, with a suitable number of Peons and other servants."

This year 1687, was distinguished by an extraordinary monsoon, which is thus described.

"Sunday, 9th October 1687. The monsoon breaking up sooner this year than is expected or usual, there happened great damage to the ships and vessels in these roads. It began on Tuesday, the 4th instant, when there ran a great sea and surf all day, and in the afternoon a flurry of wind and rain. On Wednesday, the same great sea and surf continued, with a flurry of wind and rain in the forenoon. On Thursday, the wind blew ships were driven from their anchors, and some were forced on shore. (Particulars of ships omitted.) On Friday, a very great storm of wind and rain all day. Saturday, the wind blowing very hard last night forced the "Loyal Adventure" and "Borneo Merchant" from their anchors; the former being found this morning broke to peices at St. Thomas's Point, the latter a little to the southward. During the fierceness of this storm, the winds continued between east and north east, which brought the sea very near the bulwark and wall; but this morning the wind and sea abating, we hope the danger is past.

"Ordered that a strict watch and guard be continued to be kept at the sea-side to prevent embezzling anything, that may be driven ashore; also that ten peons be sent along the coast to Pulicat and ten to Covelong, and inquire all the way for goods driven ashore; and if find any to secure them for the Right Honorable Company, and give us present advice thereof, lest the Country Governments seize them as forfeitures."

The following extract, referring to the number of peons assigned to each official, will explain itself.

"Saturday, 29th October, 1687. There having been some discourse about settling attendance of peons to the Council, which is agreed and ordered as followeth. To the Governor 20 peons; to the second 6 peons; to the Judge 5 peons and 2 talliars; to the Warehousekeeper 4 peons; to the Chief Justice and Customer 3 peons and 2 talliars; the rest of the Council 2 peons 1 talliar each; to be constantly at their disposal, except some extraordinary occasion requires them to other service."

In September of this year, the Fort of Golconda was taken by Aurungzebe, and in October, the news reached Fort St. George, as appears from the following entries.

"Saturday, 29th October, 1687. Having received a letter from Potty Khan, Commissioned by the Mogul to be Soubadar of this part of the country, and Governor of Chingleput Fort as formerly, who advises us that the Mogul has certainly taken Golconda Castle, and the king prisoner; and that all the considerable Forts and Towns in this country have already admitted the Mogul's colours and government, the Towns of Pulicat and St. Thomé our nearest neighbours having also submitted thereto; he also intimating to us the ceremony and solemnity that was generally performed at the news of the conquest, implicitly desiring and expecting the same from us; which being a matter of no great weight or charge, and may oblige them, and the neglect do us a prejudice:—It is agreed and ordered that the servant that brought the letter be tasherift with perpetuanos, and that 15 guns be fired at the delivery of the President's letter to them, and 20 marcalls of paddy given among the poor, in respect to their customs in such cases."

"Saturday, 7th January, 1688. This evening the Right Honorable Company's Chief Merchant acquainted the President that one of the Mogul's life guards, sent down into these parts to receive his rents, desired to wait upon him to-morrow; but doubting he might be too prying and inquisitive of the garrison, the President excused his coming then, as being Sunday, and desired it may be at nine this night. Three other Members of

Council were sent for and were present at his coming, when after a long discourse of the Court and Government, he declared the occasion of his coming was, that he had received about a lakh of Rupees and 6000 Pagodas for the Mogul's account, and had left it at Poonamallee; but in regard Sevajee's flying army was foraging those parts, and robbing and plundering, desired our assistance, supply him with 300 horse, 500 soldiers and 500 peons to guard it as far as Kistna River; which he pressed hard, and that it would be most acceptable to the King to serve him in his danger. But the Governor considering the unreasonableness and dangerous consequence of undertaking such a charge, or intermeddling with things of that nature, returned him for answer, that we should be always ready to serve the Mogul, but that he well knew Sevajees's forces, and that he had lately taken three Forts and a hundred Towns very near us, and done many other mischiefs in the country, and that this place was also threatened by him, and that he was within twenty-four hours of us: therefore we could not spare our forces from our guard. Besides that, three or four hundred horse would signify little to Sevajee's three or four thousand in the field, though we feared not ten times so many here; but there it would run the King's money and our people into great danger. Thereupon desired him (the Mogul's life guard) to consider well of it. Whereupon he desired permission to bring it into Town; but hearing of our war in Bengal he requested that the President would give him his word and hand that he and his treasure should be safe, and have liberty to carry it away when he thought convenient. Which being agreed to by all, he was told by the President that the Town was free to all persons, and that no prejudice should be done to him by the English, but that they should fare as we did, and that he might choose what place he pleased to reside in; desiring him to send no more people than necessary, and those to be sober and civil. Whereupon he was dismissed with rosewater and betel, and seemed pleased with the discourse and the entertainment."

"Friday, 13th January. Letters last night advise that Sevajee's forces had plundered Conjeveram, killed about 500 men, destroying the Town, and put the inhabitants to flight, dispersing themselves about the country, and many of them run hither; and about twelve this day came a letter from Chingleput advising the Governor that they had certain news from the Mahratta camp, that they had drawn out a party of about 2000 horse and 5000 foot under the command of a General, to assault this place, giving them encouragement that the plunder should be their own. Upon which advice the Governor and Council ordered that the Portuguese and Gentoos should be summoned to their arms; one man from each family that had two therein, and two from each family that had six hard with rain most part of the day, and many therein, from 15 to 60 years of age. Copy of said summons is as followeth.

"By the Governor and Council, these are to give notice and summons all persons whatever, inhabitants of or dwellers in this city of Madras, to send one man in arms from each house or family that have two men therein, betwixt the ages of fifteen and sixty years, and all families that have six men to send out two with arms. The Portuguese to meet before their Church, and the Gentoos at the Town Choultry, by four of the clock to-morrow evening, being the 14th instant; where they shall be commanded and disposed to such guards and watches, as shall be judged most necessary. The default of any person herein to be punished or fined at the pleasure of the Governor and Council. Dated in Fort St. George, the thirteenth day of January, one thousand six hundred eighty and eight.

The following extract is interesting for reasons which will be presently explained.

"Thursday 26th Jany. 1688. The Council did not meet this day, the President's only son dying last night, was interred this morning to their great grief and sorrow."

This is but an every day incident; a little boy, an only son, carried away to the great grief and sorrow of his desolate parents. But this small event possesses an interest still. On the north wall of the mausoleum on the Light House esplanade, may still be seen the granite slab, which was set up in memory of the only son, nearly two centuries ago. We copy the inscription.

"Hic jacet DAVID
Filius Honorabilis ELIHU YALE
Presidentis et Gubernatoris Castelli
St. Georgii et Civitatis Madrassae natus
Fuit 15 May 1684 et obiit 25 January Anno 168$\frac{7}{8}$.

For the sake of our lady readers we append a translation.

"Here lies DAVID
Son of the Honorable ELIHU YALE
President and Governor of Fort
St. George and the city of Madras
Born 15 May 1684 and died 25 January in the year 168$\frac{7}{8}$.

On the south wall of the same mausoleum is a slab in memory of Mr. Joseph Hynmers, who had been a member of Council during the governorships of Sir William Langhorne and Mr. Streynsham Master.

The following circumstance does not speak much for Madras Society in the old times.

"Thursday, 8th March, 1688. Mrs. Francis, wife to the late Lieutenant Francis killed at Hoogly by the Moors, being sent hither from Bengal very poor, she made it her petition that she might keep a Punch house for her maintenance. But she being a notorious bad woman, it is agreed that she be not permitted to keep a public house, lest it be the occasion of many debaucheries and disorders; she having lived very scandalously formerly here. It is therefore ordered that she go on the "Royal James" to the West Coast, and that according to the Right Honorable Company's order, she be allowed something out of the proceeds of the prizes, to provide her necessaries, in consideration of the loss of her husband in the late unhappy Bengal expedition." From a subsequent entry we learn that this lady was afterwards sent home to prevent "further scandal in our city."

The following extracts indicate the great danger the Agency was in about this time.

"Monday, 16th April, 1688. Captain Freeman is ordered to summon his Company of Train Bands to a general training upon the Island opposite to the Fort, on Wednesday next being Easter Week; and that the chief of the Moors and Gentoo inhabitants be invited to dine with the Governor and Council there, and that a handsome preparation be made for it accordingly, this being the first general appearance and will make a great report in the country."

"Sunday, 6th May, 1688. Letters from Mr. Chardin at Golconda to the Governor, of April last, give the following account. That the Mogul would free his son Shah Allum from his long confinement, but the Prince generously refused it except he would also enlarge Abul Hassan, the king of Golconda, because he (the Prince) was instrumentally the ruin of the king; having formerly engaged his word that neither the Mogul nor he, should ever come with power to trouble him; and that he would rather choose to lose his life, than break his faith and word with the king of Golconda, which was confirmed by his faith. That Sevajee's troops, joined with Siddee Masson's, are within six leagues of Golconda, burning and destroying all before them, they expect them there in a little time. That Nabob Rowalloo Khan had sent his jewels and treasure into the castle, and he and his family are on the following thereof. That there are no soldiers in the Fort (of Golconda), nor provisions fit to withstand an enemy, so that if the enemy comes, he may with great facility take the Fort. That the Dutch and French are much in the Mahratta's favour, and all roads are full of robbers. That the King of Persia marcheth in person with a great army after Sultan Akbar, to give him help, in case the 60,000 horsemen he hath already sent be not sufficient; and sworn upon his beard that he will set him upon the Indostan throne."*

This year the Union Jack was ordered to be hoisted at Fort St. George; and the following is the official account of the ceremony.

"Tuesday, 12th June, 1688. According to appointment for the solemnity of hoisting his Majesty's Flag in this Garrison, the Governor made this evening a handsome collation upon the Fort House Terrace, where he was accompanied with the Council, and chief of the Right Hon'ble Company's servants, and most of the eminent freemen and inhabitants of the city of all nations and casts; the Garrison three Companies being in arms, also the Trained Band consisting of near 100 Englishmen, commanded by Captain Robert Freeman and Lieutenant John Afflœck; when after an orderly march round the Fort, the Garrison soldiers drew round within the Fort and the Trained Bands without; when upon hoisting the Union Flag upon the Standard on the English bastion, the Go-

* This extract would prove useful to the general historian. Elphinstone merely records that Akbar, the revolted son of Aurungzebe, had taken refuge first in the Court of Sambajee the Mahratta, and afterwards in Persia, and that he died at the latter place in 1706.

vernor began a glass of Toby to our gracious King's health and Royal Family's, and his happy long reign; which was duly performed by all there, and honoured with three vollies of small shot, and as many cheerful huzzas from all the soldiers; and by thirty one pieces of ordnance, which was answered by all the ships in the Roads; also one and twenty pieces of ordnance with hearty wishes of success and prosperity to our Right Honorable Masters the Right Honorable East India Company, and nineteen pieces to their Honorable Governor Sir Josiah Child; and the more to honour this occasion there was several persons freed and generous contributions to the poor; and the soldiers as merry as Punch could make them, till night silenced all in repose."

The following account of an exchange of visits between members of the Dutch Government at Pulicat, and members of the Council of Fort St. George, will be found very interesting.

Monday, 16th July, 1688. Being advised from Pulicat of the arrival of the Heer Van Readen, Commissary General for the Dutch East India Company, with an unlimited power for the settlement of their affairs in these parts, and being also in place equal to the General of Batavia; and it being customary upon all alteration of Governors either here or at Pulicat, to send two of Council to welcome and congratulate them to the place, to preserve a fair and friendly correspondence with them; but this person being in an extraordinary employ and authority, it is thought requisite and accordingly ordered that three of our Council be sent with a letter from the Governor to compliment him at Pulicat, viz., Mr. Nathaniel Higginson, Mr. Robert Freeman, and Mr. Thomas Wavell."

According to this decision the three gentlemen started for Pulicat on the following Monday evening, and returned to Fort St. George on Wednesday morning; and the next day being Council day, they gave the following account of their journey to Pulicat and entertainment there.

"That on Tuesday the 24th instant, about seven of the clock in the morning, arriving at a Garden near Pulicat, they sent the Commissary General word that they were coming to wait on him; on which he desired their longer stay there, that he might send some of his people to conduct them to town. About ten of the clock came six of the Council, also many attendants with them, to meet them there; and after a welcome salute were conducted to the Fort Gate, where they were received by the Vice Commissary; and thence through a guard of soldiers passed to the stairs foot, where they were received by the Governor Pitt, and so conveyed up to the Commissary, who kindly received them; and, after the delivery of the President's Letter, welcomed them with twenty-one guns. Some time after went to dinner and were handsomely treated, and, as it was always customary, began the King of England's health with twenty-one guns, and then the Parliament's, the Right Honorable Company's, and the Presidents. About nine they parted with the same salute of guns as they had when they came in. During the whole time they were courteously treated and entertained, the Commissary General often expressing his kind resentment of our visit and respects, promising suddenly to return it, assuring them of his readiness to serve the Honorable Company's interest in all places he had an opportunity for it.

The very next day the visit was returned, and the Dutch visitors were duly entertained at Fort St. George. But we extract the account from the consultation book.

"Thursday, 28th July. This morning about seven o'clock, the Herr Commander Johannes Bacherus, successor to the Commissary General, sent the President word by the Chief Dubash, that he was come to the Garden to acknowledge and repay his late visit and civility to the Commissary General: Upon which the President appointed Mr. John Biggs, Mr. John Littleton, Mr. R. Freeman, and Mr. Thomas Wavell with a handsome retinue to meet and bring them into the City and Fort; where Mr. Higginson met them at the Gate, and so led them up stairs to the President then at the stair head. After the delivery of the Dutch Commissary General's letter, and his message (being return of thanks for the late visit at Pulicat), they were kindly welcomed with twenty-one guns. After some time and discourse of the Commissary his proceedings, and other public affairs, went up to a handsome dinner in the Consultation Room, where the usual healths, to equal their entertainment, were began to the Prince of Orange with twenty-one guns, the States General, Dutch East India Company, and the Commissary's. After dinner about three o'clock the President, the more to oblige and divert them, carried them by boat to the Hon'ble Company's new Garden, where they were also handsomely entertained. After supper about ten o'clock the President delivered him his Letter of thanks to the Commissary General, and acknowledging the honour and kindness he was pleased to do him, with thanks also to their several troubles of the journey, excusing the slenderness of their entertainment; which they acknowledged to be very generous and kind, appearing greatly satisfied thereat, requesting leave to return to the place from whence they came. They parted with kind salutes, accompanied to the Garden by Mr. Littleton, Mr. Wavell, and Mr. Robert Freeman."

The following entries illustrative of the slave trade formerly carried on in this Presidency, will tell their own story. We have deemed it advisable to place them together, as they possess an interest by themselves.

"Monday, 1st August, 1687. The trade in slaves growing great from this Port, by reason of the great plenty of poor, by the sore famine, and their cheapness,—it is ordered for the future that each slave sent off this shore pay one Pagoda custom to the Right Honorable Company, and that the Justices do receive no more for the usual fee for registering and passport, than two fanams a head till the Council shall think fit to alter it as formerly."

In the same month we find the following entry

concerning the black slave of an English Captain who had died in the Madras Roads:—"Captain Richard Warner having by his last will and testament given his black slave Francis Carwar aged about 14 years, his freedom, the present commander is ordered to discharge him the ship, and permit him to stay ashore."

"Thursday, 29th September, 1687. We do now order that Mr. Fraser (who being Land Customer has the best opportunity for it), do buy forty young sound slaves for the Right Honorable Company, and dispose them to the several Mussulaes, two or three in each, in charge of the Chief man of the Boat, to be fed and taught by them, and to encourage their care therein, it is ordered a short red broad cloth coat be given to each Chief man; and that the Right Honorable Company's mark be embroidered with silk on their backs, with the number of their rank and the boat, which are also to be so numbered, whereby we shall have them at better command, our business go more currently on, and easier thereby discover their thieveries."

"Thursday, 2nd February, 1688. In consideration of the several inconveniences that have happened by the exportation of children stolen from their parents, to prevent which for the future,—it is ordered that no slaves shall be shipped off or transported, except such who are first examined by the Justices of the Choultry, and their several names registered in a book for that purpose; for which the Justices are to receive two fanams for each slave. And whosoever shall offend against this same rule, and shall be convicted of stealing people, are to pay for the first fault five Pagodas, and for the next to lose their ears in the pillory. And this order shall be fixed upon the several gates and in the Choultry."

"Monday, 14th May, 1688. The custom by the exportation of slaves here, being now of little advantage to the Right Hon'ble Company by their scarcity, and it having brought upon us great complaints and troubles from the country government, for the loss of their children and servants spirited and stolen from them, which being likely to increase, by the new government of the Mogul's who are very averse, and prohibit all such trade in his dominions, and has lately expressed his displeasure therein against the Dutch for their exporting of slaves from Metchlepatam. To prevent which prejudice and mischiefs for the future, and we having received a late letter from the Seer Lascar about it,—it is agreed and ordered that, after the 20th instant, no person inhabitant of this place, either Christian or other, do directly or indirectly buy or transport slaves from this place or any adjacent Port (whereby the Government may be any ways troubled or prejudiced) upon the penalty of fifty Pagodas for each slave bought and transported against this our order. But in consideration that several persons in town have formerly bought slaves which still remain by them, by reason of their sickness or want of opportunity to transport them:—It is agreed that they be permitted to ship off such slaves, provided they give a list of them to the Justices of the Choultry, and produce them publicly there, to be duly examined and registered. And the better to prevent any demands upon them hereafter, the Justices are ordered to proclaim the same by beat of Drum ; that no person may pretend ignorance thereof, and that all may come and make their demands for children and slaves stolen, and upon due proof, they be delivered to them free of charge."

CHAPTER IX.

GOVERNORSHIP OF MR. ELIHU YALE.

(Continued.)

1687—1692.

The great domestic event in the Governorship of Mr. Elihu Yale, was the institution of a Mayor and Corporation. The political significance of the municipality has hitherto been but dimly apprehended. Mill, the most philosophic of all the historians of India, passes it over as a matter of slight importance; whilst his commentator H. H. Wilson offers no remark upon it whatever. The originator of the scheme was Mr. Josiah Child, the great Governor of the Board of Directors. The genius of this man is stamped upon the records of the time. Here and there we alight upon passages from his pen, so pregnant with political wisdom, that we frequently regret that our task is confined to unfolding the domestic annals of the Madras Presidency, rather than to reviewing the whole history of British India. In confirmation of our judgment, and before describing the origin of the Madras Corporation, we will extract the following remarks from a General letter dated 28th September, 1687, which have reference to the appointment of Mr. Nathaniel Higginson to be second in Council, and which are as applicable now as they were nearly two centuries ago.

"Let none of you think much or grudge at the speedy advancement of Mr. Higginson. We do not do it out of any partiality to him, for he has no relation here to speak for him, nor ever had the ambition to think of such a thing himself; neither have we done it out of any ill feeling or disrespect to any others now being of our Council, but sincerely as we apprehend for the public good; knowing him to be a man of learning, and competently well read in ancient histories of the Greeks and Latins, which, with a good stock of natural parts, only can render a man fit for Government and Political Science, martial prudence, and other requisites for ruling over a great city. This, we say, with some experience of the world and knowledge of the laws and customs of nations, can alone qualify men for such a Government, and for treaties of peace or war, or commerce with foreign Princes. It is not being bred a boy in India, or studying long there and speaking the language, understanding critically the trade of the place, that is sufficient to fit a man for such a command as the second of Fort St. George is, or may be in time; though all these qualifications are very good in their kind, and essentially necessary to the well carrying on of the trade; and little science was not necessary formerly, when we were in the state of mere trading merchants. But the case is altered from that, since his Majesty has been pleased, by his Royal Charters and during his Royal will and pleasure, to form us into the condition of a Sovereign State in India, that we may offend, or defend ourselves, and punish all that injure us in India as the Dutch do.

"The great trouble we labour under is, that you cannot get out of your old forms, and your cavilling way of writing, or perverting or misconstruing, procrastinating or neglecting our plain and direct orders to you; as if you were not a subordinate but a co-ordinate power with us; which has and will (till you conform to our known minds and intentions) forced us to make more changes in your Council than anything else could have induced us to; of which we hope we shall have no more hereafter, but that your well understanding and performance of our orders will cause us to change the style of our letters to you, as we hoped to have done before this, for which we more earnestly desire a fit occasion than you can yourselves."

The man that wrote these pregnant sentences may have had a hard heart, and an ungovernable temper, but we say emphatically, that his head was the head of a statesman. His reproofs were sharp, but they were the dictates of genius, and not the impertinence of a mere official.

But to proceed with our main subject. The idea of a municipal government was not directly borrowed from English institutions, as many might suppose. It was originally taken from the Dutch governments in the east; and the object Child had in view was to bring the Dutch form of government into conformity with the English traditionary idea. But we shall leave Mr. Child to explain his plan in his own words; so that our readers may be able to admire the clear headed practical way in which the wise old merchant of Leadenhall Street explained his views to the Agency at Fort St. George. The directions are given at length in the same General Letter already quoted of the 28th of September, 1687.

"We observe in the book containing the Dutch methods sent us by Mr. Yale, not much more than some of us understood before of their affairs; but as there appears in this, great wisdom and policy, so since that time they have much bettered their constitutions, and refined their politics, and created many kinds of incomes, to increase their revenues, which they thought not of when those papers were first digested some thirty years since. However, we recommend to you the frequent reading and consideration of what is contained in those papers, which the oftener you read, the more you will discover the wisdom of those persons which contrived those methods.

"Their having all Lieutenants in their Garrisons to command their Companies, and a Major without a Company to command under their Governor, we may initiate in due time, but think it not proper at present, until your civil power be as well established and obeyed at Fort St. George as theirs is at Batavia.

"But if you could contrive a form of a corporation to be established, of the Natives mixed with some English freemen, for aught we know some public use might be made thereof; and we might give the members some privileges and pre-eminencies by Charter under our seal, that might please them (as all men are naturally with a little power); and we might make a public advantage of them, without abating essentially any part of our dominion when we please to exert it. And it is not unlikely that the heads of the several castes, being made Aldermen and some others Burgesses, with power to choose out of themselves yearly their Mayor, and to tax all the inhabitants for a Town Hall, or any public buildings for themselves to make use of,— your people would more willingly and liberally disburse five shilling towards the public good, being taxed by themselves, than sixpence imposed by our despotical power (notwithstanding they shall submit to when we see cause), were Government to manage such a society, as to make them proud of their honour and preferment, and yet only ministerial, and subservient to the ends of the Government, which under us is yourselves.

" We direct nothing positively in this, but refer it to your consideration, and, if you think it may redound to the public good, and that you may the better adapt it to the good of the place, and establishing of our absolute power over it, and unto some similitude to the forms of such like Corporations in England where there is always a Governor, a superior power, and a Garrison, we have thought fit to send you a copy of the late Charter granted by his Majesty to the Borough of Portsmouth, where Sir John Biggs (Judge of the new Court of Admiralty at Madras) was Recorder, and understands well not only that constitution, but the practical way of proceeding it.

"We know this can be no absolute platform for you. You may make great alterations according to the nature of the place and the people, and the difference of laws, customs, and almost everything else, between England and India; but this will serve as a foundation from whence to begin your considerations and debates concerning this affair; which will require great wisdom and much thinking and foresight, to create such a Corporation in Madras, as will be beneficial to the Company and place, without the least diminution of the sovereign power his Majesty has entrusted us with, and which we are resolved to exercise there during his Majesty's royal pleasure and confidence in us.

"Upon the whole matter, if you think any such constitution beneficial, and shall send us a Charter filled up with the names of the first and modern Mayor, Aldermen, and Burgesses,—the proper habits and ornaments we shall enjoin them to wear in the Court house and upon all other solemn occasions,—and what maces, or ensigns of authority, we shall admit to be carried before them by their proper officers or serjeants,—we shall consider of it, and probably return it to you, engrossed under our larger seal, with none or very little alteration.

"We conceive their Court Books must always be kept in the English tongue; and the Town clerk must always be an English man, that can speak Portuguese and Gentoo; and their Recorder must be the same. The habit of the Aldermen in that hot country, we think ought to be thin scarlet silk gowns; their number twelve, besides the Mayor; that they may be allowed to have Kettysols over them. The Burgesses to wear black silk gowns; their number to be limited to 60, 80, or 100, as you shall find most convenient. The serjeants attending them, to bear silver Maces gilt, not exceeding one yard in length. All officers to be elected by the Mayor and Aldermen, with the approbation of our President, and to be paid by the corporation such reasonable salaries as the Mayor and Aldermen shall think fit; and to have such fees established by the Mayor and Aldermen as shall be settled and appointed by them with approbation of our President and Council. And, to give the Mayor and some of the Aldermen power to be always Justices of the Peace, as in the Portsmouth Charter, and to have power to try all causes that shall be brought before them,—to erect a proper prison for the use of the Corporation, and to award judgment and execution in all causes that shall be exhibited before them. The judgment to go always according to the sense of the Mayor and major part of the Aldermen present. But if any party thinks himself injured in a cause exceeding the value of twenty shillings by the sentence of the said Mayor and Aldermen,—the party offended may appeal for a rehearing to our Judge and Judicature of the Admiralty; who shall determine any cause brought before them by appeal, within two Court days next after the appeal brought; and their determination shall be final. In all civil causes, any party grieved by the sentence of the said Mayor and Aldermen, or any Mayor or Justice of the said Corporation, may appeal to our President and Council for redress, who shall determine thereof the very next Council day ensuing, to the end that Justice be not delayed.

"We think it may be convenient that in the said Court of Aldermen, being twelve beside the Mayor, there should never be above three English freemen, and three Portuguese; the other seven to be Moors and Gentoos. But if you find any inconvenience or inconsistency, in the particulars we have propounded, you may correct or alter them in the draught you send us for such a Corporation.

"All fines levied in the said Corporation shall be half to the use of the Company, and the other half to the use of the Corporation; and in regard Sir John Biggs went over so well instructed as to the raising of some petty duties for the Company's new Court of Admiralty, we shall need to say no more of that now, but expect to hear from you and him, how you have regulated that matter for the benefit of the Company, and use of the inhabitants.

"If you should find such a Corporation as aforesaid advisable to be instituted, it would be most convenient that all debates in the Court of Aldermen should be in English (if it were possible); but if that cannot be at present, you must contrive methods to bring it to that in time.

"If the officers of the Court of Aldermen should seize any Englishmen for drunkenness or any such like crime, they are not to be resisted; but every

Englishman is to be carried before the President, or some English Justice of the Peace, and not to be judged or censured by any foreigner in a criminal cause. But in an action civil or personal, between an Englishman and any foreigner, the Court of Aldermen, by the Mayor's vote, shall judge and determine without appeal, if the value be under three Pagodas; but if it be above three Pagodas any party aggrieved may appeal to our Court of Admiralty as aforesaid.

"The Mayor and two Aldermen shall be a quorum for the trial of petty causes; but no duty shall be levied upon the inhabitants for public structures, officer's salaries or other ornaments, but with consent of the Mayor and at least six of the Aldermen.

"The Mayor, Aldermen, and Burgesses, and all their officers, before they enter upon their respective trusts shall take an oath to be true and faithful to his Majesty, to the Company, and to the Company's General of India for the time being.

"The Court of Aldermen may, by virtue of the powers granted by our intended Charter, assess and levy a rate upon the inhabitants for the building of one or more free school or schools for teaching the English tongue to Gentoos, or Moors, or other Indian children; and for salaries to the Schoolmasters, and by degrees for many other public good works, their constitution being to be so framed, that our President and Council shall always influence their debates and resolutions.

"Your three English Aldermen are always to be the Company's servants, and when any of them, for any cause, cease to be the Company's servants, they are to cease to be Aldermen; and our President and Council are to nominate and appoint some other of the Company's servants to be Aldermen in the room and stead of such English Aldermen so removed from the Company's service.

"If any doubt arise concerning the true meaning or exercise of the powers intended by such a Charter, our President and Council are to determine all such doubts; and all persons are to conform to their determination until our own minds be further declared therein.

"Besides the copy of the Portsmouth Charter to help your invention, we have drawn a similar form of Charter with such alteration as we apprehend necessary at present, which you may alter and add thereunto as you see cause, and then return another draught to us, with the blanks filled up with the names of all such persons as you think fittest to be the first and modern constitution.

"In your nomination of the first Aldermen, and for ever hereafter, you must observe not to make two brothers at the same time Aldermen, nor any that are near kindred; but so mix the heads of all castes in that Court that you may always hold the balance. Many other particulars of this and other kinds, you may find wisely provided for in the Dutch papers before mentioned, which will be worth your studying and frequent perusal.

"Our design in the whole is to set up the Dutch Government among the English in the Indies (than which a better cannot be invented) for the good of posterity, and to put us upon an equal footing of power with them to offend or defend, or enlarge the English dominion and unite the strength of our nation under one entire and absolute command subject to us; as we are and ever shall be most dutifully to our own sovereign. But this distinction we will make, that we will always observe our own old English terms, viz. Attorney General instead of Fiscal, Alderman instead of Scepin, Burgesses instead of Burghers, Serjeants instead of Bailies, President and Agent instead of Commander, Director, or Commissary, etc. And this with his Majesty's approbation we are resolved to pursue steadily, and throw everything out of the way that obstructs or retards this good and great reformation."

Such was the plan proposed by Mr. Josiah Child to the Madras Council on the 28th September, 1687; and which we believe is now published for the first time. It is a curious coincidence that at this very moment a similar plan is being laid before the Madras Government by the Sanitary Reform Committee in this Presidency; a circumstance which will not diminish the interest of the above record. Mr. Josiah Child however was far more prompt in carrying out the scheme, than modern authorities are likely to be. Though he had invited the Agency at Madras to offer any suggestions they pleased, yet within three months, the maces and sword were sent out, together with orders for the immediate formation of a Corporation, and within a year the Corporation itself was in working order. On the 12th December, 1687, the Agency was informed that Mr. Child, as

Governor of the Company, and Mr. Bathurst, as Deputy Governor, had been admitted to an audience with his Majesty James II and the Cabinet Council; and that the audience had resulted in a determination to send out a Charter under the Company's seal. In September, 1688, the Corporation was fairly established, as will be seen by the following extracts.

"Thursday, 13th September, 1688. According to yesterday's summons, the President and Council met at the Fort Hall, to advise about the establishing of the Corporation of this city, where were present all,—the Mayor, Recorder, Aldermen, and Burgesses in town; when it was agreed to meet in their Gowns and Ornaments at the Town Hall on the 29th instant. The Aldermen in scarlet serge gowns, and the Burgesses in white China silk, to consult about the choosing whom they shall think fit to make up the number of Aldermen appointed by the Charter.

"Saturday, 29th September, 1688. According to this day's appointment, the President, Mayor, Recorder, Aldermen, Burgesses and chief of the inhabitants met at the Fort Hall; before whom the Right Honorable Company's Charter was publicly read by the Secretary. After which the President administered oaths to the Mayor and Recorder for their due performance of their places; and then the Mayor and Recorder did the like to the Aldermen and Burgesses, in their several manner and forms. A while after went to dinner, and about three in the evening the whole Corporation marched in their several Robes, with the Maces before the Mayor, to the Town Hall."

"Monday, 29th October, 1688. Mr. Nathaniel Higginson, Mayor, having the care and charge of the General Books of Accompts and the Mint upon him, which will take up so much of his time that he cannot attend the Court so often as may be requisite,—it is therefore agreed and ordered that the Mayor's Court be held once a fortnight, and that any two of the three English Aldermen Justices, or what other Aldermen are willing to go to the Choultry as formerly twice a week, to hear, punish, and determine all small offences and complaints to the amount of two Pagodas fine or award, all greater to be deferred to the Mayor's Court to be examined and decided there."

Before leaving this subject we may mention that in consequence of the troubles arising from the war with the Mogul, and the presence of Aurungzebe in the Dekkhan, no direct Municipal assessment was made for some time afterwards, and that consequently, the Mayor and Aldermen delivered in the following petition, dated 5th August, 1689.

"To the Hon'ble Elihu Yale, President and Governor of Fort St. George, and Council.

"Whereas the Right Hon'ble English East India Company having been pleased by their Charter under their larger seal, bearing date the 30th day of December, 1687, in the third year of our Sovereign Lord James the 2nd, King of Great Britain, etc., to make this their city a corporation, by constituting and erecting a Court, consisting of Mayor, Aldermen, etc., not only for the ease of the Hon'ble President, etc., as also for hearing and redeeming all complaints and grievances of the inhabitants according to to equity, good conscience, as well as the Laws of the English nation; and because the Corporation have not as yet any stock, or found able to defray the necessary charges and expences of such officers and servants as must unavoidably be employed for the public good of the place; and seeing the circumstances of the times are so that we cannot impose yet any taxes upon the inhabitants, either to support the Corporation by building a Town Hall, Schools, Sewers, etc., for ornament and heathfulness of the place,—

"The Mayor and Aldermen, etc. do humbly request the Honorable President and Council would please to grant and assign over to the Corporation, the petty dues of Banksall Toll, measuring of grain, weighing of goods, as is usual in all Corporations in England."

This request was granted at the consultation held on the Monday following.

We now turn to the general history of the Presidency. In August, 1688, an Assurance Office was established in Madras, according to the plan laid down in the following notice.

"These are to give notice to all persons, that the Right Honorable Company have ordered and established an Assurance Office for the greater encouragement and security of trade, where all persons may be rightly informed therein, both as to assuring and being assured, according to the several voyages and premiums the parties shall treat and agree upon; where also they may have authentic Policies drawn and registered, the fees whereof being only one quarter per cent. to the Right Hon'ble Company, and nine fanams to the register for each Policy; and those who have occasion may repair to Mr. Thomas Gray at his office in the Custom House; no other Policies being held legal but which are registered by him. Dated at Fort St. George in the City of Madras this 23th day of August, anno 1688."

The following extracts will speak for themselves.

"Monday, 12th November, 1688. Some rogues to the northward having falsified and conterfeited our Pagodas Coin, making Pagodas of the same stamp but not three quarters the value of ours, which has raised great doubts and scandals upon our coin, to the depreciating it two or three per cent. below Pulicat Pagodas, even in our city by the Merchants and Shroffs to the great prejudice and discredit of our Pagodas, and loss of our Mint custom:—it is therefore agreed and ordered that Proclamation be made in several parts of the town and city, prohibiting all persons whatever from advancing anything upon the Pulicat Pagoda by exchange; and whosoever shall offend herein, to pay twenty Pagodas for the first fault, and double for the second, and a twelvemonth's improvement for the third.

"Also that all persons be forbidden to send Gold from hence to be coined at Pulicat Mint, upon forfeiture thereof upon due proofs; and that the Justices of the Peace do appoint the publishing and affixing these orders in English, Portuguese, and Gentoo at several public places of the City."

"Monday, 4th February, 1689. The miserable bad times and trade occasions great complaints about the collecting and paying the ground Quit Rents, and Mr. Thomas Wavell, the appointed Collector, and his assistants, having been stricter and larger therein than was required by the Right Honorable Company or is,—he is therefore ordered to keep to those rules, and to receive no more than 9 fanams for a great house, and fanams 6 and 3 for small houses in the Gentoo town, except such as belong to the Christians, which is according to the Company's express orders."

Mr. Wavell, who was present at this consultation, protested against the rebuke as follows:—"There was never any rate or rule given me to collect the Quit Rents by the Governor and Council, while making their consultations. As to my strict collection of the aforesaid Quit Rents, I am sure if guilty of anything it was of too much lenity to the inhabitants."

The following entries refer chiefly to the war with the Mogul, which had been commenced at the instigation of Mr. Child, and was persisted in by him with his accustomed ardour and obstinacy. Notwithstanding the failure at Chittagong, the following remarks appear in a General Letter, dated 27th August, 1688.

"The subjects of the Mogul cannot bear a war with the English for twelve months together, without starving and dying by thousands, for want of work to purchase riee; not singly for want of our trade, but beeause by our war, we obstruct their trade with all the Eastern nations, whieh is ten times as much as ours, and all European nations put together. Therefore we eonelude Fort St. George is now mueh more worth and secure to us, than ever it was in the mean King of Goleonda's time; for he had little at sea for us to revenge ourselves upon; but now if new injuries should be offered us, we have a fat enemy to deal with, from whom something is to be got to bear our charges. Therefore we conelude that the Mogul's governors will never give us fresh provoeations, nor deny you St. Thomé, or anything else you shall reasonably and fairly request of him.

"No great good was ever attained in this world without throes and eonvulsions, and therefore we must not grudge at what is past."

The state of Madras during this period may be inferred from the following extraets. It will be seen that the expedition against Bengal had so far failed, that all the Company's servants there had been compelled to take refuge at Fort St. George.

"Thursday, 7th March, 1689. Agent Charnock, his Council, and the several Factors and Writers to the number of twenty-eight persons, being arrived from Bengal, who, having from their disturbances and sudden surprising departure thence, laden the Right Honorable Company's concerns and remains in great eonfusion upon the several ships, of which we have received neither Invoices nor Bills of Lading:—it is therefore ordered that each Commander shall give a list of what they have on board."

"Thursday, 14th March. There being two Companies of soldiers in the Garrison and four more now brought by the Bengal shipping, with many supernumerary officers at very great charge to lessen,—the Governor proposed that the Portuguese and Topasses formerly in the Garrison, who refused serving the Honorable Company anywhere but at this place, that they be disbanded; but that the Portuguese and Topasses that returned from the Bay should be continued in service for their encouragement, having by their character of their commanders discharged their duties readily and well."

"Monday, 18th March. Letters from Basherad Khan, the Mogul's Dewan, wherein he descants upon the smallness of our rent and present, in consideration of the great profits and revenues we made of the place, which now was under the Mogul's dominion, and therefore not to be as in the King of Golconda's time. His chief design herein being to get a great present from us, which being well considered of, it is resolved not to concede to, since it can do us little kindness and may encourage their exactions.

"The Dewan's messenger, a great Moorman that was sent with the letter and to discourse more particularly in this occasion, was sent for and civilly treated; who, after many stories and magnifying his Master's interest and power in the Mogul's Court and this country; the President told him that we were and should be very desirous to continue the Dewan's friendship, which we hope he would not deny us, in consideration of the many great advantages our settlements and trade brought to the country; and that he was misinformed of our profits by it, the Revenues not defraying half the charge we were at in maintaining it and the poor; however it was our own, given us by the grant of several Kings, and solely raised and built by the Right Honorable Company's charge from a barren sand; which we should defend against all opposers of our right; and so dismissed the Moor with calmer thoughts and expectations than he brought."

"Monday, 15th April 1689. The Court Martial upon the 12th instant, having tried the nine Englishmen sent us by the Dutch Commissary from Pulicat, and finding them all guilty of piracy, though not all equally culpable; therefore it was concluded by majority of votes to condemn two to death, and six to be branded in the forehead with a "P.;" which six was to have been branded to day, but the Marshall being sick, it is ordered to defer the execution till to-morrow; and that two of them be branded at the execution post under the Fort point, and that the guards be drawn up to be spectators of the sad examples. The other four, to make their punishment more exemplary and to terrify others,—it is ordered that two be branded aboard the "Williamson" and the other two aboard the "Resolution;" and the said offenders do proceed on their ships to the West Coast."

"Friday, 27th September, 1689. Last night the President receiving a letter from Pulicat, advising that the Mogul has ordered the beseiging this place and destroying all the English in his dominions, and to seize their concerns, with many other severities against us; assuring us they received late letters from Golconda of the certainty thereof, as also the continued differences at Bombay which had exasperated the Mogul to this cruel order; but that we may not be surprised, the Paymaster Storekeepers (in their several employs) are ordered to fit and repair the defences of the town, and walls of the Garrison, and make provision of Powder, Shot, etc., sufficient against a seige."

"This evening was informed with the sad news of Haja Rajah's death (i. e. Sambajee, king of the Mahrattas); but no account who is like to succeed." In an entry of the 4th December, we find that Rama Raja had succeeded.

"Monday, 7th October, 1689. The "Pearl" frigate arriving yesterday from Vizagapatam, and by her came Bengal peons, who brought us several letters and a firmaun from the new Nabob of Bengal, Ibrahim Khan to the President, dated 2nd July, very kindly inviting us to return and resettlement, with assurance of a just and fair usage to the Right Honorable Company's servants and trade, and upon the former privileges, and to assist us in the recovery of our debts owing to us in those parts; much blaming the late Nabob's injustice and cruelty to our people; which notwithstanding it is most acceptable news to us, as we doubt not it will also be to the Right Honorable Company; but our resettlement being a matter of great weight and importance, it is ordered and agreed that the Agent, etc. of the Bengal Council be summoned to a Council with us.

"Thursday, 10th October. Agent Charnock and Council being this day joined with us in Council, the Nabob's letters and firmaun from Bengal to the President were perused and long debated on, and being concluded to be a happy good opportunity to return and settle in Bengal, that Government being under that famously just and good Nabob Ibrahim Khan, who has so kindly invited us to it, and faithfully engaged our peace and safety, of his honour the Agent has had long experience at Patna; . . but the war continuing still at Bombay . . . . . it is agreed that the General of Surat be advised as soon as possible thereof, and copies of the firmaun and letters sent him, with our opinion thereof, desiring his advice and orders therein, and that a small vessel be fitted for that purpose, the overland passage being very uncertain and dangerous."

The danger of the Agency at this time may be gathered from the following account of the seizure of the English Factory at Vizagapatam, by the order of the Mogul.

"Thursday, 15th October, 1689. Letter from Maddapollum confirming the sad disaster at Vizagapatam, giving us a relation thereof as follows. That on the 13th ultimo, the Seer Lascar by the Mogul's orders had sent his Rashwar to our Factory in order to seize and bring away the English and all their concerns. The said Rashwar with his forces coming nigh the town in the night, where he had pitched his Tent, etc; and about nine did surround the Factory with his men, and acquainted the English with the Seer Lascar's orders. To which was replied, they could not go up without their Master's orders. Then as the first Rashwar was taking the Chief by hand to pluck him out of the house, Mr. Hall fires his blunderbuss and kills three of their men; upon which they murdered Mr. Stables, Mr. Hall, and Mr. Croke, taking the rest prisoners, and seizing upon all the Right Honorable Company's concerns. No further news of Mr. Dubois and Mr. Fleetwood, who were gone up the country for provision of paddy for the Right Honorable Company's account."

We shall conclude the present chapter, with the following account of a plan for relieving the poor, which was proposed in a General Letter dated 11th September, 1688.

"Upon perusal of your Consultation Books, we find in several places you pay money out of the Company's Stock, for relieving of some poor English, and other charitable uses, which is more than we can justly or dare do ourselves; we being not entrusted with the Adventurer's Stock as the Governors of Hospitals, but to trade with it, and to fortify and defend our trade by treaties or arms. Yet since there will in all Colonies be a necessity sometimes to relieve distressed poor, we would have you raise a fund or stock for that purpose, which you may intrust in the hands of two or three of our Council, and two or three of the best, most charitable, and ablest of your Inhabitants, whom you may commission by themselves or their proper officer, to ask and receive upon all Pay days, and every Lord's day, or once a month at the Church, what shall be freely contributed towards the relief of the poor; and you may entitle those so commissioned by the name or style of "Fathers of the poor," as the Dutch call them "Fathers" or "Masters of the West houses."

In another part of the same letter we are told that the Dutch were confessedly, by the whole world, the most considerate, prudent, and foreseeing of any people in Europe in affairs of this kind, and that the poor's stock in the city of Batavia had already become of the value of thirty thousand pounds.

CHAPTER X.

GOVERNORSHIP OF MR. ELIHU YALE.

(Continued.)

1687—1692.

The annals of the years 1689 and 1690, which are included in the present chapter, are marked by two important incidents, namely, the rise of the Armenian Community, and the breaking out of the war with France. Before however noticing these interesting events, it will be as well to draw attention to the following extracts which are valuable as exhibiting the relative position of the English, French, and Dutch in Southern India, as well as their attitude towards Aurungzebe the Mogul, and Rama Rajah, the new king of the Mahrattas. It may here be remarked that the French had purchased the village of Pondicherry, together with a small adjacent tract, as early as 1672, from the king of the now extinct kingdom of Bijapore. Consequently the French settlement was dependent on the Mahrattas, whilst the English were partly dependent on both the Mahrattas and the Mogul.

"Monday, 4th December, 1689. Having received certain advice from the Chief and Council at Conimere (?) that Rama Rajah, king of the Mahrattas, is come overland from his kingdom and army at Poona to the government and castle at

Ginjee, and that the French and Dutch have already sent persons with considerable presents to congratulate him into the country, each reported to be to the amount of nearly 1400 Pagodas; and it being also expected that we should likewise pay our respects to him in the same nature, as well for the favourable assistance done the Right Honorable Company at Bombay, as also for the protection of our Garrison and trade in his country; and though he may expect to be visited by one of our Council, yet lest that should give suspicion to the Mogul government and army in these parts and exasperate them against us, which they seem now inclined to from the late news and troubles at Bombay:—we therefore conclude it more safe and expedient that the Chief of Conimerc, with a suitable retinue, do go and visit Rama Rajah at Ginjee, with a present from thence, wherein not much to exceed the amount of Pagodas 600. Since the French circumstances and ours in those parts are different, where they having their chief residence and settlement in that government, and lately built a considerable Fort at Pondicherry. The particulars of our present to be one of the Right Honorable Company's Persian horses, with handsome furniture; three or four pieces of broadcloth, fine and ordinary; fire arms; with some other varieties that may be most pleasing and acceptable to him.

"Tuesday, 10th December, 1689. This day came news from Conimere that the Mahrattas had besieged the French at Pondicherry, demanding great sum of money from them, notwithstanding they had lately received a considerable present from them; and that the Conimere Government and the Dewan's peons have likewise been very pressing with our merchants there for 1000 or 500 Pagodas a man loan from them.

"Thursday, 12th October. Ordered that the out town (i. e. Black Town) and bridge river be trenched and fortified with turf and clay work as well and soon as possible; it being reported that a considerable force from the Mogul is coming against us."

This measure appears to have excited considerable discussion in the consultation room, and four out of the seven men recorded their protest against it, in their own hand writing. Mr. Thomas Wavell wrote,—"I except the trenching and fortifying the out town with bulwarks, it being in my opinion rather a battery against the Fort, than any defence to it." Mr. William Fraser wrote,—"I approve of the walling in of the Black-town with a substantial brick wall, as well for strength as for securing the Honorable Company's Customs; but not with mud or turf which will soon moulder away; and that the Honorable Company be not at six pence charge thereon." Mr. William Cowley wrote,—"I except the fortifying and entrenching the Black town, being of opinion that mud walls and bulwarks will neither answer the charge or end proposed." Mr. Thomas Gray simply wrote, —"I consent to fortify upon the Governor's promise to reimburse the Company if they disapprove of it."

"Wednesday, 18th December, 1689. There being a black fellow and slave named Francisco, alias Chow, condemned to death in the Mayor's Court for theft, who appealing to the President and Council, and there appearing no evidence against him at trial, more than his own confession under punishment before his trial, at which time he pleaded not guilty; notwithstanding which, the Jury brought him in guilty only upon his former confession; which being a hard case, and this offence too common amongst our slaves, and usually punished with a corporal punishment and banishment:—it is therefore agreed and ordered that the said Chow be pardoned the sentence of death; and that he be stigmatized on the shoulder with the Honorable Company's mark with a hot iron, and banished to the West Coast (of Sumatra) the Right Honorable Company's slave, where he may do them service and be more exemplary than by his death."

We now arrive at one of the great events in the domestic history of Madras, namely, the first appearance of the Armenians. The Armenians, as our readers are aware, originally inhabited the great mountainous region on the upper courses of the Euphrates, Tigris, and Araxes, and at an early period were converted to the Christian faith. Subsequently they fell under the rule of the Persian kings, and suffered severe persecution from the followers of Zoroaster. At length they were scattered by the advancing tide of Mussulman conquest; and, like the Jews, they spread over Asia and became the great merchants and brokers in the eastern world. Some made their way to India, and the Directors of the Company sent out explicit directions that they should be encouraged to reside within the English settlements, and invested with certain privileges and rights, which were guaranteed by a special contract made between some representatives of the Armenians who visited London, and the Directors of the East India Company. This contract is briefly noticed by Mr. Mill, who however acknowledged that he was ignorant of its terms. His commentator Mr. Wilson, however, boldly insinuates that there is no reason for supposing that there was any contract at all. This is only another instance of the mistakes into which the historians of India have not unfrequently fallen, from neglecting to go through the necessary drudgery of perusing the voluminous records. It has been our good fortune to find a copy of the contract, the existence of which was doubted if not denied by so distinguished a scholar as Mr. Wilson. It is dated 22nd June, 1688, and though our space will not permit us to give it entire, we append the most important clauses.

The preamble declares that after long conferences between Sir Josiah Child on behalf of the Company, and Coja Panous, Calendar, an Armenian Merchant of Ispahan, and Sir John Chardin, Knight, both on behalf of the Armenian nation, the East India Company had agreed,

"1st, That the Armenian nation shall now, and at all times hereafter, have equal share and benefit of all indulgences this Company have or shall at any time hereafter grant to any of their own Adventurers or other English merchants whatsoever.

"2nd, That they shall have free liberty at all

times hereafter to pass and repass to and from India on any Company's ships, on as advantageous terms as any freemen whatsoever.

"3rd, That they shall have liberty to live in any of the Company's cities, garrisons, or towns in India, and to buy, sell, and purchase land or houses, and be capable of all civil offices and preferments in the same manner as if they were Englishmen born; and shall always have the free and undisturbed liberty of the exercise of their own religion. And we hereby declare, that we will not continue any Governor in our service that shall in any kind disturb or discountenance them in the full enjoyment of all the privileges hereby granted to them; neither shall they pay any other or greater duty in India than the Company's Factors, or any other Englishman born do or ought to do.

"4th, That they may voyage from any of the Company's garrisons to any other ports or places in India, the South Seas, China, or the Manillas in any of the Company's ships, or any permissive free ships allowed by the Company; and may have liberty to trade to China, the Manillas, or any other ports or places within the limits of the Company's Charter, upon equal terms, duties, and freights with any free Englishmen whatever."

Again on the 10th August, same year, we find that all liberty previously granted to private persons to send India goods home during the war against the Mogul, was annulled and made void, except the liberty granted to the Armenians.

There can be no doubt but that Coja Panous,

Calendar, was thus entitled to the lasting gratitude of the whole Armenian community, though truth compels us to say that he took advantage of his position to obtain a nice little monopoly for himself. That Coja Panous thereby exhibited great presence of mind, and did infinite credit to his Armenian descent, will be acknowledged by all; but we think that some credit is also due to the wide awake Londoner, Sir Josiah Child. It seems that Coja Panous had agreed that his countrymen should pay a considerable number of duties even on goods belonging to the overland trade; and in return he obtained from Sir Josiah Child the following little favour which speaks for itself.

"Whereas Coja Panous, Calendar, etc. hath taken great pains in making an agreement with the said Company for a great trade to be carried on in English shipping by himself and others of the Armenian nation, the said Governor and Company in consideration thereof do by these presents (at the request of the said Coja Panous) freely grant unto him and his family the sole trade of Garnets, etc. And the said Company do hereby declare, that they will neither trade in the said commodity themselves, nor suffer any other persons, English or strangers, for the future to trade or traffic in that commodity. Given under the Company's seal, etc."

We cannot however avoid noticing one other engagement on the part of the Directors, which is somewhat remarkable, considering the general intolerance of the time. The following extract will explain itself.

"We (the Company) by these presents, declare, grant and agree, that when over forty or more of the Armenian nation shall become inhabitants in any of the garrisons, cities, or towns belonging to the Company in the East Indies, the said Armenians shall not only have and enjoy the free use and exercise of their religion, but there shall be also allotted to them a parcel of ground to erect a Church thereon for the worship and service of God in their own way. And that we will also at our own charge cause a convenient Church to be built of timber, which afterwards the said Armenians may alter and build of stone or other solid materials to their own good liking. And the said Governor and Company will also allow £50 per annum during the space of seven years for the maintenance of such priest or minister as they shall choose to officiate therein."

Copies of these contracts were sent to Fort St. George in a General Letter, dated 27th August, 1688. We append an extract from the Letter, which shews that Sir Josiah Child had formed a good opinion of Coja Panous.

"Copies of our contracts with the Armenians we send you enclosed, and desire and strictly enjoin you to perform every part and article thereof, that they may have no cause to complain of the least discountenance or discouragement from you in any respect. . . . They are an innocent harmless people, that will not be apt to contend or plead law with us, and are certainly sober, frugal, and very wise in all the commodities and places of India."

We shall probably have many occasions to return to the Armenians in future issues; but we make the following extract from the consultations, as it appears to be the earliest notice of them preserved in the Madras records.

"Thursday, 6th March, 1690. Senor Gregorio Paron, and other Armenians, in a Petition to the Council, representing the privileges they agreed upon in England with the Right Hon'ble Company, wherein they are to be equal with all other English as to the liberties and customs of the place; they likewise requested to be free from all petty duties to the Pedda Naik, Town Conicopolies, etc, as the English are; they paying nothing more than the appointed custom of five per cent, with the accustomary fees; and though this grant will be a great discouragement and lessening to the Pedda Naik's duty, whereby he will be disenabled to maintain the usual guards and watches he is obliged to, but it being the Honorable Company's orders and agreement, the Customers are ordered for the future to exempt them from their petty duties."

The following extract illustrates the mode of electing Aldermen in the olden time.

"Wednesday, 26th March, 1690. There being several of the Aldermen's places vacant in the Corporation, it is agreed that Senor Alvaro de Fonseca be elected in the room of Senor Domingo de Porto deceased, and in the room of the Portuguese that have refused standing, they make choice of the ablest Armenians they can get in the city, and Timmapa in the place of Chinna Vencatadry deceased."

About this time the news reached India of the great events which had transpired in Great Britain. The revolution of 1688 had been accomplished. James II had "abdicated" his throne, and William and Mary had become the sovereigns of England. The event was duly noted to the Agency at Fort St. George, in a General Letter, dated 15th February, 1689, as follows.

"You will hear of the great change that it has pleased God by his wonderful providence to make in the government of this nation; and before the ship departs we may have occasion to write you more thereof, when the Lords and Commons have finished the intended settlement of the Prince and Princess of Orange, whom the Lords have voted to be King, and Queen of the Realm."

Another General Letter, dated a fortnight later, contains the following advice.

"We send you herewith 20 Proclamations of our new King and Queen, to whom we wish all happiness, and hereby require to make solemn Proclamation of them according to the usual form in such extraordinary cases, and cause the like to be done at our chief Factory in Bengal, and at our Forts upon the West Coast with all due solemnity."

England now became an ally of the Dutch, and was at once involved in a war with France. But the following extracts tell their own story.

"Monday, 21st July, 1690. Receiving late advices from the Agent and Council at Surat of the 10th ultimo, enclosing their Majesties (William and Mary) Declaration of War against France, also a warrant for our hostility in these parts, both which are ordered to be solemnly proclaimed to-morrow morning at the Fort Gate, Choultry, and Sea Gate, accompanied by Captain Thomas Gray and Mr. William Hassell, and attended with a company of soldiers, the Secretary and Town Clerk, etc., formalities as usual in such cases. It is likewise ordered that their authentic copy be sent to Bengal."

"Thursday, 1st August, 1690. The Heer Lawrence Pitt, Governor of Pulicat, having some days since passed this port with three ships bound with Pulicat stores and ammunition for Negapatam, but being the way surprised with the news of a French fleet arrived on Ceylon, who had taken a fly boat of theirs, and was supposed to be bound for this coast; which occasioned the Dutch Governor's return and sending a letter to the President of Fort St. George to desire our permission for his fleet anchoring in this road under our protection, and to join with our ships against the enemy, and to consult with the President what shall be most expedient in this affair; whose letter was accordingly answered and liberty granted. He came to an anchor, paying all accustomary civilities to the place, and it is agreed that upon his coming ashore, he be entertained according to his quality and business, and that we unite our forces as well as for the defence of our ships as the garrison. There being a report that the French fleet sent out consists of seventeen men of war, which is a very considerable force for us to dispute with all, it is therefore ordered that the Paymaster do entertain as many European soldiers and gunners assistants as he can, as also Mustesees and Topasses, till this alarming danger be past; and Gunner Ivory being lately deceased, Captain Putsham is appointed and ordered to succeed in that employ as Gunner of the Fort, being well qualified therein."

The remaining portion of the consultation book for the year 1690, is chiefly occupied by the uninteresting details connected with the purchase of Tegnapatam from Rama Raja, and an obsolete controversy between Mr. Yale and the members of his council. The approach of the French fleet however, and the engagements which took place with the French, are matters which will be read with interest. The Dutch fleet, under Herr Lawrence Pitt, anchored in the Madras roads on the 1st of August; the subsequent entries tell their own story.

"Monday, 4th August. The Heer Lawrence Pitt, being designed to come ashore this day, Mr. Thomas Wavell and Mr. John Cheney were ordered to attend upom him aboard, and conduct him ashore.

"This evening the Dutch Governor landed and was kindly received by the President at the Sea Custom House Gate, and thence conducted to the Fort, welcoming him with 21 great guns, with all other due respects and civilities suitable to his quality and the great alliance of the nations.

"Tuesday, 5th August. This morning received news of the French fleet's arrival at Pondicherry, consisting of eight sail of ships, two of which is reported to have been taken from the Dutch, with considerable treasure aboard of them, betwixt Ceylon and Negapatam, being bound thither from Batavia. Also reporting to have met and destroyed a Europe ship of ours at the Island of Johanna, but what she was, or the certainty thereof, is not yet known.

"Wednesday, 6th August. An entertainment made for Governor Pitt and the rest of the Dutch people.

"Thursday, 7th August. This evening Governor Pitt returned on board to order and put his fleet in a posture of defence against the French.

"Friday, 8th August. Some French fugitives lately running away from their fleet at Pondicherry, give us the following relation of the unhappy loss of Ship "Herbert" at Johanna (in the Mozambique Channel). That in February last, the French fleet, consisting of six men of war, set sail from France, and on their way at Johanna most unhappily under Dutch colours, surprised the "Herbert;" but soon discovered their disguise by surrounding and fighting her; she making a brave resistance against all six for three hours; when upon approaching darkness she endeavoured to quit herself from them and put off to sea, but being overpowered, she was fatally cleared from her cruel enemies by the blowing up of the ship, supposed rather by choice than accident. And they also report her to be a very rich ship, and that near 300 souls perished in her destruction; the inhuman French giving no quarter to the poor creatures that were blown up through the flames into the sea, but basely murdered them as they were crawling half frosted up their ships for life, merely declaring that they would nowhere give quarter to the English. The French report the Captain and many of her men escaped in a boat to Johanna. God grant it proves true, if so they will soon get conveyance for Bombay, where we think they were bound. From Johanna the French fleet steered for Pondicherry, and in their way at Ceylon took two Dutch ships with money and goods to the value of 50,000 Pagodas. From thence they sailed to the coast, cruising from Tranquebar to Pondicherry the 3rd instant; they arrived there with eight sail of ships, where they were victualling and fitting them, putting their treasure and sick and wounded men ashore, making great preparations as they report for Siam, Tenasserim, or Bengal.

"Saturday, 9th August. The French being still at Pondicherry, making great preparations for some design or voyage, which they sometimes report to be for Tenasserim, other times for Bengal; but lest their intention should be for this place, the Paymaster and Storekeeper are ordered, with the Officers and Gunners, to get all things in readiness for the defence of the place; the Governor also giving them a role, when the Council, etc. are ordered to the charge and command of the several Gates, Bulwarks, and Points in the Garrison, and quartering our soldiers and gunners; ordering each person to visit his post to-morrow morning, to repair or supply the wants and defects of each place; and there being now little charge or business at Conimere, it is ordered that all but 12 soldiers and gunners do, with their Captain James Lesly and officers, hasten hither with all expedition to strengthen our garrison and ships which are in great want of them.

" Wednesday, 14th August. The French fleet being still at Pondicherry, making great preparation for some hostile design, and there being great reason to suspect their assaulting the Dutch and our ships in this road ;—it was therefore proposed to hire and man some of the ablest country vessels in the road to join with the Dutch fleet ; and that the Governor and the Heer Pitt consult thereon, and draw up rules and orders for the fleet in case of an engagement, that we may not be surprised into a confusion.

" Tuesday, 15th August. The French fleet of seven sail appearing about eight this morning, the garrison was alarmed, the gates shut, and orders given for all persons to repair to their several posts, the gunners to get the guns in readiness, and all possible preparations made to offend the enemy and defend the place. Captain Heath ordered aboard his ship with sixty soldiers, besides officers, and reformadoes ; and notice and assistance given to all the other ships to prepare for an engagement if they assaulted us. Advice also to the Dutch Governor and fleet that one of the French fleet was a fire ship, therefore to prepare against her ; who courageously returned the President answer, that he was in readiness and feared them not. God grant us success.

" A Relation of this Day's action and engagement of war, betwixt the enemy the French fleet and ours in this Road.

"This (Tuesday) being St. Lewis's day, the French fleet appeared in sight about eight in the morning, consisting of seven sail,—six men of war and a fireship,—all making as near the shore as the land wind would permit them. At eleven came to an anchor in St. Thomé road, calling there a council of war; the Portuguese welcoming them with several guns and their flags abroad, a respect not usually paid amongst them to any other European nation. About one of the clock they came so near that we sent a shot from the Fort to forbid their approach, which they took so little notice of that they immediately fired on the headmost Dutch ship, all theirs and ours ranging as near the shore as possible. Soon after, their whole fleet being come within shot of ours, they let fly with that sharpness and fury as is usual to a French onset; which was considerably returned by ours, as also played what guns from the Fort we could bring to bear upon them, which, though at great distance and random, did some execution and prevented their coming nearer, or within our fleet. In this heat they entered their fireship upon the Dutch Admiral, fixing their hooks and grapplings upon her leeward bow, and so blew up immediately into a flame; but was, by the courage and dexterity of the Dutch, as soon cut off from them, driving by the rest of the fleet, a great escape and mercy, which, if it had taken place, would undoubtedly have destroyed all the ships in the road; the French fleet being all ready to prosecute the confusion of the rest, and were much baulked at their disappointment. However they plied their guns with great quickness and little execution, and after three hour's hot dispute; they grew weary of the visit; returning with greater speed than they came, not allowing themselves time to weigh their anchor, but fairly cut and nimbly marched like Frenchmen, bringing their fleet to an anchor about five leagues to the Southward, where they rode civilly till about ten the next day. The same evening the Governor gave strict charge and command to all the captains and officers round the garrison, to get themselves prepared and a good watch kept, great guns loaded and mounted, lest the enemy should assault us. The same was recommended to all our fleet in the road; to which was answered that they were in a better posture of defence, and fitter for an engagement than they were before.

"Wednesday, 16th August. This morning about ten of the clock, the French fleet weighed, sailing gently to the northward, and in their way at Trivatore valiantly took an old deserted country vessel belonging to some Pulicat inhabitants. But whither they are bound God knows, but it is concluded to Bengal.

"The Dutch and our loss in this fight were but eleven men killed and about ten wounded, and but little prejudice to our ships. Undoubtedly the French have suffered much more, and their sudden weighing is an argument of it. Besides it is reported that their Admiral was killed, and several others of note, with many seamen, in all said to be

187 men, with considerable damage to their shipping and rigging. We also hear that there were several men sent ashore and buried in St. Thomé church, when the town late at night fired several guns, supposed to be in respect to the deceased.

"Monday, 28th August. The Herr Lawrence Pitt being designed this afternoon with his retinue on board, in order to their proceeding to the Fort at Negapatam,—the President made an entertainment for him and the rest of the Dutch people, showing him all the respect and civilities imaginable due to his quality and employ; and about four in the evening he embarked, carrying off with him the large treasure of 100,000 Pagodas which was secured for them in the Fort."

The French do not at this time appear to have made a second appearance in the Madras roads.

CHAPTER XI.

GOVERNORSHIP OF MR. ELIHU YALE.

(Concluded.)

1687—1692.

The concluding years of the governorship of Mr. Elihu Yale, which will be included in the present number, are chiefly occupied by the proceedings connected with a serious rupture between the President and his Council, but they were nevertheless distinguished by some incidents which will be found of considerable interest. A remarkable missionary effort in behalf of the Indo-Portuguese was made by the Directors about this period; and some important plans were sent out from home for the improvement of the town. Before however touching upon these matters, it will be as well to notice the quarrel in the Council. It appears to have arisen in consequence of some irregularities said to have been committed by a Mr. Thomas Yale, brother of the President, during a trading voyage to the Chinese seas. The matter in dispute is however of little consequence in the present day. The great point of interest is the manner in which the quarrel was carried on; and the correspondence that passed is so strikingly illustrative of the period, that we cannot forbear extracting some of the most racy passages.

The first important letter that was entered in the Records is the following. The paper alluded to in the opening paragraph, is a mere statement of commercial transactions, made by Thomas Yale and supported by the President, of no interest whatever to modern readers. The present letter was written by the Council to the President. It is dated 10th November, 1690, and plainly shows that the writers were suffering from a painful attack of "superabundant vigour."

"To the Honorable Elihu Yale, Esq., President and Governor of Fort St. George.

Hon'ble Sir,—You delivered us a paper last Council day stuffed with evasive arguments and false affirmations, to blind the Right Honorable Company and cloak your brother's frauds. It doth not require our saying anything to prove your several assertions wholly malicious and untrue, they evidently appearing so to all impartial unbiassed men, and doubt not our Hon'ble Masters will rightly discern them, notwithstanding your endeavours to cast a mist before their understandings," etc. . . . .

"That confused flashy pamphlet, being a mixture of froth, lies, wind, nonsense, and insolent abuses, signed to by Mr. Thomas Yale, and delivered us by Your Honour, we shall take no farther notice of, than to tell your Honour that we expected something more to the purpose, after that paper so long lying under your Honour's correction and amendment. Your brother's abundant ignorance so puffed up his vain mind with the hopes of being esteemed a wit, that he had the simplicity to divulge his folly to the world, by giving a copy of his infamous libel to all he met of his acquaintance, by which means half the men in town could repeat his senseless story before your Honour delivered it to us . . . . The respect and honour due to your place, has kept us from writing in your own abusive strain. We are, honourable Sir, your most humble servants." Signed by four members of council. Dated 10th November 1690.

No answer appears to have been received to this letter; accordingly on the 6th of January, 1691, the four members wrote again, requesting President Yale to summon weekly councils according to the Company's orders. "It is a long time," they said, "since you were pleased to summon us to Council, and permit our examining the Company's cash, which you have by an assumed, unwarrantable and arbitrary power, made use of as suited best to your own profit, converting it to your own use and purposes." . . . . . "We must confess that your continual affronts, abuses, and ill language is somewhat unpleasant to us, but we are willing to bear with that, and as many more ill names as you are able to contrive, rather than to let the Company's business suffer. . . . . We do therefore declare our readiness to promote their interest, which if we find Your Honour still resolved to oppose, we must make it our study to prevent their approaching ruin."

Three days afterwards President Yale sent a long and powerful reply, from which we make the following extracts:

"To the worshipful Council of Fort St. George,

I have been thus long silent to your scurrilous paper of the 10th November, as well to conceal your insolent malice, as to silence your turbulencies; but I see such mildness rather emboldens than calms them, as by your new venemous production, whose audacious falsities and threats provoke me to a plainer answer than I intended; that the Right Hon'ble Company and the world may judge betwixt me and you as to our duties, actions, and services. . . . .
. . . . You first mind me of the Right Hon'ble Company's orders for the calling a Council once a week, which till very lately I have duly performed twice a week, as sufficiently by the consultation books, where you will also find the great neglect and contempt of my summons, by the often wilful absence of some of you, who publicly declared their slights and aversion to them, and the reason why I have not troubled you are many. First for want of business. Secondly that I went to my Garden house for my health and diversion, as some of you did to the Mount and elsewhere; but mine is so near the town, as was no impediment to my inspection of the place or the Hon'ble Company's affairs; daily giving the usual orders for the garrison, and duly corresponding with all places which had occasion; and when any other business offered, I proposed it to you in writing as appears by the entries in the consultation book, and our several letters, so that there has been no neglect in the Right Hon'ble Company's business I know of; the Secretary also acquainting you by my order that if you had

anything of moment to offer, you might signify it to him, and I should summon a council for it, but heard nothing from you thereof. This quiet method I proposed as an expedient for the more unanimous carrying on the Right Hon'ble Company's affairs without interruption, and to avoid the usual disturbances our meetings were noised with; where instead of reasoning upon business, I met with nothing but obstructions, provoking affronts and cavils; and what we then agreed on was either cancelled next day, or blotted with abusive, malicious, or senseless exceptions, which made me both weary and ashamed of them . . . . You next asperse me with making use of and employing the Right Honorable Company's Cash to my own profit, which the Almighty God knows is as false as he is true, I having often freely supplied their occasions with many thousands Pagodas, but I thank God had never any inclination or occasion to make use of theirs. . . . And the more to prove the idleness of your charge, I must tell you, that for near two years past I have had near a hundred thousand Pagodas of my friends consignments laying dead by me for want of an opportunity to invest it, besides some of my own. . . But this is like the rest of your scandalous forgeries, which in the end will make you infamous amongst all loyal honest good men. . . . And I cannot but wonder at your last strange and dangerous expression that you expect a sudden ruin to the place and the Honorable Company's affairs, since I cannot see or hear any reason for or the least fear of it, excepting you design it from yourselves; since otherwise the place was never in a more peaceable state than now, as to outward enemies; I having a fair correspondence with all our neighbouring forces and governments, I doubt not the Almighty will still continue his blessing upon my care and conduct, which in our greatest troubles and dangers preserved the place free from injury, or molestation, during the whole war with the Mogul, when nothing but destruction was expected, and too heavily fell upon our other settlements; we were also preserved from threatened dangers of the Mahrattas and late assaults of the French; but if there are any inward private enemies, they may be more dangerous, and indeed I know not how to construe your threats; it too much confirms me in some reports I have had of your insinuating and making parties with the officers and soldiers of the garrison; but I hope God will divert you from any such horrid crimes as rebellion, or the seeking my life and estate, which if you do, believe it will cost you dear; therefore for God, our king's, our country's, our Hon'ble Master's, and your own sake, desist from all such wicked attempts which you will certainly fall in; remembering the sad consequences of rebellion everywhere, and particularly the former one here, as also at Bombay and St. Helena. But I hope you have better principles and designs, than to let our personal disagreements run into a general ruin, avoiding that hellish conclusion of "Scelera sceleribus fuenda."

The members of council replied on the 16th of the same month. It is unnecessary to reproduce the whole of their epistle. It contains however one taunt which led to an important disclosure. It will be seen that President Yale had referred to his own money, as well as to the money he had belonging to friends. The council noted this, and in referring to some of their charges against him, they wrote,—"it is possible when we have an impartial hearing, your mighty condition will be found too mean to compensate." Mr. Yale's wrath now fairly boiled over. He declared that he would neither receive nor answer any more of their abusive papers; but with reference to his insufficient estate, he wrote,—"I think you are a little unreasonable, that my twenty years diligent service in India and trading, above five hundred thousand Pagodas should be too poor a crop for you is hard; but I cannot help it, having used all honest endeavours to do better, so pray be contented." This enormous sum is equivalent to about £175,000 sterling; but in comparison with the ordinary fortunes of the time must have approximated to nearly a million. President Yale had undoubtedly made this fortune by private trade, a share of which was at this time allowed to every servant of the Company, and the profits of which were enormous. A salary commencing at £5 a year and never exceeding £100, until he became governor and received £300, could only have been a drop in the ocean in comparison with so vast a sum.

This quarrel continued down to the end of the Governorship of Mr. Yale. It involved another quarrel between the President and the Mayor's Court, and at last terminated in the arrival of Sir

John Goldesborough to act as Governor General of all India, and to settle all differences. These events will be discussed in the order in which they occurred. The following extracts will explain themselves.

"February 8th, 1861. The Court of Aldermen desire that the judgment of their Court might be absolute and final in all causes whatever, some of the members being unwilling otherwise to sit or act there ; to which the President told them, that if any of their members, were dissatisfied with the constitution of the Charter and Corporation, they might ease themselves of the trouble for 5 Pagodas, and others more agreeable elected in their room ; but that to give a greater power to the Court than the Charter did was to alter the Charter."

"March 27th. The President sent the following note to the Mayor's Court, and ordered to be registered.

"To the Worshipful the Mayor
and Aldermen,

The Right Honorable Company, Lords Proprietors of this place, expecting by their constituting a Corporation an advantage and benefit both to themselves and the place, as also the erecting a Town Hall, School house, Hospital, Walling the City, etc., none whereof are yet done or anything towards it or designed that I know of,—I, therefore, in the Right Hon'ble Company's name and for their account, require you to restore their revenues of measuring and weighing and duties to them as formerly ; as also what you have received on those accounts, since if they are not benefitted, there is no reason they should be losers by the Corporation.—ELIHU YALE.

The Corporation protested against this resumption on the ground that it was carried out by the President alone, and without the concurrence of his Council.

Some further light is thrown upon the working of the Corporation by the following extract from a General letter, dated 22nd January, 1692.

"In our late President's letters dated the 31st October 1690, we observe the intimation he gives us of their being at present eight English Aldermen in our Corporation. It is a thing we do not well approve of, and do recommend it to the care of our now President and Council that for the future most of the Aldermen may consist of the Heads of the several foreign castes, namely, one Armenian, one or two Hebrews, one or two Portuguese, one or two Gentoos, and one Moor if you have a sufficient number of that caste. Though we would have you effect by gentleness and persuasion, rather than by exacting the utmost of that power which in the Charter is reserved to our President and Council, because we hope that Corporation consisting of the Heads of all Castes, and representing them in a subordinate manner, may induce all the Inhabitants to contribute cheerfully to some Public Works, such as a Court House, Public Schools, Hospitals, and other things for the good of the place, and several nations therein inhabiting; which a wise Council may invent of their own accord, and may be of great use in the punishing of small criminal offences to our standing supreme authority there, our President and Council; as will also be their determining of small controversial matters among the Inhabitants, who will be the better satisfied with their judgment, as they have one of their own Caste to represent them."

The following extract will be interesting to some of our engineers.

"June 2nd. The Gunner was ordered to try the several guns on the several points to see how far they carry, who gave the following report.

"Our Guns carry into 6 fathom upon a level, and into 7 fathom at 2 degrees elevation, and into 8 fathom at 4, and into 9 fathom at 5½, and into 10 fathom at 7½ with the whole Culverin and Demiculverin; and 8 with a Sacar* and into 11 fathom at 10 degrees and into 12 fathom at 14 degrees elevation.—THOMAS MEDDOWS, Gunner.

The next entry exhibits the woful state of ignorance in which our forefathers were as regards free trade.

"August 1st. The following Proclamation was by beat of drum proclaimed at the several gates of the city. "Whereas of late several unreasonable and exacting people have made and engrossed quantities of bricks of the Right Honorable Company's clay without our license; notwithstanding which they take the advantage of their present occasion, and the necessity of the in-

* The Sacar, or Sacker, was a gun inferior in size to the Culverin, and about the same calibre as a Falcon, carrying a ball of from five to eight pounds.

habitants to finish and repair their houses before the rains, selling them insufferably dear to the ill example and prejudice of the place; to prevent which the future ill consequences thereof:—We, the Governor and Council, do hereby strictly forbid such exactions, ordering that no person whatever shall sell bricks within our Government for less than two thousand for one Pagoda, upon penalty of forfeiting the same; since at that rate they will be sufficient gainers."

Some time before this, President Yale succeeded in obtaining a Firmaun for the Factories under the superintendence of Fort St. George, but we need scarcely add that it was opposed by his Council. The war had continued raging between Aurungzebe and the Mahrattas. Aurungzebe had sent Zulfikar Khan, who had already distinguished himself in the war, to attempt the reduction of Gingee; appointing him at the same time to be Subadar of the whole district. Mr. Yale accordingly negociated with Zulfikar Khan, and the result may be gathered from the following extract.

"Translation of the Cowle or Firmaun of Nabob Zulfikar Khan Bahadoor, sent to the Hon'ble Elihu Yale, President and Governor, received the 28th December, 1690.

"Whereas in the time of the late shameless and faithless rebellion, the President of the English, Elihu Yale, Governor and Captain of Chinnapatanam, protected and assisted Mahmoud Ali and other servants of the Mogul, and supplied me with Powder with other services: in consideration whereof I made and given this my Cowle or grant.

That the rent of the Fort and Factory of Chinnapatanam with accustomary privileges, the English Factories of Metchlepatam, Maddapollam, Vizagapatam, etc. within the territories of the Golconda country, also their settlements and Factories of Devapatnam, Cuddalore, Porto Novo, Trimlevassil, etc. within the territories of Ginjee, according to the former custom and the usual practice of the English, let it remain undisturbed in Sallabad."

During the following year a still more favourable arrangement offered itself, and was concluded. The Mogul's army had encamped in the neighbourhood of Ginjee, and Mr. Frenchfield and Mr. John Pitt were sent with a petition to the Vizier. Here the extracts will again explain themselves.

"Translation of the Petition presented to the Vizier Assid Khan, by order of the Hon'ble Elihu Yale and Council, in behalf of the Right Hon'ble Company, per Richard Frenchfield and John Pitt.*

"1. That we may receive the king's firmaun for our affairs, under the kingdoms of Golconda and Bijapore.

"2. That the annual rent of Pagodas 1200 for Madras and Triplicane may be taken off.

"3. That Tandore, Pershawauk, and Egmore, three small towns near Madras, whose produce is about 300 Pagodas per annum, we desire may be given us as a gratuity to the Company rent free.

"4. That we may have liberty to coin rupees with the king's stamp at Madras.

"5. That at Vizagapatam the Poligars and

* Some uninteresting clauses are omitted.

thieves, killing our people and plundering our houses of a great amount in goods and money, we request that this may be considered of, and a small fortification be permitted us, that for the future we may live without fear."

On the receipt of the firmaun embodying the above clauses, a present of fifteen thousand rupees was to be given to Zulfikar Khan. On the 19th April, 1692, Mr. Frenchfield and Mr. Pitt with Native ambassadors arrived from Gingee at Madras, with the firmauns which are far too many and lengthy to be recapitulated here, but which seem to have been in accordance with the petition. Presents were exchanged, guns were fired, and Mr. President Yale arrayed himself in a habit sent by the Mogul, and rode horse in that guise "the more to honour and please the Prince and his people that accompanied the firmauns and nishans, who take particular notice and account of all such actions." Translations of the several documents are given at full length in the consultation books, but would prove too tedious to the general reader to permit of our reproducing them here.

We now have to notice the early Missionary efforts of the Court of Directors, to which allusion has already been made. From a General Letter, dated 18th February 1691, and evidently from the pen of Sir Josiah Child, we make the following extract.

"We would likewise desire our President Mr. Yale, whom God hath blessed with so great an estate in our service, to set on foot another generous charitable work before he leaves India, that is, the building of a Church for the Protestant black people and Portuguese, and the slaves which serve them, who have now no place to hear the word of God preached in a language they understand, and therefore are necessitated to go to the Popish Churches. Whereas if they had God's word preached to them in the Portuguese language, according to the Potestant Doctrine, and the Prayers of the Church of England, they would as readily frequent the Protestant Church as the Popish Chapels. In order hereunto we shall get our Common Prayers, and other Offices of our Church, translated into the Portuguese tongue, and send you some written copies thereof, after which when your Church is built, and you have corrected the copies we send you to the Portuguese dialect of India, and returned one copy to us with the amendments, we will cause it to be printed here, and return you divers printed copies thereof; and not only so but we will send you what benevolence we can collect here for the ornament of the Church intended. In the mean time we are now inquiring after some able Minister that can preach in the Portuguese tongue; and also a Domine as the Dutch call them, which in the style of our Church is a Deacon, that can read our Prayers in Portuguese."

Again, on the 22nd January 1692, the following advice was transmitted to Fort St. George, by the Court of Directors.

"We shall send you by the following ship two Ministers who have applied themselves to the learning of the Portuguese languages, and have made considerable progress therein; we designing them to be Ministers for the new Portuguese church which we have desired you to cause to be built by the bounty of such as shall be inclined to forward so good a work. Both Ministers are sober, able, and learned men."

Early in 1692 the Court of Directors determined on sending out Sir John Goldsborough as Governor General, to act as first member of council at the different settlements in India. It would seem from the following extract, as though orders for the suspension of Mr. Yale had already been sent out. The General Letter is dated 22nd January, 1692.

"Mr. Yale, our late President, we would have continue at Madras until the arrival of our supervisor, Captain Goldsborough; that all differences may be fairly adjusted there by the wisdom and moderation of Captain Goldsborough; and that upon Mr. Yale's return hither we may have nothing to say to him but to bid him welcome home."

The following extracts from a General Letter dated 22nd January, 1692, from the Directors to the Agency at Fort St. George will explain themselves.

"We have desired Captain Goldsborough to go in hand immediately with the building of a steeple to your Church, with the money collected for that purpose, according to dimensions given him; and by our next ship we intend to send you a ring of six tunable Bells to fix in our steeple, which the founder tells us cannot be cast at this season of the year."

"We have discoursed Sir John Goldsborough

about enlarging our Christian town to a Quadrangle, so as it may be done without detriment to the Company, with handsome stone bridges over the River; in which designed new moiety of the city, one Quarter of that moiety may be set apart for the Armenian Christians to build a new Church (for the worship of God according to their own Rites), at their charge, with stone and other durable materials, and also convenient dwelling houses for their merchants, they paying as such ground rents as will fully defray our charges. And that Quarter so set apart for their use you may call "Julpha," that being the town from whence Shak Abbas the Great brought them, when he conquered Armenia, and settled them in a suburb of his new made metropolitan city of Ispahan, and called the Quarter he allotted there to the Armenians "Julpha," the name of the city from whence he brought them, and they are increased there to be the richest people and must expert merchants in the universe."

"We being now in full peace, would have but two full Companies of soldiers maintained there besides what inferior force you may think fit to raise of Cofferies; and in those two Companies we would be at no further charge of Officers, but only of Lieutenants and Ensigns, Sarjeants and Corporals, Captains being needless in times of peace. But you may entertain an aid Major, who is to have no Company, but to Superintend over all our officers and soldiers, under the Command of our Commissary General when he is present, and under our President when our Commissary

General is absent. This is the Dutch method in all their Garrisons in India, and it is the best that can bc invented in peaceable times. Our aid Major, Captain Hilton, at Bombay, hath four shillings a day, besides twenty shillings a month as aid Major; and that we resolve shall be his standing pay, and the standing pay of all aid Major's in India in every garrison where there is need of such officers.

"But we would have you by all means to keep on foot your Troop of Volunteer horse, and to increase the number of them, under the immediate command of our President; and our Artillery Company of all the Company's English servants under the command of Captain Thomas Grey. And sometimes for recreation we would have you to exercise both horse and foot in the field, that the men may be perfect in the use of their arms, and the horses be used to abide the sound of Drums, Trumpets, and report of Guns, without starting. Being always in such a posture of defence, is a sure way to preserve your peace, and draw esteem and report, honour and obedience from the natives, with little or no charge to the Company."

The following extract from the consultation book, describes the final retirement of Mr. Yale from the Governorship.

"Wednesday, 23rd October, 1692. Ship Berkely Castle came into this road, and at one o'clock the Purser brought ashore the Hon'ble Company's packet, and a General Letter from Sir John Goldesborough, advising that a duplicate of Mr. Higginson's Commission was contained therein, who immediately gave notice thereof to President Yale advising him to meet at the Fort at three o'clock, when the packet being opened a duplicate of said Commission was found therein; and the Hon'ble Company's servants and commissioned officers being called up was publicly read before them, and after the usual ceremonies Governor Yale delivered the keys of the garrison and city to President Higginson, and a General Letter was returned by the Purser to the Hon'ble Sir John Goldesborough to give him advice thereof."

Sir John Goldesborough landed in Madras on the 5th December, 1692, and was sworn in as first member of council.

The close of the governorship of President Yale, offers a favourable opportunity for reviewing the progress of the Black-town of Madraspatanam, and the White-town of Fort St. George. It appears from a letter dated 12th December, 1687, that the population of the whole of the English Presidency, including the city of Madras, the town of Fort St. George, and the villages within the Company's bounds, amounted to three hundred thousand; and a more exact enumeration was then required to be made, for the information of James II, distinguishing the English, Portuguese, Moors, and Gentoos, both male and female, and their several professions, or occupations. Whether this more exact enumeration was ever made, we have not as yet been able to discover; but the statement of the aggregate population will be sufficient for all general purposes.

As regards the population at Fort St. George, or White-town, we have the most minute information. In a previous chapter it was shown how White Town was only half the size of the modern Fort. In the seventeenth century the river Coom ran much nearer the sea than at present. In fact it ran parrallel with the Coast right through the centre of the site now occupied by the present Fort. In the last century, the channel of the river was diverted into its present course, and the Fort considerably enlarged.

The old Fort or White-town, only extended about 400 yards in length, from north to south parallel with the sea; and about 100 yards from east to west, that is from the sea to the old channel of the river. This little space was however divided into twelve streets and alleys, and included altogether one hundred and twenty-nine dwelling houses and godowns, producing altogether a yearly rental of only one hundred and twenty-four Pagodas, and nine fanams. The streets were respectively named—Middle Street, Choultry Street, Choultry Alley, Gloucester Street, York Street, York Lane, Charles Street, James Street, James Alley, St. Thomas Street, St. Thomas Lane, and Church Street. As a matter of local curiosity we print the following Directory or Rent Roll, verbatim et literatim, of which the original may be found in the consultation book under the 2nd of August, 1688. Some of our readers may here find the names of their ancestors, probably spelt in a different manner to those of their descendants.

"Rent Rowle of Dwelling Houses, Goedowns, etc.

within the Garrison or Christian Town, with the names of their several Owners, Tenants, and Yearly Rents.

MIDDLE STREET.

Owner.	*Tenant.*	*Rent.* Pags.	Fans.
The Honorable President Yale's House ...		3	—
Captain James Betts house...	..	1	18
Martad Consason :	William Dixon...	—	27
Paul Cardozo... ...	... ...	—	27
Padre Ephraim's... ..	... ...	—	28
Martin Lope's	... ...	1	—
Mr. John Afflack	... ...	2	—
Richard Monk	John Strangway...	1	—
Widow Heathfield... ...	... ...	2	—
Mr. Peter Large... ...	... ...	1	18
Mrs. Ursula O'Neal... ...	... ...	1	—
Mr. Affiack : ...	Mrs. Ursula O'Neal...	1	18
Mr. Afflack :	Mr. Troughton ...	1	—
	Pags.	17	28

CHOWLTRY STREET.

		Pags.	Fans.
Richard Monk's house ...	... ..	2	—
John Coventry... ...	... ...	1	18
Como Lorenso...	... ...	1	18
Emmanuel Morley ...	Widow Haddock	1	18
Emmanuel Morley	... ...	—	27
Padre Theodosia... ...	... ...	—	27
Mr. John Nicks...	Sir John Biggs...	2	—
... ...	John Hill......	2	—
Thomas Greenhill	... ..	1	18
John Parera	... ...	1	—
	Pags.	14	18

CHOWLTRY ALLEY.

		Pags.	Fans.
Joan Lopus	... ...	1	—
Ditto	Ana : d'Andrada.	1	—

		Pags.	Fans.
Nath : Bonus.. ...	Gab : Roberts...	1 :	18
Ditto	John Voter ...	—	27
Ditto	... ...	—	18
Charles Metcalf. .	... ...	2 :	—
John Callender ...	... ...	1 :	—
	Pags.	8 :	18

GLOUCESTER STREET.

		Pags.	Fans.
Panchecu Viera ..	Mrs. Field ...	—	27
Mr. Henry Alford ...	... ...	2 :	—
Arthur Tilbury ...	.. ..	—	27
Madam Pavia ...	Mr. Alford ...	1 :	—
	Pags.	4 :	18

YORK STREET.

		Pags.	Fans.
Mr. Miller ...	Panchecu Viera ...	—	27
Panchecu Viera ...	Padre Lopus ...	—	27
Ditto	Andre Garmast ...	1 :	—
Ditto	Frans Tessera ...	—	18
Ditto	Marmad Consasou...	—	18
John Inch ...	... ...	1 :	—
Renou Perera ...	... ...	—	27
Tilman Holt... ...	... ...	1 :	—
John de Soza ...	... .	—	27
Domingoes Mendes ...	... ...	1 :	—
Mr. Mead... ...	John Meverell...	—	27
Mr. Mead	... ...	1 :	18
Monsieur Chardin	... ...	2 :	—
Martha de Consason...	... ...	—	18
	Pags.	12 :	27

YORK LANE.

		Pags.	Fans.
William Dixon	Mr. Glover	2 :	—
Domingo Joan...	... ...	—	18

		Pags.	Fans.
Emmanuel Rosaira		—	27
Mary Ware		—	18
Emmanuel Rosaira		—	18
Mr. Miller	Amu Dunkly	—	27
Jane Taylor		—	27
Widow Ryley		—	27
Mr. Freeman's Godown		1 :	—
	Pags.	7 :	18

CHARLES STREET.

		Pags.	Fans.
Mr. William Jearsey		2 :	18
Mr. Jearsey's several Godowns		1 :	—
Mr. Bridger		1 :	18
Mr. Bridger	Mr. Mose	1 :	18
Mr. Bridger	Mr. Constable	1 :	18
Mr. John Davis	Mr. Styleman	1 :	18
Mr. Bridger's Godown		—	18
Mr. Bridger		—	18
Mr. Bridger	Mr. Parkers Childn.	—	18
Robert Bulfield, a Godown		—	18
	Pags.	11 :	18

JAMES STREET.

		Pags.	Fans.
Gimar Peniora		—	18
Joseph Perera		—	18
Mr. Gray Smith's Godown		—	18
Robert Ray Mr.	Mr. Pitt	1 :	18
Robert Ray		—	27
Pois		1 :	—
Alexander Woodall		—	18
Mr. Bridger's Godown	Prt. Gyfford	—	18
Phillipa		—	18
Thatcher		—	18
Black Franck	Padre Bastian	—	18
Robert Bulfield		—	27

		Pags.	Fans.
Maria de Sure...		—	18
Company's Merchants Godowns		3 :	—
Nicholas Westborough		—	18
Pois new Hospital		—	27
Pois		—	18
Forrow		—	18
Padre Lorenz Parera...		—	18
Sicillia Mendes		—	18
Maria Madera...		—	18
	Pags.	15 :	9

JAMES ALLEY.

		Pags.	Fans.
Antony Caldera		—	18
Thomas de Clara...		—	18
Lisu de Cuni...		—	18
Antonio Rosada		—	18
Alexander Woodall... ...	John Moor...	—	18
Bastian Severa.., ...		—	18
Attesa Reposa		—	18
Theodosius Gregory		—	27
John Parera...		—	18
Matthias de Silva		—	18

ST. THOMAS STREET.

		Pags.	Fans.
John Stevenson...	Mr. Liddell...	1 :	18
Nichola de Silva..		1 :	—
Tarnantony...		—	27
Mrs. Griffiths... ...	Mr. Cheney	1 :	18
Senora Alvada		—	27
Emmanuel de Silva ...	Jas. Meelenen	—	27
Ditto		—	27
President Yale, a Godown		1 :	—
Maria Zebo...		—	11
Pasquall Gallon		—	18
President Yale		1 :	—
Emtanuel Navis.		1 :	—

		Pags.	Fans.
Romber Ray...		—	27
John Baptista...		1 :	—
Bernardo Medows ...	Mr. Barron	1 :	—
Antonio Qualis...		1 :	—
Clara Botalia...		—	18
Gaspar de Monte... ...	Mr. Betsworth	2 :	—
Mr. Gray, a Godown..		1 :	—
Padre Salvadore... ...	Mr. Ivory	1 :	—
Joan de Coasta		1 :	—
	Pags.	20 :	0

ST. THOMAS LANE.

		Pags.	Fans.
Donna Issabella		—	18
. . . . Pois	Elizabeth Poulter	—	27
Emmanuel Vass		—	27
Duarty Figarado		—	18
	Pags....	2 :	18

CHURCH STREET.

		Pags.	Fans.
Antony Gonsalis		—	27
Donna Phillippa		—	27
Catherena Passania		—	27
John Stevenson		1 :	—
Mr. Rodrigoes	Mr. Burton	1 :	—
	Pags...	4 :	9

The sanitary condition of this crowded little settlement may be inferred from the following startling announcement for the year 1688.

> "Christenings this year........... 11
> Marriages this year............... 13
> Burials this year.................. 101

CHAPTER XII.

GOVERNORSHIP OF MR. NATHANIEL HIGGINSON.

1692—1698.

The accession of President Higginson, followed up closely as it was by the arrival of Sir John Goldsborough as Commissary General, seems to have been a great event in the history of Madras. The Consultation books are once more filled with incidents of general interest, and are no longer encumbered with the records of an obsolete quarrel. In other respects the retirement of Mr. Yale was followed by the usual results. He was compelled to remain in Madras until all the claims of the Company were settled; but he was not prosecuted with the severity which was practised towards some of his predecessors.

The history of the first year of Mr. Higginson's administration is marked by many incidents. The progress of the war between the Great Mogul and the Mahrattas is largely illustrated; and the matter now published for the first time, will be of value to all future historians. Then we have some notices of the capture of Pondicherry by the Dutch; also a curious account of the first possession of Egmore and Pursewaukum by the Agency at Fort St. George; together with some interesting notices of the Roman Catholic Church in this country, and the relation of the Bishop of St. Thomé to the English Government. These are combined with domestic incidents which serve to throw additional light upon the lives and manners of our predecessors in this Presidency, and which we shall continue to arrange as nearly as possible in chronological order, leaving our extracts in many cases to tell their own story.

The first incident relates to a strong minded lady of the olden time, and as it contains a slight flavour of scandal, like the sensation of onions in Sidney Smith's salad, it will still be read with interest.

"Tuesday, 20th December, 1692. John Dolben, Esq., Judge Advocate, acquaints that information hath been given in before him against Mrs. Katherine Nicks of several notorious frauds by her committed in Connimere, whilst her husband was Chief there; particularly that during the late investment, she caused the Right Hon'ble Company's godowns to be broke open, and forcibly took from thence great quantities of cloth of the first sort, which she applied to Mr. Elihu Yale's private use, who was then President; notwithstanding the Merchants declared that the said cloth was brought in upon the Company's account, and positively refused to consent that it should be otherwise applied.

"That upon this he (the Judge Advocate) wrote her a letter requiring her, being a woman notoriously known to be a separate Merchant from her husband, to put in bail to answer the damages the Hon'ble Company had sustained by her illegal proceedings; which she not complying with, he issued out a warrant to arrest her. But she refusing to obey, was returned in contempt; he therefore prays the assistance of the military power to secure her in her house, being under suspicion that she designs privately to fly from justice.

"Ordered that the Captain of the Guard do send a file of Musqueteers with a Corporal to the house of Mrs. Katherine Nicks, who are to obey such orders as the Judge Advocate shall think fit to give."

The kindness of Mrs. Nicks towards Mr. Yale was not appreciated by his successor. The lady was forced to submit and pay up for the cloth she had taken; and shortly afterwards returned to England.

The war between Aurungzebe and the Mahrattas was still lingering in the Dekkan. The army of the Mogul was beseiging Ginjee, at that time occupied by Rama Rajah and the Mahrattas. But the siege languished, and one of the generals of the Mogul's army, named Alimerdy Khan, was taken prisoner by the Mahrattas; and many of the Mogul's officers fled to Madras as appears from the following entry.

"Saturday, 17th December, 1692. There being, upon the defeat of Alimerdy Khan lately received from the Mahrattas, several of his Officers and other persons of good quality, privately fled hither for good security: it is thought convenient that they be used very kindly while they lie in disguise, and treated with small presents of necessaries as the President shall find necessary and requisite: some of them being persons that may prove useful to the Right Honorable Company's affairs, not only to the Vizier but to the Mogul himself."

Subsequently an attempt was made to induce the Madras Government to become security for the payment of the ransom for Alimerdy Khan.

"Friday, 23rd December, 1692. The President acquainting us that this morning Cojee Gregorio (an Armenian merchant) came to him, and told him that he had received a letter from Pulicat from the brother in law of Alimerdy Khan (the Nabob lately taken by the Mahrattas and imprisoned in Gingee) to signify the Mahrattas having offered Alimerdy Khan his liberty for a lak of Pagodas; he does in the Nabob's name desire that the Governor of Madras would receive jewels and money to that amount into his custody, and then write to Rama Rajah engaging to pay that sum to his order upon the arrival of Alimerdy Khan in Madras; for which purpose a letter is written to the President, but it being a matter of great moment, the President has only put off the receiving of the letter, and the returning of any answer, till resolved in consultation how to act; and it is resolved not to commit ourselves in that affair."

About a month afterwards Cojee Abanus and Cojee Gregorio, Armenians resident in Madras, made another effort to induce the Government of Fort St. George to interest themselves in the release of Alimerdy Khan, by engaging to see the amount of ransom paid to Rama Rajah, on the arrival of Alimerdy Khan at Madras. It seemed however very probable that when Alimerdy Khan reached Madras, he would demand his own immediate release in the name of his master the Mogul; whilst the Presidency would be responsible for the amount of ransom to Rama Rajah and the Mahrattas. Accordingly the Presidency still persisted in its policy of non-intervention; but the following entry in the consultation book is worthy of record.

"It does appear that these Armenians have a correspondence with the Mogul's officers, and to serve themselves in strengthening their own interest would draw so great an inconvenience upon the Right Honorable Company, by engaging us to intermeddle in such an affair."

Meantime, the army of the Mogul was commanded by the Nabob Zulfikar Khan; by Assad Khan, father of Zulfikar Khan and Vizier to Aurungzebe; and by Prince Cambakhsh, who appears in the records under the barbarous name of Cawn Bux, a name which we have taken the liberty to reproduce in a modern form suitable to the eyes of those who are familiar with the modern historians of India. The following entry throws some light upon the state of the Mogul's army.

"Monday, 30th January, 1693. Lewis Forrill, one of the Soldiers that went up with Emam Cooley six months since to serve Zulfikar Khan in the siege of Gingee, returning, and with this account. That two months since, Zulfikar Khan ordered to split all the Great Guns, and the brass

Guns that were sent from hence for presents; which he supposes was occasioned by the Mogul's death, whereof he heard report.* That at the same time Cawn Bux attempting to go over to Rama Rajah, was seized by Zulfikar Khan, and ever since kept prisoner. That the camp being reduced to extreme want of provisions for men and cattle, so that if they had stayed longer they would have been starved, they made a truce with Rama Rajah for twenty-four hours, in which time Zulfikar Khan removed to Wandewash, but for want of camels and oxen was forced to leave much of their baggage behind to the discretion of the Mahrattas, which gave occasion to the report that a peace was made. Whereas the Mahratta army watches and follows the motion of the Mogul's army; so that the issue of the war remains very uncertain."

The following extracts, referring to the great Pagodas of Black Town and Triplicane, will be interesting to our local antiquarians.

"Thursday, 29th December, 1692. The Gentoo Pagoda in the Black Town, being built by Timina the former Chief Merchant, and from that time kept in repair and maintained by the Chief Merchants, who also received the custom of the said Gentoo Pagoda, voluntarily paid by all but Europe nations and Armenians, wherewith they ordered the maintenance of their Brahmins, etc.: and also the more famous Pagoda of Triplicane, which is

* The retreat from Gingee was not caused by the death of Aurungzebe, an event which did not take place until 1707, but by the dissensions between Cambakhsh and Zulfikar Khan.

mentioned in one of the King of Golconda's firmauns, dated the 23rd February, 1676, to be granted to the Company, which was obtained at the special instance of Verona, and hath been ever since under the management and care of our Chief Merchants, who applied the profit of the adjacent grounds to the maintenance of their Brahmins, etc.; amount yearly to from Pagodas fifty to seventy, until lately President Yale took both the said Pagodas out of the hands of the Chief Merchants, and made Rangia Chetty, Collavimatadre, and Child Conacoply the Overseer and Governor of the Pagodas. Though nothing doth appear in any Consultation of the reason which moved President Yale to do it. Since which time the inhabitants have entertained jealousies of diabolical arts practised in those Pagodas against some of the merchants and Sheah party. The Merchants being present it was declared to them that for their encouragement and the better satisfaction of the inhabitants, we do give them liberty to make the same use of their Pagodas, and to receive the same Income from both as formerly; but reserve to ourselves the power of recalling that liberty when we shall see cause. And also that the ground belonging, as they say, to Triplicane, is to be disposed of by us to such inhabitants as we shall think fit to settle there; and that it is not in their power to lay any tax upon such inhabitants without our consent. And further, that they are to give an account yearly on every New Year's day of the account of the Incomes of Triplicane and how the same does arise."

Our next extract refers to the arrangement of Church sittings, which has evidently been a delicate matter from time immemorial.

"Wednesday, 4th January, 1693. It is ordered that the Churchwardens do herewith cause a handsome seat to be made in the Church for the Mayor, next below the Clerk's desk in the said aisle, with a place for a Mace to lie on each side of him best to be seen. And that the Mayor's wife be placed next below him on the same side. And take care to seat those Gentlewomen, that will be displaced by that means, where best it may be to their content, having due regard to their qualities."

The arrangements as regards the payment of sea customs and clearing out ships were much the same then as now; but some strange laws were in force, as the reader will now sec.

"Wednesday, 4th January, 1693. The Right Hon'ble Company have made it a law in their City and Port of Madras, that all goods exported or imported (their own goods, and all jewels, plate, and money only excepted) shall pay towards the charges of the Garrison and Fortification five per cent Custom." Here follow the rules for collecting the Customs and for clearing out ships, of no interest now. The following regulation however is curious.

"And all ships or vessels that shall go away out of the Road, before they have paid all duties and cleared out of the custom house, as is appointed, shall be forfeited, one half to the Right Hon'ble Company, and the other half to the seizer, suing for and condemning the same in the Admiralty

Court. And the Customer, or his Deputy, shall use all means to stop them,—by ordering the gunner to fire at them without farther order from the Governor. And after the first shot, to hit them if they can. And in case the ship cannot be stopped or afterward seized, the master shall stand fined for a thousand Pagodas, to be sued for and recovered in the Admiralty Court as before, when and wherever he can be taken or come at, or his estate."

Our next extract shows that Mr. Yale had got into difficulty in the matter of walling Black Town.

"Saturday, 14th January, 1693. The Commissary General (Sir John Goldsborough), finding the mud Points and Walls about the Black Town cost several thousand Pagodas, and that Governor Yale had made them at the Right Hon'ble Company's charge against their positive order and the most of the Council's express exceptions,—did desire Judge Dolben to make demand of President Yale for three thousand four hundred and eighty-three Pagodas with interest, being the cost of them and of a Physic Garden. Judge Dolben returns answer that he hath demanded the same, and that President Yale saith he hath not done anything of that nature, but what was either ordered by the Right Hon'ble Company or agreed to by the Council, or of absolute necessity, and desires to be heard about it before any farther demand be made."

The next entry will explain itself.

"Thursday, 19th January, 1693. There being complaints made by Taliars and Peons appointed to watch the Black Town, that many people, inhabitants and strangers, do walk up and down in the streets all night, which is the occasion of many disorders, thefts, and violences committed :— it is ordered that to-morrow morning the Choultry Justices do cause the Tom Tom to be beat through all the streets of the Black Town, forbidding all persons to walk in the streets after eleven of the clock at night, under penalty of one pagoda to be paid into the Choultry, or severe corporal punishment, as the Justices shall think fit.

The following notices are interesting as illustrative of the form of Hindoo oaths.

"Wednesday, 25th January, 1693. Judge Dolben reports from the Admiralty Court that in a trial this day between the Right Hon'able Company and the late President Yale and others for wrongs and damages done them, that the said late President has objected against the manner of giving the Gentoo oath, by the usual ceremony of fetching water and flowers from the Pagoda into Court, affirming that there was a late order of consultation by which the ceremony of taking Gentoo oaths was for the future established to be done before the Pagoda. Upon which report we have made enquiry of Choultry Justices and members of Council, who all declared the way of swearing the Gentoos hath been in the Court before the Jury, by causing water and flowers to be brought from the Pagoda; the flowers are put upon their heads, and they drink some of the water before or in the Court; and both are given and done by the Brahmin of the Pagoda, and in the presence of the eternal

God who they believe in a more particular manner to be in all Courts of Justice, are required to speak the truth. . . . We likewise sent for a dozen or fourteen of the ancient Brahmin priests, the most eminent in the place, and asked them of the same matter, who all unanimously gave it as their opinion and knowledge that this is the way of their own Gentoo Government, swearing witnesses in the Carnatic country, when evidence was not believed without an oath; but that their Governor did never send or force any of them to be sworn at the Pagoda, but did cause water and flowers to be brought from thence and swear them in Court: for, say they, what is the Pagoda? it is an Image or Stone: where a Governor is, there is God; where ten men are, there God is present. . . . We therefore order the continuance of this way of swearing."

The following proceedings in the Court of Admiralty are amusing enough.

"Thursday, 18th May, 1693. Judge Dolben reports from the Admiralty Court that Captain Freke having a cause determined there between the Right Hon'ble Company and himself, about 50 tons of lead of the Right Hon'ble Company laden in England, which the said Captain refused to deliver according to Charter party; Captain Freke flew out into scurrilous language against the Government here, and the authority and justice of the Court, upon which the Judge gave him a civil caution to be more moderate. But when the decree of the Court was pronounced against him, and an appeal which he tendered was rejected, he repeated his scurrilous expressions, viz. that he had behaved himself like a man, and was used like a beast; that he knew before he came he should have no justice here, but would have it in another place; upon which the Judge ordered him to be taken into custody, which the officer going to do, he cocking his hat laid his hand upon his sword, and turning upon the Court in that posture said, that in England he was as good a man as Judge Dolben though not here, holding up his hand in a threatening posture, swore he should meet him there where he could have satisfaction; upon which the Judge, seeing the Captain of the Guard present in Court, ordered him to take him and carry him to the Cock house, but sent the crier after him and ordered him to be secured in the Fort. Since which two days ago Captain Freke came to the Commissary of his own accord all alone, and said his ship was in danger by one cable being broke, and the other wanting servis. The Commissary told him the best way to secure the ship would be to set himself at liberty by acknowledging his error in Court, and asking pardon of the Court and Judge. To which he replied, he never would do it as long as he had breath in his body, with many vindications of himself and expressions of inveteracy."

Captain Freke subsequently submitted, but sent in a protest, which is still on record.

We may here mention that the Commissary Sir John Goldsborough proceeded to Fort St. David in June 1693, and returned in July. Shortly afterwards he again proceeded along the coast, and died suddenly in November the same year.

From the next entry we learn that Alimerdy Khan had obtained his release from Gingee.

"Friday, 4th August, 1693. A Dutch ship with the Mogul's flag on the maintop mast head, passing by this road, two Dutchmen came ashore from Nabob Alimerdy Khan to give notice that he was upon the ship going for Pulicat. And the ship firing 13 guns, the Fort answered as many, in respect to the Nabob. And his brother-in-law Ali Caldera, (who has for six months past resided here) coming to the President for leave to go off to the Nabob, the President desired him to take with him two chests of Rose water, and present to the Nabob. His releasement has cost him 300,000 Rupees, thereof the Dutch have remitted part by Bill of Exchange."

The next extract will explain itself.

"Wednesday, 16th August, 1693. Percolla Chinna Warka having obtained Zulfikar Khan his Perwanna for the Government of Trivatore and Tripatore, countries adjacent, called in his way to see his family (whom he has kept here two or three years) and visiting the President, do assure him that Assad Khan is alive and well, and in the king's favour, notwithstanding all the current reports to the contrary. And on the 11th instant, Mahmood Aniffe, Zulfikar Khan his adopted son about twenty years of age, coming here with fifty horse and a hundred peons, to take his pleasure and see the place. It being judged necessary to treat him civilly, in respect to Zulfikar Khan, we appointed him the Garden for the accommodation of himself and servants; and he sending word that he designs to take his leave to-day, and to depart to-morrow, the warehousekeeper is ordered out of the stores to get ready a present to be made him of such things as may be best spared, viz. 1 Tonquen chest with 6 cases of Dressing Boxes, and 6 Bemdczas, 2 small prospective glasses, 2 looking glasses, 1 pair Pistols, 1 piece of China silk, 1 wax Image in glass and 2 glass globes, 1 chest Rosewater, 5 Swords, 2 Pictures covered with glass."

The siege and capture of Pondicherry by the Dutch is thus noticed.

"Monday, 21st August, 1693. Received a general letter from Fort St. David dated the 18th instant, advising that the Dutch had landed several great guns and three mortar pieces, and were raising batteries against Pondicherry Fort, but had not as yet fired any shot; and that Governor Pitt had sent to Monsieur Martin to surrender their Fort, which might prevent the shedding of much blood, but he returned this answer that he was there to defend it for his king's glory, and their own honour, which he was resolved to do to the last drop of his blood."

Pondicherry was taken a few days afterwards, and a congratulatory letter was accordingly sent to Heer Pitt, the Dutch Governor of Pulicat, by the Agency of Fort St. George.

The next entries illustrate the early progress of Roman Catholic Missionaries in this country.

"Monday, 28th August, 1693. Padre Don

John de Clerici delivering a Petition as entered next after this consultation, and also producing to us his letters Missionary from Don Salvador Gallus, Prefect of the Regular Priests at Goa, by which it does appear that he is not dependent upon the Padre Governadore at the Mount; and the Deputy Governor and Council of Fort St. David having in their general letter, dated 18th instant, expressed themselves satisfied in the character they have received; it is agreed that a license be granted unto the said Padre Clerici to officiate at Cuddalore in the room of Padre Paulo, who was before appointed from hence, but is lately removed from thence to Porto Novo by the order of the Padre Governadore of the Mount."

"To the Honorable Nathaniel Higginson, Esq., President and Governor of Fort St. George, Fort St. David, etc., and Council.

The Humble Petition of Padre Don John de Clerici.

Humbly Sheweth,

That your Petitioner is a Priest of the order of the Theatine Missionaries, by which being obliged to travel into remote countries to endeavour the conversion of Infidels to the Christian faith, your Petitioner humbly requests your Honour, etc., that he may by you be appointed the Padre Resident of Cuddalore for the service of the Portuguese inhabitants of that place; which employment he will to the utmost of his power endeavour to perform with all loyalty and fidelity to the Hon'ble Company and their interest, and to the satisfaction of your Honour, etc. for whom as in duty bound he shall ever pray.—D. JOHN DE CLERICI."

In the following December the worthy Padre returned to Madras with his license. The story will be interesting to all our Roman Catholic readers. We quote from an entry dated 16th December.

"Padre Clerici returning hither from Fort St. David, bringing with him the license formerly granted him, and alleging that not understanding the English language, he was not sensible of the import of some articles, which upon consideration he finds directly contrary to the strict rules of his order, and that his acceptance thereof will render him liable to the ecclesiastical censure of his superiors, and therefore chooses rather to leave that place and repair to Madapollam, whither he is invited to succeed the Padre lately deceased, than to accept. But it not being thought convenient to alter the articles upon his objections, and yet more requisite to admit him at Cuddalore, than either a French or Portuguese Padre, he being of a different order and nation from them both:—it is agreed that Padre Clerici be permitted to reside there, and perform the office of a Priest so long as he shall behave himself well, and that the matter of the articles be further referred to his Excellency the Commissary General's coming, and that a letter to that effect be writ to the Deputy Governor and Council of Fort St. David, which Padre Clerici being acquainted with was contented therewith, and delivered up his former license."

The honest Padre died a few months afterwards,

a circumstance which gave rise to a slight discussion between the Bishop of St. Thomé and the Presidency at Fort St. George regarding the power of nominating a successor. On the 11th February 1694, the following letter from the Bishop was received by Mr. Higginson.

"SIR,—Whereas I arrived in this place but a few days since, I had no time to come and kiss your Honour's hands, to whom I wish long life and health, for the relief of the Portuguese who live in these parts.

"I have had advice that Padre Don John, whom the Governor my predecessor placed near Cuddalore, is deceased, and whereas I determine to send to that Church Padre Paulo de Saa who has been there; and to content the English gentlemen there I would not do it without advising your Honour thereof, whom I believe will approve of my election.

"If I am worthy of serving your Honour, I am ready to obey your will whom God keep.

I kiss your Honour's hands,

FRYER RAYMUNDO DE MERVAIS.

The President did not approve of a Vicar being appointed in a place under the English by the Bishop of St. Thomé. Moreover he preferred Padre Gulielmus a Valle, who belonged to the order of the Theatines. Accordingly he directed the Presidency at Cuddalore to order Padre Paulo to cease from executing his priestly functions within the English boundaries; and dispatched the following letter to the Bishop of St. Thomé.

"Reverend Sir,

I received your letter dated 11th February,

wherein you advise me that you determine to send Padre Paulo de Saa in the room of Padre Don John, whom the Governor your predecessor had placed Vicar at Cuddalore. I acknowledge your civility in giving me notice of your determination; but admire at your usurpation of an authority which did not belong to your predecessor, nor to yourself nor successors, viz. to appoint Vicars in any place under the English government. You have made a wrong account, and if you would reckon right you must begin again. In this case I ought to deal plainly with you, that no foreign Episcopal authority can be admitted within the limits of our jurisdiction, and that you are not Governor or Bishop of Cuddalore no more than of Madras. But as your reverence is Bishop or Governor of Meliapore, I congratulate your accession to that authority, and desire and embrace your friendly and neighbourly correspondence; in pursuance of which I acquaint your reverence that I have determined to permit Padre Gulielmus a Valle, of the order of the Theatines, to reside at Cuddalore, in the room of Padre Don John de Clerici deceased. I am your friend and servant,

NATHANIEL HIGGINSON."

The following incident is worthy of record so far as it is strange.

"Wednesday, 30th August, 1693. Word being brought us while at Consultation on the 28th instant, that Mr. Wheeler, Member of Council and Sea Customer and Chief Justice of the Choultry, was very sick, and soon after about 11 o'clock that he was dead, we went forthwith to his house, and appointed Mr. Mildmay and Mr. Vander Anker to take account of the Right Honorable Companies' books and papers which were in Mr. Wheeler's hands; but on the way thither the following note was delivered into the hand of the President.

Honorable Sir,—I have murdered Mr Wheeler, by giving him arsenic. Please to execute Justice on me the malefactor as I deserve. Your Honour's unfortunate obedient Servant, SAMUEL BROWNE.

"Whereupon Doctor Browne after examination, and his particular relation of the circumstances of his fatal mistake, was by warrant of the Judge Advocate committed, as also his servant, who negligently powdered pearl in a stone mortar wherein arsenic had been before beaten, the mixture whereof with the pearl is supposed to be the occasion of his death; and there being symptoms of poison, Doctor Bulkley, the Surgeon of the Hospital, was ordered to open the corpse and make his report.

"Yesterday at eight o'clock in the forenoon Mr. James Wheeler was buried, with the solemnity accustomed for his high station."

The following report of Dr. Bulkley will be interesting to our medical readers.

"May it please your Honour with the Worshipful Council.

According to your orders I did on Monday the 28th instant in the afternoon open the dead body of Mr. James Wheeler about five hours after his death, and upon viewing the viscera or bowels, found them not much altered from their natural temper and colour. The parts that seemed to suffer most were the stomach and intestines, which were a little inflamed, and almost wholly bared and stripped of the mucous or slimy covering with which those parts are commonly invested. The lungs also were a little inflamed. The blood that I gathered out of several vessels all appeared blacker than usual. But the suddenness of his death, and the severe symptoms he laboured under before he died, were greater arguments of poison received, than anything I could trace out by dissection. This from, Sir, Your Honours most humble and obedient servant,

EDWARD BULKLEY."

This following incident refers to the Roman Catholics of Madras.

"Monday, 25th September, 1693. The French Padres having represented to us that Padre Ephraim is by age disabled, and that there remains only Padre Miguel to officiate in the Portuguese Church, whereunto there are belonging about eight thousand Christians, as they call them, within the bounds of this city; and therefore request that a French Padre may be admitted to reside here as an assistant to Padre Miguel. It is considered that the said Padre was formerly of Pondicherry, but left the same before it was invested by the Dutch; and that he is of the same order as Padre Ephraim, viz. a Capuchin; and that while the Church is permitted to continue it is reasonable to allow a sufficient assistance for discharging the Church Office, which is too much for one. And upon the whole, it is resolved that the said Padre may reside in this city as an assistant to Padre Miguel; approving himself true and subject to our government; not holding intelligence to the prejudice thereof; not drawing our soldiers or Protestant inhabitants to the Romish profession; not marrying or burying any but those of their own Church; and rendering a due account yearly of Marriages, Christenings, and Burials, and number of communicants; and this permission to continue till he be ordered to depart the place."

The following extract will explain itself.

"Friday, 3rd November, 1693. The Junkamers of Ypere (? Vepery), having received orders from Zulfikar Khan to cause a town to be built there, and to draw inhabitants to build and dwell there, and to receive 5 per cent custom on all goods carried in and out of Madras; and several of our discontented Chitties and shopkeepers having been drawn into a compliance with the design, and treated with the Junkamers in order to their settlement there: the Chief Dubash was ordered to treat with the Junkamers for putting a stop to their proceedings; and the Junkamers having thereupon promised him to suffer goods to pass according to sallabad, and to forbear building, and to write accordingly to Zulfikar Khan,—upon condition he shall privately receive 200 Rupees, a chest of Persia Brandy, and Broadcloths:—it is thought more convenient to take off these stops by that way, than to use force upon the Dewan's officers; and the Warehousekeeper is ordered to provide and deliver the Rupees etc. to Narrain, who is to deliver the same privately according to agreement."

Our next extract refers to a domestic incident belonging to the old Fort life when all the members of the Agency dined at the General Table.

"Thursday, 16th November, 1693. Having been informed that Mr. Edward King late Steward, had made a bargain with John the Butcher for 50 Pagodas monthly during his Stewardship, which is justly suspected to be the reason why the Butcher's meat in his time is charged in his account so much dearer than by the present Steward, to the great increase of the charges of the General Table. The Attorney General is therefore ordered to take the examination of the Steward's servants then employed, and to report the same on Thursday next."

On the Thursday following the Attorney delivered in his report on this important affair, in which the evidence of one Summoodro, a Conicopoly, forms a story which may find its parallel in every European's household in Madras.

"Summoodro declares that in February last John Arts alias John the Butcher told this deponent that he had given Mr. King 20 Pagodas; that in March he gave him 30 Pagodas; then in April, May, and June this deponent knows Mr. King received 50 Pagodas each month, which was thus: when John asked for 200 Pagodas at a time, Mr. King paid him but 150 Pagodas, and took receipt for 200 Pagodas; when the month was almost expired and

John brought in 200 Pagodas worth of provisions, they then cleared their accounts."

Our next extracts refer to the possession of the Agency of Fort St. George of the then neighbouring towns of Egmore, Persewaukum, and Triplicane.

"Monday, 25th December, 1693. Received a letter from Ramdas Tarriffdar of Poonamallee under Arsimo Naik, requiring the delivery of Egmore, Persiwauk, and Triplicane to Appogee Puntalo for the use of Arsimo Naik, to whom he alleges the Nabob has granted them.

"Tuesday, 26th. This day we are informed from the Brahmin at Egmore, that an officer with ten Rajpoots are come thither to take possession by tying leaves. It is ordered that a serjeant with eight soldiers and six peons be sent thither to hinder their proceeding; and an answer was written and sent to Ramdas, to let him know that Triplicane was granted to the English at the same time that Chinnapatanam was, and Egmore and Persewaukum were lately granted us by the King's Hoosbull Hookum, and Grand Vizier and Nabob's Purwannas, and therefore cannot deliver them."

"Friday, 5th January 1694. The Town Conicopolies and chief inhabitants of Egmore, came to make their salaam to the President, and presented him with a patch of cloth, and brought sheep, fowls, cocoa nuts, with a basket of orange, limes, and plantains, which were delivered to the Steward for the use of the General Table, and made their acknowledgments of the great satisfaction and security they enjoyed under our Government.

"Tuesday, 30th January. Appogee Puntalo being come to Vepery Junkum with 50 Horse and 50 Rajpoots to take possession thereof by order of Arsimo Naik, and it is probable he has also orders for taking possession of Egmore and Persewauk which he has already demanded by letter:—it is therefore ordered that Alexander Del Gardiner, Ensign, do forthwith march thither with 10 Centinels, with whom the Serjeant and 20 Centinels there already are to join, and to prevent the Moors taking possession of those towns."

The Agency had a considerable deal of trouble before they fairly obtained the possession of the towns; at last the perwanna arrived from Zulfikar Khan as appears from the following entry.

" Monday, 19th March, 1694. A Perwanna being this forenoon received from Zulfikar Khan for holding the new towns in our possession,—it is ordered that Captain Seaton go this afternoon with the Chief Dubash and Brahmin, and cause the said perwanna to be publicly read for the satisfaction of the inhabitants, who before not daring to cut their Paddy for fear of Arsemo Naik's people, are forthwith to go about the cutting it to prevent further loss."

CHAPTER XIII.

GOVERNORSHIP OF MR. NATHANIEL HIGGINSON.

(Continued.)

1692—1698.

The years 1694, 1695, 1696, which are treated in the present chapter, are marked by a number of incidents, none of which however require any lengthened introduction. Accordingly we at once proceed to lay our extracts from the records before our readers, interspersing a few explanations as occasion may arise.

The way in which firmauns could be obtained from Native Governors is illustrated by the fact that Dr. Blackwall, a surgeon in the Company's service, actually obtained for himself the Governorship of Porto Novo. Suspicions however had been excited of his having entertained the design of betraying Fort St. David; and his papers were seized by Mr. Hatsell the Chief at Cuddalore, and full reports, together with the delinquent, were dispatched to Fort St. George. We extract the following entry in the consultations.

"Friday, 9th February 1694. The General Letter from Mr. Hatsell being perused, with the paper of the examinations of Dr. Blackwall's servants, and also one letter from Dr. Blackwall to his wife, which gives an account of his having received a firmaun for Porto Novo, whereof he and his heirs are to be Governors, where he is to maintain one or two hundred horse, and as many Europeans as he can get. Dr. Blackwall being sent for and examined, he confessed it, and delivered in a narrative of his transactions with the Nabob and Arsema Naik, but does utterly disown any design relating to Fort St. David or Cuddalore, and allegeth in his own justification that after he was acquainted that Mr. Hatsell had seized his papers, he notwithstanding came to the Council, as he intended, to disclose the whole matter, and have their approbation before he did engage in it. But it being a matter of dangerous consequence, requires further enquiry and consideration. In the meantime Dr. Blackwall is committed to the charge of the Lieutenant of the Guard, to be kept in a chamber in the Fort under a Centinel, and none to speak to him till further orders." This matter lay in abeyance for some years afterwards, but Dr. Blackwall obtained his release on giving security.

Complaints respecting provisions on board ship have frequently appeared in the public journals, but we think that the following memorial against Captain Buck of the "Royal James and Mary" is unique in its kind. It is entered in the Consultations of the 22nd March, 1694.

"To the Hon'ble Nathaniel Higginson, etc, May it please your Honour, etc.

We have in pursuance of our petition formally delivered, proceeded to particularize our grievances, which with all due submission is offered to your Honour and Council's consideration.

1. The first and chief thing that we shall allege against Captain Buck, is that of our want of fresh provisions most part of the voyage, he not considering the great and unusual rate paid for our transportation.

2. That we neither ate nor drunk of the ship's provisions so well as the Mates during the voyage.

3. That we thought it very unreasonable to allow us but one meal a day, and that of the ship's provisions, for three, four, or five weeks together, when the Mates had breakfast and supper allowed them.

4. That when there was fresh provisions killed we had not our share, the Mates having a breakfast and supper out of it, the Captain declaring it was their fees.

5. That when we had anything to eat, we ate more like beasts than men, having neither trencher nor table cloth, but after we were forced from his table, we had a table cloth and plates constantly.

6. That upon our request by Mr. Connell and Mr. Hearne that he would supply the defect of fresh provisions by allowing cheese or butter for breakfast, he granted one small cheese amongst twenty-six persons, which when expended, and we desiring more, he retorted the ship's sides were not made of cheese.

7. That the Captain was so uncivil to us, that if any person came on board, he either took them into the Roundhouse, or turned us down into the Cabin.

8. That when at St. Jago he was so uncivil to us as to deny us his boat (unless we would go in his long boat with the cattle) to get on board, his yawl and pinnace being both on shore to wait on him and his boys, forbidding his men to let any passenger come into the boats, so that those that were ashore were forced to wade up to their necks to get into the long boat.

9. That he suffered the Right Hon'ble Company's servants in general to be abused by his officers."—(Signed by seven persons.)

Captain Buck received from the Government of Fort St. George "a very severe check for the said miscarriages, which he promises to amend for the future."

The following entry explains itself.

"Monday 26th March, 1694. There having been some disorders in the entry of consultations, it is ordered for the future that all resolves of the President and Council be written by the Secretary in a foul consultation book, which are to be signed by the President and Council with the letters of their names before parting, which is the Secretary's warrant for entering the same fair; and the Secretary is ordered the next consultation day to bring the same fair entered, which is to be signed first before any other business be considered."

In perusing the following extract the reader must bear in mind that the Mogul army was still opposed to the Mahrattas in the neighbourhood and Ginjee.

"Wednesday, 20th June, 1694. Suliman Khan, brother to Davood Khan, Captain of three thousand horse in Zulfikar Khan's army, came to town (Madras) with 6 elephants, 14 camels, and 50 horsemen, and brought a letter from his brother and from Zulfikar Khan, desiring accommodation and a Doctor for curing him of his distemper. Word was sent to Suliman Khan that he was welcome, and that he might order his servants to seek out an accommodation, and the best Doctor in the place should attend him; but that he should not bring his horsemen into town with him, but keep whom necessary for his service and send the rest out of town; and accordingly his followers pitched their tents to the west of the Fort beyond the river, and himself hired a Juliar house to the northward."

The following extract refers to the condition of the Mussulman Priests or Moollas in Triplicane.

"Tuesday, 3rd July, 1694. The two Moor Moollas, Morkai Subbah and Abou Bekker, having for many months past been at great variance concerning the division of the fees accustomed to be given them by that caste; during which time of their difference some of the Moormen have called in another Moolla to officiate in a new intended Mosque. There being two already, one built by Verona within the Black town, and the other in President Yale's time in the Pettah, sufficient for the whole caste, and for all parts of the town:—it is resolved not to admit the building of any more." The dispute between the two Moollas was settled by President Higginson, who required them to share the Mosque revenues equally; and a cowle was granted confirming to them and their children the sole right of officiating in the two Mosques.

In September this year, Judge Dolben who sat in the Court of Admiralty was dismissed from the Company's service. In the action between the Company and President Yale, he had declared that the Company's claims were set aside by the Statute of Limitations; and was moreover found guilty of receiving bribes for favouring causes. Accordingly cn the 14th September it was resolved that "he is hereby dismissed from the Right Honorable Company's service till their Honour's pleasure be further known; and that in the meantime due respect be given to a person of his quality and abilities, in consideration of which it is a trouble to us to part with him."

We may here remark that Mr. Yale continued at Madras for some years after his recall, endeavouring to evade the Company's claims against him. In February 1696 he dispatched a strong petition to the Court of Directors, in which he complained of the mode in which he had been prosecuted, in a style of which our readers have already had a sample in the letters which he wrote during his quarrel with his Council. The following extract, in which he attacks both the Commissary and the Governor and Council, will be sufficient here.

"That notwithstanding your Petitioner gave sufficient bail and security to answer all the pretended charges against him, yet did the said Commissary, new President, and their accomplices seize on and sell your Petitioner's ships, goods, and estate (from time to time as they could reach the same) to the value of thirty thousand pounds or thereabouts, being almost five times as much as they had given Judgment for against your Petitioner in their own arbitrary court and illegal way of proceeding.

"That your Petitioner being intolerably oppressed as aforesaid, did make several formal protests against such their illegal practices and proceedings, and did appeal therefrom to the Justice of England;...but contrary to all manner of Justice.........your Petitioner has been imprisoned in the Fort ever since November 1692, without hopes of liberty or relief; and with design (as your Petitioner believes) not only to stifle your Petitioner's just complaint of their unchristian usage towards him, but to enforce him into despair, or otherwise to bring on him some distemper that may hasten his death, which not long since by poison was near effected."

This insinuation of Mr. Yale's that he was in danger of poison of course called forth an indignant denial from the Presidency; a denial which gives rise to some painful suspicions that there must have been dark doings in those days, and at the same time throws further light upon the scandal appertaining to Mr. Yale's acquaintance with Mrs. Nicks. President Higginson and Council, in a general letter to the Court which appears to have accompanied the Petition, explained that they had proceeded in exact conformity to law; and that Mr. Yale had never been imprisoned one minute, but that liberty had been granted him to go home, at the only time he had ever asked for such permission; an assertion which is to some extent confirmed by the consultation books. But the original record is here so interesting that we will extract the words of the general letter:—"Therefore, his (Mr. Yale's) assertion that he hath been imprisoned in the Fort ever since 1692 without hope of liberty, is utterly and apparently false; and consequently the reflection is not only groundless, but basely scandalous, when he affirms he hath been imprisoned to enforce him into despair, and to bring on him some distemper that may hasten his death. Which reflection is heightened by an instance he gives of his death being not long since near effected by poison. The meaning of all which must be (if it hath any) that he is afraid the President and Council of Fort St. George will make away with him by poison or otherwise. They that know him will doubtless conclude with us, either this bold reflection is no more than the accustomary strains of wicked policy, or a salvo for his own credit against the common reports of the unusual deaths of several of the Council of Fort St. George when he was President; concerning which we do not accuse him, being compelled by the rules of Christian charity to suspend a censure, the most material evidence being dead; but if they had been living to declare themselves, what others have since their death declared as from them, some of Mr. Yale's aforementioned instruments must have been prosecuted, and he would have been put hard to it to clear his own reputation."

"The baseness of the reflection about poison will further appear. . . There never was a report that ever we heard, of anything that would give him the least colour for such a suggestion since the year 1691, when there was a story told all about the town of a rogue that tempted Mrs. Nick's slave wench to poison her mistress; and because Mrs. Nicks then lived with Mr. Yale at his Garden house (when she and Mrs. Pavia a Jew, with their children, have and do frequent, to the scandal of Christianity among heathens) therefore he takes occasion to suppose the design was against himself, and to insinuate that the now President and Council of Fort St. George had a hand in it."

We shall probably learn something more of Mr. Yale in a future record. We now quote an entry illustrative of the current history.

"Saturday 10th November, 1694. Zulfikar Khan suddenly removed his army from Wandewash, and it was reported that he went to take Chungamon Fort (?) At the same time came various reports of quarrels between him and the other principal officers of the Mogul's army, and it was said they had orders from the king (Aurungzebe) to seize him. Whereupon the President ordered a spy Brahmin to go and attend the motions of the Camp, and send intelligence by four Peons appointed as Tappies; from whom this day received a letter advising that Zulfikar Khan is encamped to the northward of Chungamon Fort; the Mahrattas make daily incursions in the camp and plunder them of five or six horse. At Wandewash the inhabitants by reason of the Moor's army have left their habitations, and taken to the hills nigh Chungamon Fort, for their protection.

The Mogul's horse has lately harassed and plundered the country, carrying with them both people and goods. Davood Khan and others design to seize the Nabob (Zulfikar Khan) when they shall see a fit opportunity. The Nabob sent Rama Rajah (king of the Mahrattas) ten camels loaded with rupees, but they were intercepted by Davood Khan. They (the Mogul's officers) hourly expect an opportunity to seize on the Nabob Zulfikar Khan. The Mahrattas have poisoned the waters, and have mixed milk hedges in some of the tanks, which has killed abundance of people."

The Hindoo law against putting a Brahmin to death is illustrated by the following extract.

"Saturday, 15th November, 1694. One Jugga of the Brahmin caste being found guilty of robbery and felony, and condemned to be hanged, upon the earnest intercession of the Right Honorable Company's merchants and some of the principal Black inhabitants, was reprieved, alleging it was contrary to the custom of the country to put a Brahmin to death, requesting he might be punished as accustomary among the Gentoos. It is agreed that the said Brahmin be pardoned his life; and the Justices of the Choultry are ordered to cause him to be punished in the most disgraceful way practised among the Gentoos in like cases, after which turned out of town under the penalty of being hanged whenever he returns."

About this time two nice young gentlemen, Mr. Henry Pullein and Mr. Thomas Walton, appear from the following accounts to have given some trouble to the Governor of Fort St. George.

"Saturday, 13th April, 1695. Mr. Henry Pullein, a young gentleman who came out of England as passenger in the "Defence," but not agreeing with the Commander left that Ship at the Cape, and came hither in the "Hawke," intending by the first opportunity to return to England; but before the "Princess" went home in February last, he had so far run in debt for his maintenance and extravagance, that he could not satisfy his creditors, some of whom about a month ago taking warrants out of the Court to arrest him, he to avoid their execution withdrew to St. Thomé, and in a short time fell into the acquaintance of Emaum Beague, a Moorman. The President having notice thereof, and that he was engaging himself in the Moor's service in the Camp, ordered several persons to watch his going abroad; and being advised that he was come to a Choultry near the Bar, ordered Captain Seaton with soldiers and peons to go round it and bring him in. Mr. Pullein was of his own accord coming into the town in the dusk of the evening, when Captain Seaton overtook him and brought him to the President, who finding by his examination that he had treated with the Moors in order to enter into their service, and that some of the soldiers of our garrison had also offered to go with him, though he pretends that he only gave it out to bring his creditors to reason,—the President ordered the Marshall to take him into custody till the matter can be fairly examined in Council on Monday.

"Monday, 15th April. The President doth acquaint the Council with the foregoing, and Mr.

Pullein being sent for declared the occasion of his leaving the place to be his being in debt, that he was often with Emaum Beague at St. Thomé and had discoursed concerning the Moor's service, but denies to have actually engaged therein,—it is ordered that he be confined in the room in the Fort next to the guard, and have the liberty of the Fort, with a Sentry to attend him night and day, but to keep his chamber from six in the evening till six in the morning, until he can come to a composition with his creditors."

Mr. Pullein appears to have belonged to a respectable family, who had sent him to Madras in the hope of getting rid of him, or of effecting a reformation. He was shortly afterwards sent to England, by the ship "American Merchant," as appears from the following advice in a general letter:—"We have given the Commander an order for his passage, knowing no other way to prevent his running to the Moors, and to prevent the young man's utter ruin. For if he stays he can get no employment, and will be forced to desperate courses for a maintenance, and satisfying his creditors, who must get their money where and when they can. The President is one of them, having furnished him at his first coming, to defray his charges at several times, eighty Pagodas, besides which he run into debt among the Public Houses two or three hundred Pagodas."

Mr. Walton is not noticed in such terms as can lead us to suppose that he was regarded with the same consideration as Mr. Pullein. He came out as a writer, whilst the latter was a passenger. In fact Mr. Walton was more of a type of Hogarth's idle apprentice; but we quote the official record.

"Friday, 10th May, 1695. Thomas Walton, writer, who was sent hither from Fort St. David because he was refractory and idle, and could by no means be there kept in good order; since and here for eight months being appointed to write under the Secretary always neglected to do what was ordered him; after which he was appointed about three months ago to copy over a Ledger, and all this time has done but eleven folios; though upon information that he used to lie out of the Fort, and spend the nights in wandering up and down about town in Moor's habit, and corrupted several young men to accompany him in debauchery, the President ordered him not to go out of the Fort without leave, and strictly enjoined him to finish the books; and upon further information that Mr. Walton had a design to leave the place and run into the Moor's service, having by his extravagant run in debt beyond his ability to pay, the President gave orders to the Lieutenant of the garrison not to permit him to go out of the Fort without leave. The whole matter being now represented and discoursed in Council, and Mr. Walton sent for to bring his book, it appears that he has not written one word since he was last ordered, and does declare that he cannot write, but desires to go home. Being thus incorrigible, it is resolved that he also have leave to go by ship "Armenian Merchant," and in the meantime to prevent his further debaucheries and running to the Moors, that the officers of the guard room do not permit him to go out of the Fort."

The dispute between the Government of Fort St. George and the Bishop of St. Thomé seems to have subsided for a time as appears from the following entry.

"Monday, 3rd May, 1695. After much contest with the Bishop of St. Thomé, he having declared his consent (because he could not help it) for Padre Gulielmo de Valle his proceeding to Cuddalore, the Padre (that difficulty being removed) is ready to go. It is therefore ordered that a License be granted him as follows.

"The President and Council of Fort St. George and city of Madras, for account of the Right Hon'ble English East India Company, do hereby for ourselves and successors give and grant unto the Reverend Padre Gulielmo de Valle, License to officiate as a Priest of the order of the Theatines in the Church erected at Cuddalore for the use of Roman Catholics and within the bounds of Fort St. David,—Provided that in temporal matters he faithfully obey the English Government there, aiding and assisting the worshipful Deputy and Council for the time being in peace and war as occasion shall require, neither shall he maintain any correspondence by letters or otherwise to the prejudice of the Government, nor shall he endeavour to draw the Protestant soldiers or inhabitants into the Romish religion, nor shall he marry, christen, or bury any of them without leave from the Deputy Governor; and once every year he shall deliver a list of all

Roman Catholics, men, women, and children within the bounds of Fort St. David. And further we appoint and order that no other Priest, religious or secular, besides the said Gulielmo de Valle, do perform any religious office without the express leave of the Deputy Governor. And that the said Gulielmo de Valle do not publish, or cause, or permit to be published, either by reading or fixing on the doors of the Church, any decree, order, or letter from the Bishop of Meliapore." (The remainder torn out).

The following entry records a mere domestic incident.

"Friday, 9th August, 1695. Last night Lieutenant Seaton at about twelve o'clock, being in drink, drew his sword upon the Choultry Guard, and run a Portuguese soldier through the arm. Dr. Bulkley being ordered to view the wound, reports that it is not dangerous; and Lieutenant Seaton being sent for, answer was brought that he was sick of a fever."

It is curious to compare the above notice with the following extract from a general letter to England:—

"Among several children born here, whose parents send home for education by this ship, is Ann Seaton, the daughter of Lieutenant Seaton, who has served your Honour nine years in Bengal and this garrison, and is a very able and useful officer. He hath paid Pagodas twenty-six permission, as the rest have done, and humbly begs your Honour will please to remit it."

The next entry explains itself.

"Wednesday, 15th January, 1696. This day being appointed for the solemnity in memory of our late deeeased sovereign Queen Mary. In the forenoon a Company with Drums and Colours covered with black, and Pikes trailing, attended the President and Couneil to Chureh, where Mr. Richard Elliot preached a sermon suitable to the occasion, all the Right Hon'ble Company's servants and the English inhabitants being met in decent mourning, and the principal parts of the Chureh covered with blaek. About twelve o'elock, the flag being lowered at half mast, the Fort began to fire at St. Thomas's Point, and continued by half minute glasses from Charles Point, River Battery, Caldera Point, York Point to the batteries towards the sea, from where the ships in the roads took it, and ended the firing about two o'cloek."

This ehaplain who preaehed on this oeeasion died a few months afterwards. The Company were apprised of the event in a general letter to the Court dated 19th Oetober, 1696. "The Reverend Mr. Riehard Elliot died here on the 17th instant. He hath left his books to the Library, and 250 Pagodas to the Chureh. He hath been the instrument of great good in this place. Mr. Lewis (the co-chaplain) hath not so firm a health that he ean go through the necessary serviee of the Chureh, and the frequent instruetion of ehildren and slaves, whieh he performs here both on Sundays and week-days."

The following notice is historieal.

"Monday, 20th January, 1696. The Mahrattas

army increasing at Ginjee, and frequently sending parties into several parts of the country near Tegnapatam, it is judged necessary that the Agent and Council at Fort St. David accommodate the demands of Rama Rajah and his officers; and it is our opinion that there ought to be a fair correspondence kept with them from that place, during the present uncertain position of things between them and Moors; the Mahrattas by all advices appearing to be in all probability of being masters of all their country, unless the Mogul shall speedily send a very considerable army to the assistance of Zulfikar Khan."

A curious intrigue on the part of Zulfikar Khan, the Mogul General, is recorded at very great length in the Consultations, but may be told in a few words. On the 3rd March, 1696, Emaun Cooley and Ali Bux, two of the servants of Zulfikar Khan, carried a letter from their master to President Higginson demanding a loan of a lakh of Pagodas, offering a number of jewels as security for the repayment. The President and Council refused to comply with the demand, as the money would never be repaid and the jewels might be demanded by the Nabob's successor. Meantime they were advised by an Armenian that the Mogul had ordered Zulfikar Khan to march against Madras, and therefore supposed that he only designed to pick a quarrel. Accordingly presents were made to Emaun Cooley, but the loan was refused. On the 30th of the same month they received a letter advising them of the return of the messengers to Zulfikar, with the statement that on their arrival the Nabob sent for the chief men of his army and divided twenty thousand Rupees among them, much commending the Government of Madras for their liberality. From this circumstance it would appear that the Mogul army was mutinous for want of pay, and that Zulfikar Khan only sent to Madras to gain time until he could get some money elsewhere. Fears however were entertained that notwithstanding the politic commendations he had made in the presence of his army, that he would still resent the refusal of the loan.

Our next extract refers to a domestic incident. It will be seen that Dr. Brown, the unfortunate surgeon who poisoned Mr. Charles, is again at large.

" Monday, 27th April. Complaint having been made by Madremtala in a letter received by the Governor last night, that Dr. Brown had gone to the house of Ananta Terterra his Junkameer of Vepery, and carried him away by force, and robbed him to the value of six thousand Pagodas as by a list sent. Dr. Brown being sent for gives this account. That on Saturday having rid out to Egmore in Company, in their return by the Vepery Choultry the Moor Peons called him names ; and he riding up to them to demand the reason, there followed more aggravating words and they beat him. When he came home, being informed where the Chief man of the Choultry lived, he took his sword and pistol, and being followed by his boy with another pistol, and his horsekeeper, went to the house and by force took out Ananta Terterra, and brought him to the Bridge Gate; where understanding that that was not the man which had abused him, let him go.

"Ananta Terterra doth also further complain that Dr. Brown broke his face with a pistol, pulled his beard, etc., and that he was robbed to the value of six thousand Pagodas; which though there is no reason to believe, yet the Dewan's officers will take occasion to make a demand as accustomary, and give us trouble by complaining to the Nabob. And Dr. Brown being apparently guilty of a breach of the peace, it is resolved that he be committed to the custody of the Marshall, that others may be deterred from the like, and that the inhabitants may understand that such practises are not allowed."

A week afterwards Dr. Brown was discharged from his confinement, in consideration of his patients suffering for want of his assistance, he giving security to the Judges satisfaction.

Our next extract illustrates the occasional difficulty of collecting Quit Rents in the olden time.

"Monday, 13th July. There having been many pawns taken the last year for Quit Rents charged upon several inhabitants, who either refused or were unable to pay, the Rental General was ordered, in pursuance of the Right Hon'ble Company's orders, to sell the said pawns, which was accordingly done; but the clamour and complaints made by the poor among the inhabitants, and the reports thereof in the Nabob's camp, caused the Governor to order him not to take pawns, but to proceed in the collecting of the Quit Rents so far as he could without, and then to produce an account of Quit Rents to be received for September 1695." Subsequently it was resolved to sell the pawns by private contract, and not by public outcry, or auction.

As old traditions are afloat that the sea has greatly encroached upon the Coromandel coast during the last few centuries, we have made a point of extracting such entries as will illustrate such encroachments. The following one may be compared with other notices published in previous chapters.

"Monday, 20th July. The sea having for three or four days past gained very much upon the shore and approached near the walls, and this day broke down part of two piles before the sea gate, it is propounded to consideration by what means the encroachment may be prevented, and in order thereunto resolved, that the principal inhabitants of the place be summoned to meet on Thursday next at four of the clock in the Fort to view the outworks and receive their advice.

"Thursday, 30th July. The principal inhabitants and Senior merchants having with the Council on the 23rd instant viewed the sea side. The result is, that the sea doth plainly increase and may in time hazard the walls; yet it is not admirable to stake it from Point to Point, partly because the charge will be so great (supposed to amount to if well done to at least Pagodas five thousand), and partly because it is generally doubted that it will not answer the end."

The following incidents illustrate the progress of public affairs.

"Saturday, 8th August, 1696. Madrantula having seized 250 cattle in the country belonging to the shepherds of Madras, he had caused all to be delivered to the owners except 60 belonging to the shepherds who serve the Fort with butter and milk. Upon complaint made to the Nabob, Madrantula caused them also to be delivered, and the shepherds returned this night with an answer that they had received all but three which were for the present lost."

"Letters received weekly from the spy Brahmin at the Camp (at Ginjee) give an account that the French and Portuguese continue their solicitations there concerning St. Thomé, and distribute their presents among all the considerable officers, but do not give any distinct account of their business and design."

We make the following extracts, not from their possessing any intrinsic interest, but because they illustrate the mode of procedure in the Choultry and court of Admiralty.

"Monday, 3rd August. The Choultry Justices having produced examinations taken by them concerning the murder of a child in the Black town, and the robbing of a godown within the walls :— it is ordered that the Judge Advocate do cause a session to be held on Tuesday the 11th instant, for the trial of the criminals, and that the examinations be delivered to the Attorney General in order to their prosecution.

"Thursday, 13th August. The Judge reports

from the Special Court of Admiralty held on the 11th and 12th instant, for the trial of several criminals, that on the 11th the Grand Jury found both the bills, viz. Chinandree and Nulla Tombee accused of breaking into a Godown and stealing a considerable quantity of Quicksilver; and Hosana and Pochera for murdering of a child in Black town:—the Court adjourned their trial till yesterday the 12th. Chinandree pleaded guilty to his indictment and Nulla Tombee pleaded not guilty. The Court proceeded in their trial and the Petit Jury withdrew and returned and gave their verdict, viz. Nulla Tombee guilty of petty larceny, and Hosana and Pochera not guilty of the murder. The sentence was accordingly that Nulla Tombee should on Friday next have one of his ears cut off and be whipped and turned out of town. Chinandree to be executed next Wednesday at the usual place of execution, between the hours of eleven and twelve in the forenoon, being the 19th instant, and Hosana and Pochera to be discharged."

"It is upon the question resolved in Council that Chinandree be reprieved from the execution of sentence of death, and that he be sent to Anjango (in Travancore) to work there in irons. In the meantime to remain in the custody of the Marshall; and that the Choultry Justices see that the sentence of the Court be executed upon Nulla Tombee."

The Native Agency through which the Presidency of Fort St. George made their investments in Company's goods, is largely illustrated by a very long entry in the consultations of the 23rd April, 1696, which may be summed up in a few words. At an early period, as we have already seen, Cassa Verona was the Chief Merchant through whom the Presidency transacted its business. On the 27th November, 1678, it was agreed that Cassa Verona should pay only half the custom of 5 per cent, which was levied on all goods passing into the Company's territory by sea or land; and this privilege was granted him during his employment as Chief Merchant, in return for he and his partners making themselves responsible to the Company for all the Joint Stock Merchants. Cassa Verona died on the 28th March, 1680, and on the 5th April following Pedda Vencatadry was appointed Chief Merchant, and the business was managed in the same manner as in Verona's time. But in June, the same year, the Agent and Council resolved upon making a Company of Merchants in a Joint Stock, and offered the Chiefship of the Company to Pedda Vencatadry. He refused for a long time, but at length consented; and on the 12th July the regulation of the Joint Stock was finished, consisting of one hundred shares, "nine being appointed Chief Merchants whereof Pedda Vencatadry was the first; and on the 16th September following, it was resolved by Consultation that Pedda Vencatadry and his partners do pay whole custom upon all goods and provisions imported or exported by sea or by land." This change led to long discussions and disputes, which have long since lost all interest.

The following extract will be interesting to our Roman Catholic readers.

"Tuesday, 8th September, 1696. The French Padre having hitherto avoided the paying of any Quit Rent for their Garden, and the Rental General now demanding their Quit Rent and arrears, and in case of nonpayment threatening to distrain;—the French Padre came this morning to the Governor, and plainly declared that their order of Capuchins cannot pay any tribute or Quit Rent for the Garden or for anything else; that the reason is, because their order doeth strictly and expressly forbid them to possess anything in property, and therefore if the Company will require Quit Rent for the Garden they must quit it; and if the Garden had been first offered under conditions of paying, the Padres then neither could nor would have accepted on it. The Governor argued that small matter was laid only as an acknowledgment of the Right Hon'ble Company's dominion. He answered that they readily acknowledged the dominion and property of the Company, and will readily subscribe to such a paper when desired; and that they are ready to quit the Garden, Church, and place when required so to do; both their residence and possessions here depending solely on the pleasure of the Right Hon'ble Company. It is resolved that the Rental General forbear making any further demands of Quit Rent of the Padre, and that the case be stated to the Right Hon'ble Company in our next General letter, and their orders awaited."

CHAPTER XIV.

GOVERNORSHIP OF MR. NATHANIEL HIGGINSON.

(Concluded.)

1692—1698.

The events of the concluding years of the Governorship of Mr. Higginson, which are recorded in the present chapter, throw considerable light upon the progress of the struggle between Aurungzebe and the Mahrattas, as well as upon the contemporary condition of St. Thomé, and the general progress of affairs at Fort St. George. Our readers will bear in mind that the Nabob Zulfikar Khan still continued to command the army of the Mogul, which was attempting the reduction of the Mahrattas at Ginjee. This interminable seige is but briefly noticed by Mahommedan historians, and is only interesting to the modern reader so far as the fortunes of the Madras Presidency were affected by the proceedings of the rival armies.

The very first extract is a review of the relations between the Presidency and the Nabob Zulfikar Khan.

"Monday, 14th September, 1696. The Nabob (Zulfikar Khan) is disgusted, the only apparent reason thereof is, that we did not comply with his demand of lending him one hundred thousand Pagodas when Emaum Cooley came for that purpose in March last; since which he hath been very unkind; whereas before he never denied, he has since never granted anything asked, and sought all occasions of quarrel, hearkening to every story and encouraging accusers, which not only increases the number of troublesome accusations, but emboldens his other officers to stop and seize our goods, exact unusual customs, and to do all things that tend to the lessening of the trade and destroying our privileges. From this doth proceed the stop put upon the wrecks at St. Thomé, and detaining of fugitives."

"The Portuguese of St. Thomé have sent Domingo d'Coa to the Nabob to solicit the renting of the adjoining Aldeas (?), and the confirming of the King's Firmaun for enjoying St. Thomé with privileges according to salabad, and liberty of the Nabob to fortify. The Nabob has given them a Perwanna in pursuance of said Firmaun, though he has not granted anything according to their request.

"Hadji Mahomed Ali, the Havildar of St. Thomé and Pulicat, hath been with the Nabob, and is confirmed in that office with the addition of the rent of the Poonamallee country and Junkum, though under the name of another. He was a merchant and understands and considers trade, and by a moderate Government has endeavoured to promote it at St. Thomé and Pulicat; and though he has hitherto carried it fair to us, we ought to esteem him a dangerous man, who will take all opportunities to lessen the trade and reputation of this place; in order to which he hath gained so much credit and acquaintance with many merchants, Armenians, Moors, and Gentoos, and doubtless would draw them if he could to St. Thomé.

"Our spy Brahmin at the camp advises of a Frenchman and thrée Gentoos and Brahmins, who have been there two months treating with the Nabob for a fortification at St. Thomé; but their real design is not known, nor who the persons are nor whence they came, but whoever they are the Nabob doth receive and hear them.

"It is known that the King (Aurungzebe) did at first give sudden and rash orders against Madras, and they were revoked; but whether the Nabob hath received any since is uncertain, but his carriage to us gives some reason to suspect that his demand of one hundred thousand Pagodas was the first step in order to a quarrel."

The following is a mere domestic matter. A century and a half ago beggars would appear to have been as great a nuisance in Fort St. George, as they now are in Blacktown.

"Monday, 2nd November, 1696. There being many inconveniences in admitting beggars to go up and down within the walls, being many of them diseased persons and sometimes forty or fifty in a Company,—it is ordered that henceforth no person be admitted to beg within the walls of the Christian town, and if they do the inhabitants are forbid to give them anything, and the officers of the Garrison and Peons and Corporation Officers are ordered when they meet with any within the walls to turn them out. But that the charity of those who are so disposed may not be obstructed, it is recommended to the Mayor and Aldermen to cause a list to be made of the subscriptions of said inhabitants as are inclined to give weekly, and to collect the same every Saturday; and on the Monday following in the afternoon to cause the same to be distributed at the Choultry among such as really want of those who live here and have used to beg within the walls, whose names are to be written in a list and called over at the time of distribution."

We again return to the constant intriguing going on at the camp of Zulfikar Khan.

"Saturday, 17th October. The Nabob being within four leagues of this place to the northward, and there being several reports which makes it credible that in his return to Arcot he will visit the sea coast,—it is resolved that a present be sent him and Wottom Chund, to the amount of about three hundred Pagodas in such things as can be procured and most acceptable to them.

"Friday, 30th. Two letters received from Narrain Brahmin wherein he adviseth that the present carried to the Nabob was kindly accepted, but that Wottom Chund refused his. That there is discourse in the camp of the Nabob's giving orders to Hussan Khan (Foujdar of Trivalore) concerning Madras. Also a letter from Hadji Mahomed Ali (Havildar of St. Thomé and Pulicat), which he hath received from the Nabob's servant at the Camp, and which was written by the orders of Zulfikar Khan." This last letter from the Nabob's servant to the Havildar is interesting, but the opening paragraph is partly torn away. It appears however that the Mogul army under the Nabob Zulfikar Khan, had been reduced to such a miserable condition, that the latter had in the previous February, demanded the loan of a hundred thousand Pagodas already alluded to. Here we can quote the words. "He (the Nabob) had sent by Emaum Cooley Beague, a parcel of jewels to the Captain of Chinnapatanam as a pawn for one hundred thousand Pagodas, but he did not comply. At that time the Nabob was fixed against the Mahrattas, and therefore passed it by. On receipt of this letter I would have you go to Chinnapatanam, and procure the above mentioned sum of money, which will be for their benefit, but if they cannot pay the whole sum at once, you may allow them some time to pay fifteen or twenty thousand Pagodas. Those people were much to blame in not considering rightly of it before, but you may soon make them sensible of their error. In case they do not take your advice and come into the right way, write me of it. Then that place shall be taken into the King's custody, like as Pulicat and the Sea Port towns, and only the Fort shall remain under theirs. The Nabob has left at Trepassore Hussan Khan about this business. After I have received your answer the Nabob will send a party to assist Hussan Khan in the taking of the said Sea Port town; that same town produces yearly above one hundred thousand

Pagodas ; it is no great matter to lend a year's revenue to the Nabob. I would have you send me an answer with all speed. What can I write more ?"

An extraordinary consultation was held on the next day, October 31st, to take this important demand into consideration. Timapa, who had been Chief Merchant to the Presidency, had run away from Madras, and had probably conveyed dangerous information to the Nabob. Moreover a party in Madras itself were suspected of intriguing with Timapa ; whilst grave suspicions were entertained of Narrain the spy Brahmin. The only decision however at which the Council arrived, was to put the place in the best possible defence. Two days afterwards it was resolved on further consideration that "we cannot pay or lend the Nabob the sum of a hundred thousand Pagodas, either out of the Right Hon'ble Company's chest, nor by imposing a Poll tax on the inhabitants ; nor can we admit of a Thasildar over the Black town ; and if the Nabob shall send an army as threatened to beseige the place, and compel us to compliance, we ought to defend the place as well as we can. But that it is better to prevent a seige, and the ill-consequences that will follow it, if the same can be done by spending a reasonable sum without rendering the place liable to. a tribute."

Three days afterwards the general position of the Presidency was taken into consideration by the Council, both as regards the French and Portuguese as well as the Native powers. We extract the whole of the Consultation in question, merely requiring our readers to bear in mind that the

English and Dutch were in allianee against the French; in other words that Willlam of Orange was still engaged in that tremendous war against Louis XIV for the restoration of the balance of power, which has been duly celebrated in the history of Lord Macaulay.

"Thursday, 5th November, 1696. Upon the matter of the Consultation the 31st past. The intelligence received from the Right Hon'ble Company coneerning the French designs in India is considered. They advise a great quantity of ammunition and warlike preparations proper for land service, which is a demonstration that these six French ships* come upon a design against some place in India; and though the intelligence mentions Malacca, yet it may be rationally supposed that the Commanders in Chief have their private instruetions for proceeding upon several designs if one fail; and whatever we may guess concerning their return for Europe, it seems more probable that those six ships are not returned without any attempt or lading; and it is safer to suppose that they are still in India, and that they have some design still to execute. There are some arguments may be urged against the probability of their having any design against this plaee or Fort St. David, as that the Dutch have ships of war in Bengal, which with the northerly monsoon can easily and speedily come upon them on any part

* No previous notice of these six French ships have been found in the Records. The case appears to have been that these ships were sent out, but that it was doubtful what their designs really were.

of this coast. If the French have any regard to future trade they ought not to invade this place, because seated in the Mogul's dominions. But there are also some other circumstances which are matter of caution. It is notorious that the Portuguese are friends of the French. Their intentions do appear by the ready assistance given them at Goa, and the behaviour of our neighbours at St. Thomé ever since the arrival of Francisco Luiz under the character of Captain General, and with a private Commission; but there doth not appear any business he had to do here, unless he came to serve the French designs; and if there be any reality in what the spy Brahmin has so often wrote from the Camp, concerning a Frenchman running up and down privately to the Nabob, and his officers soliciting against Madras, it may be easily thought that the St. Thomé Portuguese are joined in the Council. Besides, the Right Hon'ble Company's instructions that in case the French coming against us to procure assistance from the Moor's armies. But if the French shall prevail with the Moors, either to join with or connive at their attempting against the Place, between ourselves and the Mogul, our case would be much more the worse against two enemies. It may be objected that it is very probable that the Nabob cannot make war against this Place without the King's order. But it may be also considered that he (Zulfikar Khan) hath frequently done greater things than that, not only without but against the King's order. He has imprisoned Cambuksh the King's son; and though the King for a time did express resentment, yet there followed no effect. He hath been frequently ordered to take Ginjee, and it hath been in his power to do it and destroy all the Mahrattas in the country; but instead of that it appears plain that he hath joined council with them, and notwithstanding all the endeavours of his enemies, his father still prevails at court to keep the Nabob in his Government. And if he hath an interest to defend himself against so potent enemies, he can more easily baffle any complaints that we can make to the king. And it is in his power, if he be so inclined, to trouble and plague us, and to raise new impositions to the stopping all business; and it will not be in our power to procure a remedy at last, but by the same means that he and his officers now aim at, that is by a more considerable present."

"Thursday, 31st December. Letters and travellers that came from the King's camp fifteen days past, advice that the King is, by reason of a plague which had destroyed 95,000 men, removed with his camp to Collaburriga, standing in the midst between Vizagapatam and Golconda. That Sultan Akbar is come with an army from Persia on this side Candahar, upon which the King hath sent orders to Shah Allum to stop his further proceeding; and hath order Dider Bukhsh to Ginjee, and Zulfikar Khan to follow after Santojee into the Mysore country; in pursuance of which Zulfikar Khan is already gone as far as Punnigunda, 50 leagues from hence."

Before proceeding farther it will be as well to glance at the contemporary condition of St. Thomé, which may be fully gathered from the following extracts from general letters to England, dated 1695.

"The inhabitants of St. Thomé continue under their subjection to the Moor's government, and are generally reduced to great poverty, having to no purpose spent large sums for getting the government into their own hands, and are miserably divided among themselves, but yet retain their great pride, which makes them talk pertly upon every slight occasion. Their present great news is that the King of Portugal has made a Company at Goa, to whom is limited the trade of India; . . . but the opinion here is that the stock is French money, and the chief design is the provision of saltpetre, which the Dutch will not suffer the Portuguese, nor any other nation, to export from Bengal except the English."

"In the latter end of May 1695, arrived a ship from Goa at St. Thomé, upon which came a Fidalgo, Francisco Luiz, a relation of the Viceroy's, who is called Captain General of the coast. Upon the 1st June he summoned the inhabitants and read his commission, the purport whereof is said to be that the Viceroy gives him power to manage all business on the coast of Coromandel, and requires all the subjects of the king of Portugal to obey and assist him in the execution of his instructions which are hitherto kept private. Two things are reported, the setting up of an Inquisition Office at St. Thomé, and the calling all Portuguese to St. Thomé under pain of treason. He has brought with him commissions for a Captain of war by sea, and a Captain of the land forces. So that the Fidalgo's greater business is supposed to be the gaining of an addition to the stock of the new Company at Goa. The inhabitants of St. Thomé are greatly disgusted and much divided among themselves; and the wiser sort laugh at these bravadoes, while they see themselves so much under the power and strict watch of the Moors, that a few days since the Havaildar made a Proclamation round the town, that no Portuguese should wear a sword without the walls of St. Thomé. There appears no reason yet to take any public notice of their proceedings, but knowing their good will to us we shall watch their motions."

Upon these matters the Court of Directors commented in a general letter bearing date, 26th January, 1698.

"The account you give us of the Portuguese Fidalgo, and their servile condition under the Moor's government, is an unanswerable proof that St. Thomé is not likely to prejudice Fort St. George by its neighbourhood, or that any person under our protection worth any thing, would, to escape paying our duties, desert Madras to inhabit there. It is the free enjoyment of liberty and property that makes our territories worth courting, were the taxes double what they are; there being no danger of the capricious and changeable humours of every domineering Havildar; and doubtless the Moors are the same perfidious, insulting, imperious tyrants in all places as at St. Thomé."

The reader will now be in a position to understand the progress of events at St. Thomé, as illustrated by the following extracts from the consultations.

"Friday, 8th January, 1697. Yesterday the King's Dewan, and this day the King's Buxee from Arcot, arrived at St. Thomé; to each of whom sent two bottles Rosewater and a glass Hubble bubble with a compliment.

"Monday, 11th. The Dewan and Buxee this day employed Coolies in pulling down three of the points at St. Thomé; the reason whereof is said to be because the Portuguese have not presented them since their arrival.

"Sunday, 17th. Spies from St. Thomé have ever since the 11th instant daily advised, that the Moors go on in pulling down the fortifications, whereof five points and the gate demolished; and to-day they begun upon the wall, carrying the brick and stone to a place where the Havildar is going to build a house; they have also taken down the Flag staff, and this day visited one of the churches. The Dewan this day sent ten camels and a coach to fetch to St. Thomé his household staff and lumber, which he lodged here about seven months ago.

"Monday, 8th February. The Dewan having from St. Thomé sent a present to the Governor in silks to the value of about thirty Pagodas, and he being to depart for the camp to-morrow morning,—it is ordered that a present of about sixty Pagodas value be returned, whereof the Governor pays thirty Pagodas, and the rest on Right Hon'ble Company's account."

The next incident is one which will interest our local antiquarians.

"Monday, 25th January, 1697. The Choultry by age extremely decayed, and the walls so weak that some prisoners have made their escape by breaking through, and the Prisons being too few and small for that service,—it is resolved that the whole Choultry be taken down and rebuilt, viz. upon the ground the Choultry now stands upon, and the ground of a house belonging to an old Committee widow, adjoining to the north side of the Choultry; which house and ground Mr. Barwell and Mr. Wright are ordered to purchase, by causing the house to be valued, and the value to be paid her, or laid out in building another house for the widow in some spare ground near the burying place. And that in the meantime the Choultry business done in the large shop over against the middle Gate, which about five years ago was rented by Mulla Mossum, and is the place of the daily rendezvous of many Persians and Moors; and that so many of the small shops adjoining be made use of for prisons as occasion requires."

The next extract shows that the missionary effort of the Directors, in behalf of the Portuguese and slaves, was proceeding but slowly.

"Thursday, 25th February, 1697. The Right Hon'ble Company ordering that the Portuguese Common Prayer Books be distributed for the use of the Portuguese inhabitants in such a manner as will best tend to the propagation of the Protestant religion, it is ordered that the same be all delivered to Mr. Lewis (the Chaplain) to be kept in the Church Library, and by him distributed to such of the Portuguese as desire and understand them; and because there are at present but few such, it is ordered that he lend one of them to any of the Right Hon'ble Company's servants or married inhabitants, especially such as have in their families Portuguese servants or slaves who speak the language. But there being but seventy-two books now sent (the rest being to follow) Mr. Lewis is to keep a list of the persons to whom they are lent, who are to subscribe their names in the list under a title obliging them to return the books when demanded under the penalty of paying one pagoda each."

The following incident illustrates the habits of some of our predecessors in the matter of drinking and duelling.

"Monday, 1st April, 1697. Mr. Cheesely having in a Punch house upon a quarrel of words drawn his sword (but were parted and put up without any mischief done) and being taxed therewith, he doth both own and justify the drawing of the sword, and alleges that he had received provoking language which he thought himself obliged to resent. Mr. Cheesely is thereupon ordered not to wear a sword while here, and acquainted that by the law of this place whoever gives or receives a challenge is to pay 200 pagodas."

During this year, and during many previous years, the proceedings of Interlopers had caused great anxiety and irritation at Fort St. George. Many were seized and tried as pirates in the Court of Admiralty; but the proceedings are so briefly recorded that we have hitherto found none worthy of extract. The following entry however illustrates the anxiety of the President and Council to prevent such trading in India; and further on the reader will also find a lengthy detail of the proceedings which followed the arrival of an Interloper at St. Thomé.

"Friday, 4th June, 1697. The Armenians having promised in Consultation to sign a writing for not trading with interlopers, which being deferred for two days, the Lieutenant General (Higginson) sent the Dubash to remind them of their promise; and after several consultations and debates among themselves, this morning they brought one paper in Armenian signed, and afterwards another in English signed, the copy whereof follows, viz.

"We, the subscribers Armenians here present this day in Fort St. George, by these presents, do give our word and promise unto the Hon'ble Nathaniel Higginson Esquire, Lieutenant General of India and Governor of Fort St. George, and Council, that we are obliged from this day forward in whatsoever Port we shall meet with any interloper, we nor none of us here under subscribed will by any manner of way, or by any means, have any dealing, trade, traffic, or contract, with any such interloper nor any of their people. And in respect to the Right Hon'ble English East India Company, in whatsoever Port we or any of us shall encounter with any interloper, we hereby oblige ourselves and every one of us, to give advice and notice to all other Armenians not to deal, trade, traffic, or contract with them; but whereas there are many people of other nations who obey not their King, so we Armenians, having no King, Company, nor Superior, but are free trading Merchants independent of any, so we conceive ourselves no ways answerable for the actions of others of our nation to which we are no ways liable." (Signed by nine Armenians.)

The following extract will explain itself.

"Thursday, 2nd September, 1697. The Nabob (Zulfikar Khan) being lately returned from his victory over Tanjore to Wandewash, and since his return taken old Ginjee, and being about marrying,—it is thought a convenient time to send him a present; and the rather because our frequent advices and reports from several parts, of the Nabob's design to send an army to visit the sea coast, and hath now sent Ali Buksh his own servant to be chief Junkameer and Renter of Poonamallee country, who doth already discover his intentions to be troublesome, pretending special orders from the Nabob. Resolved that a present be forthwith sent to the value of one thousand Pagodas, and two hundred Pagodas for Emaum Cooley."

In October this year, the Junkameer attempted to collect large customs from goods passing through Triplicane and Tandore for Madras; and some spy Peons gave information to the President and Council that he was supported by the head Poligar of the neighbourhood, and that a ground for quarrel was anxiously desired. On the 11th of the month we find the following entry in the consultation book. "By daily complaints of merchants and others going and coming, it appears that this Junkameer doth at all his meets demand from 5 to 20 per cent for money and jewels, for which they search all travellers; and for all sorts of provisions that pass to the Camp; and the half a quarter value of provisions that are brought from the country this way; and hath caused an account to be taken of all trees, gardens, and fruits, and demands the half; and also demands half of the calicoes made by the weavers; and hath killed three or four men by beating with clubs; upon which many country inhabitants are fled.

"Resolved to await till we see the issue of the letter and present sent the Nabob; and in the mean time to avoid all acts of hostility except forced thereunto for our own defence; and that sixty peons be sent to guard Tandore, and forty to Triplicane, with the like orders."

"Tuesday, 12th October. The Governor having yesterday wrote to Mr. Barwell to bring his family and all the English from the Mount, this evening at nine o'clock received a note from him advising that, as he was coming with his family to town, they were stopped by the Junkameers a little beyond Triplicane, and that he would retire to a neighbouring town and await for further orders.

"The Governor thereupon ordered 40 peons and 30 soldiers to go and conduct him to town, but as they were ready to go, Mr. Barwell came to the Gates, being by order of the Chief Junkameer permitted to come, but adviseth that the rest could not come from the Mount for want of Coolies. At the same time came a letter from a servant of the Junkameer to Ramapa advising to a reconciliation; in answer to which Ramapa was ordered to write that when he returned the Company's goods which he had robbed, his proposals should be delivered to the Governor."

Some days elapsed before the matter was accommodated, but meantime President Higginson was advised that the present to Zulfikar Khan had been received, and that consequently he might rely to some extent on the favour of the Nabob. At length the Junkameer returned all the goods he had taken, and the roads to Madras were once again open for the passage of travellers and merchandize.

The following is historical.

"Tuesday, 26th October, 1697. The Spy Bramin from the camp of Zulfikar Khan adviseth that the Nabob hath sent the Mahratta prince, Rama Rajah's son to Ginjee, and hath sent Rama Rajah word that the Mogul doth not approve of his proposals, but hath ordered him to take Ginjee and that he intends to go in a few days. Reported that Rama Rajah being lately dead, the Mahrattas are going to conquer the country, which may delay their coming into these parts." In January, 1698, advices reached Madras that Zulfikar Khan had taken Ginjee, and a congratulatory letter with presents was accordingly dispatched to the Nabob.

The following incidents which befel the Factory at Anjengo, and Fort St. David, will illustrate the dangers which occasionally befel the smaller Agencies of the Company. Anjengo is a small sea port on the Malabar coast, about eighty miles to the north of Cape Comorin. Attinga, the chief residence of the Tamburretties, or Princesses of Travancore, lay in the immediate neighbourhood. In 1684 the Company had obtained permission from the Queen of Attinga to fortify Anjengo, and a small strip of land round it. The following extract from the consultations of Fort St. George tells its own story.

"Monday, 15th November. Letters from Anjengo received yesterday advising that they have had two engagements with the Queen's forces sent to turn them out of the country as pirates; in the latter whereof they slew the Nair Captain, routed his men, proceeded to burn the Moors town, and all the houses between that and the Fort, and retreated without the loss of one man. That they expect a further assault, and if the Natives can at any time, in peace or war, by fair means or foul, enter the Fort, they will cut all off; and therefore for security of their lives and of the Fort, they desire a supply of soldiers, guns, ammunition, and provision and stores." The request was granted.

"Sunday, 20th February. General letter from Fort St. David received this day giving an account, that Selim Khan sent a letter to the President of Fort St. David, desiring that nine ox load of the King's treasure passing to the Camp, might remain one night in Cuddalore for security, which being brought in by some horsemen on the 17th in the afternoon, said horsemen next morning seized Porto Novo Gate, wounding a corporal; and another party coming to their assistance, they also seized on Chellumbrum Point, robbed the Bazaar, and carried away three elephants. But a party of men being sent from the Fort to the assistance of the guard at Cuddalore, the Moors were beaten out of the town with the loss of eight men killed, five taken prisoners, and six horses; there being killed one Dutchman a soldier, and Captain Tracy a volunteer, and five or six soldiers wounded; and that Selim Khan was in person with the routed party about seven miles off."

The President and Council had now to consider whether this design of Selim Khan had been attempted with or without the knowledge of the Nabob Zulfikar Khan; but they do not appear to have arrived at any definite conclusion, and simply resolved to send assistance to Cuddalore and a letter of complaint to the Nabob. Shortly afterwards, news arrived that Selim Khan had made a second attempt upon Cuddalore, and had been again repelled; upon which the President and Council then arrived at the following conclusion. "The second, attempt gives ground to suspect that it is done by the Nabob's order; though reports give a probable account of an irreconcilable quarrel between the Nabob and Dawood Khan (the brother of Selim Khan), who carries on the conquest of Ginjee country in opposition to the Nabob."

The following curious record of the happy results of drinking a bowl of punch with a pirate crew is worthy of preservation.

"Wednesday, 5th April. The "Sedgwick," Captain Watts Commander, arrived from Anjengo. The Master acquaints that in going to Anjengo he was pursued by Kidd the Pirate three days and three nights, and with great difficulty escaped, it being calm and Kidd outrowing him; and that in his return from Anjengo he was taken by another pirate, Chivers a Dutchman, in the Algerine Galley near Cape Comorin, which with her excellent sailing and rowing fetched up the Sedgwick in nine hours. The cargo of pepper not being for their turn, they dismissed the ship, after they had robbed her of her two courses, sheet cable, anchor, cordage, pitch, tar, and other stores; though several of the ship's Company, being mightily taken with the "Sedgwick's" build and usefulness for a cruiser, Captain Watts with great difficulty prevailed to save her by a merry management of a bowl of punch among the ship's Company, upon which they said he is an honest fellow, let him go."

The following record of the lengthy proceedings which followed the arrival of an Interloper at St. Thomé is so illustrative of the times that we give it in extenso.

"Friday, 10th June, 1698. A ship came into St. Thomé road with an English ancient, but showed no jack; and in the evening the Doctor and Purser came ashore to the Captain More. Lucas Luiz his house, and gave out that they came from Batavia and the South Seas, were bound for Bengal, and called at St. Thomé for wood and water, the ship's name being the "Resolution," Captain Etherington, Commander. But a letter from a Portuguese at St. Thomé advises that she was suspected to be a Pirate. Several peons and spies were ordered to bring intelligence of what passed at St. Thomé, and to observe who had correspondence with them, and the chief peons ordered to keep a good watch.

"Sunday, 12th. In the evening advised that Joache John Domingo Mattor, and Francisco de Saa, had been this day aboard the ship to treat about trucking saltpetre for sugar.

"Several Fort St. George dubashes having been at St. Thomé, were, as they returned in the evening, brought by the peons to the Governor and sent to the trunk to deter others.

"Monday, 13th. The following advices have been received concerning the English ship at St. Thomé, viz. That on Sunday the Doctor and Purser were treating with Francisco Mendez for saltpetre, who sent two Portuguese aboard with musters to truck for sugar. The Doctor and Purser returning in the evening brought two hats and a basket of wine as a present to Lucas Luiz at whose house they lodge, and a bag of dollars. Some Portuguese have also written that they suspect them to be Pirates, because they refuse to bring goods, or to let people go aboard, and offer 30 great guns for sale, and the Captain keeps aboard.

"Resolved that the following orders be published in English, Portuguese, Gentoo, and Malabar.

"That no European inhabitant go out of the bounds of Madras without leave of the Governor or second of Council.

"That all European strangers, coming by sea or land, do repair to the Governor immediately, and in the case of omission, to be secured in the Guard till examined.

"That no inhabitant do entertain any stranger whatsoever in their houses, without notice given and leave obtained from the Governor, or Chief Justice of the Choultry.

"That no person whatsoever, inhabitant of this place, hold any correspondence, directly or indirectly, with any person belonging to the ship now in St. Thomé road, which arrived there on the 11th instant with English colours, under pain of a month's imprisonment, or so long as the said ship shall remain on this coast, and fine not exceeding 500 Pagodas. And it is further declared, that if any of the Right Hon'ble Company's servants be guilty of a breach of this order, they shall forthwith be dismissed the Company's service."

"Cojee Gregorie, Cojee Peinûs, and Cojee Saffur, the principal Armenians of this place, being sent for were acquainted that, they having formerly given a writing not to deal with Interlopers, and there being now a ship come to St. Thomé wearing English colours, not known whether Interloper or Pirate, but she not belonging to the Company,—it is expected that in compliance with said writing, they hold no manner of correspondence with them, and that they take care the rest of their nation observe the said orders,—which they promised to comply with.

"Antonio Feriera de Silva, commonly called Joache, a Portuguese inhabitant of this place, having been on board the ship at St. Thomé yesterday, and being suspected by the slight account he gives, that he designs to drive a trade with them, and the likeliest man to carry it on for himself and others, to prevent which he was committed to the custody of the Marshal till further order.

"Joache Domingo de Mattor, a Portuguese inhabitant of St. Thomé, having been yesterday aboard the ship treating about sugar and saltpetre, and coming to town, being concerned in a ship in this road and bound for Bengal,—came and acquainted that he went upon the request of the Havildar (of St. Thomé) to know whether the ship was a Pirate, and also upon Mr. Styleman's (second of council) orders to him to enquire news; whereof he gave him notice on Saturday night by a letter, and now came to give a further account. That he pretended to treat for trucking saltpetre for sugar, but observed that few men did appear, and no arms above deck; and being desirous to buy a fowling peice, they would not suffer him to go down to see them, but caused them to be brought up, and that by many circumstances he suspected them to be Pirates. That he made no bargain, nor did not intend it, though he and his uncle are concerned 2-5ths in 3000 maund of saltpetre now lying in St. Thomé, wherein Francisco de Mendez and Francisco de Saa (son in law of John Battista) are also concerned. And he now gave a writing in 500 Pagodas penalty, in behalf of himself and uncle, that the saltpetre should not be sold to said ship.

"It is upon this occasion resolved that if Francisco de Mendez, or Francisco de Saa, or any other Portuguese inhabitant of St. Thomé, shall buy or sell with the said ship, they shall not be admitted for the future to come into Madras, nor have any dealings with any inhabitant of Madras.

"Mr. Merevell and Mr. Lovell having been on Saturday last at St. Thomé in company with some persons belonging to the ship, they were sent for, and upon examination give the following account.

"That Mr. Mayor, Captain Parham, and themselves, about five o'clock on Saturday in the evening, went out in palanquins to take the air; and going through St. Thomé were invited by Senhor Lucas Luiz to drink a glass of wine; which invitation they accepted of, and at their coming into his house found two Englishmen (strangers to them all) there; and upon enquiry what ship it was and from whence she came, they answered the "Resolution," Captain Etherington, Commander, from the South Seas and Batavia; they thereupon, imagining them to be Interlopers, immediately took their leaves and came away."

"Colloway Chetty, Rugga Chetty and Servoria, were sent for, and particularly admonished not to have any dealings with the people belonging to the ship at St. Thomé."

The same day two letters were dispatched by the Presidency of Fort St. George, one to the Havildar of St. Thomé and the other to Senhor Lucas

Luiz, Captain More of St. Thomé. We give them at length.

"TO THE HAVILDAR OF ST. THOME.'

I am informed that two days past a ship came into St. Thomé road with English colours, and that the St. Thomé people do trade with them for saltpetre and provisions. I know not what they are; or who they belong to, or whence they came. But I know they do not belong to the English Company, and therefore if any damage shall follow to the King's people or their ships, the English Company is not answerable. You have heard of Pirates upon the sea, whose evil intentions have been unjustly charged to the English Company, who have suffered more by them than any others. You will do well to consider. I write this that neither you nor I may be blamed.

NATHANIEL HIGGINSON.

"TO SENHOR LUCAS LUIZ, CAPTAIN MORE OF ST. THOME.

We are informed that two days past a ship came into St. Thomé road with English colours; and that you entertain the people belonging to that ship in your house; and that they are buying saltpetre and provisions of your people. We know not what they are, or who they belong to, or whence they came. But we know they do not belong to the English Company, and therefore if any damage shall follow to yourselves, or the Mogul's people, or their ships, the English Company is not answerable. But we hereby declare you, and all those that do abet and assist them, answerable for all damages. And if you shall now do the Honorable English Company so great mischief by entertaining trade with and assisting that ship, we shall hold ourselves discharged from the rules of friendship which we have hitherto observed; and shall further think ourselves obliged to prosecute such methods as are proper towards those who openly act so injuriously to the

Right Hon'ble Company, and to those who are much inclined to be

Your ready friends
NATHANIEL HIGGINSON,
JOHE STYLEMAN,
&c. &c.

"Tuesday, 14th. Received a letter from the Captain More of St. Thomé, dated this day, wherein he excuses the reception of the English belonging to the ship as a matter of common hospitality to a nation in friendship with Portugal, coming for water and provisions; and denies that the natives have trade for saltpetre, but if they shall trade it will be with the natives or the Governor."

"Brought ashore from the "Resolution," and carried to Lucas Luiz his house, a newry and four yards of broad cloth for a present for the Havildar, a hamper of wine, bundle of white paper, and muster of sugar; and sent 14 or 16 butts of water.

"Received a general letter from Francisco de Mendez and Francisco de Saa, from St. Thomé, promising not to truck saltpetre for sugar with the English ship at St. Thomé."

Two days afterwards the excitement produced by the arrival of the Interloper appears to have been nearly over; for on the 16th we find the following short entry in the consultation book:—"This afternoon the English ship sailed out of St. Thomé road to the northwards." On the 18th a peon brought word that the "Resolution" had anchored in Pulicat road; but the Dutch refused to trade with her, and she disappeared from the coast.

The last few months of President Higginson's governorship were occupied by a long and tedious effort to get satisfactory purwannas from the Nabob Zulfikar Khan, but before they were obtained, Mr. Higginson had made way for Mr. Thomas Pitt, as appears from the following entry.

"Wednesday, 6th July, 1698. At nine o'clock this morning, a ship with a pennant came to anchor in the road, which being taken down and a flag hoisted, Mr. Empson was sent a board to know the meaning. Some time after the Cattamaran brought a letter directed to the President and Council of Fort St. George signed "Thomas Pitt," acquainting he was appointed President and Governor for the Right Hon'ble Company's affairs in these parts. Whereupon the Council being summoned it was agreed to defer giving an answer till Mr. Empson's return."

CHAPTER XV.

GOVERNORSHIP OF MR. THOMAS PITT.

1698—1702.

Mr. Nathaniel Higginson seems to have been the first Governor of Madras on record, who retired from the Presidency without a stain upon his name. After a careful perusal of the many volumes of records referring to his government, we can find none of those charges and insinuations which were so frequent during the administration of his predecessors. He was however violently opposed by one of the members of his council, a Mr. William Fraser;* and in consequence of the abuse which he received from this gentleman, he prayed the Directors to permit him to retire from the government. The prayer was granted, and in July 1698 he handed over the keys of the Fort to his successor, after holding the Office of President for six years.† The event is thus noticed in the

* This gentleman was subsequently appointed Chief at Fort St. David, and eleven years after the retirement of Mr. Higginson, he became President of Fort St. George.

† Mr. Higginson and family returned to England in February 1700. His predecessor Mr. Elihu Yale set sail in 1699.

consultation books; by which also it will be seen that the desired purwanna from Fort St. David had at last been procured from the Nabob Zulfikar Khan.

"Thursday, 7th July, 1698. The Honorable Thomas Pitt Esq., coming ashore about nine o'clock this morning produced his commission, dated 5th January 1688, appointing him President for the Right Honorable Company's affairs on the coast of Coromandel and Orissa, and of the Ginjee and Mahratta countries, and Governor of Fort St. George and Fort St. David; . . . which being read, the late Lieutenant General Higginson did resign the Chair, and deliver the keys of the Fort to the said Thomas Pitt Esq.

"The council acquainted the President of the treaty depending with the Nabob relating to Fort St. David, and of the necessity of a speedy resolution. Amir Jehan the Armenian vakeel having by his two last letters acquainted that the Nabob had condescended to the granting of the desired purwannas, and that the purwannas were ready, and desired that ten thousand Pagodas might be presently sent, otherwise the opportunity of getting the purwannas will be lost, because the Nabob is designed in a few days against Tanjore, and Amir Jehan himself is sick and cannot stay." "It was accordingly resolved that Amir Jehan should proceed in the matter, and that eight thousand Pagodas should be sent to him."

The next incident refers partly to the administration of Mr. Higginson and partly to that of Mr. Pitt. It is a curious instance of interference in private affairs, concerning which some of our readers may possibly form conflicting opinions.

"Monday, 27th June, 1698. There being a report that Mr. Henry Dobyns was privately married to Mrs. Rachel Baker, he was sent for and examined, and doth declare that he is married to her by a Romish Priest; who he is informed is now gone to Bengal, but refuses to tell time, place, or person, or produce a certificate; whereupon he was ordered not to go out of the Fort without leave.

"Thursday, 30th. Mr. Dobyns being further examined concerning his private marriage, doth allege that he is under the obligation of an oath not to discover the persons present at this marriage; and that the Priest who married them is gone for Bengal, and therefore cannot prove his marriage by witnesses or certificate, and offers their own oaths.

"Resolved, that till Mr. Dobyns doth prove his marriage he be not permitted to live with the woman as man and wife; and to prevent their cohabitation, he now declaring his request that he may return to England by the first ship. That in the meantime he either proceed for Fort St. David, or remain in the Fort without liberty of going out into her company till the marriage be proved, which is referred to his own choice.

"The foregoing being read to Mr. Dobyns, he chooses to remain in the Fort."

"Saturday, 9th July. Mr. Dobyns being sent for and further examined concerning his marriage, doth now produce two witnesses, Mr. John Sewell and Mrs. Anne Masters, who do both affirm upon oath that they saw Henry Dobyns and Rachel Baker married by a person in the habit of a Portuguese Padre, some time within two months past. He is therefore ordered to be discharged from his present confinement, but what punishment to be inflicted is referred to further consideration." The matter seems to have been afterwards dropped.

The war with France had been concluded in 1697 by the Peace of Ryswick, and in 1698 the news reached Fort St. George, as appears from the following entry.

"Monday, 11th July. Resolved that to-morrow morning at eleven o'clock, the proclamation of Peace between England and France be read with the usual solemnity at the inner Fort Gates, and afterwards at all the Gates of the city. And that the Right Hon'ble Company's Commission appointing the Hon'ble Thomas Pitt Esq. President, etc., be read at the new Garden after dinner, all the Right Hon'ble Company's servants and freemen being invited to a treat there by the Governor."

Our next extract, is one of many which illustrate the bad characters of the soldiers brought out from England.

"Friday, 15th. Ordered that Richard Okell who came out a corporal, and was formerly a soldier in this garrison, where he killed a man in exercising, and stabbed another at Fort St. David, and afterwards endeavoured to entice the soldiers to run away to the Moors, be sent home by the first ship, and that in the meantime he remain in the custody of the Marshall."

The purwanna obtained from the Nabob afforded considerable satisfaction to the Presidency of Fort St. George, as will be seen by our next extract.

"Saturday, 10th September. At four o'clock this afternoon the President and Council went to the Garden, accompanied by several of the Right Hon'ble Company's servants and inhabitants, English, Armenians, and Gentoos; where, upon the receipt of the Nabob's purwanna, and the purwanna from the Dewan, was fired 15 and 11 guns."

The following account of a quarrel between two of the officers of the garrison is not without interest.

"Saturday, 1st October. There arising some words this afternoon between Lieutenant Sinclair and Lieutenant Seaton which at last came to blows, Lieutenant Sinclair came now and acquainted the Governor and Council that Lieut. Seaton called him coward and struck him. Lieutenant Seaton being sent for, and the reason of their difference demanded, answers that there did pass some foolish language between them, but disowns that he did strike Lieut. Sinclair. Mr. Stone and Mr. Matthews who were present, being also sent for, were enquired of whether they knew the occasion of their difference; but both declared that they only heard some words pass between them at the Sea Gate, and that afterwards near the inner Fort Gate they saw some blows pass, but know not which struck first." Lieut. Seaton was accordingly dismissed the service, but was subsequently reinstated on petition. A similar punishment and reinstatement had befallen this officer on many previous occasions. He appears to have been a brave man and a good commandant, but to have been somewhat addicted to drunkenness and eccentricity.

The following case of desertion is by no means a solitary one in the early annals of Fort St. George.

"Thursday, 13th. The Governor acquaints that on Tuesday last about eight o'clock at night, Captain Sinclair came and acquainted him that a Corporal and Sentinel were run away from their guard at St. Thomé Gate with their arms, and with them a Piper. Whereupon he ordered eight soldiers and a Serjeant with twenty peons to pursue them; who returning between ten and eleven the same night, brought the three soldiers back with them, having taken them near Triplicane after some resistance, wherein one man was wounded by a shot in the thigh, and another with a sword." The prisoners were committed to the custody of the Marshall, to be tried by Court Martial, but the result is not recorded.

The history of Roman Catholic Missions in the East is illustrated by the following extract.

"Saturday, 14th January, 1699. Padre Joanni Francisco Fouquet, a Jesuit, appearing before us this day in Council, did make a demand of 1300 dollars which was carried by two of their Order with them on ship "Loyal Captain," Captain Elred Commander, bound for China; but the said two Padres going on shore at Malacca, were there seized by the Dutch and sent to Europe; but the dollars were carried on the ship for China, and afterwards delivered by Captain Elred to Captain Heath of the "Defence." He was desired to acquaint us what power he had for making said demand. In answer to which he produces a commission, dated 22d January 1698, signed by Jacobus Le Picart, Chief of the Order of Jesuits in France; which being read, it doth thereby appear that he is appointed Chief of all the Mission of that Order in China, and consequently has thereby a sufficient power to demand and receive said dollars, as being a part of the stock of that Mission." It appeared that Captain Heath had only mentioned the receipt of 800 dollars; accordingly that amount was paid over to the Jesuit Padre, and a request for further instructions as to the remainder of the sum claimed was sent home to the Court of Directors.

About this time the Danish settlement at Tranquebar was in considerable peril, as appears from the following entry.

"Wednesday, 1st March, 1699. A general letter from the Governor and Council of Tranquebar being translated was read; wherein they give an account of their being close beseiged by the King of Tanjore's forces, consisting of 14,000 horse and foot, which daily increased; taking the advantage of their Fort being weakly manned, by sparing so many of their garrison soldiers to their ships for their security against the Pirates; and therefore earnestly request us to assist them with men, arms, and ammunition, the charge whereof they promise thankfully to repay.

"The same being taken into consideration as a matter of great importance, and may prove of ill consequence to the Right Hon'ble Company's interest in these parts; if once these Princes should take a garrison from Europeans, it may induce them upon every slight occasion to attempt the same upon us here, or at Fort St. David, the latter having been lately assaulted and is near Tranquebar. Therefore in consideration, not only of the strict alliance between the two Crowns of Great Britain and Denmark, as well as the strengthening the Right Hon'ble Company's interest in these parts, expecting suitable returns from them if ever this place or Fort St. David should fall under the like circumstances:—it is unanimously agreed and resolved that we give them our utmost assistance, and in order thereunto that the ship "Sedgwick" be hired to carry them aids, provisions, and ammunition, and that five thousand Pagodas be sent them by peons overland." Two months afterwards the Governor and Council at Tranquebar dispatched a general letter to Fort St. George "wherein they express a grateful acknowledgment of our kind assistance, and promise on all occasions readily to retaliate the same; and advise to having returned such part of the ammunition sent them as is unspent, and to have ordered Mr. Afflack to make full satisfaction for what sums expended on their Company's account."

The following misdemeanor could scarcely have occurred in our own time.

"Monday, 20th March, 1699. Upon some words yesterday at the General Table, Mr. James Eustace called Mr. George Shaw son of a ——, of which he complained to the Governor, who was then present at the Table; and the Governor promised that he would this day hear their difference in council, and punish him that was found guilty of giving occasion for so rude and uncivil a behaviour at the Company's Table. But Mr. Shaw going from Evening Service to the Sea Gate struck Mr. Eustace, of which the Governor being informed confined both to their chambers. Which being considered it is agreed that Mr. Eustace was guilty of great insolence in calling Mr. Shaw son of a —— at the Company's Table, and Mr. Shaw of great disrespect to the Governor in striking Mr. Eustace after he had declared he would examine and punish the offender.

"It is unanimously resolved that for the future prevention of offences of the like nature, Mr. Eustace and Mr. Shaw be each of them fined their half year's salary payable in India, and confined to the Fort for one month, and neither to wear sword or cane for twelve months, which resolve they were both forthwith acquainted with." Mr. Shaw's fine was subsequently remitted.

The following particulars of visits from distinguished natives will be read with interest.

"Monday, 3rd April, Mortupha Khan, Foujdar of the Poonamallee country, coming to town desired leave to come and see the Governor. He was invited to the new Garden, where he was entertained with Rose water and Betel; and after some discourse promised to give a Cowle (and did send one to the Governor) for the free passage of our goods through his Government according to salabad. Whereupon it was judged necessary to make him a present."

"Tuesday, 25th. Rajah Rama Sing, General of the Rajpoots in Zulfikar Khan's army, coming to wash in the sea and pay his devotions at Triplicane Pagoda, sent a horse to the Governor about fifty pagodas value. Whereupon it was resolved that Mr. Fraser and Mr. Empson should in the Governor's name give him a visit; and his father (Cassa Singara) having always appeared a friend to the English, to oblige him to be so too, to present him with some broadcloth, rosewater, and toys to the value of a hundred pagodas; which was done this evening by Messrs. Fraser and Empson, who report that he seemed extremely well satisfied, and promised to give his assistance on any occasion."

The following particulars respecting Dawood Khan derive their chief interest from the fact that four years afterwards Fort St. George was blockaded for a considerable time by this very general.

"Thursday, 27th. The Governor acquaints that he has received a purwanna from the Nabob informing that Dawood Khan (General in Zulfikar Khan's army) designs to come and see the sea; and that Dawood Khan's servant that brought the purwanna, desired that his master might have some accommodation in the town; and that he (the Governor) returned answer Dawood Khan should be very welcome, but desired that he would not bring too great a number of men with him; and hath borrowed Mr. Styleman's Garden house for his reception, esteeming it more proper for him to reside on that side of the Fort.

"It not being known what Dawood Khan's designs may be, or what orders the Nabob may have received from the King, probably to beseige Madras and stop all trade; and considering that it was Dawood Khan's brother, Selim Khan, who plundered and burnt the villages at Fort St. David, there is great reason to suspect him, as well as his being a Commander who is generally employed on difficult attempts.

"It is thought necessary that the Garrison and out town be put into the best posture of defence it can be." (Subsequently a levy was made upon the inhabitants of Black Town for building a wall and constructing other works for the defence of the town. In June 1700, the levy amounting to 1051 pagodas was paid by the President into the Company's cash to be applied to the purpose specified.)

"Friday, 28th. Yesterday Dawood Khan came to St. Thomé, and this evening to Mr. Styleman's Garden house, from whence he sent a horse to the Governor valued about one hundred pagodas, which was carried to the Company's stable for their account.

"Saturday, 29th. Mr. Styleman and Mr. Fraser went this day in the Governor's name to visit Dawood, who they report entertained them very civilly.

"Sunday, 30th. This day Dawood Khan returned to St. Thomé, where the Portuguese entertained with their music in the Church.

"Saturday, 6th May. Dawood Khan set out for the Camp, to whom there has been presented at several times to the value of about three hundred pagodas.

"Sunday, 7th. Bahaudar Khan, a younger brother of Dawood Khan, and Commander of 1500 horse, came to St. Thomé, whose servant brought the Nabob's purwanna for shewing him the varieties of the place. Bahaudar Khan likewise received a present of the value a hundred pagodas, and returned to camp three days afterwards."

The following entry affords us another instance of the frequent bad conduct of the officers of the garrison.

"Monday, 8th. There having been several complaints of Ensign Gardner's misbehaving himself in being drunk upon his Guard, and beating the men without occasion, of which having often been continued and promised amendment, and growing worse rather than better, it is resolved that his Commission be taken from him." Two months afterwards Ensign Gardner was reinstated in consideration of his mean circumstances and promise of amendment.

We are now approaching a critical period in the history of the English Company. The war with France had been followed, as usual, by a financial crisis. The Company had offered to lend £700,000 to the government of William III. provided their Charter should be confirmed, and the monopoly of India secured to them by Act of Parliament. But their commercial rivals had by this time formed a new Company, and the latter offered to advance two millions at eight per cent. provided they should be invested with the monopoly. The offer of the latter was accepted, but the rights of the old Company were confirmed until 1701, when the two Companies became united into one. Meantime however a fierce spirit of rivalry broke out between the servants of the two Companies at home and abroad; and the new Company sent out a Consul and an Ambassador, claiming the supreme power over the whole of the English factories. The following extracts will illustrate the nature of the controversy which ensued on the coast of Coromandel. We may premise that Mr. Consul Pitt was the cousin of the President of Fort St. George.

"Wednesday, 28th July. Ship 'Degrave,' Captain William Young Commander, belonging to the new Company, came to an anchor in this road about eleven o'clock this morning, on board of which was Mr. John Pitt, from whom the President received the following letter.

"To the Worshipful Thomas Pitt Esq. President for the affairs of the Governor and Company of Merchants of London trading to the East Indies yet by permission on the Coast of Coromandel.

"Sir,

I did by some of your early ships let you know that I had engaged myself in the service of the Honorable English Company trading to the East Indies lately settled by Act of Parliament, which determine your Government in three years commencing last Michaelmas; and having gained the Coast, could not pass by without dropping an anchor in Madras road; and would salute you had I not the honour to bear his Majesty's Commission, which constitutes me his Minister or Consul for the English nation in general on the whole coast of Coromandel including all your settlements. If you think fit to pay the respect that is due to the character with your flag lowered, your compliment shall be returned you by, Sir,

Your affectionate kinsman and servant,

JOHN PITT."

Whereunto the following answer was returned by the President.

"To Mr. John Pitt,

Sir,

I received yours, the purport whereof seems very odd, as well as the superscription. If you had read the Act of Parliament and well considered it, you will find that it establishes my masters in all their rights and privileges in these parts till 1701, and afterwards it is secured to them by their subscription. Therefore you can have no power in any place of their settlements, nor shall I own any until I am so ordered by those that intrust me.

"I am not unacquainted with what respect is due to the Kings Consul (whether you are one I know not); but you cannot, or even have heard, that an ancient Fortification wearing the King's Flag, should lower it and salute a real Consul; but I take it to be your obligation to have saluted the Flag ashore at your coming to an anchor, which we should have answered according to custom and good manners.

"What liquors you have for me I desire you to send ashore in these boats. You must expect to find me no less zealous for my masters interest than you are for yours, and as you act the same will be returned you by

Your affectionate Kinsman and Servant,

THOMAS PITT."

To which Mr. Consul Pitt returned the following answer.

"On board the "Degrave" in Madras Road,
28th July 1699.

"I shall answer your scurrilous letter from Metchlepatam, (Masulipatam) and believe me you will wish you had never wrote in such a style. I will take such measures to make you sensible that my Commission reaches over all your settlements, and that you yourself shall be forced to own and publish it in all your Forts and Factories, and beg pardon for the affront offered to the character of his Majesty's Consul.

JOHN PITT."

Towards the latter end of August, the Government at Fort St. George was apprised that Mr. John Pitt had landed at Masulipatam, announced that he had been made President of the coast of Coromandel by the new Company, and that his Majesty had honoured that character with his Commission; and that he had required the servants of the old Company at Masulipatam to repair to the new Factory whilst he opened and read his Commission. Accordingly the Government passed an order that none of the English in the old Company's service, or under their protection, should obey any summons they might receive from Mr. John Pitt, under the pretence of his being a President for the new Company or Consul for his Majesty.

In December, 1699, Sir William Norris arrived at Masulipatam as Ambassador from the new Company to the Great Mogul, and addressed the following notification to the Agency established there by the old Company.

"This is to require and command you, not to presume to make any address or application, either in your own person or by any other, directly or indirectly; to any public minister or officer of the great Mogul, without my knowledge or permission, as you will answer the contrary at your peril. Given at Masulipatam, December 26th 1699.

WILLIAM NORRIS."

The following letter addressed to Sir William Norris by the President and Council of Fort St. George in January, 1700, will better acquaint the reader with the heads of the controversy, than pages of explanation.

"To his Excellency Sir William Norris Bart. Embassador to the Great Mogul at Masulipatam,

Sir,

We having been informed by Mr. Thomas Lovell, our Company's Factor at Masulipatam, that upon the approaching of the new Nabob (Meddo Khan,) who is come to govern that country, you sent for him, (Mr. Lovell) and delivered him a paper, requiring and commanding him in a most extraordinary manner, not to make any application to any of the Mogul's officers for the carrying on of our affairs, without your leave and permission; threatening to do no less than send him home in irons; from which we imagine you resolve the útter ruin of our Company, hoping thereby to promote the interest of your employers, the new East India Company.

"We having no orders or instructions to govern ourselves in this matter but the Act of Parliament, which in perusing we find, that there is five per cent laid in all goods for the maintaining Ambassadors and Consuls, from which our Company is excepted till September, 1701; which Ambassadors and Consuls are to be nominated and elected by the Directors of the new Company, and sent to such Emperors or Princes as they please; and they to pay the charge out of the five per cent, and the remainder to be divided amongst the adventurers. And in a subsequent clause it is said, that nothing in this Act shall be construed to extend, or hinder, or restrain our Company's trade till the 29th September 1701. So that they being excused from contributing to the charge of Ambassadors, Consuls, etc., it certainly never was intended that their affairs in these parts should be subjected to the direction or control of the new Company's Ambassadors, Consuls, or Agents during their limited time; we being possessed, as the rightful and lawful proprietors, of all Firmauns and Grants necessary for supporting the trade, which have been procured at vast expenses; and without corresponding with the Government, it is impossible to support our privileges or trade.

"Sir, we think your proceedings not only destructive to our masters at present, but will also prove fatal hereafter, if not entail perpetual ruin on the trade. To prevent the mischiefs that may attend us, and preserve the interest for which we are concerned, we must acquaint you that we resolve to persist in the corresponding with the Government as formerly, for the carrying on of our Government during the time limited by Parliament; and to order all our Company's Chiefs and Factors to do the same, until his Majesty commands the contrary, or we receive orders from our Company.

"As for the injuries you have already done our Company, and others of the king's subjects, by embargoing their ships who traded here under their protection, we doubt not but that they will represent it in such places where they may find a remedy or justice. In confirmation whereof, we have hereunto set our hands and the seal of our Company at Fort St. George in the city of Madras this 16th of January 1700."

(Signed By Thomas Pitt and the
other six members of Council.)

Subsequently the Presidency of Fort St. George found reason to suspect the integrity of Mr. Lovell and other Company's servants at Masulipatam and Madapollom, and to believe that they had especially betrayed the interests of the Company, by submitting to the orders of Sir William Norris and Mr. Pitt. Accordingly on the 12th July 1700 it was resolved "to settle a Chief and Council in each place, and make our Factories as formidable as possible, in order to preserve our masters interest, and to protect the persons of their servants from any injustices." Twenty-four soldiers, with a Lieutenant, Serjeant, and Corporal, were placed under the command of the Chief and Council of Masulipatam.

We now return to the ordinary run of events. The following extract refers to another case of desertion, in which an officer was concerned.

"Friday, 6th October, 1699. This morning Ensign Thomas Salmon and eleven men more run away off their guard with their arms. Upon notice whereof the Governor sent out 200 Peons after them, and wrote letters to the Dutch chiefs of Pulicat and Sadraspatam, and to several of the country Governors, desiring them to stop them." About four weeks afterwards the men were recovered, as appears from the following entry.

"Thursday, 2nd November. Receiving advices that Ensign Salmon and the eleven soldiers deserting this garrison the 6th past, were detained by Chinnatumbee Moodelliar, Naik Poligar, in the woods about sixty miles inland; who interceding to us for their pardon, Mr. Thomas Harris proceeded the 18th past with a letter and small present to said Naik, which they accepting, four returned the 31st past, four yesterday, and the remaining four this morning, accompanied by the Poligar's Chief Officer (delayway) who brought a mare, sheep, etc. for the Governor, expressing their willingness to hinder all fugitives passing through their woods, and assisting otherwise as we should have occasion." A tasheriff to the value of 75 pagodas was given to the Poligar and his servants. Ensign Salmon was kept in prison until October, 1700, and then send to England. The others appear to have been restored to the service.

The following present to Dawood Khan does not speak much for the temperance of the Mogul's officers.

"Monday, 8th July, 1700. Dawood Khan having wrote the Governor to buy him some liquors, and supposing his interest may be of advantage to the Company in these parts, it is ordered that six dozen of French Brandy, six cases of Spirits, and two chests of Syrash be provided."

The following characteristic letter from a Captain of a ship to the Governor and Council, complaining of some mutinous proceedings amongst his crew, is the worthy of preservation.

"Honorable Sir and Council.

In or about the 13th of July 1700, one of my seamen Richard Cook committing a misdemeanor by knocking down one Lovelace Green, Midshipman, had raised a bump on his forehead as big as an egg, and in some other parts of his body. Upon which I ordered the said Richard Cook to be seized to the gangway. One Lewis a soldier, who then standing by this Cook and seeing his hand seized, swore .... he would cut him loose, and immediately before my face did so. With this I ordered him to be seized on the other side, in which time of standing there till the irons were ready, he abused me very grossly, called me villain, and desired but one minute time and he would do my business. These abuses were heard before the face of my officers and seamen. After having secured them both, I ordered one of my seamen to take hold of them to help them down on the deck; and he refused my command and would not touch them, for which I ordered him to be seized to the gangway, intending to have him drubbed, but he not being very well I remitted doing of, but in the time of his standing it was heard spoke that if I had him drubbed, I should drub all of them. After this I had an account given me by my Boatswain and Carpenter that some of my seamen when night came on would set the prisoners at liberty, and that I must have a case of further mischief; upon which I was forced to secure my Gunroom and Steerage. They took off their handcuffs that very evening, and that very night broke their irons from their legs and hove them overboard. About midnight my chief Mate told me of it, so I secured them again. My humble request is that this Lewis the soldier may not remain any longer on board; for who knows but in my going down to the Bay, I may meet with a Pirate, and such a fellow as this which sticks at nothing, but ready for all mischief when the first opportunity will permit, is of ill consequence. I am

Your Honours most humble
servant to command,
WILLIAM BRIDGES."

Lewis the soldier was subsequently brought on shore and committed to prison, as it was intended to make an example of him.

The following resolution as regards gaming will explain itself.

"Wednesday, 4th December. We being informed that cock fighting and other games are very much used and practised by the handycraft tradesmen of this place, wherein they consume the half of their time to their great impoverishment, by which they are rendered unable to provide for their families: besides it prevents the making of many manufactures in this place, and many other ill consequences attending it, destructive to the very being of trade itself. Wherefore to avert so great an evil as will in time ensue thereby, we the Governor and Council do prohibit and forbid all manner of gaming for money or money's worth by all merchants, shopkeepers, and all sorts of handicrafts of this place and the bounds thereof, upon penalty of twenty-five pagodas every time it is proved upon them before the Justices of the Choultry that they have gamed, five pagodas whereof to the informer and the other twenty for the use of the Company. And in case upon proof it appears that any one has gamed for a trivial sum, and that not to the loss of time in his profession, it is then left to the discretion of the Justices of the Choultry, to inflict such punishment by fine or otherwise as they shall think fit. And this we order to be published in the country languages by affixing the same at the several gates."

In the foregoing chapter we have passed from one century to another: and it will not be uninteresting to exhibit the state of the European community as regards population, at the end of the year 1699. From a "list of persons in the service of the Right Hon'ble Company in Fort St. George and other places on the coast of Coromandel," at this date, we obtain the following statistics.

GENTLEMEN.

Company's Servants at Fort St. George	30
Company's Servants at Fort St. David	13
Company's Servants at Vizagapatam	3
Freemen	35
Seafaring men not constant inhabitants	38
Total...	119

LADIES.

English wives of Company's servants at Fort St. George	4
Castees wives at ditto	2
English wives at Fort St. David	3
Castees wives at ditto	1
English at Vizagapatam	1
Castees at ditto	—
Wives of Freemen, English,	4
Do. French	1
Do. Mustees	2
Do. Castees	4
Do. Georgian	1
Wives of seafaring men, English	14
Do. French	1
Do. Mustees	2
Do. Castees	7
Widows, English	14
Single English young women	10
Total...	71

Thus out of one hundred and nineteen Englishmen, only twenty-six were married to English wives, fourteen were married to Castees, four to Mustees, two to French women, and one to a Georgian. It will be seen that only forty-seven were married at all, and that the remaining seventy-two were bachelors. The English ladies were fifty in number, viz. twenty-six wives, fourteen widows, and ten young unmarried ladies. It seems a great pity that ten young ladies should have been unable to find husbands amongst so large a community of unmarried gentlemen.

CHAPTER XVI.

GOVERNORSHIP OF MR. THOMAS PITT, AND DOINGS OF NABOB DAWOOD KHAN.

1701.

The events which are recorded in the present and succeeding chapters, form perhaps the most interesting and important portion of the early annals of the Madras Presidency. Mr. Thomas Pitt, grandfather of the great Earl of Chatham, was Governor of Madras. Dawood Khan was appointed Nabob of the Carnatic and Ginjee countries by Aurungzebe, the great Mogul. Dawood Khan, like his predecessor Zulfikar Khan, was bent upon getting a large subsidy from the Presidency of Fort St. George. In 1701, he tried threats, intrigues, and cajollery of every kind. In 1702 he fairly blockaded the Fort, and endeavoured to reduce the English to submission by stopping the passage of all goods and provisions. Under these circumstances the domestic incidents were few and insignificant, and if introduced in chronological order would only interrupt the current of the narrative. Accordingly both the present chapter, and the one immediately succeeding it, will be exclusively devoted to recording the proceedings of the Nabob Dawood Khan as regards Fort St. George.

No extracts from the official records, which we have as yet published, possess more intrinsic value than those we are about to lay before our readers; and yet strange to say they have been hitherto almost entirely unknown to history. The fact that Dawood Khan blockaded Fort St. George is barely stated, and that is all. The diary which we have drawn up from the Madras consultation books, thus supplies an entirely new page of history. On the one hand the intrigues, the meannesses, and the drinking propensities of the Nabob and his Durbar, are depicted with a startling truthfulness; and the working of the mind of the artful Mussulman is described in these simple entries with a power exceeding that of any other Indian historian whatever. On the other hand we see a display of Anglo-Saxon pluck and commercial sagacity which throws an entirely new light on the proceedings of our forefathers in this country. Hitherto Thomas Pitt has only been known as that Governor of Madras who brought home the Pitt diamond which the Regent Orleans purchased for three millions of livres; who bought estates and rotten boroughs, and sat in the House of Commons as member for Old Sarum; and above all who founded that illustrious family, two of whose sons are reposing in Westminster Abbey, and whose honoured names will be for ever bound up with the greatness and glory of England. But now the reader will perceive that the germs of that lofty pride, untiring energy, and stern consciousness of power, which formed the great characteristics of two of England's greatest war ministers, are discernible in the proceedings of their more humble progenitor, who from the little Fort of St. George, defied the insulting threats of the grasping Nabob, and proved more than a match for the low cunning and courtly dissimulation of the oriental. Our readers therefore will not complain of the space we have devoted to these curious details, which are not merely dry chronicles of forgotten events, but are living pictures of a political status which has long since passed away.

With this brief introduction we now leave the extracts from the Madras consultations to speak for themselves.

"Friday, 17th January, 1701. Dawood Khan being ordered by the King (Aurungzebe) Nabob of the Carnatic and Ginjee countries, who has been several months on his march from the King's Camp. Two days ago we were advised, by people that we keep in his Camp to give us intelligence, that he was come to Arcot above four days march from hence. We have had several letters of compliment from him, wherein he has desired sundry sorts of liquors, which accordingly have been sent him; and it being the custom of all Europeans to present all Nabobs and Governors when they come first to their Government, in order to procure a confirmation of their privileges, besides at present we are carrying on a great investment here and at Fort St. David, and have a great deal of money spread up and down the country; further, a few days ago we have advice from Surat by Armenian letters that our affairs are embroiled there; all of which induces us to consider of a considerable present for the Nabob and Dewan and their officers, and fitting persons to send with it; though before we heard the news from Surat, we intended to have sent two Englishmen, but altered our resolution, not knowing but that the troubles there may affect us here. So there being one Senor Nicholas Manuch, a Venetian and an inhabitant of ours for many years, who has the reputation of an honest man, besides he has lived at the King's Court upwards of thirty years, and was a servant to one of the Princes, and speaks the Persian language excellently well; for which reasons we think him the properest person to send at this time with our Chief Dubash Ramapah; and have unanimously agreed with the advice of all capable of giving it, to send the presents; so in order to their setting out to-morrow on their journey, we have delivered them our instructions and letters as entered after this consultation.

"Instructions to Senor Nicholas Manuch and Ramapah.

"The great hopes we have of your fidelity and prudence induces us to send you to the new Nabob with considerable presents. The Nabob's present and Dewan's we have allotted here, and deliver you several things for presents to dispose of as you see occasion. We also deliver you letters of compliment for the Nabob, the Dewan, and the most considerable persons in the Camp. (The presents to the Nabob Dawood Khan were valued at 1700 Pagodas; those to Mahomed Seid, Dewan, at 190

Pagodas; and the provisional presents at 830 Pagodas.)

"We have nothing to ask of the Nabob and Dewan but the confirmation of our privileges here and at Tevenapatanam, and that all our business in the country may go on according to salabad; and that you may not forget, we here mention some particular grievances which we would have provided for in the Nabob's perwanna.

"That no moneys be extorted from our merchants in the countries where they provide their goods, which ought to pass all places according to salabad; and that no Governor be permitted to make stops and demand new customs as the Governor of St. Thomé has done of late.

"That the Junkameers about us demand nothing for provisions or goods in and out, but according to salabad; and that when the King's duty is paid, it shall be lawful for any to take away their goods, whereas they often make stops to extort money for themselves.

"That if we have any ships, boats, or goods cast away in any of the Kings dominions, no Government shall make any pretence to it, but that we shall have liberty to carry away whatever is saved.

"Our merchants goods to pass secure from being robbed or plundered, and whenever it so happens, that the Governor of that country shall make it good.

"What Perwannas you procure, remember to get three or four copies attested by the Cojee in the Camp.

"From the various reports that have been and

are still going, we have reason to believe several things will be objected against us; knowing that this place is not only envied by the Country Governors, but by all Europeans too. We therefore as a memorandum give you the following advice.

"If any thing be said about our revenues, which are generally magnified four times as much as they are, it is to be answered, that it is paid by none but our own inhabitants, who are enriched by our trade solely, and are daily getting money from us; which had long ago ruined us, had not we set up revenues to regain some money from them towards defraying our great charges.

"If any thing be said in relation to our making fortifications, it may be answered that we are always when new Governors come, pulling down one thing and building another and reparing.

"Remember to procure an order for our Peons and people to travel unmolested between this and Tevenapatam, whereas they now stop all our peeple at Boomypollum (?) and force money from them, besides offering insufferable affronts; which being complained of to Jemsheer Khan, he made them restore moneys, and prevented further troubles during his time." Dated 16th January 1701.

President's letter to the Nabob to be delivered with the *public* present.

"To Dawood Khan Nabob,

I have with great impatience waited for your arrival at Arcot, which being informed of two days ago, I celebrated with great joy, preparing my people to wait on you with such acknowledgements of respects as I was capable of providing. A list of which comes enclosed, whereof I humbly request your Excellency's acceptance, and what I add to it is, my hearty wishes for your good health and prosperity, and a long continuance in your Government. THOMAS PITT."

Second letter to be delivered *privately* to the Nabob with 3000 Rupees.

"To Dawood Khan Nabob,

I congratulate Your Excellency's arrival at Arcot, and have sent Mr. Manuch and our Egyb (Dubash) Ramapah to confirm the same, and to give me an account of your good health, and to request Your Excellency's favour to us in confirming our ancient privileges at Chinnapatam and Tevenapatam. I wish your Excellency all health and prosperity, and a long continuance in your Government under whom I doubt not but all will be happy. THOMAS PITT."

Similar letters were sent to the Dewan Mahomed Seid, and other officers.

"Thursday, 30th January. Senor Manuch and Ramapah advising us that the Nabob, hearing of a Persian mare that was to be sold in our town, ordered them to write us about it, he being desirous to buy it; but we well knowing their manner of buying and what is meant by it, and not being willing to disgust him for so small a matter, we bought the mare for two hundred pagodas, and it is ordered that the Steward forthwith provide furniture, in order to her being sent our Agents at the Camp to-morrow."

A few days afterwards the two messengers returned, their mission having been unsuccessful, as sufficiently appears from the following entry.

"Monday, 3rd February. Last night Senor Manuch and Ramapah returning from the Camp, this day they appeared before us in Council to give an account of their negociations which is as follows. That when they came to the camp they waited on the Nabob, he having sent ten horse and fifty foot to conduct them, who received them kindly, and ordered them to send for their present, which he accepted of; but the next day he returned it, except some trifles, he giving broad hints that that was not a sufficient present for him, and that his predecessor had ten times as much;* he also inveigling against us in scurrilous language, reaping up the business of Fort St. David's, how we had killed Selim Khan's brother, and threatening revenge upon it. But two days after, our agents having by their application to some of the principal officers in some measure pacified the Nabob, Dewan, and Buxie, he sent again for his present, but still told them it was not near enough for him, he having been at Court, where it had cost him a great deal of money for his employ, which he must and would raise by some means or other; telling us that he had an account of our revenues, calculating them at about a hundred thousand Pagodas per annum; but we had nothing to do with Black town, in which he would put a Governor and constrain us to keep only to our

* It will be seen in a previous chapter that the Nabob Zulfikar Khan obtained 10,000 Pagodas in return for his perwanna.

Fort. He also daily encouraged unjust complaints against us, telling them that he would first go to Tanjore, Tevenapatam, and then come to St. Thomé, when he would ruin this Port and set up what. After all which he dismissed our agents without any Perwanna or Tasheriff to the Governor as usual, and writ only a letter referring to that they should tell us, and the Dewan the same, the Dewan also signing an insignificant Perwanna.

"Our people meeting with the mare we sent the Nabob in the way, brought her back with them. They also inform us that they were told by several at the Camp, that this dislike of the Nabob to us is occasioned through informations of some people of our own town, who not only make their court by it, but also participate a part of what can be extorted from us, who when discovered, we resolve shall pay not only for the present mischief, but what has passed in former times.

"So having well debated and considered of what we have now been informed as to the demands and expectations of the Nabob, it is unanimously resolved that no further present be made to him, unless it be so trivial a sum as not worth our disputing; otherwise we shall entail an excessive charge upon the Company for ever, for if a new Nabob should be sent every month, they would expect the same. It is further agreed that our Garrison be put and kept in the best posture of defence it is capable of, resolving to stand the event, and advise Fort St. David to do the same."

The following short note was received from Dawood Khan, in which the anxiety of the Nabob as regards the health of President Pitt will be duly noted.

"From Dawood Khan to the Governor of Chinnapatam.

"I wish the Governor all health. I received the friendly letter you sent me by Doctor Manuch and your Vakeel, and observe the contents thereof, and have likewise heard their request, and have given them my answer thereto, which they will acquaint you with. Pray write me often of your health."

The letter of the Dewan Mahomed Seid to President Pitt was also to the same effect. The Council of Fort St. George accordingly prepared for resistance, but meantime wrote to Assid Khan Grand Vizier at the Court of Delhi, and also to Zulfikar Khan "representing the ill-treatment of our Agents sent to Dawood Khan, and his unreasonable demand upon this place."

Six or seven weeks passed away, when we find the following entry.

"Thursday, 20th March. We not only having the news from our own people at the Camp, but it being the general report of the whole country that Dawood Khan intends to come to St. Thomé, who we are confident has ill designs against us, and to prevent the same it requires our utmost endeavours. Therefore we order that the Paymaster entertains what Rajpoots offer their services (they being people most to be relied upon in time of troubles) and that he turns out as many Peons in the room of them."

In the following months Dawood Khan appears to have entertained some designs on Fort St. David as appears from the following extracts.

"Thursday, 24th April. The Governor acquainting the Council that this morning he received advice from Mr. Fraser at Fort St. David, that the Dutch had been at Conimeer a viewing, surveying, and measuring a Factory there that was formerly ours; and that Dawood Khan's Mauldars were with them. So it is rational to believe that the Dutch have a design to purchase it of this Nabob. To prevent which, for that it would not only be a great inconveniency to our affairs at Fort St. David's, but likewise a great discredit to see a Dutch Flag hoisted upon our English settlement; it is resolved that the Governor writes a letter to Governor Conans, who is still at Sadraspatam, to acquaint him with what he hears, and if possible to prevent his making any further progress therein." This journey was postponed till after the departure of Dawood Khan.

"Thursday, 27th May. We being informed that Dawood Khan is coming to Chillambaram, near Fort St. David's, against which place we have just reason to fear he has ill designs; it is proposed by the President that he himself goes thither on the "Advice" frigate, with two of the Council of this place and the Secretary, and carry with them thirty men of this Garrison, and stores and necessaries for presents, which accordingly are ordered to be provided."

At the beginning of July the Nabob Dawood Khan returned to St. Thomé, within four miles of

Fort St. George, and now the entries begin to grow exciting.

"Tuesday, 1st July. We being credibly informed of Nabob Dawood Khan coming to St. Thomé, and that he will be there in a few days, being now upon his march,—it is agreed that a present be prepared for him and the Dewan and Buxie, the particulars to be hereafter concerted.

"Wednesday, 2nd. This day Dawood Khan coming to St. Thomé, we sent Narrain to wait on the Dewan, to know when would be the properest time to attend the Nabob with our present; who in the evening returned and brought us word, that the Dewan advised us to-morrow morning.

"The Garrison being in good order, the Governor gave out necessary directions to be very strict in their duty and keep both companies to their arms, to prevent surprise, and ordered the Gunner to shot all the Guns upon the works toward St. Thomé.

"Thursday, 3rd. We having agreed the amount of the present to the Nabob, Dewan, and Buxie, and Mr. Ellis offering himself to go with it, it was agreed that he and Mr. Davenport should go, with Captain Lambert; the latter out of curiosity, being desirous to see the Nabob. And it is ordered that Narrain and the Moollah should go with them as Linguists. So about ten this morning they set out, attended with a Serjeant and three Files of Grenadiers.

"The Linguists going directly to the Dewan to give an account of the presents for himself, the Nabob, and Buxie, he complained that the ready money for the Nabob was too little; so desired that the Persian mare might be returned, and two half pieces of yellow cloth, and that the Nabob might have one thousand Rupees in the room of it. Of which Mr. Ellis acquainted the Governor by note, who with the advice of the Council sent him one thousand Rupees.

"About eight this night Mr. Ellis and the others returned from St. Thomé, acquainting us of the odd sort of reception they had from the Nabob, and that he had returned all his presents except two parrots; and that the Dewan accepted of the cloth and other things, but the money intended for him was brought back, they having not an opportunity to give it him after their visiting the Nabob. All the Buxie's present was likewise brought back, and one of the Grenadiers died so soon as returned hither.

"The Council to be summoned to meet at seven o'clock to-morrow morning with the Commanders of the Europe ships, to consult what is most proper to be done to reinforce the Garrison and prevent the Nabob from doing us any mischief.

"Friday, 4th. We being informed by people that we keep at St. Thomé, that after Mr. Ellis and the others came away last night, the Nabob at his Durbar, in discourse about this place, was saying that ten thousand Pagodas should not excuse us;* reflecting upon the amount of our revenues, and particularly upon the Tobacco and Betel,

* Dawood Khan was evidently bearing in mind the amount received by Zulfikar Khan.

and our building the Black town wall, and several other things. From which we infer, as likewise from all his actions since he was Nabob, that we must expect no favour from him; for yesterday of his own accord, he told our Linguists that he had sent four Chobdars and twenty-five men as a safe guard to prevent any of his army plundering our villages (Egmore, Pursewaukum, and Triplicane). Notwithstanding which they fell in upon one of them this morning, and carried off a great quantity of straw and firewood. Whereupon the Governor wrote the Nabob and Dewan the two following letters.

"To Nabob Dawood Khan, at St. Thomé.

"Your Excellency on coming to St. Thomé was so just and generous as to appoint your own people to guard our towns, to prevent their being plundered, which occasioned my not sending any of our own people; but I am just now informed that your men have fallen in on the towns and plundered them, which is contrary to the trust reposed in your Excellency's word and justice.

THOMAS PITT."

"To the Dewan Mahomed Seid, at St. Thomé.

"It is a great satisfaction to me that we have a person of your honour and worth to be our friend; for which acknowledgements shall never be wanting.

"The Nabob out of his own generosity appointed guards for our towns, which prevented our sending some of our own; but this morning, contrary to his word of honour, his people are plundering them. I am unwilling to occasion troubles in the

King's country, therefore I write to your honour, his Majesty's Dewan. What can I write more?

THOMAS PITT."

"We considering that if there be not a stop put to these unseasonable demands of Nabobs, that the ill consequences will in a little time be no less than a vast annual charge to this place; and we all unanimously concluding this to be a proper time to withstand them, being informed that his army consists of no more than three thousand horse and seven thousand foot, we think ourselves in a condition, with the force we have and can raise, to baffle him if he offers to make any attempt upon us. So by order of the Governor and Council, and advice of the Commanders of the Europe ships and Commission Officers of the Garrison, it is resolved that the following measures be taken.

"1st. That the Europe ships to-morrow morning land men according to charter party, viz., fifty out of the "Bedford," thirty from the "Duchess," thirty from the "Phœnix," which will make a good Marine Company.

"2nd. That the Trained Bands of this place be to-morrow raised, and that Captain Heron be appointed Captain, Mr. Berlu be Lieutenant, and Mr. Wigmore be Ensign.

"3rd. That about one hundred and twenty of the Portuguese inhabitants are to be immediately raised and armed and formed into a Company, and be commanded by Captain Emmanuel de Silva.

"4th. That the Paymaster entertains one hundred Peons to lie out as scouts for intelligence, and reinforce our best watching places.

"5th. That all the Company's cloth be brought in from the washers, washed and unwashed, to prevent its being plundered; and that the likeliest men of the watches be armed and posted in our out villages.

"So all the preparations we are capable of being made for the defence of the place, we resolve that if the Nabob will not accept of the present we first proffered him that he shall have nothing."

"Monday, 7th. The Governor and Council, with the advice of the Commanders of the Europe ships and Commission Officers of the Garrison, quartered the men and appointed their particular posts, it being very hotly reported that the Nabob is making great preparations to come against us."

The determined attitude of Governor Pitt seems to have made a deep impression upon the Nabob. He saw that his threats were disregarded, and that the little English Garrison were prepared to come to blows. The following extracts are more illustrative of the character of Native governments in India, than any history we have ever perused.

"Monday, 7th. *(Continued.)* Our Moollah at St. Thomé advises that in conference with the Dewan this day, the Dewan told him he feared some ill event if we sent not ten thousand Pagodas; and that sum would effectually procure all we requested. Whereupon answer was returned the Moollah, to be imparted to the Dewan, that we expected no new grants, only a confirmation of our perwannas in possession, and that we could not add anything to what first sent."

"Tuesday, 8th. The Governor receiving this day a letter from the Dewan, acquaints the Council therewith, translate whereof is entered after this consultation; the purport being to advise us, that he had appeased the anger of the Nabob, who would now accept our present, which we intend shall be sent him to-morrow morning."

"From Dewan Mahomed Seid.

"My constant prayers to heaven is for peace and quietness to the whole world, and it is my endeavours to forward the same when it lies in my power. Accordingly I did the utmost to appease the Nabob, which is now effected and he satisfied. You may now send one of your trusty Englishmen with Narrain and Moollah and the present which was returned, which I will see presented and procure their dispatch; as it is my temper to make up all differences, so your Honour may rest assured of me for your mediator. What else material Coja Ahmed will inform you."

"Wednesday, 9th. The Governor and Council being met, dispatched away the presents that were returned, with Narrain and our Moollah; adding to the Nabob's present a Looking Glass, a China lanthorn, two China Chests, and a Dog to a Dog (? pair of dogs); the Governor answering the Dewan's letter as follows.

"To Dewan Mahomed Seid at St. Thomé.

"I heartily join with your Honour in wishing peace and quietness to the whole world, and shall always do and contribute what lies in my power to effect the same, when it is to be had on honourable and just terms. I have sent Narrain and Coja

Ahmed with the present that was returned, desiring that it may be delivered as was first designed. I shall always acknowledge your Honour's favour, and proclaim you to the world to be a man of honour and justice. July 9th, 1701.

THOMAS PITT."

"Thursday, 10th. Narrain and the Moollah returned about one o'clock this morning from St. Thomé, and give us the following account.

"That the Nabob received his present very kindly with great expressions of friendship, and sent a Horse and Tasheriff to the Governor. That the Dewan had received his present, but told them, that he had added 1,500 Rupees of his own to the Nabob's to make it acceptable to him, (the meaning of which we well understand), and told them that if Coja Ahmed and our Moollah should come to-morrow, he would give him Perwannas for confirmation of our privileges.

"This sudden alteration happening makes us fear a snake in the grass, and resolve that we will not disband any of our forces till his army marches.

"Friday, 11th. This day the Nabob sent us word that to-morrow himself, the Dewan, and Buxie would dine with us, and desired to know with what attendance we would admit him. We would fain have evaded it, but the messenger he sent, pressing us so hard for a direct answer, we sent him word that the honour was too great to desire it, and greater than we expected; and if he pleased to come, he should be very welcome, and we be ready to receive him in the Garrison with one hundred horse. So all imaginable preparation is ordered to be made, and Messrs. Marshall and Meverell (two of the Council) attended with ten Files of Grenadiers ordered to meet and receive him at Mr. Ellis's Garden to conduct him into town.

" Saturday, 12th. About twelve this noon, the Nabob, the King's Dewan and Buxie were conducted into town by Messrs. Marshall and Meverell ; the streets being lined with soldiers from St. Thomé Gate up to the Fort, and the works that way manned with the Marine Company handsomely clothed with red coats and caps, and the curtains of the Inner Fort with our Train Bands, all which made a very handsome appearance. The Governor attended with the Council, the Mayor, the Commanders of the Europe ships, and some of the Principal Freemen, received him (the Nabob) a little way out of the Gate of the Fort; and after embracing each other, the Governor presented him with a small ball of Ambergrease cased with gold and a gold chain to it, and then conducted him into the Fort and carried him up to his lodgings ; when after sitting some time, the Nabob was pleased to pass very great compliments upon us, commending the place as to what he had hitherto seen of it, and gave us all assurance of his friendship ; after which the Governor set by him two cases of rich cordial waters and called for wine, bidding him welcome by firing 21 peices of Ordnance. Soon after the Governor drank to him the Mogul's health with 31 pieces of Ordnance; and the principal Ministers of State (our friends), as also the Nabob, Dewan, and

Buxies, with 21 pieces of Ordnance each; all which healths the Nabob pledged in the cordial waters. So, soon after, the Dinner being ready, which was dressed and managed by a Persian inhabitant, the Governor conducted the Nabob into the Consultation room, which was very handsomely set out in all respects, the dinner consisting of about six hundred dishes small and great, of which the Nabob, Dewan, and Buxie and all that came with him, eat very heartily, and very much commended their entertainment. After dinner they were diverted with the dancing wenches. The Nabob was presented with cordial waters, French brandy, and embroidered China quilts, all which he desired. The Dewan upon his promising us a Perwanna had a Ruby Ring. The Buxie had one likewise offered him, but refused it, and seemed all day out of humour, occasioned, as we are informed, by some words that had passed this day between the Nabob, Dewan, and him before they came hither.

"About six in the evening they returned to St. Thomé, the Governor and Council, and gentlemen in town, with the Commanders of the Europe ships, waiting on them without the Gate of the Fort; where they mounted their horses and were attended by Messrs. Marshall and Meverell to the place they received them, and at their going out of St. Thomas's Gate were saluted with 31 pieces of Ordnance.

"Messrs. Marshall and Meverell returning, acquainted the Governor that the Nabob desired to-morrow morning to go aboard one of the Europe ships, and in order thereto that six Mussoolas might be sent to Triplicane; which was accordingly done, and the English ships boats ordered to attend him.

"Sunday, 13th. About seven o'clock this morning Messrs. Marshall and Meverell went to Triplicane, in order to wait on the Nabob aboard the English ships, and the Commanders went off to receive him, but the Nabob having been very drunk over night, was not in a condition to go, and deferred it till to-morrow morning.

"The Breakfast we intended aboard ship for the Nabob, was sent to St. Thomé, which he accepted very kindly.

"This day the Buxie sent to the Governor to desire leave to come into town, to dine with a Persian of his acquaintance, and afterwards that he might see the Company's Garden, which was accordingly granted; where we sent Narrain to wait on him and see whether he was in a better humour than yesterday, and to present him with the Ring which he refused, with a gold Snuffbox, both to the value of about seventy five Pagodas; both which he accepted, declaring that he had no resentment against the English, but should be ready to serve them upon all occasions, but he thought in the management of these affairs the Dewan had not done fairly by him.

"The friendship of this Buxie is not so much desired for the Post he is now in, but that he is of very good family, and has many relations near the king.

"Monday, 14th. We had several alarms from St. Thomé that the Nabob was going on board ship, but his mind altered, and then he desired to see the Company's Garden, which we used all means to divert him from, by reason in going to it, he must have had a view of all the weakest part of the town. This day he sent word to the Governor that he was informed from Abdul Labby Governor of Chillambaram, that our Deputy Governor of Fort St. David protected the King's enemies ; and desired that we would take care that the like be not done for the future. The Governor answered that he would immediately write away to Fort St. David about it, which was accordingly done.

"Tuesday, 15th. This morning the Nabob sent word to the Governor that he would make him a visit at the Company's Garden ; whereupon Narrain was sent to endeavour to divert him from it, which if he could not do, that then to advise the time of his coming. So Narrain about twelve at noon sent to the Governor to acquaint that the Nabob was coming with a great detachment of horse and foot with all his elephants, and what he meant by it he could not imagine. So the Governor ordered immediately to beat up for the Train bands and the Marine Company, and drew out a detachment of a hundred men under Captain Seaton to attend him and those gentlemen of the Council who went to the Garden to receive the Nabob. But Narrain seeing the Nabob coming in such a manner, told him it would create a jealousy in the Governor, and desired him to halt until he sent the Governor word and received his answer. But before the answer came, the Nabob was got into a Portuguese Chapel very drunk and fell asleep, and as soon as waked, which was about four o'clock in the afternoon, he ordered his Camp to march towards the little Mount, where he pitched his tents, and sent to the Governor to excuse his not coming to the Garden, and desired him to send a dozen bottles of cordial waters, which weie sent him.

"Wednesday 16th. This morning our spies writing us that the Nabob with his army continued encamped at the little Mount; made us unwilling to disband any of our forces.

"Thursday, 17th. This day the spies from the Camp advises that the Nabob was marched with his army about a mile on the other side of Poonamallee."

Thus Dawood Khan disappeared for a while; the remainder of his proceedings will be recorded in our next chapter.

CHAPTER XVII.

BLOCKADE OF FORT ST. GEORGE BY DAWOOD KHAN IN THE GOVERNORSHIP OF MR. THOMAS PITT.

1702.

The events connected with the blockade of Fort St. George by the Nabob Dawood Khan, will form the conclusion of the first portion of our sketches and illustrations of "Madras in the Olden Time." They are recorded so fully and clearly in the consultation books, that a few explanations inserted here and there, are sufficient to render them easily apprehended by the general reader. Accordingly with these exceptions we leave the Government diary to tell its own tale.

"Wednesday, 7th January, 1702. We being jealous from the reports of the country, as well as cautions given us from Surat, that the Mogul government design us troubles; and being apprehensive the worst they can do is to stop trade and provisions by land, and commit devastations upon our towns, which lie a small distance from us; and considering we are not able to protect them by detaching foot forces on all occasions, for that by the extremity of heat they are incapable of marching and doing service afterwards, experience of which hath already cost many lives. Wherefore we have resolved to give encouragement as formerly to all the Company's servants to keep horses, and to allow them fifty fanams per mensem towards the charge thereof, to commence from the 1st of February next. In consideration of which, all such horses and their accoutrements shall be for the service of the garrison, and to be sent upon any expedition as the Government shall think fit; but if such horses shall be killed or spoiled in the service of the garrison, they are to be paid for by the Hon'ble Company, and to be valued by the Governor and Council, or such indifferent persons as they shall appoint to do the same."*

"Wednesday, 28th. Early this morning set out our Moollah for the Nabob Dawood Khan's Camp, (he having wrote the President to send him and Narrain), to remain there as our Vakeel; who had verbal instructions to answer the complaints, should any be made against us, of what kind soever. It being advised by our spies that the Nabob with his army are near, and upon their march to St. Thomé, but their design not known. Also sent in our Moollah's company, the Nabob's Gusbadar, whom he had sent to us some days past for liquors, and carried forty bottles of brandy distilled here with all manner of spices.

"Thursday, 29th. Nabob Dawood Khan, De-

* The troubles at Surat had been occasioned by certain piracies committed on the high seas, which the Mogul's Government charged against the Company, and desired to make the Company responsible. The evil had been aggravated by the rivalry between the Old and New Companies; the latter charging the former with being implicated in the piracies.

wan, and Buxie arriving this night at St. Thomé with considerable forces of horse and foot; and the occasion of their coming being variously reported, and we being jealous that there are ill designs on foot against this place; to prevent their effecting which, we resolve to make ourselves as formidable as possible, for which end have taken the following resolutions, viz.

"That the Trainbands of this city be immediately raised.

"That to-morrow morning the Portuguese Militia be raised and posted at the outworks.

"That both our Company soldiers lie at their arms night and day during the encampment near us.

"That two hundred Rajpoots be taken into service, to guard our out towns and the Company's cloth at the washers.

"That what Lascars, not exceeding 60 or 70, be entertained to assist the Governor.

"That to-morrow morning our Brahmin Paupa be sent to our Moollah in the Nabob's Camp; and both of them go with a compliment from the President to the Nabob, Dewan, and Buxie, and carry with them a small present of Rose water, Acheen oranges, and sweetmeats."

Very late the same night the following event was entered in the consultations.

"About eleven o'clock this night received advises from our Moollah that he had waited on the Nabob, who seemed very pleasant but the Dewan otherwise; and that the Nabob had something to say to him to-morrow."

"Friday, 30th. This day our Moollah and Brahmin Paupa waited on the Nabob, Dewan, and Buxie, as was yesterday ordered, who were very kindly received; from which we infer, it being the opinion also of many of the Natives, that they are working some ill designs against us.

"Saturday, 31st. The Nabob sent his Chobadars as a safeguard to Egmore and our other new towns.

"Wednesday, 4th. Gopal Naick, a considerable man in the country, coming to make the Governor a visit, it was thought fit with the advice of the Council to present him with five yards of fine scarlet broad cloth, a sword blade, and two looking glasses; his relations being the persons that procured the king of Golconda's firmaun for the settlement of this place; and the chief of his retinue being tasheriffed with five yards of red perpetuances, and the rest rosewater sprinkled with betel, they all went away, after passing great enconiums upon the place and justice of the English Government.

"The Nabob Dawood Khan having been several days at St. Thomé, and our Moollah attending him, whom he sent for before he arrived there, pretending great business of importance, and having not as yet imparted anything; he was ordered yesterday to wait on the Nabob to receive his commands, and know the occasion of his being sent for; who received for answer that he (the Nabob) expected some Englishmen to come to him, and that too not without a present; pretending how much he had been our friend, having never wrote against us to Court, nor informed the king of our revenues, to whom was due a great sum for arrears thereof. The Moollah returning this morning to carry an answer to what the Nabob demanded, it was resolved as follows. That whereas he (the Nabob) had sent for the English, French, Dutch, Danes, and Portuguese, (from which we infer and are jealous that he has an order from the King to oblige all Europeans on this side the country to give security for all Piracies committed in these seas, as they have forced them to do at Surat), it is resolved that no English go; besides should any be sent, we could not avoid a present going with them, which would be of ill consequence to the Company's affairs for the future, we having given him a present about six months since, which would not only be pleaded hereafter as customary by himself, but by all succeeding Nabobs. And as to our revenues, we ordered our Moollah to tell him they were only raised upon our own people, and such acquired considerable fortunes in our service; and that we were ready to demonstrate, not only that we daily gave subsistance to at least two hundred thousand people subjects to the Mogul, but that there also arose yearly by the trade of the place, a vast sum to the King's treasury; and whereas we imported to a great amount of silver and gold, we exported nothing but the produce of the country and the labour of his people; and that rather than be subject to such frequent presents, it would be more to the Company's advantage that the King gave us some years to get in our effects, and then demolish our settlement and quit his country. And this message the Moollah is ordered to deliver, resolving to send no English nor present."

The receipt of this peremptory message appears to have determined Dawood Khan upon blockading both the city of Madras and Fort St. George. Little time was lost. On Wednesday, as we have indicated, the Moollah was sent to St. Thomé. On the following Friday the result was recorded in the consultation book.

"Friday, 6th. This morning early we had news brought us, that the Nabob had stopped all provisions and all goods coming in and going out of this town; and particularly some cloth of the Company's coming, which soon after, we were advised he had carried to St. Thomé, before we could draw out our forces to rescue it; and we discovered several bodies of horse marching at a distance without our bounds. About noon our Moollah returned from St. Thomé, advising us the Nabob had sent for him, and showed him the King's order, and given him a copy thereof, translate of which appears after this Consultation. So we immediately raised our Trainbands and Portuguese Militia of the place, and appointed them their particular posts for the defence thereof.

"Translate of the Hosbulhocum from the King, with Assid Khan's seal, dated 16th November, 1701, in the 45th year of the King's reign.

"To Dawood Khan, all health.

"The English and other Europeans having entered into a contract to defend our subjects from Piracies committed on the seas; notwithstanding which they have seized and plundered Moor's ships: therefore I have wrote all Subahs and Dewans, that all manner of trade be interdicted with those nations throughout our dominions; and that you seize on all their effects whereever they can be found, and take them carefully in your possession, sending an inventory thereof to me; and it is likewise further ordered that you confine their persons, but not to close imprisonment. I write you this by the King's command, which you are to obey, and know that this is a firm decree for so doing; an answer to which, with the news that relates hereunto, we demand with all expedition."

"Copy of the Moollah's declaration, delivered here upon his return from St. Thomé.

"This day (Friday, 6th February, 1702), the Nabob, Dewan, Imaum Beague, and Mahomed Amin Mersheriff, sent for us to the Dewan's house; where the Nabob told me that the great God knows that he ever had a hearty respect for the English, and did never wish them any hurt, saying, here is the Hosbulhocum which the King has sent me to seize Factories and all their effects; which, as I style myself the King's slave, I must obey him, though, says he, we do not care to fight them, but in case they begin we are ready. The Nabob likewise told me, that we had received of the late wreck* ("Advice" frigate) seven hundred thousand Pagodas, which appertains to the King, and we

* The Mogul's Government claimed all wrecks as the property of the King.

must be answerable for it, or if we had any firmauns to this purpose we must show them him, which is the reason your effects are seized by the King's orders, whose command we must obey.

"I did see the two Hosbulhocums, one to the Nabob and one to the Dewan, the one sealed with wax the other with ink, to which the Nabob bid me send an answer. The Dewan at the same time telling me I should not be dejected, for they would be answerable for double what should be lost."

The same Friday the proceedings of Dawood Khan and the receipt of the Hosbulhocum were duly debated upon in Council; and it was resolved that the President should send the following letter to the Nabob.

"To his Excellency Dawood Khan,

"This morning our Moollah came to me, who shews me the copy of an Order said to be from the great Assid Khan, charging all Europeans with Piracy, and that by a writing they are answerable for the same. We have been informed that there was such a writing extorted from the English, French, and Dutch at Surat, which amongst us is of no value, being forced from us; nor will the same be regarded more particularly by us, who have been so great sufferers ourselves; and besides, our King have not been at so little charge as two hundred thousand Pagodas to extirpate those villains.

"The goods you have seized to-day, I doubt not but you were advised what value was thereof.

"And as to what your Excellency was pleased to say relating to the wreck, we have the law of

God and all nations on our side; for no ship is a wreck, whilst her proprietors keep possession, and had you taken the least thing of her, you must have been accountable, as you will be for many other things you have already done.

"Your Hosbulhocum says, we are not to be close confined; and your Excellency said to the Moollah that you care not to fight us, but are resolved if possible to starve us by stopping all provisions. We can put no other construction on this, than declaring a war with all Europe nations, and accordingly we shall act. Dated in Fort St. George, 6th February, 1702.

THOMAS PITT."

A letter to the same effect was also written to the Dewan, Mahomed Seid.

The next day, Saturday, the forces of the Nabob began to plunder Egmore, Pursewaukum, and Triplicane; and many of the inhabitants of Madras began to desert the place. A full account of these events, and a copy of letters which were this day received from the Nabob and the Dewan are entered in the consultations as follows.

"Saturday, 7th. This day the Nabob's forces plundered our out towns of some straw and paddy, and drove away the inhabitants; and the poor people that lived in our suburbs and Black-town, being so intimidated by the approach of the Moors army, and the preparations we made for our defence, several thousands deserted us; and the Farmers of the Tobacco and Betel complaining that they could not collect the revenues by reason of these troubles, and more particularly Betel being stopped, which would in a few days occasion great clamours amongst the inhabitants; so that for the encouragement of all to steal it in, we have ordered that the Farmers cease from collecting these revenues till the troubles are over."

The letter from the Nabob was as follows.

"From Dawood Khan Nabob to the Governor of Chinnapatam.

"I received your letter and observe the contents thereof; and as to what you write about stopping provisions and goods and your trade, it is done by the King's order, as a means to interdict your trading. You say that the King of England has spent 200,000 Pagodas to destroy the Pirates, which was our King made sensible of, it would redound to your advantage.

"You also wrote something else, but as for me I have no other order from the King than mentioned to you; but if you have any ill designs, I know how to deal with you; but I give you my best advice because I wish you well."

The letter from the Dewan was to the same effect. President Pitt replied to both in similar terms. We need therefore only extract his answer to the Nabob.

"To Nabob Dawood Khan,

"I received your Excellency's letter and observe the contents; and, as I take it, in that paper you call the King's order, there is nothing about stopping provisions, for that, in all parts of the world, is publishing a war between nation and nation; though we have sufficient for our people for two years, besides the sea open to us.

"That our King has been at 200,000 Pagodas charge to suppress Pirates, is a thing known to all nations, as also to yours, for four of his men of war were in this road.

"We have lived in this country nearly one hundred years, and never had any ill designs, nor can your Excellency, or any one else, charge us with any; and it is very hard that such unreasonable orders should be issued out against us only, when they relate to all Europeans, none excepted as I can perceive; and whether it be for the good of your kingdom to put such orders in execution, your Excellency is the best judge.

"We are upon the defensive part and so shall continue, remembering the unspeakable damages you have not only done us in our estates, but also in our reputation, which is far more valuable to us, and will be most resented by the King of our nation.

THOMAS PITT."

The same day the Presidency of Fort St. George despatched general letters to Fort St. David, Masulipatam, and Vizagapatam, "enclosing translate of the Mogul's Hosbulhocum, and giving leave to the two latter places to withdraw hither, if they apprehended that the order would any ways affect them."

"Sunday, 8th. About noon we had news brought us from our out guards, that a party of horse were drawing down towards our Washers, who had cloth in their hands to a very considerable amount; upon which we sent out a party of horse and foot to protect the same, whose appearance caused them to march off.

"Monday, 9th. Last night the Governor received a letter from the Dewan, the purport of which was, that matters were not to be accommodated by letters, but by sending some judicious person. Whereupon the Governor summoned a Council, with the Mayor, Military Officers, and chief inhabitants of the place, to consider what was most proper to be done. Upon which it is resolved to send our Moollah, who by reason of his caste they dare not affront or abuse, who is to hear what they have to say, but answer to nothing till he has direction from the Governor. Accordingly this night he is ordered to go to St. Thomé.

"This day again, we had many thousands of the inhabitants deserted their habitations, being mostly women and children. We heard that the Nabob had taken four Englishmen prisoners at St. Thomé coming overland from Fort St. David, being some sailors belonging to the "Advice" frigate and soldiers of that place, who had leave to come hither.

"Tuesday, 10th. The Merchants acquaint that the Moors have seized 40 ox loads of the Company's cloth, and carried it into St. Thomé, being come away before their orders could reach their Factors for not sending more; and they further acquaint us, that they understand the Nabob has sent to seize all cloth in the Weavers hands with their accompts.

"Wednesday, 11th. This day again the Governor summoned a General Council, and produced a letter he had wrote to the French, Dutch, and Danes, to advise them of our circumstances and the occasion thereof; also the necessity of our joining together in this matter; which was debated and agreed that it should be translated into Portuguese, but to defer the sending of it till to-morrow night, in expectation to hear some news from our Moollah before that time." (As the letter is merely a brief recital of circumstances with which the reader is already familiar it need not be published).

"Thursday, 12th. This day the Governor summoned a General Council to acquaint them with what message the Moollah had brought from the Nabob at St. Thomé, which was such rhodomantade stuff that we could hardly give credit to it. He demanded possession of our Mint; that his people should come into our Town and view our Godowns, and take an account of our estates; and that we should put one hundred men of theirs in possession of the Black town; and that then he would write to the King that we had obeyed his order, and make an attestation in our behalfs, unto which we must wait an answer. Otherwise he would fall in upon us, and make us surrender by force of arms, and cut us all off. He also told the Moollah that if we were merchants, what need had we of such a Fortification and so many Guns; which is an argument which has been much used by the New Company's servants, since their dropping into this country; and, as we have been informed, the same has been urged to the

King and the great men of the Kingdom at the Camp.

"It was agreed that no answer be returned to this message, as not being worth our taking notice of, but tacitly to defy their threats.

"There being a report of our sending some ships into St. Thomé road to batter that place, the Nabob making it his refuge; which so intimidated the Portuguese there, that the Bishop sent us a letter and protest, the translates thereof are entered after this consultation, and the Governor's answer thereto.

"Sir,—Supposing the advice that I had to be true, that your Honour was resolved to send a ship or two to this Port to bomb the City, with intention to destroy it, was the reason of my writing this, and to present your Honour the enclosed protest; in the first place, humbly desiring your Honour to desist from your intent, since the inhabitants have not deserved it, who on all occasions have behaved themselves as true friends, and thankful for the kindness your Honour has treated them with all. But when your Honour will not desist, I offer the enclosed protest in the name of the King of Portugal, whose city this is. Your Honour ought not to think strange of this protest, for in writing according to our justice and right, it is not against the rules of friendship and good will, which I owe your Honour; and from thence I hope your Honour will accept of it, with the courtesy wherewith I offer it.

God preserve your Honour. St. Thomé, 12th February, 1702.

Your Honours humble servant and friend,

BISHOP OF MELIAPOOR."

"To the Governor of Madras,

"Don Gaspar Alfonso, Bishop of the city of St. Thomé and Meliapur, and of his Majesty's Council, by the absence of the deceased Captain More Lucas Luis de Oliveira. We understand by a constant report from Madras, that your Honour with the advice of your Council has made ready one or two ships with instruments of war to come to this Port and destroy this City of St. Thomé; and supposing that we persuade ourselves that this is only a report, and that your Honour will not put in execution what is said, this being a city of the King of Portugal's, and under his flag, wherein there is a Bishop, Captain More, Ovidore, and other officers accustomary to a city, made by him; and that your Honour will not break nor act against the Peace observed so many years past between the crowns of the most serene Kings of Great Britain and Portugal; chiefly since the inhabitants of this city have not given any cause thereof, but rather have showed themselves on all occasions as true friends. But when your Honour does resolve to act against these reasons, and break the friendship between the two crowns, we do protest against your Honour once and many times, as to the rights and customs of this place in behalf of the King of Portugal, and as to this city for all the evils and damages that shall thereby succeed; of all which your Honour is to be accountable to the most serene King of Great Britain, to whom shall be represented all the prejudice you do to the King of Portugal and this city; and we desire you to accept of this Protest with the courtesy we offer it unto you, for the good of our justice and right. St. Thomé, 12th February, 1702.

DON GASPAR ALFONSO, BISHOP OF MELIAPUR."

The following letter in reply was dispatched the same day by President Pitt.

"To his Lordship the Bishop of St. Thomé.

"I received your Lordship's letter with the Protest and observe the contents thereof, and shall take care to preserve the good union between their Majesties the king of Portugal and the king of Great Britain, and the friendship that is between your Lordship and us, for which I have a great value; not in the least doubting that your Lordship, or any of your nation, would by advice or otherwise give any assistance to our unreasonable and unjust enemies. So craving your Lordship's blessing for success to our arms against them, and wishing you all health and prosperity,

I am,
Your Lordship's most obedient
humble servant,
THOMAS PITT."

"Friday, 13th. Our Moollah returned to St. Thomé, and ordered to remain there to advise us of all occurrences from time to time.

"Dispatched per Cattamaran for Fort St. David (to be forwarded thence) our letters to Pondicherry,

Negapatam, and Tranquebar, enclosing also translate of the Mogul's Hosbulhocum.

"Mr. Chardin acquaints the President he has received per Cattamaran a letter from the French Governor of Pondicherry, which advises that a Gusbadar with six horse were come there from Dawood Khan, to desire their assistance of ships and men against this place; but the Governor pleading great business, excused hearing their message upon their arrival; and that night dispatched their three ships for Europe. Also advised that the Nabob had sent for the French second to come to him, and they were told, he being sick could not go.

"Saturday, 14th. News brought from St. Thomé that one thousand Poligars are come down to Dawood Khan's assistance, and now in St. Thomé.

"Sunday, 15th. Sent the Moollah at St. Thomé, to be delivered the Nabob, Dewan, and Buxie, forty-eight China Oranges, there being no more good brought; which were kindly accepted, but the Dewan bid the Moollah write the Governor for a hundred more, that he might send them to Court; which is understood to be one hundred shoes of gold, or so many thousand Pagodas or Rupees.

"Monday, 16th. Information being brought, that a boat of the Company's goods from Kistnapatam was seized by the Moors in a Cattamaram off Pulicat; a Musoola was immediately sent hence that way in pursuit of them, and four Portuguese soldiers well armed, with orders to destroy such who oppose the bringing away the goods.

"Friday, 20th. This day our Moolah acquainting us that he had been discoursing the Buxie about the troubles we are now under, who outwardly seems to be our friend, and was telling him that there was no other way to get clear of them but by a Petition to the king, and that the Nabob, Dewan, and himself would likewise send another in our behalfs. So the Moollah desired that he would be pleased to advise the method of those Petitions, which he immediately did. So after perusing of them, we concluded to give no answer as not worth our taking notice of; but agreed to send for our Moollah hither to-morrow morning to give an account of his negociations."

The following draughts of the proposed Petitions to Aurungzebe, which President Pitt declined to take into consideration, are worthy of preservation.

"The method for the Governor of Chinnapatam to write his Majesty the Mogul, drawn by the Buxie.

"Dawood Khan and Mahomed Seid Dewan have received your Majesty's Hosbulhocum to them, the purport whereof, is to seize our effects, stop our trade, and confine our persons. We humbly lay our lives and estates at your Majesty's mercy, and are always obedient to your commands, nor are we blame worthy; being altogether innocent of any Piracies committed either to Mussulmen or any others, but on the contrary have made it the utmost of our endeavouring to destroy those rogues. Our ships are continually going and coming on this side, and to this hour never robbed or plundered any ship whatever. I hope your majesty will take this into your gracious consideration and lay no blame upon us."

"From the Nabob, Dewan, and Buxie to the king.

"The English of Chinnapatam humbly lay their lives and estates at your majesty's mercy, whom we have invested round in order to seize their effects, and have already taken what goods we could find, nor are they disobedient to your Majesty's commands.

"We have made strict enquiry, and find that they have ships always coming and going to and fro in these parts, and to this hour it was never known that they have plundered either Mussulmen or others. Besides they have been very serviceable to your Majesty's armies in assisting Khan Bahadur against your enemies with their lives and fortunes; by whose means the Carnata Country came to abound so much in wealth; and as to presents [*here the Nabob is getting artful*] they will pay into your Majesty's Treasury in the term of four years, the sum of . . . . and will keep the seas clear in these parts.

"We humbly entreat your Majesty to be favorable to them, and lay no blame upon them."

As we have already indicated, the Government of Fort St. George failed to appreciate the kind mediation of Dawood Khan. But we proceed with our extracts.

"Saturday, 21st. The Moollah returned this evening from St. Thomé, and acquainted us with abundance of discourse he had with the Nabob, etc., from whom he had great intimations that they wanted from us a very great sum of money; to all of which we bid him answer, that we owed them nothing, their king nor his country, nor would we give them anything.

"Tuesday, 25th. The Governor sent to our Moollah at St. Thomé two hundred China Oranges, half for the Nabob, the other half equally between the Dewan and Buxie; and in the evening received a letter from the Moollah that he had accordingly delivered them; and discoursing the two former about several matters touching our present troubles, all seems to hang on the Dewan for accomodation, the Nabob declaring to what the other does."

On the 26th, advises reached the President from Fort St. David, that Abdul Labby at Chillambarum was preparing to besiege that place, and that the Moors had already seized a quantity of Company's cloth to the value of 30,000 or 40,000 Pagodas. On the 1st of March the blockade had commenced, but the place was not closely invested. Shortly afterwards President Pitt received letters from the Dutch and Danes, as appears from the following entry.

"Wednesday, 4th March. Received a general packet from the Dutch at Negapatam, and another from the Danes at Tranquebar, in answer to our letters wrote them the 12th past. The former makes a specious excuse for not assisting us with men, saying they are under fear of troubles from the Tanjore country; and to shew they want their complement in Garrison, sends us abstracts of letters wrote by them to Ceylon and Batavia requesting recruits; and that the late storm having damaged their magazine of provisions, they cannot supply us with any; concluding with a feigned strain of sorrow and wishes for a happy issue from our troubles. The Danes allege their circumstances are at this time very weak, having had great mortality amongst their Europeans both ashore and belonging to other ships, which we have reason to credit; but they sent a Sloop of provisions which arrived this evening.

"Thursday, 5th. Our spy Brahmin from St. Thomé brings advice that the French Secretary from Pondicherry arrived there yesterday, and had this day presented the Nabob, Dewan, and Buxie in liquors and rarities to the amount by calculation of about eight hundred Pagodas.

"Friday, 6th. The Portuguese Trainbands, having lain at their arms ever since the Nabob's coming to St. Thomé, and most of them consisting of poor seafaring and handicraft men, who have families to maintain; we think it reasonable and necessary for the Company's affairs at this time, to allow them pay from the time they took up arms for defence of the place. Accordingly it is ordered that the Paymaster forthwith give them their pay.

"Thursday, 12th. Our spy Brahmin from St. Thomé acquaints that the Dutch arrived there this morning from Pulicat, with a present for the Nabob."

The same day important information reached Fort St. George, that the dispute between the English at Surat and the Mogul's Government respecting the Piracies, had been finally accommodated, "the English having paid for the two ships taken by the Pirates in the Straits of Malacca, upwards of 282,000 Rupees in broad cloth and other goods."

"Friday, 13th. Our Moollah from St. Thomé acquaints that this day the Dutch attended the Nabob with their public present, consisting of scarlet cloth, silks, China and Japan ware, and spices; what given privately is not known. The Dutch after some small discourse, and having been commended by the Nabob for obeying his commands, took leave and went away; when both he and the Dewan asked our Moollah why the English did not also come. Our Moollah answered, that their repeated indignities to them was a sufficient reason. In the end the Nabob told our Moollah we did not well consider our fault; and that if we regarded the welfare of our trade (he having a kindness for us) did by way of advice offer to make up the business; we paying 30,000 Rupees. To which the Moollah replied, he had no power to assure so much; and wondered he should insist on it, satisfaction having been made at Surat.

"Friday, 20th. Our Moollah remitted hither from St. Thomé, a copy of news arrived there from Court, which agrees with our Vakeel's advices that restitution is made for the Moor's demands at Surat. And the Moollah acquaints he has been very industrious to make it known in all companies; also that he told the Nabob it now behoved him to withdraw his forces, who answered that he could allege a thousand things against us beyond our power to defend; from which it is to be implied what he wants.

"Monday, 23rd. Sent the Nabob some Pegu Oranges, who returned them with an answer that they were only fit for children.

"Tuesday, 31st March. Our Moollah from St. Thomé advises that he is informed, yesterday arrived there Assid Khan's letter, confirming what done by Dawood Khan in seizing all goods belonging to the English, which we believe is only given out to hasten our complying with their demands, the Nabob often bidding the Moollah apply himself to the Dewan, who says they must have 30,000 Rs."

Matters now began to take a favourable turn. The patience of the Government of Fort St. George was nearly exhausted; whilst the Nabob seemed inclined to moderate his terms. About a week after the foregoing entry we find the following.

"Wednesday, 8th April. The Nabob and his army having lain here a considerable time, stopping all trade and provisions, and very much increasing the Company's charges, which has not only been very prejudicial to the Company in their trade and revenues, but likewise to the whole place in general; and finding now that they decline very much in their demands, which we impute to the advice they have that the merchants demands at Surat are satisfied; we have thought fit, to prevent greater inconveniences, to employ our Selim Beague, an inhabitant of this town, to offer them the sum of 18,000 Rupees; provided they deliver up to our merchants the goods and money they have seized belonging to this place and Fort St.

David; which sum of 18,000 Rupees, considering the very long time they have been here, we believe will be no inducement for him to come again, or any of his successors hereafter; and accordingly it is agreed that the President pays the said sum upon the terms aforesaid, and not otherwise."

The matter stood over for nearly a month longer, during which no entries upon the matter appear in the consultation books. At last definite proposals arrived from the Nabob, and on the first Sunday in May an extraordinary consultation was held to take them into consideration. We extract the particulars.

"Sunday, 3rd May. The Nabob and king's Officers having lain before this place upwards of three months, and interdicted all manner of trade and provisions coming into this place; the latter growing dear make it uneasy to the inhabitants; and there having been some overtures of accommodation from the enemy, which the Governor has been daily importuned by all sorts of people to accept of, occasions his summoning this General Council; whom he acquainted with every particular as entered after this consultation. Which being debated, it was agreed much by the majority that the proposals be accepted of; and that the same be negociated and settled by Chinna Serapa and Narrain, acquainting the Governor from time to time what progress they make therein.

"The proposals made by Kisnojee Dodojee, by order of the Nabob and Dewan, to the Governor of Madraspatam for an accommodation of the present differences.

"Whereas by a late order from the king all trading and provisions with the English has been interdicted at Fort St. George and Fort St. David, we the Nabob and Dewan do now reverse the said order, and do grant them free liberty to trade in all places as heretofore they have done, without let or molestation; and to confirm the same to our people, do promise to give them our perwannas directed to all Foujdars, Killadars, Corrodees, Deshais, Destramokys, Poligars, and inhabitants of all places whereto they trade, to be carried by our Chobdars.

"That whatever moneys, etc. have been taken away, either upon the roads or in towns, or in any place whatever, said moneys, etc., shall be returned to the value of a Cowry, and our merchants set at liberty.

"That the Villages, and all that has been taken from them, shall be returned, and due satisfaction made for all damages according to account.

"And whereas their trade has been stopped by the King's order, goods and moneys seized, it is requisite that an order from the king be procured to revoke the former, which we oblige ourselves to do; and upon compliance with the aforesaid articles, twenty thousand Rupees is to be paid by the English to the Nabob, and five thousand privately to the Dewan; of which sums half is to be paid upon clearing the Villages, returning the gram they have their seized, taking off the stop on trade and provisions, and sending the Chobdars to the aforesaid officers with perwannas to all parts of the country; whereby to order our trade to be as free as formerly, and to restore all goods which were seized, and now lie in St. Thomé; and when the whole business is completed the English to pay the other half."

"Tuesday, 5th. The seige raised!"

Thus this notable blockade of Fort St. George was brought to a conclusion. A few days afterwards a further present was made to the Nabob of liquors and rarities to the value of one thousand rupees; the Nabob then marched away with his army; and lastly the Portuguese militia was disbanded, and a treat was given to each Company by his Excellency the Governor.

FINIS.

MADRAS IN THE OLDEN TIME

MADRAS IN THE OLDEN TIME:

BEING A

HISTORY OF THE PRESIDENCY

FROM

THE FIRST FOUNDATION OF FORT ST. GEORGE.

1702-1727.

J. TALBOYS WHEELER

IN THREE VOLUMES

VOL. II

GYAN

Published by

GYAN

Gyan Publishing House
5, Ansari Road
Daryaganj, New Delhi-110002
Phone: 011-47034999, 9811692060
E-mail: books@gyanbooks.com

Distribution Network
gyanbooks.com
India, USA, Canada, UK, Australia, France

ISBN: 978-81-212-8395-3 (Set)
978-81-212-8393-9 (PB)
First Published, 1861

2nd Impression 2023

Printed at: Gyan Press, Delhi.

MADRAS IN THE OLDEN TIME (VOL. II)
Author: J. TALBOYS WHEELER

MADRAS IN THE OLDEN TIME.

MADRAS IN THE OLDEN TIME:

BEING A

HISTORY OF THE PRESIDENCY

FROM

THE FIRST FOUNDATION OF FORT ST. GEORGE:

COMPILED FROM OFFICIAL RECORDS,

BY

J. TALBOYS WHEELER,

Author of the "Geography of Herodotus," &c. &c. and Professor of Moral Philosophy and Logic at the Madras Presidency College.

VOL. II.

1702—1727.

MADRAS:

PRINTED FOR J. HIGGINBOTHAM, MOUNT ROAD,

BY GRAVES AND CO., SCOTTISH PRESS.

1861.

PREFACE.

In issuing a second volume of "Madras in the Olden Time" as it is depicted in the old records of the Madras Government, the Compiler has little to add to the Preface which was appended to the former volume. He has continued to adhere to his design of endeavouring to convey to the reader all the pleasure and information to be derived from a perusal of the original records, without the painful labour of wading through a mass of obsolete detail. The present volume brings the annals down to the year 1727. The third volume will so far complete the undertaking, as to fill up the blank which has hitherto existed in the history of the English Settlement, between the first foundation of Fort St. George and the period when Mr. Orme's history may be said to begin.

According to the plan here sketched out, the present series of annals of the Madras Presidency will be brought to a close about the middle of the last century. But it may not be premature to add that the compiler has no intention of bringing his labours to a conclusion at so important a crisis in the history of British India. From 1640 to 1750 the annals comprise little more than the story of a commercial settlement; and may be best gathered from selections from the early records, such as we are now placing before our readers. But the half century immediately succeeding to that period is a period of conquest, of which only a small portion of the history has been told by Mr. Orme, and to which modern historians generally have only done partial justice. India as it was in the days of Clive and Hastings, Hyder and Tippoo, of Coote and Wellington, of Cornwallis and Mornington, is almost a blank so far as a living narrative of the times is concerned. The politician, the moralist, and the military annalist have done their best, but it still remains for the antiquarian to exhume from the records of the time, the story of that eventful period written by the hands of the actors themselves. Such a task however involves far more than an examination of the records of a single Presidency; and the writer must therefore defer placing any definite plan before his readers, until the third and concluding volume of "Madras in the Olden Time," which is nearly all ready for the press, shall have been fairly brought to a close.

MADRAS,
July 10*th*, 1861.

CONTENTS OF VOL. II.

CHAPTER XVIII.

GOVERNORSHIP OF MR. THOMAS PITT, 1701—3.

Page.

CHAPTER XIX.

GOVERNORSHIP OF MR. THOMAS PITT, *(continued)* 1703—4.

CHAPTER XX.

GOVERNORSHIP OF MR. THOMAS PITT, (continued) 1704—7.

CHAPTER XXI.

QUARRELS BETWEEN THE RIGHT AND LEFT HANDS IN THE GOVERNORSHIP OF MR. PITT, 1707.

CHAPTER XXII.

GOVERNORSHIP OF MR. THOMAS PITT, (*continued*) 1708—9.

CHAPTER XXIII.

GOVERNORSHIPS OF PITT, ADDISON, MONTAGUE, AND FRASER, 1709—10.

CHAPTER XXIV.

GOVERNORSHIP OF MR. WILLIAM FRASER, 1710—11.

CHAPTER XXV.

GOVERNORSHIP OF MR. EDWARD HARRISON, 1711—12.

Page.

CHAPTER XXVI.

GOVERNORSHIP OF MR. EDWARD HARRISON, *(continued)* 1712—13.

CHAPTER XXVII.

GOVERNORSHIP OF MR. EDWARD HARRISON,

(continued) 1714—17.

CHAPTER XXVIII.

ENGLISH MISSION FROM CALCUTTA TO DELHI, 1715—17.

Page.

CHAPTER XXIX.

GOVERNORSHIP OF MR. JOSEPH COLLET, 1717—18.

CHAPTER XXX.

GOVERNORSHIP OF MR. JOSEPH COLLET, *(concluded)*, 1719—20.

CHAPTER XXXIII.

GOVERNORSHIP OF MR. JAMES MACRAE, 1725—26.

CHAPTER XXXIV.

GOVERNORSHIP OF MR. JAMES MACRAE.

1726-27.

HISTORY OF THE MADRAS PRESIDENCY.

CHAPTER XVIII.

GOVERNORSHIP OF MR. THOMAS PITT, 1701—3.

In the previous volume we brought down the annals of Madras to the siege of Fort St. George by the Nabob Dawood Khan. Before however proceeding with the annals chronologically, we shall bring forward a few extracts for the years 1701 and 1702, which refer to domestic incidents, and which could not have appeared in their chronological order without interfering with the history of the siege. After the date of the raising of the blockade, the events will be arranged as before in order of time.

The first extract refers to the old struggle for the exercise of independent power by the Roman Catholic Bishop of St. Thomé, against the Governor of Fort St. George.

"Thursday, 8th May, 1701. The Secretary is ordered to deliver Padre Friar Michael Anjous, the following paper translated in . Portuguese, and he to be present at the reading of the same in their Church on Sunday next.

"Whereas we, the Governor and Council of this place, have been credibly informed that on or about the 12th March last, the Right Rev. Father Don Gaspar Alfonso, Bishop of St. Thomé, as he styles himself, did send a paper to the Padres of Madras belonging to the Church, for the exercising the Roman Catholic Religion, commanding and requiring them to publish the same; the purport of which paper being to require and command the delivering up of sundry papers to the Provisor and Vicar General of St. Thomé; which papers wholly relate to a cause depending in our Court of Admiralty; and upon their non compliance with the same, they were to undergo the greatest excommunication.

"In order to publish these our highest resentments against the Right Reverend Don Gaspar Alfonso's proceedings, and the Reverend Padre Friar Michael Anjous compliance with the same, we hereby declare that no Bishop whatsoever of the Roman Catholic religion hath any power or jurisdiction over the Clergy or Laymen of that persuasion, residing under this our government.

"And to prevent the like irregularities for the future, we strictly command and enjoin you Padre Friar Michael Anjous, or whoever shall succeed you as Chief Padre in this Church, not to publish, read, or permit to be read any paper directed to you from any Bishop or ecclesiastical functionary whatever, without first acquainting the Governor of this place, and obtaining his leave for the same, as you will answer the contrary at your peril. And we further require you to publish this our order in your Church in a full congregation on Sunday next. Given under our hands and the seal of the Right Honourable Company. Dated at Fort St. George in the city of Madras, this eighth day of May, 1701.

(Signed by the President and Council.)

Our next incident is quite a domestic one.

"Tuesday, 9th May. Whereas Ensign William Read on Sunday last coming drunk into Church and challenging his fellow officers, it is therefore resolved for such offences, that one month's pay be stopped by the Paymaster, and he be severely reprimanded by us."

The following little anecdote illustrates the commercial rivarly which prevailed between the Dutch at Pulicat and the English at Fort St. George.

"Saturday, 28th June. Serapa and the Joint Stock Merchants informing us that the Dutch, who have now made great contracts all along this coast, are tampering with all our Weavers to seduce them from our service. And whereas it has been the custom in such considerable contracts as have been lately made here, to deposit in the Weavers hands five Pagodas for each loom, to be delivered in cloth at the last payment; the Dutch now, to engross the Weavers and get them from our Merchants, have offerred to deposit in the Weavers hands ten Pagodas for each loom. So considering the ill consequences if we should not enable our Merchants to do the same, aud that they will inevitably lose their looms; we order that forthwith fifteen thousand Pagodas be advanced to Serapa and the joint Stock Merchants."

The next incident illustrates the Native idea of the hereditary nature of all public appointments.

"Wednesday, 24th December. Angerapa Naik, our Watchman, dying the 29th October last, there has been great application by letters from several Poligars to us in the behalf of Timapa Naik, who contended several years for the place with the deceased Watchman; but finding upon enquiry that it was not his right, besides having murdered some inhabitants of this place, he was rejected. And whereas the late deceased Watchman has left a son an infant, who upon enquiry of the most knowing inhabitants of this place say, that the infant has the right of succession: so that to prevent any more application to us, and fearing that Timapa Naik may procure the Nabob's perwanna, which may occasion disputes between the Government and us; we have thought fit to grant our Cowle to the infant, during whose minority his uncle Tegapa Naik is to officiate and to be Chief Watchman of this place; and accordingly it is agreed that the infant be tasheriffed with the usual ceremony, and a Cowle drawn out."

The losses entailed upon the Company's Government by the proceedings of the Arab Pirates have been already alluded to, and are sufficiently represented in the following extracts. Our readers will bear in mind that it was at this same Judda or Jedda, the Port of Mecca, that the massacre of Christians took place in 1858.

"Saturday, 24th January, 1702. This place Madras having suffered much by ships unjustly seized by the Arabs of Muscat and the Bashaw at

Judda, which has occasioned great clamours amongst the inhabitants of all sorts in this placc, chiefly through despair of any assistance from the Government, for procuring satisfaction, for the same; the Governor and Council, to pacify them for the present, proposed the sending a Petition to the king of England, and a Letter to thc Company, setting forth their grievanccs and great losses thereby. Which Petition and lettcr was read and agreed on as entered after this Consultation.

"To the king's most Excellent Majesty in Council.

"The humble Petition of your Majcsty's most dutiful and loyal subjects, inhabitants of the city of Madras on the Coast of Coromandel in the East Indies.

"Humbly sheweth,

That we, your Majesty's Petitioners residing in this place, having liberty of trade in these parts gal, and thence to Persia, where she arrived safe; but on her return, 14th April, she met three Arab ships off Muscat, and took her and carried her into that Port, and made prize both of ship from the East India Company* Merchants of London trading to the East Indies, did in June 1695 equip out a ship called the "London," burthen about 120 tons, Richard William Master, to Ben-

* Our readers must bear in mind that the Company's servants at this time had permission to trade on their own account between different ports in the East, so long as they did not interfere in the trade with Europe. This permissive trade they generally carried on with the assistance of the principal Native Merchants of Madras on the principle of a Joint Stock Company.

and cargo, valued at about £5000 sterling. She had ten Europe men on board of her, three of which made their escape, and the others miserably perished in prison, who were most part your Majesty's subjects. And on the 18th June 1700 did send hence a ship called the "Friendship," burthen 100 tons, William Morrice Master, to Surat, who from thence went to Persia, and meeting with two Arab ships in the Gulf, was seized on by them and carried to Muscat, where they sold the ship and cargo, amounting to about £8000 sterling, besides Armenian goods of great value; and imprisoned after a most barbarous manner her ship's company, the master, mates, and several Officers being your majesty's subjects.

"We also in October 1699 sent a ship called the "Diamond," burthen about 100 tons, John Cockroft Master, to Bengal, and there to lade for Judda in the Red Seas; who accordingly did, and proceeded to the aforesaid Port; but losing her passage wintered at Acheen, so that she did not arrive at Judda till March 1701. They were promised by the Bashaw freedom of trade, and the protection of the Port; upon which they landed their goods and sold to the Bashaw and his officers good part thereof; but soon after they were possessed of the goods, they seized the ship and the remaining part of the cargo, which they made sale of; so that with what they had before in their hands, amounting to at least £30,000 sterling. They also seized the Supercargo and Commander, and what other Europe men did not make their escape, and murdered some of them by their barbarous imprisonment, and threaten to sell the persons of those living. All which was upon pretence, that this was the ship that took an Arab's ship off the high land of St. John's near Surat the year before. At which time this ship "Diamond" was at Mocha, and returned thence into this road in September, whilst your Majesty's four Men of War were here; and being informed that this place Judda is in some measure under the Government of the Grand Seignour, we have represented this great injustice by letter to your Majesty's Ambassador at Constantinople and your Consul at Grand Cairo.

"These our misfortunes, we know not what cause to assign for them, unless it be as is reported through this country, that some of our nation have most industriously endeavoured to fix all piracies committed in these parts on the Old East India Company and their Factors, and on such as reside in their settlements; inculcating likewise into the Natives, that let them seize what they will of ours, that we have no power to make ourselves restitution, nor will there be any trouble come to them thereon.

"We having here most humbly represented to your Majesty, the most notorious injustices we have suffered from the Arabs of Muscat and Bashaw of Judda, all amounting to at least £43,000 sterling; for the restitution of which we humbly implore that your sacred Majesty will be graciously pleased to extend your Royal protection to us, in granting us your letters of reprisal, or in such manner as in your great wisdom shall be thought meet.

"And your Petitioners as in duty bound shall ever pray, etc.

The Letter to the Company covering the Petition to the King, contains little more than a request that the latter might be forwarded. The following extract from it is worthy of preservation as exhibiting the feeling of animosity which prevailed against the New East India Company.

"We have too much reason to be jealous that that unhappy misfortune at Judda may be justly attributed to the infamous and hellish contrivances of some of our own countrymen (i. e. New East India Company), who have stuck at nothing in endeavouring to fix the Piracies upon you and your Factors abroad. And if that Bashaw of Judda does what we are advised of, in selling the Commander and Supercargo, why may it not be a precedent for the Arabs of Muscat, and the Moors throughout India, to do the same, and then what will become of all your subordinate Factories. These are also many more dreadful consequences to be inferred from the late resistencies of these nations; and if they be not speedily called to an account, and forced to restitution for what is passed, it will most certainly end in the utter ruin of your trade in these parts."

We now return to the domestic annals of the Presidency. During the actual blockade of Fort St. George, no other entries of any importance appear in the consultation books excepting those connected with the siege. In May however, matters returned to their old channel. The following extracts explain themselves.

"Thursday, 21st May, 1702. We finding that gardens within a mile of the works of Black town to be very inconvenient, they giving great advantage to an enemy for Lodgements, and erecting Batteries against us; for which reason it is ordered that Messrs. Empson and Marshall do take a view of what Gardens have been planted these five years, and report to the Governor and Council the distance they are from the works, and whether any ways incommodious.

"It is ordered that the Paymaster provide scarlet coats and beaver hats for the Portuguese Officers, as a gratuity for their readiness to serve the Garrison, and the same for the English Officers, viz. Lieutenants and Ensigns."

The departure of Dawood Khan was celebrated with four days successive feasting as appears from the next entry.

"Friday, 22nd May. On the 19th instant the Portuguese Militia, on the 20th one Company of Soldiers, the next day the other Company, and this day the Gunroom crew, were handsomely treated with dinners under a large tent spread in the Inner Fort; and the Commission Officers of the respective Companies those evenings supped with the Governor." Again on the 25th, "the Governor and Council and Trainbands were splendidly entertained with a supper at the Company's Garden; they having also been under arms in our late troubles."

The following complaint brought by a crew

against their Commander and Chief Mate is worthy of preservation.

"Wednesday, 8th July. The Governor yesterday receiving a sort of a Letter, with a Paper signed by twenty-nine of the *Phœnix* Ship's Company, commonly called a Round Robin; the purport of the Letter consisting chiefly of complaints against Captain Carswell and his Chief Mate, Mr. Abbis. The Governor immediately sent for the Captain and Purser of said ship, who seemed to be surprised at it, saying that they knew nothing of the matter. Upon which the Governor sent off an order to the Chief Mate, about which the Captain, Chief Mate, and five of the men appeared before us this day; two of the five being the Boatswain and Gunner of the Ship, who complained chiefly of the disability of the Chief Mate, that he knew not how to discharge his duty in that employ, as also of his abusing the men. Their complaints chiefly against their Commander for pinching them in their provisions; he confessing before us that their allowance three times a week is but a quart of rice and gram together for five men a day, but promises that for the future it shall be rectified. So upon the whole examination of this business, we find that the Gunner has been the ringleader, who seems to us to be an impudent, saucy, insinuating fellow, and believe has been the sole occasion of stirring up the men to complain in this malicious manner. The Round Robin as well as the Letter, as he himself confesses, was wrote with his hand; so that to prevent the ill consequence that may attend such clamours, it is resolved that the Gunner and Boatswain are discharged the ship, as also Daniel Bulfinch and Peter Middleston; the two latter, as the Captain tells us, have been very active in this villany; and for the present that the four aforesaid persons be committed to the main guard, till we consider of inflicting such punishment as they deserve."

On the 8th March, 1702 died William III, and in September the same year the news reached Fort St. George, as will be seen from the following entry.

"Thursday, 17th September. In pursuance to an order of Consultation, the Flag was early this morning hoisted, and at eight o'clock was lowered, when there was two volleys small shot and one hundred cannon discharged by the half minute glass, for the death of our late gracious King William the Third of blessed memory. Then the Flag was again hoisted up, when the Mayor, and all the Aldermen in their gowns on horseback, with twelve Halberteers and a Company of Grenadiers marching before them, Proclaimed our gracious Queen Anne at the Fort Gate, Town Hall, Sea Gate, and Choultry Gate, with many huzzas and great demonstration of joy, with three volleys small shot and one hundred and one pieces of cannon discharged. And in the evening the Governor, attended by all the Gentlemen of the Council, with the Mayor and Aldermen and several other gentlemen in palanquins and horseback, to the Company's Bowling Garden, where there was a handsome treat provided; all Europeans of fashion in the city being invited to the same, where they drank the Queen's health, and prosperity to old England, with many others.

The following very disinterested act on the part of a Native Chief deserves especial notice.

"Saturday, 26th. Abdul Labby Khan, Governor of Porto Novo and the country about it, came last night to St. Thomé, having been lately at the Camp at Vellore; unto whom the Governor sent this morning the Moollah with a compliment, and two bottles of rosewater, which he kindly received, and intimated to him that he was desirous of seeing Madras, which the Moollah was ordered to evade if possible, but not to give a flat denial. And whereas we have always found the Governor of Porto Novo a friend to our Company's interest, and to preserve his friendship, it is agreed that we make him a present of Gold Chains to the value of about 450 Pagodas.

"Sunday, 27th. The Moollah and Brahmin did this day attend the Nabob Abdul Labby at St. Thomé, with the present of Gold Chains, which they privately offered; but he refused to accept them, telling them he was a true friend to the English, so would take no present, but would always continue the kindness he had for us, and make it his study to do us all the good services that lay in his power."

Our next extracts explains itself.

"Tuesday, 20th October. During the time Dawood Khan lay before this place, we were continually straightened for provisions, at which time the weather being very hot we could not salt up any; so were forced to keep a great number of

Hogs, the meat for which was very chargeable, besides the great inconvenience of keeping such a number. So to prevent any future danger that may happen from the Garrison wanting Provisions, it is agreed that between this and January next, that the Steward be ordered to kill three hundred Hogs, to be salted up as the Governor from time to time shall direct. And if it should so happen there be no occasion for them, that then they be disposed of to the shipping as opportunity offers."

"Wednesday, 4th November. The President is advised from Masulipatam that the Mogul pitching his Camp near some great mountains, from which of a sudden came so great fall of waters, that it swept away about 150,000 people, with elephants, horses, camels, and baggage, he himself narrowly escaping." (This event is noticed by Elphinstone, who however reduces the number of people who perished to 12,000.)

The following incident furnishes an extraordinary illustration of the administration of the law.

"Friday, 6th. The 29th ult. it was ordered that the three black fellows apprehended, and found preparing to coin Pagodas, should be brought on their trial to-morrow; but finding the evidence against them is so insufficient that they will most certainly be acquitted, and they offering six hundred Pagodas to be acquitted without a trial, it is thought much better to accept the same; not only in regard to the six hundred Pagodas, but likewise their being acquitted on their trial would encourage others to attempt the same; and accordingly it is agreed to receive the said six hundred Pagodas, and banish them the place.

The news of the war of the Spanish succession had now reached the Presidency, and preparations were made to improve the defences. The following entry will illustrate the state of affairs.

"Saturday, 16th January, 1703. Here being a report that there is coming a strong squadron of French and Portuguese men of war for India, against which we are informed the Dutch are making great preparations, and putting their garrisons in a posture of defence; and we fearing our nation is engaged in the war in Europe, and well knowing that the Dutch will give us no manner of assistance, so think it necessary to keep our Garrison in the best posture of defence we are capable of."

This year another series of attempts was commenced for obtaining possession of the Company's out towns of Egmore, Persewaukum, and Triplicane. The first, it will be seen, was checked by a very decided action on the part of Governor Pitt.

"Friday, 12th March. The Governor having news brought him last night, that there had been six or eight Peons, who had tied leaves in the Company's towns, which is the custom of the country when they take possession of any place; Peons were sent out immediately to seize them, but could not find them; but this morning three of them came to the Governor at Egmore, and produced a paper which is an order from the Foujdar of Poonamallee, grounded upon an order he had received from the King's Dewan Mahomed Seid. The Governor ordered them to be carried prisoners to the Fort, where they were put in irons, and intended to be punished for executing an order within our jurisdiction, without first acquainting the Governor therewith." Four days afterwards the three Peons were released, "in consideration that they were but servants, and obeyed only their Master's order; but were severely checked for the same, the Governor telling them that if they or any others presumed to do the like again, they should most certainly lose their heads."

The following entry of the same date explains itself.

"Mr. Richard Pearson writer, who came out in the *Phœnix*, and immediately sent to Masulipatam, where he behaved himself very insolently to his superiors, for which they sent him hither in January last, where soon after he behaved himself very impudently to the Governor, who confined and punished him for it; and afterwards upon his submission, and acknowledging his fault with promises of amendment he was set at liberty; when in few days after, he quarrelled at the Company's General table, where he gave opprobious language to several, and blows to boot. So finding him an incorrigible and debauched fellow, and that keeping him here may tend to the ruin of several of the young men in the Company's service;—it is agreed that he be confined to the inward Fort, and sent for England by the first opportunity; and that he be permitted to come no more to the Company's Table, but that the Steward shall send him such Provisions as the Governor directs."

We have already seen, on the occasion of the visit of the Nabob Dawood Khan to Fort St. George, that the General Table could be magnificently served. The following extracts will prove that even in the matter of silver plate, the show was by no means despicable for those days.

"Thursday, 8th April, 1703. The Company having no plate for their General Table, or any other use, but what is very old and battered, and but very little of it too, which is now agreed to be melted down, and the President who brought out a set of plate with him, and has used it ever since at his own charge: it is agreed that the same now be taken on the Company's account; allowing for the same, as the Company's silver was lately sold, sixteen Dollars weight for ten Pagodas English standard; and for the fashioning thereof as it cost in England; and that the same be weighed off to the Steward, and an account of it brought into Consultation, that so it may be brought into the Books. From the particulars of an account which is given at full length in the Consultations, we learn that Governor Pitt's silver plate weighed 2240 oz. 17 dwts.; that the metal was valued at £700 sterling, and that the fashioning cost £65. The old plate which was melted down was valued at less than £100. Mr. Pitt's new plate included 66 silver plates, 6 salts small, 1 salt large, 3 castors and mustard spoon, 3 porringers, 16 spoons, 6 forks and 6 knives, 1 ladle large, 12 dishes, 1 teapot, 1 sauce pan, 2 salvers large, 2 salvers small, 1 Monteith, 4 large candlesticks, and 7 covers.

CHAPTER XIX.

GOVERNORSHIP OF MR. THOMAS PITT.

1703—4.

The great event which distinguished the period in our annuals now under review, is one which can be stated in a few words, viz. the union of the old and new Companies into one. With this event the quarrels of the two Companies naturally terminated, and attention was once more directed to the prosecution of trade, the progress of domestic affairs, and occasional communications with the Nabob.

The first incident to be noticed furnishes another illustration of the old difficulty of collecting new taxes from the natives. It will be remembered that on the advance of Dawood Khan a brick wall and other works had been erected for the defence of Black-town, and arrangements were made to meet the expense by collecting a special tax from the inhabitants. It will be seen from the following extracts, that many abuses had occurred in the collection, which were charged upon Serapa Naik, the Chief merchant who had been appointed to superintend it.

"Friday, 9th April, 1703. The Chiefs of the Castes having met daily for some weeks past at the Pagoda to consider of ways and means for raising the money for building the Black-town wall and works; and having acquainted the Governor a few days past that they had perfected the same; we summoned all the Castes this day before us, and called over the Roll of how much every Caste was assessed. With which they all seemed to be satisfied, and declared they had given their assent thereunto. Upon which we ordered it forthwith to be collected in such a method as they themselves desired; which was to be by their own Conicopolies, and two Peons to each Caste.

"Wednesday, 28th. There having been a scandalous paper dropped in the town, relating to the assessing of the Town wall money, written in a counterfeit hand in English; which we judge to be by some European who has had some insight in the Company's affairs; the drift of which can be for no other than to raise mutinies and insurrections to prevent the collecting the money for building the Black-Town wall and works; and there being some particular charges against Scrapa the Chief Merchant;—we summoned all the heads of the Castes before us this morning, and examined them to every particular, when they positively denied they knew anything of it. Which paper is entered after this consultation.

"To the Council of Fort St. George,

"Gentlemen,

"Finding personal application to some of you, to mediate matters with the Governor about a due regulation in assessing for the Town wall, has been fruitless; we have in concert with many others, taken this method to lay before you the sentiments of the inhabitants; hoping your justice in compassion to us, zeal to the Hon'ble Company, and regard to the welfare of this place, will induce you to consider the following.

" That the building of the Town wall was by the Hon'ble Company's order, some of us have been made sensible of, and we believe it; also that they expect the charges for the same should be borne by the several Castes, which we think a very great hardship; considering the benefit of Customs the Honorable Company reaps by our Sea and Land Trade; also the Farms of Betel, Tobacco, and Arrack (which fall sensibly heavy), not to mention the Ground rent of our houses, Pedda Naik's Duty, etc.

" Although these, as aforesaid, are hardships, yet by length of time, being become Sallabad (as we esteem them) there is no great demur made now, and are not recited here as grievances; so much as an introduction to inform you, that we are wholly dissatisfied in Serapa Naik's being intrusted with the collection of the town wall money, lately ordered by the Governor and yourselves to be received of us; for his audacious injunctions publicly made to the Conicopolies and Peons (who go about to gather the money) to beat and pull us by the necks with cords to the Choultry, upon refusal of payment; which has been committed on some who were not in a capacity to launch out so much as demanded.

" Such outrages and insults are seldom inflicted under the Moors, therefore we are amazed at Serapa's presumption in giving such orders under the

English Government ; but they have been redressed (upon a complaint made to the Honorable Governor) by punishing two Peons ; though we are since served almost as ignominiously ; being constrained by those sordid Collectors to stand before our doors a while in the sun, till wrought into a compliance ; and if such sufferings are caused by our backwardness to pay, please be referred to our reasons that makes us so.

"First, Serapa Naik, at a General Meeting upon his summons, told us the Honorable Company having been at a great charge for raising a wall round the Black Town for our security, must be reimbursed, and three thousand Pagodas more added to repay the said Serapa's charges of presents, etc. during Dawood Khan's stay here last.

"Second. Having well considered the Honorable Company's indulgent care to protect us, we shall most willingly acquiesce to refund their cost of the Town wall, but then humbly request may be granted, viz.

"1st. That only the first costs thereof be assessed.

"2nd. That an Englishman be appointed receiver or Collector.

"3rd. That no pretence of presents, etc. made by Serapa Naik, be interwoven with the Town wall money.

"4th. That every caste, knowing what each are to pay, have liberty of themselves to bring the same, which they promise to do within any time limited.

"Third. These four requests being granted

will give a general satisfaction, and save the hire of so many Conicopolies and Peons employed as now appointed in this affair.

"Fourth. And what further induces us to insist on the four requests as aforesaid, are, because we are under some jealousy, that besides the Town wall money, and the 3,000 Pagodas for Serapa Naik, more may still be taken, and appropriated to the present manager's use.

"Ourselves, and fathers before us, have long experienced the quiet and moderate English Government, and hope our children's children after us may enjoy the like. But when some by their characters assume to it abuses; under a presumption that their being favourities will protect them against all clamours (which we find too true); we have only this expedient left, viz. To represent our calamities. And having so done now, we hope a short time will show us the effects of your wisdom, by interposing in matters so destructive to the public good; otherwise we propose to apply ourselves to the Honorable Company, by sending them a copy hereof, with another memorial of farther complaints of this nature. Dated Madras, April, 1703. In behalf of the Native inhabitants of Madras."

Notwithstanding the denial on the part of the Natives, of any knowledge or participation in the paper, it is certain that subsequently the amount was only partially collected, and that with the utmost difficulty, as may be gathered from many allusions, which need not be reproduced here.

The following quaint but graphic narrative of

an engagement with Pirates is entered in the consultations, dated 31st May, 1703, and is well worthy of preservation as illustrative of the times.

"A Relation of the taking of the Ship "Pembroke Frigate," by the Pirates at Mayotta, March 10th, 1703, by Mr. Edward Fenwick, the Supercargo.

"On the 9th of March last we made the Island of Mayotta, and as we were standing in with the land about three leagues distance, we discovered two ships under sail close under the land. They had sent their boats off before we could see them to make out where we were; they were full of men, and kept rowing about half a mile to windward of us. After we showed our colours and fired a gun to windward, they each of them put out a flag, which we at first thought to be the King's flag, not plainly distinguishing it; but they would not come near us to acquaint us which was the road or the way in; which we were obliged to endeavour the finding ourselves, being in extremity; and with this consideration concerning the ships, that if they should prove Pirates our loading would be of no use to them, so consequently we might expect good treatment from them, as has formerly been shown to others. We steered west and west by south till we came into five fathom water about a league from the shore, and there anchored; which we had no sooner done, and veered away a little cable, but the most frightful and greatest of dangers presented themselves to us, both of the ship and our lives; breakers on all sides within half a ship's length, which, because it was dark and just high water, we did not perceive till we were so near them. Whilst we were in this consternation and hurry what to do, the two boats hailed us, lying at a Grappling right ahead within eall; but would by no means come to our assistanee, exeept we first sent our boat to them. Then we immediately sent our Yawl with four hands, two of which they took into their boat, and put two of their own people into our boat. When they eame on board they thought we had been fast ashore, and said they were sorry to find us in so bad a condition; the loss of our ship being unavoidable as they thought; we lying on a reef of roeks which run out two leagues on each side of us, and would be dry in half an hour's time, and all round us nothing but breakers. They advised us to let the ship lie till morning dry, and they would all come off then, and see what possibly might be done to save her; so little hopes had we from them of getting off again; and indeed we soon pereeived they told us nothing but the truth; for by this time the tide had ebbed very much, and at every hollow of the sea the ship began to strike. Therefore Captain Weoley considering that delaying longer was but running ourselves into greater dangers, and that there was no other remedy but to cut and stand the same way out as we eame in; so desired the two men to go and send our people on board which were in their boats, which they presently did. Then all hands turned to, and immediately hoved a peek and eut away, having a spring upon the eable to east her. By these endeavours it pleased God everything answered our expectations; and before we could cast the lead six times were past all danger, receiving no other damage than the loss of our best bower, and about ten fathom of cable. Now after our ship was out of danger, we began to consider the answers made by the two men that came on board, to a few questions we asked them. They said their great ship was a Permission ship bound for Muscat, laden with guns, anchors, cables, etc.; Captain Hillyard Commander. The little ship they said belonged to the Scotch Company, one Captain Drummond Commander, and was bound for Madagascar, to trade for slaves, with small arms, powder, etc. That they had lain there nearly three months before to repair and clean their ships; and that just as they made us coming in, they were standing out to proceed on their voyage. We acquainted them the great necessity we were in for provisions and water, and that several of our men were down; to which they answered, they did not doubt but their Captain could assist us with everything, and send their boat betimes to us in the morning. We did not give much credit to what they said, yet there was no way to get clear of them but by fair words and entreaties; so kept standing off and on all night; and at 12 o'clock next day, being the 10th, we came to an anchor about a mile from the shore, being low water, at which time we see their two boats lying dry upon the sand. About an hour after, when the water floated them, they rowed towards us; and being come with pistol shot under our stern, they hailed us, asking if they might be suffered to come on board, that they were friends and had brought us fresh provisions. Captain Weoley answered, one of them might come, yet they both came rowing on; and when they were under our quarters, one on each side, they all started up with their arms guarded, swearing if any of us fired a piece they would give us no quarter, and if we did not fire they would do us no harm, nor take any thing from us. Captain Weoley ordered every one to fire, which we all did, and they at us; Captain Weoley jumping down the after skuttle at the same time, and bidding every one to their close quarters, some into the cabin and some between decks. But we not able to keep either of them long, they firing six shot to our one; and then perceiving it was impossible for us to do more, they having two ships very near us, we called for quarter; which they gave us, disarming us, and turning us into the head. Then they began to rummage and rifle the ship everywhere, until their heat was over. In this scuffle we had two men killed, Mr. Gold our Chief Mate, and Cornelius Browne a Foremost man. Of their men they had two wounded; one of them mortally, the other shot through both his arms. The rest of the day they spent searching about the ship, and swearing to revenge themselves on Captain Weoley, for first bidding them come on board, and then firing upon them as they came along our side; likewise to burn the ship. The next day they carried Captain Weoley on board one of their ships, and kept him prisoner there; about forty of them staying on board us till Friday the 12th, when they put it to the vote whether to burn her or to give her to us again. If this had been done the next day after they took her, she had certainly been burnt; but putting it off three or four days gave us time to make many friends to give their votes in our favour, that we carried it by seventeen votes more to save her than to burn her. After taking several things out of her, they delivered the ship to us again that night about seven o'clock; they making the best of their way to Madagascar and we for Johanna, giving us six old small arms in lieu of what they took out of us. But they would by no means clear Captain Weoley; forcing him to go along with them to serve as a pilot for the Straits of Malacca, swearing to shoot him if he refused it. They likewise detained by force Francisco de Cruz our Carpenter; yet one of our men, Martin Hogendirk a Dutchman, entered himself and went voluntarily with them.

"These two Pirates are very strong, full of men, and one sails excellently well. The biggest carries 40 Guns and near 200 men; she is called the "Prosperous," and was (as they told us first) a Permission ship upon a trading voyage, but surprised and taken about six months before at Madagascar. The then Commander Hillyard died soon after of the wounds he received then, but the new Pirate Captain of her is called Howard. The little ship is called the "Speedy Return," and was formerly commanded by one Captain Drummond, but now by one Bowen. She carries 12 Guns and 70 men, and is about 100 tons. She with another about the same burden were sent out by the Scotch Company."

In consequence of this extraordinary relation, those ships in the Madras Roads which were bound for the Straits of Malacca did not proceed on their destination; "which tends," says the consultation book, "to the great detriment of the Port and lessening of the customs; besides it is to be feared that if these Pirates take any of the country ships, it will bring us into new troubles with the Government, out of which we have but a few months past extricated ourselves." It may be mentioned that Captain Weoley made his escape from the Pirates a few months afterwards.

Our next extract is worthy of record as illustrating the mode in which the political department of the Company's administration was carried on in these primitive times.

"Thursday, 12th August, 1703. It being the general report of the country that there will be sudden alterations in the Government by the removal of the Nabob, or Dewan, or both, and we having but two spy Brahmins in the Camp, and here being ——— who tenders his service, being son to Vinkettee Puttee, who procured the firmaun from the king of Golconda for this place, and he seeming to be an intelligible person:—it is agreed he be entertained, if he will serve for five or six Pagodas per mensem, to reside as a private person in the Camp, to give us intelligence of all affairs of importance, but not to be there as a Vakeel."

The following entry illustrates the stringent nature of the laws against duelling.

"Monday, 23rd August, 1703. The Governor having confined Captain Seaton and Mr. Stratford for going out yesterday to the Company's old garden to fight a duel, he ordered them to be brought up this day before him in Council to examine into the occasion of it; when it was found that Captain Seaton gave the challenge without any manner of provocation, so that it was resolved their confinement should be continued till we had considered what punishment we should afflict on them to deter others from doing the like." The confinement lasted ten days, at the expiration of which Captain Seaton was fined 200 Pagodas and Mr. Stratford 50 Pagodas. Captain Seaton, however, as we have seen on former occasions, had a happy knack of getting out of a scrape as easily as he got into it. Three weeks afterwards we find the following significant entry:—"Captain Seaton delivering in a petition setting forth his contrition for his offence, for which he was fined 200 Pagodas, and prays that we would remit the same; which, in consideration of his great charge of children, and his promises of not doing the like, is granted him, and ordered that the Secretary do return him the same."

In November this year rumours of coming troubles appear to have reached the Presidency. The Steward of the Fort was ordered to buy up 300 hogs, and feed them up, "so that they may be fit to kill and salt up during the cool weather for the service of the Garrison." We also find the following entry.

"Tuesday, 2nd November, 1703. The Governor received advices this day from the Nabob's Camp, that there was orders given out to the Foujdar of Tripassore to raise forces to come and seize our towns; which we are resolved to defend; and in order thereto, it is agreed that the Paymaster forthwith run up a brick wall round the Choultry at Egmore, in such manner as the Governor shall direct, to lodge such forces as we shall send on all occasions to defend the place; and when the wall is done, to pull down the present Choultry, which is thatched and ready to tumble, and to build a commodious one for that purpose."

Eleven days afterwards the news was confirmed by the receipt of the following letter from the Foujdar.

"Translate of a letter from Tahir Khan, Foujdar of Tripassore, received November 13th, 1703.

"I wish your Honour all health. About three months past I received a letter from Khan Bahadur to take possession of those villages you have, which are under the Poonamallee country. I was loth to acquaint you with this unwelcome news by reason of our friendship; but fresh orders are arrived to the Dewan and myself; and your Honour is sensible that the servant must obey his Master's orders; so that I can defer it now no longer. The occasion of my sending you this is to let you understand that if you will send one of your Vakeels to me, my friendship shall not be wanting to accommodate the matter."

Mr. Pitt's reply was cautious, but sufficiently firm.

"To Tahir Khan Foujdar of Tripatore, November 15th, 1703.

"I received your letter and observe the contents, and can only return this answer. The towns you mention were given us by Assid Khan, the Grand Vizier, whose purwanna we have, in consideration of the good services we had done your king; which was much to the satisfaction of Khan Bahadur who afterwards gave order for the delivering them to us. When we thought it had been in this country, as in all other parts of the world, that whatever the Grand Vizier granted, the king always made it good; or what reliance can there be on the favour of such great men's purwannas. I esteemed you always as you write yourself our friend, and am sorry you are commanded to execute such unjust orders; which will occasion no less than a difference between the two nations—Who is the aggressor let the Great God judge. Our Vakeel is sick; if you send one hither, I will immediately give my answer to what he shall propose."

The following incident of the war with France respecting the Spanish succession, is interesting from the fact that the Mr. Dolben here mentioned, was our old friend the Judge Advocate in the Court of Admiralty, who had been dismissed from his Office, and engaged in a profitable trade. Notwithstanding the report of the Pirates in the Straits of Malacca, he had boldly set out there in the Canterbury, in the pursuit of commerce under difficulties.

"Friday, 14th January, 1704. Last night the Governor received news by a Portuguese letter from Pondicherry, that the two French ships were returned with an English prize called the "Canterbury," belonging to the New East India Company; having met her and Mr. Dolben in the "Chambers" Frigate in the Straits of Malacca; which is this day confirmed to us by a letter from Pondicherry, copy of which is as follows, viz.

"The two French vessels met the "Chambers" Frigate, and another of the New Company's called the "Canterbury" of more than 300 tons, commanded by Captain Kingsford, came from England and bound to Surat. The 19th December, near the Island of Sambelan in the Straits of Malacca at night, they gave each other broadsides. The "Chambers" Frigate had her mainyard disabled, which he got repaired in the night. The next morning she fought again during four hours against the lesser French ship; after which he made all the sail he could to the bank of Parsola. The "Maurepas" (French ship) fought against the "Canterbury" which he took immediately. Monsieur de Fontenay was sent against the "Chambers" which seemed the least, but proved the biggest and best man. We hear from those we have taken, that Mr. Dolben gave 50 guineas to each man, and a promise to each that should be wounded to provide for them, to the end they should behave themselves well."

About this time a Roman Catholic Patriarch of Antioch arrived at Pondicherry, and subsequently, like the Bishop of St. Thomé, executed not a little opposition by endeavouring to interfere in ecclesiastical affairs in the Presidency. In the previous November, a messenger arrived from this Presidency with a complimentary message for Governor Pitt, as will be seen from the following entry in the consultations, dated, 22nd November, 1703.—

"There being arrived at Pondicherry a Patriarch and several Padres, said to be missionaries from the Pope to inspect into ecclesiastical affairs in China; one of which came this day into town, sent with a compliment from the Patriarch to the Governor, with a small present of Jocoles, oil, and wines; who was civilly received, and afterwards took up his lodgings in the Portuguese Church."

The following extract shows a determination on the part of the Patriarch to interfere.

"Saturday, 22nd January. Padre Michael having applied himself to the Government for leave to go to Pondicherry, for that he that calls himself the Patriarch of Antioch had summoned him thither, and he feared that if he did not go it would tend to his ruin; the Governor deferred giving him leave till he had consulted his Council, which was this day summoned and Padre Michael sent for, who earnestly insisted for leave to go. Whereupon he was asked by the Governor whether the Patriarch sent for him as Chief Priest of this Romish Church, or on any other account. He answered that it was as he was Chief Priest. To which it was replied that we could allow of no persons to have any authority over the Priests of this place, so as to send for them away, or return them or any others at their pleasure. And supposing the Abbot to have a hand in this matter we sent for him; who Jesuitically evaded, and denied that he knew anything of the matter. Whom likewise we acquainted with our resolutions that the Patriarch, nor none else, should exercise any power over the Priests that live under our Government. So dismissed them both, strictly enjoining Padre Michael not to stir out of the town; besides that orders should be given the officers not to permit him to go without the gate."

In our next chapter we shall have occasion to produce further illustrations of these intrigues.

The following entry will explain itself.

"Monday, 3rd February. Ensign Harris, who has often been found drunk, insomuch that he has been incapable of doing his duty, for which he has been frequently reprehended; but finding it to no purpose, he was this day broke; but in regard he has a wife and several children, we have permitted him to serve as Serjeant, but that no longer than he abstains from drinking to excess."

Early this year a dispute arose between Governor Pitt and the Foujdar of St. Thomé, concerning an Armenian inhabitant of Madras who had been imprisoned by the latter. It appears that one Coja Timore, an Attorney for an Armenian in Persia, had great demands on an Armenian named Coja Awan who was an inhabitant of Madras. The case was carried to court, but meantime Coja Timore the Attorney had business at St. Thomé, and was followed there by Coja Awan; and the latter by some means unknown, but which we may reasonably infer to have been bribery, prevailed on the Foujdar to imprison the Attorney. Governor Pitt of course sent to the Foujdar to deliver up both as inhabitants of Madras; but the Foujdar insisted not only that a free pardon should be granted Coja Awan, which would have been granted, but also that the papers lodged in the Court should be delivered up to him. To have granted the latter demand, would have been to establish a most awkward precedent; as it would virtually admit of an interference for the future on the part of the Foujdar of St. Thomé in all cases pending in the Madras Court of Admiralty. The following letters will throw some light on the dispute.

"From Mirusman Foujdar of St. Thomé.

"I have power over Chinnapatam, and likewise over St. Thomé, as it belongs to the king whose grant of Chinnapatam ground to the Company was on no other intent than to make the place fruitful, and bring riches into his kingdom, but not to act anything that should prove unjust or prejudicial to the Merchants interest there. I cannot help putting you in mind of the Governors of Golconda and Bijapore, who for their unjust actions and ill behaviour were instantly turned out of their Province, notwithstanding all their resistance, and clapped into irons. What reason therefore has the king to value any one, seeing he turns out whosoever he pleases; and who by his great kindness and justice towards his people, has obtained power of God to conquer wheresoever he comes; and knowing me to be one of his Officers, I wonder at the style you write me. What can I say more?"

The following was Governor Pitt's answer.

"To Mirusman Foujdar of St. Thomé.

"I received your impertinent and insolent letter. —We all know your king to be great, wise and just, and many of his nobles to be persons of great honour; but most of his little Governors, amongst whom I reckon you, to be very corrupt and unjust. We would have you to know we are of a nation whose sovereign is great and powerful, able to protect his subjects in their just rights over all the world, and revenge whatever injustices shall be done them, of which there will be speedy instances given. I am not a little surprised at your saucy expressions, as well as actions in imprisoning my inhabitants, when you know that I can fetch you hither and correct you for both. This is an unswer to your letter.

THOMAS PITT."

Meantime the matter had been represented to the Nabob Dawood Khan and his Buxie. A guard had been plaeed by Governor Pitt over the house of Coja Awan, who had procured the imprisonment of his Attorney, and who of course remained at St. Thomé; and both the Nabob and Buxie declared that this Coja Awan, was indebted to them for jewels, and required that he should be no further meddled with. Governor Pitt sent very long explanatory letters in reply. Subsequently, as Coja Awan owed a great deal of money in Madras, Governor Pitt resolved to open his house, and to take an inventory of his goods, in the presence of the Armenians, Moguls, and Patans of the place. Accordingly the latter were summoned to appear on the 6th April, 1704; but on that morning, instead of going to Coja Awan's house, a number of them appeared before the Governor. The Armenians begged to be excused on the ground that they had goods at St. Thomé, which the Foujdar would seize directly he heard of their participation in the matter. The Moguls on their part stated that the Buxie's servant had been with them that morning, and charged them in the name of his Master and in the name of the Nabob, not to concern themselves in the matter. The Patans made no appearance at all. Acccordingly they were all ordered to the Town hall, whilst the Governor and Council took the subject into consideration. After a little while the following decision was arrived at. The Armenians and others were told that if they would become security for Coja Awan's debts, or for the delivery up of his person within a reasonable time, well and good; but otherwise they must assist at the opening of the house and godowns, and at the taking an inventory of the furniture, or depart from the place altogether within three days time. This decisive measure ensured compliance; and it was agreed that eight Armenians, eight Moguls, eight Patans, and eight Gentoos should meet on the following Monday at Coja Awan's house, and assist the Registrar of the Court in taking an inventory of his goods. The whole matter seems to have been ultimately settled without further difficulty.

CHAPTER XX.

GOVERNORSHIP OF MR. THOMAS PITT.

1704—7.

The Governorship of Mr. Pitt extended over the unusually lengthy period of eleven years, and, as we have already indicated, was marked by some extraordinary incidents. In the years now under review it will be seen that though apprehensions were still entertained of Nabob Dawood Khan, yet the foreign relations of Fort St. George were tolerably tranquil. This state of things may be generally ascribed to the extreme old age of Aurungzebe, and the inability of the Mogul to subdue the Mahrattas; and it may here be noticed, what is scarcely noticed in the consultations, that Aurungzebe died on the 21st of February 1707, in the eighty-ninth year of his life and fiftieth of his reign. The internal events of the Presidency are however unusually interesting. Mr. Pitt had very great trouble in putting a stop to some disastrous conflicts between the Right and Left Hand castes, which for a long time occasioned an entire stoppage of the country trade, besides leading to the flight of many necessary handicraftsmen from Madras. Mr. Fraser also, who had rendered himself so obnoxious to Governor Higginson as to induce the latter to resign, took advantage of the caste dispute to engage in a quarrel with Mr. Pitt. We however leave our extracts in general to tell their own story.

The first refers to the failure of an attempt to rear silkworms and obtain raw silk in Madras.

"Monday, 1st April 1704. We finding that the experiment of making of raw silk to be very chargeable, the success of which depending entirely upon the well growing of the Mulberry trees, and this country being so excessive hot and dry, there is little hope of effecting the same. It is therefore agreed that all the Necauds except two, be returned to Bengal."

The next entry illustrates the losses experienced from the claims of the Native Princes to seize all ships wrecked upon their coast; and sometimes to seize vessels which were not sufficiently manned without any pretence whatever.

"Thursday, 22nd June. In the year 1702, when Dawood Khan was besieging this place, the Governor sent the "Bedford" sloop to Tranquebar for provisions, but meeting with a long passage, was straitened for water, so that they anchored in the king of Tanjore's country, where the people seized the vessel and all the men, and put them in prison, where they lay several months and were used barbarously. The vessel they hauled into a small river, and took out her guns which were four, and also ten candy of China root, and sent it to the king. Upon this the President wrote several letters to his Chief Minister demanding satisfaction; but all the answer could be had, they pleaded the vessel was a wreck, and so of course their right. At which time the Merchants of Tanjore had several effects here, which the President would have seized, but that a Merchant here, one Sanka Ramana who has great dealings to Tanjore, pretended that he would accommodate the matter and procure satisfaction; but not having hitherto done anything in it, the President acquainted the Council that he had a few days back seized goods that came from Tanjore for the aforesaid vessel and cargo. Unto which the Council unanimously assented, hoping thereby to discourage those country people, and those adjacent to us from doing the like."

The Patriarch at Pondicherry and Bishop of St. Thomé still continued their attempts to exercise ecclesiastical authority within the English government.

"Friday, 15th September. The Capuchins here of the Portuguese Church, being under interdictions from the Patriarch and Bishop of St. Thomé, who design to put upon us what Padres they please, which may be the worst of consequences. To prevent which it is agreed, for the satisfaction of many of our inhabitants of that persuasion, that Padre Lorenso a Capuchin, be admitted into town to exercise his functions in their Church."

A serious emeute at St. Thomé between the Moorish Governor and the Portuguese Governor, is thus recorded.

"Monday, 25th. Yesterday in the evening we heard that the Portuguese and Moors' had had a quarrel wherein was killed a Portuguese gentleman Senor John Rebeiro of good fashion, and two

Moors; occasioned chiefly by the Moors Governor going after a treacherous manner to his house who they call the Governor of the Portuguese, whom he had designed to have murdered, or used him barbarously by imprisonment. The Governor of the Portuguese received a slight wound, but upon firing some arms, the Moors' Governor and his people fled; two more of whose people we hear this day died of their wounds, and three or four it is said are in danger thereof.

"Tuesday, 26th. About five this morning the Governor here received a message from the Governor and Portuguese inhabitants of St. Thomé being come to the place of our out guards; who desired admittance and protection, which was accordingly granted them; and in the evening one of their chief inhabitants, Senor Matthias Cavallo, waited on the Governor and acquainted him with the whole matter; being much as before recited, only that the original of the quarrel arose from a Moor offering to take a candle from a young woman as they were walking in procession at their feast."

The following incident is very curious, as illustrating the proselyting spirit that prevailed.

"Saturday, 12th May 1705. There being never an Ensign now in the Garrison, the Governor proposes Serjeant Dixon and Serjeant Hugonin for Ensigns, one in each Company. The objection against Dixon is from an obsolete order of the Old Company that no Roman Catholic should bear command in the Garrison; but in regard that they have since employed Commanders Supercargos to India that have been professed Roman Catholics, we hope it may warrant us in making this person an Officer; he being likewise one of the best soldiers we have in the Garrison; and it is not unlikely but his preferment may make him return to the Protestant religion. It is therefore agreed that the two aforesaid persons be made Ensigns, and that the Secretary draws out their Commissions accordingly." If Ensign Dixon did turn Protestant on account of receiving an Ensign's commission, he must have proved a valuable convert.

The next extract will prove interesting to local antiquarians.

"Monday, 30th July. The President proposes the hedging and ditching of the Island round, in order to the improving of it for pasture for cattle, which may be of great use to this Garrison at all times, and more especially in times of trouble from the country."

The following entry will explain itself.

"Tuesday, 28th August. We having had for above two years past great complaints of ships losing their anchors in the road, and galling their cables: which we impute to the road being very foul by the many anchors lost, which the muckyard men and all others are discouraged from sweeping for, by reason of the Company having half salvage, and they at all the charge. So to prevent so great a misfortune of any ships driving ashore, it is agreed that all people are free to sweep the Road, and to have whatever they can take up, of anchors or anything else for their labour; and no pretensions whatever to be made upon them for account of the Company or any other; which is to be notified by the Secretary putting up a paper in all languages at the Sea Gate."

The following curious incidents in reference to the wills of Roman Catholics are very significant. The Roman Catholic inhabitants of Madras had been accustomed to prove their wills before the Capuchin Friars; but complaints had reached the Governor and Council that advantage was taken of this circumstance to convey a large portion of the effects of deceased Roman Catholics to the Partriarch of Antioch at Pondicherry. Accordingly it was ordered that for the future all wills should be approved at the Company's Court. The following successful attempt to evade this law, may be best described in the words of the original entry in the consultations.

"Tuesday, 7th May, 1706. This day was read a Petition of Donna Johanna Teseira, widow of John Baptista deceased, who was many years an Alderman of this city; who, by the instigation of the Padres, a little before his death removed to St. Thomé; and leaving a will which his widow proved in the Portuguese Court there, and the estate divided according to the tenor thereof, and the Portuguese customs and laws. But since his death his daughter having married a Portuguese inhabitant of this place, who supposing that his wife had not her just dividend of her father's estate according to the English laws; her husband Gregoria De Arangeo has commenced a suit against the widow in the Mayor's Court, and has attached some moneys in this place, against which she prays relief. And that whereas her husband died at St. Thomé and the will proved there, and that all papers and accounts relating thereto remain in that Court according to custom, which they will not permit to be sent hither to make her defence. So upon mature consideration of the whole matter, and the apprehensions we have of the ill-consequences of interfering with the proceedings of the Courts of other nations; and considering that the daughter of the deceased was content with her dividend before she married, and gave discharges for the same:—It is unanimously agreed that an order be directed to the Mayor's Court to dismiss the cause, and withdraw any attachment they may have issued out against the effects of John Baptista deceased, and leave the whole matter to the Portuguese Court at St. Thomé, where all relating to this affair has been hitherto transacted."

The eccentricities of the Natives with regard to deeds and bonds, are fully illustrated by the following entry of the same date.

"There often arising in this place great disputes and demands upon accounts and bonds of ten, twenty, and thirty years standing, so that it is next to impossible to decide the same; and it being generally amongst the Natives, most of which stick at no manner of villany, for swearing, lying, forging, or any other vile action to gain their end; to prevent which it is ordered that from the 1st of January next ensuing, no bond, bill, or account shall be sueable for in any of the Courts of Justice or the Choultry of this city, that are of a longer standing than seven years; provided it can be proved that within the space of the aforesaid seven years, both parties have been resident on the place six months at one and the same time, and no demand has been made of the debt in the Mayor's Court and an action commenced for the same."

We must now retrace our steps a little to describe the movements of the Nabob Dawood Khan. In June 1705 advices had reached Governor Pitt, that Dawood had been on a visit to the king Aurungzebe, and had returned to the Carnatic with additional honours and powers. In March this year the Nabob was in the neighbourhood of Fort St. David, and a letter was received from the Agent and Council there expressing their apprehensions of Dawood Khan, and requesting to be informed whether they should make him a present. Governor Pitt replied,—"We believe it necessary to give the Nabob a present if he comes to your place, and hope to the amount of three or four hundred Pagodas may do, and we would not have you to exceed five; but if you hear he intends to come to St. Thomé, it would be very well if you could evade it, and send him only a present of some liquors; telling his people that you have no orders from Madras, and that the Governor of Madras will be grateful to him for his civility to you; for if you should present and we too, both may be considerable, whereas good part of one, if not all, may be saved if you can manage it as before directed."

In April Dawood returned to Arcot and Governor Pitt complimented him with one hundred bottles of liquor. Five months aftewards we meet with the following entries in the consultation books which will explain themselves.

"Monday, 23rd September. The King's Dewan who is now at St. Thomé, who has all along shown great friendship to the Company's affairs; and now being sent for up to the Court to supply the place of his brother deceased, who was Lord Steward of the King's Household:—we think it for the interest of the Company to make him a present to the value of about two hundred or two hundred and fifty Pagodas in gold chains, or other things that may be most acceptable, leaving it to the Governor to advice therein.

"Thursday, 31st October. This day the Governor received advises that Nabob Dawood Khan was come to Poonamallee, and from thence designed for St. Thomé; upon which we immediately despatched our Moolla and Brahmin to him with a compliment.

"Saturday, 2nd November. The Nabob arriving yesterday at St. Thomé, and this morning our Moolla and Brahmin returning to us, saying that the Nabob receive dvery well the Governor's compliment, and did intend to come and stay some days at a Garden house a little to the southward of the town; which was ordered to be cleaned up for his reception if he continued that resolution, which we were resolved should not be encouraged to by any invitation. They likewise told us that they believed he came not with a design to give us any trouble, which they infer from the small force he brought with him, which were not above five or six hundred horse and foot. He also showed an earnest desire to dine with the Governor."

This intelligence was not wholly satisfactory. Dawood Khan had the whole country at his command, and might have ordered other forces to follow him from Arcot. Moreover he spoke many kind things of the English nation, which the Moors "usually do of all people, when they are carrying on the worst of designs against them." Accordingly two members of Council and the Secretary were sent to pay their respects to him at St. Thomé; but were directed to give no answer about the dinner, and to say they had no instructions upon the subject. The next day, being Sunday, the three gentlemen proceeded to St. Thomé, and met with "extraordinary kind reception." Dawood Khan presented them each with an emerald ring, worth about thirty or forty Pagodas a piece; and also sent a jewel to Governor Pitt of the value of a hundred or hundred and fifty Pagodas. But amidst all this ostentation he ardently pressed for an invitation to dinner; and though the deputation postponed their answer, yet Governor Pitt considered it expedient to send an immediate invitation to the Nabob, upon the condition however, that he would not bring with him more than twenty of his guards. Dawood Khan made the necessary promise, and the Governor made the necessary preparations for the dinner. The result is fully recorded in the consultations as follows.

"Monday, 4th November. Narrain and the

Moolla went to wait on the Nabob at St. Thomé as ordered this day, and the gentlemen of council to the Garden, whither he came about noon; when Narrain discerning that a considerable part of his forces followed him, at least 200 horse and foot, told him he hoped he did not expect the Governor should admit them all into the Fort, who he was confident would not admit any more than what was agreed on. Therefore he desired the Nabob to keep his promise, to which he answered that if he went all those must be admitted with him. So lighted at the Garden and bid Narrain go and acquaint the Governor with his resolution, and that if he would not be received with all his Company, it should be the same thing to him if we sent the dinner to him where he was at the Garden. With which message Narrain came, and soon after the Secretary confirmed the same; when the Governor positively refused to receive him with more than twenty men. So ordered the dinner immediately to be carried to him to the Garden, with all other necessaries; whither the Secretary and Narrain returned, who were to acquaint the other gentlemen with the Governor's resolution; and that the Guns he intended to fire they should acquaint the Nabob were for the King's health, his own, and such of the Great Ministers of State as were his friends. About five in the evening the English gentlemen returned from the Garden and gave the Governor the following account. That the Nabob first seemed out of humour at the answer that was sent him, when it was believed he would not dine there; but after some pausing he dissembled his resentment and sat down to dinner, and ate heartily, and tasted the liquors sent him which he liked very well. After dinner the present was set before him, which at first he seemingly refused, but afterwards accepted of it; and soon after he rose up and returned to St. Thomé."

The following entry records another scrape of Captain Seaton's.

"Thursday, 27th February, 1707. The Governor lays before the Council the insolent action of Captain Seaton, who on Sunday last marched part of his Company (and had all had not the Governor commanded them off) over the Company's calicoes that lay a dyeing; notwithstanding there was much more than room enough to have marched the men clear of them as usual. And afterwards when the Governor sent for him to demand his reason for doing so base an action, he had the impudence to tell him he did not understand it. Upon which, when he came for the word in the evening, the Governor told him that he was suspended till he had advised with the Council; for that he thought him not fitting to serve the Company any longer, nor would he bear any more with his insolencies. It is agreed that he stands suspended, and that the consideration of breaking him be referred to another time." A year afterwards Captain Seaton having appealed to the Directors on the strength of his twenty years service, and pleaded some extenuating circumstances, was reinstated in the command of the garrison.

The following curious entry will explain itself. "Tuesday, 17th June. The Governor produces a letter from Robert Berriman of Fort St. David, wherein he declares that he had contracted marriage with Mrs. Wilson who lately died here, to whom he had made several presents, which were found in her lodgings at her death, when the Paymaster took an account of her effects. So considering the low circumstances of Berriman, it is agreed that upon his taking his oath to the list of the things he demands, that they were presented her upon account of the intended marriage, that the Paymaster delivers him the same."

We now have to draw attention to the quarrel which broke out between the Right and Left Hand Castes,* and which is fully described in the following extracts.

* The distinction between the two Hands is said to be of recent origin, as no mention is made of them in any of the ancient books. Moreover it is almost unknown in the North, and is indeed chiefly confined to a part only of Southern India. In the latter districts, most of the Hindoo castes are thus separated. The left-hand includes the whole tribe of the Vaisya or merchants, the Panchala or five castes of artisans, together with some other mean tribes of the Sudras, and especially the caste of Chakili or cobblers. The Right-hand includes the most distinguished castes of the Sudras, but its strongest bulwark is the Pariah caste, which still glories in the title of "Friends of the Right-hand."

The opposition between the two hands arises from certain privileges to which they both lay claim. The matter is generally some trifling violation of mamool or custom, but not unfrequently leads to bloody disputes. Dabors mentions a contest so dreadful, that many of the

"Thursday, 26th June, 1707. There having been lately a dispute between the Right and Left Hand Castes, that live in the Pettah, about passing some streets on occasion of their weddings, insomuch that the Governor was obliged to order Guards to lie out to keep the peace. To prevent further disturbance it is agreed that Mr. Raworth the Paymaster takes with him the Gunner, and Serampa and Narrain, Heads for the Right Hand Caste, and Colloway and Vinkettee Chitties Heads for the Left Hand Caste; and that they survey the Pettahs, and consider of what method may be taken to prevent any further disputes of the like nature, and report the same to the Governor and Council.

"Thursday, 17th July. Mr. Raworth and the Gunner, as also the Heads of the Right and Left Hand Castes, report that they had surveyed the Pettah, and produced a draught of all the streets and buildings in the Pettah, which showed us what streets were chiefly inhabited by the Left Hand Caste, being Bridge Gate street, and that which is called the Chief Peons street; wherein lives but few of the Right Hand Caste. So to preserve the peace between the two aforesaid Castes for the future, we hereby order that those few of the Right hand Caste in the aforementioned

peaceful inhabitants began to leave their villages, just as if a Mahratta invasion were impending. This terrible commotion arose from a member of the Left-hand sticking red flowers into his turban. To this day nothing but the strong arm of the police prevents Madras itself from being frequently the scene of similar disturbances.

streets sell their houses, and go and live in the streets amongst their own Caste; and that those two streets are peculiarly appropriated for the Left Hand Caste to pass in at their making their weddings and Festivals; and that none of the Right Hand Caste give them the least disturbance in that precinct at their utmost peril. And it is further ordered that neither Caste may pretend ignorance of these limits, that the Paymaster sets up four Stones at the cost of the Left Hand Caste, according as we have directed him in the draught, and insert thereon in English and Gentoo the purport of this our order."

"Thursday, 14th August. The Governor acquaints the Council that on the 12th at night some disaffected persons to the Government had placed papers on the Stones set up in our Pettah, which stinted the bounds of the Left Hand Caste; which papers were wrote in the Malabar language and now produced.

"Since the foundation of this city no such thing has been known. By the authority of the Government and prevalence of money this Pillar was erected, in contempt and derison of the Right Hand Caste, who will forfeit the rights of their caste if they do not destroy the others like dogs and tumble them down. If it be demanded by whose order this was written, it is by the will of the King of England and the Company, who will not fail to bring these things to pass; and this by way of caution."

"The persons unknown also laid at the foot of the Stone, a sort of an enchantment as is esteemed in this country, pieces of skulls with rice and other mixtures. From the translate of the paper it is easily to be inferred that some Europeans have had a hand in it; there being expressions that these people are wholly strangers to. Of which we having considered are come to the following result, that a paper be fixed on each stone in all languages, as also on the Gates in the English and Black town; that if any person shall come and inform us of what person or persons have fixed the aforementioned paper on those Pillars, they shall have one hundred Pagodas reward, and his pardon if concerned therein. The Heads of the Right Hand Caste were sent for before us, who being charged with having a hand in writing these papers, which they denied; agreed that a month's time be given them to find out the person or persons who wrote them; and that if they do not find them, they are to be fined such a sum of money as the Governor and Council think fit; and this they were acquainted with.

"Tuesday, 19th August. The Governor acquaints the Board that on Sunday last, being the 17th instant, that the Right Hand Caste with a Wedding went in great pomp through the street which was ordered lately by the Governor and Council for the Weddings of the Left Hand Caste; and that upon hearing of which, he sent out a party of soldiers who seized nineteen of them, who are now in prison in the Choultry, who he resolves to punish and make examples.

"The Right Hand Caste came to the Fort this day in a considerable body, and delivered in a Petition as entered after this consultation; with the heads of which we had a long debate, and what they said tended, as well as the purport of their Petition, for us to retract what we have done, and that we would give up the Left Hand Caste a sacrifice to them.

"The Petition of the eighteen sorts of people of the Right Hand Castes belonging to Chinnapatam.

"Humbly Sheweth,

Whereas upon the first settlement of the English in this place, the liberty was granted your Petitioners' Castes to have their streets and habitations from Tom Clarke's Gate and the Bridge Gate, both within and without; and to the Left Hand Caste was granted from Mud Point Gate, both within and without; two streets which was kept and observed by each Caste till broken by the troubles which happened to the French at St. Thomé. At which time several people retired hither, and without knowledge or permission from the Government, built their houses one amongst the other in both the Pettahs; which being complained of to Sir Willliam Langhorn, and the ill effects of the falling out of the two Castes being taken into consideration, it was ordered that they should not live together; but that the Right Hand people should go to the place that was first granted them to inhabit, and that the Left Hand should go to theirs. Accordingly to which order the Right Hand people did obey, and likewise some of the Left Hand people; but others did desire leave to stay till the rains was over, which was granted, but after to retire to their own streets; which to this day they have not done, but rather have encroached more upon your Petitioner's liberty. Likewise the Weddings that were made by the Left Hand people that lived amongst your Petitioners, were ordered to be kept always in their own streets; but if it happened that they did make any Weddings in your Petitioners' streets, it was to be done privately in their own houses, without any music, or any such ceremony. But they now very unreasonably desire your Petitioners' streets, which never was done before; and they having complained to your Honour, but upon what account or reason we do not know. Now in the streets wherein the Stones are erected, there are one hundred of your Petitioners houses, with several Wells, Churches, Gardens, and Choultries; all which belong to your Petitioners the Right Hand people. Being very many, being twenty-one Castes in all of these people, we cannot tell every one's mind. The country people have sent letters to us, but what they can do for us we do not know. We all living under your Honour's protection, are afraid to disoblige your Honour, therefore stay very quiet. From the beginning of the world to this day it never was known that any Government did take away your Petitioner's streets, and give them to the Left Caste people, which they know to be true. Now they (the Left Hands) having made many false complaints to your Honour, which is the occasion of all this trouble; for the streets where the Stones are erected are the first streets of the Right Hand Castes for all strangers that come from the country. For these streets that your Honour has given to the Left Hand Castes is a very great dissatisfaction to all the Right Hand Caste people. Therefore your most humble Petitioners desire your Honour would be pleased to take into consideration, and they shall as in duty bound ever pray."

"Friday, 22nd August. The foregoing consultations of late mention several passages relating to the Right Hand Caste and Left. Of the former many have deserted us, and the others have locked themselves up in their houses in town; which, chiefly consisting of Boatmen, Washermen, Fishermen, and other necessary handicrafts, the Governor summoned all his Council except Mr. Fraser; who he was jealous had betrayed us in what we had done, as to settling the dispute between the Castes. And the Governor gave us this instance of it. That when on the 19th past, he acquainted the Board of the insolence of the Pariahs who went through the Left Hand streets with a Wedding and what he had done thereon; when immediately Mr. Fraser according to his custom made a long senseless speech, the purport shewing that he was now against what had been transacted in consultation about the Castes; which no notice was taken of, as coming from him. But then the next minute the Right Hand Caste delivered their Petition, which was presently read, and entirely agreed with the purport of what just before Mr. Fraser spoke. When the Governor immediately charged him with making or reading of it, which he then denied in great confusion, and the same was taken notice of by Messrs. Raworth and Frederick present in Council. So the Governor this day laying before the Board the worst of consequences that might attend the Company's affairs, as well as our own persons, to have one amongst us to betray our counsels; of which the Council being equally sensible, desired Mr. Fraser might be sent for; which was accordingly done. When he was charged with what before mentioned, and told by the Governor that it was impossible that he could make a speech so coherent with a Petition that was just after delivered in, without having made or read it; to which he made no other defence than that we should prove it if we could. The Governor at the same time charged him with directing the Malabar inscription that was put upon the Stones, which he denied with strange asseveration and execrations, but to the making or reading the Petition only a plain denial. So after he told us he had no more to say in his defence, the Governor desired him to withdraw, which he refused to do, but afterwards obliged him to it.

"When we debated the nature of his offence, and the ill consequences of any of the Council encouraging Petitions against our proceedings in general, or such in particular as he himself seemingly agreed to, without the least hesitation to anything that was done relating to the castes:— the Governor to prevent his doing further mischief, pressed the necessity of his being suspended the Company's service ab officio et beneficio; alleging that no inconveniency could accrue from it, for that his abilities were so little considerable, that all of us knew in our consciences that he never merited rice and water from the Company; but yet with his malice, pride, and envy, he has often made strange progress in mischief, and wholly incapable of doing good. And it is not amiss to insert one or two passages, though foreign to this present matter. Some time past, upon a suspicion that there was a difference between the Governor and Mr. Raworth, an impudent Dubash, that was often trusted with Mr. Fraser's whispers, came up to Mr. Raworth in his chamber, and told him that he heard there was a difference between the Governor and him, and that he treated him as he did others; but if he would stand against him and come and join with Mr. Fraser and his party, he was sure they would be able to suppress him: upon which Mr. Raworth treated him as became him by kicking him down stairs. About five years past there came from Goa a Theatine Padre, an Englishman, Milton by name, who often passed between this place and Fort St. David, and several times came to the Governor for leave to build a Chapel here or at Fort St. David; which he positively refused him, considering that the worst of consequences must attend it, or that it would be to the great dislike of the Company to have an English priest here of the Popish religion, for that being such he ought to die by our law. Yet nevertheless one Joseph Hiller, a great consort of Mr. Fraser, bought a piece of ground here (without any leave or knowledge of the Governor) for Milton; on which he immediately erected a fabrick after the model of a convent, and had made considerable progress therein, before the Governor, who was going to the Garden one morning, knew anything of it. When he immediately sent for Padre Milton, and demanded of him how he came by that ground, and who gave him leave to build on it; who answered Mr. Hiller bought it for him. Upon which the Governor ordered him immediately to desist from building, and by six at night to depart the place; which he accordingly did to St. Thomé; where a little time after, Mr. Fraser and others went to dinner with him, and has often been seen conversing with him at that end of the town. Thus whenever the Governor has frowned upon any one for crimes and misdemeanors, whether white men or black, it is well known they were always cherished by Mr. Fraser; who has been the pest of the Government, as well as the ridicule and scum of the place. Yet notwithstanding all before mentioned is well known to be great truths to every man that sits at the Board, who desired the Governor to leave him out in the sorting Summons, for that he was so impertinent and troublesome that no business could be done; yet they were generally unwilling to suspend him the service, till the Governor solemnly averred that he would sit no more with him in Council, nor give his opinion in any affairs more of the Company's where he was present; which induced the Council unanimously to suspend him the Company's service officio et beneficio till their pleasure was known in this matter; which the Secretary is ordered to acquaint him therewith, and that we will give him a copy of what we write home to the

Company relating to him, that so his defence and answer may go therewith."

The following extract from a General Letter from the Court of Directors, dated 4th February, 1708, will show how Mr. Fraser fared, notwithstanding the abuse bestowed on him by Governor Pitt.

"The charge against Mr. Fraser we have considered, and would hope no Englishman, especially none of our servants, would be guilty of such pernicious practices, which strike at the root of the well being of the place; and are more inclined to this opinion, because we find in the consultation of the 22nd August, that the Council were generally unwilling to suspend him, which we cannot think they would be if they apprehended he was justly taxed; and that it was Mr. Pitt's solemn averring he would sit no more with him, that prevailed with them. We have therefore reinstated him, as thinking it not fit to give so much countenance to any Governor whatsoever, as to approve his single opinion, against all the rest of the Council, in a case of this nature, which if it was true does not fully appear to us to have been proved; though we shall always lodge a power in our President and Council to suspend any of the Council or other subordinates, when they have or think they have a just reason; and if it be of great crimes they are charged with that deserves confinement, we shall approve it."

For the sequel of the dispute between the Right and Left Hands we must refer our readers to our next chapter.

CHAPTER XXI.

QUARRELS BETWEEN THE RIGHT AND LEFT HANDS IN THE GOVERNORSHIP OF MR. THOMAS PITT.

1707.

The quarrel between the Right and Left Hand Castes, which resulted in the flight of the former to St. Thomé, is one so extraordinary in its nature, and so illustrative of the character of the people, that we have deemed it advisable to tell the whole story as much as possible in the language of the Records, only abridging those portions which are mere recapitulations. These extracts are all taken from the consultation books during the latter half of 1707, and are arranged in strict chronological order

"Monday, 25th August, 1707. This morning early the Governor summoned twelve of the principal of the heads of each Caste, who were shut up in a room to adjust matters now in dispute between the Castes; which they acquainted him about noon they had done. Upon which at four this afternoon the Council was summoned, when the number of each Caste appeared; when unanimously and in a most solemn manner they declared they had agreed on the following terms.

"1st. That none but the Right Hand Caste

should live in the Pettah commonly called the Pedda Naik's Pettah.

"2nd. That the Pettah called Mootel Pettah should be inhabited by none but the Left Hand Caste.

"3rd. That whereas there are a great many of the Left Hand Caste in the Pedda Naik's Pettah, and so likewise of the Right Hand Caste in Mootel Pettah, it is agreed that each Caste commence removing their Houses on or before the 1st of December to their respective Pettahs before mentioned; and that the same be all completed on or before the 1st of June, 1708; and if any that have houses in either of the Pettahs can agree upon the sale or exchange thereof, they are at liberty to do it, or pull down and carry the materials to the Pettah appointed for them to live in.

"4th. That no Weddings by either Caste shall be made in the streets in the Pedda Naik's Pettah lately in dispute between them, till that Pettah be wholly inhabited by the Right Hand Caste.

"5th. That in Mootel Pettah they shall keep their Weddings there according to custom, till the Right Hand Caste are removed out of it.

"6th. That in neither of these Pettahs before mentioned, no one shall sell his house but to one of his own Caste.

"7th. That whereas there are Boatmen, Laskars, and Fishermen that have their houses by the sea side in Mootel Pettah, it is agreed that they remain there as they now are, without giving any molestation to the Left Hand Caste.

"8th. That as we ordered in Consultation of the 17th July Stones to be erected for stinting the limits of the Left Hand Caste making their Weddings in the Pedda Naik's Pettah, and a suitable inscription thereon;—we now at the request of both Castes agree that the inscription be cut out; but the Stones remain for such inscriptions to be made on them as the Governor and Council shall think fit hereafter.

"To all the foregoing articles the Governor and Council do now agree; with which the Right Hand Caste are ordered to acquaint their people that are now withdrawn, that they now return to their obedience without further delay; which they readily promise to do.

"Wednesday, 27th. Notwithstanding that all matters seem to be so fairly adjusted before us on the 25th past between the two Castes, we have seen no good effect of it by the people returning to their duty. So the Governor ordered this day to to be brought before him in Council, Serapa, Nara Verona, Sunka Rama, and Andee Chitty, —and charged them as chief instruments in raising the present rebellion; and the information of which he had had from one of their own Caste, who was in the conspiracy, who said they had a great difficulty to stir up the poor Handicrafts; and that the Pariahs who are the most numerous, refused to stir unless they sent with them one of their heads of the Caste with one thousand Pagodas to pay their subsistence, which they accordingly complied with; and the Governor was informed who had contributed thereto;

and when they proposed it to the Boatmen, Washermen, and Fishermen, they likewise refused, saying they would not leave the livelihood they had there for an uncertainty; but with much persuasion they prevailed with them, upon giving them a note under their hands that they would pay them in proportion for the days they were absent, according to what they usually got here; and that they would allow Batta or subsistence money to all that should desert us (of which the Governor had daily intelligence from St. Thomé) which was paid them. They (the four Natives summoned) denied all; knowing that whoever of their Caste came in as evidence against them was in no small danger of their life. So the aforementioned prisoners the Governor ordered to be kept in safe custody, and used suitable to their crimes.

"Friday, 29th. This day were before us Serapa, Ñara Verona, Sunka Rama, and Andee Chitty of the Right Hand Caste, and Colloway Chitty, Vinkettee Chitty, Petombee Chitty, and Cornapa Chitty of the Left Hand Caste; when having a Brahmin present, they swore to be true to the Company's interest, and to lay aside all animosity between them relating to their castes, or any other dispute; and that they would use their utmost influence to compose the present differences on that account; as also to stand by the agreement made in Consultation the 25th instant; and for the security of Serapa and the other three, four of the Right Hand Caste, the Pedda Naik, and ten Cuomities were bound for their personal appearance.

"The Governor acquainting that none that had deserted were come in since the agreement between the two Castes, which he imparted to their fear as well as shame. So advised that a paper might be published in the nature of a general pardon; which he now produced, and was read, and accordingly agreed to, and ordered to be set up in the Gates and Mettows in the Gentoo and Malabar, and one in English at the Sea gate as follows:

"Whereas some wicked and evil designing people of the Right Hand Caste, seduced by others as wicked in the Government,* have went about for some sinister ends to make an insurrection and rebellion in this Government; and the better to effect their hellish designs, have deluded the poor and ignorant with a false notion that we, the Governor and Council, had favoured the Left Hand Caste to prejudice theirs; whereas nothing was done by us but by the advice and consent of the principal of their heads; and since this dispute has happened, matters have been thoroughly canvassed by twelve of each heads of the Caste, and all differences adjusted and finally ended before us in Council; yet nevertheless, we hear that some people are still carrying on their ill designs to disturb the peace and tranquillity of the Government, which induces us to publish this our order and intentions.

"That whereas we have always showed great tenderness of the welfare of our inhabitants, and

* A hit at Mr. Fraser.

took especial care to provide for the poor and labouring people, who three or four of the rich and crafty have imposed upon them, so as to make them desert us, and to terrify them from returning to their duty, give out the Government will punish them suitable to their crimes.

"We therefore have thought fit to publish this our General Pardon to all such who have been concerned in this insurrection; promising and declaring that such who return to their habitations and duty on or before the 10th of September next, are pardoned hereby to all intents and purposes, as if they had not been concerned therein; and such as do not comply herewith, their houses and estates shall be seized for the Company's use, and their persons when and wherever apprehended, within the Company's jurisdiction, shall be proceeded against with the utmost rigour; and more particularly such who shall after the date hereof contribute any money or otherwise towards the upholding, maintaining, or employing any that shall not come in by the time herein limited. Sealed with the Company's seal, and dated at Fort St. George, this 29th day of August, one thousand seven hundred and seven."

Nothing appears to have transpired between the 29th of August and the 10th of September specified in the General Pardon; but on the latter date we find the following significant entry.

"Wednesday, 10th September. The Governor summoned the Council to acquaint them, that he was just then informed that in the night the Stones were stolen away; which we considered of, and though the impudence of the action deserves the strictest enquiry and punishment, and the immediate erecting others, yet it was unanimously agreed that we desist from doing either till these troubles are over; though obliged the Pedda Naik to give twenty thousand Pagodas for his personal appearance, who must doubtless have a hand in it, or at least knows of the taking away the Stones.

"Those of the Right Hand Caste that have deserted, retiring to St. Thomé, have sent for the heads of their Caste out of the country, who wrote us this day a most saucy and impudent letter, the translate of which is entered after this consultation, wherein is a clause that they cite former Consultations; which is a plain indication that some of our people had the penning of that letter; and though they quote is as a precedent for us, it is a sign they do not understand it, we having acted in this matter exactly according to that clause.

"From Dellaway Donne Paulo Chitty, etc., of the Right Hand Caste, of the four corners and fifty six countries of the world, to the Hon'ble Thomas Pitt, Esq. and Council.

"From the first foundation of Madras it was never known that the Left Hand Caste should be adhered to by wrongly informing your Honours to the prejudice of the Right Hand Caste; upon whose assertions you have erected Stones in our streets, and given the same from us; concerning which an address was made to your Honours by way of Petition, upon perusal whereof you directed that your Petitioners were at liberty to stay or go where they pleased, which you repeated three times. Accordingly they came to St. Thomé, from whom they wrote your Honours; and we hearing the matters are come hither.

"From the beginning of the world it was never before known that the Left Hand in the fifty six countries thereof, ever erected a Stone in the Right Hand Street, nor was it ever allowed by any Government.

"One of your predecessors with Timmia and Verona did appoint certain streets for the Left Hand Caste, and directed how they should act, as upon your Consultation does appear; upon examination whereof advantage would accrue to the Company, which you have hitherto omitted to do.

"From your first settlement justice and equity have been distributed with an equal hand in your place; which has occasioned many to resort to you, and to increase in wealth under your protection; but upon this occasion of erecting Stones we must have recourse to the customs of the country; this we write to a charitable people who we know will observe the same.

St. Thomé, September 9th, 1707.

"Sunday, 14th. The Armenians, Persians, and Patans, perceiving that the Governor and Council was not fairly dealt with in this dispute between the Castes; and that the persons who are employed and confided in to accommodate it, are of the Right Hand Caste, all of whom had been either active or passive in raising this difference; and knowing we had no other, they came in a body of fifty or sixty, and tendered their service. When the Governor summoned what of the Council were to be found, and we accepted of their service and mediation; who promised to-morrow to go some of them to St. Thomé, to which place the Right Hand Caste have retired and sent for several of their heads out of the country, who are come to them; and they promised to take with them Narrain our Brahmin and Moolla, when they will demand of them the reason of their desertion, and accommodate matters as well as they can, and as soon as possible.

"Monday, 15th. The Governor with the Secretary being writing a General Letter to the Company in the Consultation Room, there came a Gusbardar, or messenger, to him from St. Thomé, who was sent by the Nabob to turn out the old Governor there, and put in a new one. He had been here two or three times before, and seemed to be concerned at the troubles we had about the Castes; which he said were frequent in the country, and sometimes grew to such a pitch that the Government found a great deal of trouble and difficulty to quell them; and he said that, by some discourse he had had with them, he found them very impudent and saucy; and that the source of our troubles was not from them in St. Thomé, but from our own inhabitants that remained in town, who not only gave them directions, but also sent them their subsistence. He also added, saying to the Governor, you are likewise betrayed by some people that sits with you at this Table. So asking him by the Linguist what he meant, he answered that yesterday, talking with three or four of the heads of Castes, they told him that the Second of

Council (Mr. Fraser) was of their side; and that without he was restored to his employ they would not return on any terms; but if he would come they would meet him anywhere, and return with him without insisting on any pardon; for that they were assured he was their friend, and that he never consented to what the Governor and Council had done in favour of the Left Hand Caste, and that he was against putting up the Stones; which belief in them had gained him such a reputation amongst the mob, that they went up and down the streets in his hearing, crying out "Chinna Captain," "Chinna Captain," which implies in their language the Second. On which the Governor asked him (the Gusbardar) whether he had heard such discourse more than once from the heads of the Caste. He answered three or four times, and the mob crying out as before mentioned. Upon which the Governor told him that in the evening there would be several of his people there to talk to them, when we desired him to aver what he was told before by the heads of the Castes; to which he readily answered he would. This man seemed to be a very sober judicious person, a stranger in these parts of the country, and could have no manner of interest in saying what he did. There was present at this discourse the Secretary whom the Governor ordered to take Minutes; and for Linguist was present the Moolla Narrain, and Paupilia Brahmin; who all averred that whereas they had been several times to St. Thomé about this business, they had often heard the mob cry out for the Chinna Captain.

"Tuesday, 16th. The Governor summoned this Council, when he reported to them what discourse he had with the Gusbardar, as entered in a diary note of yesterday, in the presence of the Secretary, Moolla, Narrain, and Paupilia Brahmin, who all confessed the same. The three latter now acquainted us that yesterday in the afternoon they accompanied several of the Persians and Armenians to St. Thomé, in order to accommodate this difference between the Castes; who were stopped by the mob at the Gate, whilst they sent in word to their heads for admittance; where they continued near two hours, and no answer but several affronts; and whilst there heard the mob cry out, as the Gusbardar told us, for the Chinna Captain, and who asked Narrain and several of our people why he did not come, for nothing could be done towards their return without him. The heads of the Right Hand Caste at St. Thomé wrote several letters to those of their Caste remaining here (at Madras); threatening their lives and being turned out of their Caste, if they did not come to them. This much intimidated the poor people, but those of any substance little regarded it, since that we kept so good guards to defend them from the threats; and what is to be observed and generally believed that all the people who have left us are not worth five thousand Pagodas. Narrain likewise acquainted us that all the heads of the Right Hand Caste remaining in town, met last night and wrote a letter to our inhabitants of their Caste in St. Thomé; the purport of which was to let them know they were satisfied in all matters relating to their Caste; and therefore whatever ill consequenees attend further disputes, they cleared themselves of it and laid it wholly at their doors. The messenger that earried the letter just now arriving was brought in before us, who acquainted us that they at St. Thomé had returned no answer to their Caste in writing, but bid him tell them that they would aecept no Cowle than what was signed by Mr. Fraser, and that the Stones must be brought to St. Thomé or put into the Pagoda. We were also at this time speaking of a report that had run about town for two or three days, that the Castes were rose one against the other at Fort St. David, where several had been killed, amongst which four or five of our soldiers and an officer mortally wounded. The Governor said he believed it not, though he had heard of it. Mr. Frederick said he had heard it from several, but being also told it by his dubash, who said he had it told him from Mr. Fraser's dubash, who was sent for, when denied it. But the other eonfronting him with naming the time and plaee, where and when he had told it him, eaused the Governor to give credit to it, and punished him immediately for spreading false reports. This was done to encourage the Right Hand Caste, and doubtless by order of his master, or some of his aecomplices; whose ehief dubash one Fango, a crafty profligate villain, is actually now at St. Thomé, holding with the Right Hand Caste in all their eounsels. So hearing all before mentioned in this day's eonsultation, and what passed yesterday with the Gusbardar, rivets in us a belief that the

Right Hand Caste has got Mr. Fraser among them for their tool, or they durst not have adventured to have done what they have. So considering that if this quarrel between them increases, it will be an unspeakable prejudice to the Company, and effectual ruin to the place; and to agree to their insolent and saucy demands may in futurity be attended with the like ill consequences:—to prevent all which it is agreed to send for Mr. Fraser, when the Governor charged him with what before mentioned, and telling him, from which we are sufficiently confirmed, that he was at the head of this vile and base action, which occasioned the dispute between the Castes, that no less than threatened the destruction of the place. To which he answered that it was all a grand suppose, and flatly denied all. So being ordered to withdraw we considered of the whole matter; when it was unanimously agreed that Mr. Fraser, who is now removing out his lodgings in the Fort to a house in the town, that he be continued therein and confined, without permitting any one to come to discourse him, but in the presence of the sentinel. The Captain of the Guard was sent for, to whom the Governor gave a charge accordingly."

"Tuesday, 23rd. The Governor and Council having granted a pardon to the Right Hand Caste (now at St. Thomé) being at the request of several Persians and Armenians, who desired that Doctor Lewis and Padre Michael may go with them to deliver the pardon and accompany them in their return. Accordingly the refractory members of the Right Hand Caste came out of St. Thomé all together about nine this morning. But when they came near the town, they took disgust at something or other, the certainty unknown to us, and returned again to St. Thomé; the Pariahs surrounded the inhabitants and forced them to go with them. So Narrain, being in hopes of giving them satisfaction, went with them, who they abused in several respects and confined; but was the next day discharged upon a threatening letter from the Governor that he would fetch him by force."

The pardon which had proved so nearly successful in bringing the Right Hand Caste from St. Thomé was as follows.

"A Cowle granted by Thomas Pitt, Esq., Governor of Fort St. George, and Council to the Right Hand Caste.

"Whereas you deserted us by reason of our giving your streets to the Left Hand Caste, which we have again returned to you; and whereas you say we have given a writing to them on that account or any other, we say it is forged and false, if any such one be produced. Therefore you may depend upon this Cowle, and return to your duty, and enjoy your ancient privileges according to salabad; giving this before the Great God above and Jesus Christ that we will righteously perform, and that none shall be punished on this account hereafter. Given under our hands and the Hon'ble Company's seal in Fort St. George, this 22nd of September, 1707."

The failure of this pardon seems to have driven Governor Pitt frantic, if we may judge from the following extraordinary resolution, which he arrived at the following day.

"Wednesday, 24th. We finding no likelihood of putting an end to these troubles between the Castes, for that the insolency of the Pariahs daily increases, a particular instance of which we had yesterday by their forcing the inhabitants to return, and imprisoning and abusing Narrain. The Governor proposed the attacking of St. Thomé the 26th at break of day (where they are harboured) and put as many of them as possible to the sword, but no inhabitant of any Caste else; which was unanimously agreed to in Council, and preparations immediately made accordingly; resolving to march two hundred and fifty soldiers, two hundred talliars, and two hundred peons, as also eighteen hundred peons which the Left Hand Caste have raised since the troubles for their security; and the Governor disposed matters to effect the same.

"Thursday, 25th. The preparations being made for attacking our Pariahs in St. Thomé to-morrow morning, which alarmed several inhabitants, more especially Armenians, Moors, etc. who nightly importuned us to desist; for that many ill consequences would attend it, and that they were sure we could not effect our ends in cutting off the Pariahs, who would certainly fly into the country; besides our Pedda Naik who pressed us to desist from our intended enterprise; saying that the new Governor of St. Thomé would be there to night, with whom he was well acquainted, and could prevail with him to turn them out of the town, or else he would be obliged to bring the Governor twenty or thirty of their heads. So considering the numerous importunities, we deferred our design two or three days to see whether milder means would oblige their return.

"Wednesday, 1st October. The Governor acquainted the Council that he observes the new Governor of St. Thomé is weary of our mob, and seems to endeavour what he can to persuade them to return. Yesterday our people going in hopes to have brought them back, they then insisted upon signing a paper amongst themselves, and that those we sent should join them; which they refused, telling them they could not do it without the Governor's leave; the purport of which paper is that they may have leave to rebel when they please; the translate of it is as follows.

"All the inhabitants of the Right Hand Caste of Chinnapatam have entered into an agreement in the presence of the Right Hand Caste of the country, viz.

"Whereas the Left Hand Caste have broke the sallabad by erecting Stones in our streets, upon which we deserted the place, and are come hither; since which the Governor and Council have taken away the Stones, and given us their Cowle that all shall be settled and go according to sallabad, which we will unanimously endeavour to maintain; and notwithstanding, should the Governor act contrary to his Cowle, or that the Left Hand Caste should take upon them more than their duty, we jointly agree to stand by one another for the saving our credit; and whoever of us act contrary to which herein mentioned shall be turned out of the Caste, and the iniquities shall light upon them as befalls such who sacrifices a cow, woman Brahmin, and their mother before the River Ganges. Dated October 1st, 1707."

" So upon our shewing a detestation and abhorrence to give leave to their signing such a paper, it was laid aside; and, as the Governor is credibly informed, that that paper, as well as others we have received during these troubles from the Right Hand Caste, were drawn up and framed by that notorious miscreant Timapa, a fellow adapted to all manner of villany, and always a great favourite and privy counsellor of Mr. Fraser, and a companion of his chief dubash."

" The heads of the Castes and mob which deserted us, having accepted of our pardon the 22nd last month, and still every day starting new demands, and refuse to return, we unanimously agreed this day to send to them our Moolla and Brahmin, to demand of them their final answer, whether they would return upon our pardon or not, and if not to demand it of them.

" Thursday, 2nd. The Moolla and Brahmin returning last night from St. Thomé, acquainted us that according to our order they had demanded our pardon given our inhabitants that are fled there; who have refused to return it, promising that they would come back to-day, but that it was not a good day; but to-morrow or next day they would not fail, if those of their Caste here came to meet them. At last, as will be seen by the following entry, the refractory Right Hands were induced to return.

" Saturday, 4th. This evening about seven o'clock the Governor of St. Thomé, being a Gentoo and of the same Caste that deserted us, came with our people that went hence this morning, and brought back all the deserters. The heads appeared before the Governor and were dismissed to their habitations, with assurances that their pardon should be kept inviolable.

"Monday, 6th. Muttombee, the Governor of St. Thomé, having to all appearance taken a great deal of pains to effect the returning of those that deserted;—it is therefore agreed that the following present be made him; the amount of which, in a seasonable time, to be paid the Company by the Right Hand Caste.

"Scarlet 1 piece... Aurora, 1 piece... Ordinary Red, 1 piece.
Green 1 piece... Looking Glasses... Swords 4.
1 Pair Pistols..... 6 Pair Spectacles. Knives and penknives.
1 piece of Serge.

"The deserters or rebels returning the 4th at night, who for some time refused to accept our pardon, or any proposals but what should be made by Mr. Fraser; for which reasons therein he was confined; after which they never so much as mentioned his name, so that none can believe but that they moved by his direction; but being returned again, agreed that his confinement be taken off, and he set at liberty; when the Captain of the Guard was sent for, and the Governor acquainted him therewith."

A fortnight's quiet passed away, and the storm having subsided, we find the following entries.

"Monday, 20th. The Washermen that deserted upon the late dispute between their Castes, who on their return freely declared that they were forced away by the heads of their Caste, who had combined with the Belljawarr; besides they complained of great injustices that they had received from the heads of their Caste, and desired they may have other four heads; and they would not only pay what the Washers pay, but also sign a paper that they would not desert again on any pretence whatever. Upon which they presented four heads of their own choosing, which we approved of and tasherift them when the whole body signed the paper as agreed on.

"Tuesday, 21st. The officer at Bridge Gate bringing in this morning to the Governor a Cajan letter that he found hung upon a post near the Gate, which when translated seemed to be from a body of the Right Hand Caste; the purport of which was to disown the villany which had been done in the name of their Caste, and charging the contrivers of it to be Narrain, Serapa, Timapa, Sunka Rama, and Andee Chitty; upon which we sent for the five persons before mentioned, to whom our Brahmin read the letter, which as we expected they disowned knowing anything of it. So we agreed that they five should go to the Pagoda with our Brahmin, and there send for the heads of all their Castes, to whom they should read the letter, and find out if possible the truth and author of it. But in the evening the five persons with the Brahmin returned, and acquainted the Governor that they had all been at the Pagoda, where the letter was read to their Caste, who disowned they knew anything of it.

"Wednesday, 22nd. This morning was brought in four papers that were fixed on the outside of the bastions of the inward Fort; the purport of which being full of the most opprobious language against the Governor; charging him to be the author of the Cajan letter read yesterday. The authors of which are doubtless the five persons, Narrain, etc., who we in our consciences believe were the sole contrivers of the late rebellion, and are not a little nettled in fearing that that villany will in a little time be proved upon them.

"Thursday, 30th. The Governor produces a paper in the Gentoo language signed by President Baker, Agent Greenhill, and Mr. Gurney, dated in the year 1652,* for composing differences amongst the Right and Left Hand Castes; which he had from the latter, and doubtless the other had the same; by which it appears that the Governor and Council now acted as they did then; the translate of which is as follows.

"In Fort St. George belonging to the Right Honorable English Company, before the Honorable President Baker, agent Greenhill, and Mr. Gurney, were present Connaree Chitty, and Sheshadree Naik, inhabitants of Chinnapatam. There having of late been several differences and disputes between the Castes about their streets, which this day is settled; and in case it be not observed by each Caste in regard to their Weddings and Burials, the first breaker of it shall forfeit a thousand dollars.

* This reference is worthy of especial notice. It refers to a period within thirteen years of the foundation of Fort St. George, and of which no records are preserved in the Madras Record Office. The earliest record in Madras bears date 1670.

"The Right Hand Castes are to reside in the particular streets appointed for them, where are to live or come none of the Left Hand Caste; and the same with the Left Hand Caste, where are to be none of the Right Hand Caste.

"The Great street from before the Fort as far as Taggapa Chitty's Garden, and all the streets to the westward of that street, are allotted to the Right Hand Caste; and the Great street from Mr. Porter's reaching to Malley Carjun's old Pagoda, with the New street (being two streets) are allotted to the Left Hand Caste.

"The Market street opposite to the Choultry as far as the Committee's shops, is appointed to the Right Hand Caste; and as far as the Chitties shops in the same street to the Left Hand Caste; where either Caste may pass with their Weddings or Burials; and if either of the Castes act contrary to this Agreement shall pay one thousand dollars.

"The Pattnawars and Carialwars are to pass with their Weddings and Burials from the back side of Mr. Porter's house to the middle of the Quarter Porter's house, and so to proceed to the Portuguese Church; they may likewise go through the Great street.

"Before the Fort is free for all.

"Sheshadree Chitty is mediator to each Caste. His servants, nor the Company's servants and painters, cannot pass these streets. Dated November 5th, 1652.

"Signed by

Aaron Baker.	Cannaree Chetty.
Henry Greenhill.	Sheshadree Naik."
William Gurney.	

We have thus reproduced in full the more interesting papers connected with this remarkable dispute between the Right and Left Hands. There are however other entries, far too lengthy to be extracted here, from which we gather that the dispute was aggravated by other circumstances, which were not permitted to rise to the surface. In the first instance there had undoubtedly been a fierce quarrel between the two Hands about the streets in which each Hand might celebrate its Weddings and Burials. But about this time a commercial rivalry arose. The Merchants belonging to the Right Hand had generally purchased the Company's goods exported from England; but now the Merchants of the Left Hand contrived to outbid them. As the Right Hand was said to be favoured by Mr. Fraser, so the Left Hand was evidently favoured by Governor Pitt. The virulence of the hatred between Governor Pitt and Mr. Fraser seems to imply something more than a mere difference of opinion as regards the mode of mediating between the two Hands. That Mr. Fraser was the champion of the Right Hand is sufficiently proved by what has gone before. That Governor Pitt was the champion of the Left Hand seems also proved by a Petition presented by the Left Hand after the return of their enemies to Madras. We are sorry that this Petition should be far too long to be reproduced in these columns; but a careful perusal of it has strongly impressed us with the idea that though it may have been presented by he Left Hand it was originally from the pen of Mr. Pitt. It recapitulates at very great length the whole history of the disputes, and employs exactly the language and style which Mr. Pitt would himself have used to clear himself before the Court of Directors; and it contains a petition that the Left Hand might be permitted to leave Madras peaceably at the end of six months, and seek for employment elsewhere; and that a notice of their intention of doing so might be made public, so that they might have the opportunity of paying up every debt they owed before leaving the town!

In December matters were restored to tranquillity; and during the following year a final arrangement was made between the two Hands for removing into separate streets. But the quarrel between Governor Pitt and Mr. Fraser continued to be as virulent as ever. Mr. Pitt drew up eight charges against the latter, with which however the reader is generally acquainted; but we make the following extract for the sake of its style. "That it is well known by most upon the place, as also by what appears upon the Consultation Books, that he (Mr. Fraser) has ever been found a person of a factious and turbulent temper; and though weak in contriving, yet industrious in promoting mischief and confusion; of a capacity unfit for any business or advice; impatient of peace, and only pleased when factions run high; wherein he has always made one to the great prejudice of the Company's affairs; during the time of our present Governor always herding and siding with such persons as are under the frowns of the Government let their crimes be ever so black; and at the beginning of these troubles it was observed he was very intimate with his old acquaintance Timapa, a profligate and wicked wretch, but a bird of the same feather, notorious for mischief, and one of the chief contrivers of the rebellion."

Mr. Fraser was promised a copy of the whole of the charges, but notwithstanding his repeated applications, he could not get one till just before the ships were about to sail for England, and then it was only signed by the Chief Secretary. Accordingly he wrote a short protest couched in tolerably decent terms, but which led to the following entry in the Consultation Book.

"Saturday, 6th December. Fraser this morning sending an impudent and saucy paper to the Governor and Council, it was agreed that it should be delivered to the Marshall to be burned under Gallows, which was accordiugly done."

In our last chapter we recorded the opinion of the Court of Directors upon the conduct of Mr. Fraser; and we here extract from the same General Letter, a copy of their judgment upon the quarrel between the two Hands. After some remarks on the investments, the Court wrote as follows:

"This naturally leads us to the many and long paragraphs in your letters relating to the differences between the Right and Left Hand Castes; because the heads of them are the men by whom you make your investments; and without entering into a particular detail of the matter, we say in general, that the generality of men in all countries are naturally disposed to be at ease and live peaceably, if they have a quiet possession of liberty and property; and the most turbulent spirits will in a good measure lie still unless they have a specious handle given them on account of hardships done or offered to be done them. Nor does it appear probable to us that either of the two Castes would have ventured to fly in the face of Government, which is or should be power, without a real or apprehended great provocation; nor can we think that the Right Hand Caste would have carried things to that extremity on the single quarrel of the Left Hand Caste making a wedding in their own streets. It seems to us that the seeds of discord lay deeper, and that things growing ripe for a rupture, this handle was taken to begin the quarrel and set fire to the fuel that was before preparing for it. We should have esteemed it a praiseworthy management in our President and Council to have foreseen and prevented this mutinous disposition before it broke out, or at least to have quenched it when it first began to flame.

"Nothing more does better bespeak the ability and diligence of Governors than keeping their subjects and dependents in quiet; and they can never do that without an impartial administration of justice to all under them; for whether they themselves, or others by their authority or connivance, oppress or injure the subject, it comes to all one in the upshot; that is to say, first the people secretly murmur and complain, then they break out into more open reproaches, and at last into down right mutinies and rebellions ; and this seems to us to be the true reason why those scurrilous papers were fastened upon the Stones set up, and afterwards on the walls of the town ; whereas the Wise Man's remark will be found to be eternally true, "That the Throne can only be established in righteousness."

"It was very surprising to us to read that so many of the handicrafts, and other useful hands, went away on this quarrel ; and gave us but ordinary apprehensions of the conduct of the then administration. Surely they were too valuable to be parted with without the last extremity. All nations and times have agreed in this, that useful people are the riches as well as the strength of a city or country ; and although we readily agree that neither the one or the other Caste are over honest, or will scruple laying hold of any handle for their own benefit ; yet it seems plain to us there must be something more than ordinary at the bottom, that should make the Right Hand Castes go away in general in a body, and the heads of them consent to be at the charge of maintaining the handicrafts people at St. Thomé.

"On the whole matter we heartily recopmmen to you all to endeavour in your stations to reventd such like quarrels in future ; and to that ned to take care the established ancient privileges of both Castes be preserved to them, and the like to all other the inhabitants ; and that all of them have the free possession of their liberty and property ; that justice be administered equally and impartially, and no real cause given of discontent; and then if you find any makebates that would be putting the people in a ferment, make them public examples as their faults deserve, and remember in such cases "too much pity spoils a city."

CHAPTER XXII.

GOVERNORSHIP OF MR. THOMAS PITT.

1708—9.

The Governorship of Mr. Pitt, which extended over the unusually long period of eleven years, was suddenly brought to a close in 1709. The later years of his government are distinguished by events which emphatically belong to the history of the British rule in India. Hitherto the English Governors had only carried on their communications with the Nabobs in their neighbourhood, but circumstances now brought them into more immediate communication with the Great Mogul. During the later years of the reign of Aurungzebe the Governor of Madras had been brought into communication with the Grand Vizier Assad Khan, and with his son Zulfikar Khan. After the death of Aurungzebe, circumstances, as we shall presently see, brought Mr. Pitt into direct communication with the new Emperor himself, Shah Aulum, known in Mahomedan history under the title of Bahadur Shah.

Before however noticing these events, we lay before our readers the following extracts illustrative of the internal state of Madras. The first is a copy of agreement between the Right and Left Hand Castes, dated 14th January, 1708, which appears to have settled for awhile the dispute between the two.

"Whereas there has lately been differences in the Streets between both parties occasioned by a wedding going in procession in the Pedda Naik's Pettah; and it being brought before your Honour, who ordered us to chose out twelve Heads of each Caste to meet in the Gentoo Pagoda, and make matters up, and then report what done to your Honour. (Names of the twelve Heads of each Caste omitted). These twenty-four agreed and confirmed as follows.

"The Left Hand Caste co-habiting in several streets that belong to the Right Hand in the Pedda Naik's Pettah, so that they cannot safely make their weddings; therefore from this day all the Left Hand that live in the Pedda Naik's Pettah, shall have the following streets to live and make their weddings, viz. Eastward of Eccombre Sheraloo Pagoda, as you go in the back side corner street of Vencata Narnapa's stone Choultry, and go from that place along the Southward Street as far as the well before Gulla Annitches house, where besides the South Street there is another North Street as you come from Brahmin Appelia's Garden which joins to the Well; and from the well westward as far as Dubash Ruggana's house; thence as you go northward of Nautowary Pillary Pagoda as far as Mr. Empson's Garden; in which streets the Left Hand Castes shall live and make their weddings. But if the aforesaid streets are not enough to hold them all, some of those houses that lie to the westward which belong to the Right Hand, we will supply them with; and in case those are not enough too, we will find some houses out either of the east, north, or south; and Eccombre Sheraloo's Pagoda, and Vencata Narnapa's Choultry, shall belong to both Castes. And the Left Hand shall carry their dead towards the westward of Bangana Rama's Garden Street. Those of the Right Hand that were living in the abovesaid streets shall now change with the Left Hand that did inhabit the Right Hand street, and henceforward live there. Both parties having thus agreed, we shall keep our Customs and weddings in our own streets. The Left Hand shall not buy those gardens to the westward of the street that fronts Mr. Empson's garden, without the owner's consent, nor shall the Right Hand build any houses there. If any of the Castes act contrary to this agreement, shall be fined twelve thousand Pagodas to the Hon'ble Company, and receive punishment according to the custom of their Caste. To this we both agree and confirm. All the eastward from Nautowarry Pillary Pagoda shall belong to the Right Hand: all the westward to the Left Hand."*

The following curious account of the knaveries of the Madras boatmen, and the strong measures taken in consequence, will be found very illustrative of the character of the times.

"Tuesday, 20th. The Governor this morning summoned this Council to acquaint them, that just then the Pedda Naik informed him that he discovered a villainy in the Boatmen, in opening the Company's bales sent on board the Duchess; which he hearing of in the night immediately secured the head Boatmen and two Peons, at the watching places by the sea side, on whom he found two pieces of middling longcloth. The Governor immediately sent for the Conicopoly of the Godown to enquire what peons were sent off in the boats, that day they loaded fifteen boats; which to his great surprise he told him no Peons at all; though often at the Council Board he ordered that no goods of the Company's should go off or come

* This agreement was recapitulated and confirmed on the 23rd June, 1708.

ashore without Peons in the boats; and the same he had often ordered the Conicopoly when with him, and twice or thrice thrashed him himself when that he found he neglected it.*

"The Chief of the boatmen were before us when the Pedda Naik charged them with the knowledge of this villainy, and brought one of their servants to their face to prove it; who did not only do that, but sent some of his people with their servant to one of the Chief's houses, and found four pieces of Bettelees buried underground. Upon which orders were given to apprehend all the Boatmen that were ashore, and those that were gone off in boats when they returned; and as soon as the Governor was informed of it, and knowing four boats were gone off this morning with bales, he sent for Captain Raymond, whom he desired to write to his Mate to search the four boats as soon as come on board, to see whether they had not played the same tricks with those bales. When some of those boats off returned near the surf, their associates in this villany made them some private sign, so that they returned again as far as the Paddy boats, and there consulted one another; from which we apprehended they would run away to the northward or southward. So presently sent two boats with the Vizagapatam boatmen with soldiers to prevent it; which as soon as they discovered, ten boats run away

* We wonder what would be said now if a Governor of Madras gravely recorded in the Consultation Book, that he had more than once thrashed a Conicopoly with his own hand for neglect of duty.

to the southward; upon which the Governor ordered the Gunner to fire shot from the Battery and sink them if possible; several of which fell very near, but had not the good luck to do execution†; and the ship observing it sent their Pinnace, who cut off the flight of four and brought them back, but the other six got to St. Thomé, whither the Government sent Peons with our Brahmin to secure them as they came ashore and bring them hitherto; which, if the Governor refused, to charge them with them; both which they (the St. Thomé authorities) refused; upon which it was thought fit to fetch them with a Company of soldiers; but upon consideration, we then heard the Nabob was at Conjeveram and expected every day at St. Thomé, we desisted, believing the consequence would be embroiling the Company's affairs for the present. Upon which it was agreed to write the Nabob a letter, and another to the Governor of St. Thomé, who is now at Poonamallee; and if we have not immediate redress, then to apply ourselves to other courses to procure it.

"Wednesday, 21st. This morning the Governor severely punished all the sea side Peons, and we ordered the two Peons that were taken with the pieces of cloth to be whipped round the town, and to-morrow morning to be put in the Pillory with ears nailed thereto, and at twelve o'clock at noon to be cut off.

"Though we are apprehensive that these vil-

† From this and other allusions, Governor Pitt does not seem to have been very fond of the natives.

lains have stole out of the bales on board the Duchess to a great amount, and that we cannot come at the certainty without unloading the ship, which will not only augment the demurrage, but lose so much time as may endanger her passage. Upon which consideration we have resolved to dispatch the ship, and to take an obligation from the Warehouse and Sea gate Concopolies, sea side Peons, and Boatmen, to pay what shall be found wanting when opened in the Company's Warehouses in England."

The following little piece of horsedealing on the part of Governor Pitt, appears to be rather a doubtful transaction. The Nabob was at this time at St. Thomé.

"Tuesday, 16th February. The Nabob being very pressing for a Persia horse of the Governor's for which he has been often offered 450 Pagodas; but the Nabob being willing to give no more than 400, it is agreed the Company allows the 50 Pagodas."

Mr. Pitt's quarrels were about this time very much on the increase. Mr. Frederick, member of Council, incurred his wrath, from the following circumstance. Captain Seaton had been cashiered for marching his troops over some cloths. Mr. Pitt subsequently nominated a Mr. Roach to the vacant commission. Mr. Frederick, who had married a daughter-in-law of Captain Seaton, objected to the appointment on the ground that Mr. Roach had been in France without leave, and was subject to certain penalties. Thereupon Mr. Pitt made a rather warm entry in the consultation book, in which he upheld the character of Mr. Roach, and thus commented on the objection of Mr. Frederick. "We cannot but think it a severe reflection on us, the Governor and Council here, that we should not be thought by Mr. Frederick to be better judges of those matters than himself; and that he should be the only person amongst us that is fit to judge of men and their capacity, when it is notoriously known by all in this place, that profound ignorance and pride are his only qualifications."

We have now to narrate the progress of events which brought Mr. Pitt into more immediate communication with the Great Mogul. Aurungzebe expired in the camp at Ahmednuggar on the 21st of February, 1707. He left behind him three sons, viz. Moazzim, better known as Shah Aulum, who was Governor of Cabul; Azim Shah, who was Subahdar of Guzerat; and Kam Buksh, who was Governor of Bijapoor. By his will he recommended that Shah Aulum should be recognised as Emperor, but that he and Azim Shah should divide the empire; Shah Aulum taking the northern and eastern provinces, with Delhi for his capital; and Azim Shah taking all the country to the south and south-west, including all the Dekkan excepting Golconda and Bijapoor. These last mentioned kingdoms were assigned to Kam Buksh.

The decease of Aurungzebe was followed by a war between his sons. The moment the second son Azim Shah heard the news of his father's death, he had hurried to the camp at Ahmednuggar, and was immediately proclaimed Emperor of all India in perfect disregard to the will of Aurungzebe. Meantime Shah Aulum had assumed the imperial crown at Cabul. Azim Shah marched against him, and a bloody battle ensued in the neighbourhood of Agra, in which Azim was slain.*

Shah Aulum was now joined by Zulfikar Khan, and Assad Khan; both of whom, as we have seen, are frequently mentioned in the records connected with the later years of Aurungzebe; Zulfikar Khan as commander-in-chief of the army against the Mahrattas, and as predecessor of Dawood Khan in the Nabobship of the Carnatic; and Assad Khan, as father of Zulfikar Khan, and Grand Vizier of Aurungzebe. Another contest still remained. Kam Buksh was not contented with Golconda and Bijapoor, but aspired after the imperial throne. Shah Aulum attempted to win him over by concessions but in vain. At last Shah Aulum marched an army into the Dekkan to oppose him. After a considerable delay a battle took place near Hyderabad in February, 1709,† at which Kam Buksh was mortally wounded.

In 1708, when Shah Aulum was anticipating a conflict with his younger brother Kam Buksh in the

---

* Elphinstone dates this battle in June 1707.

† Elphinstone says the battle took place in February 1708, but it must have taken place in January 1709, or rather in January 1708-9. The exact date we are enabled to give from the records. It is very probable that the previous date of the defeat of Azim Shah, is fixed a year too early; and indeed Mr. Elphinstone appears from the records to have confounded the old and new styles. In the present publication we have invariably given the new style for the sake of clearness.

Dekkan, the Steward of his household dispatched a letter to the Governor of Fort St. George, "professing great kindness and tendering his service in any affair." The reason for this advance is obvious. Kam Buksh was then in command of the Dekkan, and the continued allegiance of the English might prove of importance to Shah Aulum. Governor Pitt determined to take every advantage of the crisis to secure a better understanding with the Mogul's Government. Accordingly he wrote an answer to the Royal Steward, requesting that Shah Aulum would be pleased to confirm the privileges granted the English by his father Aurungzebe. The progress of affairs can now be best explained by the following extracts from the Consultations.

"Saturday, 31st July, 1708. This evening at four o'clock the Governor summoned the Council, and most of the Company's servants, with the chiefest of the European inhabitants, to accompany him to the garden, where he was met by all the Armenians, Persians, Moguls, Patans, and Head Merchant Gentoo inhabitants of this place, there to receive a Husbulhookum from King Shah Aulum to the Government here, procured by Zoodee Khan, Lord High Steward of said King's household, which was received with all ceremonies usual on such an occasion, by firing of great guns, etc.

"Saturday, 7th August. The purport of the Husbulhookum from Shah Aulum seems to invite us to make our addresses to the King for a confirmation of our privileges; which opportunity we resolving to take hold of, believing we shall accomplish it for a much less to the Company, than if we defer it till the contests between the brothers are over; wherefore it is agreed that the Governor draws out a petition to the King, a letter to the Grand Vizier, and another to Zoodee Khan, and lay them before the Council for their advice therein.

"Zoodee Khan's Lady (by whose Husband's means the Husbulhookum was sent us) living still at St. Thomé, to whom it is agreed to send a present of Persia fruit, rosewater, etc. and some fillagree work of Manilla, with a piece of Persia cloth of gold, all to the value of 120 or 130 Pagodas, or thereabouts."

The Husbulhookum was said to be from Khan Khanan Bahadur the Grand Vizier; but the real Vizier at this time was Monaim Khan. Khan Khanan merely signifies "Khan of Khans."

"From Khan Khanan, Bahadur Zephir Jung, Grand Vizier.

"The Governor of Chinnapatanam may depend upon his Majesty's Royal Favour.

"The good and faithful services you have done his Majesty's subjects has been represented to him by some of his Chief Ministers of State, upon whose recommendation of your merits, a mark of his favour to you, he has ordered this Hosbulhookum to be sent you to certify the same; not doubting but your deportment will continue to be such as to increase in fame and reputation; and according as you observe this Husbulhookum you may expect further marks of his Majesty's grace and countenance. Dated June 1st. Received July 31st, 1708.

"Friday, 13th August. The Governor lays before the Council this day for their opinion and advice, a Petition he had drawn up to King Shah Aulum, a Letter to the Grand Vizier, a letter to Zulfikar Khan, and another to Zoodee Khan; which were all read, and agreed to be put in the Persian language, and to be dispatched with all expedition, that so they may arrive before the King comes to Golconda."

Petition to the King Shah Aulum.

"God grant the great King Shah Aulum may live for ever, is the hearty Prayers of the Governor of Chinnapatam, and of all the English Nation in your Majesty's Dominion, who have been here lately blessed with your Majesty's most Gracious and Royal Husbulhookum; and for your Majesty's commands therein, they shall always be kept as sacred as they were in the time of your Majesty's Royal Predecessors, who were pleased to bestow their Royal favours on us in granting us several Privileges to encourage us in our trade; for a confirmation of which we humbly Petition your Majesty to grant us your royal Firmaun, with what additional favours your Majesty in your Royal Wisdom shall think fit; which we shall not only record in our books but in our hearts also; and as in duty bound shall ever pray for your Majesty's long and prosperous reign, and that you may be always so victorious as to lay your feet on the neck of your enemies."

"To his Highness Khan Khanan, Bahawdee Zephir Jung Grand Vizier.

"Your Highnesses noble qualifications and

virtues being known to all the world, which increase by your daily giving instances of your justice and mercy, and particularly your favours and protection which you so liberally bestow on all strangers in your King's dominions; of which we here have a late instance in receiving the blessing of his Majesty's royal Hosbulhookum; which we must attribute to your Highness's favour and great care of us; for which we return our most humble thanks; and humbly request that as we now send our Petition to the great King Shah Aulum, humbly desiring his royal Firmaun for a confirmation of our privileges according to Sallabad throughout his dominions; that your Highness would be pleased to countenance and assist us in procuring the same; for which you shall not only find us grateful but dutiful; and shall always pray for your Highness's health and prosperity, and for ever to be blessed with the favour of your great king."

"To Zulfikar Khan, etc.

"The many obligations we lie under to your Highness are never to be forgotten, being rivetted in our memories as well as recorded in our books; which we should have often acknow ledged, but prevented by the great distance and troubles of the country; yet nevertheless we never failed to enquire after your Highness's health, which God continue.

"Your Highness is well acquainted with the privileges our nation enjoyed in the reign of the great Aurungzebe of blessed memory; which we are endeavouring to get confirmed by a royal Firmaun from the great King Shah

Aulum; that we and our trade may go on in all parts according to Sallabad; to effect which we humbly petition that your Highness will continue your constant favours to us in speaking in our behalves as an opportunity presents, for which we shall be always grateful, and pray for your Highness's health and prosperity."

"To his Excellency Zoodee Khan Lord High Steward of the King's Household.

"It is your noble and generous mind that have drawn this trouble of our application to you; and as I wrote you in my last Letter, which I delivered Aga Makeem, I now send our humble Petition to the King, and Address to the Grand Vizier; copies of which I here enclose to Your Excellency; humbly requesting that you will favour us with the management thereof.

"We are not ignorant of what should accompany such Petitions and Addresses; but the hazards and troubles in the way prevent us from performing that part at present; in which I humbly desire your Excellency's advice and direction as to what would be acceptable to his Majesty, the Grand Vizier, and such others where you think it is necessary; and we shall endeavour to procure it if possible.

"Your Excellency will see that we desire a Firmaun to confirm our privileges according to Sallabad in all his dominions; unless his Majesty shall, out of his Royal bounty, bestow some new favours on us. Your Excellency cannot but know that Miliapore (St. Thomé) is a troublesome neighbourhood to us, creating always disputes and quarrels, of little advantage to the king nor will it ever be more; which could we obtain, and the town of Trivatore on the other side of us, it would make us easy, and increase the riches of the king's country.

"And whereas the goods we import are generally carried to the capital cities of Golconda and Bijapoor, etc., which trade we should much increase if there was no custom paid upon them between this place and those cities; and that the Mettas about us, which of late years have been increased to the plague and ruin of trade, were laid aside; which only find employs for some little people, who destroy trade by their vexation and extortion, and in the main very much lessen the King's revenue.

"And we humbly desire that you would get it inserted in a Firmaun, that whenever we are so unfortunate as to lose any ship in any part of his Majesty's dominions, we shall have the liberty to preserve what we can of the wreck, without any molestation from the Government; which is not only practised throughout the world, but the inhabitants are generally commanded to assist therein. For it is a great hardship that, after the great risk that our people have run of their lives, they shall not be at liberty to save what they can of their estates. We must own with great thankfulness that this justice have been granted us by former purwannas from Khan Bahadur and the present Nabob; but as it has been formerly disputed it may again, which nothing but the King's gracious grant can prevent.

"We extremely want the King's blessing and favours to give new life to our trade; for since your Excellency went hence this place has lost nearly three lakhs of Pagodas by misfortunes and most by pirates; so that it is become poor; and nothing can contribute to the retrieving our losses but God's blessing, the King's favour, and Your Excellency's continuance in assisting of us.

"Here are ships in a few days that will depart for Pegu, when we shall write the King what you advised in your former letter, that an Ambassador was coming to him. Khan Bahadur always showed himself a friend to our nation; whose favours we cannot but retain with great thankfulness; so have wrote him a letter which comes herewith, and a copy of it for your Excellency; we leave it to your pleasure whether it shall be delivered him.

"If please God we are so fortunate as to be blessed with the King's favour, as to obtain his Royal Firmaun, we humbly entreat Your Excellency to appoint some able person to see it so fully penned as that it may not admit of any dispute from Nabob's and Governors, where the same is to be executed. Our dependance is entirely on Your Excellency's friendship, for which we shall be always full of our acknowledgments, and heartily wish Your Excellency and all your family health and prosperity."

The following extracts will explain themselves.

"Thursday, 19th August. There having come some people belonging to Zoodee Khan, our great friend at the King's Court, to acquaint the Governor that his Lady at St. Thomé extremely wanted money for her charges; not being able to get bills upon her husband, nor could he remit any, by reason of the great troubles in the way; so desired of the Governor to lend 500 Pagodas for his account; who answered them that it was the Company's positive orders to lend none of their money to any people whatever; nor that their Governors nor any in their service should lend any money to any in the country Government, upon the penalty of being discarded their service; but considering our dependence to procure a Firmaun is upon the friendship of the aforesaid Lady's husband, the Government acquaints the Council that he promised to procure a merchant to lend that money, if Aga Makeem, a merchant of this place, would give his bond for it, which he had done for 500 Pagodas to be repaid in four months without interest; which bond being now produced, it was agreed that the 500 Pagodas be on the Company's account and repaid the Government out of the cash; being a thing absolutely necessary at this time, though not to be drawn into a precedent for the future."

The following entries are in the Consultations of the same day; and are worth preserving though they do not illustrate the current history.

"The Company having a sorrel Persian horse good for little, and there being some people about to buy him, it is agreed the Governor sells him for what he can get."

"We having lately more thefts and robberies committed in this city than usual, and finding they daily increase, to prevent which it is agreed that all persons as soon as convicted shall be punished by being whipt at a cart through all the streets in Black Town, and afterwards lie in prison till an opportunity presents to send them to the West Coast, where they are to be the Company's slaves for ninety-nine years; and this order to be published by setting it up on every Gate of the Black town.

"The Governor being advised from Pegu that a Conicopoly, one Ansapal, that went hence on one of the ships hither, had the impudence to counterfeit a letter to the king of that country, as if it came from the Governor here, and with it sent a present; for which he had an advantageous return in Elephants as usual; so to prevent the pernicious consequences which attend such vile practices, the Governor seized him as soon as he returned, and put him in prison, and intended to have punished him severely; but having been there a Factor for several Merchants of this place, to whom he had not yet rendered any account, and it is thought he never would if he is disgraced by a punishment; it is therefore agreed that he be fined for his crime 200 Pagodas, to be paid into the Company's cash, and give security he never more goes to Pegu."

In September this year, the Government of Fort St. George was informed that the Nabob was about to proceed to join the King Shah Aulum at Golconda, and accordingly a member of Council and the Secretary were sent to him with a present of about 200 Pagodas. In return the Nabob presented the Company with a Perwanna for the five following towns, the names of which are spelt as follows.

"Trivetore town itself.
Vasalawada under Perumbore.
Santunganda under Trivetore.
Lungumbaca (? Nungumbaukum) under Egmore.
Cutteewauca under Trivetore."

These Towns were valued at fifteen hundred Pagodas. Subsequently the King's Officers at St. Thomé raised a clamour against this present of the King's towns, and declared that their real value was as much as three thousand Pagodas; upon which the Nabob ordered the King's books to be searched, and the real value to be laid before him. From the following entry it will be seen that the dispute was hushed up in the Oriental fashion :— "It is agreed that our Moolla and Brahmin return again to St. Thomé with about two hundred Pagodas, which is ordered to be distributed amongst the King's Officers who keep the Records in order to settle this matter."

The next extract is also interesting.

"Saturday, 16th October. We having large experience that it is impossible for us to manage the income of villages, so as not to be imposed upon, and lose at least half the produce; to prevent which it is agreed this day to let or to rent the five villages, lately given the Company by the Nabob, for twelve years to Colloway and Vinketty Chetties, at 1200 Pagodas per annum, to commence from this day; who are obliged to repair all tanks belonging thereto, which have been let run to ruin, as customary, by those who have been lately the renters of them; and the Secretary is ordered to draw out a lease for them."

Towards the end of the year another Husbulhookum arrived from the King Shah Aulum, with answers penned in the usual oriental style from the Royal Officers to the letters sent them by Governor Pitt. It would be wearisome in the extreme to reproduce these compositions here. In return Governor Pitt engaged to forward the necessary presents to the King Shah Aulum and his principal Officers; and sent numerous fulsome letters to the various Ministers of State, all of which are recorded at full length in the Consultation. The following extracts from a letter to the Royal Steward will sufficiently illustrate the tone of the whole.

"To Zoodee Khan, Lord High Steward of the King Shah Aulum's household, January 5th, 1709.

"By your faithful Chobdar Cossae, by whom Your Excellency sent the Royal Husbulhookum, and Vest, and Purwannas, I now send this humble address, which doubtless you expected sooner, and had been sent but for the two following reasons. Your Excellency enjoining secresy, I was obliged to commit the translating of them to some particular friends, which took up fourteen days. When fully apprised of the purport thereof, I could not but be surprised at your unparalleled expressions of friendship and invaluable honours you have done us; which so confounded my thoughts for some days that I almost despaired of being able to acknowledge them by my pen or otherwise; but then considering what a generous friend I had met with, who had been so lavish of his favours to one who had as little power as merit to oblige you; I could no longer refrain from blessing my stars, who were so propitious to me as to give me the honour of your first acquaintance; which I esteem the happiest fate that has attended me through the whole course of my life; which I shall ever remember, and that posterity may do the same, I humbly request that when you come to Golconda you will honour me with sending me your picture; which I will send to England and have copied by the most exquisite limner in the world, and order it to be sent me hither; beside I will erect your effigy finely cut in marble, with such an inscription on it that the world may know the author of our happiness in these parts. . . . . . Your Excellency writes that there must be presents for all the princes and some of the great men. If you mean such as are suitable to their birth and quality, it is impossible for us to purchase them with our Company's estate; who you know are merchants who run great risk to get a little, and who often meet with loss instead of gain. We hope as the presents we intend are suitable to our circumstances, that they will meet with a gracious acceptance from the great king and princes; which puts us in mind of what we read in history that upon many persons making very rich presents to a king, there happened a poor man to come with a drop of water, which was acceptable as any of their presents, being according to his ability."

Shortly afterwards the following Firmaun arrived from King Shah Aulum, by which it will be seen distinctly that the conflict with Kam Buksh was the cause of such demonstrations of friendship.

"Let the chosen of his Caste and Nation, the Governor of Chinnapatam, know that he may be in hopes of the King's favour. Seeing that Kam Buksh doth purpose to fly from the powerful arms of our victorious army; for that reason the command of the sovereign of the world, worthy of all submission and obedience is due, is issued forth; that in case he, Kam Buksh, should come wandering, not knowing where to go, into those parts, and desire to embark himself on some ship in order to get away; that the chosen of his nation shall use his utmost endeavours to procure that he be either killed or made a prisoner; and to effect this let him know that the command from the Royal Throne is strict in the strictest manner. Written the 17th of the moon Ramazan the Blessed in the second year of the King's Reign."

In reply Governor Pitt's promised obedience in general terms, but on the 18th January, 1709, intelligence was brought to Madras that Shah Aulum had obtained a complete victory over his brother, and that Kam Buksh had died of the wounds he had received during the battle.

CHAPTER XXIII.

GOVERNORSHIPS OF PITT, ADDISON, MONTAGUE AND FRASER.

1709—10.

The period upon which we are now about to enter will be interesting to all who are fond of historical coincidences. The rapid succession of Governors, in the years 1709, 1710, and 1711, bears a curious resemblance to the similar changes which took place in 1859, 1860, and 1861 after the exact interval of a century and a half. Within two years Fort St. George saw five successive Governors, viz. Mr. Pitt, Mr. Addison, Mr. Montague, Mr. Fraser, and Mr. Harrison; and now within the last two years of our history we have seen the same event repeated in the rapid succession of Lord Harris, Sir Charles Trevelyan, Mr. Morehead, Sir Henry Ward, and Sir William Denison.

In the middle of the year 1709, Mr. Pitt's government was fast drawing to a close; but though it is apparent from the records that he had some suspicions of the probability of his being recalled, yet he evidently had no idea of the sudden way in which the recall would be carried out. Before however noticing this event, we make the following curious extracts which seem to have some reference to the great Pitt diamond to which allusion has already been made.

"Wednesday, 3rd August, 1709. The Governor this day acquainted the Council, that he having lately heard of some villainous and scandalous reflections that had been made upon him by the late Lieutenant Seaton, who he yesterday sent for from the Mount, and examined thereon; who with his usual impudence averred to him the most notorious falsities that ever could be thought or imagined. Upon which he (the Governor) said, he had confined him, Seaton, to the Ensign's room; and he desired that he might be sent for up, and examined thereto. Which accordingly was done, and when he came into the Consultation Room before us, without first hearing what the Governor had to charge him with, and the reasons of his confinement,—he immediately addressed himself to the Council, saying, "I am come here to accuse the Governor for buying a great diamond to the Company's prejudice." When the Governor answered and told him, "we would discourse of that by and by;" and demanded of him whether he had said, that he had received of Paupia to make him Chief Dubash, five hundred Pagodas; and that Ramapa offered seven hundred to be continued, which was refused. This he acknowledged to have said, but being commanded to prove the same, he answered he had it from a black fellow, but could not remember who he was. After which the two Dubashes before mentioned declared they never gave the Governor a Pagoda, or that ever he asked or hinted to them of any such thing; and to this they took the most solemnest oath in the Pagoda. Then the Governor demanded what he knew of his buying a diamond. He answered in general terms, that he knew every particular of it; when he was commanded to acquaint the Council with it, which he said he would then do, knowing that there would be a change of Government this month, and therefore for what this Governor said to him did not signify a farthing, with many such insolent and villainous expressions. He further said that to his knowledge the Governor was betrayed by all the Black servants about him; insomuch that he knew every thing that was done and said, nay as much as in his Counting house; and to give an instance thereof, said, that the great diamond he had bought was entered in his books folio 64. He further told us that one Rogers, who went hence in October last for Bombay, had carried papers along with him, signed by Black people, that would do the Governor's business; which Sir Nicholas Wait had got translated and carried home with him.

"The Governor also acquainted the Council that he had very good reason to suspect that this Seaton was turned Informer to the Government, and held a correspondence with them, and promised in a few days to prove the same; in expectation of which, and what the Governor charged him with, and he confessed before us,—we now unanimously confirm his confinement till other means can be considered of; and for what discourse passed between the Governor and him yesterday in the Consultation Room after his coming from the Mount, is as entered as follows, the truth of which we shall always be ready to justify by oath or otherwise."

Copy of what passed between the Governor and Lieutenant Seaton in the Consultation Room on the day before.

"This evening being the 2nd of August about five o'clock, I discoursed Captain Seaton in the Consultation Room, when charged him with his having said that I had 500 Pagodas given me to make Paupia Chief Dubash; which he owned, and he told me that I was betrayed in whatever I did or spoke by all my servants about me; and that I had not a friend upon the place, whatever I thought.

"Then I asked how he durst presume to talk up and down of what I bought or sold, and how it was possible for him to know anything of it; to which he answered that he had so good intelligence that there was not the least thing said or done by me, but that he knew; and to convince me desired leave to ask me some questions, which I permitted him to do and were as follows. "Whether Mr. Roberts did not write to me, requesting that he might be concerned in a great diamond I had bought?" Answered: "False." "Whether a person did not come and wish me joy of its being sold for 500,000 dollars?" False. "Whether two persons did not come from the Dekkan to demand a great diamond, and that I gave one of them at coming eleven rupees, and the other at going away, a hundred and fifty." All false, only that one man came. Upon which I told him that I found him (Seaton) a villain; and as I found him endeavouring to betray me, doubtless he would do the same to the Government; so ordered the Captain of the Guard to confine him to the Ensign's room, none to come to him but the Council.

"Thursday, 11th August. It is unanimously agreed that Lieutenant Seaton be confined till the first ship goes for England, and on her to be sent home a prisoner to the Company."

In the following month Governor Pitt was suddenly recalled, as will be seen by the following entry.

"Sunday, 18th September. Yesterday evening appeared a ship to the northward of this Port, and about nine at night came ashore Captain Tolson, who acquainted the Governor that he was commander of the Ship "Heathcote" come directly from England; and that he had brought the Company's packet which he produced directed as follows:—

"TO THE HON'BLE GULSTONE ADDISON, PRESIDENT, MESSRS. FRASER, MONTAGUE, MARTIN, RAWORTH, FREDERICK, HUNT, BULKLEY, AND JENNINGS, FORT ST. GEORGE."

And withal told him there was great alterations here, and that he was dismissed the service; therefore pressed that the Council might be immediately called. The Governor told him that it was impossible to be done, not only from the lateness of the night, but that several of them were at the Mount; so desired the Captain to strictly observe in what condition he delivered the packet, and be here to-morrow morning at eight o'clock, against when the Council should be summoned, that so he might see it in the like condition he delivered it. This morning accordingly all the late Council met, when the Governor refused to surrender the Government by virtue of the superscription on the packet, but demanded a supercedent to his Commission, by virtue of which he had been Governor of this place upwards of eleven years. So after some hesitation the packet was opened, wherein there was a Commission which superceded his. He also demanded the reading of the General Letter, which was refused him; but in the packet there being a Letter from the Managers to him, wherein it was fully expressed his dismission from their service, the constituting Gulstone Addison, Esquire in his room, so he immediately read the cash and tendered the balance thereof; but the new Governor desired the payment for that time be deferred, for that he was very much indisposed. So the Governor just as he left the Chair, challenged the whole Board, or any upon the place, to charge him with an unjust action during the whole time of his Government, or that he had ever refused a kindness to any one that asked it, and that it lay in his power; or that ever he acted arbitrary in any one matter, notwithstanding some villains of this place have had the impudence to represent him otherwise; so rose out of the chair and placed the new Governor in it."

The recall of Mr. Pitt, at the moment he had succeeded in establishing friendly relations between the Company and the court at Delhi, proved anything but advantageous to the English; and the Directors on more than one occasion had cause to regret their precipitancy, and quoted the government of Mr. Pitt as an example to his less politic and less energetic successors. The following extract from a general letter of this period will alone warrant this inference.

"We read with pleasure that when Messrs. Raworth and Davenport visited the Nabob at St. Thomé with a present of two hundred pagodas, he gave you for us the grants of five towns adjoining to ours, worth about fifteen hundred pagodas a year, which you are now in possession of; and that you preserve a good understanding with the government, notwithstanding some little jangling. This we take to be the effect of your good conduct and President Pitt's interest with the great men; and shall be glad you, our present President and Council, will follow in the same steps, which is now so much the easier because the path is ready trodden."

The administration of Mr. Gulston Addison, who was brother to the greatest of English essayists, did not extend over a month. On the Sunday morning that he succeeded to the government, he was too much indisposed to receive the balance of the cash from Mr. Pitt; and his signature is wanting to the proceedings. On the Monday he made his appearance and stated that he had "laboured under most severe pains, which almost rendered his limbs in a manner useless to him;" and the trembling signature which appears in the consultation book seems to indicate that he was still suffering from the attack. He only attended five consultations afterwards; and at the last one to which his signature is appended, he signed the instructions to the Captain of the "Heathcote" to receive Mr. Pitt on board, and to treat him with all the respect due to an ex-Governor during the voyage to England. Mr. Addison died at noon on Monday, the 17th of October, 1709. The event is interesting from its connection with the fortunes of his more celebrated brother. Whilst Gulston had been toiling away in the Company's service at Fort St. George, the fame and fortune of Joseph had been rapidly rising in England. Literature in those days was on a different footing to what it is now. The Battle of Blenheim in 1704, had been celebrated with a chorus of such wretched poems, that the government had actually routed out Joseph Addison from his little garret in the Haymarket, to write "The Campaign." The poem met with vast applause, and the subsequent promotion of its author was rapid. In 1708 he was chief secretary to the Lord Lieutenant of Ireland on two thousand a year, and keeper of the Irish records on four hundred a year. About the very time that Gulston died, Joseph furnished his first contribution to the Tatler. But shortly afterwards the Whigs went out and Joseph lost his chief secretaryship. This was unfortunate as he had deemed it expedient to fall in love with the dowager Countess of Warwick; a lady of mature charms, who considered Mr. Addison as the chief secretary and Mr. Addison as the mere literary man, to be two totally distinct individuals. Accordingly though she had smiled on the secretary she now frowned upon the author. It was at this juncture that Joseph inherited his brother's fortune, and the inheritance seems to have won back the heart of Chloe. In due time the pair were married; but poor Gulston's wealth had better have been left at Fort St. George. Henceforth, as the story goes, Mr. Joseph Addison was far happier over a bottle of claret at a tavern, than in the company of his magnificent countess dowager at Holland House.

But to return to Madras. The succession to the Governorship belonged to Mr. William Fraser, the enemy of Pitt and Higginson; but as Fraser was at that time Deputy Governor of Fort St. David, Mr. Edward Montague took the post of provisional governor until his return. The administration of Mr. Montague only lasted a fortnight, and was distinguished by only one incident worthy of notice. The government had at last resolved to send Captain Seaton to England on board the "Heathcote." The Captain however refused to leave his house, and the Governor was obliged to send Ensign Dixon with a file of soldiers to carry him on board. What transpired is best described in Ensign Dixon's own narrative of the proceedings, addressed to the Governor and Council on the 25th of October, 1709, which was follows:—

"Honourable Sirs,

According to orders, I carried your prisoner Captain Seaton alongside of the Ship "Heathcote," and laying there some time I found no person appear to hand us a rope or any to assist us. Then I went on board and delivered your Honor's and Council's order to Captain Tolson, desiring him to receive the prisoner. I informed him that the said prisoner was carried from the Sea Gate, and that he refused to come on board, unless he were hoisted in. Captain Tolson replied that all his passengers came on board willingly, and would not hoist him in, nor suffer anybody else to do it, nor would he overhale the least tackle in his ship; and that he would not suffer any gentleman lying alongside of his ship to be forced on board or ill used. Captain Tolson asked the prisoner, if he would come on board, which the said prisoner refused. Then the prisoner demanded of Captain Tolson, whether he had any further commands for him. Captain Tolson answered no. I waited for a note, but at last he told me I might go, for he would give none." Subsequently Captain Seaton appears to have left the Presidency of his own accord.

On the 2nd of November the new Governor, Mr. Fraser, reached Madras from Fort St. David; the members of Council and other English Gentlemen, together with the chief inhabitants of the place, going out as far as St. Thomas' little Mount to receive him. The next day a council was held, as will be seen by the following extract.

"Thursday, 3rd November, 1709. The Council being duly summoned met in Consultation, and having taken their places, the President, rising up from the chair, exhorted the Gentlemen of the

Council to forget and forgive whatever hitherto had given cause and occasion to the difference that had formerly happened amongst them; and that all such piques might for ever be buried in oblivion, and that they might henceforward agree amongst themselves, in the Unity of Love and firm Friendship, with all reciprocal respect to each other; in testimony of which they were desired to shake hands all of them; which was accordingly done with all promises of sincerity to the performance of the promises."

The Governorship of Mr. Fraser lasted little more than eighteen months, being brought to a conclusion on the 11th of July, 1711, when Mr. Harrison came out as President of Fort St. George. The records connected with the administration of both Mr. Fraser and his successor are much occupied with two or three discussions which it is impossible to treat in detail. In the first place there was an interminable correspondence with Zoodee Khan, concerning the present intended for the Court at Delhi, and which was detained for years on its way. It seems that Governor Pitt had intended to forward it to the King whilst the latter was staying at Golconda after the victory over Prince Kham Buksh; but part only was sent by sea to Masulipatam, and there got no farther; the King having by that time been called back to Delhi and the North-west in consequence of the rising of the Sikhs.

Many consultations were held, not only with the members of Council, but with also the chief merchants and inhabitants of the place, as to how the present was to be conveyed. To send it overland to Delhi was declared to be a Herculean labour, the imperial city "being little less than 2000 miles off," which would occasion "an immense charge to the Company." Subsequently it was determined to send the portion that was at Masulipatam to the Subah at Golconda, there to remain until the King's pleasure could be known; whilst the remaining portion was to be sent on to Bengal, thence to be forwarded to Delhi. Very many months however after this decision was recorded, we still find Zoodee Khan applying for the present, and the Governor of Fort St. George sending every kind of excuse and apology for the delay.

Another subject of endless correspondence between the Governor and the Nabob of the surrounding country, was the five new villages which had been granted to the Company by the Nabob Dawood Khan. Notwithstanding the present to Dawood Khan, and the judicious bribe administered to the keepers of the records, the Mogul government determined to recall the villages, on the ground that they belonged to a jaghire which had been granted to Zulfikar Khan, now styled Khan Bahadur. There were also troubles both at Vizagapatam, and Fort St. David; but these subjects will be sufficiently explained as we proceed. We shall now produce our extracts in chronological order.

The first refers to a severe storm which broke out about a fortnight after Mr. Fraser's accession, and is thus described in the consultation book.

"Saturday, 19th November 1709. Saturday

in the evening, it rained very much, and about 8 at night began to thunder and lighten, which was very violent (for about an hour), by which the Flag Staff was rent and shattered from the top to the ground. Some pieces flew near 600 feet, and thousands of small pieces strewed the curtains and other places. A large iron hoop was burst from the mast, and flew near 200 feet, and two holes struck through the truck as though it had been with a shot.

"The Company's house at the Garden was likewise damaged at the Southernmost end, one leaf of a window being shattered to pieces and one side of the Frame much rent; the door pierced through in several places, and the upper part of the Frame much scorched, whereby it was rendered unserviceable. The wall was pierced through in two places; one hole just above the Terrace, being about 5 inches diameter; and the other, which went beneath the beams that bear up the Terrace, was about 7 inches diameter, and the beam next the wall was likewise pierced through in two places, and all this with little or no wind."

We may here add that the season of 1709-10 proved in other respects a remarkable one. The monsoon rains returned in January with considerable violence, a circumstance which we believe is of very rare occurrence on the Coast of Coromandel.

The next extract will be interesting to our Armenian readers, for notwithstanding the complaints recorded against one of their community, the following story plainly indicates that the Armenians had gained considerable wealth and were aiming at independent power.

"Thursday, 13th January, 1710. Lewis Melique, an inhabitant of this place, presents a petition setting forth the abuses and insolencies of Cojah Saffur, an Armenian, also an inhabitant here, who hath for some years past lived at St. Thomas' Great Mount, where he hath impudently assumed a power to himself, as if he was Havildar there; insomuch that in a controversy between the said Lewis Melique and Antonio Soares about a piece of ground, the said Saffur concerned himself so far, though not belonging to him, that he threatened to beat the said Lewis Melique, and send him a prisoner to the Catwall of St. Thomé; which he had certainly done, had not the said Lewis Melique made his escape.

"On which the Governor sent for the said Saffur yesterday, who appeared before us this day, and the matter being put close to him did stiffly deny every thing, notwithstanding the evidence that was brought against him; and it being well known that the said Saffur has been an insolent troublesome fellow to all the English in general, who have resorted to the Mount for their health; of which there has been several instances, too many to be enumerated here.

"And that there is cause to believe, that the said Cojah Saffur, with others of his nation, intend to associate and form themselves into a Factory at the Mount, and make St. Thomé their port, as appears by their having in the late Governor Pitt's time bought and built several houses there, which they ought not to have done without leave of the Governor and Council; and that they intended to build a Gate at the end of the lane to stop up all avenues, and prevent all others having any entrance there but themselves; to prevent which growing evil, it is thought expedient to pull up their insolent weed of ill humour by the root.

"Agreed and ordered that the said Cojah Saffur be confined to the Fort, until he give security of Pagodas 5000, for his forthcoming and good behaviour for the future; for which none of his own nation would engage for him, and therefore was committed."

The following entry illustrates the war between Great Britain and France which had extended to the Bay of Bengal. The false intelligence by which Governor Fraser proposed to deceive the French will be found creditable to that gentleman's invention. It will be seen that Mr. Montague, the late provisional governor of Fort St. George, was now Deputy Governor of Fort St. David; and that he and his Council were anxious to dispatch the ship "Somers" to Europe, but were afraid to do so whilst the French ships were at Pondicherry. Accordingly the design of Governor Fraser was to induce the French ships to leave Pondicherry, so as to leave the coast clear for the "Somers."

"Tuesday, 31st January. This morning received a general letter from the Deputy Governor and Council at Fort St. David, dated 28th instant, and the President found matter enough contained therein to summon the Council to meet immediately. They, at Fort St. David, advise the Ship "Somers" to have been full laden that day. They likewise advise of their great fears and apprehensions they have of the St. Malo's ships at Pondicherry, of their having some ill design in agitation against the "Somers." For which reason they think it not adviseable to despatch her though full laden, and therefore do earnestly desire our orders and directions in that matter.

"The President propounding to the Council what they thought might be the best ways and means to be used to prevent the "Somers" being in danger of the French. Upon the whole we come to this following resolution, that a letter should be devised as from Bengal, advising the great troubles the English were in there, by reason of the country Government stopping their goods from coming down the river; which occasioned a warm skirmish, in which a great many Moors were killed and some English; and that the Council there thought the Company's affairs in great danger, and forthwith desired our utmost assistance. As also to write the Deputy Governor and Council (and send them copy of said devised letter) for to send for Captain Peacock and endeavour to agree with him on further time according to a New Charter party, that he might be unladen and sent to Bengal; with the intent that the same might be industriously diffused and spread abroad, in hopes it might occasion the French Ships departure the sooner thence, who had lain full laden for some days. It was also agreed, we should write our joint letter to Deputy Governor Montague, Mr. Raworth, and Captain Peacock to unravel and explain to them the mystery of our general letter to the Deputy Governor and Council, and that it was only feigned with a design in hopes, it might hasten the despatch of the French."

By subsequent entries we learn that this device proved unnecessary, but it nevertheless received the warm approval at the Court of Directors.

The following petition will explain itself.

"To the Honorable William Fraser, Esq. etc.

"The petition of the Ministers and Churchwardens of the Parish of St. Mary's in Fort St. George.

"Humbly representeth,

That whereas the monuments of the dead, and the ground where they are interred are held by most people in some measure sacred, and not lightly applied to any common or profane use, yet it is our misfortune that the English burying place in Fort St. George (where so many of our relations, friends and acquaintants lie buried) is not kept in that decent and due manner it ought to be, but every day profaned and applied to the most vile and undecent uses; for since the year 1701, when an old building that stood in the burying place (and in which the Buffaloes used to be shut up) was taken down to build lodgings for the soldiers at the Gate adjoining, the Tombs have been made use of for stables for the Buffaloes; which is not only a thing very undecent, but also a very great damage to those buildings, by having so many stakes drove into the pavement and with the walls to fasten the Buffaloes to.

"Another occasion of our complaint on this subject is the Cocoa-nut trees standing in the burying place; the profit arising from them, we know is inconsiderable, but the nuisance accruing to the place thereby, we are sure is very great. For the Toddy men have people employed there all the day and almost all the night in drawing and selling of Toddy, so that we are obliged on their account to keep the Gates always open, both by day and by night. And there about eight o'clock at night after work is done, is such a resort of basket makers, Scavengers, people that look after the Buffaloes, and other Parriars, to drink Toddy, that all the Punch houses in Madras have not half the noise in them; and by reason of the gates lying open, beggars and other vagabonds (who know not where to go) make use of the tombs to lie in, and what unclean uses the neighbours thereabout do make of that place we forbear to tell. We hope, what is here urged, together with the reflection it must cast on our Church and nation to have so little regard to the repositories of our dead, when all other nations who live among us have so just a regard to theirs, will prevail with your Honor &c. to take this matter into your consideration, and to find out some method to redress these abuses. And your petitioners as in duty bound shall &c.

GEORGE LEWIS. } *Ministers.*
ROBERT JONES. }
EDWARD BARKHAM. } *Church Wardens.*"
FRANCIS COOKE. }

FORT ST. GEORGE, }
February 19*th* 1710. }

We are glad to inform our readers that the matter was taken up by Governor Fraser, and the profanation removed. The Rev. George Lewis, who has signed his name to the above petition, appears to have been an active Chaplain, and we shall have occasion to mention him in a future issue in connection with some Missionary proceedings.

The following letter from Zoodee Khan to the Governor of Fort Saint George, is not only interesting as illustrative of the new relations which at this time began to spring up between the Mogul's government and the English, but it seems to indicate the commencement of a new commercial policy on the part of Shah Aulum.

" From Zoodee Khan, Ameny and Phoujdar of Hooghly and other seaports under the Subah of Bengal, as also of Orissa, Masulipatam, Peddipolle, Chinnapatam, St. Thomé, Pulicat, Chicacole, &c., under the Subah of Golcondah, received May 16th 1710.

" I lately wrote your Honor by your peons that the King had granted me the above mentioned Ameny and Phoujdarship, and therefore I have appointed Mirza Mahomud Zaman, son-in-law of Aloudabeeg, and Mahomed Salaubeeg, Deputies under me for Masulipatam and Peddepolle and my friend Aga Mookeem, Deputy at Chinnapatam, St. Thomé, Pulicat and Chicacole, and have sent them their commissions with a copy of mine attested by the Codjee at Court.

" As there is a great friendship between us, and you have often informed me that it was your opinion that if all the seaports under the King's dominions were under the Admiral (as a Company) he might settle the sea affairs, destroy the pirates, enrich the seaports and encourage the sea Merchants to come and depart, which will increase their profit; and you desired me to use my utmost endeavours to obtain this; which I have done; and on account of our friendship have undertaken this great business myself, and if it happens otherwise, the discredit will be the same to us both. For I have no other hopes than the safety of all subjects, the security of ships and merchants going or coming by sea, extirpation of pirates and the enrichment of the King's seaports. So your honor must use your endeavours in this matter likewise, and advise all your Gomastas and merchants every where to trade freely, without suspicion of any danger, and augment their trade.

"I want your advice if you think it proper to send some of the King's ships to bring Elephants from the other coast."

"The King has ordered me to build a Fort at Ballasore and enrich your Factory."

"After I arrive at Hooghly I will observe how affairs are managed and advice your honor."

"And now I must desire you to think of means, how things may best be carried on for the King's advantage and your Company's; that so all persons may live happy and serve their Maker. For I have neglected other business, and undertaken this on your account, in hopes to get a great name by it; and within 5, 6, or 12 months' time, if it is your request that I should take in the other sea ports, as also Surat, I can procure it; and we must endeavour to promote both our fames. For if we agree we can conquer the whole world, and clear the seas of all dangers for the merchants.

"As to the present, I have wrote you lately to send it to Bengal, according to the king's order, which be sure you do. For it is very necessary that you send a present, and when I come to Hooghly, I will advise you of all other matters; and you should send a Vakeel to be with me; which if you approve of, you may send such a one as Cojah Hamud, or Surapa, or write your people at Calcutta to send one. For I shall want him on several occasions. I heartily wish you all health and prosperity."

We are sorry to add that this arrangement proved to be only a temporary one, and that after a few months the seaports on the coast of Coromandel were again placed under the ordinary jurisdiction of the Subah of Golconda.

We now return to the subject of the five new villages which had been obtained by Governor Pitt. It must here be remarked that the purwanna for the out towns had been received from the Nabob Dawood Khan, and subsequently confirmed. The Nabob had also given to the Company a piece of ground of about forty acres at the Mount, in order that a house with a garden attached, might be built there as a sanatarium for the Company's servants. In April 1710 the Nabob recalled the villages, and ordered them to be delivered to Zulfikar Khan's* officers, on the ground that they belonged to his Jaghire. About the same time Dawood Khan was himself recalled to Delhi, in consequence probably of the rise of the Sikhs. The Government of Fort St. George suspected that the Nabob had been persuaded to this action by Yeavellappa, the Manager of Poonamallee, otherwise the Renter of the country surrounding the English dominions; and for a long time they deferred giving them up. In May the same year, a letter arrived from Dewan Sadatulla Khan at Arcot, who is described as the new Nabob, demanding not only the five villages recently granted, but also the three old towns of Egmore, Tandore and Pursewaukum, which had been granted some years previously by the Nabob Zulfikar Khan. The following letter from President Fraser to the Dewan Sadattulla Khan, puts the whole matter in a clear light.

"To DEWAN SADATULLA KHAN, HEALTH.

Fort St. George, May 25th, 1710.

"About some three days ago a servant of yours by name Muzzadeen brought me a letter, said to be from you, which I gave my Brahmin to be translated, at which I desired your servant to go and rest himself after his journey, until I had given answer to said letter; when he insolently and very pertly, as void of all manners and respect, insisted on the delivering up the villages. Else he would carry back your letter; which he did. I told him

* We continue the old name to prevent confusion; but henceforth Zulfikar Khan is styled Khan Bahadur in the records.

my business was not with him but with his master yourself.

"But, supposing the purport of said letter was to demand back the new villages, because they belong to Zulfikar Khan's Jaghire, which may be true. But you cannot but at the same time know that my noble great friend, the late Dawood Khan, gave an equivalent out of his own Jaghire to the great Zulfikar Khan which makes that matter even, and thus far I am in the right; and you likewise know that I gave away more than those villages brought in, so that the English here lived in all friendly tranquility with the late Nabob, until Yeavellapa, that plague of the poor and Cockatrice of all venom, when at Cudapa, never let the Nabob be quiet till he had gained his point to revoke the several former as well as late Perwannas, which confirmed those villages to our Company. So that one Perwanna is not sufficient to take away the force and power of all our former grants under the Nabob's signature and great chop; by which you would make the promise, faith, and truth of a great man of no more value than that of an ordinary man; which is a great derogation to the honor of a great personage.

"Yeavellappa deals treacherously with Madras, a place he is so much beholden to, where he stores up so much paddy and grain to await a scarce and dear season to increase the misery of the poor; and borrows large sums of money at the same time to enable him to pay his rent at the time due, else he must have been necessitated to sell at the market price which would be cheap.

"As for the four old villages, they were granted and confirmed to us about twenty years ago by the then Prince Khan Buksh, the great Assad Khan, and the then Zulfikar Khan, now Khan Bahadur, under their several and respective larger seals.

"My friendly council and advice to you is that you would consider and value the English as being the king's friend and in his favour, as may appear by his Royal Hosbullhookum from the throne to my late predecessor; and that you would keep the king's peace, by not committing any manner of hostility. I hope you will do nothing misbecoming, so wise a man as yourself, in so great a post and place of trust; and then you and I may come to have a better understanding at least till I hear from the Great Zulfikar Khan to whom I am now going to write, and have his answer; till when I shall be awake I need say no more."

About the same time Governor Fraser wrote another letter to Zulfikar Khan reminding him that the old villages had been granted to the English in consequence of the services rendered to the army of Aurungzebe by President Yale during the siege of Ginjee, and that the grant in question had been signed by his Zulfikar Khan's father, namely Assad Khan, the grand vizier. The remonstrance however was of no avail. Zulfikar Khan merely sent a short purwanna ordering that the villages granted by the Nabob Dawood Khan out of his jaghire should be delivered up to the Manager of the Poonamallee district.

CHAPTER XXIV.

GOVERNORSHIP OF MR. WILLIAM FRASER.

1710—11.

The administration of Mr. William Fraser was short and unhappy. It only lasted from November 1709 to July 1711, and was distinguished by circumstances which excited much animadversion from the Directors or Managers at home. It was through Mr. Fraser's intrigues and inveterate opposition, that Mr. Nathaniel Higginson had resigned and Mr. Thomas Pitt had been recalled; and now that he had obtained what appeared to be the object of his ambition, disorders arose at the Presidency and out-stations; and whilst quarrels broke out between the subordinate chiefs and the country authorities, the accounts were neglected, the consultation books were badly kept, and the advantages obtained by Mr. Pitt as regarded the out-villages were wholly lost, and the latter were retained for a while by the Renter of Poonamallee.

In the first place we must notice the troubles at Vizagapatam, which had their origin in circumstances that took place twelve years previously, but which reached a climax during the Governorship of Mr. Fraser. It seems that about the year 1698, two neighbouring Rajahs, Ananterauz and Pycrow, had borrowed large sums of money from Mr. Holcombe, the Deputy Governor of Vizagapatam.

Mr. Holcombe had been induced to enter into these transactions by a Brahmin named Juggapa, who had been largely bribed by the Rajahs to exert his influence in this direction. Unfortunately Mr. Holcombe had not lent his own money, but had borrowed for the purpose 44,000 pagodas of Fuckerla Khan, Nabob of Calinga. Seven years elapsed, but Mr. Holcombe had only repaid 37,500 pagodas, leaving a balance of 6,500 pagodas of the principal; and thus the debt due to the Nabob, inclusive of arrears of interest, amounted to some sixty or seventy thousand rupees. The following letter, written to Mr. Holcombe by Fuckerla Khan as far back as 1705, exhibits the then state of affairs.

"From Fuckerla Khan to Mr. Holcombe chief at Vizagapatam dated the 10th May 1705.

"You wrote me that you have received Pagodas 44000 principal of me.

"An account of what paid.

To a merchant upon my bill and order for a Jewel I bought of him Rs. 16,000 is Pagodas...	4600
Sent me to Vellore..............................	28000
To a bill payable to Govindaus and Veresedaus	4100
To Sundry bills amounting to.................	800
The total amount of what paid is...	37,500
The balance is Pagodas................	6500
Together is...	44000

"It is true you have receipts under my seal for all the above mentioned accounts, excepting the balance 6,500 Pagodas out of the principal money lent, which amounts to Rs. 23,000.

"Other people in the world allow 3 or 2½ per cent., but you gave me a bond allowing me but one per cent (? per mensem); notwithstanding that being pretty tolerable interest, I agreed to it, and now it is above six or seven years past; for which time there is due to me 60 or 70 thousand rupees with principal and interest. Likewise 10 or 15 thousand rupees more or less, which together amounts to a hundred thousand rupees.

"I have showed a great esteem for you, and had that confidence in you as to intrust my estate into your hands. Therefore I am satisfied that no person of any other religion would have dealt so uncivilly and unrespectfully by me as you have acted. Likewise now you unreasonably defer the payment in telling me you will discharge the debt as soon as you receive money, and at my arrival in your place; but in the meantime you have traded with the money, and make at least 25 or 50 per cent. profit. Besides is it proper or handsome you should occasion me so much trouble in perpetually writing to you, and sending my people up and down, who always return without satisfactory answer? . .My money is like bread as hard as iron, so not easily digested. Perhaps you may imagine I cannot come to your place, so intend to wrong me of my money. But if I live I will certainly come into that part within the space of 4, 6, or 12 months, if I meet with any convenient opportunity; and then how can you hope or expect to have my favour, having rendered yourself so unjust and uncivil. Perhaps you may intend to give me the slip, and go for Madras or some other sea port town; but go where you will, you are still in king Aurungzebe's country. So I can procure order-sent by the Gusbadars to the Subah of that counstry, and seize upon your house and goods, and therewith clear my money or debt. Then afterwards take no further notice of you, which you will not digest, or well approve of. For according to any law I can demand my money, and will have it by fair means or foul. Therefore fear God and consider I must have my money. So draw bills upon Masulipatam, or else you shall repent it as long as you live. I write you this, as likewise I wrote you before by Phauntee Mahomed, which pray peruse and consider well of it. You must not think I only threaten you. For God knows, I am very impatient so expect a full and satisfactory answer; or else you shall find I will send orders with Gusbadars to Meida Khan and will wait no longer."

Shortly after this Mr. Holcombe died without paying the remainder of the debt; and Fuckerla Khan claimed the amount from the Company, as Mr. Holcombe had actually affixed the Company's seal to the obligation. The question was still unsettled when Mr. Fraser succeeded to the Governorship of Fort St. George. Meantime there had been a competition between Fuckerla Khan and another chief named Habib Khan for the Nabobship; and the successor to Mr. Holcombe had been imprudent enough to acknowledge the latter, and thus to increase the exasperation of Fuckerla Khan. The following extracts from the consultation books shortly after Mr. Fraser's accession will exhibit the progress of affairs.

"Monday, 27th March 1710. From the

chief and Council at Vizagapatam dated the 2nd and 7th instant, advising the great troubles they have had with Fuckerla Khan, by their having been so closely besieged by his people stopping up all avenues of their bounds. For remedy of which they advise us that they resolved to make proposals to accommodate matters in a friendly way with him, intending him a present of 5000 rupees in Europe goods; in order to which they sent a Portuguese Padre and a Dubash, in hopes thereby to appease him, or obtain his patience for some days. But he refused their offer, and sent back the messengers in a very angry manner, and wrote the chief that he must immediately pay the money (due from Mr. Holcombe), or leave the place or prepare to fight."

"Tuesday, 15th August. General letter from the Chief and Council at Vizagapatam read: wherein we observe that their troubles are rather suspended than any way accommodated, by Fuckerla Khan's being gone up to the Dasheroon's country to adjust accounts, and agree with Habib Khan for the Government of those countries; and they still continue to urge their arguments for the Company's paying that debt of Mr. Holcombe's. They advised that they have supplied Habib Khan with ten candy of country gunpowder and five candy of lead, and that the said Nabob desires a further supply of thirty candy of powder and twenty of lead, which they desire may be sent them down."

"Monday, 11th December. Received general letter from the Deputy Governor and Council at Vizagapatam assuring us that they had sent the Moollah and a Brahmin to Fuckerla Khan's camp, to have a sight of the seal affixed to Mr. Holcombe's obligation. But after waiting for some days they returned with answer that Fuckerla Khan was enraged to the last degree, and would not hear any more proposals about his money without prompt payment, but was coming himself within a day or two with guns, ammunition &c. to besiege their town; and had placed guards on the roads to prevent their sending or receiving any letters and provisions coming to them; and that Fuckerla Khan refusing to show the obligation, they are of opinion and believe that Mr. Holcombe's seal is affixed thereto and not the Honorable Company's.

"That on the 8th past the said Nabob with his army, consisting of about 7000 foot and 800 horse, encamped behind a great sand hill near the Town, and the 9th at night fired on their out guards; which being returned again by the English, made the enemy retire further and turn their siege into a blockade by stopping all provisions of which they were in great want; that they have made a Brigantine of the "Rising Sun" smack, and fitted her up in order to secure what may be put aboard in time of extremity."

"The foregoing being a recital of their said general letter almost verbatim.

"First. We observe that the Chief has strangely erred in his politics (not to say worse); that he having by his former frequent letters advised us, what he had then foreseen, as what might be the result and issue of not paying Mr. Holcombe's old debt to Fuckerla Khan, as the event now proves,— that the Chief in that case should not sooner and earlier get sufficiency of provisions for the use of their Garrison, at least until the monsoon should serve for our sending them supplies hence.

"Secondly. That the Chief should supply Nabob Habib Khan and Fuckerla Khan with so large a quantity of gunpowder and lead, when the said Nabobs and the Chief were on so precarious terms; and not only so but by their general letter of the 27th July last write us to send them 30 Candy of powder and 20 Candy of lead for a further supply to the said Nabob; notwithstanding the frequent cautions we gave them, or without ever considering they were strengthening the hands of said Nabob, who were then contriving of the means and ways of laying that siege, they have since formed against that Factory.

"Thirdly. It being now the Northerly monsoon, it is strange that the Chief should not have wrote to Bengal to the President and Council there to be supplied thence with whatever they wanted.

"Fourthly. That Juggapa the Brahmin, that arch knave and villain, who was the chief cause and instrument by the powerful bribes he received from time to time from the Rajahs Ananterauz and Pycrow, by whose means and persuasions he prevailed so far with Mr. Holcombe, as to induce him to lend those large sums of money at high interest to those said Rajahs; which is still a debt, which we may reasonably suppose to have been most or all Fuckerla Khan's money, and has been the original cause and first spring, whence all these troubles are derived and devolved upon us; and notwithstanding our having so often or frequently wrote to Mr. Hastings, the Chief there, to send us up the said Juggapa either by sea or by land, which has never been complied with; and being credibly informed Fuckerla Khan does demand of the Chief the said Brahmin, and that on the delivery up of him all the causes of their troubles shall cease.

"And now upon the whole, it is unanimously agreed that we write the Chief and Council, that upon the reading the said intended letter to them, that they had that instant seized the said Juggapa, and put him in irons, and secure all his books, papers and accounts; which if the Chief should oppose or hinder the same, it is our positive and peremptory order that the Council, or any one of them, do execute this our order, and that the military and peons be assisting to him or them in this matter.

"It is likewise agreed that the President write his letter to Fuckerla Khan relating to the premises, and desire him to send us up a person fitly qualified to accommodate all matters and that in the meantime to withdraw his forces from the Factory."

Next year this troublesome business was brought to a close through the mediation of Habib Khan; the money demanded being paid to Fuckerla Khan, and the obligation which was found to have the Company's seal affixed, being forwarded to Fort St. George. The record is chiefly remarkable as exposing the evils which arose at this early period from pecuniary dealings between the Company's servants and Native authorities; and it is worthy of note as being the origin of a standing order which strictly prohibited all such dealings for the future.

We now turn to a curious entry which is very suggestive.

"Monday, 4th December. They having wrote us from Fort St. David that it has been usual for us at the festival times of the year to send them one of the ministers of this place, and Christmas being now approaching they request that one may be sent. It is, therefore, agreed and ordered that Mr. Jones do proceed thither, as soon as conveniently he can; and that the paymaster do take care to fit him out for his journey accordingly."

Cases of breach of promise of marriage are always interesting, but we are rather inclined to regard the one we are now about to place before our readers as somewhat unique in its character. The matchmaking tendencies of the mamma and daughter, and the "interested" nature of the gentleman's affection, are plainly evident throughout the papers. Moreover the record is valuable as illustrating social life as it actually was at the commencement of the last century. The extracts will explain themselves.

"To the Honorable William Fraser, Esq. Governor of Fort St. George and to the Gentlemen of the Council.

"The petition of Anne Foquet and Elizabeth Brown doth humbly set forth the unworthy treatment your Petitioners have met with from Captain Henry Cornwall, Commander of the "Sherborne." Your Honor is no stranger to this story, nor the rest of the Gentlemen at this Honorable Board; therefore shall be as brief in relating it as we can. In the year 1707 and before he went last for England, Henry Cornwall aforesaid, and your Petitioner Elizabeth Brown, did enter into a contract of marriage, and that in as solemn a manner as such contracts usually are, or can be done; for we plighted our faith either to other in the most binding terms, and changed rings in the presence of competent witnesses; Anne Foquet your petitioner, Mr. James Wendey, then one of the ministers of this place, and Mr. Bernard Benyon, merchant being present. And for the due performing of the aforesaid contract, the said Henry Cornwall and Elizabeth Brown did enter into articles in writing, and did both of them sign and seal the same in the presence of the Rev. Mr. James Wendey and Mr. Bernard Benyon aforesaid, who hath been sworn in Court. And moreover, the said Captain Henry Cornwall did bind himself in a bond of one thousand pounds sterling for the due performance of those articles; and further to confirm us in the reality of his intentions, he made a gift to your petitioner Elizabeth Brown of what estate he had in India and left a will in her hands; wherein he bequeaths her his whole estate and makes her sole Executrix. But notwithstanding all the vows, ties, and obligations he had brought himself under, Captain Henry Cornwall in a short time after his arrival in England marries himself to another woman; and after all this injurious and unfair dealing towards your petitioner, the said Henry Cornwall, to prove himself the same man throughout, would have his bonds and obligations under his hand and seal to go for nothing, and to be of as little force and validity as his words and vows. We, therefore, your petitioners humbly apply ourselves to your Honors for redress, hoping you will oblige him to satisfy his bond for one thousand pounds, which he hath forfeited; a poor reparation for all the injustice he hath done us. There hath been a suit commenced upon this Bond, for some time depending in the Mayor's Court, but deferred to be brought to a judgment upon advice that Captain Henry Cornwall was designed for this place; presuming, as may be supposed, he would either comply with his bond, or offer such terms as would be accepted of; and the Revd. Padre Lewis did before and since the arrival of the "Sherborne," speak to your petitioners to accommodate matters amicably with Captain Cornwall (if it might be done) and not drive things to extremity. To which your petitioners did not seem averse. But instead of offering to come to an accommodation, Captain Henry Cornwall, the second day after his arrival, sent a letter to your Petitioner Elizabeth Brown, of which she cannot better, nor more modestly give you the contents, than by saying, it was made up of all the ill nature and ill language he is master of; and after so much unworthy and base treatment as we have met with from this man, for him to think at last to run us down, and to carry his point by calumny and slander is so vile a thing, that no man who hath the least sense of honor or the least grain of honesty would be guilty of. We shall not be further troublesome to your Honors, but only beg leave to observe, that if such principles and such practices be connived at, no man's honour, person, or estate can be any longer safe. We hope your Honors will take things into your serious consideration, and do us that justice which to your wisdom shall appear our due. The reason of our addressing your Honors at this time is, that Mr. Mayor hath refused his warrant to arrest Captain Cornwall in an action of one thousand pounds, at the suit of your Petitioner Elizabeth Brown, and we as in duty bound shall ever pray. Fort St. George, February 12th, 1711."

Captain Cornwall's answer to these charges is still more interesting.

" Monday, 19th February. To the Honorable William Fraser, Esq. Governor of Fort St. George and Council.

" Gentlemen—" You were pleased on Thursday last to summon me to answer to a petition, preferred by Mrs. Elizabeth Brown and Anne Foquet of this place, touching a designed marriage between the said Elizabeth Brown and self, a perfect account of which I gave at that time, and comes inserted in this narrative.

" The motive that induced me to enter into an obligation of that nature was the assurances Mrs. Anne Foquet gave me of preferment from England by her and her friends' recommendations home; which proved no ways serviceable, but rather the contrary. I often repeated to her and daughters, if I could not better myself by post or fortune, I would by no means think of complying with that obligation. When Mrs. Foquet's friends proved of no use, I solicited my own relations, that entirely refused all merchandize, being strangers to trade. Then the time drawing near for the India Shipping to depart that year, I petitioned the Honorable United Company to come abroad a passenger on Captain Phrip, which they granted and he refused, being full and my circumstances not able to permit me to pay for my passage. I then solicited both the Captain Hudsons who refused the same. I then advised with my friends what method to take that might be of service to Mrs. Elizabeth Brown, and a sufficient acquittance to me. First, I declared my circumstances, so miserable when in England, I was forced to run in debt and that considerably. Secondly, I had no interest in the Company then governing to serve me by recommendation abroad. Thirdly, I presume the most of this place knows Mrs. Foquet not able to better any one's circumstances by interest or fortune. Notwithstanding her present encouragement in this affair, these circumstances considered on both sides, if any one gentleman can see the least appearance of any thing but complete misery, in case of that marriage, I should willingly submit to the several sentiments. I cannot perceive that Mrs. Anne Foquet ever designed a marriage, because she declared to Robert Raworth Esq., Mayor of this place, that she refused me marriage before I went home, because she was assured I would marry in England, when she would have the opportunity of prosecuting this obligation. Further, why did Mrs. Anne Foquet and Brown give me an obligation of Captain Lee's, now Commander of the "Litchfield," to prosecute him for not complying with the marriage according to his obligation, not out of date at the commencing of mine, if she designed her daughter my wife. I can give several instances wherein Mrs. Foquet has showed herself a designing woman of no sincerity. She and her daughter are pleased to term the penalty of the obligation, a poor reparation for injuries I have done them. If they were as just in their aspersions as I have been in this proceeding, they would not have troubled your Honor and Council with their petition on this occasion.

"I think, since I could not procure a passage out occasioned by my miserable circumstances, Mrs. Foquet and daughter are under obligations to me, that I advised them of it in order to Mrs. Elizabeth Brown's not refusing any offer to her advantage. I did at my first arrival at the West coast, order my attorney here to make Mrs. Elizabeth Brown a considerable present for the favours received when last here. But since my arrival at this Port, I found so many malicious reports from her, that it has entirely removed the thoughts of any such thing. My circumstances are miserable enough, having lost all I was worth, by my misfortune in Ceylon; and the balance of my accounts for four years' service in this place amounts to so small a sum that I fear

I shall go off a debtor from this place. I am ready to make oath in every particular here inserted; hoping your Honor and the Council will take it into your serious consideration; then doubt not but you will perceive my actions on my side justifiable; otherwise I must refer myself to the Courts at home, by whose verdict I must rest satisfied. I am, with due respect,

Your Honor's and Council's most humble Servant,
HENRY CORNWALL."

The Judgment of the Governor and Council upon this case is worthy of record.

"Monday, 19th February 1711. Pursuant to the order of last Consultation, Mrs. Foquet, and her daughter Elizabeth Brown, as likewise Captain Cornwall appear now before us; where after all parties were fully heard, more especially Captain Cornwall, all persons being desired to withdraw:—it is the unanimous opinion of the Board (Mr. Raworth excepted), that Captain Henry Cornwall, having married a wife in England notwithstanding his preengagement with Mrs. Brown, he has forfeited his obligation and thereby become liable to the penalty therein expressed; but in regard we ought to weigh matters in the scales of Equity and right reason, and considering the present circumstances of Captain Cornwall which are but moderate, having met with great losses, and he generously offering a moiety of what he has in the world, and he having cleared the reputation of said Mrs. Brown; both parties being called in, were reconciled and made friends, and the said Captain Cornwall's proposal accepted of."

About this time the King of Pegu appears to have been very anxious to obtain some articles, of European workmanship, particularly clocks, as appears from the following letter to the Governor of Fort St. George, dated 24th February, 1711.

"In the jurisdiction of Sunapranda and Thamadiha, the precious kingdom of Ava and Golden Court, Rajah of Ni and king of twenty and three kingdoms and Monarchies, Lord of Silver, Gold, Amber, Ruby mines, and red and gold Palaces 12 in number made of Gold, Lord of the Elephant of great value, Lord of many horses of great price, Lord of all nations, Lord of all manner of arms, Lord of many armies, Lord of this world, the excellent High and Mighty Lord,

"His order to the Governor of Madras, being informed, that amongst the English nation, there are many able men, and that without much trouble a clock may be had. I desire that it may be thus, viz. that it strikes the hours distinctly, beginning in the morning by one and so on till twelve; having two images to strike the hours on the bell or clock. This and another clock of Malta, with a woman's image pouring oil in a vessel which runs all the hour; and when it is out the said image fills it again and so every hour. The king having heard of these things will have much to be done to get them; and if not to be got, to send a man here to make them and shall then return to his country. I have sent by the Captain of my Ship, Cojah Simon, to the Governor of Madras two Ruby rings; if amongst the English or Portuguese there is any curiosity to be got, let it be sent. If my desire is accomplished there shall be great rewards according to my piety, &c."

The governorship of Mr. Fraser was, as already indicated, brought to a sudden close by the arrival of a successor, as appears from the following entry.

"Wednesday, 11th July. This morning about 8 o'clock, came ashore the Honorable Edward Harrison Esq., who produced his Commission, dated the 22nd December 1710, appointing him President for the Right Honorable United East India Company's affairs on the coast of Coromandel and Orissa, and of the Ginjee and Mahratta country, and Governor of Fort St. George, Fort St. David, and the Island of Sumatra. Which being read, the late President William Fraser Esq. did resign the chair, and deliver the keys of the Fort to the said Edward Harrison Esq."

CHAPTER XXV.

GOVERNORSHIP OF MR. EDWARD HARRISON.

1711—12.

The commencement of the Governorship of Mr. Harrison is a fitting moment for reviewing the contemporary state of Southern India and the Dekkan. The declining condition of the Mogul power had led to the establishment of new relations between the English and the Native authorities; and at the same time we are approaching the period when our historians generally have commenced what they have been pleased to term the history of the British empire in India. Henceforth therefore the new facts we shall bring forward from the official records will rapidly increase in value. They will serve to throw a clearer light upon one of the most obscure portions of the history of the Mogul rule; and thus they will form a connecting link between the dry Native annals of Southern India, and the delightful and picturesque history of Robert Orme.

The death of the great Aurungzebe in 1707, and the subsequent struggle between his three sons which led to the establishment of Shah Aulum on the throne of Delhi, have already been noticed; and it will be remembered that a large portion of the Mahomedan conquests in the Carnatic, including the country round Madras, had been granted as a jaghire to the celebrated general Zulfikar Khan. The rising of the Sikhs to the west of Delhi had called away Zulfikar Khan to the assistance of his royal master Shah Aulum. For a brief period Dawood Khan had acted as Soubah of Golconda, in behalf of Zulfikar Khan; but in his turn was called away by the troubles in the North West.*

In 1710 the Dewan Sadatulla Khan was appointed Nabob of the Carnatic, and appears to have retained the government until his death in 1732. He is briefly mentioned by Orme as having been a regular and acknowledged Nabob of the Carnatic; and appears to have been noticed by that historian in consequence of his being the first Nabob who attempted to render the office hereditary. Orme says that Sadatulla Khan, "having no issue, adopted the two sons of his brother; appointing the elder, Dost Ali, to succeed in the Nabobship; and conferring on the younger, Boker Ali, the government of Vellore." This Sadatulla Khan has already been mentioned as having required Governor Fraser to deliver up the five out-villages to the Renter of Poonamallee; and his further intercourse with the English will be fully illustrated in future chapters.

As regards the general state of the Mogul em-

* From entries in the Consultation Books, respectively dated 2nd of October and 24th of November, 1710, we learn that Isuph Khan held the post of Subah of Golconda at this time, but that in consequence of some troubles caused by the Mahrattas in the neighbourhood of Golconda, Dawood Khan was again appointed Subah in his room.

pire during the reign of King Shah Aulum, but little need be said. Shah Aulum sacrificed the prestige of his sovereignty for the sake of a hollow peace. He effected a compromise with the Rajpoots and Mahrattas, but though he thus appeared to secure his throne from their attacks, he was wholly unable to repress the growing disorders, which in the end produced the downfal of the Mogul dynasty. He died in 1712, after a short reign of five years.

The great event in the governorship of Mr. Harrison, namely the rupture between the English at Fort St. David and the Mussulman Governor of Ginjee, is strikingly illustrative of the contemporary state of Southern India. Sixteen miles south of Pondicherry and a hundred miles south of Madras, was the English settlement of Fort St. David, to which we have already had frequent occasion to allude. In 1691 the English had bought the settlement, previously named Tegnapatam, of Ram Raja, the Mahratta sovereign who was at that time in possession of Ginjee. The plot of Dr. Blackwell to deliver up Fort St. David to Zulfikar Khan in 1693 has been mentioned in its proper place. The celebrated fortress of Ginjee is worthy of a passing notice. It is seated on the declivities of three detached rocky mountains, of very difficult ascent and from four to 600 feet in height, which were connected by lines of works enclosing an extensive triangle in the plains between them; and for centuries this place had been regarded by the natives of Southern India as the strongest Fort in the Carnatic. Its origin dates far back in immemorial antiquity. Somewhere about the time of the wars of the white and red Roses, it appears to have been the great stronghold of the kings of Chola (Tanjore) against the famous old Hindoo sovereigns of Bijanugur. At length about D. 1500,—about the time of the battle of Bosworth Field and the accession of the house of Tudor,—the kingdom of Chola, and with it the fortress of Ginjee, was transferred to the possession of the Rajahs of Bijanugur; and long after the kingdom of Bijanugur had been overthrown by the Mussulman sovereigns of the Dekkan, the Hindoos still retained possession of Ginjee. About 1669 the Fort was captured by the Mussulman king of Bijapore; but in 1677 it was taken by Sevajee the great Mahratta. For four or five years it held out under Ram Raja against the whole force of the army of Aurungzebe; but was finally captured by Zulfikar Khan in 1698. A series of Rajpoot governors were then appointed by the Mogul, and ruled the surrounding country in his name; but during the anarchy which followed the death of Aurungzebe, these Rajpoots affected independence and assumed the rank of Rajahs.

At the time of Mr. Harrison's accession to the Government of Fort St. George, Serope Singh was Governor or Rajah of Ginjee. It is difficult to assign the exact limits of the country under the jurisdiction of Serope Singh; but it was probably bounded on the north by the territory under the Nabobs of Arcot, and on the south by the Hindoo principalities of Trichinopoly and Tanjore. Fort

St. David was thus included in the country under Serope Singh, in the same way that Fort St. George was included in the country of Sadatulla Khan. It appears that a former Deputy Governor of Fort St. David, Mr. Roberts by name, had in some sort of way, not sufficiently explained in the records, become security to Serope Singh for the sums collected by the Renters. Subsequently the Renters had run away with the money, and Serope Singh held the English Company responsible for the amount. By way of expediting a settlement, Serope Singh had carried away two European Officers of the garrison of Fort St. David, and confined them and treated them with the greatest barbarity at Ginjee. In February 1711, an attempt was made by the Government of Fort St. David to seize some Chief men of the Ginjee government, who happened to be in the neighbourhood of Fort St. David. No prisoners were taken, but three Moormen, and one of the Fort St. David Garrison were killed on the spot. Great troubles were therefore to be anticipated from this direct act of hostility on the part of the English; and as it appears that the Government of Fort St. David had acted in many cases most injudiciously, and that the utmost disorder prevailed in the Garrison, Mr. Raworth, a member of the Council of Fort St. George was dispatched to the scene of action, accompanied by five European ships whose presence it was hoped would bring the enemy to terms. Mr. Raworth set off in July 1711. The following extracts will illustrate the state of affairs. The enemy's force from Ginjee had blockaded Fort St. David by land, so that ammunition and provisions could only be forwarded by sea. The first extract is entered in the consultation on Sunday evening 19th August, 1711, and is entitled "A true narrative of an action that happened between Captain Roach's party and our enemy this day, being the 11th of August, 1711." It is related in Captain Roach's own words, and describes a desperate encounter in which he was engaged with the forces of Ginjee. The narrative is as follows :—

"I was ordered to possess myself of a part of the bounds, where the enemy were seen to be firing very briskly from last night; which I did this morning by break of day. I ordered about 200 peons that belonged to the outguards to attend me. The coolies began to work about the demolishing the walls by six in the morning, and continued till 12 at noon; but could not hear of any of the enemy's to be near our bounds, only a few peons about a mile off. But about 12 o'clock, intelligence was brought that Mahobat Khan, with all the force of Ghinjee, was within a mile of our bounds. Upon which I despatched immediately a peon to the Governor and Council, who was not arrived in two hours. In the interim, before I had any relief from the rest of the bounds, they attacked me with about 400 horses and 1000 foot. It was a great misfortune to me their attacking the party Captain Coventry had the command of, and Ensign Somervile; the latter proved such a coward, that he was the occasion of the ruin of the whole party, in showing them an example by running away first, which cost him his life, and abundance more of the same party. But I must do Captain Coventry that justice, that he behaved himself extraordinarily well, and would have made a very good officer, if please God he had lived. He received several wounds before he dropt. I had my horse shot under me, and was charged several times by the whole party of horse upon both flanks and rear, and kept them in play till they were glad to leave me master of the field with less than forty men. There was not one of the 200 peons I carried with me, would stand, neither officers, nor peons ; but when the horse charged me, they presently ran away. If they had but stood by me, I would have mounted as many horses of the enemies as would have made a good troop for the Company. For there was not less than seventy or eighty of them running about the field, without riders, their masters being dismounted. We compute that the enemy could have lost not less than 140 and 150 men killed and wounded, besides horses. I have buried the dead all in the field of battle, excepting Captain Coventry and Ensign Somervile whom I sent to the fort. I leave any impartial person to judge what the loss of the enemy must be, when they were at the push of the pike for two hours together, and applied with our bullets and swan shot as fast as possibly we could. This is the true narrative of what happened."

The next extract, dated 10th September, 1711, will show the disorders which prevailed at this time amongst the soldiers of the garrison. It is entitled

"An account of the murder of Thomas Parsons, Serjeant, by Jacob Vanbashayson, Centinel, one of the Bengal men, but at present belonging to Captain Roach's party."

"Thomas Kirk, John Buck, and Abraham Clark, belonging to Captain Viver's company at Cuddalore, by his permission came to the Fort to visit some of their comrades, particularly Thomas Parsons who had the command of the party at Tevenapatam Gate. On meeting him they went in company to a punch house near the said gate, where they found several more of their vocation drinking; but being none of their acquaintance, they passed by them, saluting them with their usual ceremony, "Good morrow to ye brothers," and so went into another yard, where they stayed no longer than to drink a dram each man. Then they were returning, when Jacob Vanbashayson, a Dutchman, without any manner of provocation given, attacked the said Serjeant Thomas Parsons with his naked sword, and struck him several blows over his head. Secondly, without giving him time to defend himself, he gave him a thrust into his body, on which he immediately fell. John Kirk abovementioned was the person next to the Serjeant, who the said Jacob Vanbashayson attacked in the same manner he did Parsons. But seeing the fate intended him, he defended himself so well with his sword (which was not drawn), that though he cut his scabbard in six places and made several thrusts at him, yet he received no harm; but had certainly been murdered, had not John Buck stept into his assistance. John Buck immediately called Jacob Vanbashayson, and seized his sword, which—notwithstanding he drew through his hand and gave him some strokes over the head, and at last made a stab at him which just touching his thigh,—for safety of his life he was obliged to quit his hold; when the said Jacob Vanbashayson still pursued him, and to save his life, having no weapon, he was forced to dodge him round some pillars which were in the yard, till he found an opportunity to go out of the door; which he immediately embraced, but as he was going over the threshhold was prevented by Derrick Johnson, who pulled him back by the coat and likewise knocked down John Kirk. By this time the guard from Tevenapatam came, and made the two Dutchmen prisoners. Though they resisted some time with sword in hand, before they would surrender, and the murderer was so very desperate for fear of condign punishment, that had he not been bound he would open breasted have run upon the bayonets on the muzzle of the guard's pieces.

"Jacob Vanbashayson says nothing more in his defence than that he was drunk and knew not what he did, that he had no malice at all against the Serjeant, and repented sincerely of the fact. Notwithstanding, as he had imbrued his hands in a fellow soldier's blood, he thought he deserved to die; but begged if we could not be merciful, as he had good relations (though he now was no more than a Centinel) that he might not die the death of a rogue, but a soldier, and be shot to death by a file or two of men of the party he belonged to.

"Derrick Johnson who was with him, is a fellow that has been publicly scourged at Batavia, and wears the cross on his back. He denies he was accessory to the murder, and that he only interfered when he knocked Kirk down, to part the persons engaged. But all circumstances make the contrary appear, and shows his inclinations as good. But it was not in his power to commit as heinous a crime as his companion.

"Thomas Parsons was brought speechless into the fort; but at that juncture more occasioned by liquor than his wound. The Doctor had some hopes at first; but in six hours they ended with the fellow's life. Upon opening his body we found the wound, very near direct down, and that the sword had penetrated his midriff and wounded several of his intestines.

"This is what the three persons first named have declared upon oath before the Deputy Governor and Council.* THO. GRAY. Secretary."

"Fort St. David, September 11th 1711.

About this time a Lieutenant and Ensign were found drunk and incapable whilst on guard at Cuddalore, at a time of imminent danger. Accordingly they were sent to Madras, and the following remarks upon their case, as well as upon the murder of Parsons, are entered in the consultation book as follows:—

"Thursday, 20th September, 1711. Lieutenant Viver and Ensign Williams being sent for up, and

* The murderer appears to have been subsequently executed.

the charge against them being read by the Secretary, they were asked by the President, what they had to say in their vindication; who making many frivolous excuses, but at last confessing their crime and begging pardon, were ordered to withdraw, and the President offered to the board as follows. That the military in general under this Presidency are, by slack discipline for the past two years, become so intolerably sottish and disorderly that it is high time a reformation should be made for the security of our settlements, and the Honorable Company's estate committed to our charge.

"The barbarous murder lately committed on Serjeant Parsons by a drunken Dutchman at Fort St. David, is testimony sufficient to what a height of insolence matters are grown; and it is well known that Mr. Farmer when Deputy Governor of Fort St. David durst not go out of the Fort for fear the Guard should shoot him as he passed the gate.

"Add to these instances the daily disorders of drunkenness in this garrison, which though severely punished, yet the seeds still remain, and the cure is not thoroughly perfected.

"If the officers themselves, whose business it is by strictness of discipline and good examples to preserve their command and keep their people within the bounds of their duty; if they shall be found dead drunk upon their posts in a time of service when surrounded by the enemy, what can be expected but ruin and destruction to the affairs of those that employ them.

"Offered further that the crime in our European Armies is punished in a capital manner; and then the question was put and unanimously agreed that Lieutenant Viver and Ensign Williams be cashiered, and that Lieutenant Viver do prepare to go for England by the Halifax."

Whilst Fort St. David was thus in danger of falling into the hands of Serope Singh, Mr. Harrison thought it advisable to lay the whole matter before Zulfikar Khan, in the hope that the interference of so great a man might have its effect upon the Rajah of Ginjee. The letter to Zulfikar Khan is dated 11th October, 1711 and is as follows :—

"To His Excellency Zulfikar Khan Bahadur, Nurzerat Sing, Backshee of the whole Empire, &c.

"Sir,—Understanding how great a share your Excellency bears in the Government of this mighty Empire, I thought it my duty to acquaint you of my arrival here to preside over the English affairs in these parts; and I think myself obliged more especially so to do, in regard that my predecessor in this Government (Mr. Pitt) have informed me, before I left England; that as your Excellency was one of the Chief pillars of the Empire, so you had upon sundry occasions manifested your good inclinations to the English in these parts; and that it was under your shadow and by your good countenance that they enjoy those privileges and security in their trade, which now they do. While Your Excellency lay with your army at Ginjee, I understand you were pleased to issue out your Purwanna for securing to us our privileges at Tevenapatam (Fort St. David). Upon my arrival here I found that place in trouble; Serope Singh having seized some of the English there and carried them prisoners to Ginjee, on occasion of some disgust given him by a former Governor. We are but a small handful of people, and our business is trade; and, therefore, all quarrels with the Government is extremely prejudicial to us, and distroys the end for which we settle in these parts. Since my coming I have laboured all I could to compose this difference, but to my great trouble, it hath hitherto proved ineffectual. If this affair comes to be represented at Court, no doubt but Serope Singh's agents will do it as much to our disadvantage as they can. I, therefore, humbly beg of your Excellency, that if any complaint be made against us on this subject that you will be pleased to excuse the matter, and that we desire nothing more than to live in tranquility and peace in our small Factories. And if Your Excellency would be pleased to procure us his Majesty's Hoosbullhookum to Serope Singh, to let us live in quiet and mend on trade, it will be a singular service to your petitioner, and which he shall always retain a grateful sense of."

To this letter no reply appears to have been received. Zulfikar Khan, now the great Bahadur Khan, was far too much engaged to trouble himself about the affairs of a small Factory of foreign merchants, like those at Fort St. David and Fort St. George.

Our next extract is a still more curious one.

Mr. Raworth on arriving at Fort St. David to take up the duties of Deputy Governor, discovered that his immediate predecessor Mr. Farmer had ordered the destruction of a great quantity of grain and a large number of villages belonging to the Ginjee government, simply because he had heard that Mohabat Khan, the commander of the beseiging force, had boasted that the English "dared not make another attempt by marching out into the country belonging to Serope Singh." This needless act of destruction and ravage naturally increased both the exasperation and the demands of the Rajah of Ginjee, who at that time had sent ambassadors to Fort St. David with the terms on which he was prepared to conclude a peace. When these terms were communicated to Fort St. George, together with the cause of their being so much in excess of the Renters debt, the matter was warmly commented on by Governor Harrison and Council as follows:—

"Monday, 29th October. A general letter from Fort St. David was read; in which to our great surprise, we find that Mr. Farmer and the Council in his time have set their hands to the following paragraph.

"It is most certainly true that Serope Singh could not before in justice demand more of us than the Renters debt, and not that neither because Mr. Roberts was their security when they run away, not the Company; but the destruction of fifty or sixty thousand pagodas worth of grain, about fifty two villages and towns, among which was his favorite town Yembollum, and killing the

Pandarrum: these are things which really make his demands carry too much justice with them; and we heartily wish the differences may be composed, and so happily settled as before the commencement of this war. Without your permission though to disburse something considerable out of the Company's cash, we shall not ask it till we find an absolute necessity."

"We (the Governor and Council of Fort St. George) cannot but observe with a great deal of concern the unaccountable folly and ill-management of these gentlemen through the whole course of this affair; but most particularly in this article. For after they had sent out all their forces, without any orders from hence, to burn and destroy all the country and grain round about them, empowered by a single order signed by Mr. Farmer only,—they now as good as tell us in so many words, that the unlawful depredations they have committed really make Serope Singh's demands carry too much justice with them; and shamefully confess that they are afraid they shall be necessitated to ask us to disburse something considerable out of the Company's cash. Mr. Farmer and his then Council would have done very well to have considered this inconvenience before they proceeded so rashly on their own heads."

A few days afterwards some further progress was made in effecting a settlement with the ambassadors of Serope Singh, as will be seen by the following extracts.

"Tuesday, 6th November. The President

communicates to the Board a letter from the Deputy Governor of Fort St. David; the substance of which is as follows:—

"That the enemy cannot be brought to more moderate demands than thirty thousand Chuckrums, which is sixteen thousand six hundred pagodas. In consideration of which they will give us three towns, Trevandrum, Padre Copang and Coronuttum, besides their half of all the towns that lay part within and part without our bounds. They likewise agree for ever to renounce all claim to our bounds, and all pretensions upon us whatsoever, with the usual presents of horses and vests upon the like occasion. To all which the Deputy Governor desires a speedy answer; this being their last result, and that he keeps the ambassadors with very much difficulty from returning to Ginjee."

"Then the state of the Fort St. David war was taken into consideration and fully debated.

"Agreed that our Honorable Masters are at four thousand pagodas charge more or less per month for maintaining the war, besides several stores and provisions sent from hence; and no rent was received for the villages in our bounds since the beginning of the war, which is an intolerable charge; and no hopes of any ease as long as the war continues, amounting to forty-eight thousand pagodas per annum.

"Agreed that if the war continues, our people will be shut up in their bounds, and we must supply them with grain from hence and all other necessaries. Most of their inhabitants out of fear would desert them; and our merchants, though they have made a large contract, will never be able to bring in their goods; and consequently we shall have our broad cloth left upon our hands when the next year's shipping arrives.

"Agreed likewise unanimously that let us continue the war never so long, we can never hope to be reimbursed one farthing of our vast expenses. It would indeed have been well, if all these things had been duly considered before our predecessors were so far engaged in it. But it is never too late to repent of wrong measures, and now we must make the best of a bad market; wherefore we have agreed that a letter be wrote to the Deputy Governor and Council of Fort St. David as follows:—

"To Robert Raworth, Esq., Deputy Governor of Fort St. David and Council.

"Sirs,—This morning the Governor has laid before us Mr. Raworth's letter of the 3rd instant, wherein he writes that the enemy will not come to any agreement unless we consent to pay thirty thousand Chuckrums, which we take to be sixteen thousand six hundred and odd pagodas. In consideration of which they will give the villages of Trevandrum, Padre Copang and Coronuttum, besides their half of all the towns which lie part within our hedge and part without, and that they will entirely renounce all claim to our bounds on any pretence whatsoever.

"We have very seriously considered the first article and find it to be so unreasonable a sum of money that we can never consent to pay it on our Honorable Masters' account.

"We cannot judge if it be worth while to buy the three villages before mentioned, and the half of the towns that lie part within our bounds and part without, till you send us a computation of what revenue they will annually yield, and what security we can have we shall continue in quiet possession of them hereafter. For we must be of opinion we have too much ground already at your settlement to defend against an enemy. If Serope Singh dares dispute a grant confirmed to us by Zulfikar Khan Bahadur, what value ought we to put upon his grant, (or what else he will call it) who is no more in comparison with the other than his Buckshi is to him, and may be not so much. Pray let this point be urged home, and let us have a speedy answer.

"An entire renounciation of claim to all things within our bounds is a tender point to be handled; for his pretending to a claim, after Zulfikar Khan Bahadur's grant, is an undeniable reason why we should buy no grants of him; since by the same rule the next Governor of Ginjee may dispute our title to all we possess, and, by the same forcible means may compel us to pay what sum he pleases, so that our title will always be precarious.

"We should consent to paying off the Renter's debt; and if we could have good security that even he himself and the rogues about him would not molest us in the possession of these grants he offers, we might though unwillingly consent to pay a sum of money for them, but never the sum they insist upon. Since upon the best account we can get of the villages here, the rent will be but inconsiderable.

"We shall wait your answer to these material points, and in the mean time desire that the treaty may go on in the manner we have mentioned; that is to say that the Renter's debt be kept apart and made up by itself; and if we give any thing more that it may be for some thing that you are satisfied will bring in an equivalent in a few years, or otherwise we can never consent to buy till we have orders from England.

"We leave this management as we did formerly to the Deputy Governor, with the same directions that he lay the treaty before the Board, ere the agreement is perfected."

Immediately afterwards further intelligence was received from Fort St. David to the effect that the Company's merchants and all the chief inhabitants, were determined to leave the bounds if the treaty should break through; also that the towns offered by Serope Singh were worth six thousand chuckrums per annum; and that if the ambassadors were once suffered to return to Ginjee there would be no hopes of getting them down a second time; and if the English should be forced to send their own ambassadors to Ginjee for a peace, it would cost at least double the money. Accordingly another letter was dispatched to Mr. Raworth, from which we make the following extracts.

"We are still of the same opinion for a speedy and honorable peace. We agree that Serope Singh ought to have satisfaction for the Renter's debt, and we should as readily agree to make Mr. Roberts pay it, if it was in our power. But since it is not, we must by the necessity of affairs submit to pay it for him; because he was the Company's Governor, and it being always customary for the Governors to treat singly with the great men of these parts, that whatever is transacted between them, they look upon it as firm as if done with the Company themselves. We shall apply the money we have attached belonging to Mr. Roberts, for the payment of this matter as far as it will go, and shall take care to debit him for the remainder.

"We think this article of our treaty ought to be first settled; and as to the remaining part of the sum demanded, we had much rather let his precarious villages alone than have any thing to do with them; though we must confess six thousand chuckrums per annum is a sufficient rent for the sum we are to pay.

"If you can make good what you write in your letter, and can have good security that we shall enjoy the villages peaceably, and be unmolested in our affairs, we are content that you make a peace upon the terms that you mention; though we hope you will show your dexterity in procuring an abatement.

"It will behove you to be very circumspect in the Articles of the treaty, and to part with no money till you have some security. For there is not a more faithless wretch upon earth than the man you have to deal with. We desire that there may be an article inserted for the ease and security of passengers at Tanapollum, which we think is the place where Mr. Raworth formerly met with so much trouble in going to Fort St. David.

"You will do well to lay these matters now before your Council; and before you conclude the treaty, it will be proper that you protest in form jointly against Mr. Roberts as the author of all these troubles, and the person that ought to be accountable for all the damages sustained thereby.

"As for your merchants offering to leave the bounds, we cannot but think it a great piece of insolence at such a juncture; and since they would seem thereby to necessitate you to a compliance, it was a very proper time to ask them how much they could contribute to a peace. When they made their contract, they knew the war was a afoot; and though you have not yet sent us a copy of your contract, we do not remember you ever mentioned that you had obliged yourselves to buy a peace.

"It is a great sum of money we now consent to, and should never have done it upon any terms but the equivalent to re-imburse us. We shall impatiently expect your answers."

We gather from the following graphic account of an attack on the enemy's entrenchments, that the negociations were for a while broken off.

"Friday, 25th January, 1712. A general letter from the Deputy Governor and Council of Fort St. David, dated the 20th instant, was read; acquainting us that they had made an attack upon an entrenchment of the enemy's at a place called Crimumbaukum, about half way between that place and Pondicherry, in the following manner.

"Mr. Raworth being advised that a party of about three hundred Moorish foot detached from their entrenchment at Crimumbaukum, used in their rounds to pass between Coniquile and our hedge. Ordered Captain Courtney and Captain Howson, with sixty Grenadiers, to lay ambuscade for them on the 19th, in a place that was thought the most convenient, and if possible cut them off. Accordingly at nine they went to the place appointed, where they waited till one o'clock, when perceiving none of the enemy appeared they marched directly to their entrenchment, which was immediately alarmed, about forty of them being without the door, who repairing in with a great deal of precipitation on their approach, excluded about twenty-two of their comrades. All which were immediately put to the sword, and then they (Captains Courtney and Howson) ordered Serjeant Aulin with two file of men, to mount the wall on the opposite side; which he did with a great deal of bravery, and forced them to retreat where the two captains were with the main body of the party; who immediately upon it ordered forty grenadoes to be flung in, which did wonderful execution. And while they were in this consternation, the grenadoes flying in pieces amongst them, and the serjeant on the other side firing upon them with swan shot, they forced open the door and entered sword in hand; where they met with a good stout repulse. But the execution done upon them before had so dispirited them, that in the end every man began to shift for himself; some making for the door, and others flinging themselves over the wall into the ditch, in order to make their escape ; till what with those that got away, and those that fell, they had in a short time free possession of the place without any molestation ; when they had an opportunity to view the slain which amounted to more than one hundred. Besides which they say the ground was all strewed with pieces of skulls, hands, and legs, which to be sure was the effect of the grenadoe shells."

The disorderly state of the garrison of Fort St. David has already been illustrated, but still we cannot avoid bringing forward the following particulars as giving us an insight not only into the affairs of Fort St. David, but into military life in general as it was a hundred and fifty years ago.

"Wednesday, 28th January. The President acquaints the Board that the Deputy Governor and Council of Fort St. David have sent up Lieutenant Courtney, Ensign Brooks, and Serjeant Peterson prisoners in two Mussulars, for several crimes set forth as follows in their general letter.

"On Tuesday last Captain Courtney having dined with the Deputy Governor (Mr. Raworth) went as he was accustomed into Mr. Weld's room, where was sitting Ensign Paddle. He walked backwards and forwards for sometime without speaking a word. But at last attacked him in a very odd sort of a manner, telling him he was an impudent fellow, son of a Skip Jack, and used abundanee of other epithets, very improper for a man that carries a commission, to utter or take ; but Paddle it seems, regarding the place he was in, and not caring to make any disturbance under

Mr. Raworth's roof, bore it very patiently, till Courtney at last drew and assaulted him; and before the guard could come in to quiet the disturbance, had wounded Paddle about an inch and a half deep in the belly and stabbed him in the left temple. The Deputy Governor immediately secured them both under guards in different appartments, and yesterday acquainted us with it in consultation; when they were both sent for up, and heard what they could say for themselves, and the declarations of Messrs. Matthew Weld and Henry Cottrel taken. The one of which was present when some words past between them on Sunday last; and the others not only there but likewise the greatest part of the time they were scuffling together. The copies of which we enclose for your Honor's perusal."

"*The Declaration of Mr. Matthew Weld.*

"Sunday the 20th in the Afternoon. Captain Hercules Courtney and Ensign Joseph Paddle being at my lodgings, where also was Mr. Henry Cottrel, when Captain Courtney asked Ensign Paddle to give one Richard Pain, a Centinel on the main guard and a drunken abusive fellow, liberty to go out of the Fort for two or three hours in a day about some business he had for him. To which Ensign Paddle replied, he could not. Thereat Captain Courtney paused a little, and then flew into a passion, saying, "What do you mean Ensign Paddle, D— me, I will have him without asking you." To that Ensign Paddle said, "If he is a man belonging to your Company you may have him, but as he is upon this guard, I must have another in his room to do his duty." Hereat Captain Courtney grew very abusive to Mr. Paddle the Ensign of the guard, giving him the lie, calling him an impudent saucy fellow, and threatened to beat him and thrust his cane down his throat, which he shook at him in a menacing manner, uttering many other abusive expressions. To all which said Ensign Joseph Paddle made civil replies and mild, and gave his reason, why he could not permit said Pain to go out of the Fort; he being so frequently guilty of misdemeaners when at his liberty, that he feared, he should be blamed if he suffered him abroad; desiring Captain Courtney not to treat him so scurvily, and that he would not strike him, for he would not suffer it. When their difference grew to this height I desired them both to forbear quarrelling in my house. Whereat, they then gave over, and I thought all would have been past by.

"But Tuesday the 22nd of January 1712, about three in the afternoon, Captain Hercules Courtney came into my lodgings, where Mr. Joseph Paddle was with me at a table smoking a pipe of tobacco; and after taking some few turns in my room seemingly in a passion, stood by me and demanded of Ensign Paddle, how he came to write so saucy and impudently to him in the parole note; telling him that his superiors used him with more respect than barely to conclude after the word with his name only. To this Ensign Paddle replied he wrote it in haste and designed no affront by it, and hoped he would not make this omission occasion of quarelling with him, on account of their late difference about said Richard Pain; adding that Captain Courtney had then very grossly abused him, who answered he had not, but he very much deserved it; and immediately flew into a passion, and said he was a saucy impudent fellow and would make him know his distance, and let him see he did not make such as him his companion, with several such like scornful expressions. To which Mr. Paddle replied in a very calm manner, "Sir, I bear a Commission so well as you;" and then desired he would curb his passion, for he could not bear such abuses.

"Upon that Captain Courtney flew into a more violent passion, and stepping back into the middle of the room immediately drew his sword. Whereat Ensign Paddle (whose sword lay with the belt and scabbard about two steps on one side of him upon two chairs) got up and took hold of it. But before he had completely drawn, and putting himself into a posture of defence, whilst the point of his sword was scarcely out of the sheath and pointing downward, Captain Courtney who drew first and was in a readiness, advanced on him and struck a forcible blow on Ensign Paddle's sword, which beat it up backward and so struck it out of his hand, pushed Ensign Paddle into the belly who notwithstanding readily got hold of his sword again. But in the very instant as he stooped to recover it, Captain Courtney closed in with him, and shuffled him down into the window; where Captain Courtney had him under, with his left hand on Ensign Paddle's sword arm, and his own sword pointed at Ensign Paddle's breast, bidding him deliver his sword and beg his life. Upon this I left them, and made what haste I could to call a guard; and on my return found Captain Courtney with both swords in his hands and Ensign Paddle asking for his sword, which Captain Courtney returned. After this a dispute arose about the difference, when Ensign Paddle told Captain Courtney that he used him very scurvily in drawing on him in the Fort and unawares; but that now he was so good a man as himself. With that Captain Courtney said "D—— me Sirrah, what after I have given you your life and sword, you have the impudence to prate:" and immediately run furiously upon him, and catching hold of Ensign Paddle's sword, broke it in two pieces; and then they fell to cutting, but were parted by Serjeant Wanton. Soon after came the Captain of the Guard, in whose presence Captain Courtney continued to abuse Ensign Paddle in very scurrilous language, calling him "skipkennel," "sorry fellow," "just come from waiting at a table;" and treated him with abundance of such like insufferable expressions; though at the same time Ensign Paddle desired him to shake hands and be friends. To which Captain Courtney replied, he would not concern himself with any such fellow as he is."

MATTHEW WELD."*

* The other deposition is little more than a repetition of the above. Captain Courtney was subsequently recalled.

The troubles at Fort St. David were at last brought to a conclusion in April 1712, through the mediation of M. Hebert, French Governor of Pondicherry; but the peace appears to have cost the Company a sum of 12,000 pagodas in direct payment to the Rajah Serope Singh and his officers, in addition to the other charges and losses attending the war. This mediation of the French was only accepted after some deliberation, as the war with France was not brought to a final close until the treaty of Utrecht in 1713. It may be mentioned here that the fortress of Ginjee was captured in 1715 by the Dewan Sadatulla Khan.

CHAPTER XXVI.

GOVERNORSHIP OF MR. EDWARD HARRISON.

(Continued.)

1712—13.

During the troubles at Fort St. David recorded in the last chapter, but few incidents of importance appear to have taken place at Fort St. George. In 1711 the celebrated Danish Protestant Missionary, Bartholomew Ziegenbalgh appears to have arrived from the Danish settlement at Tranquebar on a visit to Madras; and in the consultation book of the 13th August, 1711, we find the following entry.

"The Danes Padre, Bartholomew Ziegenbalgh, requests leave to go for Europe on the first ship; and in consideration that he is the head of a Protestant Mission espoused by the Right Reverend the Lord Arch-Bishop of Canterbury, and the rest of our Episcopal Clergy, and that our Masters were pleased to send out their money freight free, we have presumed to grant him his passage without paying permission money."

A few days afterwards a member of the Danish Council at Tranquebar arrived at Madras on his way to Bengal, and requested that this permission might be rescinded, as a dispute between Ziegenbalgh and the Danish commandant which had been referred home to the king of Denmark. Accordingly the passage was refused until the said

Missionary had obtained the consent of the Governor of Tranquebar.

The following extract from a General Letter, dated February 2nd, 1712, and addressed by the Board of Directors to the Governor and Council of Fort St. George, containing some further information respecting any Missionary proceedings in Northern India.

"It is proper here to tell you that since the entire union of the two Companies, we act on the foot of the new Company's Charter, which directs, that the Company shall constantly maintain, in every of their garrisons and superior factories, one Minister; and that all such Ministers as shall be sent to reside in India shall be obliged to learn, within one year after their arrival, the Portuguese language; and that they shall apply themselves to learn the native language of the country where they shall reside, the better to enable them to instruct the Gentoos that shall be servants or slaves of the Company or of their agents in the Protestant religion. That in case of the death of any of the said Ministers residing in the East Indies, his place shall be supplied by one of the Chaplains out of the next ships that shall arrive at or near the place where such Minister shall happen to die; and that the Company shall from time to time provide School Masters in all their Garrisons and superior Factories, where they shall be found necessary.

"We are further to acquaint you that the Society for Promoting Christian Knowledge, which is composed of many of the Reverend Bishops and other Clergy, together with divers well disposed Gentlemen have addressed to us in behalf of the Protestant Missionaries (at Tranquebar), to give them our protection and encouragement, and to permit them a Charity School or Schools at Madras. They find it difficult to get any English to undertake this service, but hope to be able to do it in another season. We have consented to their sending three persons by this shipping, viz. Mr. Berlin to be a School Master, Mr. Adler a printer, and his brother. They are not certain whether he will reside at Madras, but wherever it is, he is to instruct children there gratis. They have printed some small Tracts in Portuguese of prayers, the Catechism, and other pious collections, for the use of the scholars. We recommend to you to give your countenance and protection to the said persons, and other Protestant Missionaries; and to supply them with a few of the Portuguese Liturgies as you find it necessary, and do whatever you think proper for the strengthening their hands in this difficult but honourable work of spreading the Gospel among the heathens. Some other requests they have made us, among the rest, that you should be empowered to prefer such as they shall instruct, preferable to other natives; which will be time enough to pronounce upon, when we hear the success of their endeavours, and whether you have any and what objections thereto."

About a year after receiving the above, Governor Harrison and Council replied as follows in a General Letter, dated 16th September, 1713.

"The design of erecting a Charity School or

Schools at this place is a very noble one, and worthy that Honorable Society for Promoting Christian Knowledge. We will not only be ready to adjust them with the power you have given us, but also with our purses; and do not doubt but many of your inhabitants will do the same, if the persons they send out are of tempers and qualifications fit for the undertaking. But we hope they will be English and not foreigners. The Danish missionaries have not wanted for our assistance on all occasions, though we must still continue of opinion that they spend a great deal of the Society's money to little or no purpose; and though there may be some good men among them there is one very turbulent person, of whose principles you may please to judge, by his contriving the escape of Mr. Abendana's widow from her creditors here to Tranquebar, and marrying her though a Jew to a Christian by the way." To this letter the Directors replied by the next ships as follows. "The Society for Promoting Christian Knowledge have presented to us, that they have not as yet been able to prevail with any of the British nation to undertake the Service of the Protestant Mission to the East Indies. But are advised to make an experiment of two Malabar Christians, educated at Tranquebar under the Danish Missionaries, to be employed as masters of two Charity Schools, one to be kept at Fort St. George and the other at Fort St. David, subject to the inspection of yourselves and direction of our Chaplain at Madras, and of the Deputy Governor and Council at Fort St. David; and desiring we would approve thereof, and protect the persons that shall be employed therein. We have promised to recommend this, as we hereby do, to your consideration; and to give them all proper assistances for propagating the Protestant religion in the way they propose. We have also allowed the Society to send the Missionaries three hundred pounds' value in pieces 8-8, and fifty-five reams of paper, with a chest of Books, a chest of Beer and a cheese, Freight free."

We must add that the Charity School was not founded in Madras until the Governorship of Mr. Collett, the successor of Governor Harrison.

From the two following extracts from the consultation books, it would seem that at this time the morals and manners of the Company's servants themselves were very far from what they ought to have been.

"Thursday, 2nd August, 1711. The Right Honorable Company's Servants, Factors, and Writers being summoned, according to an order last Consultation do now attend, and being called in, were severally checked by the President, for not giving their attendance at Divine Service; and told that for the future, whosoever shall be absent on Sundays from morning and evening service shall not only be fined nine fanams to the poor but be under the displeasure of this board and be treated accordingly."

"Monday, 30th June, 1712. Several disorders having been committed at the General Table, which we find to be partly occasioned by the absence of those persons in the service, that are of a superior standing and might awe the young ones into better behaviour;—we have thought fit to appoint Joseph Smart head searcher, and five others, to take their turns, either weekly, or monthly, or as they shall agree among themselves, to be present at the Table, and to take care that no indecencies or disorders are committed."

We must now turn to the history of the Presidency. Whilst Fort St. David was warring against the Mussulman chief of Ginjee, Fort St. George seems to have maintained tolerably peaceful relations with the Dewan Sadatulla Khan, now Nabob of Arcot. The Dewan sent Governor Harrison the customary vest, turban, and purwanna, all of which were received in public with the usual solemnities. It is a noticeable fact that at this time the authority of the Mogul was declining, whilst the distant authorities were become more independent in the exercise of their power. The following story of the arbitrary conduct of the Foujdar at St. Thomé fully illustrates this state of things.

"Monday, 21st January, 1712. Pier Zudda, Foujdar of St. Thomé, is a Moollah of the Serad Caste, which is the chief of all the Moor's castes in these parts. He is likewise chief priest to the Dewan Sadatulla Khan; and has such an influence over him that whatever he says is a law, and the Dewan does nothing without his advice. When Pier Zudda visits him, he rises from his seat, and meets him at the door; and when the Dewan goes to him he receives him sitting, and frequently suffers him to kiss his feet.

"This priest has his Jaghire in and about St. Thomé to the yearly amount of nine thousand pagodas; and has by his cruelty to the Portuguese inhabitants of that place forced most of them to quit it and retire hither, the Bishop among the rest. They found means by a Christian woman in Shah Aulum's Seraglio to lay their complaints before him; who ordered Zulfikar Khan to send down a Perwanna immediately to the Dewan, commanding him to restore the Portuguese to their habitations and privileges, and to see restitution made them. A copy of the said Perwanna was sent by the Christian woman to the Bishop of St. Thomé, who sent several persons with the same to the Dewan at Arcot. But he received them very roughly; charging them with accusing him falsely to the King, put them in prison, and threatened them till they paid a sum of money for their release; withal obliging them to sign a paper in the Persian language without reading it, wherein it is said they own all their former complaints to be false and scandalous. This is a piece of roguery that we cannot forbear taking notice of, to show the weakness of the present Government under Shah Aulum, and the great power of Zulfikar Khan, whose creatures the Dewan and Pier Zudda are; and undoubtedly he has directed them what to do in this affair. However the Portuguese are preparing for a second complaint by the same hand, by which we shall see if the King will exert his authority or no."

In April the news of Shah Aulum's death had reached the Presidency, as will be seen from the following extract.

"Monday, 7th April, 1712. The news of King

Shah Aulum's death being duly confirmed, we find the neighbouring countries round about us under a great apprehension; all the Poligars having long waited this opportunity to set up for themselves, and assert their ancient rights and privileges; and our Dewan, who is at present Soobah (Nabob) of these parts, being marched away towards the Tanjore country to raise money, which is what he chiefly minds, and neglects the welfare and security of the Government committed to his charge. We have just reason to fear advantages will be taken of his absence by the petty Governors, to the prejudice of trade and our investment; and several considerable persons and inhabitants of Arcot, and other neighbouring places inland, have within these few days past sent considerable sums of money to be lodged here for security against the expected troubles. Wherefore it behoves us to put ourselves into as good a posture of defence as we can, for the security of our Master's Estates, our own inhabitants, and all such as shall have recourse to our protection."

It will here be necessary to glance at the events which immediately followed the death of Shah Aulum; and we cannot do so better than by extracting the account sent home by the Governor and Council of Fort St. George, in their General Letter to the Court of Directors. It records some circumstances which have not yet been published in reference to the accession first of Jehander Shah, and secondly of Feroksere; together with the first appointment of the Nizam of the Dekkan.

The first extract is dated October 14th, 1712, and is as follows.

"On the 3rd of April 1712, we received advices by way of Golcondah that king Shah Aulum died at Lahore on the 17th February, after very few days sickness, and most people are of opinion that he was poisoned. All his four sons being present when he died, immediately put themselves at the head of their friends to dispute the Empire. Azim-oos-Shaun, the second of the four who had the Government of Bengal many years, where he amassed vast treasures, was much more powerful both in men and money than any of the other three. For which reason Zulfikar Khan the Vizier, who was entirely in the interest of Moiz-ad-deen, the eldest brother, found means by fair promises to unite the elder with the two younger brothers against Azim-oos-Shaun; a verbal agreement being made between them, that Ruffeh-oos-Shaun the third brother should have the kingdom of Cabul, and Kojesta Acktar, the fourth, the kingdom of the Dekkan. Upon these terms they joined their armies and fought a bloody battle with their second brother; in which after, a stout resistance, he and his eldest son were slain. Moiz-ad-deen, having gained so complete a victory, and being proclaimed king, the two younger brothers sent to him to make good their agreement by a firmaun, that they might depart to their several kingdoms. To which Moiz-ad-deen returned answer (as it is said by the advice of Zulfikar Khan) that he was ready to put them in possession of their several Governments; but that he would reserve to himself the stamp of all money coined in his reign, and the Duroy,—for which we have no word in English, but the sense of it is that he would retain a Supreme power and command over them. These new terms enraged the two younger brothers to such a degree that they immediately joined their forces and invited the elder to a battle; declaring that they would be either real kings or die in the dispute. In this second battle fell the two younger brothers and their sons after a very sharp engagement; and it is said that of the youngest brother, who was a very valiant prince, had not been killed by a chance shot just as he had surrounded the eldest, he had taken him prisoner and won the battle. Zulfikar khan having been the main instrument in promoting the interest of Moiz-ad-deen, and behaved himself with wonderful courage in both battles, he was immediately confirmed Prime Vizier and received other unusual Honors, one of which was permitting him to have a seat in the king's presence. As soon as he had established the Government he slew several great Omrahs, who had been in his brother's interest, and imprisoned them. After this he marched with his camp away to Delhi, having disgusted most of the great Omrahs, by the honors done to Zulfikar Khan.

"Azim-oos-Shaun, upon leaving Bengal to go to his father Shah Aulum's court, left the Government of that kingdom in the hands of his second son Feroksere; who no sooner heard the death of his father, but he immediately set up for himself, raising forces and coining money in his own name, and endeavoured to seize upon the king's treasure in possession of the Dewan, but we do not hear he has yet effected it. The last adviees we had from Bengal were dated the 26th July, and give us an account that he was then at Patna with a considerable army; where he waits for Moiz-ad-deen's son, who is marehing against him; and they were in hopes the affair would be decided before the rains were set in, but that we believe is impossible."

The next extracts are taken from a General Letter to England, dated 18th September, 1713.

"We wrote your Honors by the last year's shipping the great Revolution that had happened in this Empire upon the death of Shah Aulum. We added that Prince Feroksere, son to Azim-oos-Shaun that governed Bengal, had passed Agra with his army and defeated the king his unele Jehandar Shah,* which has been sinee eonfirmed as follows.

"This young prince, hearing the sad fate of his father, by adviee of an old Seiad called Abdulla Khan, whom Aurungzebe had given him for a Tutor, immediately caused himself to be proclaimed king; and with his father's treasure, and what he raised in Patna among the merehants of all nations, he got a pretty good army altogether; and hearing his unele had disobliged most of the great Omrahs, by his barbarous cruelties and vicious course of life, he marehed directly for Agra, near whieh city the king's army gave him battle and was entirely defeated, many great men going over

* Jehandar Shah was the title assumed by Moiz-ad-deen on ascending the throne.

to Feroksere's side. The king with Zulfikar Khan fled to Delhi; but Feroksere with his victorious army followed them close at their heel and surrounded the city that immediately surrendered and took them prisoners. Few days after they were both murdered, and Feroksere now remains the peaceable possessor of the Empire. He has made Seiad Abdulla Khan his prime Vizier and Gousdeen Khan, who came over to him in the battle, Nabob of all the Dekkan country, which includes this Carnata, Bijapoor, and Golconda; he has the character of a brave generous man, and a friend to the Europeans.* We have news of his (the Nizam-ul-Mulk's) arrival at Aurungabad, and expect him to take his residence near Bijapoor, at a place called Burhampoor, where when arrived it will be absolutely necessary for us to address to him, because he has a very great interest with the present king and indeed throughout the Empire. Whatever we are obliged to do shall be managed with the greatest frugality. Your Honors will have heard from Bengal that our old friend Zoodee Khan came early into this new king's interest, and made a very brave defence in Hooghly against

* The father is here apparently confounded with the son. Gousdeen Khan (more properly Ghazee-ud-din Khan) was the father of Cheen Kulich Khan (Chicklis Khan in the records); and it was the latter who was appointed Viceroy of the Dekkan under the title of "Nizam-ul-Mulk, or "Regulator of the State." Cheen Kulich Khan, the "Nizam," was the founder of the great independent kingdom of the Dekkan, whose sovereigns still bare the name of their illustrious ancestor.

a much superior force on the side of the former king. He is now rewarded by being made Dewan of all the Dekkan country under Gousdeen Khan (i. e. the Nizam); which is a very great employment. The gentlemen in Bengal, who were very assisting to him under hand at Hooghly, seem to have their chief dependance upon him for introducing our present to the new king.

"Zulfikar Khan being cut off, there came immediate orders from Court to re-assume all the lands and villages that were granted him in these parts by Aurungzebe, in consideration of his good services in the conquest of the Gingee country. Accordingly the Dewan Sadatulla Khan sent us a summons to deliver up Egmore &c., villages granted us by Zulfikar Khan on account of the assistance we gave him with ammunition, and what else he wanted to carry on his designs. We have hitherto staved this business off with good words and pleading our rights; and when the new Nabob (Nizam) comes nearer, we will endeavor to get our grant confirmed. In the mean time, if any force is used to take them from us we resolve to defend them as well as we can. We are in daily expectation that our Dewan Sadatulla Khan will be turned out, as having been a Creature and Vassal of Zulfikar Khan. For which reason, we avoid purchasing his friendship in this matter by presents.

"The new king Feroksere is a young man of about twenty-six years of age. He has the character of being brave, prudent and generous; and is the last of the race of Aurungzebe except some young children imprisoned in the fortress of

Gwalior, where when once they have entered they never came out, and have potions given them to destroy their senses. This seems to be the King for whom Providence has designed your present, which leads us to touch upon that affair."

The following extract from a General Letter to England dated 14th October 1712 is curious as showing the changes in the trade which attended these revolutions in the Government, as well as the nature of the Native demand for the more important articles of English manufacture.

"In obedience to your commands we shall lay before your Honours, the best account we can get concerning the consumption of Broad Cloth and other manufactures in the Mogul's dominions. The coarse red and green broad cloth is chiefly used among the soldiers and ordinary Moormen for saddles, saddle cloths, sumpture cloth, covers, beds and cushions, for palankeens, carpets to sit upon, mantles to cover them from the rain and sometimes covering for their tents of pleasure. The fine broad cloth as scarlet, aurora, some blue and yellow is used for the inside of tents for vests or mantles in the rainy season among the great men; covering cloths for the Elephants and hackarys cloths to hang round their drums; for shoulder and waist Belts, scabbards to their swords and Jimdars or daggers; for slippers and for covers, beds and pillows, and for palankeens. The embossed cloth is used to hang round the bottom on the inside of the great men's tents three feet high; for spreadings to sit upon, and cushions to lean against; and for cloths to cover the Elephants and horses. Perpetuanos are only used among the meaner sort of people for caps, coats, and covering cloths to sleep in during the rains.

"And now we are upon this subject, we must inform your Honors that at least nine-tenths of the Woollen manufactures vended in these parts is among the Moors; the Gentoos making very little or no use of them. The greatest consumption is in the Mogul's camp, which when at Lahore or Delhi is supplied wholly from Surat and Persia; but when at Agra, partly from Surat and partly from Bengal by way of Patna, from which ports the conveyance to the camp is easy and safe. But what is disposed of hereabouts is dispersed among the Nabob's flying armies in the Carnatta country, Bijapore and Golcondah, seldom reaching so far as Aurungabad, because the carriage is very chargeable, and the roads are difficult and dangerous to pass. When king Shah Aulum came down to Golcondah with his army in the year 1708 to destroy his brother Kam Buksh, we immediately found a quicker vent than ordinary for our broad cloth; and indeed for all other sorts of goods consumed among them. And when Dawood Khan was formerly Nabob of these parts, he always kept a good body of horse in pay, which obliged the neighbouring Governors to do the same, being always jealous of each other. And among these horsemen by much the greatest quantity of our broad cloth then imported was consumed; the trade from this place to their camps being very considerable. But now our Dewan, who is Subah of all this country, seldom keeps above five hundred horse with him; and the Government in general being grown much weaker than in Aurungzebe's time, none of the great men keep up the number of horse allowed by the king, but apply the money to their own use; and this has brought a considerable damp to our trade in general, but more especially upon the sale of your manufactures. For we have not only lost the camp trade, but the roads are become impassable for want of these horsemen to scour them as usual; so that the merchants are discouraged from coming down with their money and diamonds to buy up and carry away our Europe and other goods as formerly; and we cannot see any likelihood of better times till the Government is well settled and some active man employed on the Government of these parts."

We now proceed with the general current of events at the Presidency. The troubles which accompanied the death of Shah Aulum and Jehandar Shah, and the accession of Feroksere, had induced a number of wealthy persons to take refuge in Fort St. George. Amongst others came the Nauvajee, or Collector General of the revenues of Zulfikar Khan, with treasure estimated at five or six hundred thousand pagodas. The following extract respecting this individual will explain itself.

"Thursday, 26th March, 1713. The President produces a Purwanna from the Subah Sadatulla Khan, wherein he demands by virtue of an order from Court, that the Nauvajee Collector of Zulfikar Khan's revenues in this Carnata country (who came down hither upon the beginning of the late troubles for the security of the treasure under his charge) be delivered up with the said treasure into the hands of Fire Khan his Deputy Governor at Arcot.

"The reason of this demand, we take to be, because the new King Feroksere has cut off Zulfikar Khan and his father Assid Khan, and would now seize upon all their treasure.

"The President further acquaints the Board that immediately upon receipt of the Perwanna, he sent it to the Nauvajee, with the slight intimation that we could not think of engaging ourselves in any disputes with the Country Government, by protecting persons employed under the King, contrary to his positive commands. To which he returned answer that he was ready to go directly to the Subah with the treasure, acknowledging the many civilities received during his residence here.

"Agreed that a proper answer be returned the Subah, acquainting him that as the Nauvajee came here a stranger upon his master's business, we were under an obligation to receive him with civility and distinction, but know nothing of the treasure he brought with him, it not being our custom to search strangers. But finding him very willing to return upon the first summons, we had no occasion to use any compulsion; and whatever he might bring with him he carries back under charge of the person that brought the Perwanna."

Our next extract is a further illustration of the disorderly character of the times.

"Wednesday, 16th September, 1713. The President acquaints the Board that Fleet Aynsworth writer did, on the 14th instant in the evening upon rising from supper at the General table, draw his sword and made several passes at Thomas Wilford writer, one of which entered his body, just under the left pap about three inches. Dr. Robson being sent for and examined, declares he has hopes the said Wilford may do well but that he is not yet out of danger. Ordered that Fleet Aynsworth writer be kept under strict confinement till further order." A few days afterwards it was agreed "that the said Aynsworth always behaved himself in a very disorderly manner, continually drinking, quarrelling with one or other, for which he has frequently been reprimanded to no purpose, as appears by this last bloody action;" and he was therefore dismissed the Company's service and sent to England by the first ship.

The following Will, which is entered in the consultation book of this period, furnishes a curious picture of social life.

"In the name of God, Amen, this thirteenth day of May in the year of our Lord one thousand, seven hundred and twelve, I, Thomas Saunders of Bengal, mariner, make this my last Will and Testament, in manner and form following. First, I commit my soul into the hands of God that gave it, and my body to be decently buried as my Executors shall think convenient. As for those worldly goods it has pleased Almighty God to bestow upon me, I give and bequeath in manner and form following; viz.

"To my Uncle Richard Saunder's Children, on

account of an adventure which was lost in the ship that I came to India, valued at one hundred and ten pounds sterling or thereabouts, sixteen hundred rupees, if they give no further trouble to my estate. Otherwise no more than the Law will give them.

"To a slave girl, named Clara, her liberty, with all her jewels and five hundred rupees; and if brought to bed within eight months and a half after my leaving Bengal, being the twenty-third day of January one thousand seven hundred eleven twelve, I bequeath unto the said child four thousand rupees and to be under the care of my Executors. A slave boy named Pompey I give his liberty, and five rupees per month during his life. A slave boy named Anthony, his freedom. If the said child that I bequeathed four thousand rupees dies afore it comes to age or married, then the said four thousand rupees shall go to my son John Saunders.

"The remainder part of my estate I bequeath unto my son John Saunders, after my debts are paid. If my son should die I give my wife, that was now Mrs. Martha Bingley, four thousand rupees, and each Executor four thousand rupees; the remainder part of my estate after the said Legacies above and my debts are paid unto my loving brothers John and Richard Saunders.

"I appoint executors to see this my last will and Testament executed, my esteemed friends Mr. James Williamson of Bengal and Mr. Charles Boone of Madras; and to manage my estate to the best advantage till my son comes of age. I allow my said Executors the power of remitting money to England for the use of my son, if there, and employing my estate to sea, if they shall think convenient for my son's best advantage; I put my son wholly under the care of my said Executors till of age. In witness whereof I have hereunto put my hand and seal in Gombroone the day and year above mentioned."

THOMAS SAUNDERS.

Our next extract will explain itself.

"Thursday, 8th October, 1713. The present Nabob Sadatulla Khan, having received a firmaun from the new King Feroksere, confirming him in the Government of these parts; upon which the French and Dutch have presented him each to the amount of a thousand pagodas or thereabouts; and having lately received a message by a horseman from him, that if we do not forthwith deliver up the villages he intends to come and take possession of them."

"Agreed that a present be sent to the amount of about five hundred pagodas, and lodged in the hands of Sunka Rama at Arcot, to be presented the Nabob by way of congratulation on account of his new dignity; but that it be a clause in the instructions to Sunka Rama, not to part with it before he gets assurances that we shall have no further troubles about the villages; and this to be done as from himself, because we will insist upon the goodness of our title and reserve a right to defend them upon occasion."

The year 1713 closed with a singular rebellion at Fort St. David. Our readers will remember that Mr. Raworth, the Deputy Governor, had gallantly conducted the defence of the place against Serope Singh, Rajah of Ginjee. They will now be surprised to hear that this same Mr. Raworth, openly rebelled against the authority of Governor Harrison. The story is best told in the following extracts from the consultations.

" Monday, 5th October. The President offers to the Board that the Method established by the Right Honorable Company for carrying on their mercantile affairs, and for the Government of their Garrisons and Factories, has been entirely neglected and despised by the Deputy Governor of Fort St. David, who has assumed to himself a liberty of acting as if he was independant of this Board. Consultations are neglected; Paymaster's and Cash accounts are fictitious and irregularly passed; and our strictest orders have been contemned. He has promoted and commissioned officers of the Garrison unknown to this Board. He has considerably increased the pay and allowances of several persons, particularly in Diet money to the Gentlemen of Council, three pagodas per month each, and almost all other expences in general. He has laid out considerable sums in building, and has let out the Company's bounds to rent without our knowledge or consent. He has used the Company's merchants very barbarously, whereby they have been necessitated to seek protection and redress from this Board. He returns no answers to such persons as have large and just demands upon him; with many other irregularities, which this Board ought not to bear with any longer, lest the Honorable Company's affairs should be brought into irrecoverable confusion.

"The President further offers to the Board several paragraphs of their general letters, as also a copy of a paper or protest signed by Mr. Raworth and Council, which were read and considered; and the Board came to the following Resolution.

"That whereas the Deputy Governor in his name, declares our proceedings (in sending for the Company's merchants up hither at their repeated request) to be highly prejudicial to the Company's interest, and that of this place; we are obliged to justify ourselves in as plain and public a manner as possible to our Right Honorable Employers; though we cannot but think it an inexcusable piece of presumption in Mr. Raworth to send us such a charge in a general letter from a subordinate Factory, which is giving encouragement to those under him by his example to dispute and disobey our orders hereafter.

"Agreed that a charge be brought in against Robert Raworth Esq. Deputy Governor of Fort St. David, containing such articles as can be fully proved without any room for dispute.

"Monday, 5th October. All the foregoing premises having been fully considered and debated the following question was put:

"Q. Whether this Board is not obliged upon the charge now read, and other circumstances concurring, to remove Robert Raworth Esq. from the Government of Fort St. David?

"Agreed in the affirmative nemine contradicente.

"Q. Whether he shall be suspended or dismissed?

"Agreed unanimously that he be suspended, that his commission be revoked and superseded, the same to be signified in a general letter to him with orders for him to repair hither when his charge shall be delivered him."

"Agreed and ordered that Mr. Henry Davenport be commissioned as commissary and Provisional Deputy Governor of Fort St. David, to set out this evening, in order to receive the Government from Mr. Robert Raworth.

"Sunday, 11th October. The President communicates to the Board a letter from Henry Davenport Esq., advising us, that, upon his arrival at the edge of the bounds of Fort St. David, he dispatched Lieutenant Porrier before with our letter to Mr. Raworth, and a short one from himself. To which Mr. Raworth in a short time returned answer, that he would not allow him any authority to rule there by whatever commission he could receive from us. All the outworks were alarmed with the usual signals for enemies when Mr. Davenport entered the bounds; and when he came to Tevenapatam gate, he was denied entrance by shutting it upon him, and the officer's declaring he had an order not to let him in. All the Council came in to Mr. Davenport, except Mr. Richard Harrison. Ensign Hobbs being posted at the Garden with a hundred men, Mr. Davenport sent to him for admittance there; but he sent word that he would obey no orders but Mr. Raworth's, and that if he offered to come into the Garden with any peons or soldiers, he would fire upon him. Upon which, finding the whole Garrison debauched from their duty (except old Captain Hugonin and some other of the officers which were confined before hand), he was forced to retire out of the bounds to a choultry about five miles distance, for the security of his life and the treasure he has with him ; Mr. Raworth having given out several unaccountable orders to some of the officers, and publicly threatened to cut him off.

"This affair being debated, with the greatest concern to see a whole Garrison of five hundred men and upwards, seduced by some false persuasions from their duty to our Right Honorable Employers, and commanded openly to resist our orders which may be of very ill consequence hereafter.

"Agreed that it is not safe for Mr. Davenport to remain where he is, considering the small guard he has with him and the threatening expressions Mr. Raworth has used.

"Ordered that he do forthwith return hither and bring with him the Gentlemen of the Fort St. David Council (that cannot safely return into the Bounds), to inform us of several necessary points before we can come to any further resolution."

"Monday, 12th October. A general letter from Henry Davenport Esq. and Council dated the 10th instant from Monapa's choultry ; read also a private letter from Mr. Davenport to the President ; advising that Mr. Richard Harrison is as active in this rebellion as any officer in the Garrison ; that the council now with him (Mr. Davenport) affirm that by the promotion of several officers and increasing their pay, Mr. Raworth has the majority entirely at command, and that he openly declares he will stick at nothing to be revenged. They add further that he has held no consultation, since August; transacting the Company's affairs wholly by himself.

"The President's private letter being wrote after the General advices, that Ensigns Paddle and Handlon were come over to Mr. Davenport, and acquainted him that the Garrison was in great confusion and most of them would follow, if they were sure of a place to resort to; that they had received no pay for two months past, which is very surprising to us considering that we know they are in cash, though they have kept the account so long from us.

"Agreed that orders be immediately sent to Mr. Davenport to remain where he is, and see what the Garrison will do; that a party of sixty chosen men be forthwith sent away to be landed at Pondicherry for a guard to Mr. Davenport and the others, against any sudden attempt of the desparadoes; and that a protest be drawn up against Mr. Raworth for this unwarrantable way of proceeding."

"Thursday, 15th October. A general letter from Henry Davenport Esq., dated the 13th instant read, advising that he has dropped declarations and copies of his commission at the several guards, which has had a very good effect and occasioned many men coming in; that whole Garrison seem inclinable to return to their duty, and that he has now so many men with him that he is forced to draw towards Pondicherry for assistance to maintain them.

"Agreed that it be an instruction to Henry Davenport Esq., and Council to avoid as much as possible coming to blows; and not to attack any party or post, unless obliged to it for their own safety; but to use all peaceable methods of recovering the men to their duty, promising them full pardon and their arrears.

"Agreed that Mr. William Warre and the Revd. Mr. George Lewis be immediately sent down with proper instructions to persuade Mr. Raworth to reason, by representing the ill consequences that are likely to attend his rash way of proceeding."

"Monday, 19th October. The President lays before the Board several letters from Henry Davenport Esq., advising that finding himself strong enough he marched into the bounds on the 17th very peaceably, finding all the out guards deserted; and that he put a serjeant with twenty men into one of the most considerable to protect it from the country enemy. After which he marched to the Garden, where he found Ensign Hobbs posted with about fifty men, whom he summoned to their duty. But they absolutely refused to surrender, and he would not force them, though it was very practicable, for fear of shedding blood. But while they were parleying, they were saluted with a twenty-four pounder from the Fort that fell within twenty yards of Mr. Davenport. After which he marched away and took possession of Cuddalore, that was also entirely deserted; in their way being open to the Fort, they were again saluted with a twenty-four pounder, which fell among them, but by God's good providence did no harm.

"Agreed that Henry Davenport Esq. and Council remain at Cuddalore, endeavouring to save our bounds without committing any acts of hostility, whilst Mr. Warre and Mr. Lewis are endeavouring to terminate this unhappy affair; and that they do set the merchants to work as fast as possible to procure Long Cloth and Sallampores."

"Wednesday, 21st October. The President communicates a letter from Henry Davenport Esq., advising that he has put men into as many of the out guards as he can spare from Cuddalore. But that on the 18th instant Mr. Raworth sent a party of horse to beat the men out of Condapah Choultry, who dismounted and summoned them within to surrender; which being refused they fired upon them and threw in several Granadoes, which wounded some of the men and killed one outright. The Serjeant that commanded immediately fired a field piece with partridge shot, which killed two and wounded three more of the attackers. Upon which the rest fled, leaving five of their horses behind them. The Serjeant being so near the Fort, and at least six miles distance from Cuddalore, dreading a more dangerous attack in the night, when he could not be supported, withdrew in time to Cuddalore and the five horses with him. Mr. Raworth just before the attack was made, fired three great shots at the Choultry from Tevenapatam, which fell very near them."

Friday, 23rd October. "A general letter from Henry Davenport, Esq., and Council, dated the 19th instant read, advising that those who remain in the Fort and at the Garden with Mr. Raworth, are already reduced to such necessities that many of them would get away if they could.

"A letter from Messrs. Warre and Lewis, dated the 20th instant, read, advising their reception by Mr. Raworth; that they had fairly laid all matters before him as recommended in our instructions. Upon which he desired sometime to consider thereon, and he would give them an answer in the evening, seeming in very good temper; that they went to Cuddalore and returned to him about five o'clock, when he very briefly answered that provided the Governor would come in person, he would immediately resign, upon condition that those who had been faithful to him (as he calls it) should be treated with superior respect to such as deserted. Upon which they desired time to receive our answer, and got his consent to forbear all acts of hostility till then. This matter being debated,

"Agreed that as matters now stand here with the Nabob, and considering the necessary preparations to load our shipping that are expected early from Bengal, it is no way convenient for the President to leave this place; especially when Mr. Raworth insists on such terms as are impossible for us to consent to; since it is no better than confessing ourselves in the wrong, and encouraging others hereafter to follow this wicked and pernicious example.

"It was also considered that if the Nabob should come to St. Thomé, as is credibly reported, the President cannot come back hither till February by sea; nor can he come by land without passing through his camp at his mercy, since he can have no body of men with him fit to force his way.

"Agreed that a letter be wrote to Mr. William Warre and the Rev. Mr. George Lewis, requiring them to see Mr. Raworth once more, and offer him every thing that is in our power to grant, provided he will surrender quietly without any further troubles or mischief.

"Agreed that a short commission be given Mr. William Warre to receive the Government at Mr. Raworth's hands, if he should consent, and to make all easy, insisting only upon not seeing Mr. Davenport before he comes away hither.

"Agreed that if Mr. Raworth does not accept the terms offered him in our letter of this date, Mr. Warre and the Rev. Mr. Lewis be permitted to return."

"Wednesday, 28th October. General letter from Messrs. Davenport: Warre and Lewis, dated 24th instant read, advising that the two latter having been with Mr. Raworth that same day, found him in much worse temper than ever peremptorily declaring that he would resign the Fort to none but the President himself.

"A letter from Henry Davenport Esq. singly of the same date read, wherein he says, he is very well assured Mr. Raworth will not deliver up even to the President himself, and that there is no way but to starve him out.

" Sunday, 1st November. The President produces a letter from Mr. William Warre and the Rev. Mr. George Lewis, dated the 27th, wherein they say that though they must acknowledge themselves mistaken as to Mr. Raworth's sincerity, they are still of opinion, the Governor's presence would soon put an end to all disputes. The foregoing words being considered and debated, and the President acquainting the Board that by the last advices from Sunka Rama at Arcot, matters are likely to be fairly accommodated with the Nabob about the villages,

" Agreed that there seems an absolute necessity for the President to set out for Fort St. David, as soon as the rivers will permit, in order to put an end to the present troubles if possible before further mischief is done.

" Agreed that a party of sixty men be despatched away before hand to Pondicherry, for a guard to wait the President's arrival; and that a hundred Pagodas be advanced the ensign to defray their expenses."

" Wednesday, 4th November. This evening the Honorable President attended by the Rev. Mr. Stevenson, Lieutenant Roach, and Messrs. Theobalds, Bulkley, Maubert, Nanney, Langlier, Turner, and Richardson set out overland for Fort St. David.

" Friday, 6th November. A general letter from the Honorable President and Mr. William Warre, dated the 5th November, read, enclosing several letters and papers the Honorable President met upon the Road, and advising that they have fired six shots into Cuddalore from the Fort in one day, but it pleased God they did no damage; that some deserters daily came in, and that Henry Davenport Esq. has possessed himself of Condapa Choultry and Horse tail point, in order to facilitate the Honorable President's entry into the Bounds.

"A general letter from Henry Davenport, Esq. and Council dated the 3rd instant read, wherein they acquaint us that they were in great hopes Mr. Raworth and his adherents, would by this time have been reduced to a very low condition for want of provisions. But that contrary to their expectations, and to the promise made to the Deputy Governor from the Gentlemen at Pondicherry no ways to assist them, of which he reminded Governor Dusivier in his letters dated 29th ultimo and 3rd instant; notwithstanding which there was a chelinga sent them full of provisions. They further advise the sloop, that was sent down with stores for Cuddalore, as she passed by Fort St. David they fired three shots at her; but that she continued her course for the road and that Mussoolas were gone off to bring the stores ashore. They also remit us their account cash for the month of October, balance being six thousand three hundred and ninety-five pagodas.

"Thursday, 12th November. Another of the 10th informs that after the hopes they had of bringing matters to an end that they found Mr. Raworth the same fickle and unfaithful man as veer; that they had sent the same persons in that morning with such terms as they thought he neither could nor would refuse; but were strangely surprized at their return to find he absolutely refused what he gave under his hand the day before; which was that if the Governor insisted he would bring the keys of the Fort where he pleased; that they had offered to venture into the Fort if he would permit Captain Road to go in first with fifty men for the Governor's Guard. For which his answer was under his hand, that he would not suffer the Governor to enter with any guard, and several other extravagancies; so that they can see no hopes of his being brought to better temper whilst he is able to hold out."

"Sunday, 22nd November. General letter from the Honorable Edward Harrison Esq., Messrs. Davenport and Warre dated 20th instant read, wherein they acquaint us that having perused the Fort St. David cash accounts from April 1712, and by what they can learn from the Council &c., Mr. Raworth ought now to have a balance by him of seventeen thousand pagodas, which they took to be one of his chief reasons for acting in this unaccountable manner; that Mr. Raworth and his adherents being cooped up in the Fort and in want of provisions are very uneasy; that some desert him daily, but not without the risk of their lives. They add that on the 18th in the morning Mr. Raworth saluted them in the Garden with a fourteen pounder; but afterwards made an apology that a drunken Dutchman fired the gun, between sleeping and waking, that happened to be pointed that way; that on the 19th at night the President, being accompanied with all the Madras Gentlemen, went into Tevenapatam to visit the men posted there; and having been for sometime in the streets, they were briskly entertained from the batteries with all the guns they could bring to bear, besides their small shot, in the reach of which they happened to be; but by Good Providence no mischief was done; that they returned them a Culverin salute from Patcharee hill, which went through Mr. Raworth's lodgings, as they learn from deserters; that several of the men sallied from the Fort, but were warmly received, and two very dangerously wounded, which made them return faster than they came out."

"Tuesday, 1st December. General letter from the Honorable Edward Harrison, Esq. and Mr. William Warre, dated 29th ultimo read, wherein they acquaint us that they have not as yet brought Mr. Raworth to an accommodation; and that they are fearful they must be obliged to consent to his going to Pondicherry to reside there and settle his account; and if so Governor Dusivier is to give his parole that in case satisfaction is not given us in fifteen days he will deliver Mr. Raworth to us at Fort St. George."

"Monday, 7th December. From the Honorable President and Mr. William Warre, dated the 2nd instant, advising but that that morning the Honorable President entered the Fort, according to articles of agreement passed between him and Council and Mr. Raworth; who received him at the head of his rebellious crew in such a manner as none but Mr. Raworth could be capable of;

seeming no ways concerned for the many ill actions he has committed in this affair. There was a hundred and thirty men under arms in the Fort, of whom eighty Europeans, who seemed to be as stout men as any in the Company's service. Every thing was found in confusion; which will require the President's longer stay than he expected; as also to settle the Garrison and separate those he found in the Fort, that it may not hereafter be in their power to act the like again."

"Monday, 7th December. Henry Davenport acquaints the Board, that he this afternoon received a private letter from the Honorable President, dated the 5th, advising that Thomas Frederick, Esq. arrived at Fort St. David that night; and that the next day in the evening the Honorable President designed to depart thence for Fort St. George, expecting to reach the Mount to-morrow night, where he desired the Gentlemen of the Council would go and wait upon him.

"Monday, 21st December. The following general letters read. From the Governor of Pondicherry dated 30th instant (new style) advising that Mr. Raworth, having publicly demanded their king's protection and passage upon their ships for France, which they cannot refuse him without exposing themselves to their king's displeasure.

"The President likewise produces a letter from Father Thomas de Poictiers, Capuchin of the Church here, whom he has employed at Pondicherry to solicit the Governor and Council on this affair; wherein the said Father Thomas advises that one of the principal reasons why Mr. Raworth refused to come hither and settle his account with us, was that he had seen a letter from a member of this Board to a person at Fort St. David, mentioning that it was resolved to have him assassinated. Every member now present solemnly declares, and offers to take his oath if required, that he never gave him any such advices, nor ever heard the Governor say any thing tending that way.

"The Governor for himself solemnly protests before God that he abhors the very thought of so barbarous an action; though he can bring sufficient proof that Mr. Raworth, when Deputy Governor of Fort St. David, did more than once threaten the same to him.

"It being debated what measures are most proper for us to take upon this extraordinary proceeding of the Governor and Councils of Pondicherry; agreed that we defer coming to a resolution thereupon till Father Thomas returns from Pondicherry."

"Thursday, 24th December. Mr. Raworth's answer to the proposals made him in the Governor's name by Padre Thome read which is full of notorious falsities and calumny without any manner of ground or proof and of a piece with all the rest of his behaviour, and upon the whole it appears very plain that he will do or suffer anything rather than come to a fair account for what he has had under his charge."

This extraordinary affair ended shortly afterwards in Mr. Raworth's departure to France; and it is a singular circumstance that he died at Paris, just as the Directors of the Company were preparing to prosecute him in England.

CHAPTER XXVII.

GOVERNORSHIP OF MR. EDWARD HARRISON.

(Continued.)

1714—7.

Before proceeding further with our extracts from the records of the Governorship of Mr. Edward Harrison, it will be necessary to glance at the contemporary state of India. Shah Aulum, eldest son of Aurungzebe, had died in 1712; and a struggle ensued between his four sons which terminated in the establishment of Jehandar Shah on the throne of Delhi. Jehandar Shah owed his elevation to the support of Zulfikar Khan, but his vices rapidly lowered him in the eyes of his subjects, and excited the religious hostility of all who respected the precepts of the Prophet. A drunken sovereign, ruled by a concubine who had once been a public dancer, and frequently appearing in the streets of Delhi in a condition which but too plainly indicated his vices, was not the potentate who could long hope to maintain his authority over a distracted empire like that of the Moguls. Two Seiads, or descendants of the Prophet, advocated the cause of Feroksere, a nephew of Jehandar Shah. Forces were raised, the imperial army was defeated, and Jehandar Shah and his minister Zulfikar Khan were both taken and put to death.

Feroksere now ascended the throne at Delhi, and ruled the empire from 1713 to 1720. His reign thus corresponds to about four years of the Governorship of Mr. Harrison, and three years of his successor Mr. Collett. It is remarkable from the fact that a mission was at this time sent to Delhi by the English Governor of Calcutta; and many advantages, including the disputed out villages near Madras, and the Zemindarship of some villages in the neighbourhood of Calcutta, were at that time obtained from the Mogul. Fortunately copies of most of the original dispatches from the English envoys at Delhi to the Governors of Calcutta and Madras, have been preserved in the Madras records; and these documents throw a flood of light upon the intrigues of the period, and enable us to obtain a clear picture of the court of the Great Mogul. This mission arrived in Delhi in 1715 and left it in 1717, and thus extended over a period of two years. As it is a subject of imperial interest rather than of local interest, we shall not incorporate the narrative embodied in the dispatches with the history of Mr. Harrison's administration, but reserve it for a future and separate chapter.

As regards the changes more immediately effecting the Madras Presidency, we may remark that Cheen Kulich Khan, variously spelt in the records, had been appointed Subah of the Dekkan under the title of Nizam-ool-Moolk; an individual who is remarkable in the history of Southern India as the founder of the present kingdom of the Dekkan. Our old friend Dawood Khan obtained the Soubahship of Guzerat in place of Golconda, but was killed in a battle a year or two afterwards. At the same time Sadatulla Khan continued Nabob of the Carnatic, and effected the reduction of the great fortress of Ginjee, which had been defended by the son of that Serope Singh, who has already been introduced to our readers as the Rajah who nearly succeeded in capturing Fort St. David.

We now turn to the local annals of the Presidency. The records of the remaining period of Mr. Harrison's Governorship contain but few matters worthy of interest. The reduction of Ginjee in 1714 is thus noticed in the consultation books.

"Saturday, 9th October 1714. General letter from the Deputy Governor and Council of Fort St. David, dated the 6th instant, advising that our Nabob Sadatulla Khan had drawn all his forces round Ginjee, and summoned Serope Singh's son to surrender, upon pretence of an order from Court to take possession of that place ; which he refused to do, and making a desperate sally with about 300 Rajpoots, was very near killing the Nabob, having cut the harness of his Elephant with his own hands. But timely succour coming into the Nabob's rescue, Tejah Sing, Serope Singh's son, with Mohabut Khan and several others of the principal men belonging to Ginjee, were overpowered and cut off, so that it is believed Ginjee will surrender in a few days." On the 15th of November the news arrived that Ginjee was captured by Sadatulla Khan.

The following strange revelation appears in a

petition addressed by one Dr. Thomas to the Governor in Council, dated 9th November, 1714.

"The humble petition of Doctor Thomas.

"Showeth,

"That your petitioner's father-in-law Lewis de Melho in his life time held a converse with one of his slaves named Ignacia near the space of thirty years; living with her in a separate house, and entrusting the greatest part of his estate in her hands, and taking no notice of his wife or daughter. But upon his death bed repenting himself of the ills he had done, he asked pardon of his wife for his ill usage of her; and declared that the said Ignacia had been the cause of it by the power of medicines she had given him, and that he had delivered into her charge 2600 pagodas in money, besides jewels and medicines of value. And he did appoint and constitute his said wife and daughter heiresses to his estate; as appears by a certificate under the hand of the Rev. Padre Paschall Perciva de Cuntra. But now so it is, may it please your Honor that the said Ignacia refuses to deliver up or give any account of the said estate; though it can be proved by witnesses that she has divers things of a large value as well as money in her possession. Wherefore your petitioner, in behalf of his mother-in-law Francisca and his wife Isabella, humbly prays that your Honor will oblige the said slave to make a true discovery and surrender of all those things in her possession, belonging to the estate of the deceased Mr. Lewis de Melho, that so they may have their right, and he as in duty bound shall ever pray."

The Governor and Council ordered that the goods should be secured, but referred the matter to the decision of the heads of their Castes.

On the 1st of August, 1714, died Queen Anne, and the crown of England thus descended to George I. The event passed off quietly and more than eight months passed away before the news reached Madras. It will be seen from the following entry, that the Presidency still kept early hours.

"Friday, 8th April, 1715. The letter read advising the unfortunate death of Her late Majesty Queen Anne, and the happy accession of His most serene Highness the Elector of Hanover and Brunswick to the Imperial crown of Great Britain under the title of King George; at nine o'clock this morning the Mayor and Aldermen, attended with the proper officers and a company of soldiers belonging to the Garrison, proclaimed his Royal Majesty King George; and at noon there was an entertainment made for the council and all the chief inhabitants of the place, at which his Royal Majesty, the Prince of Wales, the Royal family and the Honorable Company's healths were drank and guns fired at each."

The following extract concerning the Capuchin Friars, is a curious testimony to their character at this time.

"Monday, the 12th December 1715. "Edward Harrison Esq., President of and for all the Right Honorable United English East India Company's affairs on this coast of Coromandel and Orissa, in the Ginjee and Mahratta countries, Commander in Chief of all the forces, which now are or hereafter may or shall be employed for the Service of the said United Company under this Presidency, and Governor of the Fort St. George, St. David, and Council. To all to whom these presents shall come Greeting.

"Know ye, that the Reverend the Capucin Fathers of the French nation that officiate in the Portuguese Church of this place, and others of the same nation and order at Pondicherry that formerly resided here, having made application to us for our assistance to justify themselves from several aspersions that have lately been cast upon them in France by their inveterate enemies, in order to blast their reputation and render them contemptible in these parts of the world, and having in order thereto humbly proposed the following queries.

"1st. Whether the Capucin Fathers that have dwelt and officiated in this city of Madras from the first settlement to this time, viz. Ephraim de Nevers, Zenon de Bauge, Cosme de Gien, Jacques de Bourges, Esprit de Tours, Laurent d'Engouleme, Michael Ange de Bourges, Rene d'Engouleme, and Thomas de Poitiers; they or any of them ever behaved themselves otherwise than became their sacred function as Missionaries and persons in Religious orders, or whether they have given any cause for scandal by their deportment.

"2nd. Whether they have ever had any quarrels or differences among themselves, which obliged them to have recourse to our Tribunal for an accommodation, and particularly Father Esprit de Tours with Father Michael Ange before mentioned.

"3rd. Whether the Capucin Fathers of Madras or those of Pondicherry, particularly Father Esprit de Tours, either now have or ever had any money at Interest or otherwise in the Cash of the Right Honorable Campany our Masters.

"4th. Whether Father Thomas de Poitiers, now residing and officiating here, ever bought or sold 500 chests of Persia wine, as he is accused of having done in the year 1713, or before or since that time.

"To the first article we are obliged to declare that the Capucin Fathers above named, who have had the care of the mission in this city of Madras from the first establishment thereof to the present time by permission of our Right Honorable Masters, have always demeaned themselves in so handsome a manner, both in spiritual and temporal affairs, as to give no just cause of complaint to us their representatives; their conduct has been regular and agreeable to their profession, nor have we ever heard of or remarked any action of theirs that could occasion the least scandal to their order.

"To the second article, we never heard, nor can we find upon examining our Registers, that any of the said Capucin Fathers, particularly the persons before mentioned in this article, ever had any difference, which obliged them to have recourse to this or any other Tribunal here for a decision.

"To the third article, we must declare it to be a notorious falsity that the Capucin Father of Madras or Pondicherry, or of any other place, ever had any money or effects at Interest or otherwise in the Right Honorable Company's cash that we know of.

"To the fourth article, we know it to be very false that Father Thomas de Poitiers bought or sold 500 chests of wine in 1713, either he or any other of the same order; and we further certify that none of the Capucins before mentioned have ever been known to be concerned in any sort of commerce whatsoever. In witness whereof, we have at their humble request given them this our certificate, which could not in conscience be refused. Done in Fort St. George this 12th day of December 1715, and sealed with the Right Honorable Company's seal."

From this testimony to the character of the Capuchin Fathers we turn to the proceedings of the Protestant inhabitants. The scheme set on foot for a Charity School in Madras has already been noticed; and the following copy of the Rules will be found curious and interesting.

"Rules for the better establishing and management of the Charity School, erected by the unanimous consent of the Vestry of St. Mary's parish in Fort St. George, on the 28th October 1715.

"That in some convenient place within the English town, there be proper accommodation made at first for 30 poor Protestant Children, dict and education gratis.

"That the Scholars be trained up to a practical sense of religion, and bc particularly instructed in the doctrines of the Church of England as by law established; and therefore no person shall be capable of being master of the School unless he be qualified according to the acts of Parliament.

"That the children, whether boys or girls, shall be taken into the School house at five years of age or thereabout; and be put out to service or apprenticeships when they are about 12 years old. And while they are entertained in the School, the boys shall be taught to read, write, cast accounts, or what they may be further capable of, and the girls shall be instructed in reading and the necessary parts of house wifery.

"That no scholar shall be taken in, nor any matter of moment transacted, without the previous consent of the Honorable Governor for the time being.

"That besides the Ministers and Church wardens, who shall always be overseers of the Charity School, there be three others chosen yearly by the Vestry for the better management and more careful inspection of the affairs of the School; and in order thereunto, that the said overseers (or at least four of them) meet every week at the Vestry, and keep Minutes of what they agree upon (if it be of any moment) to be laid before the Governor for his approbation.

"That one of the overseers annually chosen by the Vestry shall at the same time be nominated Treasurer to the School, and be obliged to keep exact regular accounts of the School stock and expenses; to be laid before every Vestry, and before the other overseers, or any of the contributors, when they require it at any of their weekly meetings or otherwise.

"That when the Cash belonging to the School stock shall amount to the sum of 1,000 pagodas, it shall be employed at sea, or let out at interest, by the treasurer, with the advice of the rest of the overseers, and the consent of the Governor; and if the money cannot be thus employed, that it be lent to the Church at the usual interest.

"That all Bonds, Deeds of conveyance, and other writs for the use and benefit of the Charity School, shall be drawn and granted in the name of the Treasurer and other overseers for the time being.

"That all Legacies, Gifts, and Benefactions to the School, whether of money or other things, be duly entered by the Treasurer in a Book to be kept for that purpose, which he shall sign at the foot of every page.

"That no part of the School stock shall on any pretence whatsoever be employed to any purpose, or in any manner, but what is agreeable to the original design and institution above expressed.

"That in all difficult cases and disputes about any matter of consequence, the overseers shall make application to the Governor for calling a vestry, wherein all such matters shall be determined by the majority of the contributors.

"That the aforesaid articles shall be the standing rules and fundamental constitutions of the Charity School, according to which the overseers shall always be obliged to act. And therefore that the said rules shall be registered in the beginning of a

Book, wherein the said overseers shall enter all the subsequent orders and regulations which they may have occasion to make hereafter concerning the said school; providing that such subsequent orders shall be first approved by the Governor and Council for the time being."

In connection with this subject we make the following extracts, respecting the library in Fort St. George, from a general letter received from the Board of Directors about this time.

"We understand that the Library in Fort St. George is worthy our notice, as consisting not only of a great number of Books, but of a great many that are choice and valuable. John Dolben Esq., Mr. Richard Elliot, and others having made a present of their Books (which were considerable) to the Library, besides other augmentations it hath lately received from the Society for Promoting Christian Knowledge. We therefore recommend the care of the Library to our President and Ministers; ordering that the said Books (such at least as are of value) be put up in close presses to keep them from dust and vermin; and that none of them be lent or carried out of the Library, without the consent of both Minsters, if two shall be on the place; and the Books so carried out shall be entered in a book kept for that purpose, inserting the day and year when the person to whom it is lent on one side of the folio, and on the other the day and year when returned.

"And we order our Ministers to sort the said Books into proper classes, and to take a catalogue of them to be kept in the Library, of which they shall deliver a copy to our President, and send a copy home to us ; and we desire our President to order two of our Servants, together with our Ministers, to examine the Books by the Catalogue once a year ; that is to say some few days before the Vestry is held and make their report at the Vestry. It would be very proper also to put our chop on the said Books in the title page or first leaf, to show to whom they belong, if they should any of them happen to be stolen, and to stamp our arms on the cover."

The next extract refers to an incident already recorded, from which it seems that at one time the Mussulman inhabitants contributed to the support of the Hindoo pagodas ; an arrangement which was finally abolished during the Governorship of Mr. Harrison.

"Monday, 16th January, 1716. Petition of the Patan Merchants Inhabitants of this place, and several others that trade hither annually from Bengal; wherein they set forth the hardship of being obliged, contrary to the rules of their religion, to contribute to the maintenance of the Gentoo Idols.

"This affair having formerly occasioned great disputes and troubles, particularly once in the time of Governor Pitt, and again since the arrival of the present Governor ; at which time it was decided in favour of the Gentoo Pagoda upon account of its having been a custom of long standing, and that our Honorable Masters approved of what was done in the time of Mr. Pitt ; but now the Board being sensible it has occasioned a great heart burning among the Patan merchants aforesaid, who annually import great quantities of rich goods from Bengal; insomuch that we find they begin to leave us and land their goods at St. Thomé, where the present Nabob has granted them a Cowle with several valuable privileges, and particularly that they shall pay no more than 2 per cent. custom:—it is thought high time to use all means in our power to make these people easy and prevent their forsaking us to settle at St. Thomé.

"Accordingly agreed that the President make for them a Cowle for collecting that duty themselves, Kanakapillâ, of 25 cash for every pagoda, to be applied to the maintenance of their own Mosque; and to promise them all manner of favourable usuge, and encouragement, if they continue to trade hither as usual."

The following extraordinary story of a common soldier, who passed himself off as a Chaplain, and married himself to the daughter of his Captain without her father's consent, is worthy of preservation.

"Tuesday, 12th June, 1716. The worshipful the Mayor acquaints the Board that Captain William, having entered an action against John Mitchel in the Mayor Court for defaming his daughter and deluding her by a pretended marriage, in which he officiated himself as Priest and husband. Upon which a trial ensued, and due proof being made by several sufficient witnesses, as well as from the said Mitchell's original letters; the Court had respited judgment on account of his being in the Military service, till the pleasure of this Board be known, what punishment shall be inflicted in such a case.

"The Board taking this matter into consideration, it appears that the forementioned John Mitchel came out a soldier upon the last year's ships to serve the Honorable Company the usual term of years. But pretending himself a regular clergyman in Holy Orders, and that he had served some years Chaplain of one of her Majesty's ships of war, but was forced to abscond and fly for these parts upon account of a debt contracted by being bound for a brother in England; which circumstances inclining every body to compassionate him (though he brought no Orders with him) he was taken off is duty as a Soldier, and employed as Master to the Charity School lately established in this place, at a handsome salary, with all fitting encouragement, besides a recommendation to the Honorable Company in our last general letter. But since that time he has been guilty of many irregularities and scandalous actions, altogether unbecoming the profession he pretends to; many of which appear under his own hand, and others are proved by undoubted testimony, and particularly his unwarrantable action of marrying himself clandestinely. Wherefore the Board thinks fit to come to the following resolutions concerning him.

"That the said Mitchel, if in holy orders (as he pretends but cannot prove) has basely scandalized the priesthood by an irregular and unheard of way of marrying himself to a woman, and absolutely against her father's consent.

"That the Board is not obliged to regard him otherwise in this case than a soldier, enlisted in the Honorable Company's service upon the usual terms, and that he ought to be punished accordingly.

"That however as he has appeared under the notion of a clergyman, and been entertained as School Master, it will not be proper to expose him to public punishment in the eye of the natives; and not having wherewithal to make just satisfaction to the persons he has injured, it is agreed that the said John Mitchel, Centinel, do give sufficient security for his good behaviour; or else that he be kept under confinement till opportunity offers to send him off the place for Europe."

Mr. Edward Harrison left the Madras Presidency on the 8th January 1717, upon which the governorship fell to Mr. Joseph Collett. The last months of his administration and the opening months of the administration of his successor were occupied by another of those strange disputes between the Right and Left Hands, which furnish such curious illustrations of the character of the people. We have already brought forward the narrative of more than one of these caste riots; but some curious particulars are recorded in connection with the present disturbance which are worth preserving.

It may help the reader somewhat if we mention that in olden times the Chetties and Comatees had separate streets and separate idols; the Chetties belonging to the Left Hand Caste and the Comatees to the Right Hand. A Comatee could never enter a Chetty street except by permission of the Chetties, and then he could not enter it in a carriage, or a palanquin, or even with shoes on his feet. A Chetty was also prohibited in the same manner from entering a street belonging to a Comatee. The present dispute seems to have arisen in consequence of a Comatee having presumed to offer ceremonies to an idol belonging to the Chetties.

"Friday, 12th October 1716. A dispute having arisen between the Chetty and Comatee or Banian castes, about some ceremonies at their feasts, the former pretending that the latter have usurped several titles belonging to them, and performed some ceremonies before an image that they have no right to do. The heads of the Right and Left Hand castes were called in, and acquainted that the Board is very unwilling to intermeddle in any business of this nature, which they cannot pretend to understand; and therefore they are strictly enjoined to keep the peace among themselves, and by no means to disturb the quiet of the place, upon pain of forfeiting the 12,000 pagodas mentioned in the agreement between the castes in consultation the 21st of June, 1708. They were further required to choose a number of persons out of the neutral caste to decide their differences without further delay by fair arbitration; which the Left Hand side readily agreed to, but the Right Hand insist to choose out of their own caste, and a number of Brahmins* besides; which the Board judges to be unreasonable and therefore orders them to choose ten Brahmins for each party, and to enter into arbitration bonds without further delay."

"Monday, 15th October. The President acquaints the Board that upon summoning the heads of the Comatee and Chetty castes to sign their arbitration bonds according to order of last consultation, they flew off from their agreement; the Comatees insisting to choose out of all the Right Hand castes, which are of their own side. Consequently the Left Hand would be over-powered by numbers, and therefore refuse to comply. Whereupon we were obliged to confine them all to the Merchants Godowns till they can come to some agreement among themselves; the disturbance daily increasing in the Black Town; and the Painters of Triplicane, that had the Honorable Company's work in hand, having deserted their habitations."

"The Heads were again called in, and the ill consequence of this foolish dispute fairly laid before them; but all persuasions being to no purpose, they were again remanded to the Godown."

"Thursday, 18th October. Colloway Chetty appears as the Head of the Chetty caste, and makes an offer of having the difference between them and the Comatees decided among the heads of all their castes in the country; by means of

---

* The Brahmins are the neutral caste; they belonging neither to the Right Hand nor to the Left Hand.

Deputies to be sent from hence; which appearing to be a reasonable expedient, it is agreed to let the parties concerned have their liberty, in hopes they will come to an accomodation in this way."

"Thursday, 25th October. The President acquaints the Board that when all things seemed in a fair way towards an accommodation between the castes, the following accident happened on the 21st instant.

"A young lad of the Left hand caste having done hurt to a Pariah woman of the Right hand castes (big with child), the whole caste got together and came in a tumultuous manner to demand justice. Upon examining the matter, he ordered the offender to close confinement, promising the heads of the caste to do them justice when it should appear whether the woman would die or live. They seemed satisfied, and the crowd was dispersed. But in the night, without any further provocation, they got together again; and all such as serve under the Honorable Company and the English Inhabitants, deserted their Employs; such as Cooks, water bearers, coolies, palankeen boys, roundel men (umbrella carriers) and other useful servants; and arming themselves with pikes, daggers, and long staves, made a grievous uproar in the Black Town; stopping all the water from coming in, and committing many other disorders. The Captain of the Guard, with the Steward and several others, were sent to them to demand their reasons for making such an uproar; and finding they were headed by several peons in the English service, they seized two of the ringleaders and brought them to the Governor, who are secured in irons till further order.

"The Heads of the Right Hand Caste are ordered to go immediately and acquaint them that we will make any shift without them rather than submit to such usage; and not a man of them shall ever be taken into service again, if they do not forthwith disperse and return to their duty; also to let them know that orders are given at all the guards to fall upon them if they commit any disorder, or draw near in a body where the guards are posted."

"Thursday, 1st November. The Painters that deserted Triplicane, as mentioned in consultation the 15th ultimo, on account of the caste disputes, have made some overtures towards returning to their habitations; but at present insist on such unreasonable terms, that the Board cannot comply with them, considering that they ran away without any just provocation, and on purpose to distress us in our affairs."

"Friday, 16th November. The President acquaints the Board that he has intercepted a vilainous letter or Cojan, wrote by some of the Right hand castes to the Painters that deserted Triplicane and now reside at St. Thomé; wherein they are encouraged to insist upon unreasonable terms, and promised to be supported with money for their expenses, in hopes of creating further disturbances. Those that write the letter are inconsiderable persons, but he hopes to discover those that set them to work. In the mean time all possible diligence is used to reconcile those unhappy disputes and prevent future trouble."

"Monday, 10th December. The President acquaints the Board that though he hoped all things would have continued quiet between the castes, upon a resolution formerly taken to have the controversy decided by the heads of them that reside in the country; the Chetties have this day shut up all their shops, and called all the coolies from their work that belong to their caste; and that he has employed proper persons to enquire into the meaning of it, which he will lay before the Board in next consultation."

"Thursday, 20th December. The President produces a petition delivered last night by the heads of the Chetty caste, that have for sometime shut up their shops and refused to do any business. The substance of the said petition is, that they have already complained of the Comatees singing their Naggarum before the idol named Chindadry Pillarry (Ganesha, the "Belly God");* and that their caste people in the country have heard of it, and threaten to turn them out if they suffer such abuses. Wherefore they desire the matter may be decided by the Brahmins (who are the fittest persons to do it); otherwise they cannot continue in this place; and that a bond of 12,000 pagodas on

---

* The Naggarum is the verse which is addressed to Ganesha "the remover of hindrances," before undertaking any kind of business or engaging in any affair. Naggarum is properly the name of the language rather than of the verse. The complaint here made was that the Comatees recited their verse before a Chetty Pagoda.

both sides may be signed to stand to the said Brahmin's award.

"Agreed, that since the Comatee and Chetty castes cannot be persuaded to reconcile their differences by the heads of their own or any other castes, the Board will on Monday morning next hear the opinion of all neutral persons among the inhabitants, and endeavour to determine the matter in dispute so as will best secure the peace and quiet of the place.

Monday, the 24th December, 1716. "The heads of the Chetty and Comatee castes being summoned made their appearance, and a great number of witnesses were examined concerning the ceremony in dispute, whether the Comatees have a right to cry out their Naggarum (Sanscrit hymn) before the Chindadry Pillary Pagoda or not. After three hours spent in vain endeavouring to persuade them to come to some agreement among themselves, the Board deferred the affair till next meeting."

"Monday, 7th January 1717. The President (Edward Harrison Esq.) being ready to embark for Great Britain, proposes to the Board the best method that he can think of, after having discoursed with all the principal inhabitants of the place that are not actually engaged in the dispute now afoot between Comatee and Chetty castes, for putting an end to all future trouble; and the Board upon reading them came to the following resolutions.

"That for anything that has yet appeared the Comatees, may cry out their Pennagundoo Naggarum at their houses, feasts, weddings &c. according to Salabad, but not before the Pagoda of Chindry Pillary, till that matter can be decided in the manner hereafter mentioned."

"That whereas the Comatees did agree before this Board to defer the matters in dispute to 20 Brahmins, which are the neutral caste; ten of which to be chosen by the Comatees and ten by the Chetties; though they went from their word next morning, and insisted upon joining some of their own Right Hand caste, when they found the Chetties were willing to comply; the Board think it just for the Company's and their own honour, that the Comatees shall be obliged to make good their promise by referring the ceremonies in dispute to 20 Brahmins as before mentioned.

"That in case of any foul play by the 20 Brahmins that shall be chosen on this occasion, upon full proof thereof being made, the parties aggrieved shall have justice done them.

"That in case the Comatees refuse to comply with their first promise of a reference to the Brahmins, the image of the Chindadry Pillary Pagoda shall be removed to the great Gentoo Pagoda; and to prevent all future disputes the Chindadry Pillary Pagoda shall be shut up for ever.

"That, whereas great numbers of these small Pagodas have been clandestinely built without the knowledge or permission of the Government, and more are daily begun, which tend to raise disputes among the castes, none shall be built henceforward without the permission of the Governor and Council.

"That no colours for the future shall be used at any feast in Madras, but the English, commonly known by the name of St. George's colours, with a white field and a red cross.

"That the Pedda Naik shall be Overseer of the Pariah caste, and take care to keep them in due obedience; and that no other person shall pretend to summon or have any command over them.

"That whoever shall hereafter presume to stir up the castes to mutiny or desert on account of the disputes between the Comatees and Chetties, or any other such frivolous pretence; such person or persons, upon full proof being made before the Board, shall forfeit the Honorable Company's protection, be rendered incapable of any employ in their service, and fined at the discretion of the Board.

"These resolutions will be pursued by the succeeding President and Council, unless any unforeseen difficulty should arise to occasion an alteration in opinion; and there is good reason to hope that all matters will be fairly accommodated by the Brahmins."

"Wednesday, 8th January, 1717. Early this morning the Honorable President, Edward Harrison Esq., embarked upon Ship "King George," for Great Britain; upon which the Government of this place fell to the Honorable Joseph Collett Esq. pursuant to the Honorable Court of Director's appointment in their general letters by the last ships."

"Tuesday, 22d January, 1717. The President reports that he has received an answer from Colloway Chetty and Collastry Chetty to the summons affixed yesterday at the gates to this purpose: that they would not return unless we would oblige the Comatees to refer the differences between them to 20 Brahmins as formerly proposed.

"Agreed that although we had determined, if the Chetties had stayed for our decision, to have referred the matter as they propose, yet that now it is not fit to make such an agreement with them in order for their return for the following reasons.

"First, the immediate consequence would be that all the Comatees, and probably several other tribes of the Right Hand caste, would desert the place upon our making such a condescention to the Chetties, on condition of their returning; by which we should be drove to greater straits that we are or can be by the desertion of the Chetties.

"Secondly, such a condescention would so far enervate and weaken our authority, that we should never after be able to govern the several castes with any steadiness; who would be ready on every occasion to threaten us with a desertion, by which they would govern us at their pleasure.

"For these reasons we think it necessary to assert our authority, and either to force them to a compliance, or take what satisfaction we can get out of their estates."

"Ordered that the Warehouse keeper, assisted by one of the board alternately, remove the most valuable wares belonging to the said Chetties into the Fort godown; and take an exact account of them; there being large quantities to a considerable value. By which means we hope to frighten the Chetties into a submission, and return; or otherwise to obtain some satisfaction out of their estates for the damages that may accrue to the Honorable Company by their desertion.

"Ordered that an attachment of moneys due from any inhabitant of Madras, whether Europeans or others, to any Chetties now deserted, be affixed at the Sea Gate; with a declaration that whoever shall pay any such debts after this publication to any of the said Chetties, or their order, shall be obliged to repay the same to the Honorable Company."

These resolutions appear to have brought matters to a conclusion; and the President accordingly drew up the following agreement.

Thursday, 7th February, 1717. "We, Joseph Collett Esq., President and Council of Fort St. George, in order to determine and put an end to the differences which have been for sometime past between the Comatee and Chetty castes, and also to prevent all public disturbance of the like kind for the future, do hereby appoint and order for determination of the present differences, that the Comatee shall have the liberty of saying the Pennagundoo Naggarum, or any other of their titles, before the pagoda within the Pillarry or any other in the Right Hand streets; and that the Chetties shall have liberty of rehearsing their titles, or saying their Naggarum, before any pagoda in the Left Hand streets. But that the Comatees shall not say the Naggarum in the Left hand streets, nor shall the Chetties say their Naggarum in the Right hand streets. And we do hereby further order that neither the Comatees nor the Chetties shall have the liberty of saying their Naggarum or rehearsing their titles before the great Gentoo Pagoda. And for preventing disturbance of the like kind for the future, we do hereby forbid all persons whatsoever, building any new pagodas in any part of this city without leave first obtained of the President and Council. We do also forbid any flags to be used in the public procession and solemnities by any of the castes whatsoever, besides St. George's flag; that is a flag with a white field and a red cross. We do hereby publish and declare that if any inhabitants of this city do on any pretence, grievance, or any differences amongst themselves whatsoever, desert their habitations, and go out of the Honorable Company's bounds, without leave from the Governor; before they have applied themselves to the Governor and Council for redress, or before the said differences shall be determined in such manner as shall be appointed by us, and shall refuse to return being summoned; shall forfeit their estates to the Honorable Company and be put out of their protection."

Four days afterwards the termination of the dispute is thus recorded in the consultation books.

"Monday, 11th February, 1717. Colloway Chetty, Collastry Chetty and Mino Chetty, the heads of the Chetties that lately deserted to St. Thomé, being come back again appear before the Board, and ask pardon for themselves and the rest of their caste, requesting they may be permitted to live under the Honorable Company's protection and enjoy their ancient liberties as Inhabitants.

"Agreed that their request be granted, upon their depositing in the Honorable Company's cash for 12 months the sum of 4,000 pagodas for their good behaviour; and the heads of the caste signing the law lately established.

"Agreed that an interest bond of this day's date at 8 per cent. per annum be given to Colloway Chetty and Collastry Chetty for the 4,000 pagodas deposited as before mentioned; and that the warehouse keeper do deliver them up all their bonds, papers, accounts and goods as soon as conveniently he can; and the remainder of their money shall be paid them after the account of charges we have been at on their account can be made up."

CHAPTER XXVIII.

ENGLISH MISSION FROM CALCUTTA TO DELHI.

1715—17.

Before proceeding farther with our annals of the Madras Presidency, we shall devote a chapter to the consideration of an event, which is not only interesting in connection with the early fortunes of the English on the coast of Coromandel, but which marks an epoch in the history of all the English settlements in India,—in Calcutta and Bombay, as well as in Fort St. George and Fort St. David. This event is one to which Mr. Orme and Mr. Mill have each devoted a page of their respective histories, but yet which we have reason to believe is but little known to the majority of either English or Indian readers. It appears that about a century and a half ago, a mission was sent from Calcutta to Delhi, to carry a valuable present to the Great Mogul, and to endeavour to remove certain grievances which affected the several Presidencies, and procure such advantages as could be obtained by bribery or cajollery from the Durbar. This mission was entrusted to two of the English Factors at Calcutta, Mr. John Surman and Mr. Edward Stephenson; and with them were joined an Armenian named Cojee Serhaud, and a surgeon named Hamilton. These gentlemen remained at the Court of the Great Mogul for more than two years, during which they sent frequent dispatches to Calcutta, and some few to Madras and Bombay. Copies of most of them however appear to have been forwarded to Fort St. George, and were entered from time to time in the consultation books. Accordingly it has been the good fortune of the present writer to exhume these mouldering dispatches from the old manuscript records in the Government Office of this Presidency. We shall not however publish them in detail, for whilst a large portion refers to discussions which have long since lost all interest, another portion is wanting, and could only be recovered by a collation of the records at Calcutta with those of Fort St. George. We shall therefore simply review these old letters by the light of contemporary history; combining our extracts and illustrations in such a manner as will best serve to render the narrative an interesting picture of the times.

But what were the times? We candidly express our belief that in the present day there are very few who either know or care to know. Indian histories, whether of Hindoo or of Mussulman, are generally regarded with a distaste highly flavoured with contempt. The reason of this is obvious. Our historians generally fail altogether to excite our interest or enlist our sympathies. Many can dwell upon the picturesque pages of old Orme with the liveliest emotions. There the intrigues and treacheries of Native princes derive a powerful interest from the fact that the genius of our own countrymen, and perchance of our own great-grandfathers, triumphed over all. Arcot and Plassey are to us still spirit stirring names; and a host of rich associations still hang round the old Fort at Vellore, and the precipitous heights of Ginjee. But who cares to read the history of Ferishta? Who cares to peruse that dreary chronicle of Mussulman dynasties who have long since withered in their tombs? We may yet exult in the triumphs of Englishmen over Mussulman, Mahratta, or Pindaree; but neither Mill, nor Elphinstone, nor any one else, has hitherto succeeded in exciting our interest in the old wars between Mussulman kings and Hindoo Rajahs,—in old religious dissensions between Sheahs and Sonneahs, Vaishnavas and Saivas,—or even in those seraglio stories of murder and sensuality which pervade oriental history in every direction. Yet the time has been when the annals of historians like Ferishta were the delight alike of people and of princes; when every Mussulman throughout the land listened to the old annals of Ghazni and Delhi, of Bijapore, Golconda, or Berar, with an enthusiasm only to be surpassed by that with which the Jew listens to the chronicles of the kings of Israel and Judah, and to the inspired traditions of Jerusalem and Samaria. Even the very names of places and of men, names which are a positive torture to English eyes and ears, would awaken his feelings and sympathies, in the same way that the hearts of the old Scottish cavaliers warmed at the names of Dundee, Montrose, or Killiecrankie.

We believe that this evil would be remedied if an historian possessed larger sympathies as well as a larger personal acquaintance with the country and the people; if he appealed to the affections as well as to the judgment; if in a word he not only familiarised himself with those differences which are the result of a peculiar history and a peculiar culture, but also with all those complex desires and passions, in which all men can sympathize because they are common to all the great family of mankind.

The story which we are about to relate is one which ought to largely excite the interest of our readers. The year 1715, the very year that the Highlanders and the Pretender rose against king George, the two English Factors, together with the Surgeon and the Armenian, set out from Calcutta to Delhi. The character of the honest Factors is reflected in every page of their dispatches. They displayed none of the enlightened curiosity of a Clavijo at the court of Timour, or of a Bernier at the court of Aurungzebe; but they were shrewd practical business men; and they went out like members of a Chamber of Commerce, eager to obtain certain privileges, which would not only redound to the advantage of their honourable employers, but to their own credit and reputation. In Calcutta they desired some protection against the oppressions of the Nabob of Bengal, and permission to purchase more villages. In Madras they desire to recover the out villages, which had been granted in former years, but which had been since resumed by the Nabob of Arcot. In Surat they wanted to pay a fixed yearly rent in view of the customs levied by the Mogul governor. A few other similar privileges they desired to obtain, which were of considerable importance in those days, but which would excite no interest now. In a word they went, not as political envoys, but as petitioners. Neither one of them had ever been to Delhi before, but still they were not without Indian experiences. They had formed an exalted idea of the wealth and power of the Great Mogul; and they knew something of the character of the Omrahs or nobles at the Court of Delhi. Jaffier Khan, the Nabob of Bengal, was himself a good type of an Omrah; a man who rose from nothing, by that happy mixture of intrigue and audacity, which is peculiar to the Asiatic. Originally he had been a mere Tartar adventurer, who had rapidly risen in the army during the wars in the Dekkan, and had subsequently been appointed Dewan, or comptroller of finance, in Bengal. At that time, Prince Azim, the grand son of Aurungzebe, was Nabob or Subah of Bengal; and when the sovereign died, Azim and his three brothers plunged into a war for the imperial throne. Azim was slain, and Jaffier seized the happy moment for appointing himself to the Nabobship; and this post he managed to retain until it was not thought worth while to remove him. Towards the English Jaffier had acted the part of a petty tyrant. He had insisted upon searching their goods which were sent up country, and in levying exactions in that arbitrary manner which is especially offensive to Englishmen. This was one of the grievances for which Mr. Surman and Mr. Stephenson now hoped to obtain redress;

and it was therefore expected that the influence of Jaffier Khan would be exercised to the utmost to impede the success of the mission at Delhi.

But to return to the narrative of the mission. For some reason not explained, the hottest part of the year had been chosen for the journey. The envoys left Calcutta in April 1715, and reached Delhi on the 7th of July, after a three months journey. The report that they were carrying a large present to the Great Mogul, secured them an escort from the Governors of the different provinces through which they passed; and they even travelled through the district of the Jauts, who at that time were regarded as the most dangerous of robbers, without meeting with any serious mischance. The day after they reached Delhi, they dispatched a letter to Mr. Hedges, the Governor of Calcutta, from which we make the following extract.

"We passed the country of the Jauts with success, not meeting with much trouble, except that once in the night rogues came on our Camp, but being repulsed three times they left us. We arrived at Phwordabad the 3rd instant (July), where we were met by Padre Stephanus, bringing two seerpaws, which were received with the usual ceremony by John Surman and Cojee Serhaud. The 4th we arrived at Baorapoola, three coss from the city, sending the Padre before to prepare our reception, that if possible, we might visit the king the first day, even before we went to the house which was got for us. Accordingly the 7th in the morning we made our entry with very good order; there being sent a Munsubdar of two thousand Munsub, with about 200 horse and peons, to meet us; bringing likewise two elephants and flags. About the middle of the city, we were met by the Seiad Sallabut Khan Bahadur, and were by him conducted to the palace, where we waited till about 12 o'clock till the king came out. Before which time we met with Khan Dowran Bahadur, who received us very civilly, assuring us of his protection and good services. We prepared for our first present, viz. 1001 gold Mohurs, the table clock set with precious stones, the unicorn's horn, the gold escritore bought from Zoudee Khan, the large piece of ambergreese, the astoa and chelumgie Manilla work, and the map of the world. These, with the Honorable the Governor's letter, were presented, every one holding something in his hand as usual. John Surman received a vest and Culgee set with precious stones; and Serhaud a vest and Cunger set with precious stones likewise, amid the great pomp and state of the kings of Hindoostan. We were very well received; and on our arrival at our house, we were entertained by Seiad Sallabut Khan with dinner sufficient both for us and our people. In the evening he visited us again and stayed about 2 hours. The great favour Khan Dowran is in with the King gives us hopes of success in this undertaking. He assures us of his protection, and says the King has promised us very great favours. We have received orders first to visit Khan Dowran as our patron; after which we shall be ordered to visit the Grand Vizier and other Omrahs. We would have avoided this, if we could, fearing to disoblige the Vizier; but finding it not feasable, rather than disoblige one who has been so serviceable, and by whose means we expect to obtain our desires, we comply with it."

On the seventeenth of the same month, Mr. John Surman dispatched another letter to Governor Hedges, from which we make an extract showing the farther proceedings of the mission.

"We have lately sent to your Honor the good news of our safe arrival here, the visit of the King, and the civil treatment we met with, all which will without doubt be very welcome news. We have since visited several Omrahs, as the Vizier (Abdulla Khan) and

Khan Dowran, and Tuckrub Khan; where we were received with all the respect that could be expected, and gives me some hopes that all will end well; but what gives me the most encouragement (for I am well acquainted these nobles, as long as they are expecting to get any thing are always complaisant) is that the methods we are at present taking is consistent and with the advice and counsel of Zowdee Khan. We visited that gentleman the 11th current, and met with the same treatment he has always given to Englishmen, with the highest acknowledgments of the favours he has received from them, that as yet he had never been able to retaliate any of them, but hoped he had now an opportunity of doing something. He pressingly advised us to do nothing without the advice, counsel, and order of Khan Dowran (and the main instrument of our affairs) Seiad Sallabut Khan; that the turn of affairs at the Durbar obliged us to it. This, which he told us by word of mouth, he wrote me when I sent your Honor's letter to him. We are convinced he advises like a friend, and we are intent on the method, but at the same time very cautions, how we any ways disoblige the Vizier; we being very sure that Zowdee Khan was very intimate there, sent and advised him when we intended to visit, that he would use his interest for our better reception, intending to manage the Durbar by his means. He assured us that we might be satisfied as to the important Durbar. The good prospect we have of our affairs makes Cojee Serhaud very good humoured, and at present tractable, in hopes he shall obtain his promised reward and considered that every thing is come to its crisis. I take particular care that he remains so, and as much as possible persuade every one with me to do the like; which I fear gains me but little good will. But as passion must now be curbed, except we expect to be laughed at, we must be very circumspect in our actions and counsels."

Three days afterwards Mr. Surman and Mr. Stephenson dispatched another letter to Governor

Hedges, complaining of the invalidity of their letters of credit, and the difficulty they had in obtaining money, which they felt to be the mainspring of their negociations. But before following the course of their proceedings, it may be as well to glance at the contemporary state of the court at Delhi.

The Moguls were Mussulmans, but they were altogether a different race from the first Mahommedan conquerors of Asia. They were Tartars, whilst their predecessors were Arabs or Afghans. During the Afghan period the Mussulmans had established several large and independent kingdoms both in Hindustan and the Dekkan. During the Mogul period, these independent kingdoms were brought under the supremacy of one sovereign—the great Mogul who reigned at Delhi. The Afghan supremacy dates back to the time of William the conqueror. The Mogul period only commenced in the sixteenth century, about the time of Henry VIII. It reached its zenith in the reign of Aurungzebe, who conquered the last Afghan dynasties in the Dekkan, and who died in 1707, after having flourished from the time of Oliver Cromwell to that of Queen Anne. But at the very moment when the power of Aurungzebe seemed to extend from the Himalayas to Comorin, a new enemy had arisen. The old Hindoo nationality flashed out in the Mahrattas, and the Mahrattas resisted Aurungzebe until the day of his death. From that hour the Mogul empire was on the decline. It became a prey to disorders of every kind, to wars without and wars within. It was threatened by the Sikhs on one side, and by the Mahrattas on the other. Meantime the country was desolated by internal struggles. No sooner had Aurungzebe departed this life than his sons plunged into a desperate conflict for the throne, which terminated in the death of all save his fortunate successor and survivor Shah Aulum. The latter died in 1712, and then another conflict arose between his sons, which likewise terminated in the death of all, save a drunken and depraved wretch named Jehandar Shah. The new sovereign was even too bad for Delhi. A sort of religious revolution was got up by two Seiads, or descendants of the Prophet, who were brothers; and after another desperate struggle Feroksere, a nephew of Jehandar Shah, was placed upon the throne.

Feroksere was thus the reigning sovereign when the English mission arrived at Delhi. His great aim was to escape from the thraldom of the two Seiads, through whom he had obtained the empire. These two Seiads had been amply rewarded. Their names were Abdulla and Hussein. Abdulla was made Vizier, and Hussein was made Bukshi, or paymaster of the forces. We may add that the Omrahs of the Court were as ready as their royal master to procure the ruin of the two Seiads. Amongst these must be especially mentioned a particular favourite of the king, named Emir Jumla. But as we shall see, all their machinations and intrigues were defeated by the energy and genius of Hussein.

It will have been seen by the extracts already made from the despatches, that the great friend of the English at the court was an Omrah named

Zowdee Khan, the same who had carried on an amicable correspondence with Mr. Pitt, the former Governor of Madras. By his advice, the envoys endeavoured to obtain the favour both of Abdulla, the Vizier, and of a powerful nobleman named Khan Dowran. But Khan Dowran was a strong supporter of Emir Jumla, and a great enemy of the Vizier. This circumstance, and others which will be presently noticed, served to delay the negociation of the English envoys for a very considerable period.

The intrigues against the two Seiads were in full play at the moment of the arrival of the mission at Delhi. Emir Jumla had made an effort to separate the brothers, but without inflicting any blow upon their power. Hussein had been raised to the rank of Commander-in-Chief, and sent to reduce Ajeet Sing, Rajah of Marwar;—a Rajpoot prince, who had rebelled during the recent troubles, and had likewise distinguished himself by destroying Mussulman mosques and erecting Hindoo pagodas. The Court party however was not ashamed to intrigue with this worshipper of idols. Accordingly, private advices were sent to the Rajah, assuring him that the king Feroksere would be infinitely obliged to him, if he would use his best exertions to resist Hussein. But this little plot proved a failure. Hussein triumphed over the Rajah, and the Rajah did not deem it expedient to sacrifice himself for the good of the Court party. Terms were concluded between the two in a manner worthy of a passing notice. Notwithstanding the influence of caste prejudices, it had been the fashion throughout all the later conflicts between Mussulman and Hindoo, to cement every peace by a royal marriage; that is, the defeated Rajah was persuaded, or constrained, to give one of his own blooming daughters as a bride to the Mussulman sovereign. This custom was followed on the present occasion; and the Rajah Ajeet Sing gave not only a large peiscush, but promised also to give his youthful daughter to the king Feroksere. Hussein hurried back to Delhi with the welcome news, and was once again all powerful at court; and Emir Jumla was compelled to retire to Patna and undertake the Government of Bahar. Feroksere however still fretted under the domination of the Seiads, and meditated upon the best means of escaping from the constraint they imposed. At this juncture Hussein obtained the appointment of Viceroy of the Dekkan; and about the same time the English Factors reached Delhi and were admitted to an audience. Three days afterwards however, they were astonished by the news that Feroksere had left Delhi; but the following extract from a letter which they addressed to Governor Harrison at Madras on 4th August, 1715, will sufficiently explain the state of affairs.

"Three days after our arrival here, the king left the city, under pretence of visiting a sacred place, about 6 coss from thence. But the true reason (we are of opinion) was to clear himself of a kind of confinement, which he thought he suffered whilst in the Fort. Afterwards on the petition of his Omrahs to return to the city, the time of the rains being improper for travelling, he showed himself resolved to proceed either to Lahore or Ajmeer. Neither could all the arguments used avert his intended journey. This startled us, and considering with how great trouble and risk we had brought the present thus far, and how to carry it on at this time of the year, we were something at a stand. At last we concluded to give the gross of our present in, notwithstanding the king was abroad. But in delivering some of the fine clocks, they were ordered to be returned and kept in good order till he came back to the city, he having now determined only to visit a sacred place about 40 coss from Delhi; after which he would return. This stopped our presenting the remainder of our goods, but we concluded that it was necessary to attend his Majesty in this tour. We now continue in the camp, leaving Mr. Stephenson and Mr. Philips to take care of what goods remain in the city; and in case that the king should proceed further, that they may concert measures to bring the goods after us. We are in this interval preparing petitions to be delivered to his Majesty, hoping we shall do something for our Honorable Masters that has not been yet obtained. The patronage and management of this negotiation is in the hands of the greatest favourite at Court, Khan Dowran, and under him Seiad Sallabut Khan. Withal, we being no ways unmindful of an old friend Zowdee Khan, without whose advice, we enter upon nothing. But he being at present in so low a station is not able to obtain the King's ear. However we are satified that in whatever lies in his power, he does and will assist us, but particularly in the Vizier's Durbar.

Hussein Ali Khan Bahadur Ameer-ul-Omrah is lately gone into the Dekkan country, having the entire command of all that part of his kingdom. Your Honors have undoubtedly heard how great he has made himself even to vie with the command of his imperial Majesty, as lately appeared in the disputes between himself and Emir Jumla whilst at Court, when he obliged his antagonist, contrary to the King's desires, to remove from Court to Patna, whereby through the interest of Hussein, and his own mismanagement, he is quite ruined. Wherefore we humbly recommend a very good correpondence with Hussein. Otherwise, whatever we shall be able to do here will be of very little service before him."

Another pleasant intrigue awaited Hussein Ali in the Dekkan. Emir Jumla had been sent to Patna to undertake the Government of Bahar, at the time that Hussein had set out for the Dekkan. Before leaving Delhi, Hussein had assured the king, that if any mischief were aimed at his brother Abdulla, he would be at Delhi within twenty days to avenge him. But the blow was aimed not at Abdulla but at Hussein. Our old friend Dawood Khan had been appointed Governor of Guzerat; and he was instructed to pick a quarrel with Hussein and cut him off if possible. The further progress of affairs is fully illustrated in the dispatches. On the 31st August, 1715, Messrs. Surnam and Stephenson wrote as follows.

"We have advices here that Hussein Ali Khan and Dawood Khan are come to a rupture in Barrampore, so that it is likely a battle will ensue, the latter having engaged many of the Dekkan country to his party. It is whispered at this Court that this is a design laid to involve Hussein Ali Khan in trouble, and retrench his grandeur which of late has not been very pleasing.

"The king proceeding no further than Paniput,* returned to the city on the 15th, but being a little disordered in his health has not made any public appearance. So that we have not had an opportunity to

* The shrine of a Mahommedan saint of great repute, and famous in history as the scene of two of the greatest battles ever fought in India; viz. that which overturned the Afghan dynasty and established the Mogul emperors in 1525; and that which nearly crushed the Mahrattas in 1761.

deliver the remaining part of our present, or commence our negotiation, which shall be done by the 1st proxm."

On the 6th of October, the envoys wrote to Governor Hedges as follows.

"We designed to have presented our petition on the first good opportunity; but his Majesty's indisposition continuing, and Mr. Hamilton having undertaken to cure him, it has been thought advisable by our friends, as well as by ourselves, to defer delivering it till such time as it shall please God that his Majesty in some measure returns to his former state of health. Which advice, we intend to follow, considering that, whilst he is in so much pain, it can be but a very indifferent opportunity to beg favours of him. The first distemper the Doctor took him in hand for, was swellings in his groin, which thanks be to God he is in a fair way of curing; but within these few days last past he has been taken with a violent pain, which is likely to come to a fistula; it hinders his Majesty from coming out, so naturally puts a stop to all manner of business, wherefore must have patience perforce.

"Your Honors will have heard of the death of Dawood Khan in the Dekkan, slain in a battle with Hussein Ali. (This was a desperate conflict, in which a matchlock ball struck Dawood at the moment when victory had declared on his side.) This has given a great deal of uneasiness to this court, it being quite otherwise laid by the king and his favourites; and that which was designed for Hussein Ali's ruin, has proved a great addition to his former glories. The king at first seemed to resent it to his brother Abdulla, who not taking it so patiently, as he expected, he has altered his resolution to sending Hussein Ali Khan a Seerpaw and other marks of favour. We have advised in our letters to the Governor and Council of Madras to have particular regard to the friendships of that great Omrah; otherwise whatever we shall be able to do here for that coast will be of little service, unless backed with his favour."

The dispatches are here silent upon a point of considerable interest. The king laboured under a disease, which was not only painful in itself, but which prevented him from completing his marriage with the daughter of the defeated Rajah. After some months Dr. Hamilton succeeded in curing him; and according to the popular story the gratitude of the sovereign was unbounded. Ferokseré is said to have promised to grant any favour which Dr. Hamilton chose to ask; and we are told that the generous surgeon requested no rewards for himself, but simply asked that the requisitions of the Company might be complied with. The king it is added, immediately granted this favour, and also directed that all the fees of office should be remitted. No such story however appears in the dispatches; nor indeed is it likely that the envoys would have given prominence to a fact, which was calculated to deprive them of all the personal credit which would otherwise have accrued from their successful negociations. The following extract of a letter to Governor Hedges, dated 7th December, 1715, contains all they had to say upon the matter.

"We write your Honors the welcome news of the Kings recovery. As a clear demonstration to the world, he washed himself the 23rd ultimo, and accordingly received the congratulations of the whole court. As a reward for Mr. Hamilton's care and success, the King was pleased on the 30th to give him in public viz. a vest, a culgee set with precious stones, two diamond rings, an Elephant, horse, and 5000 rupees; besides ordering at the same time all his small instruments to be made in gold, with gold buttons for his coat and waist coat, and brushes set with jewels. The same day Cojee Serhaud received an Elephaut and vest as a reward for his attendance on this occasion.

"We have esteemed this as a particular happiness, and hope it will prove ominous to the success of our affairs, it being the only thing that detained us hitherto from delivering our general petition. So pursuant to the orders we received from Khan Dowran, the King's recovery was succeeded by the giving in the remainder of our present (reserving a small part only till the ceremony of his marriage should be over); and then delivered our petition to Khan Dowran, by his means to be introduced to his Majesty. Seiad Sallabat Khan, who has all along managed our affairs under Khan Dowran, being at that instant, and some time before much indisposed, we were obliged to carry it ourselves; not without taking care to have his recommendation annexed. Since the delivery Cojee Serhaud has been frequently with Khan Dowran, to remind him of introducing it to his Majesty; but has always been informed, no business can go forward till the solemnization of the king's wedding is over, when he has promised a speedy dispatch. All offices have been shut up for some days, and all business in the kingdom must naturally subside to this approaching ceremony, so that we cannot repine at the delay.

"The Rajpoots are likely to receive great honor by this wedding; the king having consented to all their desires in respect to the ceremonials; and this evening goes on his throne attended by his whole nobility on foot, to receive his spouse. All the Fort and Street, through which he passes will be made resplendent with innumerable lights; and in fine all will appear as glorious as the riches of Hindoostan and two months indefatigable labour can provide."

We are surprised that we cannot find in the dispatches any further notice of this celebrated marriage. According to Mussulman historians, the festivities on the part of the bride were conducted by Hussein Ali, and "the marriage was performed with a splendour and magnificence till then unseen among the sovereigns of Hindustan. Many pompous insignia were added to the royal train upon this occasion. The illuminations rivalled the planets, and seemed to upbraid the faint lustre of the stars. High and low shared the festivity, and joy thrilled through the veins of all. The Emperor Feroksere came to the palace of Hussein Ali, where the ceremony was performed; after which, he carried the princess in the highest splendour of imperial pomp to the citadel, amid the resoundings of musical instrument and acclamations of the metropolis.*

It was now to be expected that the cure of the king by Dr. Hamilton, would have led to a speedy consideration of the petition; but no such good fortune happened to the embassy. The king's marriage, and the general dilatoriness which prevailed,—every Omrah at the Court being far too much occupied in plotting and intriguing to pay any attention to the petition of the Feringhees,—led to a delay which threatened sometimes to imperil the success of the mission. On the 8th January, 1716, the envoys wrote to Governor Hedges as follows.

"As to the course of our negotiations, we can give but a very slender account of their progress; for although our affairs are fallen into the patronage of one of the most able men in this court to dispatch them, if he pleases, yet his dilatory methods of proceeding are such as must make us pursue our designs with patience

* Scott's History of the successor of Aurungzebe.

for the present. Our petition is returned, after having passed the examination of the books; the next that follows will be the King's signing; after which we shall take care to give your honors a particular account of it.

"We have lately been surprized with the King's designs of departing from this place, but God be thanked he is delayed for some days at least. We shall make the best use we can of the delay, if possible to effect our business before his departure, but which we cannot rely on.

"Two nights ago Emir Jumla arrived in this place from Bahar, attended by about 8 or 10 horsemen, much to the surprize of this city; for it is but at best supposed that he has made an elopement from his own camp for fear of his soldiers who mutinied for pay. The particulars of all which we are not yet acquainted with, nor what reception he is like to meet with from his Majesty."

On the 10th March, 1716, Messrs. Surman and Stephenson again wrote to Governor Hedges as follows.

"Your Honors will doubtless have heard by flying reports the troubles that have possessed this place for the past month, occasioned by the coming of Emir Jumla and all his forces, as it is said without the king's order. All the Tartars mutinously joined to demand their pay, which they gave out they would force either from the Vizier or Khan Dowran. This was certainly the grounds of gathering forces on all sides, the Vizier himself having not less than 20,000 horse; all which continually filled the streets and attended him when he went to the king. Khan Dowran and the rest of the Omrahs, with their forces and all the kings Tope Conna, kept guard round the Fort for about 20 days. The Vizier was obstinately bent not to pay the Tartars any thing, without very particular examinations and accounts to be made up for the plundering the town of Patna; which conditions the Tartars did not think to comply with till such time as they found the Vizier was not to be bullied; when they seemed to be willing to come to a composition, which was effected by breaking their party, and the king's orders for Emir Jumla's procedure for Lahore. The king ordered Chicklis* Khan to go and see Emir Jumla out of the city; divesting him of all his posts at Court, as also of his Munsul, Jageers, &c. with his glorious additional titles, which are ordered for the future never to be used. It is the general observation of this city, that this has only been a scheme laid if possible to entrap the Vizier, and take away his life; but he has been so continually on his guard, that nothing could be effected. So once more all is calmed, much to his (the Vizier's) Honors, and the entire disgrace of all Tartars in general; they being almost all turned out of service, a few great ones excepted. Emir Jumla is now 20 coss off this place in his way to Lahore, at present without any Munsul or post. But it is reported he will enjoy the former by the king's favour. These troubles occasioned the shutting up all the Cutcherries for this month, so that no business could possibly go on; in which ours met the same fate, with the rest, being just in the same state as a month ago. Khan Dowran very frequently promises that he will make an end with all possible expedient; but he is such a strange dilatory man, and withal inaccessible, that we have occasion to summon the utmost of our patience. There is no help for it, for with all this dilatoriness, he is the only reigning man in the King's Durbar, so that we hope he will at last consider and for his own honor see us handsomely despatched with all full grant to all our petitions.

"The great rebel Gooroo (Bandu the Seikh) who has been for these 20 years so troublesome in the Subahship of Lahore, is at length taken with all his family and attendance by the Subah of that province. Some

---

* This man afterwards became famous as Subah of the Dekkan, under the name of "Nizam-ool-Mulk."

days ago they entered the city laden with fetters, his whole attendants which were left alive being about 780, all severally mounted on Camels, which were sent out of the city for that purpose, besides about 2000 heads stuck upon poles, being those who died by the sword in battle. He was carried into the presence of the king, and from thence to a close prison. He at present has his life prolonged with most of his Mutsuddies, in hopes to get an account of his treasure in the several parts of his kingdom, and of those that assisted him, when afterwards he will be executed for the rest. There are 100 each day beheaded. It is not a little remarkable with what patience they undergo their fate, and to the last it has not been found that one has apostatised from the new formed religion."*

It is scarcely possible to conceive of a more wretched state of affairs than that depicted in the foregoing extracts. The leading events are already known to the historical student; but these notices, written on the spot by Englishmen who were probably eye witnesses of many of the scenes they describe, seem to bring the events more clearly to our eyes. The revolt of a Tartar army in the streets of Delhi is bad enough; but that terrible procession of 780 Sikh prisoners, with two thousand bleeding heads elevated on poles, is something too terrible to contemplate. We may add that the whole 780 were subsequently beheaded on seven successive days. We learn from Elphinstone that Bandu the chief was reserved for greater cruelties. "He was

* This religion was a sort of compound of Hindooism and Mahommedanism, in which the leading doctrines of both were reconciled by a strange kind of compromise.

exhibited in an iron cage, clad in a robe of cloth of gold, and a scarlet turban; an executioner stood behind him with a drawn sword; around him were the heads of his followers on pikes, and even a dead cat was stuck on a similar weapon to indicate the extirpation of everything belonging to him. He was then given a dagger, and ordered to stab his infant son; and on his refusing, the child was butchered before his eyes, and its heart thrown in his face. He was at last torn to pieces with hot pincers, and died with unshaken constancy, glorying in having been raised up by God to be a scourge to the iniquities and oppressions of the age."

But to proceed with the story of the English mission. The following extract from a letter dated 21st March 1716, is a singular description of the procrastination which generally pervaded the court of the Mogul.

"We have frequently complained to your Honors of the strange dilatoriness of our patron Khan Dowran. He is never known to sit out in public, and return answers to any manner of business; so that what can be said to him in the way from his apartment to his palankeen, is all that can be got; which is so very little for a man of a great business, that many days pass before an opportunity can be had even for the least answer; and that his own servant, Seiad Salabut Khan, who has the management of our affairs under him, and is as intimate as any one with him, can do as little that way as other people. Wherefore the main part of all our business has been managed by notes. This has been a great occasion of the dilatoriness of our affairs; all which we were obliged to bear with abundance of patience; still having very fair promises that our business should be done to our satisfaction. Nay Khan Dowran himself, very often both by word of mouth, and in several notes, promised to do it. A few days ago when Serhaud went to pay his respects as usual to Khan Dowran, and put him in mind of our petition, he was very surprizingly asked what petition? "Have not I done all your business?" To which Cojee Serhaud answered; but the time and place not allowing of a further explanation, he got into his palankeen and went away. This strange forgetfulness made us in very pathetic terms enquire of Salabut Khan, what we might expect after so many promises of having our business effected to our satisfaction, when we had so long and patiently waited, and been at so great an expence, to be thus answered was very surprizing, and what we did not nor could not expect in the least. We were answered that daily experience might convince us of the strange carriages and forgetfulness of that great man. Still bidding us not to despond, but that every thing would go very well after so many fair promises as we before had received. This gave us but small satisfaction, and the rather made us the more inquisitive, which gave us this further light, viz. that Khan Dowran had been advised by his own Mutsuddies that it was not his business to persuade the king to sign our petition, but that it was better to get the Vizier to advise the king what things were proper to be granted us. We were in hope that in case we would have got those petitions granted us by the means of Khan Dowran, that afterwards the Vizier would not gainsay it, as at least by a little bribery it might have passed. There has been several endeavours made to get an opportunity to speak with Khan Dowran so as to convince him; but more has been procurable. We fear the petition in this interim may be gone in, and will come out signed by the Vizier as before mentioned.

"Yesterday the King contrary to the advice of the Vizier, and purely on his own will, went out a hunting; and all the Omrahs to their tents. The place at present mentioned is about 18 coss off; but God knows what may be the designs of it, or where he will march to. This obliges us to follow him to-morrow or next day, leaving Mr. Edward Stephenson and Philips behind to take care of the Honorable Company's effects here. Should the petition come out signed as above mentioned, we shall be obliged to make a new address to the Vizier; which will not only protract this negotiation, but must lay us open to a denial, and at the best very expensive. We shall advise your Honors as soon as we have any hopes of success (which God send) or what we shall be obliged to recede from."

It would be useless to inquire into the various motives which induced Khan Dowran to hand the English embassy over to the Vizier Abdullah. Sometimes it was supposed that the bribes to the subordinate officers had been insufficient; sometimes that Khan Dowran was desirous of escaping from the responsibility of advising the king. One rumour reached the ears of the English envoys, and seems to have been more likely a cause than any of the others. It was said that the mysterious disease with which the king had been attacked the preceding year, had again made its appearance, and threatened to become annual; and that the king had given private orders that the business of the embassy should be delayed, in order that he might retain the services of Dr. Hamilton. Meantime the results were most unfortunate to the embassy. Mr. Surman and Mr. Stephenson, strongly objected to being handed over to the Vizier as the "cast-off favourites" of Khan Dowran. At this moment an incident occurred, which so plainly illustrates the disorderly state of the court, that we extract the account from one of the dispatches, dated 20th April, 1716.

"Whilst the king was encamped 14 coss from Delhi in order to hunt, there happened a quarrel between the people of Khan Dowran and Mahamud Amilkhan as they came from the Durbar; which, after their masters got into their tents, ended in a downright fight, herein they fired with small arms, boms and great guns for about 2 hours, notwithstanding the king's repeated command to forbear, yet was it at last made up after about 100 men were killed and wounded. The king was highly displeased with the liberty they took, and resented it to both of them. But the munsal of all the actors took the trumpet from his favourite; who was not admitted to his presence for three days, and threatened much more. But at present all is made up and his Majesty again reconciled to them."

The story of the delays which followed in accomplishing the business of the embassy, would be somewhat amusing were it not also interminable. Khan Dowran was at last induced to stir himself; but again the envoys were disappointed, for their petition was only in part granted, and then was only signed by the Dewan. At length the news reached the Court that the English at Bombay intended to withdraw from Surat altogether, in consequence of the oppressions of the Mogul Governor of the district; and fears were entertained that the English fleet would immediately appear in those seas, and retaliate upon the Mogul ships, as it had done on a previous occasion. This intelligence appears to have had an extraordinary effect. The Vizier Abdulla, began to take an active interest in the petition; and accordingly he is mentioned in the dispatches as the "good Vizier." All the forms of a royal firmaun were gone through as rapidly as could be expected. The petition was signed without any further demur, by the Vizier, and finally by the king Feroksere. But when the royal firmaun was an accomplished fact, and the envoys prayed to be permitted to return to Calcutta, another difficulty arose. In consequence apparently of another unaccountable exhibition of dilatoriness on the part of their patron, Khan Dowran, they could not obtain permission to leave Delhi. At length even this difficulty was apparently surmounted, and the envoys were admitted to a farewell audience with the king. But the event is best described in a letter addressed by the envoys to Governor Hedges, dated 7th June, 1717.

"The 23rd ultimo, John Surman received from his Majesty an horse and Cunger, as was pre-appointed; and the 30th ult. we were sent for by Khan Dowran to receive our dispatches, which we had accordingly; a seerpaw and culgee being given to John Surman, and seerpaws to Serhaud and Edward Stephenson, as likewise to the rest of our companions. We were ordered to pass one by one to our obeisance; then to move from the Dewan. We did so. But when it came to Mr. Hamilton's turn, he was told the king had granted him a vest as a mark of his favour, but not for his dispatch. So he was ordered up to his standing again. Whilst he was performing this the king got up. We were highly surprized at this unexpected motion, not having the least notice of it till that minute, either from our Patron or any of authority; it being near a twelve month since Mr. Hamilton had been in private with the Majesty, and in all this time not the least notice taken. We were very much concerned at his detainment, and the more because we were assured of his firm aversion to accepting the service, even with all its charms of vast pay, honour &c.; that if the king did detain him by force, if he outlived the trouble of his esteeming imprisonment, he might be endeavouring at an escape, which every way had its ill consequences. To free our Honorable Masters from any damages that might accrue to them from the passionate temper of the king, our patron Khan Dowran was applied to for leave, twice or thrice; but he positively denied to speak or even have a hand in this business, till our friend Seiad Sallabut Khan had an opportunity to lay the case open to him, when he ordered us to speak to the Vizier, and if by any means we could gain him to intercede that he would back it; nay if the Vizier refused, he would make one effort for the doctor himself. Nay Sallabut Khan promised to convince the king himself in case of any delay, pursuant to our patron's directions. We made a visit to the Vizier the 6th instant, and laid the case open to him in a petition from Mr. Hamilton, of how little service he could be without any physic, language or experience in the country medicines, or their names; besides which the heart breaking distractions of being parted for ever from his wife and children would be insupportable, and entirely take away his qualifications for the king's service; that under the favour of his Majesty's clemency, with the utmost submission, he desired that he might have leave to depart with us. From ourselves we informed the Vizier that we should have esteemed this a very great honour, but finding the Doctor under these troubles not to be persuaded, we were obliged to lay the case before his Majesty, and we humbly desired he would use his intercessions to the king, that his Majesty might be prevailed upon to despatch him. The good Vizier readily offered to use his utmost endeavours; and since the case was so, the business was to gain the Doctor's dispatch without displeasing the King; and he ordered a petition to be drawn up to his Majesty in the same form as that given to himself. It was sent him and the Vizier was as good as his word; writing a very pathetic address to his Majesty, enforcing Mr. Hamilton's reasons, and backing them with his own opinion, that it was better to let him go. The King returned an answer which came out the 6th as follows: since he is privy to my disease, and perfectly understand his business, I would very fain have kept him, and given him whatsoever he should have asked. But seeing he cannot be brought on any terms to be content I agree to it; and on condition that after he has gone to Europe and procured such Medicines as are not to be got here and seen his wife and children, he return to visit the court once more, let him go. We hope in God the troublsome business is now blown over."

Such then is the history of this curious embassy. We leave our readers to moralize upon the contrast of those days with the present; and merely conclude our narrative, by dismissing the dramatis personæ. Dr. Hamilton died of a putrid fever soon after his return to Bengal; and a curious anecdote respecting his memory was told to Jonathan Scott, the translator of Ferishta, by the celebrated Warren Hastings. The emperor Feroksere was not satisfied with the account of Hamilton's death, which he received from the Governor and Council at Calcutta. Accordingly he sent an Officer of rank to Calcutta to examine the truth from the Natives, whose solemn testimony and that of the Europeans were carried to the emperor. This circumstance was afterwards engraved on the tombstone of the deceased surgeon. The other English envoys returned in safety to Calcutta, and we trust "lived happy ever afterwards." The end of the principal actors in the Mogul court forms a part of the tragical history of the times. Three years after the visit of the English embassy, Feroksere was suddenly placed under confinement by the two Seiad brothers, Abdulla and Hussein; but the story of his death belongs to a future chapter. During the succeeding reign Hussein was assassinated by the connivance of the then sovereign; and shortly afterwards Abdulla was also thrown into hopeless captivity, and his life is said to have been only spared out of respect for his descent from the prophet. Thus ends our story of the English embassy from Calcutta to Delhi a century and a half ago.

CHAPTER XXIX.

GOVERNORSHIP OF MR. JOSEPH COLLET.

1717—18.

Mr. Collet succeeded Mr. Harrison as Governor of Madras on the 8th of January 1717. His administration only lasted three years, for on the 18th of January 1720, Mr. Collet retired in his turn, and was succeeded by Mr. Francis Hastings. The annals of those three years, 1717-20 are marked by events, which are well worthy of preservation. The English at that time possessed a great many slaves, and accordingly two Charity Schools were erected for the children of those slaves. Then again the reception and proclamation of the Firmaun, granted by the emperor Feroksere to the English envoys at Calcutta, was evidently regarded as a most important affair ; and it is interesting to note the ceremonies and rejoicings which took place on the occasion. We have also a lively account of some serious and sharp fighting which took place respecting the possession of the out-villages which had been guaranteed by the Firmaun ; together with notices of various incidents which serve to enlarge our picture of those primitive but stirring times.

Before however we proceed with the annals of Madras, it will be necessary to briefly explain the position of affairs in Southern India. Sadatulla Khan was still Nabob of Arcot; but Cheen Kulich Khan, better known as the Nizam-ul-Mulk, had been recalled from the Dekkan, and the Seiad Hussein Ali Khan, had been appointed in his room. Hussein Ali, as Subah of the Dekkan, thus exercised supreme authority over the whole of Southern India in the name of the Mogul emperor Feroksere.

We shall now place our extracts before our readers in chronological order. The first refers to a curious case of forgery, one however which appears to be more common in our own times than in the generation which has just passed away.

"Thursday, 4th April, 1717. The President acquaints the Board that on Monday in the afternoon, Captain John Powney having made a complaint to him of Mr. John Richardson, writer in the Honorable Company's Service, for counterfeiting his hand, by drawing out a false invoice of goods; pretending to have sent them by the said John Powney on Ship "Britannia" to Siam; writing a receipt on the bottom of said invoice, and counterfeiting Captain Powney's name thereunto. That he, the President, had upon the said John Richardson's acknowledging of the fact, closely confined him to his room. The said invoice, with another note, whereunto Richardson forged Mr. Benjamin Walker's hand, being given to Soondrum, a Conacapily, in pawn for the sum of 200 pagodas lent to Richardson; Soondrum is called in, and produces the true notes to the said John Richardson; who being shown the same, and asked whose hand writing the notes were of, and the names signed thereunto, acknowledged both the notes and the names to be of his own hand writing; only excusing himself, by saying he was greatly put to it for money, and hoped to have recovered his notes before they were due. The said John Richardson being thereupon ordered to withdraw, the Board came to the following resolutions in relation to him.

"That he be immediately discharged from the Honorable Company's service; that he be close confined to the cock house, and sent for Great Britain (with the consent of his creditors) by the first ship; and the Secretary is ordered to endorse the said John Richardson's true counterfeited notes on the back side of them, declaring they have passed this Board's examination, and are found to be forged."

The next extract explains itself.

"Monday, 29th April. The President reports to the Board, that he has been acquainted with very great inconveniences which the soldiers suffer, by being obliged to give their whole pay to the Steward of the Hospital, for sustenance during the time of their continuing sick in it; and being also obliged to pay half a pagoda per month towards their clothes, as many months as they stay in the Hospital for recovery of their healths. By paying so many half pagodas, they of course become in debt, which is so great a hardship upon them, that when they leave the hospital, the payment of the debts they thereby contracted takes away great part of what they should buy provisions with. To avoid which, many poor fellows have ruined their healths rather than go into the Hospital to be cured, when their distempers have been but in their infancy.

"Ordered that for the future the soldiers be obliged to pay the Steward no more than two pagodas per mensem for sustenance, during the time they continue in the hospital; it being found upon a scrutiny into the matter, fully sufficient to furnish the men with good provisions."

The next extract refers to a piece of immorality we should have hesitated to publish, were it not curious as illustrating the light in which such proceedings were regarded five or six generations ago.

"Monday, 6th May. Petition from Benjamin Skinner, Serjeant at Vizagapatam, complaining of Thomas Wilford, Factor in the Honorable Company's Service for having used too much familiarity with his wife; as fully appears by the deposition he now produces, taken upon oath before Mr. Robert Symonds, Chief, and Mr. John Emmerson, Second of Council at Vizagapatam, which is entered after this consultation.

"Agreed that the said Thomas Wilford be sent for up from Vizagapatam, and that he be suspended the Honorable Company's Service till their pleasure be known concerning him."

"The deposition of Stephen Whinship taken before the Chief and Council of Vizagapatam.

"The deponent declares upon examination in the case between Benjamin Skinner and his wife Anne, that he, the above said Stephen Whinship, with his wife, Mary, inhabiting in the house with the above said Benjamin Skinner and his wife Anne; that Mary the wife of deponent did tell him her husband, that Anne the wife of the above said Benjamin Skinner held a familiarity and an unallowable communication with Mr. Thomas Wilford, one of the Right Honorable Company's Factors; and that said Mr. Thomas Wilford used to climb over the wall at unreasonable hours, and enter into the apartment of Anne, wife to the above said Benjamin Skinner; which the deponent taxing her with, and threatening to acquaint her husband of her evil practices, when she with tears confessed the fact, entreating him to conceal it from her husband's ears. Afterwards, upon some difference between the wives of the deponent and the abovesaid Benjamin Skinner, Mary the wife of the deponent revealed it to the above said Skinner."

Our next extract is far more pleasing. It refers to the erection of the two Charity Schools for the education of the children of the slaves.

"Monday, 27th May. The President lays before the Board a paper of proposals delivered him by Mr. Grundler, one of the Danish Missionaries lately arrived from Tranquebar, for erecting two Charity Schools in this city. It is agreed that liberty be given for erecting two Charity Schools, one for Portuguese in the English town, and another for Malabars in the Black-town. The proposals are as follows :—

1. Whereas the slaves belonging to the English Inhabitants of this place have a great many children, who have no manner of care taken of

them, but are kept entirely ignorant of the Christian Religion; it is humbly proposed that a Charity School be erected, wherein such poor children shall be taught to read and write the Portuguese language (which is the only one they understand) and be fully instructed and trained upon practical knowledge of religion and the true doctrines of the Gospel.

2. There being some reason to hope that the knowledge of Christianity may also be propagated among the Natives of this country, it is likewise proposed that a Malabar Charity School be erected in some convenient place in the Black-Town, for instructing poor children in the principles of Religion, and to teach them to read, write, and cast accounts, after the way and manner used among the Malabars.

3. That these two Schools be allowed the protection and patronage of the Honorable Governor and Council, without whose consent and approbation nothing of moment relating to the said Schools shall be transacted.

4. That the immediate care and directions of the said two Schools shall be committed to two or more Trustees, to be appointed by the Honorable Governor for the time being.

5. That leave be given to such Trustees to build or buy two School houses, one for the Portuguese School within the English town, and another for the Malabar School in the Black-Town.

6. That what money, gifts or legacies shall be given by Charitable persons for the support of the said two Schools, or either of them, shall

duly be registered by the Trustees in a book to be kept for that purpose.

7. That the Trustees shall have power to make what particular orders and regulations shall be found necessary for the better management of the said two Schools, provided that said regulations shall be approved of by the Honorable Governor and Council."

We now come to the all-important event, the reception and proclamation of the imperial Firmaun. The history of the embassy from Calcutta to Delhi, by means of which the Firmaun was obtained, has already been given in the preceding chapter.

"Wednesday, 24th July. This day being appointed for proclaiming the Royal Firmaun or charter, granted by the Great Mogul King Feroksere to the Honorable English East India Company, for enjoyment of several privileges in his dominions (received from Bengal the 21st instant) the following orders for the ceremony are to be observed.

"All the Soldiers of the Garrison are to be upon duty, and one company to be drawn up under arms before the Fort gate.

"The Mayor with all the Aldermen and city officers to attend on horseback at the Fort Gate, where the Firmaun will lie in the Governor's state palankeen, till the Governor comes down and orders the Secretary to read it in the English language, and the Chief Dubash in the Moors and Gentoo languages, in presence of all the inhabitants of the city. After which, the palankeen with the Firmaun, attended by the Mayor, Aldermen, city officers on horse back, a company of foot soldiers, all the English with music, are to move forward down Charles Street to St. Thomas' Gate, where the Registrar is to proclaim His Majesty's Firmaun. From thence to proceed to the Sea Gate, proclaiming it there; and soon to the Middle Gate repeating the proclamation over again; from which Gate the Mayor, Aldermen and city officers are to return to the Governor in the Fort, and the Firmaun to be carried forward from this Middle Gate through the Black Town to Attapollium Gate in manner following: viz. First the Pedda Naik, or watchman of the city, to be on horse back with all his Taliars and the country music, then one company of the English Guards, next two trumpets, after which the Chief Dubash on horse back, the palankeen with the Firmaun guarded by six Serjeants after him; and then all the Moors and Gentoo merchants on horse back close after the palankeen to the aforementioned Attapollium Gate; where the Chief Dubash on horse back is to hold up the Royal Firmaun, and proclaim it by expressing himself in the following words.

"This is His Majesty King Feroksere's Royal Firmaun, wherein he confirms to the Honorable English East India Company all former grants and privileges, enjoyed by them heretofore; and further grants many new privileges, with the possession of several lands in many parts of India, with such favour as has never before been granted to any European nation.

"Then he, the Chief Dubash, is with the retinue to go out at the said Attapollium Gate, and enter the town at Tom Clarke's Gate, proclaiming the Royal Firmaun a second time there; and thence to proceed within the town at Bridge Foot Gate, in order to proclaim it a third time; and from the said Gate to return to the Choultry, where the Taliars and Black Music are to stay without, and the guards with the Dubash and palankeen to return to the Fort and deliver up the Firmaun to the Governor; the Black merchants being permitted on foot to attend it back from the Choultry gate: and for the more regular management of this solemnization the following orders were delivered the Gunner of the Garrison for discharging his part of the ceremony.

"To Mr. Frans Hugonin, Gunner,

"As soon as the Firmaun is read before the Governor at the Fort Gate, you shall begin to fire from St. Thomas Bastion, and proceed from thence to the Westward and on the Northward till you come round to the said St. Thomas Bastion; and then to continue firing round the walls of the Black Town to the numbers of 151 guns. As soon as the fire is gone round the White Town, Captain Matthew Martin, Commander of the "Marlborough," must take up the fire; and when he has done, all the Europe Ships in the road must fire one after another; and the country ships, upon the Europe Ships finishing, to fire altogether as fast as they can; the ships being handsomely dressed out with their colours and streamers.

"When the Governor and Company come to the garden at Tiffin, the Governor will begin the

Mogul's health, when you must begin to fire from the Garden point, and continue the fire round the town to the number of 101 guns; after which you are to prepare against Dinner to fire 101 guns at King George's health, 51 guns at the Prince and Princess and Royal Families health, and after Dinner 31 guns for the Honorable Company's health; the ships in the road to fire at drinking the Mogul's and King George's healths, in the same manner as they did upon proclaiming the Royal Firmaun.

"After the ceremony of proclaiming the Firmaun in the English and Black Town was over, the Honorable President with the Gentlemen of Council proceeded to the Garden house through the Black town, attended upon by all the Gentlemen of the city on horse back with handsome accoutrements; where all they, English, Portuguese, Armenian and Moors Inhabitants, were splendidly entertained at Dinner; and the day concluded with feasting of the soldiers, with tubs of punch, and a bonfire at night; and the Black Merchants, to show their joy at the Honorable Company's receiving so much favour from the Mogul, made abundance of fireworks upon the Island."

The next extract refers to the projected occupation of Divy Island, off Masulipatam, by the English. Possession had been granted in the Firmaun, but some difficulties rose in the way. The extract is chiefly interesting as illustrating the feelings of the Natives towards the English of that period.

"Monday, 26th August. The President delivers to the Board a translation of their letters from Masulipatam, one by Cunsum Pera, who had been formerly Chief Dubash to the New East India Company there, the other from Khan Colonoo Buggawan, an eminent Brahmin in those parts, advising and pressing us to take speedy possession of Divy Island. They both agreed that all the inhabitants wait impatiently for us, and that we may depend upon having an accession of people from the continent; the inhabitants being very desirous of living under the English Government, and that there are already eighteen towns and villages upon the Island.

"After full debating the matter, it is agreed that Cunsum Pera be sent for hither to give us a more full account of the state of affairs there; that he be taken into the Company's service and employed in that business; and that in the meantime, the President do give orders for providing all necessaries ready for taking possession of Divy Island."

The following extracts exhibit the operation of the imperial Firmaun, as regards regaining possession of the out-villages.

"Monday, 2nd September. The President produces translates of letters from the Nabob Sadatulla Khan, Sunka Ramah, and our spy Brahmin at Arcot, relating to the demand he had made of Trivatore and other villages lately granted by the Royal Firmaun. The Nabob's letter is wrote in general terms, with a great many compliments, but refers to Sunka Ramah and the spy Brahmin for an answer to the business in hand. They both advise that in conversation the Nabob told them, he could not deliver up possession of the villages without seeing the original Firmaun, but that he was desirous to maintain good understanding with the English.

"On a full consideration of the matter it was agreed that the President should write to the Nabob, rendering him thanks for the assurances of his friendship and favour, and acquainting him that 21 days after this date, he designs to take possession of the said villages; and together with his letter to send the present, usually made upon a new President's accession to the Government of this place; which has been suspended so long, that we might be assured of the Nabob's keeping his post; which has been very unlikely, and if a new Nabob had been established, we should have been obliged to have given it over again. The sum agreed on is 500 pagodas, and one piece of superfine scarlet cloth to the Nabob, and 200 pagodas with some cordial waters to Ducknaroy, the Nabob's Secretary and Son-in-law, who has the chief management of his affairs. To whom also it was agreed the President should write a short compliment. It is further agreed that the President do write to Sunka Ramah to make the several presents; and at the same time to acquaint the Nabob that it is an express grant in the Royal Firmaun, that neither he, nor any of the King's officers, should demand to see any of the original papers; but that copies, duly attested by the Cazi, shall be a sufficient claim on our parts for the several privileges and grants bestowed upon us; and that himself and all other officers are obliged to yield obedience to such attested copies."

"Thursday, 19th September. The President proposes to the Board the taking possession of Trivatore, &c. (five villages granted the English Company by the Mogul) on Monday and Tuesday next, and begin with Trivatore, and in case of opposition (which is hardly expected) to repel force by force."

"Monday, 23rd September. Early this morning the Honorable President (attended by most of the Gentlemen in the place) set out for Trivatore, whereof he took possession, stayed there and dined and returned in the evening, having in the interim taken possession of two more villages.

"Tuesday, 24th September. Early this morning Mr. Richard Lordon set out with a party of men, and took possession of the two other villages without any opposition, and returned about noon."

"Sunday, 29th September. The President represents that this morning he has received advices from the Nabob's Court at Arcot, and from Peersada at Poonamallee, that the former would not accept of the 500 pagodas present, we had sent to Sunka Ramah for that purpose; and that less than 1000 would not content him. That Peersada had stopped the roads to this city from Poonamallee, and would not permit merchandize, or the common necessaries of firewood, &c. to be brought into Madras; and that he had sent to Diaram, the Head Renter of the country under Hussein Ali Khan, for assistance to distress us further.

"On mature deliberation upon these advices it was agreed to make the Nabob's present 1000 pagodas for the following reasons.

"First, that we might divide the interest of the country Government about us, and thereby prevent their joining together to distress us.

"Secondly, the present last made by our late President amounted to that value, and might give them the fairer pretence to demand the same now.

"Thirdly, the present is conditional on his giving a letter confirming to us the peaceable possession of the villages we have lately taken."

"Wednesday, 9th October. The President produces a letter which he received from Diaram yesterday, wherein the said Diaram demands by what authority we have taken possession of Trivatore and the other villages; and adds that unless we have a sunnud under Sadatulla Khan's seal or Seiad Hussein Ali Khan's Perwanna, to warrant our so doing, we must restore the villages to his order.

"The President's answer to the aforesaid letter is also read, signifying to the said Diaram, that what we have done in relation to the villages is by virtue of his Majesty's authority; and that we will not give up our just rights on any pretence whatsoever, but on the contrary will defend them to the utmost of our power. The President's conduct on this occasion is approved by the Board.

"The President likewise communicates to the Board a letter which he lately received from some of the inhabitants of Divy Island, pressing him to despatch the Deputy Governor thither with all speed, to prevent the countries being laid waste by Apporrow the Renter, who is now plundering the inhabitants, as apprehending their desertion from him upon the arrival of our people there. The President's answer to the said letter is also read and approved; encouraging them as much as possible to wait with patience till the rains are over, when they may expect the Deputy Governor with a sufficient force to rescue them from the oppressions of Apporrow and to redress their grievances.

"Wednesday, 16th October. The President communicates to the Board a proposal which was made him by Sunka Ramah and the other late joint Stock merchants, to rent the five new villages granted by the Firmaun, viz. Trivatore, Satangodu, Catawaucha, Vezallawarrow and Lingambauca at 1200 Pagodas per annum for 12 years. Whereupon the yearly amount of that Revenue being examined into, when the said villages were granted the Honorable Company in President Pitt's time, and found to be just the same, it is agreed that they be let to the aforementioned persons for 12 years, at 1200 pagodas per annum; and that the Secretary do prepare a lease against next consultation."

Diaram the Head Renter was not disposed to see the villages taken out of his hands, without making an effort to force Governor Collet to give him a present. The following extracts in reference to these proceedings will be found very curious.

"Friday, 18th October. The President acquaints the Board that he has just now received advice from Trivatore, that Diaram's son has entered that town with 250 horse and 1000 foot, and had cut down our flagstaff and posted himself in the town. He adds that in the morning a Brahmin belonging to Diaram had been with him; and after a very long harangue wide of his purpose, delivered his errand, which was to demand a present of 1000 pagodas to Diaram, in consideration of which he would quit all pretentions to the villages we were possessed of. He declared withal that unless we would comply with that demand, Diaram's forces would take possession of them the next day. It appeared in fact that the forces were on their march to Trivatore whilst the Brahmin was delivering his message.

"The President then proposed to the Board to consider whether we should comply with their demands of money in order to buy a peace; or whether we should tamely sit down with the affront they had given us in cutting down our flag, and wait to see how much further they would proceed; or whether we should make a vigorous charge with our forces, and endeavour to drive them out of the Town by force of arms.

"After mature deliberation it appeared to be the unanimous opinion of the whole Board, that we should endeavour to drive the enemy out of Trivatore by force, for the following reasons.

"First, that Diaram has no pretence to make any demands on us on account of the said town; that we are not directed by the Firmaun to demand possession of them from him, but from the Nabob; his business being only to collect the rents for Seiad Hussein Ali Khan; and that to give him money upon this occasion would be a precedent for him to make demands on any other, or perhaps without any pretence, whenever he should think fit.

"Secondly, that to sit down quietly without resenting the affront, would but encourage the enemy to proceed to greater injuries; and give them reason to apprehend that we were doubtful of our own strength, and must submit to whatever terms they should think fit to impose on us.

"Thirdly, our men having of late been pretty well disciplined, and being now completely officered, we do not doubt their being able to drive the enemy out of the town and maintain the possession; which we hope will have so good an effect as to deter them from attacking us rashly again.

"Agreed that the direction of the Military be left to the Governor singly."

"Monday, 21st October. The President reports that after closing the consultation on Friday evening, he held a consultation with the military officers; the result of which was, that he gave orders to Lieutenant John Roach to draw out 150 men of the Garrison, to be in a readiness to march by two o'clock in the morning of the 19th to Trivatore; that he should endeavour to enter the town about break of day, and if he found the enemy there, to attack them immediately, and endeavour to drive them out of the town, and to keep possession of it till further orders. The President adds that about 9 o'clock in the morning he received advices from Lieutenant Roach, that he had entered the town exactly at the time appointed, and found the enemy in possession; but that after about an hour's dispute he had obliged them to quit the town and take to the plains. That after this they made some attacks, but were constantly drove back;

and Lieutenant Roach pursuing some of them to the plain, saw a fresh body of horse coming from the northward, which he then guessed by view to be about 500 in number. On these advices the President ordered Lieutenant Fullerton to draw out 100 men more of the Garrison, and with a sufficient quantity of provisions and ammunition, and two field pieces, to march immediately in order to join Lieutenant Roach. By 12 o'clock at noon all things were in a readiness, and Lieutenant Fullerton began his march. In the meantime the President ordered the militia of the town to be raised, who took possession of the White town; while the out-guards were strengthened by the remainder of the Garrison; and Gunner Hugonin, with the Governor's Horse Guards (being six in the whole), were ordered to patrol about the Washer town and Tondore, to prevent the enemy from burning or plundering on that side. At 3 o'clock in the afternoon, the President received further advices from Lieutenant Roach, dated half an hour after 12, advising that the enemy had kept skirmishing with them till near that time, but then were all drawn off, and marched towards Satangodu, after he had recovered the Flag Staff, and Flag, which he again hoisted in the middle of the Town. Soon after arrived further advices that Lieutenant Fullerton had joined Lieutenant Roach with his body, and that the enemy were marched off to some mile distance. On which the President sent order to Lieutenants Roach and Fullerton to march back in the evening or early the next morning; it being difficult to supply them with necessaries at that distance. They returned the same evening, and arrived at Fort St. George about 8 o'clock.

"It appeared that on Lieutenant Roach's entering the town the boors were not prepared to receive him, presuming we durst not march out of the reach of our own cannon. As soon as he gained the middle of the town, he saluted them with three vollies which did some execution. As fast as they (the enemy) got into order, they possessed themselves of the Avenues which are numerous, and endeavoured to regain the middle of the town; it being a very large square containing a Tank and a Pagoda; but in about a hour's time they were obliged to quit the town and take to the plains, though they afterwards made several attempt to re-enter the town but were obliged to retire about noon.

"In the whole action, which lasted about six hours, there was not one man of our Garrison killed or wounded by the enemy; one only of our Europeans was shot in the arm by his comrade's error in firing; three of our peons were slightly wounded, but none killed. The enemy left in the place one camel, 6 horses killed; six horses were taken alive by our men. Five men only of the slain were left, the rest being carried away; so that we do not know the certain number, but suppose there might be about 10 or 12 killed in the action.

"The President adds that he received advices yesterday from Poonamallee, that when the enemy had marched about 3 miles from Trivatore towards

Poonamallee, they encamped and continued there till 9 o'clock at night; and then marched one hour (contrary to their custom) without lights; fearing, as it appeared, to be attacked in the night; for when they thought themselves out of reach of pursuit, they light their duties and proceed on their march towards Poonamallee. Advices from thence further adds that Diaram's son, who commanded the party, was shot through the shoulder blade and his life endangered; that the commander next to him had several balls in his thigh; that thirteen more of their men were wounded, and eleven horses, besides one camel and two horses which dropped on the road.

"The President concluded that this great success without any loss must, next to the blessing of God on the justice of our cause, be ascribed to the good conduct of Lieutenant Roach, who had posted his men in such a manner that the enemy was not able to make any attack without certain loss to themselves, as at the same time they were unable to do us the least injury. He, therefore, proposes to the Board to consider of some honorary reward to be given Lieutenant Roach, who to his former merit at Fort St. David, has added this new and eminent service.

"Agreed that in consideration of Lieutenant John Roach's former services at Fort St. David, for which the Honorable Company have in their letters ordered him a gratuity, which has never yet been given, and also in consideration of his eminent service at Trivatore on the 19th instant, in defeating the enemy, with so much loss on their side, and without the loss of one man in ours;—that the President by his Commission constituted Lieutenant John Roach, Major of all the Honorable Company's forces on the Coast of Coromandel and Island of Sumatra; and that a Gold Medal, with the Honorable Company's arms set round with diamond sparks, with an inscription on the reverse suitable to the occasion, (the value about 300 pagodas) be given him.

"Agreed that his pay as Major be 20 pagodas per mensem.

"Agreed that it be left to the discretion of the President to order smart money to the wounded, and some gratuity to the inferior officers, who all behaved themselves very well in the engagement."

Thus ended this gallant little affair, which must have created no small excitement amongst the denizens of Fort St. George.

The following story of a spy is very curious as illustrating the life of an adventurer in the olden time.

"Friday, 7th February. The President informs the Board that he had for sometime past kept one Francisco Ferera, a pretended Doctor, close prisoner in the Fort, on an information he had received that the said Doctor had performed the part of a spy, and given information of our circumstances to the Moors during our quarrels with Diaram. That as to his personal character, he had formerly been a Jew in Italy, and Constantinople, and at Grand Cairo; and that in the latter place he turned Turk, and married and had children, who now reside there. That he has been sometime in these parts, and professing himself a Christian, married a Portuguese woman an inhabitant of this city. The President adds that he has been very much solicited to release the prisoner, who is not capable of doing any further hurt with respect to Diaram. He proposes to consider whether the prisoner may not be freed on giving security for his behaviour, and that he shall not go out of the English bounds without leave of the Governor. All the circumstances being considered, it is agreed, that on giving good security as above, that the said Francisco Ferera be discharged from his imprisonment.

"The prisoner proposing one Francisco Gregorio, an inhabitant of this place of some substance, to be bound with him in the penal sum of 1000 pagodas for his good behaviour;—it is ordered that the Secretary make out a bond accordingly."

The next story of a murder gives us an insight into the working of the police peons under the Pedda Naik.

"Monday, 9th June 1718. The President reports that some Guzerat Merchants had been with him this morning, to advise him that one Frivadee, a Surat Merchant Inhabitant of this place, was found this morning with his servant hanged in his own house, and that it was supposed they had hanged themselves. That on this information he had ordered the Secretary, in the presence of the Company's merchants and the Guzerat merchants, to take an account of the deceased's effects and secure them for his relations.

"Wednesday, 11th June. The President acquaints the Board that yesterday morning he had discovered that Frivadee and his servant, who were supposed to have hanged themselves, were murdered by robbers, who had carried off a very large booty in money; that he had immediately given out orders for a strict search after the murderers; and that just now three persons were brought before him, charged with that murder; that the case being extraordinary, he had summoned them together to hear the examination of the prisoners, and such witnesses as should appear against them.

"The prisoners and witnesses, with a considerable number of the principal inhabitants, Europeans and Natives, were called in; and the money and jewels which had been taken by the prisoners from Frivadee were produced, having been taken in possession of the several prisoners to the amount of five or six thousand pagodas.

"On a full examination it appeared to the whole Board that there was sufficient reason to put the prisoners upon trial for their lives for murder and robbery; and it was accordingly agreed that they should be tried in the Mayor's Court according to the charter, and that an order be given the Mayor in the following manner.

"On a full examination of Cadojee, Perseram, and Kisnados, who stand charged with the murder of Frivadee and his servant on the night between eighth and ninth instant, and several other witnesses concerning that murder,—we do find full and sufficient cause to put the said Cadojee, Perseram and Kisnados on trial for their lives; and in order thereto, we do hereby authorize you, the Worshipful John Legg, Esq., Mayor, to summon a court to-morrow, being the 12th instant, for the trial of the said prisoners, and to acquit them, or on their conviction of murder and robbery, to condemn them to suffer death in such manner as shall seem to you most proper to deter others from committing the like crimes."

Short work was made of these gentlemen, for two days afterwards we find the following significant entry.

"Friday, 13th June. This morning about 9 o'clock Cadojee, Perseram, and Kisnados were executed upon the Island."

This event directed the attention of Governor Collet's attention to the inefficiency of the Pedda Naik. We extract the proceedings at length.

"Monday, 7th July. The President reports to the Board that Pedda Naik, the chief Watchman of the town, has forfeited his Cowle by open and notorious transgressions of every part thereof; that he is become utterly incapable of discharging the duty of that post, having by his extravagance rendered himself unable either to maintain a sufficient number of Taliars to watch the city, or to make good any losses that shall happen as by the Cowle he is obliged to do; that through his incapacity as a watchman to discharge his duty, frequent robberies have happened of late, and one instance of what is unusual in these parts of a merchant and his servant murdered in their own house by robbers. The President added that if a speedy stop was not put to this mischief it would increase upon us till it become past remedy.

"The Cowle was then read, and the violation of every part thereof by Pedda Naik was notorious to the whole Board.

"The Pedda Naik being called in, and acquainted with the sentiments of the Board on his conduct, was asked if he had any thing to say in his own defence. He only replied that he was not able to do better, and left himself to the judgment of the Board.

"Agreed that Pedda Naik, chief watchman of the city, having forfeited his Cowle, and being incapable of performing the duty of his office, be dismissed the Honorable Company's Service.

"Agreed that Koonugoree Timapa, Naik of the same cast and family with Pedda Naik, be constituted chief watchman of this city of Madras, under the same obligation of duty, and with the same privileges and revenues as the former enjoyed.

"Agreed that the revenues from the Sea Gate, Choultry and Bazar appropriated to the Watchman, be to the end of this month carried to Pedda Naik account, they being mortgaged to the corporation; and the beginning of the next month delivered up to the new Watchman; and that all these other revenues be immediatcly delivered up to the new Watchman."

Towards the end of the year 1718, Governor Collet appears to have concluded a definite arrangement with Sadatulla Khan, Nabob of Arcot, as regards possession of the out-villages. The following extracts will sufficiently explain the matter.

"Monday, 10th November 1718. The President represents to the Board the present state of affairs with respect to the country Government; that he has been for sometime past, as they know, threatened with forces from the Nabob, in case he would not deliver up Trivatore and the villages granted by the firmaun. But that for about a fortnight past the Nabob had by some of his agents begun privately a treaty of peace with him. The first terms that were offered were that the villages should be delivered into the hands of Sunka Ramah till a sunnud could be procured from Seiad Husscin Ali Khan; which being rejected by the President, the Nabob proposed that the President should write to him in general terms to this purpose; viz, that he had taken possession of the village by virtue of the king's grant, and that the Company would give orders to return the king thanks for his bounty, and to procure a sunnud from Sciad Hussein Ali Khan. If not that the Nabob was at liberty to act as he should think fit. To which the Nabob was to answer, that if the Company procured a sunnud from Seiad Husscin Ali Khan, it would confirm the peace between us. The President adds that the sum insisted on for presents is 2000 pagodas for the Nabob, and 1000 pagodas for Ducknaroy his Secretary, and prime minister; of which he proposes 1000 to be paid out of the tax levied for building the choultries, and the other 2000 out of cash. The President further adds that he has not yet returned an answer to this proposal, being willing first to know the sentiments of the Board concerning it.

"After mature deliberation the whole Board unaminously agreed that the President should accept of the Nabob's proposal, and make peace with him accordingly, for the following reasons.

First. Hereby we fully assert our right to the possession of the villages by virtue of the King's grant, without entering into any engagements of receding from that right, even though a sunnud should not be obtained.

Secondly. That three years time of settled peace (as far as such a thing can be with the Moors) is hereby gained, and thereby time sufficient for the Honorable Company to give their orders for our future conduct.

Thirdly. We hereby assert the Honorable Company's right to all the grants made in the Firmaun, in which that of Divy Island is included.

Fourthly. By making peace on these terms, we effectually prevent all future demands upon us on account of our new fortifications on the Northside of the Town, and of our fortifying Egmore, which used to be always esteemed a ground of complaint and cause of quarrel. It also prevents all claim on account of the goods recovered out of the wreck of the Ship "Success," and the manner of our doing it, that is by open force. A peace being once concluded without any claim on these accounts, there can be no pretensions raised on them hereafter.

"The President then told the gentlemen of the Board that this negotiation required the utmost secrecy till it was effected. Besides that, though he does believe the Nabob to be in earnest, yet the

Moors so much affect a mysterious conduct, that it is not to be depended on till perfected. It being very usual for them to enter on a Treaty when they design a surprizing blow. He added that to prevent any danger of that kind, he had placed a sufficient Garrison in Egmore Fort, and doubled the guards at all the Choultries; and that he had employed several spies in the enemy's camp as well as in the country round about."

"Monday, 15th December. The President reports to the Board that this day the peace concluded with the Nabob was fully ratified; that Aga Mogheen, who had negotiated that affair with him, came to the Garden about 10 o'clock this morning with two elephants, fifteen horses, and about three hundred peons; that one of the elephants carried a chair of state with a canopy, in which sat two persons who brought two Seerpaws for the President, with a perwanna in answer to the letters wrote sometime since, expressing the Nabob's agreement to the terms of peace, and desiring a sunnud might be procured from Seiad Hussein Ali Khan as soon as it could be done conveniently. The Nabob sent also a horse which Aga Mogheen delivered to the President. The solemnity was greater than usual on the occasion on the Moors part. We received them with a body of nearly 500 men in arms; all the Honorable Company's servants and most of the inhabitants being present, with great numbers of the Natives. The presents being received, the Nabob's health was drank and 31 guns fired."

During this year Governor Collet was engaged in a long and troublesome inquiry into the conduct of the Governor of Sumatra, who by irregular proceedings had brought on a war with the Sultan, which had terminated in the forced retirement of the English. The particulars would afford but little interest to our Madras readers; but the following certified statement of the inhuman conduct of an English supervisor at this time, furnishes such a sad picture of the atrocities which occasionally occurred, that we cannot pass it over. The entry is to be found in the consultation book of 14th August, 1718; but the event itself had taken place at the beginning of the year. The statement is as follows.

" To whom it doth or may concern,

" This is to certify that on Sunday the 2nd of February 1718, before noon came on shore at Bantall, Mr. James Morris (supervisor from the Malborough) some thing in liquor. After dinner, he being drunk, he sent for two of the men prisoners of war out of the cock house; when having asked a few questions, he ordered them down upon the parade, himself attending, where he ordered one of them to be beheaded first, and then the other inhumanly to have his fingers and thumbs hacked off joint by joint, and at last his head cut off; after which, or next day, he obliged Sultan Cutcheel to sign their death warrants; in attestation of which we have hereunto set our hands this 9th day of August 1717 in Madras.

BENJAMIN GRAVES.
ROBERT WYNN.
AUGUSTUS WYNN.
ROBERT BARRET."

CHAPTER XXX.

GOVERNORSHIP OF MR. JOSEPH COLLET.

(Continued.)

1719—20.

The closing year of Mr. Collet's governorship seem to have passed tranquilly away; and the domestic incidents which occurred at Madras thus present a striking contrast to those tragical revolutions at Delhi which were heralding the fall of the Mogul empire. In a previous chapter, we noticed the state of the court at Delhi in 1715-17, when the English embassy was despatched from Calcutta to the emperor Feroksere. We now purpose to bring out in bold relief the contrast already indicated. First stringing together the concluding annals of Madras under Governor Collet; and then taking a glance at the contemporary events which were being enacted in the empire of the Mogul.

Our first incident is simple enough, and the extract will explain itself.

" Monday, 5th January, 1719. Augustus Burton, who came out in the Honorable Company's Service upon the "Mary" the last year, on his coming on board the ship brought with him clandestinely a young man, named Edmund Massey, his brother-in-law; without permission of the Company or Captain, who was ignorant of it till the ship was under sail, when it was too late to send him ashore. The Captain, since his arrival from Bengal, applied to the President for permission to carry the said Edmund Massey back again to England, to prevent his having to pay the penalty for bringing out any passenger to India without the Company's permission, which he is obliged to by his charter party. But the said Edmund Massey, having likewise requested to be entertained in the service here as a writer, and being a sober lad and capable of business,—it is agreed that we do give Captain Hobben a permission to leave him here, and that he be admitted into the service till the Honorable Company's pleasure can be known concerning him."

Our next extract illustrates the peaceful state of the relations between the Government of Fort St. George, and Sadatulla Khan, the Nabob of the Carnatic.

"Wednesday, 11th February. The President represent to the Board that Ducknaroy, who is prime minister to the Nabob Sadutulla Khan, and Fyre Khan the Nabob's general, came to St Thomé last Saturday, with a body of 400 horse and 1000 foot, in order to perform a religious ceremony of washing in the sea at the time of the Sun's Eclipse the next day; and that he (the President) had sent the Company's black servants and merchants to welcome him into this part of the country, and to sound the inclinations of Ducknaroy, whether he was inclined to accept an invitation to see the Fort; and that he had received a very civil answer from Ducknaroy and Fyre Khan, with assurances of their friendship, and an intimation that they were inclined to give him a visit.

"These two persons having the greatest influence both in the direction and in the execution of the Nabob's affairs, it is thought convenient to receive them in such a manner as may establish the good understanding between us and them begun on making the peace; and that presents be made them in such a manner as may be most acceptable to them to the amount of 1000 pagodas; that they may be admitted into the White Town with 20 palankeens, 100 horse, and 200 foot; that the President receive them at the foot of the stairs in the inner Fort, and lead Ducknaroy into the Consultation Room; that 51 guns be fired by the Fort; and then taken up by the ships; that on his departure out of the White Town the same number of guns be again fired, and taken up by the ships also; that the Secretary and Captain Fullerton be sent to St. Thomé to invite them to come into Town to-morrow morning."

"Thursday, 12th February. About 9 o'clock this morning Ducknaroy, the Nabob Sadatulla Khan's Prime Minister and favorite, together with Fyre Khan his General, entered the Town with 100 horse and 200 foot (in pursuance to the invitation) and came to pay a visit to the President. They were welcomed into Town with 51 guns from the Fort and afterwards from the "King George" and other ships in the road with a proportionable number. The President attended by the gentlemen of Council, covenanted servants and most of the inhabitants of the place, conducted them into the Consultation Room, where the Nabob's health was drank, and after a short confabulation, they took their leaves (being saluted with 51 guns from the Fort and afterwards by the ships as above) and went to a house in the Black Town prepared by Sunkah Ramah for their reception; where they were sumptuously entertained at the Honorable Company's Expense till 5 o'clock in the evening, when they went to take a view of the Garden house and from thence returned to St. Thomé."

The following incidents are so simple that we leave the records to tell their own story.

"Monday, 23rd February, 1719. The President acquaints the Board that being informed several Patan Merchants were come from Bengal on a ship bound to St. Thomé, he had used means to induce them to settle at Madras and to land their goods here; that he had prevailed with them, on condition they had a cowle granted exempting them from paying the Pagoda or Musqueet duty. They alledged that to pay to the Pagoda would be contributing to the promoting of idolatry; and that they cannot consent to contribute to the Musqueet in this place, which belongs to a different sect of Mahommadans.

"Agreed that in consideration the granting such a cowle will be no detriment to any part of the Honorable Company's revenues, but on the contrary will increase them by the addition of foreign Merchants becoming inhabitants, such a cowle be granted them."

"Thursday, 26th February, 1719. Chinna Chetty, one of the Chetty Caste, was brought before the Board and charged with the breach of the law made the 7th February 1717, for preventing disputes and differences between the several Castes; wherein it is provided that all the several castes shall, on their public festivals and solemnities, make use of St George's flag and no other. In violation of which law the said Chinna Chetty did hoist a Gentoo flag at Trivatore on Sunday last. He confessed the fact, but pleaded ignorance of the law, which could not be true; that law having been promulgated with the utmost solemnity, being affixed to all the gates of the town for some months, and made on so remarkable an occasion as the desertion of the Chetty caste.

"The Board, not being informed of the criminal's circumstances, fully agreed to defer pronouncing sentence till the next consultation; designing, if he be a man of some substance, to impose a proportionate fine upon him; otherwise to inflict a corporal punishment and turn him out of the bounds; it being necessary to make an example of such offenders on the first breach of that law; the preservation of which is so requisite to prevent all disturbances that may otherwise arise on caste affairs.

"Monday, 2nd March. The President reports to the Board that according to agreement in last consultation, he had enquired into the circumstances of Chinna Chetty, and found him incapable of paying a fine which would be large enough to deter others from committing the like offence.

Wherefore the Board gave sentence that he should stand in the pillory for the space of an hour the next choultry day, with a label before him to signify his offence, and that then he be expelled the Bounds."

The next incident is particularly interesting, as illustrating the growth of religious toleration in the English settlement at Fort St. George. Some of our readers will remember that in the year 1680, when Mr. Streynsham Master was Governor of Madras, the intermarriage of Protestants with Roman Catholics had excited the attention of the English Government; and the two English Chaplains being taking into Council, the following atrocious order was forthwith promulgated. "That upon the marriage of a Protestant with a Roman Catholic, both the parties to be married shall solemnly promise before one of the Chaplains of the place, before the Banns shall be published, and also in the Chapel or Church upon the day of marriage, that ALL the children by them begotten and born, shall be brought up in the Protestant religion." How this narrow-minded regulation worked for the benefit of the Protestant religion, will be gathered from the following circumstances which transpired some thirty years afterwards.

"Thursday, 2nd April, 1719. The President represents that the Portuguese priests of St. Thomé had very lately taken the liberty to marry some English people belonging to this city without leave; which practice he apprehended to be of dangerous consequence; many of the young Gentlemen in the Company's Service being of good families in England, who would be very much scandalized at such marriages as were likely to be contracted here, without the consent of the President; particularly that one Crane, late chief Mate of our ship "Falconbridge", was married to a French man's daughter of this place on Sunday last; and in order to it renounced the Protestant religion, which he had professed all his life till within a few days before. The other was one Dutton, an ordinary fellow, who was married a week before at St. Thomé to Ann Ridley, whose father was formerly Governor of the West coast. Her small fortune being in the hands of the Church, the minister, as one of her guardians, refused his consent; on which they went to St. Thomé, and found a priest to marry them there. The President adds that, to show his resentment of such a practice, he had ordered the Mettos not to suffer any of the Portuguese Padres, belonging to St. Thomé to come into the English bounds. He further proposed to the Board to consider of some proper orders to be given for preventing the like practices for the future. After some consideration, it was agreed that an order be published in the English and Portuguese languages, and put up in writing at the Sea Gate and at the Portuguese Church, that if any Christian inhabitant of Madras shall be married in this city, at St. Thomé, or elsewhere, without leave from the President; that if he be in the Company's service he shall be liable to such penalty as we shall think fit; but if the person so offending shall not be in the Company's service, and only a free merchant or inhabitant of the Town, he shall be expelled the English Government on the Coast of Coromandel. Also any parent consenting to, or promoting such marriage, without leave as aforesaid, shall be liable to the like penalty of expulsion."

"Monday, 6th April. The President informs the Board that on a full enquiry into the marriage of the Mate Crane, mentioned in last Consultation, he finds that the said Crane had been bred a Protestant, and continued to profess a Protestant religion till within a few days of his marriage; and then the woman whom he married refused to have the ceremony performed in the English Church, because all Roman Catholics married there are obliged to subscribe a declaration that they will bring up their children in the Protestant religion, by an order of Council dated the 25th of March 1680; and that on her refusal there to comply with that obligation, he had renounced the Protestant religion and declared himself a Roman Catholic in order to marry her. The President therefore proposed to the consideration of the Board, whether that order of Council, dated 25th of March 1680, should be repeated or not; which being freely debated, it was unanimously agreed to repeal the general order, for the following reasons.

"First, that the obligation is in its own nature unjust, and a violation of that natural right which all parents have to educate their children in that religion they think most acceptable to God. Secondly, that such a promise can be no obligation on the conscience of any person, being unlawful in itself. Thirdly, that the requiring such a promise may be attended with ill consequences, as in the instance now before us; the woman refusing to be married in the English Church for that reason only; the consequence of which was, Crane's renouncing the Protestant religion and declaring himself a Roman Catholic.

"Ordered that the Secretary acquaint the Honorable Company's Chaplain of the place in writing, with the repeal of the aforesaid order, and that he is not any more to require such subscription."

"The President also acquaints the Board, that the severe methods which he had taken to show his resentment to the Protugnese priests of St. Thomé, for marrying any subject of this Government without his consent, had produced a very good effect; for that the Padre Governor at St. Thomé had sent him a very submissive letter or address, wherein he obliges himself, and those of his fraternity subject to him, not to marry any persons subject to this Government for the future, without asking his previous consent."

The following entry refers to the general history.

"Thursday, 16th April, 1719. General letter from Masulipatam dated the 26th ultimo read, advising that it is reported that there is an insurrection amongst the Seiads, who have dethroned and imprisoned King Feroksere. The said letter further advises, as a confirmation of that news, that the Nabob of Golcondah who was advancing towards Masulipatam, immediately upon that intelligence returned to Golcondah, in order to draw in his effects with all possible expedition."

The Nabob of Golcondah here mentioned, does not appear to have been the Seiad Hussein Ali, Subah of the Dekkan; for he had gone to Delhi to assist his brother Abdullah, the Vizier, in dethroning Feroksere, and setting up other puppet kings in his room.. Nor could it have been Cheen Kulich Khan, better known as the Nizam-ool-Mulk; for he had retired from the Dekkan on the appointment of Hussein Ali, and was at this time merely Governor of Malwa. We therefore infer that by the Nabob of Golconda was meant Mobariz Khan, the local Governor of Hyderabad. But we shall have more to say upon this subject further on.

To return to the annals of Fort St. George. The following incident does not speak much for the philological attainments of the English inhabitants at this period.

"Monday, 25th May, 1719. The President represents to the Board that there is not any person in the Honorable Company's Service in this place, who is able to translate a letter out of the Portuguese and French languages into English; or *vice versâ*, to translate English into those languages; which has rendered it difficult for him to maintain the necessary correspondence in the Honorable Company's affairs; the Portuguese language being the common language of India amongst all Europeans. He therefore proposes to admit a young man, named George Foriano, son of Mr. Nathaniel Foriano (Super Cargo of the Honorable

Company's Ship "Hertford" to China), who is well qualified for the purpose abovementioned, being skilled in both those languages, to be a Factor in the Honorable Company's Service here.

"Agreed that Mr. George Foriano be admitted a Factor, Mr. Elwick offering to be security for him, and that the Secretary make out his Indentures for three years."

The next entry is worth preserving as illustrative of the times. Singularly enough it expresses the same fears on a small scale, as those which have been felt in some quarters in reference to the reductions which are now going on in our Indian army.

"Thursday, 9th July. The Honorable Court of Directors having, in the 5th paragraph of their letters to us by the "Marlborough," thought fit to order that the Garrison of this place should be reduced to 360 men and the Garrison of Fort St. David to 340. The manner of doing it is taken into consideration.

"It appears to us,—First, that this limitation is only designed for a time of established peace, which is not the case at present; there being by our last advices from Delhi, two princes with large armies contending for the Empire, the event of which may very probably affect us.

"Secondly, it appears dangerous to disband the whole number of supernumerary forces at once, even in a time of peace, much more so in a time of famine. Such number of men must be put upon violent measures, or else be obliged to go in a body into the service of the Moors, which may be very dangerous to this settlement.

"It is therefore agreed that the President give orders to the officers to disband gradually the worst of the Topazes, from about twenty to forty in a month as he shall think fit"

In the last chapter we noticed that the Pedda Naik, or Chief Watchman, was dismissed from his post on account of neglect of duty. It will be seen from the following entry that it was soon found necessary to restore him to his former employment.

"Monday, 17th August. The petition of Coonogozee Timapa Naik read, desiring liberty to resign his employment of Chief Watchman to Coonogozee Pedda Naik, who officiated in that office before him, and was very capable of executing it, but was dismissed for his extravagance. The said Timapa Naik being unfit to do the duty of that post any longer, by reason of his old age; and the former Pedda Naik, being very much reclaimed by the hardships which his extravagance brought upon him, promises a faithful discharge of his duty for the future, and tenders the duties belonging to the office of Chief Watchman as a security for his fidelity and good behaviour.

"Agreed therefore that Coonogozee Timapa Naik be discharged at his request from the office of Chief Watchman of this city; and that Coonogozee Pedda Naik be appointed in his stead."

Another entry occurs the same day which illustrates the summary method of proceeding with pirates in Governor Collet's time.

"The President acquaints the Board that on Tuesday 11th instant, he, with the rest of the Commissioners for trying of pirates, did bring Roger Bullmore, one of those that ran away with the "George" Brigantine, to his trial, by virtue of King George's Commission; and that having found him guilty of piracy, felony and robbery, they had passed sentence of death upon him, and that he was ordered to be executed on Wednesday next."

The hot winds this season appear to have been too much for Governor Collet and accordingly he determined to retire. But we leave the records to tell the story.

"Thursday, 15th October, 1719. The President acquaints the Board that having found himself indisposed during the last season of the land winds; so that it is with difficulty that he has been able to discharge the duty of his station; and that therefore he has determined to return to Europe on the next ship to be despatched from hence; and acquaints them with his purpose so early that there may be time for settling the Government according to the Honorable Company's standing orders.

"He then proposed that Mr. Francis Hastings should be sent for up from Fort St. David, as soon as he could conveniently, in order to take the chair upon the President's going off; and that Mr. William Jennings, second of Council here, should go down thither with a Commission for Deputy Governor, and that Mr. Nathaniel Elwick, who will then be second here, take on him the office of accountant.

"The President then produced a letter wrote to himself separately by the Honorable Court of Directors, dated the 8th January 1717, and read the first para; by which it appears that they designed Mr. Elwick for the Export Warehousekeepers employ particularly, as being well skilled in the sorts of calicoes sent from hence to England. He therefore, proposed that Mr. Elwick should keep the Export Warehousekeeper's employ, and that Mr. Richard Horden Sea Customer should take the Import Warehousekeeper's employ upon him; and that this regulation should continue in force till the arrival of the next letters from Europe.

"To all which proposals the Board agreed unanimously."

The last measures of Governor Collet are of such a simple character that they require no preliminary explanation, and it will be sufficient to lay the entries themselves before our readers.

"Monday, 2nd November, 1719. According to order of last consultation, Vizago, the Choultry Dubash, was brought before the Board on his trial, for extorting exorbitant fees beyond what had ever been practiced, particularly on the register of slaves. The most that had ever been allowed was 20 fanams in the whole, including the Company's duty; whereas he had obliged great numbers of people to pay him 24 fanams, and took the 4 fanams to his own use; also in house bills registered at the choultry, where the true fees are 2 pagodas and 2 fanams per cent., he extorted 2 pagodas and 18 fanams, and in many instances a larger proportion; and also in house bills registered at the court, he extorted in general about 16 per cent above the usual fees; and that besides the above mentioned, he has been guilty of great neglect in his office, by putting off the poor people and refusing to do their business.

"A great number of persons of all ranks appeared to prove the several branches of the charge; but there was no occasion to hear any witness except to the last article, he confessing all the rest on their being proposed to him; some witnesses were called for the proof of that, who very fully convicted him of delay, and putting off their business from time to time without any reasonable excuse.

"The prisoner and witnesses being withdrawn, it was considered that the practice was in itself scandalous and abusive, and particularly oppressive to the poor; many of them being obliged in this time of famine to sell their children for rice; and the extorting 4 fanams in the fees was a considerable hardship on them; that, therefore, it was necessary to put a stop to such abuses by making the offender a public example.

"Accordingly it was resolved that Vizago, the Choultry Dubash aforementioned, be turned out of the Honorable Company's service, and disabled from any future employment therein; that he stand in the pillory the next Choultry day; and that he be fined 500 pagodas, one-half to be paid to the Charity School, and the other half to the Choultry Stock for the maintenance of prisoners.

"The criminal being called in, sentence was pronounced accordingly.

"To prevent such abuses for the future, it is ordered that the after written statement of Choultry fees, being agreeable to ancient custom, be hung up in the Choultry by the Chief Justice.

"For registering houses and land in the Mayors Court register, situated in the Black town, pettahs, or out gardens; for every bill to pay one per cent to the Chief Justice, and half per cent to the Registrar on the value of the house or land.

"And whereas most of the buildings in the Christian Town do far exceed those without in value, to prevent the charges running too high: for every bill value under 500 pagodas, is to pay the same fees as above; but all bills exceeding that sum are to pay 5 pagodas to the Chief Justice, and 2½ pagodas to the Registrar, and no more.

"For registering houses and land in the Choultry Register; for every bill to pay one per cent. to the Chief Justice, and one per cent. to the Registrar, on the value of the house or land.

"For Registering slaves; for every slave the Honorable Company are to receive 8 fanams, the Registrar 8 fanams, and the Chief Justice 2 fanams.

"And all bills, either for houses, land, or slaves, are to pay to the Choultry Dubash one anam, and to the Chief Justice's Taliars one fanam, for their trouble in getting the bills registered.

"And whereas some small houses in the Black Town, not exceeding 5 or 6 pagodas in value, are made over by bills of sale wrote in Gentoo on Cajan leaves, which are entered in the Register kept by the Town Conicoply for that purpose; for every Cajan bill the Town Conicoply is to receive 2 fanams; besides the one per cent as above to the Chief Justice and Registrar.

"The bricklayers for measuring of ground are to receive for their trouble 2 fanams for all valued at 100 pagodas or upwards, and one fanam for all under."

"Thursday, 26th November, 1719. The President acquaints the Board that he had some time since published an order for registering all houses and gardens in the Black Town, or the adjacent parts, in the Mayor's Court or Choultry, for prevention of frauds in sale and mortgages; but that some of the poor having complained to him that during the present dearness of grain it would be hard upon them to pay the charges though small, he therefore, proposes that all houses under 50 pagodas value should be exempted from the obligation of that order, till plenty returns, which the Board agrees to."

"Wednesday, 23rd December, 1719. The President being about to depart for England, demands for his justification hereafter, a certificate from the accountant that he stands not indebted upon the Honorable Company's General Books. He likewise demands a certificate from the Sea Customer that he has paid all their customs due from him; one from the Receiver to the same purpose, and another from the Land Customer. All which are ordered to be drawn out against next consultation and delivered him, the Board being satisfied that he is not in any way indebted to the Honorable Company.

"Monday, 28th December, 1719. The President delivers in a list of the inhabitants of a new pettah or town raised near Trivatore, consisting of 105 houses which are inhabited by 489 persons, male and female, besides children, ranged under the usual divisions of Right hand and Left hand Caste. He acquaints the Board, that the town, in which there is also a handsome pagoda, is called at the desire of the people "Collet's pettah;" and that the inhabitants consist of weavers and painters, which he encouraged by degrees to come and live near this place, that they might be serviceable to the Honorable Company. That in order to prevail with them to a compliance, he promised them, so soon as the town was completed, a Cowle should be given them to secure to them such privileges and immunities; and the said Town being now finished, and the inhabitants well settled, he proposes that his promise which is now claimed, should be performed, and a Cowle given them accordingly; the conditions of which being approved by the Board, as well as the President's management in this affair, the Secretary is ordered to prepare."

"Monday, 18th January, 1720. Early this morning the Honorable Joseph Collet, Esq., President, embarked on Board the "King William;" whereon the Goverment fell to the Honorable Francis Hastings, Esq.

Having thus closed the narrative of the tranquil state of affairs at Fort St. George during the last year of Mr. Collet's administration, it may be as well to take a brief glance at the contemporary state of the ruling power at Delhi. All those influences which indicate the decline of an empire, were in full play in the empire of the Mogul. Vice and sensuality at the court, frequent rebellions in the provinces, a puppet king struggling for power, overbearing ministers, a mercenary army without theslightest sentiment of loyalty, incessant intrigues ending in open assassinations;—these, and a thousand other significant circumstances, were transpiring in India. Indeed it must have been evident to all that ever since the death of Aurungzebe in 1707, the Mogul empire had been hastening to its dissolution; worn out by premature old age brought on by its political crimes, and vainly struggling to retain the appearance of strength and beauty when it was fast sinking into the grave.

It was during this gradual decay of the power of the Mogul, that a man arose, whose name, and that if his descendants, must ever take a prominent place in the history of this Presidency. This man was Cheen Kulich Khan, better known as Nizam-ool-Moolk, the first Nizam of the Dekkan. His father Ghazee-oo-deen was one of those Tartar adventurers, who had migrated into India at a comparatively recent period, and risen to eminence during the wars in the Dekkan. The future Nizam was born in 1644, and like his father had distinguished himself in the wars of Aurungzebe. During the reigns of the immediate successors of Aurungzebe,—Shah Aulum and Jehandar Shah,—he had fallen into obscurity, in consequence of his rivalry with Zulfikar Khan, —that great king maker to whom both the last mentioned princes owed their thrones. But in 1713, when he was fast approaching his seventieth year, his fortunes were again on the rise. Jehandar Shah had been dethroned by the two Seiads; and both he and Zulfikar Khan were put to death. The two Seiads set up Feroksere as a puppet of their own; and Cheen Kulich Khan, being well known as the enemy of Zulfikar Khan was first appointed Nizam of the Dekkan.

Most of the intrigues of Feroksere to escape from the thraldom of the Seiads, have already been noticed in the narrative of the English mission from Calcutta to Delhi. But the last of all, the one which led to the downfall of Feroksere, deserves especial notice; for it is one which strikingly illustrates the desperate state of public affairs, whilst it is closely connected with the rising fortunes of Cheen Kulich Khan. But the last and most and important plot of all, the one in which Cheen Kulich Khan was implicated, and which led to the ruin of Feroksere about the very time that Governor Collet left the Madras Presidency, deserves especial mention.

Very early in the reign of Feroksere, Cheen Kulich Khan had cause to hate the two Seiads,—Abdullah, the vizier, and Hussein, the commander in-chief. He had held the government of the

Dekkan little more than a year, when he was removed to the small government of Moradabad, and the Dekkan was handed over to Hussein. Under such circumstances the disappointed Nizam was likely to prove a powerful supporter to Feroksere. Accordingly he was summoned to court, and the emperor promised to make him vizier in the room of Abdullah, provided the Seiads were overthrown.

A plot was speedily formed, and was soon ripe for execution. Hussein was away in the Dekkan, and Abdullah was alone in Delhi. Accordingly it was determined to assassinate Abdullah at that great festival which terminates the Ramazan; for on that day the king went in state to the Mosque, attended by a train of nobles and troops far exceeding in number the guards of the vizier. But all went wrong through the criminal weakness of Feroksere. He had a favourite, a low profligate minion, who was naturally hated by the whole court. The influence of this favourite was all powerful. By his advice Feroksere was induced to postpone the plot. Worst of all, Feroksere forgot his promise to Cheen Kulich Khan, and actually engaged to make this wretched favourite vizier as soon as the Seiads were overthrown. Lastly the emperor was mad enough to give to this favourite the district of Moradabad as a private jaghire; being the very district of which Cheen Kulich Khan was Governor.

These circumstances came out in time, and then Cheen Kulich Khan was more exasperated against such an infatuated king than he had previously been against the Seiads; whilst the vizier Abdullah saw that Feroksere was incorrigible, and that his own life would be in constant danger so long as Feroksere continued on the throne. Accordingly he drew over Cheen Kulich Khan by the promise of the government of Malwa, and immediately summoned his brother Hussein Ali from the Dekkan.

The doom of the emperor Feroksere was now sealed. In his alarm he sought a reconciliation with Abdullah, and the vizier engaged with the emperor in mutual oaths of fidelity and attachment. Of course such oaths were utterly worthless. Abdullah merely desired to gain time for the arrival of his brother; whilst the cowardly Feroksere continued to lay plots for the assassination of the Seiads. Meantime Hussein Ali had made a peace with the Mahrattas, and at last reached Delhi with thirty thousand horse, ten thousand of whom were Mahrattas.

The whole city was now filled with dread. Every one felt, from the highest Omrah to the lowest dealer in the bazaars, that a terrible convulsion was at hand. The very appearance of the Mahrattas, Hindoo robbers as they were, suggested ideas of massacre and plunder to the Mussulmen of Delhi; whilst no one could foretell who would gain the ascendant, the Seiads or the emperor. Meantime the wretched Feroksere began to see his own folly. He was however far too weak and cowardly to attempt the slightest resistance to the two Seiads, and therefore helplessly submitted to their mercy. They demanded that the royal guards should be withdrawn from the palace, and that their own soldiers should be posted in their room. Feroksere obeyed. Hussein Ali then paid him a formal visit, and the poor miserable emperor made a desperate effort to conciliate his enemy. He received the Seiad with the greatest distinction. He burst into tears and placed his own turban on the head of Hussein; and even took the jewels from his dress and pressed Hussein to accept them. But the Seiad refused, and upbraided the fallen monarch with his ingratitude. He then left the palace without paying any of the ordinary ceremonies of respect due to the person of his sovereign.

In a few days more all was over. On the 15th of February 1719, Feroksere expressed a wish to hunt, but the Seiads suspected him of designing an escape, and obliged him to postpone the intention. The next day the Seiads surrounded the palace with their troops, and the vizier entered the presence of the Emperor, and demanded that all the offices of the palace should be given into his hands. Feroksere promised compliance, but prayed for delay; and the evasion threw the vizier into such a passion, that the terrified emperor retreated to the haram, which he hoped would be respected by the rebels.

The story of the night which followed is one of the most thrilling narratives in all the Mussulman histories. The vizier Abdullah remained in the palace, and so also did Ajeet Sing, Rajah of Mewar, whose daughter had been given in marriage to Feroksere as a token of submission to the Mogul supremacy. The army of Hussein

Ali, including the ten thousand Mahrattas, remained under arms the whole night. Early in the morning a rumour flew through the city that the vizier had been killed by Ajeet Sing, who had resolved to protect the emperor his son-in-law; and accordingly several omrahs prepared to rise against Hussein Ali. Meantime a party of Mahrattas had engaged with some soldiers whom they had mistaken for an enemy; and the still more frightful rumour spread through Delhi that the Mahrattas were plundering the city. At once the whole population of fiery Mussulmen arose as one man against the idolatrous Mahrattas. Fifteen hundred Hindoos were massacred in the streets, and the whole city was thrown into frightful disorder. Those omrahs who supported the cause of the Seiads, in their alarm at the supposed death of the vizier, were preparing to make their escape from the scene of anarchy. Plunder, fire, and massacre had already begun, when the news spread that Abdullah was still alive. Hussein Ali and his friends now recovered their spirits and restored order. The royal servants were dispersed after a brief resistance; and it was proclaimed from the walls of the citadel that another prince had ascended the throne.

Whilst these events were being transacted in the city, still darker horrors were being perpetrated in the palace. Feroksere utterly refused to leave the haram. Meantime Abdullah was informed that the people were already in revolt, and that no time was to be lost. In this extremity he commanded some Afghans to force open the doors of the haram. There was a short conflict with the eunuchs and other attendants, and then the vizier and his rude soldiery rushed into the sacred apartments. The unhappy emperor, surrounded by his mother, wife, daughter, and other princesses, was soon discovered. The royal ladies filled the air with their shrieks and prayers for mercy, whilst Feroksere himself was in an agony of terror. But Abdullah turned a deaf ear to all entreaties, and pounced upon his prey. The emperor was dragged from the arms of the half frantic women, and thrown into a dark chamber. A child was taken from the confined princes, and immediately seated upon the throne; and the booming of cannon and customary strains of music announced to the people of Delhi that Feroksere was deposed and that another puppet king reigned in his stead.

The end of Feroksere may be related almost in the very words of the Mussulman historian. For two months he was confined in a dark chamber, enduring various calamities. The hot iron, by which so many princes had been incapacitated from reigning, was drawn over the eyes of Feroksere; but strange to say it did not utterly destroy his sight. He sent the most piteous messages to the Seiads, praying to be restored to the throne on any terms they chose; but not the slightest attention was paid to his prayers. Then he promised immense rewards to his keepers, provided they would connive at his escape. The Seiads were now alarmed, for Feroksere was still lamented by the lower orders amongst whom he had squandered his treasures, and an escape might be followed by a revolt and a revolution. Accordingly they resolved on his death. On two different occasions poison was mingled with his victuals, but without effect. The third time he was thrown into violent agonies, and began to invoke God against his murderers. The bow string was then sent for, but the emperor struggled against his executioners with all the violence of desperation. He seized the bow string with his hands, and it was only after he had been beaten down with clubs, that the string was passed round his neck, and he at last expired. On the following evening the body was interred in the tomb of Humayun, followed by a large crowd, cursing the Seiads and lamenting their beloved Feroksere.

The new child emperor only reigned four months, and then died of a consumption. Another child was taken from amongst the confined princes, but he shared the same fate. At last a healthier young prince was selected, who ascended the throne under the name of Mohammed Shah. He began to reign before the end of 1719, and before the end of 1720 the power of the Seiads was entirely over. This event is so intimately connected with the final establishment of Cheen Kulich Khan as Nizam of the Dekkan, that we can scarcely avoid narrating it here.

On the deposition of Feroksere, Cheen Kulich Khan had obtained his promised reward, namely, the government of Malwa. There he found everything lapsing into anarchy;—the Zemindars asserting their independence, and the people either suffering from robbers or becoming robbers themselves. These disorders justified him in raising and maintaining troops ; but the Seiads soon suspected that he was aiming at something far beyond the mere defence of his province. Accordingly they tried every friendly means to remove him. Hussein Ali was still viceroy of the Dekkan, and they hinted to Cheen Kulich Khan, that as Malwa lay half way between the Dekkan and Delhi, so it would form a very convenient residence for Hussein Ali; inasmuch as from that spot Hussein could both superintend his vice royalty in the Dekkan, and watch the progress of affairs at the capital. Accordingly they offered Cheen Kulich Khan four other Subahs, any one of which he might have in exchange for Malwa. He sent back an insulting refusal, and then marched an army over the Nerbudda into the Dekkan, where he had many old connections both amongst the Mussulmans and the Mahrattas. There he achieved a brilliant success, and the Seiads became alarmed. An army was sent against him, but he defeated it. At the same time, the new king Mohammed Shah, saw in Cheen Kulich Khan, one who might deliver him from the thraldom of the Seiads. Accordingly he sent secret messages assuring him that he should receive royal support in his resistance to the Seiads.

In this extremity the Seiads resolved that Hussein should march against the self-constituted Nizam of the Dekkan, whilst Abdullah remained at Delhi. To make matters doubly sure, it was also resolved that Mohammed Shah should accompany Hussein. This circumstance proved the ruin of the Seiads. A conspiracy was formed for assassinating Hussein during the march. A savage Calmuck named Hyder Khan was pitched upon to strike the blow. Whilst Hussein was passing along in his palankeen, Hyder attracted his attention with a petition; and when Hussein commanded him to present it, he drew out his dagger and inflicted a mortal blow upon the Seiad. Hussein suspected the author of the conspiracy, and cried out "Put the emperor to death." But it was too late. The necessary preparations had been made for the defence of Mohammed Shah, though the assassin himself was cut in pieces on the spot by a hundred swords.

Here closes the story of the famous usurpation of the Seiads. Mohammed Shah returned to Delhi, and Abdullah was utterly defeated, and imprisoned for life. How the Mogul empire rapidly faded away, until it seemed to expire in the funeral pyre heaped up by Nadir Shah, belongs to a future episode in our annals of the Madras Presidency.

CHAPTER XXXI.

GOVERNORSHIP OF MR. FRANCIS HASTINGS.

1720—21.

The Governorship of Mr. Francis Hastings, the successor of Mr. Collett, was short and turbulent. It lasted little more than a year and a half, namely, from the 18th of January, 1720, to the 15th of October, 1721. The foreign relations were quiet enough at this time, and for some years afterwards, as both Sadatulla Khan, Nabob of the Carnatic, and Cheen Kulick Khan, Subah of the Dekkan, were far too busy in establishing themselves in their several governments to pay much attention to the little Factory at Fort St. George, so long as it paid the annual rental on the day it was due. But the internal affairs of the settlement were marked by many irregularities and disorders during the administration of Mr. Hastings, and of his successor Mr. Elwick; and thus necessitated those rigid inquiries and thorough reforms which were subsequently carried out by one of the most remarkable of all the early Governors of Fort St. George, namely, Mr. James Macrae.

The first incident under the rule of Mr. Hastings is connected with an extraordinary dispute with an Havildar in the neighbourhood of Egmore, which was brought to a tragical conclusion; the Havildar being shot dead in the midst of the quarrel by the Company's Chief Peon. The following is the official narrative of the affair.

"Saturday, 20th February, 1720. The President acquaints the Board, that last night the Havildar of the Metto near Egmore had stopped some oxen, loaden with bricks and straw, which belonged to the Honorable Company, which were coming into Town. This morning, being complained to about it by the Paymaster, as also of the people being beat and imprisoned that were driving the oxen and refused to pay some money, which the Metto people would have extorted from them ;—he (the President) sent the Chief Dubash, with some others, to know the reason of such an insult, and to demand the delivery of our people whom he had imprisoned. The President adds that instead of receiving answer to that message, the Havildar returned him a very saucy one, and refused to let the Honorable Company's goods and people pass ; though the Chief Dubash used many mild persuasive arguments with him for that purpose. At length, not being able to prevail, the Chief Dubash returned and gave the President an account of what had passed ; whereupon he ordered the Chief Peon, with some others, to go and expostulate with the Havildar further, and in case of any resistance to force the Havildar to a compliance. But when the Chief Peon went to him, he found him at the head of about 50 of his peons and people in a fighting posture ; and upon going up to him to deliver the President's message, the Havildar drew his scimctar and struck at him, which he warded off with his target, and thereby evaded being cut down. The Chief Peon immediately drew a pistol from his side, and shot the Havildar; which when he had done, he with his people fell upon the rest and killed two more, which terrified them all so much that they ran away.

"The President adds that he thinks the Chief Peon has by this action showed himself a trusty servant to the Honorable Company, and deserves encouragement; that if he had sat tamely down under this first insult, we should not have failed of receiving many more of a higher degree; and that our showing our resentment upon this occasion will have a good influence upon all the Metto people, and Junkameers for the future; that lest the matter should be represented to our prejudice to the Nabob, he has taken care to transmit an exact account of it to our Vakeel at Arcot; and for the security of the garrison has given orders to the Officers to be upon a very strict guard for fear of surprise."

"Monday, 14th March, 1720. The President acquaints the Board that he has received very friendly letters from the Nabob and Ducknaroy upon the subject of the Metto Havildar being unfortunately killed by our peons; and that apprehending no disturbance will ensue, he has ordered in the guards which he had joined to those at Egmore and the Choultries, in order to put a stop to the expence occasioned thereby."

The next event is narrated at a length far exceeding its importance, and can be best told in a few words. It seems that a discovery was made that some sort of correspondence had been going on between the principal Chetties in Madras and the Portuguese Viceroy of Goa. From a perusal of the papers it would seem that this correspondence only referred to some presents that the Viceroy of Goa wished to send to Hussein Ali, the previous Subah of the Dekkan; but Governor Hastings appears to have suspected that the correspondence had for its object the "revolt of the Chetties," or in other words their removal from the English Government of Fort St. George to the Portuguese Government of St. Thomé. The matter assumes an undue importance in the records, inasmuch as it was the cause of a tremendous quarrel between Governor Hastings, and Mr. Nathaniel Elwick, who was at that time third in Council; Governor Hastings being inclined to deal harshly with the Chetties, whilst Mr. Elwick declared that no proof whatever had been furnished that they were really guilty. Under such circumstances Governor Hastings placed the Heads of the Chetties under confinement, and then ordered the following proclamation to be posted on the Sea Gate, with the view of obtaining further evidence against them.

"Monday, 25th April, 1720. Whereas a discovery hath lately been made of a design sometime since formed by the inhabitants of the Chetty caste of this place, to revolt from this Government and to take protection under the Portuguese at St. Thomé; and whereas there is just reason to suspect, by the Viceroy of Goa's letters to the Heads of the Chetty caste, that they signified under their hands their resolution to desert this place and shelter themselves under the Portuguese at St. Thomé, in case he could have obtained a grant of that place from the Nabob; and whereas, furthermore, the said Chetties upon examination have confidently denied their engagement in any such conspiracy;—the Honorable Governor and Council have therefore thought fit to issue out this proclamation, that if any person or persons concerned in the said conspiracy will make discovery to the President, or to any one of the Council, so as that the rest of the persons concerned may be fully convicted, such person or persons shall receive a handsome reward and full pardon for themselves."

"By order of the Honorable Governor and Council."

The Proclamation had no effect whatever. No one came forward to volunteer evidence, and the Chetties themselves obstinately denied all knowledge of such a conspiracy. Accordingly Governor Hastings desired them to sign a paper, in which confiscation of all property and the forfeiture of all protection were declared to be the penalty of desertion. This however the Chetties refused to do, and then the Governor proposed that the two head Chetty merchants, who conducted the Company's investments, should be suspended from their office. The following extract from the consultation of the 30th May, 1720, will show the nature of Mr. Elwick's opposition.

"Mr. Elwick offered security for the two Chetty Merchants, as far as 10,000 pagodas, for their appearance six months hence; but being asked if he would sign the security paper in their behalf aforementioned (involving the pain of confiscation and forfeiture) ; and being also asked if he would suffer the penalty which the Chetties must suffer in case their accusation should hereafter be turned into a conviction ;—he refused them both ; and being told by some of the Board, that the security which he offered was no more than bail for their appearance six months hence, and that according to the laws of our nation all persons taken up upon suspicion of treason are forthwith imprisoned without bail or mainprize, Mr. Elwick's notion was thereupon rejected."

Mr. Elwick continued to be very earnest in his opposition to the suspension of the two Chetty Merchants, and declared that the sorting of the cloth, and the business of the Company generally, could not go on whilst they were in confinement. The records of the dispute are far too voluminous for publication, but the following extract from the consultation book of the 19th of July will sufficiently illustrate the party spirit which prevailed.

"The President acquaints the Board that Mr. Elwick, the Warehouse keeper, has been very remiss in his business in not having given in any account of the contract ever since it was made, and in not having sorted any quantity of cloth since the "Dawson's" dispatch ; though out of perverse, obstinate humour Mr. Elwick pressed him once or twice, while the merchants were confined, for their releasement in order to go to sorting. Mr. Elwick, finding his plea for not sorting proved to be nothing else but an excuse for idleness, began to be mueh enraged; and told the President that it would draw very strange stories on the stage, and that the eonsequenee must take its course, desiring those words might be minuted verbatim; to which the President made no reply, but ordered the Seeretary to minute them accordingly."

About this time the attention of the Government was exeited by the murder of a Chetty whose name is not mentioned. It was a cold blooded affair. The murderers were two soldiers, named Robert Grott and Richard Righting, who appear to have killed their vietim for the sake of drink. The depositions are lengthy, but the following extraet will suffiee to show how such cases were adjudicated on in the Council Room.

"Monday, August 1st, 1720. The affair of the murder is now resumed. The President aequaints the Board, that a Dubash boy (belonging to one of the prisoners suspected to be guilty of the murder) was apprehended at St. Thomé; who being sent for in, deposes that he went with Robert Grott, his master, from his house in company with two white men, and a woman, whose names he could not tell, to drink toddy at a toddy house; where they stayed till past 12 o'eloek at night, at whieh time the two men and the woman left them. Then the prisoners Grott and Righting went to a choultry and carried a bottle of arrack; where they saw a man covered over with a elout, fast asleep; whom soon after they awaked by giving him a blow with a eane, and at the same time asked for fanams to buy arrack. The man answered he had none. But receiving a blow or two more from them, he gave them one fanam, then another, and afterwards a third. Upon continuing their usage to him, and repeating their demands, he drew down his purse and bid them look if there was any more. Then the prisoner Righting told him if he had no more than three fanams, he would give him more if he would go with him to the Governor's Garden; but instead of carrying him thither, they led him to another garden near the Choultry, where he afterwards heard him cry out. The Dubash further deposes that when he would have followed them, they struck him and bid him be gone; and as he was going away he saw Righting take the club from Grott. After this they went to Town, and a soldier, by name Clark (whose house they were in) asked them, how came they so bloody; who said they had been fighting. The Dubash afterwards went to look for a mat to sleep on, and saw Righting look over some silver things; and upon demanding leave to go home, he denied him. Clark again asked them how came they so bloody; who replied as before that they had been fighting.

"Righting being sent for in and interrogated concerning what the boy had deposed against him, says that he never had the club in his hand, but carried the Chetty into the Garden; upon which he was ordered to withdraw; and Grott being called in says that Righting took the club away from him and killed the man.

"Righting being brought in again, and acquainted with what his comrade had alleged against him, declared that they had been drinking, and that the Dubash boy told Grott that this Chetty fellow had money; upon which Grott went to him and asked him for some, when he gave him two fanams; then he demanded two more, but he would not give it them. The deponent Righting, seeing that, took him into a garden, and told him if he would not comply he would carry him to the Governor's Garden; and as they were talking together Grott struck him with the club and killed him. Grott being called in, again denies what is laid to his charge; and being asked where the Chetty's silver girdle, his earrings, and other things were, avers that Righting took them and he has heard nothing of them since. Upon which Righting was again sent for and asked the same question; who answered that the Dubash boy took them off, which is all that he knows of the matter."

"The prisoners being all dismissed the Room, the Board debated upon the affair for some time, and then unanimously pronounced them guilty of the murder. But the Honorable Company, having not yet procured a power to bring to an Execution, it was agreed they should be continued in prison and whipped very severely every week as a punishment for the disorders they committed as soldiers."

The murder case being thus deposed of, Governor Hastings poured out the vials of his wrath upon Mr. Elwick. He brought forward a declaration that he would no longer sit at the Council Board whilst Mr. Elwick was present.

But the story is best told in the language of the records.

"Monday, 8th August, 1720. The President acquaints the Board, that he has called this consultation on a very extraordinary occasion, in order to lay before us a declaration concerning the repeated affronts that he had received from Mr. Nathaniel Elwick, a member of this Board, and also his incapacity for the service of the Honorable Company. The said declaration being read before the Board, and duly considered; Mr. Elwick was ordered to withdraw; in pursuance of the Honorable Company's orders, that no member of the Board should continue sitting while such cases relating to himself were examining.

"Mr. Elwick being withdrawn the President's declaration was more maturely considered; and most of the members of the Board agreed that one or other of them was assured of the truths of all the facts charged on Mr. Elwick by the President, in relation to his behaviour at this Board as well as in this place.

"The facts alleged to prove his incapacity were then considered, and thereupon Mr. Draper the Secretary delivered in a report, which was read and observed to prove one article of Mr. Elwick's remissness. All the other instances of his negligence were well enough known to most of the members of the Board, and therefore did require no other proof.

"The latter clause of the President's declarations was then considered, wherein he pleased to publish his full resolution to sit no longer as President at this Board, if Mr. Elwick should continue as a member of it.

"Upon recourse to the Honorable Company's letter in order to find out some directions in such out of the way cases, no such appeared; and therefore, we judged it a case of an extraordinary nature. We observed, however, that suspension is made the penalty of a refractory disorderly behaviour, as well of negligence and remissness in business; and therefore the President desired the opinion of the Board, if Mr. Elwick had not incurred the penalty of suspension.

"The matter being debated for sometime, the Board thought fit to come to the following agreement.

"That as Mr. Elwick, on account of his refractory disorderly and insolent behaviour to the President, has most justly incurred the penalty ordered by our Honorable Masters to be inflicted in such cases, as well as on account of his negligence and remissness in his business, which penalty is no less than suspension. And as the Honorable President has been pleased to put the matters upon so important an issue, as to declare to us all that he will not sit any longer as President, if Mr. Elwick is continued at this Board; we think ourselves under a necessity of suspending Mr. Elwick, who has been guilty of remissness in his business as well as of indecent behaviour to the President and to the rest of the Board; rather than to part with the President, who has so long suffered Mr. Elwick's insolence and passed by his remissness, as well as behaved himself to us all with the greatest candour, mildness and decency imaginable. It is therefore, agreed and resolved that Mr. Nathaniel Elwick be suspended forthwith from the Honorable Company's Service (officio et beneficio) till the Honorable Company's pleasure be known concerning him.

"As every Member of the Board was allowed to give his opinion on this, as well as on all other occasions very freely, Messrs. Turner and Benyon declared that they could not agree to suspend Mr. Elwick; because they thought the Honorable Company's orders did not allow of a sufficient latitude for so doing, although they could not but confess that he had not behaved himself to the President so respectfully as he ought to have done."

Mr. Nathaniel Elwick subsequently protested against the proceedings, and then the matter ended for a while.

The next incident to which we have to draw attention is a very curious one. Charles Davers, a young gentleman who came out as a writer in 1717, died this year; and left an extraordinary will so illustrative of the times that we give it at length. Mr. Davers had come out in his eighteenth year, and was not twenty-one at the time he died. He was the fourth son of Sir Robert Davers, Baronet. His salary appears to have been only £5 a year, and yet he seems to have been already engaged in several commercial adventures. The desire of the young man to have his name and memory perpetuated is very striking; but we leave the will to tell its own story.

"Thursday, 22nd September, 1720. In the name of God, Amen, I, Charles Davers, now of Fort St. George in East India, Merchant, being of sound and perfect mind and memory, do make and ordain this my last will and testament in manner and form following.

"Imprimis, I recommend my soul to God who gave it, hoping through the merits of a crucified Saviour to obtain a joyful resurrection; and my body I commit to the earth to be decently interred; and for all such worldly estates, as these which it has pleased God to bless me with, I give and bequeath as follows; viz.

"Imprimis, I leave unto the Charity School of this place 200 pagodas; and desire the boys belonging to this School may attend me to the place of burial. Item, I leave unto the Master and Mistress of said School 20 pagodas each for mourning. I wish all piety and learning may attend them, and that they may infuse the same into the children, by the help of our Blessed Lord and Saviour Jesus Christ, Amen.

"Item, I leave unto my friend Mr. Thomas Wright 20 pagodas for mourning. I wish all health may attend him in this world and happiness in the next.

"Item, I leave 200 pagodas for a tomb to be erected in the burial place in form as follows. Four large pillars, each to be six covids high, and six covids distance one from the other; the top to be arched, and upon each pillar a cherubim; and on the top of the arch the effigy of Justice. My body to be laid in the middle of the four pillars, with a handsome stone a top of me, raised about four feet; and this inscription in the stone :—" Here lyeth the body of Charles Davers, fourth son of Sir Robert Davers, Bart, who departed this life the———of——Anno Domini——-aged——." The four pillars to be encompassed in with iron rails, which are to go from pillar to pillar; and at every square, steps to be raised with stones, so as people may read the inscription.

" Item, I leave the Honourable Governor, Council, and Secretary of this place, each a Gold ring of one pagoda and a half each value, with these words to be engraved in them, " Charles Davers, obiit," etc. To whom I wish all tranquility, health, and prosperity.

" Item, I leave unto Dr. Pitchers, the sum of 30 pagodas in case I die of my present illness, and that I did not pay him before I died.

" Item, I leave unto my friend, Mr. Paul Foxley 20 pagodas for mourning; to whom I wish all health in this world, and happiness in the next.

" Item, I leave unto the Minister that attend me 20 pagodas for a ring.

" Item, I leave unto my friend Mr. John Maubers 20 pagodas for mourning.

" Lastly, I leave my two trusty and beloved friends Mr. George Sittwel and Mr. Catesby Oadham, my two executors of this my last will and testament, and desire them to see me carried to the place of burial in the manner following viz.

" My Corpse to be carried from the Town Hall

at seven o'clock at night. I desire that all the free merchants of my acquaintance to attend me in their palankeens to the place of burial; and as many of the Company's servants as I have had any intimacy within my life time; that all that attend me may have scarves and hat bands decent. I desire that Mr. Main, and the Charity Boys, may go before my corpse, and sing a hymn; my corpse to be carried by six Englishmen or more; if occasion, the minister and the rest of the gentlemen following. I desire of the Honorable Governor that I may have as many great guns fired as I am years old, which is now almost twenty-one. In case it is customary to pay the great guns firing I desire you to do it. I desire the favour of the Captain of the guard to attend me; and that you present him with a gold ring the same as the Governor and Council. And now as to my Estate. I have 1086 ounces of silver, which my father sent me out this year. I am concerned with Mr. Thomas Theobalds in a respondentia bond in the "George" Brigantine. I have also an adventure with Captain James Hurdis, the prime cost being 72 pagodas and a half. I have at this time in my escritore about 100 pagodas, besides clothes and linen; an account of which I always keep in my escritore. I desire of my two executors to accept of 30 pagodas each for mourning; and each a ring of 15 pagodas value, with my name and time of death engraved upon it.

"After my corpse is buried, which I desire may be done very handsomely, the remainder of my estate I desire may be laid out in rice, and be given to the poor at the burial place, as long as it lasts. This I declare to be my last will and testament."

CHARLES DAVERS."

In the early part of 1721, an event transpired in Black Town which appears to have given no little trouble to the Governor. The Warehouse Conicopily had seduced a Rajpoot woman residing at Madras; and the strictness of the ideas of honour prevailing among the Rajpoots, led her relations to demand the severest punishment against the offender. The story is sufficiently told in the following extract from the consultations.

"Thursday, 23rd February, 1721. Petition from Venkataranze, an inhabitant of this place of the Rajpoot caste, was presented to the Board; the import of the said petition, being a complaint against Davaroy, the Warehouse Conicopilly for seducing his sister from her lawful husband, and forcibly detaining her when she was demanded by himself and her said husband. The President thereupon acquainted the Board that this complaint had been made to him singly a few days since; whereupon he confined him to the Choultry, with a resolution to re-examine the case at the Board; the complainant being very pressing and importunate for justice; and being so much exasperated at the shame and disgrace which their family was like to suffer on the occasion, that they could scarcely be restrained from murdering themselves as well as the woman; the caste or tribe to which they belong being so nicely strict in their rules with regard to matters that concern their honour, that they choose much rather to suffer death than ignominy or reproach. Davaroy being brought before the Board, and examined upon the occasion; he replied that Venkatarauze came about ten days ago to him and told him that his sister had returned from the place, to which he sent her up in the country, but that he could not find her. Devaroy added that thereupon he sent to one Eyamoi-Villevochum a Washerman's wife and bid her look for the girl; and when she had found her she told her that her brother desired she might be carried to Davaroy's house. Davaroy added that when the girl was brought thither it was very late, and that therefore he asked the Washerwoman why she brought her at that unseasonable time of night, and bid her go away; but that they desired to lodge in the house that night, for fear of being taken up by the rounds. That in the morning, just before he went to the Fort, he enquired which was the Rajpoot woman; who when she saw him desired his protection from her friends, who, she said, would use her ill whenever she returned to them. He affirmed that he then bid her go a second time, but she replied, she was afraid and could not go; and then the Washerwoman told him that if he did not keep her from her relations she should suffer very much. Whereupon he came to the Fort. Davaroy further declared that he could not deny but that Venkatarauze came to his house the next day, and demanded his sister, as having heard that she was there; and that he replied that it was not in his power to deliver her up, but that he might go to his master. That the third day the said Venkatarauze met him in the street, and demanded his sister again; and that he replied, that he had been hard at work in the Fort, and was very much fatigued, but that he would talk with him in the morning; when the said Venkatarauze went and made his complaint to the Governor.

"Venkatarauze, the Complainant, being called in, and asked concerning the matter in dispute; he declared that about four months since, having heard that his sister frequently went to the aforementioned Washerwoman's house who bore no very reputable character, he began to be apprehensive, lest his sister should be seduced by her, if he did not timely prevent it; and that therefore he sent her up in the country to some relations there, but that lately returning again very privately (which however came to his knowledge) he sent to the aforesaid Washerman's to enquire where she was. The Washerwoman at first replied, that she knew not; but afterwards assured him she was in the house of Davaroy; whither he accordingly went, and meeting him at home, intreated him to deliver up his sister in order to prevent shame and infamy from falling upon their whole family, which the detention of his sister would unavoidably occasion. The said Venkatarauze further declares, that the defendant Davaroy then returned him for answer, that she was not in his house, but some where in the street; that thereupon being exasperated, he persisted in his demands of the girl; telling him without that if he was resolved, himself and family should kill themselves or leave the bounds; they would do either of the two. To which Davaroy replied, they might do what they would, but that he could not make up the matter in less than eight or ten day's time, when the Ships were gone for Europe.

"The Washerwoman being called in, and asked concerning this matter, she declared that the Plaintiff Venkatarauze did go to Davaroy and demand his sister; and that thereupon she herself was sent for by him, who bid her look amongst the cooly washerwomen for the girl; which she did accordingly, found her, and brought her to Davaroy's house, who bid her go away; that they replied it was late, and that they were afraid of being taken up by the rounds; for which reason they desired to lie there that night. This deponent further alleged, that then Davaroy permitted them to stay, but ordered her to take care of the girl, and stay with her. In the morning they asked Davaroy what they should do with her; who replied she might go. The deponent added that she told Davaroy, that if the girl returned to her relations they would murder her. Whereupon Davaroy gave them leave to continue in his house for three days; two of which, this deponent adds, she remained with the girl; but confesses that the third day she was absent.

"The sister to the Plaintiff Venkatarauze, being brought before the Board, was asked if Davaroy was guilty of the several particulars wherewith he now stood charged. In answer whereto, the woman declared in the affirmative and offered her oath to the same.

"The foregoing depositions being heard and fully considered; Davaroy was remanded to the Choultry, and the several persons concerned in this affair, dismissed the room."

This affair was debated at very great length, and occupies an important place in the records. The case was subsequently handed over to the arbitration of the heads of the castes, and Davaroy was sentenced to pay the sum of four hundred pagodas.

Our next extract refers to the general state of affairs in the Dekkan. It has already been mentioned that Hussein Ali Khan had been assassinated, and that Cheen Kulick Khan, alias Nizam-ool-Moolk, was Subah of the Dekkan. The entry though short may be useful to the historian.

"Tuesday, 21st March, 1721. The President acquaints the Board that he has received repeated advices from our spy peons at the Nabob's Camp, relating to Cheen Kulick Khan's coming this way with a very powerful army; that he (Cheen Kulick Khan) had summoned all the Nabobs of this country to come to him to give an account of their management; and that it is thought he will come to Ginjee. The President therefore proposes to every one to consider, whether his coming this way may not prejudice the Honorable Company's affairs, if we do not send a present, attended with proper persons to treat with him. The President further acquaints the Board that it is reported Diaram is with him; but as there is no certainty of it at present, he intends to make further enquiry."

About this time Governor Hastings was engaged in an enquiry into the murder of two Englishmen at Syriam in Pegu. The event excited considerable attention at the time, but has long since been devoid of interest. The main features however may be related as illustrative of the mode in which the British traded with Pegu about a century and a half ago

In 1720 a Captain Heron resided at Syriam, a few miles to the south-east of Rangoon, in the character of British Resident; and it had been customary on the arrival of any of the Company's ships at the Syriam river, for Captain Heron to transact all the necessary business with the Prince of Syriam, or even the King of Pegu, and to give the supercargo such aid and advice as lay in his power. About this time the Company's ship "Lusitania," with Mr. Stephen Orme as Supercargo, arrived at the Syriam river. For the first day or two Mr. Orme lodged at Captain Heron's house, and all things went on smoothly. Mr. Orme however refused the proffered assistance of Captain Heron, and acted for himself. He made his own presents to the Prince of Syriam, and rejected the aid of Captain Heron's overseer whilst conducting the repairs of his vessel. A coolness naturally sprung up between the two, which was greatly increased when Mr. Orme not only took a separate house, but hoisted the English flag in his compound. The quarrel soon extended to the subordinates; and whenever the Lascars of the "Lusitania" went ashore they were obstructed and affronted by the Lascars of Captain Heron. The former requested Mr. Orme that they might be permitted to resent these affronts; but he replied that he should severely punish any one of his crew who should make any attack upon Captain Heron's men unless he had received the first blow.

Under these promising circumstances the time came round for the Mussulman feast called "Hossein Jossen," and the "Feast of Jamsee;" better known as the Mohurrum. This festival is celebrated by dancing round large fires in the vicinity of the Mosque, together with mock fighting which generally ended in real blows. Accordingly Captain Heron had never permitted any Englishman to go near these festivities, and had very often prevented the Lascars from doing so. Above all it was strictly forbidden that any one should carry English colours on the occasion. It seems however that a number of Lascars from the "Lusitania," together with others from some Moors ships, went to the feast, followed at a distance by five Europeans. Whether colours were carried or not appears to be uncertain. But an affray broke out, in which Cojee Zackary, an Armenian merchant at Syriam, interfered at the head of his Lascars; being also accompanied by the Lascars of Captain Heron. It was in this affray that the Chief Mate and Gunner were murdered at the direct instigation of Cojee Zachary. We quote the deposition of one of the witnesses as a sample of the whole.

"I, the under written Manoel DeMonte, inhabitant and married in this city of Madras, do hereby declare that I being in Syriam in the time that the Moors made their feast; we, the Lascars belonging to the Frigate called the "Lusitania," and some Moor's Ships, joined at night and were going to the place where the feast was kept; and when we came to the Street wherein lives the Moors Calafa, we met the Lascars of Cojee Zachary and Captain Heron. The streets being very narrow, we could not pass by them in a body, and the Pilot of the Frigate (who was in our Company) went and desired them friendly to go forward, or grant us liberty to pass them. Instead of hearing his petition, one of the Moors insulted him and gave him many blows. We seeing that, we all arose against them and made them presently run away; and so continued our march to the place where the feast was kept. A little while after came Cojee Zachary on horse back, with a lance in his hand (made after the country fashion); and after him his Lascars, and some of the natives, all armed with sticks and stones. The Pilot of the Frigate perceiving Zachary, he went to him and took the reins of his bridle in his hand, and begged of Zachary not to take notice of what had happened. Zachary gave him no answer, and shaking his head he went round the fire crying, "Beat the dogs;" and immediately the quarrel began, which grew so great that our people all run away, except the Pilot and Gunner of the Frigate. Zachary, spying them out ordered his people to beat them; and he went himself to assist them, and with the lance that he carried in his hand, he wounded the Pilot, of which wound the Pilot fell on the ground. Zachary perceiving that, and that the Gunner was yet safe and running away, he ordered his people to run after him and bring him back; which they did and beat him in the presence of Zachary till the Gunner fell dead; which Zachary perceiving, and it being near the fire round which the Moors celebrated the ceremony of their feast, he ordered to bring a light; and looking on and examining the two corpses, and finding they were dead, he retired to his house. To the truth of which, being acted in my presence, I standing all the while in a house near the place, where all this was acted, I do hereby declare and certify, and take my oath on the holy Evangelist in Madras, this 8th day of May, 1721."

The next day Mr. Orme, appealed to the Prince of Syriam for justice against Cojee Zachary, but appears to have been greatly obstructed by Captain Heron. The information was transmitted to the king of Ava, and the latter ordered "that Zachary should be in the sun three days, be bored through his cheeks and cut in his back seven times, and pay a hundred viss of silver; and that each one of all the others concerned should receive one hundred blows; provided that Captain Heron would declare in the public Ronda that the whole story was true." It would seem that Zachary escaped punishment; and on reaching Madras Mr. Orme charged Captain Heron before Governor Hastings with having been bribed to screen the murderer. It will be sufficient to say that the charge of bribery fell to the ground, but that Captain Heron received a severe reprimand from the Court of Directors.

It was soon after this inquiry that the Governorship of Mr. Francis Hastings was brought abruptly to a close. The quarrel with Mr. Elwick was brought to an unfavorable termination; for instead of his suspension being confirmed, he was appointed Governor of Fort St. George and Mr. Hastings was removed. The proceedings are somewhat obscure, the General letters from the Court of Directors being missing. We can therefore only extract the following entry, after which Mr. Nathaniel Elwick took his seat in the President's chair.

"Sunday, 15th October, 1721. Ships "Heathcote" and "Marlborough" (belonging to the Honorable Company), arrived this afternoon from Great Britain; by whom received two packets from the Honorable Court of Directors, directed to the Honorable Nathaniel Elwick, Esq., President and Governor, William Jennings, Nathaniel Turner, Richard Benyon, Catesby Oadham, John Emmerson, Randal Fowke, James Hubbard, and George Drake. All except Mr. Jennings immediately met in the Consultation Room in the Fort; where all the Company's servants, both Civil and Military, and other inhabitants, were summoned; and on their appearance the packet was opened and the Commission read to them, after which they withdrew."

CHAPTER XXXII.

GOVERNORSHIP OF MR. NATHANIEL ELWICK.

1721—24.

Our readers will already have remarked that during the period now under review, Fort St. George was singularly free from any interference on the part of the Nabob of the Carnatic or Subah of the Dekkan. This tranquil state of affairs continued for some years. The rent was paid regularly, and at intervals compliments and presents were interchanged, but no differences appear to have arisen like those which mark the early annals of Madras. A change also is perceptible in what may be called the domestic history of the Presidency. Much of the roughness of the early period had passed away. Manners became less quaint and simple, but more refined; and altogether there is a better tone in the consultations. Decorum was more strictly preserved, whatever doubts may be entertained as to any real improvement in the morality of the times.

The first event in the new administration was however an extraordinary one. On the very Sunday, the 15th of October, 1721, that Mr. Elwick took the place of Mr. Hastings in the President's chair, the new Governor asked the Secretary for the Cash book, in order that he might see the balance; but found that it was closed up only to the end of the previous month, and that nc entry of receipts or disbursements had been made for the month of October. Accordingly, as it was too late to examine the actual state of the cash that evening, the cash chest was sealed up, and the key of the Godown in which the silver was kept, called the Silver Godown, was delivered up; and Mr. Hastings, the late President, and Mr. Cooke, the Secretary, were requested to be present in the morning to see them both opened.

On the following morning the council assembled in the Consultation Room. Mr. Hastings was not present, but Mr. Cooke was sent for to see the Silver Godown opened. The proceedings may here be described in the language of the official entry.

"Monday, 16th October, 1721. Mr. Thomas Cooke being sent for, pursuant to an order of yesterday's Consultation, to see the Silver Godown opened and the treasure delivered, acquaints the Board that there is none at all in the Godown; he having sold the last 29 chests by an order of Mr. Hastings, since the Consultation of the 2nd instant, at 14 dollars per 10 pagodas; which he intended to have reported the first Consultation that should have been held. He was asked to pay in the produce of the silver, but he answered he had not received it. The Board then told him that, as he had sold it without any authority, they looked upon him to be accountable for it; and demanded what security he could give for the payment of it. In answer to which he desired time till the afternoon, when he doubted not he should be able to give security to our satisfaction. He was then ordered to withdraw, and acquainted we should want him by and by."

"The President then acquaints the Board that he sent to Mr. Hastings, to desire to speak with him upon the matters of his cash account. Accordingly Mr. Hastings attended the President at the Fort, where they had a private conference in the President's room; the result thereof from Mr. Hastings was, that he was deficient in the cash account, but that he would in seven days time make it good and deliver in the cash account with the balance. In the mean time he desired to reside at the garden for his health and convenience; and likewise desired leave to retire to the Mount till the next ship sails for England, on which he hopes to embark.

"Mr. Thomas Cooke was again sent for to the Board, and the money for the 29 chests of silver demanded of him. He answered he could not at present comply therewith, but that in twenty day's time he would make good the amount of what the 29 chests sold for. Upon which the Board insisted on security till he has paid the money. He answered at present he had not any to offer, but that he would go and get security. Accordingly he was acquainted we should meet again at four o'clock, and that then we shall expect he brings it with him."

Four o'clock came, when the following discussion took place in the Consultation Room.

"Mr. Cooke attends the Board (according to order in this morning's consultation), and acquaints the Board that the late President will be answerable for the amount of the sale of the 29 chests of treasure; and if the Board does not think the late President's bond for the same sufficient security, that he is willing to enter into the bond with him for the amount of the same; and being pressed for a sum of money forthwith in part, he answered, he hoped in five or six days to be able to pay in on account of the said silver about ten or twelve thousand pagodas. Upon which he was ordered to withdraw till the Board had considered further on the affair.

"Agreed that the late President and Mr. Cooke's joint bond is no security to the Honourable Company for the 29 chests of treasure; for a bond, without assets being joined with it and made over to the amount of the said treasure, is no more than an acknowledgment of the debt.

"Agreed that as the President designs this evening to return Mr. Hasting's visit to him this morning, that he does discourse Mr. Hastings on the subject of his debt on his cash account, and Mr. Cooke's debt account, viz. the 29 chests of treasure; and that the President desires to know of Mr. Hastings if he will give security for his debt on account of the cash; as also for Mr. Cooke's debt on account the 29 chests of silver; and that the Board do wait the President's return, in order to debate further on this matter which has already taken us up a great deal of time."

Late in the evening there was another consultation, the proceedings of which are thus recorded.

"The President reports to the Board, that he having been with the late President Mr. Hastings to return his visit of the morning, did according to agreement discourse Mr. Hastings on the affair of his cash account, and the 29 chests of treasure disposed of by Mr. Thomas Cooke; and that having demanded the money, or sufficient security for each, the late President did thereupon reply to him, that he would certainly on the day after to-morrow (which he said was as soon as an affair of that nature could be transacted) pay him the balance of the cash account in money, diamonds, or other sufficient security; and that as to the affair of the 29 chests of silver, he desires till the time is elapsed which the said silver was sold at; and concluded with desiring that no unkind expressions or entries be made upon our Consultation Book to slur his reputation. To which the President replied, he found no member of the Board any way inclined thereto.

"Agreed that the Board will wait till the day after to-morrow, and expect the late President Mr. Hastings' performance of his promise, unless in the meantime there should appear cause for the contrary."

During the interval Mr. Hastings was taken dangerously ill. Accordingly on the Wednesday, being the day fixed for paying the balance of the cash, the following entries are recorded.

"Wednesday, 18th October, 1721. The President reports that upon hearing of the late President's dangerous illness, he sent for Mr. Cooke, and demanded of him security for the 29 chests of treasure which he has disposed of out of the Warehouse. He replied he could not give in security for the same. Whereupon the President thought himself obliged to deliver him to the Captain of the Guard's charge; but that upon his request, he had permitted him to remain in the lodgings of the Warehouse under sentinels."

Mr. Cooke being thus confined as security for the 29 chests of silver, the next thing to be considered was what was to be done about the cash balance. On perusing a rough draft of the cash book, it was discovered that Mr. Hastings was indebted to the company more than seventy-two thousand pagodas; whilst the amount of cash actually remaining in the treasury may be gathered from the following extract of the same date as the foregoing.

"Wednesday, *continued.* Mr. Walsh brought the key of the cash chest and opened it; upon which there was found, in money one Fanam, and some Firmauns and Husbulhookums; being 29 from the Mogul, and the Commission for trying the pirates; also a paper with blue seals, said to be a purse belonging to Dalton deceased in Pegu. These were all the things found in the chest, except some empty pagoda bags. Mr. Walsh being asked if he brought any message from Mr. Hastings, answered he had none.

"Agreed that to-morrow morning the late President's cash account be drawn out, sent to him, and the balance demanded to be forthwith paid; and after having had a long debate upon the matter, it was also agreed that the President do give orders to the Captain of the Guard for securing the person of the late President from making his escape from the place till such time as that he has paid the Honorable Company, what he owes them on his cash account and the 29 chests of silver reported to be sold by Mr. Cooke."

Notwithstanding this singularly empty state of the Silver Godown and Treasury Chest, Mr. Hastings scarcely appears to have been a dishonest man; and it was only the sudden manner in which he was required to vacate the chair that caused the deficiency. On the next day he paid in ten thousand pagodas; on the Saturday following he deposited diamonds to the value of twenty thousand pagodas more, and a few days afterwards gave ample security for the remainder. Unfortunately for him the illness with which he had been attacked proved fatal. The following simple entries tell their own story.

"Tuesday, 12th December, 1721. Mr. Francis Hastings, late President, desires leave to go home on the "Marlborough," which is granted, believing the security we have on the Honorable Company's account more than sufficient to answer their demands; the very ill state of health he is in, and the little likelihood of his life if he continues here, being sufficient motives thereto. We have also permitted his servant, Thomas Newton, to go with him; he being as Mr. Hastings says a very useful servant to him, and has long since served his time to the Honorable Company.

"Friday, 15th December, 1721. This evening died the late President, Francis Hastings, Esq."

The year 1721 was rendered memorable by a great storm, which took place during the North East monsoon, and occasioned very great damage. The records describe exactly the same kind of weather which still visits the coast of Coromandel at intervals; but in addition to the terrors of the storm, it would seem that in cases of shipwreck some fears were entertained of the Moors, though not to the same extent as in former years. The following extracts will describe the commotion which attended such an event a hundred and forty years ago.

"Monday, 13th November, 1721. The Captain of the "King George" having yesterday in the afternoon received his dispatches, was this morning to take his leave of the President, who went with him to the Sea Gate to see him off; but the surf running very high, he could not get over, but hoped for meeting with an opportunity in the afternoon; but the wind and weather increased rather than abated, growing very thick to the north east. As the evening approached rain came on and wind in greater abundance, which prevented him from going off that night.

"14th November. All last night and this day the wind and rain continued with more violence than yesterday, and increased towards noon to a great storm. The rapidity of the waters out of the country was so great that it broke two of our bridges, that next to the Fort and the other on the road towards Triplicane. At the former of these there was at least two feet fall, which must be a prodigious stream to so small a bridge; and as to the other it was hardly dry, so consequently the more liable to this disaster. The whole Island was overflowed, and nothing all round us to be seen but water, tops of hedges and trees. The rains and floods have carried away most of the Macquaw and poor peoples' houses in the suburbs of Madras. The weather at one o'clock in the afternoon was so thick and hazy that we could not see a stone cast round us; and notwithstanding we are extremely alarmed at frequent firings from the ships in the road all this afternoon, yet we cannot do anything for the security either of our Honorable Masters' goods, ships or treasure; the surf flying quite up to the gates, and impossible for almost anything to live upon the sea.

"15th November. This morning the wind began to abate and the weather to clear up; but on our looking out into the road we could perceive only one ship remaining, which in the afternoon we heard was the "Heathcote." The Chief Mate writes ashore that the brigantine he had not seen all yesterday, nor the "King George," nor the "Dartmouth" since that day at noon. As for the "Marlborough" she drove about 5 in the afternoon; and he judged that ship which was then at an anchor within half a mile of the surf off St.

Thomé, to be her. Captains Elliston, Warden, and Crossing, and Mr. Bates, Chief Mate of the "Marlborough," desired horses to go down and see her, and look if any more were to be seen to the southward, but after all that they could do it was impossible for them to get over the river, so they were obliged to return. We endeavoured immediately after that to send off anchors and cables to the "Marlborough," who made frequent signals of distress; but the boat we put the cable into (and in which the Chief Mate was going) filled and split to pieces. However we with much ado got off a cable that afternoon, and the Chief Mate went aboard. As soon as he was there he hoisted his Ensign in the fore shrouds, the signal agreed upon in case of another ship in distress below there; but notwithstanding all that we could do, we were obliged to defer sending an anchor till the next morning.

"We also ordered three boats to be got ready and seven soldiers to go in each boat; Captains Warden, Elliston, and Crossing, whose ships and brigantine were missing, went one in each of them. But an accident prevented that wherein Captain Warden was from proceeding, which was her oversetting; by which misfortune a Serjeant and three men were drowned.

"The Honorable President in the morning, perceiving the ships were missing, dispatched 100 peons to the southward along the sea side to see if any wrecks came ashore; but the rivers being so very deep and rapid, and the country under water, that the peons could not pass; so that had not any intelligence till the 17th in the afternoon from the Chief of Covelong. However it was judged necessary to have an account of the above-mentioned signal, in order to send the men as before related. Captain Crossing was in the first boat that went off that evening; when he got aboard the "Marlborough" fired one gun, which was agreed to be done if the signal on the fore shrouds in the evening was not a mistake.

"A Letter from Captain Tolson's Chief Mate to him, of this day's date, giving an account of the storm is hereunder entered.

"Heathcote," November 17th, 1721.

"Captain Tolson,

"Sir,

These are to inform you that the ship has met with no further misfortune than the loss of the Long boat and the parting of our small Bower Cable; though I must confess it is less than expected. It is impossible to relate the extremity of weather we had as to the Ships. I cannot tell further of them than that ship to the Southward of St. Thomé I take to be the "Marlborough." The "Dartmouth" I see drive yesterday in the afternoon; the weather coming on so thick saw no more of her. The "King George" I saw yesterday noon. The brigantine we saw nothing of, which impute to the thickness of the weather at that time; but heartily wish they may be well, which I much doubt. The "King George", she being a very pestered ship, or indeed the rest, I cannot see what they could do by going to sea with the wind at north east, and north east by east, and such a grown sea.

I am Sir,

Your most humble Servant,

ROGER HALE."

"16th November. The Honorable President received a letter from Captain Elliston on board the "Marlborough," acquainting us she rode in six fathom water, and that since eight o'clock Tuesday morning she had seen neither of the other Ships, but she has lost four anchors, and had only their sheet anchor left; but that they had one of the Company's stocked, and desired timber to stock another, and a large Cattamaran to carry their anchors out to work further off shore. The President forthwith sent them an anchor of 25 tons weight ready stocked, on a large Cattamaran, according to their desire, and they have immediately gone out in deeper water, and now she is very safe.

"Captain Tolson also communicated to us a letter that he received from his Mate, importing the ship laboured prodigiously during all that Hurricane, which has forced all the oakum out of her upper works; that they rode almost under water which had damaged very much their provisions; that their sheet cable and best bower were both rubbed very much, and the outward cable to the best bower anchor very bad; that she had worked down all the cabins in the steerage, and the bulk head, and broke all their hen coops to pieces. Late at night the President received a letter from Captains Elliston and Crossing, two miles off Covelong, importing they had met nothing like a wreck in their way, but a Long boat and David which they believed belonged either to the "Marlborough" or "Heathcote."

"Friday, 17th November, 1721. The President acquaints the Board that, by peons sent from hence, he received advice about noon from the Chief of Covelong, that a ship is drove ashore about eight miles to the Southward of said place; and that 5 chests and 20 Europeans are come ashore and seized by the Moors; but what ship is stranded, the peons could not tell the name of.

"Agreed that the "Heathcote" be forthwith ordered under sail to the wreck; that twenty Europeans and Captain Sutherland be sent upon her to protect the wreck, with ten Lascars and ammunition, as also sixty spare arms for the Ship's Company; with all other necessaries and as many Mussoolas as can be spared, together with such as we can borrow from St. Thomé. Fourteen Europeans are already at Covelong, under command of Captains Elliston and Crossing, as also twenty Lascars."

"Friday, 17th November, 1721. Received a letter from the Chief of the Flemings at Covelong, advising that an English Ship was stranded at Mauvelipuram, and that the people that we sent down were arrived there; that the Moors at his intercession treated them very well; let them have two palankeens and a horse to go to the wreck, and enquire news of the others that were missing; that they had secured all the sailors, but upon the Captain's request had released them again; and he assures us that the Moors will not in the least hinder but rather be assisting to us in this affair."

We now turn to an incident, which is by no means without a parallel in the early history of Madras, and which at the same time is very significant. The Governors of Fort St. George appear about this period to have each had some very clever Native acting for them under the name of the Dubash; and this Governor's Dubash not only transacted all the private business of his master, such as sales and purchases, but was frequently guilty of extortion and oppression towards his fellow countrymen, of which no one can have the slightest conception who is not intimately acquainted with the native character. Of course after the death or departure of a Governor many of these acts of tyranny came out, and the Dubash was made to disgorge a portion of his ill gotten gains. Thus some time after the death of Mr. Hastings, his Dubash Mar Kistna, got into trouble; though we may remark in passing, that his evil deeds were subsequently left in the shade by another Native who afterwards acted as Dubash to Governor Macrae.

The story of Governor Hasting's Dubash is however somewhat singular from the fact of this clever extortioner being of a jocular and musical turn; and indeed seems to have been a type of a character but little known to the European, namely that of a convivial Hindoo. Dickens tells a story of a London cabman who was sentenced to solitary confinement for six weeks for having "thrashed a fare;" and who thereupon lay upon his back and sang comic songs all day. It does however seem somewhat strange that a similar character should have turned up in the records of this Presidency. We give the original entry.

"Saturday, 8th September, 1722. We have acquainted the Honorable Court of Directors that we had secured Mar Kistna, Mr. Hasting's Dubash, whom we had severe complaints against for large debts owing to sundry persons, and other indirect management. He hath now either made full satisfaction, or given security for all the demands that have appeared against him, except a debt to Amerash Tacca, a company's merchant, and to the estate of his master Hastings. His crimes are so enormous that they call for public punishment, that he may be an example to future Dubashes how they make use of their Master's power in an unwarrantable manner. He at present complains of a lameness in his limbs, how real we cannot determine ; but shall leave the determination of his case till the Europe ships are gone. He always had a lodging in the Fort, and a sentry upon him, and had the liberty of his acquaintance, till the Company's Merchants reported that he lived so jocular with his singing master attending him, that he would never think of paying him his money ; which was above two months since, when the President ordered him into the Ensign's room upon the Main. Guard, and the door to be shut ; though however he still observes a constant levee at his window every morning."

The following extract will furnish a sufficient illustration of Mar Kistna's proceedings.

"Saturday, 8th September 1722.

"A Declaration of Tombee Chetty and Moota Venkitta Chetty.

"We, Tombee Chetty and Moota Venkitta Chetty, do hereby declare that Mar Kistna sent for and told us, that as we had entered into a contract with the Honorable Company, we ought to give the Governor 5000 pagodas, which he then demanded. Upon our refusing to give the said money, he went and told the Governor some false stories, which occasioned us to be confined one day at the Gardens. About 12 o'clock that night the peons carried us to Mar Kistna's house, when we asked why we put him to so much trouble without any reason. He answered, that if we would lay down 5000 pagodas we may go free, or else we should be confined in the Choultry. Notwithstanding those threats we still refused to give any money. Then he sent us to the Choultry, and put us in a close prison, where two men can scarce stand; and ordered the peons not to let us go out without the door upon any account whatsoever, but made us eat and drink and live entirely in that little place. About four or five days after he gave orders that we should not have any provisions whatsoever, but once in four days, and then only a little rice and water, and of that not half enough to satisfy our appetites. One day we lighted a lamp in the said godown; which Mar Kistna saw, and ordered it immediately to be put out. Sometime after, we sent a man to the said

Mar Kistna to ask him how he could be so barbareous to us. He answered, that we should not be released unless we would give the said 5000 pagodas; telling the said servant that if we would give the said money, to come and tell him; if not, not to come to him again; and then he ordered the peon to push the said man out of his house. Sometime after he sent a man to us to tell us that if we would give 3000 pagodas we should be free; which we refused. Sometime after 2000 pagodas; then that we should be released for 1500 pagodas. Lastly he sent word, if we would directly lay down 1000 pagodas we should be set at liberty. But finding he could not get any thing from us he increased his barbarity to the utmost of his power, and then released us, all which was by the persuasion of Mar Kistna. Therefore we hope this Honorable Board will examine this affair."

The subsequent treatment of Mar Kistna may be gathered from the following extracts.

"Wednesday, 10th October, 1722. Agreed that Mar Kistna be, as he has petitioned, permitted to go about Town under a guard of peons and Talliars in the day time, to gather in his effects, in order to satisfy what he owes to the estates of Messrs. Hastings, Wright, and other creditors; that the Petitioners be permitted to sue Kistna in the Mayor's Court if they please, and that the peons and Talliars every night do return Mar Kistna to his confinement, till he has satisfied all his creditors."

"Tuesday, 11th December, 1722. Petition of Mar Kistna read, setting forth that being under confinement at the Fort, and not having conveniences proper to take the necessary physic for recovery of his health, it is agreed he be delivered to the charge of the Chief Peon, and Taliar, and that he remains at his own house."

After this Mar Kistna managed to satisfy all his creditors and obtained his liberty.

The following extracts regarding the Armenians will be found interesting, as throwing light upon the mode in which trade was carried on in the olden time. Our readers will bear in mind the distinction between the Company's trade, and the trade carried on by the Company's servants and merchants of the place.

"Monday, 27th April, 1724. The President told the Board that the Armenians had for a long time behaved themselves in a very insolent haughty manner; and had rendered themselves not only undeserving the great privileges granted them, but likewise obnoxious to the Government by several actions, contrary to the rules and regulations thereof; and that he had ordered them to attend the Board to answer to several facts he had to charge them with. The first was that Codejee George, and the rest of the owners of the Ship "London," had imported great part of the Ship's Cargo at Pondicherry, to the amount of 12,000 pagodas, contrary to the orders of the Company; as would fully appear from their letter of the 7th April 1708, where they order the native inhabitants to be expelled the bounds, if they carry the trade to St. Thomé to the prejudice of the customs of Madras; which by parity of reason holds the same with respect to Pondicherry, since wherever the goods are imported, still the customs are lost to them. He, the President, likewise produced the Company's letter of the 19th December 1719, where are these remarkable words, speaking of the French,—that none of our Servants, whether Europeans or Indians, nor any of our Merchants or Brokers, be permitted to buy or sell for them, or otherwise assist them, in their trade or merchandize. He added that Codejee Petrus, an Armenian lately arrived from Manilla, and an inhabitant of this place, had contracted with the French this very year for 30,000 dollars worth of goods upon freight; and that besides they had encouraged one Bassilio, a subject of Manilla, to come hither and carry away the freight from this place; all which actions tend greatly to the damage of the Company with respect to their customs, and to the place itself, by encouraging foreigners and destroying the navigation of the English. He added that this evil had been long growing to the height it now is, and that as it is daily increasing, if the Board do not take some measures to prevent it, the commerce of Madras must inevitably fall away to nothing.

"The matter being sometime debated, and the privileges granted the Armenians duly considered, they were called in and told that it was the express orders of the Company, that no inhabitant of Madras should be allowed to import goods in any foreign settlement to the prejudice of the customs of this place. Likewise that none under the English protection were to aid and assist other nations in their trade and navigation, to the detriment of the English. They affirmed that they never had done any thing of this kind; but being presssed with the importation of goods at Poudicherry, Codejee George assured the Board that he knew nothing of the doing of it till the goods were ashore and sold; and as to the contract with the French, Codejee Petrus told them that money came from Manilla for account of Spaniards there, and consigned to him and another Armenian upon the French Ship, and that his orders were to return it on the same Ship.

"They were then ordered to withdraw, and after some small debate it was agreed to overlook what was past, but to let them know that if they were guilty of such practices for the future, they should be proceeded against with the utmost rigour, in compliance with the orders of our Honorable Masters. They were called in accordingly, and told the resolution of the Board; to which they promised due obedience"

"Wednesday, 20th May, 1724. The Armenians not taking warning by the late orders given them at the Board, but growing more insolent; and having since engaged with one Agostinho Bassilio, who is a Spaniard and come to this place, where he has offered freight at a lower rate than has for many years been customary, to the vast prejudice of the trade and navigation of this place; it was proposed to put a stop to such proceedings; but this being a matter of great moment, after some debate about the methods to be used in such a case, the Board thought fit to defer coming to a resolution thereupon till they had more fully considered it."

"Tuesday, 26th May, 1724. The Board then resumed the debate concerning the Armenians, and the Manilla freight, which was deferred the last consultation day; and it was agreed by the whole Board that, if some measures were not taken to prevent it, the trade of this place would be entirely lost to the English and given to Foreigners. But as the Company have given great immunities to that set of men, it was urged that we could not, without infringing those privileges, prevent their trading on the best terms they could. To which it was replied that the contract mentioned was an obsolete one; and that even at that time it was made the Company complained that the circumstances of the times obliged them to grant greater immunities than they would otherwise have done, and that probably when those circumstances should be altered they might make some alterations therein; by which it appeared, the Company themselves did not thoroughly approve of the granting such privileges. It was added upon this side that the Armenians had long ago forfeited the privileges granted them, by carrying on their trade to and from Europe on the Danes' ships, and now more recently by contracting with the French and Spaniards, directly contrary to the conditions on which these concessions were made them. It was further added on the same side, that the Company do covenant and agree with their servants, and Free Merchants whom they permit to reside in India, that they shall have all manner of freedom in their trade, but that if ever they think fit to order any of their own ships to freight voyages, they do expect to be first served, and our ships after them. From whence it is reasonable to suppose, if they will insist upon the first plan themselves, we ought to be and are allowed the second; or otherwise we should be on a much worse foundation than any set of men in India, and obliged to leave off all trading; being under traded by the natives on the one hand and obliged to prefer the Company's ships on the other. Upon the whole of the debates, which was continued for a considerable time, it was unanimously agreed and ordered, that the inhabitants of Madras shall not be allowed to freight to Manilla any goods or money belonging to this place on any foreign ship before the English ship is laden."

The following complaint addressed to the Government of Fort St. George on the 8th June, 1724, by Mr. Drake, a member of Council, is worth preserving as illustrative of the times.

" Honorable Sirs,

" I am to acquaint you that on Tuesday night last about 10 o'clock, a Musteez belonging to ship " Moylip," did in the open street assault and most barbarously beat one of my servants. As soon as I was informed of the same, I sent a civil message to him by my Dubash, and only desired to be acquainted with his reasons; but instead of having the least reply from him he returned to me my Dubash very much beaten, and had the insolence to follow him with blows to my very door. I then could do no other than send for the Guard, who accordingly came and secured him for the remainder of the night. This no sooner was done, but Captain Hill, the Commander of the Ship this young offender belongs to, came to my house and in a most indecent manner addressed himself to me; telling me I had forfeited all good manners, and had sent a better gentleman than myself on the Guard, and that my Councellorship was my only protection for so doing, and only on that presumption I had dared to do it, and that it was well for me I had such a protection to skreen me from his immediate resentment. In short Captain Hills language and manners throughout were very foul and rude, and such as I believe your Honours upon examination will find ought neither to be given or taken, especially as I had only done my duty, and taken no more privilege than the meanest of your inhabitants may, to quell a riot in the properest manner I could. I should have been very glad if Captain Hill would have recollected himself the next morning, that I might not have given your Honors this trouble; but as he persists, and will make me no acknowledgment, I am strictly obliged to make this application, and do believe you will find I merited better usage than Captain Hill was pleased to bestow on me. But this I refer to your determination."

It may be gratifying to hear that Captain Hill, after much expostulation, was induced to make an apology.

The following entries are worth preserving on account of their historical value. They seem to refer to a confederation of different Nabobs in Southern India, including Sadatulla Khan, Nabob of Arcot, against the power of Cheen Kulich Khan, Nizam of the Dekkan. Also to a struggle between two Mussulman chiefs for the possession of Ginjee.

"Wednesday, 1st July, 1724. The President informed the Board, that yesterday he received private advices from the country that in a late engagement near Aurungabad, wherein the Nabobs of this side of the country were most of them joined against Cheen Kulich Khan, this latter had gained a complete victory. Galib Khan, commander of the forces sent against him by our Nabob, being killed; as was likewise Falum Khan son to Abdul Nabbee Khan, and almost all the Chief Officers in the Army. Sheik Mahmud Khan, Nabob of Hyderabad, was likewise wounded and his life despaired of. These letters add that a detachment of Cheen Kulich Khan's army, amounting to about 15,000 men, were on their march to seize Sattingurra, one of the passes into the Carnatta country, which had occasioned our Nabob to march to secure it; in order to which he was levying forces with the utmost expedition and at very extravagant rates. Further advices say that Abdul Nabbee Khan was marched against Fyre Khan, to take possession of the Ginjee country; and that we might shortly expect an account of the engagement from those parts."

"Friday, 16th July, 1724. The President produced another letter, giving us an account that there had happened a very bloody engagement between Abdul Nabby Khan and Fyre Khan, in which the former was killed and the latter mortally wounded, and that there were upwards of 12,000 men cut off in the engagement. That upon this, our Nabob was marched to take possession of the Ginjee country, imagining that after such a vast loss neither side will be able to oppose him; that Cheen Kulich Khan* on his march to this side of the country, and a detaehment of his army consisting of 15,000 men, is now encamped at 15 leagues distanee from Hyderabad, in their way hither, followed by himself with the main body.

"The President added that there are remaining of Abdul Nabby Khan's family, 23 persons, which are all resolved to maintain their right to the Ginjee country or die, so that there is little likelihood of these parts being settled again in peaee for a long time."

"Wednesday, 22nd July 1724. There being a large quantity of Madeira wine in the Godowns, it was proposed to dispose of some part thereof. But the Persian Empire being so much disturbed, and the Afghans† beseiging Shiraz, it was resolved, not to sell any Madeira yet, it being very unlikely that we should have any wine from Persia this year, and consequently the price of Madeira will rise which is now very low."

About this time a erime was committed at Fort

---

* In the records he is styled Nissa Mulmuloch, who is said to be the same as "Chicklys Khan." There cannot however be the slightest doubt of his identity.

† The Afghans are here entitled "Ophgoons" in the Records. Of course in this, as in other similar cases, we have modernized the spelling.

St. David, which is worthy of some notice. A Gunner was living with a Portuguese woman; and one evening an Ensign of the Garrison made the Gunner drunk apparently for the purpose of seducing the woman. The Gunner however awoke from his drunken stupor, and after much altercation shot the Ensign dead. Many of the details are unfit for our columns, but the following extracts from the depositions are curious illustrations of the Garrison life of the period. We must premise that the Gunner's name was Jens Pitterson; the Ensign who was murdered was named Edward Key.

"Jens Pitterson declares, that the 2nd of October 1724, about 5 o'clock in the afternoon, he came from shooting; at which time Ensign Edward Key asked him what game he had got; to which he replied he saw nothing worth shooting, and so came home immediately. Afterwards Jens Pitterson declares he went home to eat, and when he had done Ensign Edward Key asked him, the said Jens Pitterson, to go to his room to drink a dram with him. To which the said Pitterson replied, that he was not used to drink and could not bear liquor, and therefore desired to be excused; but after many persuasions the said Jens Pitterson declares he went to Ensign Edward Key's room, and there drank with the Ensign two drams. After which the said Jens Pitterson says he retired into his own room, and that Ensign Edward Key about half an hour after followed him to his own room; when the Ensign told him, the said Jens Pitterson, that he wanted a companion to go with him to Bengal; for that his pay was going to be reduced, and he should be obliged to ask for his discharge. To which Jens Pitterson says he replied, that he had no occasion to leave the place while he was maintained; but that if he was discharged he must seek his livelihood where he could. Upon which Ensign Edward Key shook the said Jens Pitterson by the hand, and said to him "Comrade you must go along with me;" and then they fell to drinking in Pitterson's room to such an excess; that the said Jens Pitterson declares he knows not what he did afterwards, only that some of the guard told him this morning that the Ensign had beat him.

"Gulielmo D. Rozario, Sentry from 12 to 2 o'clock over the gate, deposes that about half an hour after one o'clock in the morning, Jens Pitterson, Gunner of Trepopolore Guard, waked in liquor, and asked Ensign Key what he was doing. Sometime after Jens Pitterson took his cutlace, which the Ensign seeing, retired into his own room and shut the door. Upon which Jens Pitterson enraged called out, and fell a cutting and slashing the bars of the Ensign's windows. But Jens Pitterson finding he could not come to the Ensign with his cutlace, went to his room and brought a gun. Whereupon the Deponent declares Ensign Key threatened Jens Pitterson, that if he did not retire from the window, he would fire upon him without waiting for orders; and that he the deponent called out to the Serjeants and Corporals who awaked, but were afraid to seize the said Jens Pitterson because he had a loaded gun in his hand. Whereupon Ensign Edward Key came to the window of his room, and bidding Jens Pitterson be gone to sleep, the said Jens Pitterson fired his gun in at the window, and shot him; which alarmed the guard, but they dared not seize him because he had got another loaded piece by him; therefore they waited till he fell asleep when they seized and bound him."

It came out in the evidence that the pay of the Ensign was only nine pagodas a month, and that of the gunner only six pagodas. It will be sufficient to say that the prisoner was sent to Fort St. George for trial, but the judgment subsequently passed does not appear in the records.

The administration of Governor Elwick was now drawing to a close. The last event in his administration worth recording, is an enquiry into the barbarous conduct of some peons who were sent to St. Thomé to arrest a man named Aneonah for debt. As all the facts were fully proved, it will be sufficient if we simply publish the complaint of Aneonah, and the punishment awarded to the accused. The petition is dated 16th November 1724.

"The petition of Godee Aneonah.

"Humbly showeth,

"That on Saturday night, three of the Company's peons came to my lodgings at St. Thomé, and told me your Honor sent for me. To which I replied, I would wait on your Honor directly. But one of the peons called Annapah, took hold of my hand, and drew his sword, and wounded me in the side. After that he and the other two carried me into the yard, and one of them put my head under his arm and cut the tip of my ears and took my jewels. My mother-in-law, seeing what they did, asked them why they used me so ill. At which one of them drew his sword and cut my mother-in-law on the neck. Then one of my man-servants, seeing me so cruelly used, begged them to let me alone. One of them presently cut off his hand and gave him a wound on the head; and after that they gave me several wounds on my belly and breast; then they beat all my woman servants and brought me into the streets, kicking and beating me on the belly. Then bringing me half way to Madras they overset me, beating and kicking me very basely; and thinking that they had killed me, they put their hands to my nose to feel if I was breathing, or whether I was dead or alive. Then they brought me before your Honor, who was pleased to order Doctor Pitcher to dress my wounds, who told me that if I had stayed but four hours longer without a Doctor I had been a dead man.

"I can assure your Honor and Council that I never wronged the Company, or am indebted to any body; but am a free merchant, and pay the Company's customs for my Merchandize. I am still very weak in my body and limbs, therefore leave it wholly to your Honor and Council to see your poor petitioner righted, and the offenders punished, according to your Honor and Council's pleasure."

Governor Elwick and Council entered upon a long and careful examination of all the circumstances connected with this outrage. In the first instance they resolved that the effects of Annapah and the two other peons should be confiscated and sold, in order to recompense the man who had lost his hand; and that the three criminals should stand in the pillory and have their ears cut off, and should then be whipped out of the bounds. Meantime however Aga Mogheen, the Governor of St. Thomé, interceded in behalf of the prisoners, and begged that they might be pardoned; and accordingly, in order to prevent the affair from being represented to the Nabob of Arcot in such a way as might prove troublesome to the Madras Government, it was resolved that the sentence should only be put in force against Annapah; and that the two other peons, who had only acted under his orders, should be discharged. Annapah however appears to have been an influential member of the Left Hand Caste, and the Heads of the whole of that Caste appeared before the Board and begged that a fine might be substituted for corporal punishment. Accordingly it was determined that Annapah should pay the following. To Anconah, whose jewels had been taken from his ears but whose circumstances were good, and who desired a public acknowledgment of the crime, Annapah was required to pay 200 pagodas. The manservant who lost his hand, being a much inferior person, would have received less; but considering that he had been disabled from getting a livelihood, "it was thought necessary to give him such a sum as might maintain him, or at least put him in a way of living easy for the rest of his life," and therefore he was to receive 200 pagodas.

Two other persons who were hurt were to be paid 50 pagodas each. Finally, in order that Annapah might make public reparation for his crime, "it was agreed to fine him further 200 pagodas, to be lodged in the Corporation Cash towards keeping the bridges in repair."

On the 18th of January 1725, Mr. Elwick resigned the President's chair, and shortly afterwards returned to England; and Mr. James Macrae of Glasgow notoriety assumed the Government of Fort St. George.

CHAPTER XXXIII.

GOVERNORSHIP OF MR. JAMES MACRAE.

1725—26.

Mr. James Macrae, Governor of Fort St. George and all the English Settlements on the Coast of Coromandel from 1725 to 1730, was one of those remarkable men who rose from poverty to affluence at the time when large fortunes were still a novelty in the commercial world. The annals of his Government will thus derive additional interest from his extraordinary career, especially in the eyes of those of our readers who come from those parts of Scotland where his name and memory are still preserved in local traditions. Accordingly, before entering upon the records of his government, it may be interesting to glance at such particulars respecting his origin as may be gathered from stories which are still current in Glasgow and Ayr.*

* Some interesting particulars concerning Governor Macrae and his family, and the mode in which he disposed of his fortune after his return from India, were published some years ago in the "Ayrshire Observer," and have been placed at the disposal of the compiler of these annals. It is curious to notice that all who have attempted to collect the traditions respecting this extraordinary man, dwell especially upon the fact that his Governorship of Madras, and indeed his whole Indian career, is a perfect blank. This blank will therefore now be filled up for the first time.

Mr. James Macrae was born in Ayrshire about the latter part of the reign of merry king Charles. His parents were of the very lowest class, and he himself whilst a boy is said to have been employed in looking after cattle. His father however died whilst James Macrae was still very young; and his mother then removed with her son to the town of Ayr; where they lived in a little thatched cottage in the suburbs, and where the poor widow gained her living as a washerwoman. Here young Macrae added something to his mother's earnings by running messages; but at the same time seems to have picked up some little education by means only known to Scotchmen. He appears however to have grown tired of this monotonous life whilst still a boy. Ayr was a seaport, and it is easy to understand how a young man, endowed with the energy which Macrae subsequently proved himself to possess, should have imbibed a keen desire to embark in the adventurous trading of the time, and finally have turned his back upon the poverty of home and run off to sea.

Forty years passed away before Macrae returned to his native land; and it is generally believed that throughout the whole of that period he held no communication whatever with his relations or his home. Meantime his sister married a carpenter named MacGuire, who was also in great request as a violin player at kirns and weddings, and was consequently known as "Fiddler MacGuire." The poverty of these people may be gathered from the fact that the children of MacGuire were on one occasion seen crying for bread, whilst their mother had left the house to try and borrow a loaf. But we shall have more particulars of this family to relate hereafter. For the present we must confine ourselves to the career of Mr. Macrae.

The early events in the seafaring life of the young runaway must we fear for ever remain unknown. We can learn nothing of him till about 1720, when he must already have been thirty years in India, and is simply alluded to as Captain Macrae. Most probably he had risen to the command of a vessel in the country trade, and had undertaken voyages to Sumatra, Pegu, and China. It appears however that he had been successful in gaining the confidence of his Honorable Masters, for he was subsequently sent on a special mission to the English settlement on the West Coast of Sumatra, to reform the many abuses which prevailed at that settlement. Here he acquitted himself in such a manner as to ensure his appointment to a high post. He effected savings to the extent of nearly 60,000 pagodas, or about £25,000 per annum; and at the same time carried out such reforms as promised a very large increase in the supply of pepper. Accordingly the Directors ordered that on leaving the West Coast he should be appointed Deputy Governor of Fort St. David, and thus stand next in succession to the Government of Fort St. George. The retirement of Mr. Elwick led to Mr. Macrae's advancement to the latter post sooner than could have been expected. He returned from the West Coast towards the end of 1724, and without proceeding to Fort St. David, at once took his seat as second Member of

Council at Fort St. George. At last on the 18th of January, 1725, the son of the poor washerwoman of Ayr took his place as Governor of the Madras Presidency. The proceedings on that occasion are thus recorded in the consultations.

"Monday, 18th January, 1725. The President (James Macrae, Esq.,) opened this consultation by telling the Board that, as this was the first time of their meeting since his taking the chair, he thought it would not be improper to acquaint them of his resolutions; of which the principal was, that he would prosecute the Company's interest to the utmost, and endeavour to retrieve the abuses that had crept into the management of their affairs. He added that he was determined not to interrupt in any manner the commerce of the place, but that all the inhabitants both Whites and Blacks, the Free Merchants as well as the Company's Servants, should have free liberty of trade, and that he should expect the same freedom from interruptions in what he should undertake; that he would endeavour to be as agreeable to the Gentlemen as any of his predecessors, but that he was determined to maintain the privileges and immunities belonging to the President; and he concluded by saying, that he expected a ready assistance from them in the pursuit of the above resolutions, which was accordingly promised."

Before proceeding with the annals of Mr. Macrae's administration, it may be as well to remark that he was emphatically a commercial Governor and a most laborious administrative reformer. The relations with the Nabob of Arcot remained unaltered, and what may be called the domestic incidents of the Presidency are few in number. But in all matters connected with the trade of the place, the reduction of the expenditure, the improvement of the revenues, the supervision of the mint, and the administration of justice, his proceedings are distinguished by an indefatigable industry, a display of strong sense, and above all by a fullness of record far beyond those of any of his predecessors. Nothing appeared too large or too small for Governor Macrae. Everything received his attention in turn, from such matters of detail as the sorting of cloths and the better preparation of the consultation books, up to the most difficult and complicated questions connected with the coinage, the customs, the quit rent, or the very doubtful cases of appeal from the Mayor's Court. Like most men who have risen from nothing, he was arbitrary and occasionally harsh towards his subordinates; but he proved himself a valuable servant to the Company, whose orders he rigidly respected; and no records which have as yet fallen into our hands throw more light upon the internal administration of Fort Saint George.

Our first extract seems to illustrate the determination of the new Governor to support his own dignity.

"Monday, 22nd February, 1725. The President acquainted the Board that Pondy Chetty Kistna, a person who was formerly whipped out of Fort St. David for practices against the Government, and afterwards banished from hence for the same crime; but who had lately ventured again without leave, and had wrote a letter into the country, wherein he tells his correspondent several things of the President very much to his dishonour; which coming to his knowledge had occasioned him to confine the said Pondy Chetty Kistna. The letter was produced, and the Board unanimously agreed that he ought to suffer very severely and his imprisonment was confirmed." This letter is unfortunately not entered in the records; otherwise it might have thrown some light upon the assumed faults of the Governor.

The first important matter which received the attention of Governor Macrae was that of the coinage of rupees at the Madras mint. It seems that the Native chiefs had awakened to the profit derived by the Madras Government from the coinage of rupees; and accordingly they had not only set up mints of their own, but about this time they contrived to make more rupees out of the same quantity of silver, than were made by the Company. For instance out of every hundred ounces of silver, the mints at St. Thomé and Arcot turned out to the merchant Rupees 266, annas 14; whilst the mint in Fort St. George only turned out Rupees 257, annas 7. Thus the merchant obtained nine rupees seven annas more for his hundred ounces of silver at St. Thomé and Arcot than he could obtain at Fort St. George. In other words the Madras rupee was two per cent dearer than the rupee of Arcot or of St. Thomé. The consequence was that the merchants preferred coining their silver at the latter mints; and the Company found its customs decreasing. Accordingly Governor Macrae directed Messrs. Pitt, Benyon, and Emmerson, to enquire into the whole matter. Their report is accordingly entered in the consultations, but it is not only intricate but devoid of interest to the general reader. The substance of it, rendered as clear as we can make it, appears to be as follows.

At St. Thomé, Arcot, and Covelong the charge of custom and coinage had formerly been 35 rupees per thousand; viz. 15 rupees custom to the Nabob and 20 rupees for mint charges. Both however had been recently reduced, the Nabob's custom to 10 rupees and the mint charges to 11 rupees: thus the custom and coinage were only 21 rupees per thousand, instead of 35 rupees as heretofore. It seems however that the mint charges were only nominally 11 rupees per thousand; and that actually they were 14 rupees, as may be seen from the following table.

	Rs.
Charcoal for making the powder......	$1\frac{1}{2}$
Waste in melting..............	$8\frac{3}{8}$
Pots.................	$\frac{1}{2}$
Flatting the bullets............	$\frac{3}{8}$
Chopping...........................	$\frac{1}{2}$
	$11\frac{1}{4}$

To which was added

	Rs.
Brahmins for their care.........	$\frac{3}{4}$
Goldsmiths......	$\frac{3}{4}$
Gold washers.........	$1\frac{1}{4}$
	$2\frac{3}{4}$

Rs. 14 per thousand.

This amount was made up thus. Every 300 ounces of silver ought to have made 974 rupees, whereas these mints only paid out 971 rupees; the difference of three rupees being about the same as the difference between 11 rupees and 14 rupees per thousand. Again there was a depreciation of weight of one rupee eleven annas per thousand, and another depreciation of standard of nine rupees per thousand; making an additional profit of ten rupees eleven annas per thousand. This fraud had been introduced ever since the reduction of custom and charges from 35 rupees to 21 per thousand; and it had proved successful, inasmuch as these native mints paid out their rupees by tale and not by weight, and the difference was so slight as to render their rupee as good in the market as the rupee of Fort St. George.

The custom and charges on the Madras rupee were as follows, two per cent. or 20 per thousand to the Company, and two per cent or 20 per thousand to the mint. Thus making 40 rupees per thousand.

The 20 per thousand mint charges were distributed as follows. First $11\frac{1}{4}$ per thousand for charcoal, waste, pots, flatting, and chopping, as in the St. Thomé and Arcot mints; and the remaining $8\frac{3}{4}$ as follows:—

	Rupees.
Brahmins for their care	$3\frac{1}{8}$
Goldsmiths	$3\frac{1}{8}$
Gold washers	$2\frac{1}{2}$
	$8\frac{3}{4}$
Other mint charges as above	$11\frac{1}{4}$
	Rupees...20 per thousand.

It will be seen by the following resolution that Governor Macrae endeavoured to put matters to rights,—1st, By prohibiting the export of silver from the Company's bounds, and thus compelling the merchants to coin their silver at Fort St. George; 2ndly, By lowering the Company's custom ½ per cent and the mint charges ½ per cent, or altogether 10 rupees per thousand. Henceforth then the custom and charges at Madras would be 30 rupees per thousand; whilst the custom and charges at St. Thomé, Arcot, and Covelong would be nominally 21 rupees per thousand, but actually 31 rupees 11 annas per thousand. The original entry will serve to render the subject more intelligible.

"Monday, 8th March, 1725. Messrs. Pitt, Benyon, and Emmerson deliver in a report of the coinage, together with an account of the charges and customs collected at our Mint, and those in the country; as likewise an account of the produce of a hundred ounces of silver of the fineness of the Rupee in our and St. Thomé Mints.

"This matter being fully debated it was upon the whole agreed, that no silver except rupees shall be permitted to be exported to any part of the coast of Coromandel under penalty of confiscation, half to the informer and half to the Company; and the Secretary do give notice hereof at all the public places in the town.

"As by the calculates and reports abovementioned, it appears that our rupee is two per cent. dearer to the merchants than the St. Thomé and Arcot rupee; it was further argued that we ought to find out some method to lessen the charge of coinage, that so we may bring it nearer to a par with the country coin; and it appearing that the Brahmins actually indisburse 11¼ rupees per thousand, and that they must have something besides for their trouble, it was plain their custom could not be reduced above a ½ per cent; which not being sufficient it was agreed to strike off a half per cent likewise from the custom paid the Company; which it is hoped will be approved by the Honorable Court of Directors for the following reasons.

"First, that the present charge of coinage being 4 per cent in our Mint, and but 21 per thousand in the St. Thomé Mint, nobody will bring any silver to us, but on the contrary carry it away thither; but that when our custom is reduced to three per cent, the difference will be so much less that probably we may have the greatest part of the coinage return to us, especially since our rupee is in greater esteem in the country than theirs.

"Secondly, that we shall receive orders from Europe in two years; and if our Honorable Masters shall disapprove hereof, which we cannot believe they will, it may be laid on again.

"Thirdly, that at present the revenue is sunk to almost nothing, so that should no more silver be coined here than has been for sometime past, the difference will be very inconsiderable; whereas should we hereby regain the coinage it will be very apparently advantageous to the Company.

"Lastly, that the Company will save ½ per cent in the coinage of their own silver; which as we coin one-third generally of what goes down to the

Bay, will very near if not over compensate for the reduction of the custom on other silver.

"These being the causes why it is thought necessary to lessen the charge of the coinage, it was recommended to the President to talk with the Mint Brahmins, and bring them to an agreement for lowering the charge agreeable to the above resolve, which he accordingly promised."

How far the Government order respecting the exportation of silver was regarded by the Madras merchants may be gathered from the following entry.

"Tuesday, 30th March, 1725. Two parcels of silver having been seized last night upon some shroffs, who were carrying it out of the bounds, contrary to the late order affixed at all the gates and in all the languages, so that the proprietors could not pretend ignorance:—agreed that it be confiscated; and Mr. Hubban offering to take it at 15½ dollars for ten pagodas, the Secretary was ordered to weigh it off to him and receive the money, which is to be divided agreeably to the said order at the gates, half to the Company and half to the informer."

The following petition is interesting from illustrating the mode in which private property was originally acquired in the Madras Presidency. It was received by the Government on the 30th of March, 1725.

"To the Honorable James Macrae, Esq.
President and Governor of Fort St. George.

"The humble petition of Maria Pois, Widow, showeth, That a few years after the Honorable

Company's settlement here, a great many inhabitants, and your petitioner's grand father, planted gardens without any title thereto from the then President and Council. Some of their posterity have sold this ground and gardens as their own, some part to the inhabitants to build on, and some still enjoy it themselves; several have also since his Honor Harrison's time planted gardens without any title, and enjoy them as their own. But your petitioner's grand father, believing it proper to have a title to his garden, and having then an interest with the Honorable the President, Council, and Gentlemen in the place was promised the title; but in the interim he died, and his son his successor, being soft and illiterate, lost his father's interest, but got a cowle from the Honorable the President and Council for thirty-one years, contrary to his father's request and desire; and if he had not troubled the Honorable President and Council for a cowle, might have enjoyed it as the rest have done, him and his heirs for ever. All this your petitioner was unacquainted with till the time was expired. Your poor petitioner having built a house, planted trees, and brought the garden to a vast perfection, this your petitioner laid before the then President, how simply the son of the deceased managed it; to insist on a cowle but for 31 years, when the rest have ever since enjoyed the same as their own and heirs for ever.

"Now the Honorable President and Council compassionately took this, your petitioner's case, into consideration; and rented said house and

Garden to your petitioner; it being extremely hard, after having built the house and brought the garden into perfection, to lose all, your petitioner having no other subsistance. This Garden your petitioner has rented of the Honorable Company ever since the expiration of the cowle.

"Your petitioner is now informed that said house and garden is to be put up at outcry to rent; if so it is an immediate ruin to your poor petitioner, it being your petitioner's only subsistance; she, having no habitation or placc of abode, most humbly begs your Honor will, out of your abundant clemency and goodness, look upon this your petitioners case with compassion, and suffer her to rent said house and garden as usual, as she answers yearly the income of the garden to the Honorable Company. If not your petitioner will be reduced to extreme want and misery. Therefore humbly begs your Honor will continue your poor petitioner to rent said house and garden, and as in duty bound shall ever pray."

Governor Macrae however showed himself to be a stern man, not easily moved by petitions whether from widows or from any one else. Accordingly the prayer of Maria Pois was rejected, and it was agreed that her farm should be put up to public outcry.

Our next extract shows that the arbitrary order for prohibiting the exportation of silver was now extended to gold.

"Tuesday, 6th April. The President acquainted the Board that several shoes of gold* had been

* A "shoe of gold" was ten thousand pagodas.

lately carried out of the bounds, which he believed was to be coined at St. Thomé; and therefore he proposed that an order should be made prohibiting any gold, except what is wrought or ready coined, shall be carried out of the bounds under penalty of confiscation, the one half to the Company and the other to the informer; which is agreed to and the Secretary ordered to affix a note at the gates accordingly."

It will be seen from the following entry how the occupations of the Governors in the olden time differed from those of the more aristocratic Presidents of modern times.

"Monday, 21st June. The President and Council met in the Sorting Godown, and examined the Fort St. David Cloth, which proved pretty good. They also examined several parcels of what was brought to be sorted here, which they found for the generality amended in the number of threads, but so thin that it was not fit for the Company's use."

The following extract shows that Governor Macrae was learning a lesson in free trade.

"Saturday, 3rd July, 1725. The prohibition some time since laid on the exportation of silver and gold into the country, which was then thought for the benefit of our Honorable Masters, having been now found to occasion a general stagnation of trade, and likewise to have fallen the price of silver very considerably, which will in the main vastly overbalance the gain by the coinage.

"Agreed that the said prohibition be taken off,

and that the Secretary do give public notice thereof at the gates."

Our next extracts, referring to the renting of the three out villages, will explain themselves.

"Saturday, 3rd July, 1725. The Lease of the Farms of Egmore, Persewauk, and Tandore being expired, the President informed the Board that he had received proposals from the present Renters, who had agreed to take them at the rent of 14,000 pagodas, provided they might have them for ten years. But that if they could not have them for longer time than the former lease, they would give but one thousand pagodas per annum, because that they actually lost in the last three years, though very plentiful ones, six hundred pagodas; but that having a long lease, they might have some encouragement to improve the lands, which they shall not have in taking them only for three years, which being considered, it was agreed that they be let on the above terms."

"Monday, 12th July. The President informed the Board that he had got the old Renters of Egmore, Persewauk, and Tandore, to give 1,450 pagodas per annum for the rent of those villages for ten years next ensuing; and that Poncala Kishna, the tobacco farmer, was security for the performance of agreements; which being the utmost he could raise the rent to, the Cowle was produced and signed to Kishna Reddee Chandra Seaca, and Chittombee."

The following extract refers to almost the only difference which ever arose between Governor Macrae and the native powers.

"Monday, 23rd August, 1725. Sometime since eight bales of goods being brought hither on one of our ships belonging to a Moorman, were attached for a debt due to Mr. Sitwell from the said Moorman, who is since run away to Covelong; and the goods have been claimed by the Nabob as his, and bought for his account; which demand being now again repeated, it is agreed that since the Nabob declares the goods are his, it is better to let them go, than make any dispute thereupon. Wherefore the President is desired to write him that upon giving up the Moorman, and paying the Company's customs, the goods shall be delivered to his order."

The Nabob however seems to have refused to deliver up the Moorman, or to pay the Company's customs. A correspondence accordingly ensued which spread over the greater part of a year; and was at length brought to a conclusion on the 21st July, 1726. We give the extract from the consultations of that day.

"The President represents to the Board that he had been long importuned by Nabob Sadutalla Khan, by pressing letters and frequent messages, to deliver up the eight bales of goods mentioned in Consultation held the 23rd August 1725, to have been attached here by the creditors of Shaak Bonlaki for the payment of his debts, as belonging to the said Shaak Bonlaki; but that the Nabob continues to claim them as belonging to himself, and insists peremptorily upon their being delivered to him; and that without his demand is complied with, he, the President apprehends a breach with him unavoidable; which in our present circumstances would be of very great prejudice to the Company's affairs.

"This matter having been considered by the Board, and the consequences a breach at this time with the Nabob might produce having been duly weighed; and it having likewise been admitted that the creditors of Shaak Bonlaki might have had reasons to believe that the eight bales in question did belong to him, yet the Nabob's right to them could not be disproved; and he continuing to insist so very peremptorily. upon having them delivered to him, notwithstanding the President endeavours by repeated messages and many letters to prevail with him to suffer them to be sold for account of Shaak Bonlaki's creditors. There being no prospect of prevailing with the Nabob, it is ordered that Mr. Turner do deliver to Nabob's order the said eight bales of goods in dispute."

The following perjury cases are worthy of being preserved, as showing how false witnesses were punished in the olden time.

"Friday, 10th September, 1725. In the examination of Anconah's affair one Magdulla Kistna confessed himself perjured, by a declaration under his own hand, whereupon he was ordered into confinement; and it is now ordered that he be Pilloried to-morrow at the usual hours, and afterwards whipped at the Choultry, and then released from his imprisonment."

A year afterwards we find Governor Macrae still determined to put down perjury with a strong hand. He had been engaged upon deciding upon a long list of appeals from the Mayor's Court, chiefly equity cases connected of course with wills, bonds, and disputes about property of all kinds. These interminable and complicated cases may have been interesting to the parties concerned, but present not a particle of interest now, beyond the fact that they are marked by contradictions, palpable perjuries, forgeries, and oppressions of all kinds. Many of the cases were reversed by Governor Macrae, whilst others were sent home to be adjudicated on by the Directors, and even to be tried in Westminster Hall; from which we may infer that the old stories of corruption in the Mayor's Court, so frequent in the narratives of old travellers, were not without some foundation in truth. How far Governor Macrae was exasperated at this state of things may be gathered from the following punishment ordered upon another perjurer.

"Monday, 29th August, 1726. Ordered that Arnagery for punishment of his crime of perjury, and for terror to all such abandoned villains, be remanded to the Choultry prison, and be thence conveyed to the Pillory every first day of the month for the next six months, and set upon it from ten to twelve o'clock; and immediately after he is taken down from the Pillory to receive thirty-nine lashes each time at the whipping post, and be afterwards turned out of the bounds with order never to return again under severe punishment."

The following extract respecting the circulation of false pagodas will explain itself.

"Monday, 27th September, 1725. The President informed the Board of a complaint the

Shroffs had made to him, that vast quantities of pagodas had been brought into the place lately, which were worse than Pagodamatt, and bore the Negapatam stamp so nicely counterfeited, that it was almost impossible to distinguish them ; and therefore he proposed that some method should be taken to stop this evil, which being for some time debated, it was agreed that the Secretary do affix a note at the gates to give notice, that whosoever should be found bringing in such bad pagodas, or offering them in payment, should be punished at the discretion of the Governor and Council, and the money be forfeited, one half to the informer and one half to the Company; and that whatever shroff should find such pagodas should be obliged to carry them to some one of the Justices of the Choultry to be defaced, or if he did not, he should be pilloried and whipped out of the bounds."

Governor Macrae was far too fond of Committees of inquiry to let such a matter pass without the most searching investigation. Accordingly about three weeks afterwards we find the following report entered in the consultations, which will be found interesting as illustrating the condition of the country generally.

"Monday, 18th October, 1725. The following report was presented to the Honorable James Macrae, Esq., the President and Governor of Fort St George and Council.

"Honorable Sir and Sirs,

"The committee you were pleased to appoint,

to enquire into the business of the present current pagodas, and put a stop to an abuse which will at last be attended with such dangerous consequences, do now humbly lay before you their proceedings and opinion of the most proper remedy effectually to prevent this mischief without giving a shock to commerce.

"We find upon examining the shroffs that this has been a growing evil, introduced by the corruption of the country Government in conniving at the circulation of any sort of pagodas, provided their profits from those who have the liberty of coining them are answerable; and as this is so considerable an advantage to them it is not from the Nabob we are to expect any relief. Therefore we thought it most proper to have the opinion of the merchants in general which method we should pursue; who on a meeting came to this resolution, which we offer to your honors as what we likewise think sufficient to answer the design, without risking a stagnation in the circulation.

"That five shops shall be appointed in the most convenient parts of the town, for the exchanging of all money which is necessary for the currency of the Bazar; in each of which must be placed, two shroffs, a gold smith, and a Company's peon, whose stations are to be changed every day with power to cut or deface all such pagodas as are found to be bad. As to payments of large sums the merchants themselves will undoubtedly be cautious for their own security, and take such care as not to be imposed upon in what they receive, by employing such shroffs in whose fidelity they may confide.

"George Mortan Pitt.
"Nathaniel Turner.
"Richard Benyon.
"John Emmerson."

"The most convenient places for the shops are Jappa Chetty's Street, Choultry Street, Mutala Pettah, Pedda Naick's Pettah, Jaga Mulla Street."

Another point which attracted the attention of Governor Macrae at this time is also worthy of some notice. For some years past different sums of money had been lodged in the Company's cash chest at Fort St. George on account of the Jesuit Missionaries in China; for which the Government of Fort St. George, under orders from the Court of Directors, had allowed interest at the rate of six per cent. per annum. In September 1725, Father Moriset at Fort St. David wrote to Governor Macrae respecting a further deposit of cash, on the same terms; but the economical President, having plenty of money in hand, considered that this would be a favorable moment for reducing the yearly interest from six per cent. to five. The matter led to a Committee of inquiry into all the monies lodged in the Company's chest at various times by the Jesuit Missionaries in China. The following extracts from their report will be sufficient to explain the state of affairs. It will be seen that the sums deposited were not to be returned; the yearly interest paid being supposed to be a sufficient return, without any repayment of the principal. We must therefore suppose that the sums lodged at Fort St. George were of the nature of an endowment to provide for the perpetual support of the Jesuit Missionaries in China. Our report from whence the following extracts are taken is dated 21st July 1726.

"To the Honorable James Macrae, Esq.,
President and Governor and Council of
Fort St. George.

"Honorable Sir and Sirs,

"In pursuance of an order of Council, we lay before your Honors what orders have been received from the Honorable Court of Directors, relating to the receiving into the Company's cash money from the Jesuit Missionaries in China at interest; together with an account of the several sums that have been hitherto received into cash for their account, and what has been writ by this Board to the Honorable Court of Directors on that subject.

"We find that the sum of 10,000 pagodas was received into cash for their account the 31st August 1721, but no interest to be paid them thereupon till the Company's order should be had for that effect.

"The Honorable Court of Directors in their general letter dated 26th April 1722 say as follows.

"We have had application made us by Monsr. Labbe, agent for the French Jesuit Missionaries in China, to receive 10,000 pagodas of theirs into our cash at Fort St. George; that President Hastings had received the money conditionally to await our orders, though he had no occasion for any having a flowing cash; that said agent desires the money may remain in our cash and the proprietors to be for ever dispossest of the property thereof, on the Company's yearly allowing them a reasonable interest. We have considered of the whole, and in regard we sometimes have and at other times have not occasion to borrow money at Fort St. George; therefore we are willing to allow them a certain interest of six per cent. though it is one more than we pay here per annum, and hope it will be to their satisfaction."

"In consequence of which general letter a bond was executed by the Governor and Council, and delivered to the Agent to the said Missionaries, to pay them interest 600 pagodas per annum upon the sum of 10,000 pagodas received.

"The 25th February 1724 their agent paid into cash the further sum of 2,000 pagodas; and the same day the Governor and Council delivered him a bond for six per cent. interest per annum upon it.

The receipt of this sum was advised to England to which the Honorable Court answered as follows:

"Your letter advises that the Jesuits in China have by their attorney offered to deposit in our cash with you a sum of money, which you intend to receive and give bond to pay six per cent. per annum for it. Padre de Goville, lately returned to Europe, has by writing requested of us to receive 10,000 pagodas into our cash, and to pay the Missionaries for it 600 pagodas a year, which we have agreed to."

It would thus appear that at this time the Company had agreed to receive in all the sum of 20,000 pagodas on behalf of the Jesuit Missionaries in China, for which they were to pay a perpetual interest at the rate of 6 per cent. per annum, the principal not to be returned. Accordingly it would seem that the China Missionaries paid in that amount, and derived from the Company alone a yearly income of twelve hundred pagodas, or about five hundred pounds sterling.

CHAPTER XXXIV.

GOVERNORSHIP OF MR. JAMES MACRAE.

1726—27.

The commercial character of the administration of Mr. James Macrae has been already noticed, and the very lucid manner in which commercial transactions are recorded in the consultation books of the period, induces us to pay more attention to such extracts as serve to illustrate the mode in which the Company carried on their business with Native merchants, either for providing a sufficient number of bales of Native cloth for exportation to Europe, or for disposing of broadcloth, iron, and other articles of home produce which had been imported from England. These extracts however we shall not group by themselves, but simply arrange them, together with other selections, in strict chronological order; by which means the reader will be enabled to form a better idea of the miscellaneous character and general scope of the records themselves, than by any other method.

Our first extract refers to the supervision of native goods maintained in old time by the Government of Fort St. George.

"Thursday, 6th January, 1826. The Warehouse-keeper reported to the Board, that the chintzes being brought from painting (dyeing) had been examined at the Sorting Godown, and that it was the general opinion of the Sorters that both the cloth and paintings were worse than the musters; wherefore they had resolved, if the Board approved thereof, to allow the merchants only 35 pagodas per corge, instead of 40 for the cloth; and the painter 47½ pagodas per corge, instead of 60, which they used to have. This being approved, the merchants were called in and told the resolution of the Board."

"At the same time the Warehouse-keeper reported that the Pulicat Betillas, brought in by the merchants upon the muster, for which in the contract we were to give 120 pagodas per corge, were vastly inferior to the muster; and that it had been agreed in the Sorting Godown that 100 pagodas per corge was the value of them; so that he (the President) desired the order of the Board for bringing them to account at that price, which was agreed to, and the merchants accordingly told these resolutions."

The Native merchants appeared to have submitted to the reductions very quietly, for no demur on their part is entered in the proceedings. When however the Board desired to make a contract with the same merchants, as to the quantity of Europe cloth they should purchase, or the quantity of native cloth they should supply, it was not always found so easy to deal with them, as will be seen by the following extract.

"Thursday, 3d March 1726. Our Merchants were called in, and a proposal made, to them as follows.

"That they shall engage in a contract at Fort

St. George for 2000 bales of cloth, to be delivered to us one half in August, and the remainder by the last of January next."

"That they shall take all the broad cloth (from Europe) at the usual advance, to be kept under two keys, one of which to be left with themselves and the other with the Warehouse-keeper; that before they take any out of the warehouses, it shall be paid for in ready money; and that the whole amount shall be paid off by the 1st of April 1727. In consideration of which the Board (they were told) would abate the penalty of 30,000 pagodas, to be inflicted for breach of the last contract, to 10,000 pagodas; but if they would not do this they must expect to pay the whole amount of the penalty.

"Upon the hearing these proposals, the Merchants immediately declared they could not engage by any means, either to take the broad cloth, or contract for above 800 bales; and to this they adhered for a considerable time, but at last after near two hours debate, finding the Board determined to exact the whole penalty if they did not agree to the terms proposed, and being excused from any contract at Fort St. David, they consented; having first obtained a promise of the Board that if they complied within 300 bales, no penalty should be exacted."

Our next extract refers to a forged bond, found amongst the papers of a deceased Company's servant named Woolley.

"Thursday, 30th June, 1726. Captain Richard Upton, representing that a forged note, mentioning that he had received of Robert Woolley deceased 1000 ounces of Silver, for which he was to be accountable, having been found amongst said Woolley's papers, whereof payment had been demanded, signed as by him and witnessed as by Messrs. Samuel Harrison, and Richard Stephens; and that he and the said pretended witnesses were ready to make solemn oath, that neither he nor they ever had any knowledge of any such note, nor ever signed the same. Therefore craving that he and they might be sworn to the truth of what he affirmed, in order to prevent any demand being made upon him for the said 1000 ounces of Silver.

"Captain Upton and Messrs. Harrison and Stephens being called in, were interrogated as to the signing and witnessing the said note; and affirmed each of them that it was forged and without their knowledge; that there was no similitude of hand writing, and severally made oath to what they affirmed. Whereupon it was ordered that the said note appearing to be forged be cancelled; which was done."

The next entries which we consider worthy of preservation are still more curious. It has been seen that the revenues of Trivatore, and of the other out villages belonging to the Company, were farmed out to some of the Company's Merchants, on their engaging to pay a certain sum (1450 pagodas) per annum. The Merchants in their turn rented the villages to a man named Mahadin, and this Renter appears to have treated the inhabitants in a barbarous and oppressive manner. Accordingly two of the villagers sent in the following petition to Governor Macrae in which all their grievances are specified. The petition will be found to form an admirable illustration of Native administration in the olden time.

"To the Honourable James Macrae, Esq. President and Governor of Fort St. George, The humble petition of the inhabitants of Vessa Caward,

"Showeth,—That the Company has let out Trivatore and the other out villages to the Company's merchants, who during five years that they kept them in their own hands, allowed your petitioners all their privileges and allowances as usual, and they lived very happily. Then one Mahadin took these villages of these merchants, and promised to allow your petitioners the same privileges and allowances as the said merchants had done; but he has acted contrary, and not given them any privilege or allowance. Upon whch they asked him the reason; and he replied that the Company had sold those villages to him, and he could do what he pleased. The said privileges and allowances due to your petitioners for these six years amounts to about 100 pagodas. Besides this he has distressed your petitioners and laid many hardships on them. He set one of their Pariahs half way in the ground, where he kept him three hours and fined him. Another Pariah he chaubucked 25 blows, put him into the stocks, and kept him there an hour. He tied one of their shepherd's neck and heals, for four or five days, an hour each day, and beat him very much and fined him. He broke a Talliar's back, and turned him out of the village. He tied a shopkeeper of the village, neck and heels, putting a heavy stone on his back, and kept him so an hour and then fined him. He served another shopkeeper in the same manner. He has done too many other barbarous actions to your petitioners to give your Honor in writing an account of. Therefore they humbly implore to take their case into consideration, and order them satisfaction. They cannot go on with their business if he be continued the Renter. Your petitioners hope your Honor will do them justice, and they as in duty bound shall ever pray."

To this petition, a Native named Chandarasaha, who seems to have been the steward of Mahardin, sent in a counter-petition, denying or explaining away the charges. This also is a gem in its way.

"The petition of Chandarasaha.

"Humbly showeth,—Whereas your petitioner has been falsely accused that he has punished the inhabitants beyond reason, and as to his burying the man half under ground is utterly false; for the man having, contrary to order, let the water run the wrong course, was punished according to custom; that is by laying his hand in the water course, which filled with sand and the Company's chop put thereon. And as for your petitioner's forcing of unreasonable forfeits from the inhabitants, it is also false; for the inhabitants having complained to your petitioner that a milkman's measure was less than it should be, which your petitioner by examining found true; therefore fined him 6 fanams; and to a seller of tobacco and betel, for selling contrary to the renter's order, was fined 6 fanams. As to the Talliar, he stole away above three pagodas worth of Mangoes, for which he paid 48 fanams; and when the Talliar had found the thief, your petitioner told him that he might do what he would. Also the said Talliar (i. e. the Talliar who was the thief not the Talliar who had arrested him) took more than his right of the paddy, and took it away without leave; for which fault he was tied neck and heels two hours. And as for your petitioner's putting any body in irons, it is false; but a Pariah being taken stealing paddy, was by your petitioner's order put in the stocks. That the three persons before mentioned have sold the Company's ground, which when the Buyer came to take possession, your petitioner refused to let him take it without your Honors leave. That your petitioner for the good of the inhabitants did lend them money, and let them have paddy to the value of pagodas 260; and when your petitioner demands his money then they begin to make a disturbance. Now three of the inhabitants being come to this place, they have taken opportunity to say that all the inhabitants will leave the place. The Pedda Naik's allowance of ground in the said village is 4440 yards, but now he has taken 14,400 yards, which is more than his due by near 10,000 yards; which for these four years he has not sown, nor would he let any body else, to the loss of about pagodas 229; and now about a thousand yards which he sowed, the paddy now lies there and he refuses to divide it. Therefore your poor petitioner most humbly requests your Honor to give him justice, and as in duty bound shall ever pray."

Governor Macrae's action upon these two petitions will be gathered from the following extract.

"Friday, 26th August, 1726. The President delivers into the Board two petitions which had been presented to him; one from some inhabitant of Vessa Cawarda, against Mahadin the present Renter; the other from Chandarasaha, who acted as steward to the said Mahadin, and put his orders in execution. Which being read, the President acquaints the Board that both parties had been before him; that he had heard them separately and also given then a joint hearing; that he had examined witnesses to the truth of the facts charged against Mahadin, and heard the Company's Merchants upon the affair. That from the whole, it appeared to him, that the said Mahadin had been guilty, and was fully convicted by evidence, of the charge delivered against him in the first petition; which is even acknowledged by the said Chandarasah in his petition, who acted by order and authority from Mahadin in all these matters, as is by Mahadin owned.

"This affair being taken into consideration, particularly the presumption of Mahadin in taking upon him to levy fines and inflict corporal punishments upon the Honorable Company's subjects without authority; which had actually frightened several inhabitants out of the bounds, as the President further informs us had been proved before him, and would deter others from coming out of the country to secure themselves and properties under the protection of English Law as usual. To prevent any such violences and extortions in time to come, it is resolved that no Renters or Farmers of Villages have authority to levy fines, or inflict corporal punishment upon the inhabitants; and that for an example Mahadin be ordered to resign his Cowle of Trivatore and the other villages into the hands of the Company's Merchants; having forfeited the same by his unwarrantable actions; and for a further punishment to him and example for others, he be fined in the sum of 50 pagodas, to be paid into the Company's Cash, and that the Secretary do demand the same."

This decision was rigidly carried out, for three days afterwards we find an entry to the effect that Mahadin had given up the Cowle and paid the fine of fifty pagodas.

Perhaps few entries are more illustrative of the character of Governor Macrae, than the following attempt at reduction in the matter of Hospital charges. The decision of the canny Scot is wonderfully suggestive. How far it contributed to the comfort of the sick we leave to the judgment of our readers.

"Saturday, 17th September, 1726. The President represents to the Board that, upon reading the particulars of the article of Hospital charges, he apprehends there are several of them too large, and others unnecessary, and ought to be reduced and discontinued; which being taken into consideration, and the several particulars again read and enquired into, it was represented that the Surgeon, who has the immediate direction of the Hospital, always insists that the present charge is necessary for entertaining and recovering the sick, and that no reduction can be made of it.

"Ordered, that whereas it hath been for some time the custom for one of the Surgeons to have the immediate care of the Hospital solely, they do in future act each six months by turns; that by their acting thus interchangeably, we may make the experiment whether the one cannot reduce the charge of the Hospital lower than the other, which it is believed out of emulation to recommend themselves, they may do."

Next follows a curious entry respecting the horses sanctioned by the Company for the use of the President.

"Monday, 7th November, 1726. The President represents to the Board, that their being now remaining alive only two Chaise horses belonging to the Company, and these so weak that to save them he had been obliged for above a twelve month to make use of a pair of Manilla horses of his own for his Chaise; that the Honorable Company had allowed his predecessor three horses for his Chaise, one of which had been dead some time, and the other two so much wore that they are not now fit to do the service of one; that the Company's piebald horse was lately dead, and that the horses for his guards were very old, and some of them quite worn out, that he was now obliged to allow two Pegu horses of his own for that service. Wherefore he proposed to the Board to purchase the said two Pegu horses for the use of his guards, and the two Manilla Chaise horses for his Chaise, on the Company's account; being all of them young, well broke, and seasoned to the country.

"Resolved that the foresaid four horses be purchased for the Company for the service above mentioned, at 150 pagodas each; and that the Paymaster do pay for the same; and that one of the worst of the guard horses be sold at public outcry as soon as the season permits the usual concourse of people at the sea gate."

Whilst Governor Macrae was thus attentive to his own interests, he was by no means unmindful of the interests of the younger servants of the Company, as will be seen by the following extract, which is well worthy not only of preservation but of more general imitation.

"Tuesday, 15th November, 1726. The President represents further to the Board, that he thinks it a great discouragement to the subordinate servants, and inconsistent with that emulation we ought to excite amongst them to distinguish themselves by merit in order to their advancement, that some should be continued so long in laborious stations without any profit, while others enjoyed places of profit and that required little application. Particularly that Paul Foxley had served under the Export Ware housekeeper above five years, and discharged that trust faithfully to the approbation of his superiors; and that Edward Croke, had continued several years Writer at the Sea gate, in which station he had had but very little opportunity of exerting himself in the Service. Therefore moved that Mr. Foxley be appointed in Mr. Croke's room Writer at the Sea gate."

"Resolved that Paul Foxley do enter upon the employ of Writer at the Sea gate the first of January next, and that Ralph Mansell do succeed him in the Export Warehouse at the same time. Edward Croke being Senior in standing to all the Servants under the Council, it was judged reasonable that he should be advanced to a station of a higher trust in the Service. Wherefore resolved that he be employed in the station of Receiver of the Honorable Company's customs, and that he do enter upon the same the first of January next."

The following petition is simply an illustration of the times.

"The humble petition of Hirdaram.

"Sheweth,—That your petitioner's brother, Nundaram, brought 2773 rupees from Arcot, and procured therewith a Bill of Exchange on Bengal from Governor Collet. Your petitioner's brother being murdered by robbers on his way to Bengal, the Bill has not yet been paid; which your Petitioner hearing came to Madras with the Nabob's perwanna to demand the repayment of the said money from Governor Elwick and Mr. Benyon, attorneys to Governor Collet; who told your petitioner that if he could bring a sufficient security to indemnify them they would pay him. Your petitioner has now brought an attestation, signed by many great Gentlemen at Arcot, witnessing that your petitioner is the next heir to the said deceased Nundaram; which your petitioner hopes is a sufficient authority for receiving the said money; and that your Honor would please to give such orders therein as your Honor shall think meet."

It will be sufficient to say that the security offered by the gentlemen of Arcot, some of whom stood high in the favour of the Nabob, was deemed sufficient, and the money was accordingly paid.

Our next extract is another curious illustration of the times; like the previous one it will explain itself.

"Tuesday, 6th December, 1726. Mr. Emmerson, Chief Justice of the Choultry, reports to the Board a late instance of a woman slave having attempted to poison a whole family; that the poison had actually been given, but operating very violently quickly discovered itself, and the effect was prevented by immediately administering proper emetics, and that the criminal had confessed the fact. That in order to strike terror into such abandoned mind's and for securing the lives of the inhabitants in future from atrocious attempts, the Justices of the Choultry were come to a resolution to punish the said criminal in the most public and exemplary manner, the approbation of this Board being first had; and that he was further empowered from the Justices of the Choultry to represent to the Board that, considering how easily poisons are procurable here, as in the late instance by low miscreants, even Sublimate Mercury, it will be highly necessary to publish a prohibition of selling or delivering poisons of any sort, but under a proper regulation; that therefore they were of opinion that no person should be permitted to sell or deliver poison, without first acquainting one of the Justices of it, under the penalty of confiscation of half of their estate, and being further liable to corporal punishment at the discretion of the said Justice.

"Approved the proceedings of the Justices in their affair, and agreed with them to prohibit the selling or delivering poison without the consent of one of the Justices, and under the penalty above mentioned, and that a prohibition be forthwith published accordingly."

Strange to say we can see no entry of the punishment which was inflicted on the woman. She was probably treated in such a fashion that the Government did not care to place it upon record.

Our next extracts will be found interesting, as exhibiting the amount of expenditure and revenue at Fort St. George and the other settlements on the Coast of Coromandel. We give an extract from the consultation first, and the Accountants' report afterwards.

" Tuesday, 6th December, 1726. Nathaniel Turner, Accountant, delivers into the Board a Report of the state of the Honorable Company's expenses and customs at their settlements upon this coast, at the balancing and closing the general books ending April last; which is read and ordered to be entered after this consultation.

"The said Report being maturely examined and considered, the Board are agreed that the reduction of the charges of their settlement, and of Fort St. David, has been carried as far as it has been hitherto practicable.

"That the increase of the expense of Vizagapatam last year, was owing to the additional number of soldiers we were obliged to send and continued there, for the security of that factory, while the country round it was ravaged and they threatened by contending armies; that after the reduction made as advised by Mr. Symonds and Council in their letter to us dated 7th May last, the charge of that settlement will appear to have been considerably diminished upon the next years books.

"That we must likewise refer to next years books for the reduction of expense at Masulipatam and Madapallum.

"That the decrease of the Sea Customs, and the increase of the Land Customs here at Madras last year, are owing to one and the same cause;—they having ordered the whole 5 per cent custom to be paid at the Choultry upon goods imported from the country; whereas formerly only 2½ per cent was accounted for there and the other 2½ at the Sea gate upon exportation of said goods."

"That the decrease of the Customs is general last year, here and at Fort St. David, and from there account of the proceedings, seems indeed totally owing at Fort St. David to the five per cent charged in said preceding year upon so large a quantity of turned out cloths, that had been brought in there upon former investments; and here in part to the like five per cent custom having been charged our Merchants upon a considerable quantity of turned out cloths. Besides which the customs have been considerably lessened in this fort last year, and will more considerably this, by the great decay in the trade to Manilla, and the almost total loss of the trade of the Patans from Bengal; both which trades being principally in fine goods, and formerly to a great value, were very considerable branches of the Sea Customs."

Here follows the report of the Accountant to the Governor and Council.

"Honorable Sir and Sirs,

"The General Books of this settlement ending April, 1726 being balanced and closed, and the subordinate Factory's Books, ending April 1726 beng sent up, I am to lay before your Honors the last years expense of this settlement and its subordinates on the coast, that you may please to consider whether any part of the charges can be saved to the Honorable Company.

"The Expense of this settlement of Fort St. George on the balance of our Books ending April 1725 amounted to Pagodas..........................	.. ..	39034 34 28	
"The expense as per our Books ending April 1726 is as follows:			
"Charges Garrison.. .. Pagodas..	15779 26 77		
"Presents..	174 18 20		
"Charges cattle..	800 0 0		
"Charges Extraordinary	173 21 10		
"Fortifications and repairs	1495 29 70		
"Charges Diet	7000 0 0		
"Account Salary..	3265 34 67		
"Charges Hospital..	769 35 20		
"Charges General	6086 22 44		
		35546 8 68	
"Lessened the expense of this place this year..	.. ..		3488 25 40
"The expense of Fort St. David on the balance of their Books ending April 1725 amounted to Pagodas..	.. ..	29268 28 15	
"The expense as per their Books ending April 1726 is as follows:			
"Charges Garrison	13082 7 52		
"Charges Extraordinary.. ..	342 26 35		
"Peons and Servants wages	3285 6 0		
"Charges cattle	600 0 0		
"Fortifications and repairs.. ..	96 34 10		
"Charges Diet	2966 4 0		
"Account Salary..	941 30 40		
"Presents	12 30 0		
"Charges Hospital	219 28 26		
"Charges General..	3668 3 58		
		24215 29 61	

Lessened the expense of that place this year.. Pagodas... 5052 34 34

"The Expense of Vizagapatam on the Balance of their Books ending April 1725 amounted to.. .		Pagodas. 5838 1 61	
"The expense as per their Books ending April 1726 is as follows.			
"Charges Garrison..	2103 6 0		
"Presents	480 6 69		
"Charges Diet	578 30 0		
"Charges Extraordinary	151 33 35		
"Fortifications and repairs ..	336 33 3		
"Account Salary	422 34 19		
"Account Gardens	35 19 41		
"Account Wax	46 34 64		
"Servants' wages	1492 25 77		
"Factors' provisions	25 1 16		
"Account repairs	18 6 68		
"Charges General	373 13 39		
		6065 29 31	
"Increased the Expence of that place this year			Pagodas. 227 27 50
"Which is occasioned by 20 European Soldiers being sent down to that settlement on account of the troubles in the country in the beginning of the year; ten (10) of which soldiers are still continued there, and adds to the expense of that place; but since Mr. Symonds going down he writes us that he has in pursuance to your Honors' orders made a considerable reduction in the Peons' and servants' wages, which reduction will appear in their next general Books ending April 1727.			8313 32 24
"The Expense of Ingeram for one year ending April 1725, was		Pagodas. 1315 19 18	
"The Expense of Ingeram from April 1725 to May 1726 is		1182 13 63	
"Lessened the Expense of that place this year,..			233 5 35
"The Expense of Masulipatam and Madapollum was last year ..		Pagodas. 628 34 40	
Do. this year ending April 1726		622 28 43	
"Decreased this year in their expenses			6 5 77
"The Expenses of these two factories will next year be considerably decreased by the regulation your Honors have lately made therein.			
"Lessened this year in the expenses of this settlement and its subordinates			Pagodas. 8553 7 56

"Thus having given your Honors account of the Honorable Company's annual expenses on this coast, I shall proceed to lay before you an account of the produce of their customs in this place and at Fort St. David ending April 1726.

" The Sea Customs of Fort St. George.		
" On the balance of our Books ending April 1725 amounted to.. ..	36051 8 29	
" The amount Ditto for one year ending April 1726..	28560 7 46	
Decrease in this revenue..		7491 0 63
" The amount of the Land Customs of Fort St. George.		
" On the Balance of their Books ending April 1725 was..	4455 8 28	
Do. .. April 1726 was	10185 33 76	
Increase in this revenue..		5730 25 48
" Less this year in the Customs of Fort St. George than last..		1760 11 15
" The Revenue of Fort St. David ending April 1726 amounted to ..	11941 24 75	
Do. 1725..	9877 0 38	
" Less this year in the Customs of Fort St. David than last		2064 24 37
" The Customs of Forts St. George and St David have on the balance of our general books ending April 1726 Decreased	Pagodas.	3824 35 52

I am with respect,
Honorable Sir and Sirs,
Your most obedient humble servant,

FORT ST. GEORGE, 6th December 1726. NATHANIEL TURNER, *Accountant.*

The following record of an enterprising project in the olden time is very curious.

" Monday, 26th December, 1726. Petition read of Stephen Newcome, requesting leave to build a Sawmill, and a lease for a space of ground to the northward of the White Tower along the sea side, for building the said mill and proper sheds upon. And he being called before the Board, and heard to the benefit he proposes his mill will prove to be to the Company and the Corporation, gave sufficient reasons to believe that it will be of public advantage, and affirmed that he would saw timbers and planks 50 per cent. cheaper upon the cooly hire now usually paid. Besides that he could saw blocks of timber to much greater advantage, and prevent the waste occasioned by the unskillfulness of the present sawers."

"Granted his petition for the space of ground therein mentioned, and ordered a lease to be prepared for the same for 21 years; he paying before signing it 20 pagodas fine into the Company's cash, and annually one pagoda Quit rent during the term of his lease; and in consideration of the expence of preparing the ground, and building the mill and necessary conveniences, and the benefit it will prove to be to the Company and the place,—it is resolved that the sole privilege of sawing timber and plank by a mill be vested in him for 21 years next ensuing, and no other person have that liberty but upon an agreement with him during that time."

We hope that we shall find in future records that this Sawmill proved a successful speculation.

That Mr. Macrae was a most vigilant Governor is further proved by the following entry.

"Monday, 9th January, 1727. The President represents to the Board, that he had observed in the Sorting Godown that a great deal of cloth had been turned out this year, which he was persuaded would upon a re-examination be found as good as muster; that as he would never countenance the taking in bad cloth, so he thought it was not serving the Honorable Company well to turn out any that was as good as their musters; that all he proposed or desired was, that justice might be done our Masters and the Merchants likewise, that they may not be discouraged from contracting with us again. He therefore moves that in order to do justice both to our Masters and to their Merchants the cloth turned out this year may be restored." This was of course agreed to.

The following consultation respecting the best mode of improving the declining trade of Madras, is very interesting.

"Tuesday, 31st January, 1727. The Board having taken into consideration the declining state of the trade of this place, which appears by the customs to be greatly diminished; and if expedients are not found for its support must in consequence affect every other branch of the Honorable Company's Revenue, and utterly ruin the inhabitants;—It principally appears to be owing to the following causes.

"That whereas heretofore the trade was entirely carried on by the shipping of this port, it is now in part in the possession of the French, Armenians, and Moors, who traffic on other bottoms and import their Cargoes into other Settlements; which they are enabled to do by the money taken up here by Respondentia bonds, and without which they could not carry on so extensive a trade. It seems most probable that the preventing this evil will most conduce to the recovery of the customs, and make all other ports on this coast dependent on us, though the duties are less elsewhere; and whereas several of our English Supra-Cargoes take up large sums of our inhabitants at Respondentia, and afterwards proceed to Bengal, where they take up as much more of persons who are ignorant of their engagements here; so by thrusting into their private adventures greater quantities of goods than the markets where they are bound can possibly consume, they are forced to be in those ports two seasons to dispose of their own private effects; to the great prejudice of those concerned in the stock, and puts a stop to the quick circulation; which will effectually be prevented by letting the Gentlemen in the Bay know what engagements those Supra-Cargoes lie under here, and by degrees reduce trade to its proper bounds, which by this licentious practice has been quite overdone.

"In order therefore, to support the Honorable Company's Revenue, and to prevent the injuries this place receives from these clandestine practices;—it is resolved that in future all Respondentia bonds, notes, or writings at Respondentia for money lent by the inhabitants of this place,—Company's servants as well as others,—upon all ships trading from this or any other port in India, shall be duly and regularly registered in a book to be kept for that purpose.

"That in case of any Supra-Cargo, Merchant, Commander, Mariner, or other, shall have borrowed money at Respondentia of any of the said inhabitants proving Insolvent, all such bonds so registered shall be accounted and deemed a preferable claim to such as are not.

"That the Sub-Secretary do keep the said Book of Register, and that he shall receive 9 fanams for registering each Respondentia bond or note under 100 pagodas principal, or 18 fanams for each such bond or note for 100 pagodas or upward; that after having registered the said Bonds or notes he shall sign them registered, the day of the month and year; and that the Secretary do put up at the Sea Gate a publication of this resolution in writing in the usual languages for the notice and observation of all the inhabitants."

Our next extracts are curious, as clearly showing how the business between the Government and the Native Merchants was transacted in the Olden Time.

"Saturday, 11th February, 1727. The President acquaints the Board that, after a great deal of management with the Company's Merchants, he had engaged them to agree to a contract for taking off the woollen goods expected upon the next ship from Great Britain, and for providing goods for Europe this season; and delivers in the Contract and the counterpart to the Board. Which being read are approved, and the said Merchants being called in, were interchangeably signed and delivered; and they promise their utmost endeavours to comply with their engagements.

"The President represents to the Board, that the Merchants having received no tasharief according to custom at signing the contract with the Company the two preceding years, and that they now insisted upon their being now tashariefed for the three contracts:—it is ordered that the Warehousekeeper deliver seven pieces fine scarlet cloth for that use. Ordered also that 10,000 pagodas be advanced them out of the 20,000 promised them in the terms of the present contract."

The following is a copy of the contract as entered in the Consultation Book.

"Saturday, 11th February, 1727. A contract made, concluded, and agreed upon this 11th day of February 1727, between James Macrae, Esq. President and Council of Fort St. George in behalf of the English East India Company on the one part, and Sunca Ramah and Tomby Chetty etc. Joint Stock Merchants on the other part.

"The said Merchants do hereby covenant, promise and agree, that they will buy of the said President and Council all the Woollen goods that they shall receive upon the next expected shipping from Great Britain, for the said Company's account, at thirty per cent. advance upon the European price; that it shall be deposited in a Warehouse under two keys, one of which to be kept by the Warehousekeeper and another by the said Merchants; that before they receive any Woollen-goods out of the Warehouse they will pay the amount thereof to the Warehousekeeper, and further that they will so receive and pay for the whole quantity on or before the 1st day of October 1728.

"The above said Merchants do further promise, covenant and agree, to and with the said President and Council, that they will provide 3000 bales of cloth of the sortments; to be delivered at least 1,500 bales thereof on or before the 20th day of September next, and the remainder on or before the last day of January following. All the cloths now remaining in the Company's godown unmeasured to be counted in part of the said 3000 bales now contracted for; and the said President and Council do promise to receive the same, provided it be agreeable to our musters.

"The said Merchants do further covenant and agree that they will not demand any money upon account of this contract until the goods are delivered to the Company and embaled; excepting only the sum of 20,000 pagodas which the said President and Council do hereby promise and are obliged to advance to the said Merchants upon this contract; which said sum shall not be by them accounted for until the conclusion hereof, and the closing their accounts with the Company.

"The said Merchants do likewise covenant, and are hereby obliged in case they shall fail in complying with the terms of this contract, to pay a penalty of 20 per cent. for all the bales that they shall deliver short of the number agreed upon; unless it shall be manifestly made appear that troubles in the country have hindered them; provided always, and it is hereby agreed that in case the merchants shall comply with this contract within 500 bales of the whole 3000, that then the President and Council will remit the penalty for the said 500 bales.

"In witness whereof the said President and Council have to one part hereof set their hands, and caused the Company's seal to be affixed; and to the other part the said Merchants have set their hands and seals the day and year first above written."

"SUNCA RAMAH.
"NAIRO BALL CHETTY.
"TOMBY CHETTY.
"COLLASTRI CHETTY.
"MOODU VENKATA CHETTY."

The following story of attempted fraud will explain itself.

"Monday, 3rd April, 1727. Goodapilla Rangappah, having brought a large diamond from the mines to be sold here, and being a stranger, and recommended to Gruapah a goldsmith, to assist him in disposing of the said diamond, he had trusted him with the sale of it. But the said Gruapah, with intentions to defraud Goodapilla of the real value of the diamond, persuaded him upon several delusory pretexts to retire to Conjeveram. In the mean time, that he might carry on the fraud with the greatest security, he possessed the ignorant stranger with several groundless calumnies, to the prejudice of the President's character and to the trade of the place. Goodapilla being thus removed, Gruapah applied himself to Gopaul, a Diamond Merchant; and they entered into an agreement to have the Diamond cut without the owner's knowledge or consent, and afterwards sold it likewise without acquainting him to Mr. Parkes for 4150 pagodas, of which Gopaul and Gruapah rereceived each one half; though Gruapah had been to Conjeveram, and affirmed to Goodapilla that the President had taken the stone from him, and had given him only 1500 pagodas for it; and told him that he must not come to Madras, that if he did he would be in danger. But Goodapilla suspecting the fraud, came at last to Madras; and having information that his diamond had been sold as above, made his complaint thereupon to the President, and craved that justice might be done him. Whereupon the President had ordered the said Gopaul and Gruapah to be committed to prison; of all which he now acquaints the Board; and they and Goodapilla being called before the Board, and the whole affair being particularly enquired into, it appears evident that Gruapah had imposed upon, and defrauded Goodapilla Rungapah, and aspersed the President very grossly as above narrated. Mr. Parkes being called, declared he paid so much for the diamond. Gopal and Gruapah acknowledge that it was the same diamond that Goodapilla had trusted Gruapah with to sell for him, and that they had received each one half of the money. Gruapah affirms he had paid Goodapilla 17,000 pagodas; but the other persists to affirm that he had received only 15,000 pagodas for his diamond. It being likewise evident that Gopaul was concurring with Gruapah in this cheat, and that he knew the diamond was Goodapilla's, and had treated with Mr. Parkes about the sale of it, the Board came to the following resolution.

"That, after deducting the charge of cutting the said Diamond, and the sum already paid by Gruapah to Goodapillah, Gopaul and Gruapah do make up to him the sum it was sold for, each one half; that Gruapah being in low circumstances, the Secretary do make an inventory of his effects and sell them at the Sea Gate by public outcry, for payment of his half of the said money; and that if the amount of all his effects shall not prove sufficient, that Gopaul shall make up the sum that shall be wanting; and that he shall recover of Gruapah the sum so made good if ever he shall be found to have effects; that both be remanded to prison until the judgment is complied with, and that Gruapah be exemplarily punished for groundlessly aspersing the President's character in so gross a manner."

Here the matter ended, and we can only presume that the money was subsequently paid. It is however a significant fact that Goodapilla should be so easily induced to believe in the oppression charged against the Governor. Mr. Macrae's proceedings as regards interlopers may be gathered from the following extract.

"Tuesday, 25th April, 1727. The President represents to the Board that several persons, without indentures or license to trade as free Merchants, thrusting themselves into the several branches of the trade of India, are a great prejudice to the trade in general, and to the Company's Covenanted Servants and others that have license particularly in Pegu. That we are directed by the Honorable Court of Directors in their letter dated 7th January 1726, to send home all such Traders. Wherefore the President moves that Miles Barne and Thomas Pritchard, both now here and intended to return to Pegu, and Lewis Tornery and James

Lander, who are now there trading (though none of the four has the Company's Indentures) may be served with an order to return to Great Britain, conformably to our Honorable Masters' directions in that respect.

"Resolved that the orders for Lewis Tornery and James Lander be sent in a general letter to Captain Bereyman, Resident at Syrian, by a conveyance that now offers; with directions to him to serve the said orders and see them complied with; and that the Secretary do serve Miles Barne and Thomas Pritchard who are on the place, with the like orders."

These orders were evaded. Miles Barne and Thomas Pritchard obtained to go to Pegu for one year to recover their effects, promising faithfully to return and embark for England at the expiration of that time. However they broke their word and stayed at Pegu; and the resident at Pegu appears to have avoided taking any action in the matter.

We close the present chapter and the present volume with the following entry, which serves to illustrate the nature of the trade with China carried on by the Company's servants at Madras, and at the same time indicates the state of existing relations between Fort St. George and Pondicherry.

"Wednesday, 1st June, 1727. The President represents to the Board, that he proposes to send a ship to China this year, and is on that account in want of some silver to send on her; that as the French at Pondicherry have lately sold their silver at fourteen and three eights dollars weight per ten pagodas, he is willing to take the Company's at that price, with the allowance of a quarter more as usual for ships that go for China. Agreed to deliver the President thirty Chests of silver at those rates."

The concluding years of Governor Macrae's administration will be treated in the next volume.

END OF THE SECOND VOLUME.

them. In the meantime we have immediately to deal with Mr. WHEELER's Summary (i. e. Hand-Book) of the Records of the Presidency, which lies beside us. Mr. WHEELER has had a rich mine opened to him, and has made the best of his opportunity. He was appointed last year to search through the Government Records, and to give an opinion as to the value of them, nor could the task have been placed in better hands. His report on them has been pronounced perfectly satisfactory by the Madras Government.—*Athenæum*, March 2d, 1861.

" The Reporter has performed his task with so much ability, as we said on a previous occasion, and has so condensed the voluminous documentary matter submitted to his treatment, that, to use a pithy old Scotch proverb, we have " great gear packed in little bulk," and can make extracts invitingly short. Mr. WHEELER's toil in wading through the Records above mentioned, with a view to that re-classification of the whole effected by him, must have been enormous.—*Athenæum*, March 12th, 1861.

" We have been favoured with a copy of Mr. J. TALBOYS WHEELER's entertaining work, entitled, " *Madras in the Olden Time,*" a history of this Presidency from its first foundation to the Governorship of Thomas Pitt, Grandfather of the Earl of Chatham. This interesting work, compiled from official records in the Government Office, had already afforded us a good deal of amusement, and no little instruction, as it appeared in a fragmentary state in the *Indian Statesman*. It comprises the annals of our Madras Commonwealth during a period hitherto little known or studied, extending from 1639 to 1702: and we must confess we did not imagine that old Madras could have furnished any thing so interesting. Had the prospectus of such a work been set before us, we should have smiled incredulously at the promise of entertainment; but we can assure our readers that a perusal of this little history will amply repay them both with valuable information and amusement. Mr. WHEELER has eliminated what is dull and commercial, and has thrown a charm over the early records of our Presidency by his easy and pleasant style, whilst he has also exhibited his subject in connection with the history of the times in a most instructive manner.

"Madras has reason to be grateful for the labours of Mr. WHEELER, and we hope ere long to see a continuation of his researches into times of still increasing interest and importance.—*Madras Observer*, March 14th, 1861.

"Madras in the Olden Time," a compilation from the records of Government by Mr. J. T. WHEELER, has just been published in convenient form by Mr. HIGGINBOTHAM. The student of Indian history will find much to interest him in the old Records for the first time disinterred and arranged chronologically by Mr. WHEELER, for the *Indian Statesman*, and now placed before the public in a compact volume by Mr. HIGGINBOTHAM. The compiler appears to have laboured with great zeal and industry, wading through hundreds of volumes of consultations," and we think it must be admitted by all who perused the several chapters as they appeared in the *Statesman* that the permission accorded by the Government to Mr. WHEELER has been used very judiciously. So far as we are able to judge, we should say that no event of any importance in the history of the infant Presidency has been omitted, whilst the extracts referring to the quarrels of the Governors with one another, with their servants and subjects and with the native chiefs from the Naik of Poonamallee to the great Mogul himself, convey the most vivid description of the position, manners and character of the first settlers, and of the people by whom they were surrounded. As to Mr. WHEELER the least we can say of him is that whilst he has furnished the public with some very interesting and amusing reading, he has added a valuable contribution to Indian History.—*Examiner*, March 2d, 1861.

" The whole period about which Mr. WHEELER writes is between 1639 and 1702, corresponding, as he remarks, almost exactly with that of Lord Macaulay's History. The materials for the narrative have been collected after an amount of labour, which few would voluntarily undertake, from the old Government Records. It was well known that, amidst very much that was uninteresting and having reference only to mercantile transactions, much that was valuable and amusing might be discovered if any one sufficiently indefatigable would undertake the work. A few scraps of valuable matter had been disinterred from among the rubbish which surrounded them, but it was left for Mr. WHEELER to gather up all these fragments, separate them from the worthless material by which they are encrusted, and work them into one, continuous and readable narrative."—*Madras Crescent*, March 23d, 1861.

The *Hurkaru* writing of Mr. WHEELER's work says:—

"We have to acknowledge the receipt of "Madras in the Olden Time," from 1639 to 1702 a seemingly very interesting work, by J. T. WHEELER, Esq. Every page of it into which we have had time to look contains matter of much interest to any settler in the East."

"In conclusion, we may notice the fact two works have issued from one of the local presses of great interest to all who are connected with Madras, and of considerable importance to the student of Indian History. They are both written by Mr. J. TALBOYS WHEELER, the Editor of the *Indian Statesman*, and are deservedly spoken of in the highest terms in two reviews which we quote elsewhere. One is "Madras in the Olden Time" being a history of this Presidency from its first foundation to the Governorship of Mr. Thomas Pitt, Grandfather of the Earl of Chatham, that is, from 1639 to 1702. This Period has been almost ignored by Mill, and where alluded to by him is in many instances inaccurately treated. As the present work is compiled from the Government Records, which were placcd at Mr. WHEELER's disposal by the Madras Government, all the facts connected with the early history of the Presidency have been for the first time brought to light in a handy and well printed volume. The other work is a Hand-Book to the old Records of Madras which has been prepared for Government. It deals with the same subject of Madras in the Olden Time, but is of course more official in style: it is nevertheless highly interesting."—*Overland Athenæum*, March 29th, 1861.

" We have now beside us the publication referred to, in the form of a " Hand-Book to the Madras Records," a pamphlet in boards extending to the length of 94 pages, (with Chronological annals extending over 40 pages,) and full of most interesting matter connected with the past history of our Presidency, which we heartily commend to the notice of our readers, as a valuable addition to their libraries. They will learn from it much that even the most studious among them, and those best acquainted with extant books relative to India, never knew before, because he has wisely been permitted to open to them sources of information hitherto concealed, and the nature and value of which was unknown to the possessors of the treasure so long kept under lock and key, in the archieves of Fort Saint George. Regarding the excellence of the Report, and the amount of labour bestowed on the preparation of it, we need add nothing to what we have said already, but we must particularly mention in addition to the Report, as now printed, of thirty-one pages, which are perhaps more valuable for the purposes of reference, although less directly instructive and amusing, than the Report itself, as they contain "Chronological Annals of the British Government at Madras, from the earliest period to the present day; 1631 to 1861." In those "Annals" Mr. WHEELER has brought his work down to the 5th of March 1861, his record concluding with a notice of the late lamented Bishop of Madras. He has furnished a minute and correct chronological series of past events, not to be found elsewhere, which every one who wishes to learn the past history of Madras will do well to consult.—*Athenæum*, April 13th, 1861.

"MADRAS IN THE OLDEN TIME; being a history of the Presidency from the first foundation to the Governorship of Thomas Pitt, Grandfather of the Earl of Chatham—1689—1702;" such is the title of a work compiled from official records, by J. TALBOYS WHEELER, Professor of Moral Philosophy and Logic, Madras Presidency College. The work first appeared as a series of papers in one of the ablest of our Indian journals, the *Indian Statesman*. Many of our readers will remember that a similar work, entitled "The English in Western India," by the late lamented Phillip Anderson, a Chaplain on this Establishment, appeared as a series of papers in our own columns. The two works are the best we have on 'the Olden time in India.' They are replete with information, amusement, and interest. ... ...

... ...

We could give our readers, if our space permitted,

many more amusing pictures from the work before us. We shall, however, conclude by supplying them with a *tableau vivant* of Fort St. George at the end of the seventeenth century. "They will hear the gun fired at early morning,—and they will see the gradual stir of the inhabitants,—the measured tramp of the European soldier,—the little stately peon with his sword and buckler,—the rush of noisy and naked coolies,—the appearance of apprentices, writers, factors, and merchants in half-Hindoo costume,—the assembly for morning prayers in the little chapel, good master Patrick Warner officiating in his gown and bands, and indignant at the smallness of his congregation,—the opening of the Factory and jobbering crowd of Native traders,—the grand displays of European goods for sale, and packing up of Native Merchandise for export home,—the little school-room and long array of little boys and girls,—the orderly dinner shortly after noon, where all are assembled at the general table from the apprentices to the Honorable Governor himself,—the return to the labors of the desk and ware-house, until the joyous hour of closing has arrived, and the jaded Europeans recruit their exhausted spirits with the pleasures of punch, tobacco, and other persuits which we need not and cannot name. If it is Sunday, all would be changed; for in old times English Sundays were rigidly observed as little festivals. Then Europeans, civilians as well as soldiers dropped their half native attire, and were apparelled in the European fashion of the time. Then for a brief hour or two the Chaplain would be a greater man than the Governor. Then he would denounce vice and popery to his heart's content, and expound the Scriptures by the light of a theological learning which was almost general in those days when the Church was a living reality, but which is fast passing away now. Then the Church could boast of literary giants, such as Walton, Lightfoot, Stillingfleet, Beveridge: thousand time-honored names. She has few men to boast of now."—*Bombay Gazette.*

MADRAS IN THE OLDEN TIME

MADRAS IN THE OLDEN TIME:

BEING A

HISTORY OF THE PRESIDENCY

FROM

THE FIRST FOUNDATION OF FORT ST. GEORGE

TO THE FRENCH OCCUPATION OF MADRAS.

1727-1748.

J. TALBOYS WHEELER

IN THREE VOLUMES

VOL. III

GYAN

Published by

Gyan Publishing House
5, Ansari Road
Daryaganj, New Delhi-110002
Phone: 011-47034999, 9811692060
E-mail: books@gyanbooks.com

Distribution Network
gyanbooks.com
India, USA, Canada, UK, Australia, France

ISBN: 978-81-212-8395-3 (Set)
978-81-212-8392-2 (PB)
First Published, 1862

2nd Impression 2023

Printed at: Gyan Press, Delhi.

MADRAS IN THE OLDEN TIME (VOL. III)
Author: J. TALBOYS WHEELER

MADRAS IN THE OLDEN TIME.

MADRAS IN THE OLDEN TIME:

BEING A

HISTORY OF THE PRESIDENCY

FROM

THE FIRST FOUNDATION OF FORT ST. GEORGE

TO THE FRENCH OCCUPATION OF MADRAS.

COMPILED FROM OFFICIAL RECORDS,

BY

J. TALBOYS WHEELER,

Author of the "Geography of Herodotus," &c. &c. and Professor of Moral Philosophy and Logic at the Madras Presidency College.

VOL. III.

1727—1748.

MADRAS:

PRINTED FOR J. HIGGINBOTHAM, MOUNT ROAD,

BY GRAVES AND CO., SCOTTISH PRESS.

1862.

PREFACE.

In issuing the third and concluding volume of the annals of Madras in the Olden Time, the compiler has to do little more than express his gratification at having completed his original design of illustrating the history of the Presidency by means of the Government Records, from the period of the first foundation of Fort St. George in 1639, down to the occupation of Madras by the French in 1746-48. The facilities afforded him by the Madras Government, have thus enabled him to fill up a blank in the history of India, and to supply authentic illustrations of that century of which there had been previously no published record worthy of the name; and he sincerely trusts that the labour of love upon which he has been engaged will afford some pleasure to his readers, as well as add to their knowledge of the doings in the Presidency in the days long gone by.

The present volume, which is somewhat thicker than either of its predecessors, possesses some peculiarities to which attention may be specially drawn. Besides a complete alphabetical index of names to all the three volumes, a curious collection of quaint old rules and regulations has been added in the shape of an appendix. Above all the writer has been able to present his readers with a copy of a valuable map of "Madras and its Environs in the year 1733," representing the actual condition of the Presidency as it was about a hundred and thirty years ago. This map was originally drawn during the administration of Governor George Morton Pitt, and has been preserved in the department of the Chief Engineer. Moreover, in order to illustrate the changes which have taken place since that period, a corresponding map has been drawn on the same sheet of "Madras and its Environs in the present year of grace 1861." At the same time two plans of the Fort St. George at corresponding dates are exhibited on the same sheet. For this map, which so exactly illustrates the outward appearance of Madras in the Olden Time, the compiler and his readers are equally indebted to the Madras Government.

In thus announcing the completion of the first series of "Madras in the Olden Time," the compiler by no means wishes it to be inferred that his labours on the Records of this Presidency have been brought to a close. A glorious half century yet remains, which commences with the conquest of the Carnatic, and ends with the fall of Seringapatam, and final triumph of the British arms from sea to sea. But this period requires a different treatment from that which has been adopted in dealing with the history of the preceding century. The political and military transactions of the period have already perhaps been sufficiently narrated by Orme, Wilks, Duff, and other writers, whose names and works are alike generally known. Accordingly it has been deemed expedient to commence an entirely new work, which shall be altogether independent of the present annals. But this proposed plan is not yet sufficiently matured, and indeed, the engagements of the compiler demand a brief breathing time. However, in thus presenting the public with the completion of his first work on the history of this Presidency, he may be permitted to express a hope that but a short time will elapse before he may be able to resume his historical illustrations of Madras in the Olden Time.

MADRAS,
18*th December* 1861.

CONTENTS OF VOL. III.

CHAPTER XXXV.

GOVERNORSHIP OF MR. JAMES MACRAE, (*continued*) 1727.

CHAPTER XXXVI.

GOVERNORSHIP OF MR. JAMES MACRAE, (*continued*) 1728-29.

B

CHAPTER XXXVII.

GOVERNORSHIP OF MR. JAMES MACRAE, (*continued*) 1729-30.

CHAPTER XXXVIII.

LAST YEARS OF MR. JAMES MACRAE, 1730-46.

CHAPTER XXXIX.

GOVERNORSHIP OF MR. GEORGE MORTON PITT, 1730.

CHAPTER XL.

GOVERNORSHIP OF MR. GEORGE MORTON PITT, (*continued*) 1732-35.

CHAPTER XLI.

GOVERNORSHIP OF MR. RICHARD BENYON, 1735-36.

CHAPTER XLIV.

GOVERNORSHIP OF MR. RICHARD BENYON, (*continued*) 1741.

CHAPTER XLV.

GOVERNORSHIP OF MR. RICHARD BENYON, (*continued*) 1742-43.

CHAPTER XLIX.

CAPTURE AND OCCUPATION OF FORT ST. GEORGE, BY THE FRENCH—1746-48.

APPENDIX.

HISTORY OF THE MADRAS PRESIDENCY.

CHAPTER XXXV.

GOVERNORSHIP OF MR. JAMES MACRAE.

1727.

In the previous volume we brought the annals of Mr. Macrae's government down to the middle of 1727. The present chapter comprises extracts from the records of six months only, namely the consultation books of the latter half of the year 1727, the selections we have made are almost entirely confined to three subjects. First, to the general survey of the houses, gardens, and other tenements within the Company's territories, which was carried out this year by a Committtee acting in three divisions. Secondly, to the case of a Mr. Colin Campbell, who having lost large sums by speculating in the South Sea Company and other bubbles of the day, had betaken himself to Madras to retrieve his fallen fortunes; and who, being called upon to give his reasons for not paying the sums he owed in England, delivered in such a singularly well written explanation of his circumstances, that we have thought proper to preserve his narrative entire. Thirdly, to the remodelling of the Mayor's

Court, which was granted by the Royal Charter of 1726, and was carried out this year in the Madras Presidency.

Governor Macrae's survey of the town and suburbs of Madras, as they were some hundred and thirty years ago, may be best understood by reference to the consultation of 19th December, 1726, in which the following entry appears.

"Monday, 19th December, 1726. The President moves that a general survey may be made of all houses, tenements, gardens and grounds, within the extent of the Honorable Company's bounds, that are not formed and comprehended under a cowle from them, in order to a better proportioned assessment, and for improving and making more effectual in future the revenue of Quit rent and Scavenger's duty; which is agreed to as the most effectual expedient, and most conducive to the ends proposed. And it be an instruction to the Gentlemen appointed to make this survey, that they do make inquiry into the present value of houses, gardens, and other tenements; what quit rent or scavenger's duty they now pay; and what those that are not assessed ought to pay in proportion to the value or produce. Also to inquire into the circumstances of the inhabitants, in order that an additional sum may be raised, if practicable to the Company; and that the poor may be released by easing them, and assessing the wealthy who are able to bear it higher.

"Resolved that Messrs. Turner, Emmerson, Fowke, Hubbard, Houghton, and Pyot do make the said survey; that they act two and two together, dividing the whole extent of the bounds in three divisions; and that they report the same the 5th of April next, because the Company's immediate service will not permit them to perfect it sooner."

The reports of the three several Committees were not delivered in till the 27th of June, 1727. These reports we shall give at length, as they throw considerable light upon the condition of the Native inhabitants generally, and especially upon the state of sanitary reform in the olden time. It will be seen that the Committee of six was required to act in three divisions of two members each; each division taking up a particular part of the Company's territory. At the conclusion of their labours each division sent in a book of assessment which does not appear to have been preserved; accompanied by a separate report already mentioned. Of the three reports it will be remarked that the third and last is by far the best, and a sort of story belongs to it. The two Committee men appointed in that particular survey were both carried away by death; and Mr. Samuel Hyde was appointed to undertake their duty singly. Mr. Hyde was strongly recommended to the Madras Government by the Court of Directors when first sent out to India; both on account of his superior qualifications and the very high family to which he belonged. Mr. Hyde appears to have been a member of the great Clarendon family, which presented vicissitudes as extraordinary as those in the life of Governor Macrae. Anne Hyde, daughter of the great Chancellor, had been the first wife of James II; and if we mistake not, her grandmother was a village girl who many years before had gone to London to seek her fortune as a domestic servant. But we have no space to dwell upon the general vicissitudes of families, and at once proceed to extract the reports of the Committee of Survey.

The report of the South and Eastern division was as follows.

"To the Honorable James Macrae, Esq., and Council.

"Honorable Sirs,

"In pursuance to your orders of Council of the 19th of last December, we now lay before your Honors our Book of Assessment on the division which fell to our lot; which were all the Company's bound to the southward of the White Town, one side of the Choultry Street, and all the Black Town within the walls to the eastward of the Choultry Street.

"Our foresaid Book of Assessment will show your Honors the sums the several houses and gardens were rated as in the last Rent Roll; and in the said Book you will likewise observe what sums we have now put on the said houses and gardens, both for Quit rent and Scavenger's duty.

"In going through the several streets of the Black Town we had the cries of many poor widows and decayed people, which obliged us out of charity and compassion to ease them what we could; and that the amount of the Company's duty of Quit rent and Scavenger's duty might be made more certain and not decrease, we were necessitated to put on the rich the small sums we took of the poor. Some were so poor that we were oblig-ed to take all off; others we eased by taking off a few fanams. These persons are described in one of the columns of our Book of Assessment by the words "very poor," being wrote over against the persons' names; and those which we eased by only taking off a part of the duty, are described by the word "poor" being wrote over against their names.

"We once thought that calling in the Bills of sale for the Black inhabitants house, would have helped us in making a more proportionable assess-ment than formerly; but upon their being brought us we found most of them to be old bills of a great many years standing, amounting to small sums of money; so that on viewing the several houses, we found the greatest part of them had been made new and large houses long since the date of the bills of sale. Wherefore we were forced to proportion our assessment by the largeness and value of their houses, and ability of the possessors, as near as we could judge.

"Our new assessment within our division amount to 10 pagodas 6 fanams in the Quit rent more than in the last Rent Roll; and in the Scaven-ger's duty it comes to 15 fanams less. We should have been willing to have made a greater increase in these branches of the Company's revenues, could we have judged the inhabitants in circumstances to bear it.

"In and about Triplicane we found 67 houses and gardens which had no Quit rent laid upon them; so that we assessed each of them as near as we could judge the value of them, and it amounts to 165 pagodas 31 fanams. These gardens have most of them been made out of sandy spots of ground, and are a great improvement to the place; but are as near as we can learn more an expense to the owners than any real gain to their estates.

"We have gone through all the streets in Triplicane Town but could find very few houses to assess; the inhabitants thereof being mostly Brahmins, maintained by the merchants, and poor painters, gardeners, and other labouring people.

"Thus having given your Honors an account of our transactions in obedience to your orders of Council, we hope for your favourable approval thereof as no pains or fatigue therein have been spared by

Honourable Sirs,
Your most obedient humble Servants,
NATHANIEL TURNER.
JOHN EMMERSON.

Fort St. George, 26th June, 1727."

The second report seems to have referred to the West and Northern division, and was as follows.

"Honorable Sirs,

"The division which fell to our lot was the western part of the Black Town within the walls from the Choultry Street; also all the Mutteal pettah, and what gardens and grounds stretching out as far as the garden commonly called Addison's Garden, now Sunca Ramah's, on one side of the road, to Pulicat and Narrain's on the other. Through all which we have been, and shall give you a description thereof as we found them, and of the methods we have taken to concur with your intentions.

"In the Black Town we find 638 houses; the former Quit rent and Scavenger's duty laid thereon, both amounted to 613 pagodas and 7 fanams, which we have now raised to 687 pagodas and 9 fanams, the difference is 24 pagodas and 2 fanams.

"In the Mutteal pettah are 1405 houses, and among them we believe there are not ten worth 300 pagodas each, and the inhabitants all miserably poor. Some are Carpenters, Peons, and Coolies, and great numbers of beggars and Brahmins, who live in straw huts on the sand upon charity. Others are poor widows and children, who threw themselves at our feet as we passed along. We took off these sort of people a few fanams, and shared it among those whom we thought, by the appearance of their houses and the information we could get of their circumstances, better able to bear it. The former Quit rent and Scavenger's duty together amounted to 410 pagodas and 8 fanams; the present amount to 457 pagodas and 29 fanams. So that we have raised here 47 pagodas and 26 fanams; and we humbly offer our opinion, it is as much as possible can be done without distressing the subjects.

"To the northward of this Mutteal pettah are 26 gardens, two whereof are under cowle; viz.

Maria Pois, which pays pagodas	70	per annum.
The Company's Garden.........	351	do.
Total...	421	

by this no one thinks the renters can get any thing.

"The amount of the other three gardens was 28 pagodas and 9 fanams, which we have now raised to 51 pagodas and 27 fanams; so that the increase is 23 pagodas and 18 fanams.

"One of our Chetty's gardens produces nothing, being at present but a heap of sand; nevertheless we have laid on him but one pagoda per annum; also the garden of Chiniah Muttiah.

"We are of opinion what part of this revenue has been every year wrote off to profit and loss, which commonly amounted to 200 or 300 pagodas, happened thus: That whereas the Rental general and Scavenger has always made up his roll in August for the year following; before which is expired great numbers of people generally die in debt, and leave nothing but a poor widow and children, who are forced to suffer their pots and pans to be sold to pay 3 or 4 or half a dozen fanams Quit rent; and some there are that have nothing but the bare mat they lie on; that we cannot see how it can be avoided among such multitudes of poor people, and such a large sum of money to be collected in such small driblets.

"The care and method we have taken in this affair we hope will meet your Honor's approbation; having duly had at heart our Honorable Master's future interest whose we are, and

Your Honors

Most obedient humble servants,

RANDAL FOWKE,

JAMES HUBBARD."

The third, and most important report of all, referred to the Central division of Black Town, and was written as before said by Mr. Samuel Hyde. It was as follows.

"Honorable Sir and Sirs,

"In compliance to your Honor's order for finishing the survey of that part of the Black Town called the Pedda Naick Pettah, formerly under the direction of Messrs. Houghton and Pyot deceased, I herewith present a new Roll of rates for the same; whereby will appear such alterations as I have thought necessary for the relief of the poor and benefit to the Honorable Company: the whole amounting to 1329 pagodas 19 fanams; and the advance gained thereby 85 pagodas and 26 fanams; which I believe is the most the inhabitants can bear, and is submitted to your Honors for your approbation.

"As the annual and strenuous recommendation from the Honorable Court of Directors to this Presidency, for preventing of the bad debts yearly outstanding on the Scavenger's account, have been the chief motives for your Honor's appointing this survey; I have carefully examined how those debts have arose, and found the whole remains of the last years to be 174 pagodas, 17 fanams and 40 cash; of which above 60 pagodas arises from persons leaving their houses uninhabited; the humour of the people being such, that in cases of mortality or misfortunes they had rather go up the country, and suffer their houses to decay many years for want of repairs, than sell them out of the family. The Scavenger can have no defence against such loss, and though the said debts are wrote off for that year, yet the annual rates of these houses are continued in the succeeding Rent Roll, though it is uncertain when the owners will return. The same I may say of the many places in the Black Town and Pettah, that have continued empty without houses or improvement thereon for many years, as may be observed in the Roll now presented; all which were charged according to the old rates amounting to upwards of 35 pagodas, though the Scavenger had little probability of receiving any part of it. The reason that has been given for this custom is, that by continuing them on the Rent Roll they may the better remember the old tax that was laid on such grounds, and to endeavour a recovery of the same, when the owner shall return; though I never yet knew or heard of such debts so recovered, and it is to be feared the multiplicity of such vacant places may in time lay waste great part of the Black Town. The owners of many of them are unknown, and out of memory; and others nominally known, yet no one knows where to find them, or how to apply for the purchasing their grounds, and consequently the grounds must be useless. Whereas were these grounds publicly sold for the payment of the Company's Quit rent, and the overplus deposited in the Company's cash for the benefit of such as shall hereafter make good their claims; such places would be rebuilt or improved, and the whole Town in a constant employ.

"The rest of the bad debts arise from the poverty of the inhabitants, of whom thousands that pay the Company half a fanam and upwards per month, have no better means of supporting themselves and families than by beating rice, cooly hire, and such low business. By which the most industrious cannot gain above 18 to 20 fanams per month, with rice from their friends and relations.

"The unfortunate death of Messrs. Houghton and Pyot, late Scavengers, having prevented their good intentions in representing many inconveniences arising from the evil customs now practiced in the Black Town, and the better management of that business for the future; I therefore beg leave to mention what of them I can remember to have heard proposed, had they survived the report now made to this Honorable Board.

"It has been a frequent complaint to the Scavenger that, notwithstanding the great assessment with which the inhabitants are yearly charged, the streets are yet in a most abominable and filthy condition; which I presume will be found to arise from the insufferable custom of the inhabitants— in the streets; their perpetually throwing out of ashes and house dirt; their hogs and buffaloes and horses in the streets, all which make a constant litter, which the small number of carts allowed by the Company connot clear away. Wherefore I humbly propose that an order be issued that no person whatever be suffered to make free in the streets; or keep any hogs, buffaloes or horses, but in their compounds; and for the better and more easy carrying away the dirt and ashes which is the produce of every house, I should think it but a small trouble for the several inhabitants to carry their dirt to some one or more places that shall be appointed for a general dunghill in every street, which the Scavenger can take care to have removed every morning.

"It is a most grievous custom for every house to have a sink hole to receive the house water; which are dug in the open street, and lie uncovered in the passages, or perhaps two or three long stones cast over them, but yet not sufficient to prevent the passengers and especially children from falling into them. Besides the intolerable stench that proceed from them is so very strong, that it is justly complained of as one of the greatest nuisances in the Black Town; and yet is easily remedied by obliging such persons to cover them, and that in such a manner as to be on a level with the foot path.

"The wells have not been publicly repaired since Governor Collet's time; and are now become dangerous to young persons that draw water, and by scattering the water make a dirty kennel in the street; encouraging the hogs to wallow and vermin to breed in them; all which were formerly remedied by repairing the wells, and to which I find the neighbours are willing to contribute according to their abilities.

"The frequent encroachments in the streets grow so general, that without care be timely taken the passages will become too narrow for passengers, and pernicious to the health of the Town in so warm a climate. Almost every house lately built has encroached further into the street, by enlarging the house, or by raising pials of two and a half feet high, and other parade before the doors, of stone or brick, from 10 to 20 inches higher than the common path and from 6 to 9 feet into the street, which serve only for the makers' use and throw off the passengers. Whereas were the same stone or brick work on a level with the path (as in the White Town), they would be as a general pavement. There are innumerable Smiths, Cajan's shops and Sheds, Buttecas, and small brick houses, built against the front of other large houses which come six or eight feet into the street, and are from eight to sixteen feet long, which pay no Quit-rent to the Company. Likewise several parcels of large stones or timbers, planks and palmeiras, all which are so many encroachments upon the streets, and turn aside the passengers.

"Many persons expose to sale cloth, brass ware, and other goods, by spreading of matting &c, in the middle of the street, which pester the passage, and can be of no account but saving Butteca rent; while the Honorable Company's Buttecas remain neglected, to the loss of the Butteca farmer, and the lessening of that revenue to the Honorable Company.

"These are what have fallen under my observation, and though they may seem in themselves trifling, yet as I do not doubt but they will contribute very much to the wholesomeness, beauty, and good order of the city, I hope your Honors will excuse the presentation from

Honorable Sir and Sirs,
Your most faithful and
obedient humble Servant,
SAMUEL HYDE."

No immediate action seems to have resulted from these reports, beyond the sale by public outcry of some lands where the ownership was doubtful; but the reports themselves will no doubt be found very interesting, especially to those of our readers who are familiar with the present state of Black Town, or who have taken an active part in sanitary reform.

Our next extracts, referring to the peculiar case of Mr. Colin Campbell, will explain themselves. The name is certainly a remarkable one, at the present moment, though we believe not uncommon in Scotland; and would seem to indicate that the gentleman in question belonged to the same family as the present Lord Clyde. The circumstances of the case are best explained by the following entry in the consultations.

" Monday, 3rd July, 1727. The Honorable the " Court of Directors, having in their letters by the Princess of Wales" ordered us to assist Captain John Haye and others in the recovery of debts from Mr. Colin Campbell to a very considerable amount, the said Colin Campbell was called before us and payment demanded. Whereupon he delivered in writing an answer, importing in substance that the said Captain John Haye had no reason to treat him the said Colin Campbell in so scurvy a manner; that the whole of what he brought out with him was less than £300; that he spent a part thereof for payment of his disbursements at Deal and other places, and part for his passage money; that the remainder was most of it expended here before he could get an employ, and that when he had one, the small adventure and little advantage he made thereon did but barely pay his table expenses in the voyage; so that he hath now left scarce any thing more than to pay his passage to Europe, whither he says he proposes to go.

" The answer of Mr. Campbell was ordered to be entered; and it was agreed, that as every one of us are fully convinced of the truth thereof, that we so allow Mr. Campbell to go to Europe if he please; and that he be not molested here on account of the said demand, since he is desirous of returning to England where the claims may be demanded the same."

The letter of Mr. Colin Campbell to Governor Macrae and Council was as follows. The reader will scarcely fail to remark upon the superiority of the diction over most of the extracts we have made from the records.

" Honorable Sirs,

" Being commanded to deliver in writing an answer to some charges and demands laid against me from England, and lately transmitted hither; I shall here give as true a state of those affairs as the distance of time and remoteness from my books and papers will allow; being the same in substance with what I informed the Honorable the President and Council by word of mouth upon examination. I therefore declare to the best of my knowledge as follows.

" Captain John Haye, having presented a petition to the Honorable the Court of Directors for the affairs of the East India Company against me, wherein he has stated the affair between him and me in the basest manner, and has represented me in a very unjust and odious character; I am obliged in my own vindication to be somewhat more particular in relation to him than I ever intended. In the general I might safely appeal for a character before my misfortunes to all the Gentlemen who knew me in this army in Spain, the latter end of the late Queen's reign, and to all those of the garrisons in Minorca after that time; to the highest of whom I had the honour to be well known, and served in many different stations both in Catalonia and Port Mahon without blemish or reproach; and my character is sufficiently known in London, not to have ever given any room for such base and malicious reflections as have been thrown upon me by that Gentleman; and had I been guilty during the general infatuation in South Sea time, and in time of my greatest necessities, of contributing to the hurt of others, knowingly and wilfully, I should be the first to condemn myself, and could not find fault with such as would join in the same accusation against me. But I cannot help thinking it the severest of all calamities, to have my reputation in danger of being destroyed, by drawing me in so very bad colours; and that my misfortunes, a fate almost universal and common to thousands besides me at that time, should be charged upon me as a crime. The far greater part of persons engaged in dealings at that unlucky juncture were involved in the same ruin, and consequently proved the unhappy occasion of making many others share in their sufferings, which was also my most unfortunate case.

"A great many years are past since Captain Haye and I were first acquainted, having served together in the same Regiment for sometime at Port Mahon, where it was well known what offices of friendship I did him; but more particularly by venturing my whole fortune by my credit with Mr. Neale, then Pay Master General, to raise him from an Ensign to Captain, at a time when not one person would give him the least assistance either by their money or credit. Many years after that, I having sold out of the army and settled in London, Captain Haye arrived there in the South Sea year 1720; and hearing that I was in very flourishing circumstances, he came to me to ask advice how to employ a small sum of money, not exceeding as I can remember £600. My opinion was to put it into South Sea stock, then upon the rise; but he chose rather to put it into my hands, begging me to allow him good interest for it. To serve him I complied with his request, paying him for some months 10 per cent per month. He having gained considerably by these means, I thought it unreasonable for him to expect that I should always keep it at so high a premium, and so very much above what any body else would allow, and therefore made him take his money back again. Upon which he bought a bargain in York Buildings Stock for time; but it happening to fall considerably before the term of payment came, he complained to me that he and his family were ruined if I did not help him; and did by his importunity prevail upon me to deliver him from that bargain and to take it upon myself, which was an actual loss to me of £400; that being the difference between the price of the Stock at the time he purchased it and the time I paid for it. After this he teazed me till I took his money a second time, being about £800, but at lower usury, being at the rate of 3 or 4 per cent per mensem. If I remember right, sometime afterwards he, having raised some money by taking in subscriptions from sundry persons to a Bubble called the North Sea; which he did by giving notes promising so much North Sea Stock for money received, at the same time sinking six pence on every half crown, for his notes run only two shillings for a half crown paid him;—with money raised in this manner, he bought £330 in South Sea Stock. This happening soon to fall in a very precipitant manner, he came to me about the beginning of September, complaining in his wonted style, that he and his family would be ruined if I did not help him in this distress, by taking that Stock off his hands. I refused it on account of being too deeply concerned in Stocks already. He then proposed that I should buy it of him at time, allowing him an advance; to which he pressed me with great earnestness, and prevailed upon me to give a bond for said £330 Stock, to pay him £2600 in three months; being a very extravagant advance. Stocks falling soon after to a very low rate, involved me in utter ruin, and put it absolutely out of my power to comply with that or other bargains I had then depending. As to the sum of £800 which I had taken at the abovementioned usury, I did all that was in my power, even after I was ruined, to clear it; which my wife and I did to near £400, as by his receipts appears. She out of compassion to his family sold some of her jewels to raise him money; and sometime after, when I had no way to find more, I gave him pictures and other things to the value of the remainder of my note. But he, not waiting for a proper time to dispose of them, sold for five and twenty pounds, as he acquainted me, what cost me about four hundred pounds some years before. By all which it appears, that of all my creditors, Captain Haye has the least reason to persecute me, though the only one that has done it, and though since my misfortunes, I having often reduced myself to the last necessities to supply him. His troubles, which he maliciously imputes to me, are chiefly owing to his fraudulent management in the North Sea Bubble, as above related.

"As to his charge of my carrying large sums of money with me to India, nothing can be more ridiculous and inconsistant. Can it be supposed that any man in his senses would part with his family, country, and friends, and at my age, to live in India under dependance on strangers, and enjoy so large a fortune as £30,000, as he used to give out in all places when I was at home. Had I been possessed of so much money, could I not have retired to many parts in Europe, where I might have lived more at my ease and satisfaction, in case my creditors would not have suffered me to do so in England. But what shows the falsehood as well as malice of that charge to a demonstration is this. Had I been possessed of any sums of money, the law would certainly have given him as well as others a right to them ; and sure I am he left no methods untried to find out and seize all he could of mine while he was in England. But it is very easy for any person concerned to know, if they please, what money I brought abroad with me. All I had was delivered into Captain Charles Small's hands, with whom I came out hither ; which was a very small sum, and was lessened before I got to this place by my expences at Deal, Portsmouth, and aboard ship ; and my living out of business for above a twelve month after my arrival here exhausted the little money I brought out with me. When by favour of the Honorable Governor I went to China last year, I carried but a small sum with me, which I took up at 16 per cent Respondentia, and which produced not much more than defrayed the expence of my table and other charges to and from China. So that at present I have not more than will enable me to pay my passage back to England, and answer my expences here, till I can meet with a favourable opportunity to return.

"As to Mr. Wordsworth's and Mr. Heathcote's demands, I am very sensible that they would not have given me any trouble had not Captain Haye raised such false and malicious reports of my flying to India with large sums of money ; they having never given me any disturbance the four years I was in England from the time of my misfortunes, for which I reckon myself extremely obliged to them. I believe they were then convinced of the badness of my circumstances, as well as of my inclination to do all that was in my power; having given them for a further security all the stock I had left. There were many sums of money due to me; upon account of bargains in stocks and otherwise; but I was not able to recover above £200 of all that was owing me, and my circumstances did not permit me to carry on law suits to endeavour to recover any more. I gave those Gentlemen such securities for their money as they judged very good at that time, and which then sold above the value of the sum borrowed; and by the contracts and defeazances passed between us, they had full power and authority without my consent, to sell said securities and pay themselves at what time they pleased. But it was a great misfortune to them and me that they did not sell those securities, as they were empowered to do. I came to India with no other view than to try my last and utmost endeavour to get money, in order to give some satisfaction to those gentlemen and others; being unwilling to have any reason to reproach myself with having neglected any means, or the least probability of any that might put it in my power to do justice to those that suffer by my misfortunes. To this view I sacrificed all the ease and happiness I was possessed of, and submitted to a voluntary banishment, and to the greatest distance from my family, friends and country. It is unfortunate for my creditors as well as me that my design has miscarried; there remaining nothing now to do in these parts; so that I propose to return in some months, and shall very willingly give all my creditors a fair state of my circumstances as soon as it pleases God to bring me safe back to England.

"All the above related particulars, I declare to be true to the best of my memory and knowledge.

COLIN CAMPBELL."

Fort St. George, July 8th 1277."

We now turn to the third and last subject in the present chapter, namely the reorganisation of the Mayor's Court. A detailed account of the establishment of a municipality by the Charter of 1687, has already been given in a preceding chapter. The exercise of judicial powers however had never been based on a satisfactory foundation, but, "in 1726," says Mr. Mill, "a Charter was granted, by which the Company were permitted to establish a Mayor's Court at each of their three presidencies, Bombay, Madras, and Calcutta; consisting of a Mayor and nine Aldermen, empowered to decide in civil cases of all descriptions. From this jurisdiction, the President and Council were erected into a Court of Appeal. They were also vested with the power of holding Courts of Quarter Session for the exercise of penal judicature in all cases, excepting those of high treason. And a Court of Requests, or Court of Conscience, was instituted, for the decision by summary procedure of pecuniary questions of inconsiderable amount." With this introduction we place the extracts from the records referring to these new arrangements.

"Monday, 14th August, 1727. The President represented to the Board, that the time for putting in execution the Royal Charter was very near; and that therefore it would be necessary to come to some resolutions agreeable thereto. That the death and absence of Messrs. Higginson, Woolley, Way and Munro, having occasioned four vacancies, it was necessary to supply them according to the rules of the Charter; which was accordingly done by appointing Messrs. Thomas Weston, William Monson, John Bulkelay, and Edward Bracstone, Aldermen in the room of the said four persons.

"Mr. Higginson having been by the said Charter appointed Mayor, and it being provided therein that the President and Council should in case of his death nominate the first Mayor,—It was unanimously agreed to appoint Mr. John Powney to that station.

"Ordered that Thursday next be appointed for swearing the Mayor and Aldermen, and putting in execution His Majesty's Charter for so far as relates to the Mayor's Court."

"Thursday, 17th August, 1727. This being the day that the Honorable President and Council had appointed for putting in execution the new Charter, and the Town having received notice accordingly; the Gentlemen appeared on the parade on horse back with the Guards, Peons and country music; and about nine in the morning proceeded to the Company's Garden house in the following manner.

Major John Roach on horseback at the head of a Company of Foot Soldiers, with Kettle drum, Trumpet, and other music.

The Dancing Girls with the Country music.

The Pedda Naik on horse back at the head of his Peons.

The Marshall with his staff on horse back.

The Court Attorneys on horse back.

The Registrar carrying the old Charter on horse back.
The Serjeants with their Maces on horse back.

The old Mayor on the right hand and the new on the left. The Aldermen two and two all on horse back.	Six halberdiers.

The Company's Chief Peon on horse back, with his Peons.
The Sheriff with a White Wand on horse back.
The Chief Gentry in the Town on horse back.

" In this manner they proceeded from the parade through Middle gate street into the Black Town, and so out at Armenian bridge gate, through the Pedda Naik pettah to the Company's Garden, where the President and Council were met to receive them."

" The old and new Mayors being come to the Company's Garden house in the form mentioned, they were admitted ; where the President administered the oath of allegiance and the Mayor's oath to John Powney Esq., and the oath of allegiance and the Alderman's oath to Messieurs Abraham Wessel, Francis Rous, Luis de Medeiros, Thomas Weston, William Monson, and Edward Bracstone, being all the Aldermen that could attend on this occasion. After which the President having received the old Charter from Mr. Francis Rous, returned him thanks in the name of himself and the rest of the Council, for his careful and faithful discharge of the trust that had been reposed in him ; and expressed the great satisfaction he promised himself from the known abilities and integrity of the present Mayor John Powney, Esq., to whom he delivered the new Charter."

Our next extracts refer to the institution of the other Courts, and will explain themselves.

"Tuesday, 22nd August, 1727. It being appointed by the Charter, that the President and the five Senior Counsellors, should in thirty days after the receipt of the same, be and constitute a Court of Oyer and Terminer, and Goal delivery; the said President with George Morton Pitt, Esq., Messrs. John Roach, Randal Fowke, and Samuel Hyde, accordingly took the oaths of allegiance and of office. Mr. Robert Symonds one of the Seniors being absent will be sworn on his arrival."

"Monday, 11th September, 1727. It being necessary that there be a Court of Justice for deciding small debts; for the relief of the poor who cannot afford the charges necessarily attending the forms of proceedings in the Mayor's Court, and would therefore otherwise be defrauded of their just dues. It was agreed that the five Justices of the Peace appointed by the Royal Charter, be also appointed Justices of the Choultry, and to decide causes of that kind as far as 20 pagodas value."

"Monday, 27th November, 1727. The Committee nominated to inspect the list of fees appointed to be paid in the Mayor's Court, reporting that they think them moderate and just, it is ordered that they be copied after this Consultation, and that our approval of them be signified to the Court. Also that the same list be translated into the several languages, and hung up in the Town Hall; and that a note be affixed at the several gates of the Town, giving notice to the inhabitants of this new regulation of the fees, and that they are hung up in the Town Hall; that every one who has business in the Court may thereby be enabled to avoid being imposed on.

"The Board having on the 11th of September last ordered that the Justices of the Peace should decide petty causes of Meum and Tuum at their Sessions at the Choultry; and that method being found to occasion some inconveniences, particularly the subjecting the members of the Superior Court to an appeal to the Mayor's Court:—It was unanimously agreed that for the future all petty causes shall be decided in the Sheriff's Court; and that the Sheriff shall and may decide ultimately without appeal as far as five pagodas, and that he may likewise decide further as far as 20 pagodas, allowing the parties a liberty of applying to the Mayor's Court in case they are not satisfied with the Sheriff's award. Also that the Register of Slaves, which formerly was kept by the Justice of the Choultry, be now kept by the Sheriff, with the former fees; and also that he do keep a Register of sales and mortgages of houses as far as 100 pagodas value, as was formerly done at the Choultry; only that the fees for so doing be no more than 18 fanams for 100 pagodas value, and in the same proportion for lesser sums:—of which regulations it is ordered that the Secretary do give notice by affixing papers at the gates.

"Ordered that the Justices of the Peace do take cognisance of all breaches of the Peace, petty Larcenies, and other crimes properly belonging to their office; that for the lesser faults they do order corporal punishment to the offenders; for those of a very high nature, they bind over to the Sessions; and that for others they do commit the offenders to the Choultry, and report their crimes to the Board the next Consultation. And that the Secretary do affix papers at the gates in the several languages; giving notice to the inhabitants that all murders, breaking open of houses, or robberies by night will be punished with death, and all other thefts with the utmost severity of the law, and that all receivers of stolen goods will be punished as the thieves;—as also that all persons on whom it shall be proved that they have bought any thing from Gentlemen's servants, such as Candles, Damars, Bottles, &c., or things of greater value, shall be fined agreeable to the value of the things so purchased, and punished in the same manner as receivers of stolen goods; and in order for the better and more effectual finding out thereof, that whoever will inform against such purchasers or receivers, shall have the one half of the value of the goods, which he shall make appear to have been so purchased or received.

"A List of Fees read and approved of by the Honorable the Mayor's Court of Madraspatanam the 29th August 1727.

"REGISTER'S FEES.

For every precept, warrant of arrest and warrant of execution 18 fanams to be paid out of that to the Sheriff's Serjeants for serving the same, four fanams.

For any petition that is read or any other paper he is to charge six fanams each and for filing any petition or any other necessary paper nine fanams.

For attesting any paper, not exceeding one side twelve fanams if it exceeds nine fanams each side.

For summoning any person six fanams, to be paid out of that two fanams to the Sheriff's Serjeant.

For copying any paper not exceeding one side eighteen fanams if it exceeds, twelve fanams each side.

For affixing the Court seal to any paper ten fanams.

For every entry of Court three fanams.

For every order or judgment of Court six fanams; for a copy of the same six fanams.

For the taking of Bail six fanams.

For affixing a note at the sea gate eighteen fanams, to be paid out of that six fanams to the Translator.

For every affidavit four fanams.

For registering any paper not exceeding one side eighteen fanams.

For drawing out a letter of Attorney one pagoda.

For every letter of administration eighteen fanams.

For protesting Bills of exchange one pagoda—registering do. and protest one pagoda.

For writing and registering bills of sale or mortgage bonds without the White Town eighteen fanams per cent; the same in the White Town if the amount exceed not 500 pagodas, if exceeding 500 pagodas the Registrar to take no more than two pagodas eighteen fanams.

Upon all deposited estates and money paid with Court a half per cent.

ON WILLS.

Reading wills twenty fanams.

Registering will if not exceeding one side eighteen fanams.

Probate with the seal of Court twenty-eight fanams.

Summoning the witnesses twenty-four fanams.

Swearing each witness three fanams.

EXAMINER'S FEES.

For swearing every witness three fanams.

For examining and taking depositions for every one nine fanams.

For all copies of depositions six fanams.

For a summons to any person to appear at the Examiner's office twelve fanams; to be paid out of that four fanams to the Court Serjeant.

For a note to be delivered the Defendant's attorney before he is examined, two fanams.

ATTORNEY'S FEES.

All persons that employ an Attorney to act for them in any cause is first to deposit in his hands 3 pagodas, of which he is to give an account when the cause is ended.

Attorney fee one pagoda.

For writing petition eighteen fanams each side of a sheet of paper.

Pleading each Court day and attendance nine fanams.

Translating any paper eighteen fanams a side; to be paid out of that to the Translator six fanams.

Attendance on a Client in the White Town nine fanams.

Attendance on a Client in the Black Town twelve fanams.

For drawing out the interogatories in the whole cause eighteen fanams.

SHERIFF'S FEES.

Commission upon all Levys and Executions 5 per cent. under 200 pagodas and 2½ per cent on all above.

For executing all warrants and summons ten fanams.

N. B.—The Mayor and two cash keepers to draw 3½ per cent. upon all deposited estates and money paid into Court upon every cause that is decided; the interpreter to have nine fanams.

Upon all summons to the Blacks he is to have one fanam.

CHAPTER XXXVI.

GOVERNORSHIP OF MR. JAMES MACRAE.

1728—29.

The concluding years of Mr. Macrae's government, like those whose history has been recorded, are marked by events of a purely domestic nature. One little difficulty occurred with the French at the Mauritius, and another one with the Rajah of Travancore, but both were of a trivial nature. The remainder of the entries we have preserved refer almost entirely to the administration of Governor Macrae within the Company's bounds; and to such little incidents as serve to illustrate the internal condition of the settlement at Fort St. George.

Our first extract refers to Major Roach, who had distinguished himself both at Fort St. David, and in the defence of Trivatore. As a reward for his services, the Directors at home appointed him to a seat in Council. The entry in the consultation book will explain itself.

"Monday, 21st August, 1727. Major Roach having taken his place at the Board, after returning thanks for the honor conferred upon him, desired that he might still continue in his employ of Major of the Forces; declaring his resolution rather to sacrifice all that was dear and valuable to him, than to have it thought he had, by accepting a mercantile employ, entered into an asylum. He added that as he had for near twenty-five years faithfully served the Honorable Company in the field, he could not think of quitting that post; but should believe himself undeserving of any regard, should he not, by this additional mark of esteem conferred on him, be the more encouraged to venture his life for the defence of the Honorable Company, should an enemy come down upon us; that as for the pay he had formerly been entitled to, he had no thoughts of receiving it longer, but quitted that, though he was still desirous of the employ.

"Upon which it was immediately resolved, that Major Roach, having shown himself upon many occasions an experienced and good officer, he be continued Major; and the President expressed his satisfaction in observing the zeal the Major showed for the Company's interest, and the neglect of his own ease, in desiring to serve in a double capacity, and to take the trouble of two employs on him at once."

The subject was referred home to the Court of Directors, who decided that Major Roach could not continue a Member of Council, and a Commander of the Forces at the same time. Two years passed away before this decision was fairly acted on at Fort St. George; but for the sake of a connected narrative we insert the result here.

"Monday, 14th July, 1729. The President, agreeable to the General letter of February last, called upon Major Roach to declare which employ he would accept, whether he would continue Member of Council or Major of the Garrison;—to which he made answer as follows.

"That as he had served the Honorable Company upwards of twenty-five years in a Military capacity, and received distinguishing marks of their favour for his service in that way, he could not without some reluctance quit an employment that had given him a title to so much of their esteem; but as it has pleased them to put it to his choice, whether he will resign his title to the Military service, or have the honor of sitting at the Council Board, the late decay of his constitution, occasioned by a long fit of illness, induces him to accept of the latter; which, though it deprives him of any immediate command of Military, yet it no ways lessens his inclination to venture his life whenever he shall be commanded, and his Honorable Master's occasions call for his sword to assert their just rights and privileges. At the same time, returning his most humble thanks for this particular favour shown him, he begs leave to assure this Board that it shall be his whole study to merit his Master's esteem, by a faithful discharge of his duty in whatever station he shall be called to."

Whilst Major Roach was obtaining such an honourable recognition of his public services, his private character suffered some injury from his being concerned in the elopement of a Portuguese young lady from St. Thomé. The story will be found further on.

We have now to draw the attention of our readers to one of those documents which serve to throw a light upon the inner domestic life of the English settlers in the olden time. Most of our readers, and especially those of the fair sex, are no doubt alive to the fact that a rigid examination of all the property of an individual, including a peep into all his or her boxes, drawers, and other private receptacles, will enable us to draw a tolerably accurate conception of his or her habits and modes of life. Accordingly we here present them with a tolerably minute inventory of the effects of an Englishman who lived some hundred and thirty years ago, in the days when men wore wigs, breeches, and swords, and indulged in strong waters unknown to the present temperate generation. We print the list in full, exactly as we find it entered in the consultation book of 15th January 1728.

Inventory of the Effects of Mr. John Blunt deceased, December 1727.

Cash found in his escritoire. 21½ rupees and 124 pagodas.

In the First Drawer.

2 Gold watches.
1 Gold seal and 1 silver seal.
1 Pair of gold buckles.
1 Pair of silver gilt buckles.
1 Emerald ring.
1 Stone seal.
1 Pair of silver garter buckles.
1 Ring with Elephants hair.
1 do Tomback.
1 Pair of sleeve buttons.
1 Tweezer case and Memorandum Book.
2 Silver Cuspidores.
24 Gold buttons and Silver Chain.
2 Gold headed canes.

In the First Drawer.

2 Silver Salvers.
1 Silver Tankard.
1 Small silver mug.
7 Silver spoons.
1 do. for tea.
1 Case with 12 silver spoons and 12 knives and forks tipped with silver.
13 Horse tassels.
14 Silver buttons.
1 Silver Betel plate (the Company's.)
1 Silver rose water Bottle (the Company's.)
1 Silver hand for a fan.
2 Guglets with silver.
2 Silver hilted swords.
1 Pair of silver spurs.
1 Moor's Dagger.

In the Second Drawer.

1 Remnant of Chintz.
1 Pair of Bengal taffaty white.
2 Pairs of double thread betillas
2 Pairs of single thread betillas, white.
1 Pair of Bengal stuff, 1 Pair of issarees white.
1 Pair of Salampores.
1 Pair of Handkerchief Pulicat.
1 Remnant of taffaty.
1 Silver sash, 2 small looking glasses.
2 Pairs of brown betilas, 1 velvet Cap.
2 Pairs of Masulipatam handkerchiefs.
3 Remnants of Chintz.
16 Gold striped handkerchiefs.

3rd Drawer.

2 Pairs of Madras Gingham.
13 Moor's cloaks.
11 Turbans.
10 Sashes.
3 Pairs of flowered custanees.
11 Pairs of drawers of sundry sorts.

In the 4th Drawer.

1 Silver sword knot.
I Bag sundry trifles.
2 Pairs of embroidered slippers.
I Pair of Gingham Sheets.
I Palampore.
II White waistcoats.
1 Brass lock.
40 Pillow cases.
12 Handkerchiefs.
18 Shirts and 20 Caps.
24 Turnovers and 8 stocks.
II Pairs of white stockings.
8 Pairs of drawers.
I Red cloth waistcoat.
I Pair of brass seals.
4 Rasors, hoan and strop.
2 Pairs of pistols.

In the large Chest.

I Parcel of gloves.
9 Coats and 5 waistcoats.
II Pairs of breeches.
I Remnant of Grogram.
2 Silver Lions for a palanqueen bamboo.
I Velvet Cap.
9 Valances for a cott.
10 Pairs of silk stockings.
5 Silver tassels for a palanqueen.
II Panian coats.
3 Palanqueen Pillow cases.
2 Remnant of Brampore Chintz.
I Escritoire.
3 Pairs of blue betillas and one piece of red.

In the large Chest.

3 Hats and I Bag Empty.
3 Pairs of sail cloth.
4 Pairs of Sandal wood curtains, for a cott.
I Remnant of coloured betillas.
I Brass mounted Sword and 2 Sword blades.
2 Silver hilted swords.
I Catty tea and 2 sword belts.
2 Bandeja's some old gold buttons.
I Pair of holster and I remnant of gold thread.
Tassels for a palanqueen.
I Saddle and furniture.
2 Hangers.
I Bulker for a palanquin
Some old brass.
2 Small pillows.
I Palampore.
I Clock.
I Quilt and curtains.
1 Telescope 2 Pillows.

In the Europe Chest.

5 Elbow and 22 other chairs.
I Couch and 3 round tables.
I Close stool.
I Palanquin with silver.
I Standing Escritoire.
I China Screen.
I Old Book press.
I Bamboo Screen.
3 Cotton Carpets.
I do.
Palanquin flags.
Covers of red cloth for planquin bedding.
I Pillow.
I Quiver and arrows.

In the Godown.

I China Escritorie with 18 Bottles of Bitters and 7 Bottles of Hungary water.
I Little Box with empty bottles.
I do. with wine glasses.
1 Basket of China ware.
4 Pairs of Irons.
2 Empty dram cases.
2 Large glasses for lamps.
2 do. for candle.
I Box with some pipes.
4 Pairs of Sandal wood.
10 Small iron guns I Pair of lead.
3 Glass lanterns, I basket of shoes,
I Jar of Sugar candy.
1½ do. of Sugar.
2 Small Jar of Sweetmeats.
Some Empty Jars &c.
4 Cots, I stool.

In the Godown.

3 strip's colours.
1 Tent marquees, and Tent walls.
3 Bengal Mats.
Boatsail.
2 Roundells.
Palanquin bedding and Pingeres.
1 Small Bundle of Bengal Candles.
Iron auning for a Boat.
1 Old Iron Saw.
2 Large Looking glasses.
1 Paper press.
1 Wig box with 3 Wigs.
1 Brass dutie.
10 Brass dish covers.
6 Candlesticks and 1 Pair of Snuffers.
6 Piepans 3 Copper Pots.
1 Frying pan.
3 Brass Lamps for the Ship.
1 Library of Books.
2 Travelling boxes.
1 Small Chest.
1 Cash Chest.
1 Physic box.
2 Small dram cases 1 with white flint bottles.

In the Godown.

2 Boxes to carry liquors &c.
2 Painted boxes.
1 Hand Escritoire.
1 Old Palanquin and Bamboo.
1 Pennace and oars.
1 Teak Timber and 72 Spars.
2 Horses.
19 Geese.
33 Ducks.
6 Turkeys.
17 Hogs and pigs.
65 Goats and kids.
44 Cows, calves and Oxen.
6 Guns.
3 Bales Longcloth ordinary No. 2. qt. 4-10 F.
2 Chest Goa Arrack.
30 Bottles of Claret.
20 do of Palm wine in pints.
40 do of Madeira.
30 do of Reniah.
4 do of Soye.
52 do of Small beer.
½ of carboy of double distilled Arrack.
2 Empty Arrack cases.

Our next extract is very striking and suggestive. It seems that on the death of the Chaplain, two lay servants of the Company were appointed to perform his office, and divided the salary between them. The following entry fully illustrates the practice.

"Monday, 12th February, 1728. Upon the occasion of the death of the Rev. Mr. Wm. Leeke our Chaplain, who died on Friday last, it was agreed in order for keeping up the worship of Almighty God, that Messrs. Randall Fowke, and George Torriano, do perform Divine Service in the Church; and that prayers be read twice on Sundays, with a sermon in the morning, and also prayers on Wednesdays and Fridays in the forenoon; for which they are to receive £50 a piece salary, being equivalent to what is allowed one Chaplain."

The following entry, refers to home news.

"Saturday, 9th March, 1728. General letter from the President and Council of Bombay, dated the 23rd January, giving an account of the death of His late Majesty King George, and the accession of his son the Prince of Wales to the throne.

"Having immediately on receipt of these advices fired one hundred guns on account of the King's death, and one hundred and one for his present Majesty's accession:—It is agreed that we do on Saturday, the 16th instant, proclaim him with the greatest solemnity, by the name of George the Second; and that on occasion of the death of King George the First, this Board will go in mourning for three months."

An event occurred at this time which is curious as showing the relations between the Government of Madras and the Rajah of Travancore. The story occupies some space in the records, but can be told in a few words. Sunka Rama, one of the Company's merchants, had presumed to trade for pepper within the kingdom of Attinga; whereupon Mr. Alexander Orme, Chief of the English Factory at Anjengo, and father of Robert Orme the historian, seized a quantity of Cotton lying at Anjengo, which belonged to the said Sunka Rama. In this predicament Sunka Rama appealed to the Rajah of Travancore, and the Rajah in his behalf laid claim to the cotton. The proceedings of the Council of Anjengo were approved by the Government of Bombay; but the Directors at home decided in favour of Sunka Rama. Accordingly, as it appeared that the Rajah was indebted to the Company, the matter was settled by carrying the amount claimed by the Rajah to his credit in the accounts, and leaving Sunka Rama to obtain the same from the Rajah. Sunka Rama however was severely blamed for appealing to the justice of a country government in a matter entirely between himself and his employers.

Our next extract simply illustrates the character of Governor Macrae as a "canny Scot."

"Monday, 17th June, 1728. The President observing to the Board that the Company have several anchors and guns lying here, which are too large for the use of any of our shipping at this time, and which have lain for several years exposed to rust and spoil for want of demand; told them that he is willing to take a parcel of them to send to Manilla, provided he can have them at a reasonable rate, and that the company will take them back again, provided he cannot sell them their; which last condition he expected, because that not knowing whether they would sell or not at Manilla, he thought it was sufficient for him to risk the money without being obliged, in case they would not sell, to have the goods lie upon his hands; and that should the Company take them back, it would be only the same thing as if he had never received them, and they had laid here all the time.

"This proposal being considered, it was agreed that it tended manifestly to the Company's advantage, and therefore that it be accepted; and that the Store keeper do deliver the President as many of those large guns and anchors as he will take;

he paying for the same four pagodas for the achors and one Pagoda and seven-eighths for the guns.'

About this period a difficulty arose between the Government of Madras, and the French Government at the Mauritius, which is worthy of notice, though the original record is far too long for publication. On the 15th of October, 1727, the brigantine "Amity," under the command of Captain John Widdrington, left Madras on a trading voyage to the coast of Africa, having on board a proper pass signed by Governor Macrae. On the way Captain Widdrington touched at Port Louis in the Mauritius for a supply of provisions and water; and the French Governor M. St. Martin, having first examined his pass, permitted him to stay and obtain what he required, but strictly enjoined him not to dispose of any merchandize to the inhabitants of the Islands. At the same time a ship belonging to the French Company, called the "Expedition," under the command of Captain Marcay, was anchored at Port Louis; and this French Captain went on board the "Amity," and obtained a few trifles for himself and Officers, which could not come under the name of merchandize, and which only amounted to some thirty or forty dollars. It would seem however that this proceeding was only a ruse on the part of Captain Marcay of the "Expedition," to obtain possession of the "Amity." The story of the trading was carried to Governor St. Martin, who at once sent a guard on board the "Amity;" but Captain Widdrington explained the matter to his satisfaction, and he permitted the "Amity" to proceed on her voyage. Captain Widdrington then weighed anchor and was steering out of the harbour, when the "Expedition" fired a shot at the "Amity." As the two nations were at peace, Captain Widdrington could not understand the reason of the shot, and sent a boat to enquire; but Captain Marcay not only detained the boat, but sent some of his officers in a long boat to the "Amity," ordering Captain Widdrington to accompany the "Expedition" in a voyage to Bourbon. The latter was compelled to submit, and on arriving at St. Paul in Bourbon, sent in his protest to the Governor M. Dumas. The Government of Bourbon however seized the vessel, on the ground that he had been trading; and even disputed Governor Macrae's pass, on the ground that it exhibited two different kinds of handwriting; the body of the pass having been written by the Secretary, whilst the name of the ship and the Captain, and the signature at the foot, were in the handwriting of Governor Macrae. The result was that the "Amity" was detained at Bourbon, and her goods taken out; but subsequently, on the arrival of the French ships from Pondicherry on their way to Europe, the whole matter was again made the subject of inquiry. The result was that Captain Marcay was dismissed from the command of the "Expedition," whilst the "Amity" was permitted to return to Madras. The owners of the "Amity" resident at Madras, then represented the affair to Governor Macrae, and the complaint was forwarded to the Governor of Pondicherry; but the matter was delayed for some years, and appears to have been quietly suffered to drop.

About the same time an extraordinary outrage was perpetrated by an English Captain on board a ship belonging to one of the Company's servants. Some Patan merchants at Madras had freighted some goods on board the ship, and sent some of their servants in charge. The ship however was wrecked, and the Captain seems to have embezzled their goods, and endeavoured to get the servants out of the way. Accordingly the Patan merchants sent in their complaint to Governor Macrae. We give the petition at length. It is dated 22nd July, 1728.

"The humble petition of Sheik Mahmud Ameen, and merchants of Fort St. George,

"Sheweth,

"That your petitioners did freight on ship "James," belonging to Mr. George Torriano, a quantity of rupees, coral, rubies of different sorts, false pearl, chank, and other goods; which ship "James" on the 24th April 1728 struck on a sand bank. About two hours after the ship struck, the Captain, by name Charles Bissell, and the Chief Mate, with the Serang and Tindal, consulted together, and went under the decks and brought up some of our chests, with a design to take out the money; from which action, your petitioners' servants endeavouring to stop them, they wounded one of our people and took all the treasure, coral, pearl, &c., and put them in their own chests; at which your petitioners' servants being very discontented, and still persisting to hinder such practices, the Captain bid them not fear any thing, for that he would return their goods and money when he came ashore. The Captain went into his pinnace, with one servant and four Lascars, and carried with them a chest, two jars, and a compass, and was getting sail for Calcutta, when your petitioners' servants desired to go with him; to whom he answered he would send some sloops down as soon as possible. Three days after they made three rafts of timber, one of which was in bad case and very weak, on which the Chief Mate ordered our servants, who refused and desired to go with them; upon which they put our servants on that raft by force, and in their sight the Chief Mate, Serang, and some Lascars took the treasure and other goods, and put them in the pinnace; and put some Lascars in another small boat according to the Captain's direction, and went away with them to Hajeily in a small time; they being well provided with Oars. But your petitioners did not arrive off Sunderbund Wood till four in the evening, where they rowed backward and forward for six days; with which labour and want of provisions three of the people died; when it was their good fortune to find a vessel that was wooding, where they got some provisions and went on her to Calcutta; where hearing the Captain was arrived, your petitioners' servants went and demanded their goods and money; and received answers from the Captain that the pinnace was overset, and that all was lost. But after a long debate he brought out the rubies, which your petitioners' had packed in a chest of treasure, and said that was all that was saved of ours; when your petitioners' servants demanded to know where was the money that these stones were packed with; when after a great deal of trouble the said Captain also produced the chest of false pearl, and bid your petitioners take that, and give him the bill of lading and a discharge, which he demanded with force and threatening. Therefore your petitioners' servants, not being able to argue with the Captain, they sent one of them here; and as your petitioners have left the Moguls, which is their native country, we have now no other remedy, nor other justice to apply to but your Honors; and as we have lived well under this Government for 30 years, and have never had reason to complain, but have always found its justice bright as the sun beams, so we hope still for justice from your Honor; for that we with great confidence paid the freight of those goods, before we put them on board, to Mr. George Torriano, who is the owner of the said ship; and we doubt not but when your Honors in justice shall examine this affair, we shall recover our money, when we shall go on happily, and for ever pray for your Honors' long life, great happiness and abundant riches."

The foregoing petition was forwarded by Governor Macrae to the English Government at Calcutta, with a request that the Governor and Council there would enquire into the affair. The result is not recorded.

Another petition delivered in at this time to Governor Macrae is interesting as illustrating the way in which the trade was carried on in the olden time. It was presented by the Renter or farmer of the Paddy Fields, and complains that the inhabitants of Trivatore, Tandore, and neighbouring villages, make and export great quantities of salt, contrary to his supposed privileges. We give the petition at length.

" The humble petition of Coolecherla Veahsum Brahmin,

" Sheweth,

That a certain tract of land belonging to the Company, lying out from Tom Clark's Gate up to the Batteries, together with another tract lying along the river from Coomerapollum towards Trivatore, commonly known by the name of the Company's paddy fields, were formerly rented at 40 pagodas per annum. But when the cowle was out in Governor Harrison's time, he being desirous of raising the Company's revenue, put it up at out-cry, and promised that the highest bidder should be permitted to wear a Roundel as a mark of distinction for his endeavours to serve the Company. With which great honour, my Uncle Paupa Brahmin, being extremely encouraged, gave as far as seven hundred and ten pagodas per annum for what formerly let at only 40 ; and this for only ten years, though he knew he must lose a great deal by it, and in fact he has lost every year near 300 pagodas per annum. For payment of his debts contracted by this means, I have mortgaged my houses, gardens, etc. ; and now all in me and my father's debts, contracted on this account, amount to upwards of 2,000 pagodas.

" Now your petitioner humbly begs leave to represent to your Honors that, although the Cowle is given for lands called paddy fields, yet a very small part thereof is fit for that use, and therefore the rest hath for many years been converted into Salt pans; and by the profit arising therefrom, your petitioner and his father have hitherto been enabled to pay the annual rent; till within this little time that several persons have presumed to make salt in the Company's Bounds, and bring it into Town, and also to ship it off, to the great prejudice of your petitioner, who by giving so large a rent cannot be supposed to be able to sell so cheap as those people who pay nothing for this liberty. Nor is this all, for they even buy salt from the Moors and import it into the Company's Bounds; by which undue practices your petitioner is prevented selling his salt, and is therefore unable to pay his rent without your Honors will give him immediate redress.

"Your Petitioner doth not pretend to infringe the liberty which the inhabitants of Tandoor, Trivatore, &c. have formerly, enjoyed; but only hopes your Honors will restrain them from encroaching on his undoubted rights.

"They formerly had five pits in those parts, where they made salt, and had the privilege of selling to the country people, who brought a few oxen to carry it away; and sometimes, having first obtained leave from the Farmer of the paddy fields, would load five or ten garce of salt on board of boats; but they were never permitted more. Of late they have neglected to ask leave of me, and by the great quantities of salt they have shipped off to boats and ships, and by underselling me, they have been encouraged to increase the number of their salt pans, by which means I have now upwards of 600 garce of salt which I cannot dispose of.

"I am therefore humbly to request your Honors that you will please to order, that no body may be permitted to load any salt within the Company's Bounds, or bring it into town for sale, without leave from me; or else it will be impossible for me to continue to pay the large rent I now do.

"I am also to request that the Pedda Naick may be obliged to keep a watch over my salt, as he did in my father's time, but hath since neglected; and by that means I have lost great quantities, for which I humbly hope your Honors will please to oblige him to make satisfaction.

"And since the only inducement to my father's giving so large a rent for these grounds was the token of honour given him, I promise myself your Honors will allow me to wear the Roundel as he did, if I still pay the great rent he did.

"All these particulars are most humbly submitted to your Honor's clemency, on which your petitioner most humbly depends for ease in these his hard circumstances, and as in duty bound shall ever pray."

In reply to this petition Governor Macrae ordered "that a Committee, consisting of Major Roach, Mr. Hyde, and the Secretary, do enquire into the several allegations, and into the ancient privileges of the inhabitants of those towns." The result is thus recorded.

"Thursday, 28th September, 1728. The Committee appointed to inspect into the rights which the inhabitants of Tandore, Trivatore, etc. have to make salt, deliver in their report, by which it appears that they have equal rights with the farmers of the paddy fields. It was therefore agreed that we cannot take the liberty from them; and as Veashum Brahmin without that cannot pay his rent, for which he is now considerably behind hand, and Poncola Kistna, the Renter of Tandore and the other villages, being willing to take the Cowle of the Paddy Fields at the old rent,—it was agreed to take it away from Veashum Brahmin, who is not able to pay the rent of it, and to grant it to Poncola Kistna."

Our next extract explains itself.

"Thursday, 28th November, 1728. The tobacco and beetle Farmer, complaining that several persons have lately run into the Bounds great quantities of beetle and tobacco to his great prejudice, and praying some stop may be put thereto;—It was agreed that we do publish an order at the sea gate, that whatsoever Conacopillay, Dubash, or other substantial person is found to run into the Bounds any quantity of tobacco or beetle, or to encourage others to do it, shall be fined one pagoda for every fanam's worth so run, and to be in prison till it be paid: and that all coolies, and other poor people, who shall be convicted of the like practices, shall be publicly whipped at the choultry, and receive thirty nine lashes, and stand one hour in the pillory."

CHAPTER XXXVII.

GOVERNORSHIP OF MR. JAMES MACRAE.

1729—30.

The Government of Mr. Macrae was now drawing to a close. In May 1730 he retired from the President's chair, and his place was taken by Mr. George Morton Pitt. Accordingly the present chapter will contain the annals of the last years of his administration; whilst the next chapter will contain a supplementary account of the events which transpired between Mr. Macrae's resignation and his departure from the Presidency; together with some particulars connected with his subsequent life in England which will be interesting as general illustrations of the time.

Our first extract is curious as showing how utterly unable our forefathers were to apprehend and appreciate the first principles of free trade. The entry speaks for itself.

"Monday, 3rd February, 1729. There having been imported this year pretty large quantities of grain from the Northward, notwithstanding which the price holds up at ten maracals per pagoda for paddy, and scarce any procurable even at that rate, especially for the poorer sort of people. The President proposed to the Board to take into their consideration the settling of the prices of grain for the ensuing season; and after some time spent in considering thereon, it was agreed and ordered that the prices of grain be as follow.

Paddy Coarse......	13	Maracals for a	pagoda.
Paddy Fine.........	12	do.	do.
Natcheny............	7	do.	do.
Rice...................	1¼	measure for a	fanam.

"Which prices the Secretary is ordered to affix at the gates with the following resolves, viz. That whoever shall sell at a dearer rate than above specified, shall upon proof thereof made be fined at the pleasure of the Governor and Council; and that the person who shall make proof of his having paid more than the above prices, shall have his money returned him, and shall also keep the grain he has purchased to himself; and that whoever has more rice or paddy that is necessary for his usual annual expense, shall be obliged to sell; and whoever shall deny or conceal such overplus, upon proof thereof made, it shall be confiscated to the use of the Company. Ordered that the above be also signified by beating the tom tom."

We now come to the mysterious affair which served to throw such discredit on Major Roach. We give the petitions to the Madras Government at full length as illustrations of the times; and indeed the energetic language of the petitioners is well worthy of preservation as a combination of invective, indignation, threat, and argument which is rarely to be found even in the most impassioned novel. The petitions will explain themselves. The first is from the ostensible father of the young lady.

"The humble petition of Sebastian Texeira DeBritto.

"Showeth,

That your petitioner, who is an inhabitant of the city, did in the month of July last embark on ship "Arcot" for Manilla, and left a maiden daughter of the age of nineteen years in St. Thomé, under the care of Mrs. Maria Elveira, to remain with her till your petitioner's return; as your petitioner hath often done when going on the like voyages. Being now returned, your petitioner received the melancholy notice that the aforesaid child was missing from the said house on Friday the 14th February last, at past twelve at night; and for her there was ready at the seaside a palanqueen and several peons, which conducted the same into this city, as was found in about eight days after this insult done. Whereupon the Rev. Padre Thomas went to the house of Major John Roach, as one of the Justices of Peace in this city, and represented to him the said insult and dishonor done to the people in general; and craved that for his sake and credit he would cause enquiry to be made where the said child was, and who it was that had done this injustice. To which the said Major Roach answered there was no occasion for so much trouble; that he knew where she was, and if he pleased could produce her; and further said that the said child was not the daughter of your petitioner, but of Mr. Robert

Raworth,* and that she is now under his protection, and that he will give her five or six hundred pagodas in marriage; and that it appertaineth unto him to do that justice, for that he hath a power of Attorney to that purpose from Mr. John Raworth, and that also the child requested it of him; and further told the said Padre Thomas that he might acquaint the gentlemen of St. Thomé with this answer; that it now belonged to him to take care of and maintain the said child, and that he would have them pretend no further in this affair.

"To consider the foregoing particulars, it will appear that Major Roach was the inducer and cause of taking away the said child from the house wherein your petitioner had placed her; and the following reason will prove that the said child is not the daughter of Mr. Robert Raworth. For that the mother of the said child left this city, and went to St. Thomé more than fifteen months before her delivery of this child; the said Mr. Raworth left India for France in the year 1714, and the said child was then aged five years; and to this time what care did the said Mr. Robert Raworth ever take of the said child? Did he ever demand her? did he ever give her any subsistance? or what charge hath he been at

* Mr. Raworth was the refractory Deputy Governor of Fort St. David, who gave so much trouble to Governor Harrison. If the young lady was his child at all, she was probably the offspring of an illicit amour. The only particulars recorded concerning her, are however to be found in the entries published above.

for her maintenance? which he might well have done in the posts and power he bore in India. The said Robert Raworth's brother, John Raworth, also arrived from Europe, and stayed in India some years. What did he ever do for the child? or did he once demand her? As neither of the brothers ever did in any manner lay claim to the child, nor do any thing for her when so young, and they in these parts, it seems very unlikely that at this distance there should now come a power and letter of Attorney, as is alleged, by Major Roach, to this end; and if it was so, before what justice did he present or show such letter or power, as he ought to have done, and not to have been a Judge in his own cause. Well might Major Roach say to the Rev. Padre Thomas that he knew where the said child was, and that he could produce her; for it is notorious that he received her at his house, when she came at that time of night from St. Thomé; and seems rather that he was the taker of her; for how is it possible that a child, brought up in the close manner as is customary to bring up children of the Portuguese in India, without any acquaintance or knowledge of the world, with so much resolution and courage to go out at that time of night, and directly to get a palanqueen and peons to conduct her to Madras. It is plain, and evident to be seen, that some person might have seduced her by flattery or other means, to pass such an excess of shame and scandal. Neither is it to be believed that the child on her own head should so leave the house, and go directly to Major Roach, as a Justice of Peace, to complain of oppression received. Neither at those hours does it seem good for any Justice of Peace, so much to prejudice the honour of a maiden, as to receive her in his house; but rather for a good example, and to preserve her honour, would have sent her to some creditable house till the morning, or till he could have had an opportunity to acquaint the Governor of the affair; who, as Chief Justice, ought to have been so acquainted. Instead of which, Major Roach kept, and still doth continue to keep the said child in his house, to her great scandal and dishonour, and without the fear of any man, under pretence of being under his protection, and that he will give her in marriage. All which makes it appear plainly that Major Roach had induced the girl to leave the house, where she was placed by your Petitioner; and what man that hath any regard to his honour, and not lost to shame, will marry a woman after this scandal to her reputation never to be taken off. Lastly, to what Major Roach says, that the child is not your Petitioner's daughter. It is a thing not in the power of any man to prove. Though so many years as she is old, she has been known to all people as the child of your Petitioner; and though if she actually denies that she is your Petitioner's child, and accompanies such denial with other scandalous and injurious language, who will believe a young woman lost in error, in fear of her reputation, and incited by others. Will she not say it, and will she not throw such scandal, and yet far greater, on those that gave her being. And if she was asked, if she ever heard her mother say that your Petitioner was not the father of her, or of her brothers, or sisters, your petitioner believes she will even say that too. But that cannot hide it from all the inhabitants of Madras and St. Thomé; for, as your Petitioner's children, they were baptized and educated; and if she and they were not the children of your Petitioner, he would scarce have brought them up with so much care and love, and at these years to pass so much fatigue and trouble and risk of life, to get them fortunes to set them forward in the world, and to give them in marriage. And as your Petitioner is an inhabitant of this city, and is subject to the laws thereof, so it is but reasonable to hope for and expect their protection, and in what more than for our children.

"Your Petitioner, therefore, prays your Honors to examine of this great injustice done by Major Roach to your Petitioner, and dishonour to your Petitioner's child; for as the said Major Roach is a Justice of the Peace of this city, and a member of the Council for the affairs of the Honorable Company, and Commander of the Military, he ought to suppress such proceedings; and not himself to be the actor, and cause of scandal and dishonour, to the discredit of his nation and of his colony. No Government in the world sure will suffer such usage, thereby to give occasion for the like proceedings in others, to be the destruction of the Republic. And as you are or all may be fathers, your petitioner again prays you will take this affair in due consideration; and reflect how severe a stroke this must be to a parent, and also the scandal that will attend the place where such usage is suffered."

The second petition was signed by the Portuguese Padre and inhabitants of St. Thomé, and is equally forcible with that of Sebastian Texiera De Britto. We give it at length.

"The few inhabitants of the ruined and poor city of St. Thomé, send this their most just complaint on occasion of the scandalous affair of Sebastian Texeira De Britto's daughter; who privately in the night went out of an honest house standing in St. Thomé, where her father, according to his constant custom, had left her; and the same night she was conducted to Major Roach's house, where she has now been for a month past. Those cautions not being sufficient (which were such as a father could use when, according to the custom of the Portuguese in India, he leaves the shore) in order to secure his child. It is supposed that promises were the means that broke down the walls of her retreat and modesty. An example which these inhabitants, though poor, never met with from the Moors themselves, who rule and governor here without control; and in reality it is injurious to the community, for in future there will be no house secure, however honest it may be. This excess having opened a way to many others, as if there was not justice to be found to punish actions so pernicious to the good and quiet of the public.

"Wherefore we request of the Honorable Governor and his Council, that they will find out some remedy for what is past, and to prevent such enormities in future; and also that an authentic copy of this complaint, and of the determination which shall be made thereon, may be transmitted to the Supreme Court of the Honorable Company; of which the said inhabitants of St. Thomé, where this injury was offered, will send another copy to be delivered them by the Envoy of Portugal in England; to the end that the said court may be informed of the conclusion of the affair, and confirm the same, in order to prevent the like accidents in future."

The proceedings of Governor Macrae and Council upon this extraordinary charge are thus briefly recorded.

"Wednesday, 19th March, 1729. Major John Roach gives in answer to the charge delivered him about the daughter of Sebastian Texeira, wherein he denies the contents of it absolutely, except the receiving the woman; which he confesses he did do, as believing it a part of his duty as a Justice of Peace; she coming to him and claiming protection; and he does acknowledge himself guilty of an indiscretion in not acquainting the Government of it, and submits himself to the censure of the Board for the same. Whereupon the Board came to the following resolution.

"That such actions manifestly tend to the disturbance of the public peace and good order of this settlement. Wherefore it was unanimously agreed that the Major, for his indiscreet conduct in this affair, be fined 300 pagodas into the Company's Cash; and that the woman presuming to come into this Government, under pretence of asking protection, without making her application in a regular manner, be advised by the Secretary, that she do not continue in our Bounds longer than Friday night next, under penalty of public punishment. This time is allowed her to try if she can be reconciled to her friends on account of her elopement."

The following notice closes the record of the transaction.

"Monday, 21st April, 1729. Major John Roach pays into cash three hundred pagodas, being the fine laid on him in consultation the nineteenth of last month."

A barbarous outrage committed about this period by the Arabs at Jedda, the seaport of Mecca, on the Red Sea, is worthy of record. Early in the year two ships, the "Margaret" and the "George," sailed from India for the Red Sea. The "Margaret" from Tellicherry arrived at Jedda after a voyage of sixty days on the 18th of March 1727. Mr. Hill, the Supercargo, was courteously received by the Bashaw, and met with all the encouragement he could expect in the sale of the cargo. About a month afterwards the "George" arrived at Jedda from Bengal, and a good understanding was preserved between the two ships. It so happened that the "George" had seven Arab Lascars on board, who managed to swim ashore at Jedda, but were arrested by the orders of the Bashaw, and put into prison; but were restored to the ship on the promise of the Captain not to punish them. On the sixth of June the

"Margaret" prepared to sail. Meantime several Lascars on both ships had died, and had been buried by their comrades according to the rites of the Mussulman religion in the little islands off Jedda. Unfortunately sufficient care had not been taken to cover the bodies with the earth; and the fishermen of the islands reported at Jedda that the Captain of the "George" had broken his word to the Bashaw, and put to death the Arab sailors who had been restored to his ship. On the 5th of June the Bashaw sent a special messenger on board the "George" to make enquiries, but none of the crew had any complaint to make. On the sixth of June, being the following day, the same messenger then went on board the "Margaret," and there found no complaints; but chanced to espy the body of a Lascar who had died in the night, and who the crew were preparing to bury. He immediately left the ship and made threatening gestures from his boat. At this time Mr. Hill the Supercargo was ashore with a few other Europeans, whilst the Captain of the "Margaret" was on board preparing to set sail. Shortly afterwards Mr. Hill dispatched orders for the body of the Lascar to be sent on shore wrapped in cloth. The order was obeyed, but by some accident the corpse was exposed to the view of the people. The mob of fanatics, as excitable then as they are now, at once rose and massacred Mr. Hill and all the Europeans with him. Nothing of this was known on board the ships until some boats arrived from the Bashaw, ostensibly to preserve the ships from the fury of the mob. The matter terminated in the detention of the two ships for a period of ten months, whilst the Captains were kept close prisoners on shore, and also were compelled to make large advances to their crews of Lascars. At length the dragoman of Mr. Staman, the British Ambassador at Constantinople, arrived at Jedda, and solicited their discharge; and though the Zerrif came from Mecca and did his utmost to oppose the departure of the English ships, the Bashaw finally gave way, and in July 1728, the "Margaret" reached Madras. A formal complaint was laid before the Madras Government, but it does not appear that any further steps were taken in the matter beyond a representation to the authorities at home.

Our next extract refers to a curious coinage of pagodas with an alloy of iron; also to the issuing of Governor Macrae's order against the exportation of silver.

"Monday, 17th March, 1729. The Assay Master attending the Board and being called in, produced a bag of Madras pagodas, just coined out of some gold dust brought from Manilla; which having a mixture of iron melted down with it, it had made the coin though exactly alloyed, look of a dirty pale colour, and had made likewise the gold so brittle that the pagodas were very much cracked, and consequently ill stamped; which he told the Board he thought proper to acquaint them of, that he might receive their orders thereon before he let the remainder be coined. The said pagodas being compared with others just stamped, the difference was so great that the

Board unanimously agreed it would be a very great discredit to our coin to let them pass; and therefore resolved that the merchant should be obliged to refine the gold, and burn out the iron alloy before it was coined.

"The President reports a seizure of fifty-six and a half (56½) ounces of silver endeavoured to be run, which being produced was sold him at fourteen and a half dollars for ten pagodas, amounting to forty-three pagodas, twenty-eight fanams 43-28 the one-half of which is paid into the Company's cash and the other to the peon who seized it."

Governor Macrae appears to the last to have had considerable difficulty in dealing with the Company's Native merchants. The proceedings are so suggestive as to be worthy of record.

"Monday, 14th July, 1729. The President represented to the Board that, notwithstanding the indulgence given the merchants in February last, when it was agreed to give them till the first of September to complete the contract which should have been finished the 31st of January last: they had nevertheless been very backward in bringing cloth; and that unless some further measures are taken to oblige them to bring in cloth, he feared we should be very much disappointed in the quantity necessary for the dispatch of our ships. Which being debated, it was thought that possibly the indulging them with the broad cloth this year come and coming from Europe, might be a means to induce them to bring in goods, and accordingly the following terms were agreed to be proposed to them, viz.

"That they should provide and deliver seventeen hundred bales of calicoes on or before the 20th of January next; in consequence of which they should have the broad cloth at thirty-five per cent. on the invoice price. But if they did not comply and deliver the said seventeen hundred bales, that then they should pay ten per cent. more for the broad cloth; and that the old penalty should be forgiven them if they complied with this contract; in order to do which the better they should be advanced fifteen thousand pagodas without interest till the 20th January next.

"The merchants were hereupon called in, and the above proposals offered them; which they refused alleging that the great drought in the country, and dearness of cotton, made it very difficult to provide cloth, and that therefore they could not comply therewith.

"Whereupon they were told it was a favour to them that was designed thereby; that they had incurred a penalty of near twenty thousand pagodas by their non-compliance with the last contract; that there were now due on that contract fourteen hundred bales not yet delivered in by them; so that the seventeen hundred now proposed to be provided by them was only three hundred more than they were obliged to by their old contract; and that in consideration thereof, they were to be indulged with all the Company's broad cloth:—but these arguments not prevailing, the Board came to no conclusion with them."

"Monday, 21st July, 1729. The Company's merchants being again called in and asked whether they had considered of the offers made them the last consultation day, and would sign a contract on those terms, still urged the difficulties of providing cloth, the scarcity and famine and dearness of cotton, which made the weavers turn their hands to other work and retire into other countries where grain was to be got. Which arguments they insisted on so strenuously, that the Board came to no agreement with them, and therefore dismissed them; with an assurance that they would sell the broad cloth at outcry, and insist on the performance of the last contract, or penalty due for the breach thereof."

"Thursday, 31st July, 1729. This day the Company's Merchants being again called in; and a contract for seventeen hundred bales again proposed to them, it was at last agreed on the following terms.

"That they be advanced fifteen thousand pagodas without interest till the 30th January next; that the penalty of the last contract be wholly forgiven them, and nothing more demanded of them on that account; that they have all the Company's broad cloth at thirty five per cent; and that they shall pay twenty per cent, on the value of all the bales which they shall deliver short of seventeen hundred bales by the 20th of January. Accordingly a contract being drawn out on those conditions, was mutually signed, and the money ordered to be paid them to-morrow morning."

The following entries referring to the changes in the administration of justice are worthy of preservation.

"Monday, 21st July, 1729. Our Honorable Masters having disapproved of the Sheriff's Court, it is agreed that it be no longer continued, and that the Justices sit weekly at the Choultry for punishing of petty offences which are daily committed in the Town, and which are of too trivial a nature to be brought before the Quarter-Sessions, and that the Paymaster do make a pair of stocks.

"Thursday, 7th August, 1729. General letter from the Deputy Governor and Council of Fort St. David, read, desiring, we will give them instructions how to prevent the great inconveniences which will arise by their inhabitants being obliged to come up to Madras to get their disputes determined by our Mayor's Court.

Agreed that we write them, when such do arise to persuade their inhabitants to go to arbitration before the heads of their castes."

The one great fault of Governor Macrae, and a fault common with most men of his calibre, was an arbitrary mode of settling matters which by no means met with the approbation of the Directors. His violation of the principles of free trade were only so many instances of this arbitrary conduct; and were productive of evils, all of which will be unfolded in due time. The rule against the exportation of silver caused much dissatisfaction to the inhabitants, and was abrogated by an order from the Directors; whilst he himself found it necessary to repeal his own absurd regulations respecting a fixed price for grain. These events are duly recorded below; but in another chapter we shall have occasion to allude to far greater evils which arose from the Governor's arbitrary measures.

"Monday, 25th August, 1729. The Board taking into consideration the purport of the last general letter,—it is agreed that the Secretary do give public notice, that the inhabitants and others are at liberty to carry their silver into the country uncoined, and that the prohibition be taken off.

"Upon this occasion the President remarked to the Board that there are several very severe aspersions thrown on him in this paragraph, as if the prohibition had been laid on for private advantage, and that he had connived at the breach of that order in such as made it worth his while; and he solemnly averred that he had never, directly or indirectly, carried, or permitted others to carry, any silver out of the bounds during the prohibition, except in rupees; and adding that it is necessary for him to clear his reputation, he demanded of them all to declare at the Board, whether they, directly or indirectly, know of any silver being carried out by him, or by others, by his authority and protection. To which every member of the Board answered, by declaring they knew, neither directly nor indirectly, of any such thing."

"Thursday, 25th September, 1729. Having in consultation of the 3rd February last, fixed the prices of paddy and rice, in order to relieve the poor; it hath been found by experience that the said regulation had not its desired effect: and the season for importing of grain now coming on, and there being reason to believe that if that regulation be continued great quantities will be carried to other places, which would else come hither, it is agreed to take off the said order and to permit every one to sell as they can."

Our next extract refer to the proving of the wills of Roman Catholics. It tells its own story.

"Friday, 16th October, 1729. There being some mistakes arisen from the orders this year received from our Honorable Masters, relating to proving wills in the Portuguese Church :—it is agreed that a note be affixed in the several languages at the Sea and Choultry Gates, and at the Portuguese Church, to explain the same ; and to give notice that any person of the Romish Communion is at liberty to take out Probates of wills, or letters of administration, in that church ; but that they are not compelled to do it. Also that by so doing they are not entitled to a right of using any subject of England, or other person who is not of that communion ; and that although the priests of that Church are allowed to grant such Probates, or letters of administration, to such as request the same of them ; yet that they have no authority to examine, or decide any controversy between man and man, or to do or execute any other judicial act whatsoever."

Our next extract is simply curious. It appears that the old Chaplains of the Company were generally bachelors, and that consequently the accommodation assigned them was sufficient perhaps for a single man, but insufficient for a family. The Rev. Thomas Consett, who came out about this time, proved to be a married man with a family ; and he accordingly prayed the Governor and

Council to allow him more accommodation. The letter is sufficiently quaint to be worth preservation.

" To the Honorable James Macrae, Esq.

" President and Governor, and the Council of Fort St. George.

" Honorable Sir and Sirs,

" The inconveniences of my habitation are too manifest to be represented, and your own apprehension of them at my first coming was the reason of the proposals you were then pleased to make of enlarging it. Time does not alter but lengthen the reason of doing this, and since it is my lot to come amongst you with a family, I entreat you will so far distinguish me from a bachelor, as to allow me a habitation somewhat larger for a number, than would strictly accommodate a single person. The consideration of our healths, besides the want of several necessary conveniences in these strait quarters, oblige me to make this request; otherwise would not presume to give you the trouble of this application and desire the necessity of it may excuse.

Your Honors,

Most obedient humble Servant,

FORT ST. GEORGE, 2nd December, 1729. } and Chaplain, THOMAS CONSETT."

We are sorry to add that though Mr. Consett's family had increased since his arrival at Fort St. George, the Government was unable to give him larger accommodation.

The following petition to Governor Macrae and Council will explain itself.

"The humble petition of the French Capuchin Missionaries.

"Sheweth,

"That your petitioners, who have the honour and happiness to be established in this city under the auspicious protection of the Honorable Company, and your most favourable Government, humbly request your Honors and the Gentlemen of Council's permission to rebuild the cells and apartments belonging to our church; they being very old and ready to fall; which we design to do after the model in Tuscany, answerable to that of your Hospital and Guard house. Your condescension to this will entail an everlasting obligation on

Honorable Sir and Sirs,

Your most obedient & obliged humble servants,

FORT ST. GEORGE, } F. THOMAS.
14*th* *February* 1730. } Cap. M. Assist.

The petition was granted.

The following entry is preserved, as it furnishes historical data, which may prove of importance.

"Monday, 2nd March, 1730. A general letter from the President and Council of Bombay, dated the 11th December, was read; advising that the British ambassador at Constantinople had sent to Bussorah an authentic copy of the capitulations betwixt England and the Port for regulating the commerce in the Turkish dominions; that Persia is threatened with fresh troubles, which, with the cruelties committed by the Governor of Ispahan, has put an entire stop to all manner of trade, and that Angria's son with his Grabs had taken "the William" an English ship belonging to Bombay."

We bring the two following entries together, for the sake of the illustrations they furnish of the mode of collecting the rent or revenue from the Company's out villages.

"Monday, 22nd December, 1729. The petition of the inhabitants and renters of Egmore and the other villages was read; setting forth that for want of rain the last year, they are unable to pay their rent; and request therefore to be charged no more than the paddy fields produce in that time.

"Ordered that as we think the cowle is let at a moderate rent, and will one year with another produce the renters a reasonable profit, that they comply with the conditions therein; but if they think the term of the cowle too hard that they have liberty to resign."

"Tuesday, 24th March, 1730. The petition of Poncola Kistna was read; setting forth that as he had been bound for the renters of Egmore and the other villages, he was obliged to see the payments duly made; and that the renters having made default for the last year's rent, he had accordingly paid the amount to the Company, and that one Ecambaram who had given him a bond of indemnity in behalf of the renters, now refuses to pay. Wherefore he desires the Board to do him justice in this particular, and oblige the said Ecambaram to pay him what he has already paid the Honorable Company on this account.

"As this money has now been due upwards of

nine months, and no satisfactory reason given for so long a delay,—ordered that Ecambaram and the renters be confined to the Choultry unless they will cause immediate payment. Mr. Peers (a member of Council) dissents to their being confined.

"The rent for Trivatore and the other villages having been also due several months,—ordered that the Secretary demand the same; and in case the renters do not comply to acquaint the Governor that he may confine them or otherwise as he thinks most proper."

Here the annals of Madras under the administration of Mr. James Macrae are brought to a close. Mr. Macrae however did not embark for England until the 21st of January 1731. During that interval some extraordinary charges of corruption and oppression were brought against his Dubash, Gooda Anoona, which will be duly discussed in our next chapter, and to which we shall add such particulars of the after life of Mr. Macrae in his native country which may prove interesting to the general reader.

CHAPTER XXXVIII.

LAST YEARS OF MR. JAMES MACRAE.

1730—46.

On Thursday the 14th May, 1730, George Morton Pitt, Esq., arrived from Fort St. David, and delivered a Commission which he had received from the Honorable Company, constituting him President and Governor of Fort St. George, and of all the Company's settlements on the coast of Coromandel, in the room of James Macrae, Esq.; and accordingly Mr. Macrae vacated the President's Chair, and Mr. Pitt was installed into his new Office with all respect and submission. On the following Tuesday the complaints against Gooda Anconah, the Chief Dubash of Mr. Macrae, were first taken into consideration by the Madras Government, as will be seen by the following entry in the consultations.

" Tuesday, 19th May, 1730. The President acquaints the Board that he has had several informations of complaint against Gooda Anconah, the late Governor's Chief Dubash; some of them of extortion, and other crimes of a very heinous nature; and as there is the greatest reason to believe that Gooda Anconah will seek protection of the Country Government, to avoid the course of justice, (as he did once before) if not immediately prevented by being taken into custody; he (the Governor) desires they will consult the properest measures to be taken on this occasion. Which being debated and considered, the Board are unanimously of opinion that, if Gooda Anconah should escape, it would be of the utmost ill consequence to the Company's affairs, a great disquiet and discouragement to the inhabitants of this place, and would unavoidably draw a censure on the vigilance and justice of this Board. Wherefore agree that the Justices immediately commit him to the custody of the Sheriff, to be kept in the Ensign's room in the Fort, with permission to go where he pleases to eat, but under a guard to prevent his escaping, till the complaint can be more regularly heard and examined into."

A few days afterwards complaints and petitions against Gooda Anconah poured in upon the Madras Government in one continuous stream; and from the latter end of May until the beginning of July, appear to have absorbed public attention. We give a few extracts from the records of this period, which will be sufficient to indicate the progress of affairs.

"Monday, 25th May, 1730. A letter from Mr. Macrae was read, requesting that Gooda Anconah might be allowed to come to him at the Garden house to settle some accounts; which the Sheriff being acquainted with, he represents that he cannot be answerable for so important a prisoner in such a place. Wherefore agreed that Mr. Macrae may send his Accountant or any other to Anconah;

and if he desires to be with him himself, that a convenient room in the Fort be appointed for their meeting.

"Sundry petitions of complaint against Gooda Anconah were delivered into the Board, and read as followeth, viz.

"From Sunkah Ramah and Tomby Chetty, Joint Stock Merchants, complaining that Gooda Anconah, Chief Dubash to the late Governor Mr. Macrae, having exercised an unlimited authority over the Black Town, had by force and other ill means extorted from them upwards of 3,700 pagodas at several times.

"From Muta Muten, Comra Collati, Mooteapah Chinaan, and Andachetty, setting forth that Gooda Anconah having sent with peons several sorts of grain, and lodged the same in the petitioner's houses, did afterwards by threats, menaces and confinement oblige them to pay for at most extravagant and extortionable prices; that amongst the many instances, they set forth particularly that the complainants, having contracted and given earnest for upwards of 90 garce of oil seeds at 40 pagodas per garce, the said Gooda Anconah, against the consent of both parties, obliged them to withdraw the said earnest, and did afterwards compel these petitioners to receive the same oil seeds at the rate of 68 pagodas per garce; a great part of which they have paid at the extortionable rate, and are now vexed and distressed at his suit for the remainder.

"From Margaparam Rangapah and Mootal Mar Chetty, setting forth that they having received

12,000 Rupees from and on account of their correspondents at Arcot, the same was forcibly seized by Gooda Anconah and his peons, and carried to the Governor's Gardens; and after keeping them sometime, he obliged these petitioners to sell them at 310 Rupees per hundred pagodas, although the current price was no more than 300 per hundred pagodas; whereby these petitioners lost not only the difference of that exchange, but also suffered in their credit, and their further trade obstructed by the fear of such practices.

"From Nina Chetty, Razapa Chetty, etc. Shroffs, setting forth that they had delivered a quantity of gold into the mint to be coined into pagodas; but that after some part had been coined, Gooda Anconah put a stop to the rest, giving for reason that Governor Macrae had a quantity of gold to dispose of, which these petitioners must buy before theirs should be coined. And notwithstanding they represented to him that they were then unable to buy so large a quantity, he continued with his peons to obstruct the mint servants for above a month, and at last obliged these petitioners to pay him 130 pagodas for his consent to have their gold coined.

"From the Brahmins, Goldsmiths, and Goldwashers of the mint, setting forth that Gooda Anconah, Chief Dubash to the late Governor, having exercised an illegal and arbitrary authority over the inhabitants of the Black Town, had greatly distressed them, and inflicted many grievous oppressions and hardships; that these petitioners in particular complain that Gooda Anconah had extorted from them upwards of 1,400 pagodas, to effect which he had punished them with long and painful imprisonments, and further inflicted many cruel and unnatural tortures, and by these means forced them to comply with other unfair demands to the ruin of themselves and families.

"From Nina Comra Chetty, Mooteapah, etc., Grain Merchants, setting forth that Mar Kistna Rao, a Brahmin and servant to Gooda Anconah, sent for Nina, one of these petitioners' partners, and ordered him to buy and measure out a parcel of rice; which he refused to do, knowing it would be charged at an extravagant rate. Mar Kistna Rao, gave him very abusive language, and struck him in the face, and threatened him with the anger of his master, Anconah, and by these means did compel the petitioners to take and pay for the said rice; that Mar Kistna Rao had extorted from these petitioners, by threats and menaces at several times, upwards of 300 pagodas; that the said Mar Kistna Rao had sent a quantity of paddy to these petitioners' houses, against their consent, and compelled them to pay 60 pagodas per garce for the same, when the market price was no more than 40 pagodas per garoe, with other acts of cruelty and extortion.

"The complainants in the several petitions being called in, it was recommended to them first, to apply for justice to the Mayor's Court; and if they should not be satisfied with the determination there, they might then apply to this Board and should have a rehearing.

"It being represented to the Board, that sundry reports are industriously spread to intimidate the inhabitants from complaining of the injuries received from Anconah, and others concerned with him; insinuating that they have still influence enough to hinder their complaints being heard, or if heard and determined they will after be reversed to the prejudice of the complainer. Wherefore to prevent any ill impressions from such scandalous insinuations, and to give peace and quiet to the minds of the people;—it is ordered that public notice be put up at the Sea gate, to acquaint the inhabitants they may apply to the Courts of Justice without any fear or apprehension; and be assured of a fair and candid hearing and suitable redress for the wrongs they have suffered, and that such determinations will not be revoked hereafter, but remain in full force for ever."

"Tuesday, 2nd June, 1730. Seven petitions of complaint against Gooda Anconah were read containing in substance as followeth. (We publish one only as a specimen of the whole.)

"From Gopal and Gruapah, Merchants, setting forth that they being entrusted with the sale of a diamond did accordingly dispose thereof to the best bidder; that Gooda Anconah hearing of this sale sent for these petitioners and demanded the diamond to be brought to him, but that not being in the power of these petitioners they were sent away under a guard of peons; that the next day they were carried to the Governor at his Garden house, where after a great many menaces and threats of the pillory, and being hanged, and such like punishments for daring to sell the stone to any but the Governor, it was proposed that these petitioners should pay 3,000 pagodas as a fine for this heinous crime. But these petitioners representing their poor condition and inability to pay such a sum, it was at length brought down to 1,000 pagodas; which sum they actually paid to the Governor. Besides which Anconah insisted on a gratuity for interposing with his good offices; otherwise, as he told these petitioners, they had surely lost their ears; that Gopal, one of these petitioners, carried 75 pagodas to Gooda Anconah on this account, but he not contented therewith ransacked his cloth and found about him a small diamond of more value, which he took from the said Gopal. That Gooda Anconah did also exact 50 pagodas on account of a diamond mortgaged to Ball Chetty, and by him to the Governor; and that after this these petitioners did again fall under the Governor's displeasure, and were confined to the Choultry prison; whence they could not be released till they had further paid to Gooda Anconah the sum of 150 pagodas, which sum he has within a few days past returned.

"All which petitions are referred to the Honorable the Mayor's Court."

The following petition with many others, are recorded in the consultations. It is impossible to publish the whole, but the following selections will suffice to illustrate the general character of the charges which were brought against this corrupt and tyrannical Native.

"The humble petition of Muta Muten, Comra Collati, Mooteapah Chinaan, and Anda Chetty.

"Sheweth,

That your petitioners have been sufferers upwards of 6,400 pagodas, by several parcels of rice, paddy, grain, natcheni, oil seeds, and other species of grain, which he the said Anconah, hath forcibly put upon your petitioners; sometimes by abusive language and threatenings to go to the Honorable Governor, and by some charge and complaint against your petitioners, whereby as he said your petitioners should be put in the pillory, lose their ears, and be whipped out of the Company's Bounds; sometimes harassing your petitioners with frequent messages and attendance upon him; and in case your petitioners not coming upon such summons, frequently hath he sent his peons Pooteah, Kistnamah, Veraugo, Raganaculoo, Sangomiah and others to haul and drag your petitioners by force from their families; and having expelled your petitioners, shut up their Shops and Warehouses, to prevent their trade and livelihood, till your petitioners should submit to his impositions. Many times have his servants compelled your petitioners to be in his Warehouses, wherein his grain was measuring, as if by consent; commanding the coolies to carry such and such parcels to such and such godowns belonging to your petitioners, where the coolies would by his order set it down before the door, and leave it to rapine and the weather; at the same time commanding your petitioners to take, buy and pay for such parcels thus forcibly thrown upon their hands; and upon non-compliance, or even endeavouring to put off the payment, the said Anconah and Mar Kistna, have beat, bruised, whipped, and confined your petitioners, not only within doors, but even uncovered in the sun till payment. Yea many times have they so done, even for refusing to receive some parcels of rice and oilseeds, though at the most exorbitant prices. If your petitioners scrupled to buy or take at such prices, giving for reason the order of consultation whereby all persons were forbid to buy or sell above such limited rates; and your petitioners then saying they were afraid that the Governor should hear of such bargains, and they be most justly and severely punished, he the said Ancona would laugh and put a scorn and contempt on the said order of consultation, saying who could tell the Governor of what he does? who dare to complain of the dearness of his rice? he always would stay by the Governor, and if your petitioners would take his rice at his price, they might sell it again without fear of persecution upon the said order of consultation.

"If it should be asked why your petitioners submitted to such severities? or wherefore did not your petitioners make a regular complaint of these things before? your petitioners must appeal to the knowledge of all men, how often they have complained of these things in a private manner; and should undoubtedly have been more ready to have done the same in the most public and solemn manner, had your petitioners any hopes of relief, or could they have been secure from the resentment and revenge of this great favorite of the then Governor's, whose authority and dread servitude were so deeply implanted in every man's heart, that your petitioner's complaints were only answered by a comparison of other the like facts upon other inhabitants. No one dared to council or advise your petitioners to complain; no one could flatter your petitioners with hopes of success. Many petitions have undoubted by this time convinced your Honors that the said Anconah hath so used the greatest of Merchants, that the best families in Town have occasion to murmur at his impositions. The Company's Covenanted Merchants confess they have felt his extortions and abuses; and so far were they from complaining, that they then thought it their interest to flatter the vanity, and soothe the licentious power of this favorite, by the most servile adulation and attendance upon him all hours in the day and night. The Company's sworn Measurers made their Court to him by false measurage and perjury. The Company's peons neglected their duty, and at his beck and word, harassed and watched over the confinement of such as were so unhappy as to be the objects of his passions. Every man in the street hath seen him publicly triumph over the sacred rights and distinctions of the Castes and sects; and made the very Churches his hoards to secrete grain under a pretence of charity, when in truth he brought forth the grain privily, and sold it at midnight for double the consultation price. These and many more public and private tokens are most convincing marks of his arbitrary sway over all men and all things in the Black Town,—your petitioners hope will be thought sufficient reasons for their passive acquiescence, and non-prosecution against a torrent of power during the administration of his Master the late Governor Macrae."

"Tuesday, 9th June 1730.

"The humble petition of Moomadue Chetty Tommiah,

"Showeth,

"That your Petitioner hath for many years been a considerable trader to this port in grain and other goods from the Northward; and having duly paid the Honorable Company's customs, and other usual port charges, always met with good usage and encouragement, till sometime in the month of March 1729, when some of your Petitioner's concerns arrived at this port under the care of two Gomastas,—one named Maurollee Juggoo, the other Strepaudum Nersia,—whom Gooda Anconah of this place, servant to the late Governor James Macrae, Esq., sent for by his peon Jangomiah, and demanded of them to deliver to him two garce of rice and two of paddy; which they endeavoured to evade, and assured him they were not the owners thereof, but only employed as servants to your Petitioner to dispose of the said goods; besides which all the rice and paddy they had in their possession was already contracted for and they could not sell it to any other person. At which refusal the said Gooda Anconah was in a great passion with your petitioner's servants; and after having threatened and abused, bid them in particular take care of to-morrow. In the morning the said Gooda Anconah went to his Master, the then Governor, and framed some complaint of what your Petitioner's servants knew not. But they were thereupon ordered to be beaten with a chawbuck five stripes at every Banksall; at the hearing of which Strepaudum Nersia made his escape, but the other Maurollee Juggoo underwent that punishment; of which when your Petitioner saw him a month after he was in great torment, and the pain thereof threw him into a flux and fever, of which he died the day after your Petitioner saw him. All the rest of your Petitioner's servants, whose duty it was to look after the Banksals, fled for fear; and left your Petitioner's goods exposed to rapine; by which your Petitioner lost near the value of one hundred and twenty pagodas, which was actually stole from your Petitioners Banksals at that time. The day after your Petitioner's servants had received the aforesaid punishment, Anconah sent for them again to his house, and asked them in an insulting manner, if they were not grown wiser, and whether they would comply with his demand. To which your Petitioner's servants could answer no other than that he might do his pleasure; and he thereupon sent Marcasaya with a maracal, who after his way caused to be measured one garce and twenty maracal of rice, and three hundred and sixty maracal of paddy, which with the over-measurage, was then worth to your Petitioners Pagodas 150, fanams 14, and cash 58. For payment of which sum, your Petitioner's servants often attended on the said Anconah, and at last received from him sixty pagodas; on the payment of which he insisted that they should sign a full discharge, which they accordingly did. By which matters afore related, it doth appear that, together with the interest now due thereon, your Petitioner is a sufferer by the said Gooda Anconah to the amount of Pagodas 229, fanams 30, and cash 58; and therefore prays your Honors will please to grant a general relief and,

Your Petitioners as in duty bound shall ever pray."

The following statements appear in the Consultations.

"Tuesday, 16th June, 1730. It being observed that in the petitions of the merchants dealing in grain, there is constant complaint made of undue measurage; although there is an officer particularly appointed for that purpose, and sworn to do justice. Wherefore the Town Measurer was called for, and being examined on this head he acknowledges that of late there has not been justice done to the merchants in measuring their grain; for that Gooda Anconah gave him orders always to take over measurage; and that he represented to Anconah the ill-consequences of such a practice, but that he bid the Measurer do it, and Anconah would take the ill-consequences upon himself. That in pursuance to his orders he used sometimes to take more but never less than 40 maracals in every garce he measured for Anconah of grain, seeds, &c.; the quantity of which he says to the best of his knowledge amounts to six or seven hundred garce; but says when the same grain seeds, &c. were delivered again to others, he did not make any allowance but struck the maracals to even measure. He further saith that Anconah's peons locked up the Company's maracals, so that none could measure but as he pleased; and that they customarily measured the grain all the day, and in the night time carried it away; that after the Company's order for selling 12 maracals of paddy for a pagoda, the poor people could get none in the bazar, it being all carried to Anconah's Godowns, and sold in the night sometimes for 90 pagodas per garce."

"Saturday, 20th June, 1730. Petition of Jellapilla Naugonah, setting forth that in the year 1720 Gooda Anconah, intending to go up in the country, delivered to this petitioner a considerable sum of money to remain with him at interest; and also left with him a bond payable by Mar Kistnah. That during Gooda Anconah's absence, the petitioner paid to his order the whole amount of the money so entrusted; and that the bond from Mar Kistnah was not nor could be recovered. That after Anconah was settled in the service of Governor Macrae, he sent for the petitioner and told him that what money had been paid to his order was of no signification, and that he should be further accountable for the bond of Mar Kistnah's for 1500 pagodas; and that he did, by confining the petitioner and his whole family near 3 months, oblige him to give bonds to the amount of 3,500 pagodas. That sometime after, in consequence of these bonds being for 2000 pagodas, he was again kept a prisoner, till by selling his houses, and other means, he raised and paid the sum of 2,230; and that being again confined, Gooda Anconah obliged him to give further bond for 2000 pagodas, in lieu of the other as forcibly obtained for 1500 pagodas."

"Friday, 10th July, 1730. Two petitions of complaint against Gooda Anconah were read viz.:

"From Poncola Kistnah and Com Chetty, late renters of the beetle and tobacco farm; setting forth that during the time these petitioners rented said farm, Gooda Anconah, servant to the late Governors James Macrae, Esq., did send for and demand of them several sums of money, as well as large quantities of beetle and tobacco, which were delivered according to his order, and amount in value to pagodas 3668 and fanams 5. For payment of which sum they have several times made application to Gooda Anconah, but without effect, and they now seek redress at this Board.

"From Juddooram, setting forth that Cosheram, a Guzerat Merchant, having adopted this petitioner for his son, did in his last will and testament bequeath his effects to this petitioner; and at his decease was put in possesion thereof. That some time after, Gooda Anconah, servant to the late Governor, sent for this petition; and after many menaces and threats to dispossess this petitioner, sent him to the Choultry prison, where he was confined for three days; and being released upon bail, Gooda Anconah demanded of him the sum of two thousand pagodas to let the petitioner enjoy the said effects, under pretence that he was not the lawful heir. Which sum being denied, he fell to one thousand five hundred and at last to seven hundred pagodas; which sum the petitioner paid him, being in dread of his power. But the same being an unjust demand and illegally and arbitrarily extorted, humbly prays redress.

"Ordered that the petitioners be referred to the Honorable the Mayor's Court."

Such was the general tenor of the petitions against Gooda Ancoonah, all of which were referred to the Mayor's Court. By the 16th of July, Gooda Ancoonah had been fined 20,000 Pagodas, whilst many demands against him still remained unsettled. How far Governor Macrae was implicated in these transactions, it is impossible to say; but there does not appear to have been any direct charges brought against him personally, and there was no such investigation into his conduct of affairs, as had taken place after the retirement of previous Governors. The subsequent entries respecting Mr. Macrae are very meagre and unimportant. In August the same year (1730) we find that he was allowed a hundred and fifty pagodas a month for his table expenses; and in the following January we meet with the following entry, dated only two days before Mr. Macrae embarked for England.

"Tuesday, 19th January, 1731. A letter from James Macrae, Esq., acquainting that he could not invest his money in diamonds without a manifest loss; and Bills not being procurable, he was obliged to carry it home in current pagodas; 25,000 of which he desires to lade on the "Craggs," and 25,000 more on the "Fordwich." He also desired that the freight and custom may be left to the Company's determination:—which is agreed to, and a letter being wrote to the Honorable

Court of Directors to advise thereof, was read and signed."

On the 21st January, 1731, Governor Macrae set sail for England, after an absence of some forty years. Without a wife, and without of course any legitimate child, he appears to have returned to his native land, laden with a fortune popularly estimated at above a hundred thousand pounds. According to a tradition published a few years back in the "Ayrshire Observer," the vessel in which Mr. Macrae returned to England, was captured on its way by a privateer; and the shrewd ex-Governor, knowing the vessel to have on board a valuable cargo of diamonds, had the address to get the ship ransomed for a comparatively small sum. We are also told by the same authority that the East India Directors were so pleased with the Governor's conduct in India, that on his return they enquired how they could reward him. He is said to have replied that if he had done anything meritorious, he would leave the reward to them. We have not however succeeded in discovering what was the value of the reward conferred on the ex-Governor, or if indeed any pecuniary reward were conferred at all. The story in itself is quite in keeping with the character of Mr. Macrae. In the matter of his allowance for table expenses already noticed, it is recorded that Governor Pitt had frequently desired his predecessor to give in some account of his expenses, but that Mr. Macrae declined doing anything of the sort, and left the Board to allow him whatever they thought proper.

On Mr. Macrae's arrival in England, his first object appears to have been to enquire about the fortunes of his family. It seems that his mother had been dead some years, and that his sister, who was still living at Ayr, had married a man named MacGuire, who gained a livelihood partly as a carpenter and partly as a fiddler at kirns and weddings. Mr. Macrae accordingly wrote to his sister at Ayr, enclosing a large sum of money, and engaging to provide handsomely for herself and family. The surprise of Mr. and Mrs. MacGuire was of course unbounded; and they are said to have given way to their delight by indulging in a luxury which will serve to illustrate both their ideas of happiness, and the state of poverty in which they had been living. They procured a loaf of sugar and a bottle of brandy; and scooping out a hole in the sugar loaf, they poured in the brandy, and supped up the sweetened spirit with spoons, until the excess of felicity compelled them to close their eyes in peaceful slumber.

The grand object which Mr. Macrae appears to have had in view during the remaining years of his life, was the elevation of his sister's family, the four daughters of Mr. and Mrs. MacGuire.* The eldest married Mr. Charles Dalrymple, who was Sheriff Clerk of Ayr, and received the estate of Orangefield. The tradition is still preserved of a large box of tea, a great rarity at that time, having been presented to Mrs. Dalrymple by Governor

* The information here given has been derived from descendants or connexions of the family who are still living.

Macrae; and this box proved so large that the doors at Orangfield would not admit it, and it became necessary to haul it up on the outside for admission at a large window. This box strongly bound with brass is still in existence, and is used as a corn chest by Dr. Whitehouse of Ayr. The second daughter married Mr. James Erskine, who received the estate of Alva; and was afterwards elevated to the Bench under the title of Lord Alva. The third daughter married William, the thirteenth Earl of Glencairn. In this match Governor Macrae took the liveliest interest, but it did not come off till the year 1744; and then the old Nabob was so seriously ill that the doctor could not assure him of living until the solemnization of the nuptials. On this occasion Governor Macrae gave his neice as "tocher" the barony of Ochiltree, which had cost him £25,000, as well as diamonds to the value of £45,000. But the marriage did not prove a happy one, for the Earl had no real affection for his wife, however much he may have respected her wealth. The Earl however was not inclined to submit to any taunting allusions to his wife's family, for when Lord Cassilis reproached him at a ball with having so far forgotten his rank as to marry a fiddler's daughter, he at once replied,—"Yes, my Lord, and one of my father in law's favourite airs was "The Gipseys cam' to Lord Cassilis's yett,"—referring to the elopement of a Countess of Cassilis with the Gipseys, celebrated in the old song of "Johnny Faa." The second son of this Earl of Glencairn by the niece of Governor Macrae, succeeded to his father's title as James, fourteenth

Earl of Glencairn, and is known as a benefactor of the Poet Burns. This Earl died in 1791, when Burns wrote his "Lament for James, Earl of Glencairn," concluding with the following pathetic lines :—

> "The bridegroom may forget the bride,
>   Was made his wedded wife yestreen ;
> The monarch may forget the crown
>   That on his head an hour has been ;
> The mither may forget the bairn
>   That smiles sae sweetly on her knee ;
> But I'll remember thee, Glencairn,
>   And a' that thou hast done for me !"

The fourth daughter of the MacGuires married a young gentleman of suspicious origin, who went by the name of James Macrae. This young man was said to be the nephew of the old Governor, but he is generally supposed to have been a natural son. The barony of Houston was conferred upon the pair, but the subsequent career of this branch of the family was far from fortunate. A son known as Captain Macrae became a reputed bully and professed duellist at Edinburgh ; and is represented in one of the caricatures of the time as practising with a pistol at a barber's block. In 1790 Captain Macrae fought a celebrated duel with Sir George Ramsay, in which the latter was mortally wounded. It seems that whilst both gentlemen were escorting some ladies out of the Theatre in Edinburgh, their servants quarrelled as to whose carriage should be drawn up at the door. Each of the gentlemen took his servant's part, and the result was the duel, which occasioned the death of Sir George Ramsay and the exile and outlawry of Captain Macrae.

In conclusion we must notice the very few recorded events which are still preserved of the last years of Governor Macrae. The old Anglo-Indian appears to have passed some fifteen years in his native country prior to his death in 1746. In 1733 he was admitted as a burgess of the old town of Ayr, when his name was entered as "James Macrae, late Governor of Madras." In 1734 he presented the citizens of Glasgow with the metallic equestrian statue of king William which still adorns that city. How he employed himself during the latter years of his life is no where stated, beyond the bare fact that he lived and died at Orangefield. We can easily however imagine the old man busy in promoting the advancement of his nieces, and in superintending the estates which he purchased from time to time. One of his last recorded acts occurred in December, 1745, when he lent £5000 to the community of Glasgow, to meet the sum which had been levied from them by Prince Charles. He died somewhere about the year 1746, and was buried in Prestwich Churchyard. Such is the eventful story of Governor Macrae, the son of a washerwoman of Ayr.

CHAPTER XXXIX.

GOVERNORSHIP OF MR. GEORGE MORTON PITT.

1730—31.

Mr. George Morton Pitt succeeded to the Governorship of Fort St. George, and of all the Company's settlements on the coast of Coromandel, on the 14th of May, 1730. The first few months of his administration were sufficiently occupied in receiving the complaints against Gooda Anconah, the Chief Dubash of Governor Macrae, already recorded in the previous chapter. But the following little entry within two days of his accession, having reference to the repeal of Governor Macrae's order against the exportation of silver, is worthy of being preserved.

"Saturday, 16th May, 1730. The President observing that in Consultation the 25th August last, the prohibition against exporting silver only was taken off, and that that on gold is still continued; whereas it seems the intent of the Honorable Company that it should be taken off from both: wherefore ordered that the Secretary give public notice, that the inhabitants and others have full liberty to carry their gold into the country uncoined."

The following brief entry exhibits the punishment awarded against Gooda Anconah.

"Thursday, 16th July, 1730. The President

representing to the Board that Gooda Anconah having been fined 20,000 pagodas, which is ordered by the Company to be laid out in grain and distributed amongst the poor; but it being doubted whether there will be sufficient effects found to answer the other just demands upon Anconah, he proposes that the fine when levied shall lie in the Company's Cash till that is known, and afterwards make the distribution, which is agreed to."

In dealing with the annals of Governor Macrae's administration we have sufficiently indicated his arbitrary character. We however publish the following extract as a still further illustration of the relation which existed in old time between the President and members of Council.

"Monday, 22nd June, 1730. After reading the letter (from the Directors animadverting on the arbitrary conduct of Governor Macrae) the President told the Board that he hoped always to see such an harmony there, that every thing would go with unanimity; but as the former administration had been reflected upon for severely treating those Gentlemen who spoke their opinions freely, it behoved him to declare that, as his intention was to serve the Company in the best manner, he should be glad of their advice upon all occasions; and as he thought it to be every man's right to enter his dissent whenever he pleased, he should be far from resenting, either by his influence or power, so justifiable a practice."

The following notice concerning the origin of the "M" Pagodas is very interesting.

Saturday, 5th September, 1730. The President

observing to the Board what is recommended in the last general letter concerning the badness of pagodas, desires this affair may be now taken into consideration, and that the Assay Master may be sent for to assist with his advice. Mr. Weston was accordingly called in, and acquaints us that the pagodas grow daily worse; and that some he tried in May last were no better than eighty three and a half touch; whereas they ought to be of the value of the Negapatam pagodas, which is eighty-five and three quarters. The Board taking into consideration the danger the Company's estate is in; and that commerce must inevitably suffer if this uncertain money circulates longer unsuspected; and that though we defer taking proper measures to prevent this abuse at present, at last there will be an absolute necessity to do it (may be, when it will give a much greater shock to trade); and likewise no time can be so proper as when the Company's cash is so low, as now by the large draught sent to the Bay by the "Cadogan." We therefore come to the following resolution, in order to secure the Company's estate, which we hope will be sufficient to open the eyes of every body else, who must otherwise be undone by their credulity.

"That a new pagoda be coined of equal weight and fineness with the Negapatam pagoda, and with the same stamp, only distinguished with the letter M on each side the image; which shall be current in all branches of the Company's business, and that no other sort shall be paid or received, excepting in the Northern investments, where the old Madras pagoda is only current. But as this resolution cannot be put in practice till we have a supply of gold from China and elsewhere to make a circulation, we declare that this order of the Board shall not be in full force till the first of May ensuing; when we are in hopes the Eastern ships will be returned, and the merchants have sufficient time to coin the gold they purchase into the above said specie; which were we to insist upon before a supply arrives, they must be obliged to melt down the present coins, and be considerable losers in giving it a new stamp."

In the first chapter of the annals of the administration of Governor Macrae, we found occasion to notice at some length the steps taken to increase the business at the Madras Mint, and to put a stop to the coinage of inferior rupees by the country powers. Mr. Macrae expected to carry out his plan by preventing the exportation of silver, and reducing the mint charges. The prohibition however was repealed, as we have seen, and of course led to the reconsideration of the allowance made to the Brahmin minters in the Madras Mint. On the same day therefore that the Assay Master was summoned to give his opinion upon the bad pagodas, he took the opportunity of representing the case of the Mint Brahmins. The circumstance is thus recorded.

"At the same time Mr. Weston the Assay Master delivers a petition from the Mint Brahmins, representing the hard conditions upon which they are obliged to coin rupees; which they consented to, only because they were promised and flattered that there should be a prohibition of all uncoined silver being exported; by which means they would be so perpetually employed that their gains would be equal to, or more than what it was before; and requesting that half per cent. more be allowed them as heretofore; since we had thought fit to take off the prohibition. Upon due consideration of the matter, we agree to their request; being sensible that the prohibition of exporting silver inland was the motive that induced them to consent to coin at the present rate; and lest too great a restraint upon them who are numerous and poor, should tempt them to debauch the coin, which is well known to be the practice in foreign mints where the Arcot rupee is coined cheaper."

The regulation of the price of grain appears to have been a mania with the Madras Governors in the olden time, notwithstanding the severe lessons they had received respecting the utter impracticability of such measures. The following extracts tell their own story.

"Tuesday, 29th September, 1730. Great complaints being made that the merchants, dealing in rice and paddy, secrete the same, and withhold its coming to market; and it being necessary, in order to prevent the ill consequences of such a practice, to be informed of the quantities of grain in the place, and the possessors thereof: it is ordered that public notice be given, that all persons being possessed of more than 5 garce of rice or paddy, do declare the same within 3 days to Messrs. Hubbard and Morse, on penalty of being severely fined; and that whomsoever shall, within 3 days after, discover and prove any such concealment shall have 10 pagodas as reward."

"Tuesday, 6th October, 1730. Notwithstanding the order of last Consultation for discovering the stock of grain in the place, the Committee acquaint the Board that they received notice only of a few small parcels; whereby it appears the Merchants hoard up their grain in order to enhance the price; and the markets having been quite empty for several days, and consequently the poor grievously distressed thereby:—it is ordered that all the Merchants dealing in grain by the great, be obliged to sell their stock on hand at the rate of 60 pagodas per garce for rice, and paddy at 30 pagodas; that the retailers shall be obliged to sell it again rice at 1¾ measures for one fanam, and twice the quantity of paddy, and no dearer on any pretence whatever; that Messrs. Hyde, Burton, Peers, and Morse be appointed as a Committee to see these orders complied with, and the markets fully supplied at that rate; and that they may be the better able to do this, it is ordered that no grain be sold between the hours of six in the evening and six in the morning; and also that the Committee be authorized to seal up all godowns or repositories of grain in order to secure the same for public use."

"Ordered that the Secretary do give public notice thereof."

The following very extraordinary story is best told in the language of the original record.

"Monday, 11th January, 1731. The President acquaints the Board that a very surprising accident having happened this morning, which by a false representation might be used very much to the detriment of his character; he thinks it incumbent on him to clear that, by giving them the whole account of the affair which is thus. One Gruapa, a person frequently entrusted with the sale of diamonds, had for some months amused him with the notice of having in his custody a diamond of the most extraordinary size that had been known; which made the President very desirous to treat with him about the purchase of it; which the man seemed inclined to, and promised to bring the diamond to the President; but with a number of trifling excuses he delayed and shifted it off from one time to another till last Wednesday; when Gruapa came to him in Company with Ponchola Kistna and Permaul, and told him he had brought the diamond he promised, but could not then let him see it, the said owner not being in the way; and then delivered him a large bulse, sealed with three seals, which he said were the owner's, who would wait on the President in a few days and strike the bargain. The President observed to him that the stamp of one of the three seals was imperfect, which he immediately offered to correct with his own seal. But the President being very desirous to see the diamond, told him if he had power to alter the seal, he had power to open the bulse; on which he recollected himself, and tearing off a piece of his clout, carefully wrapped that about the bulse, and fixed a seal thereon; which was a small cornelian stone he took from his turban ; and so he left the bulse ; having at several times received before 1,300 pagodas, which he said the owner was in immediate want of. The next morning the President went to the Mount and carried the bulse with him ; thinking it more secure with himself than any where else ; but before he had been at the Mount many hours, he was surprised with the news of Gruapa's being dead; that he died suddenly in the morning, without discovering any previous symptoms of illness. Mr. John Roach and Mr. Rawson Hart were present with him when he received this news ; which he was very sorry for, and he immediately told those Gentlemen of his having received a very large diamond from the deceased, and showed them the bulse ; and further told them it had been possible to secrete such an affair ; but he assured them, though he had not agreed for the sum, he was resolved the man's family should have full as much as he could afford to have given had the man been alive. After the President's return from the Mount, he was acquainted that the same Gruapa had been with Mr. Macrae, and offered to lodge with him a large diamond upon receiving 10,000 pagodas ; but he refusing to let Mr. Macrae see the diamond they came to no agreement. This story gave some suspicion to the President, who being willing to be satisfied, and not knowing who the owner was, he sent for Mr. Roach and Mr. Hart, who had before seen the bulse ; and showing them the seal and satisfying them the bulse was in the same condition he received it, did in their presence cut it open without defacing the seals ; and all that was found therein was a large sandy stone which he delivers to the Board to view. Mr. Roach and Mr. Hart, being present at this narration, declare upon oath that the parts when they are mentioned to be present are true. Captain Eckman, who had been very conversant with this man for a long time, being examined and shown the outer seal, declares upon oath that he remembers it very well, and knows it to be a seal that the deceased Gruapa had in his custody; and that the inscription thereon is the word "Raganaculoo;" and gives this further testimony concerning it, that Gruapa once offered to give him that cornelian before it was cut, but not caring to accept of it, his dubash desired Gruapa would cause it to be cut for him, but not being done to his liking he returned it to Gruapa. Captain Eckman's dubash was called for, and asked his name, he says it is "Raganaculoo;" and being examined concerning the seal he declares he knows it very well, and gives the same account of it that Captain Eckman had done."

Our readers will scarcely know which to admire most; the wily cleverness of Gruapa, the prudence of that canny Scot Macrae, or the regular take in of Governor Pitt. The sudden death of the man at the very nick of time is not the least curious feature in the case. What further transpired, after the discovery of the sand stone in the place of the diamond, is not recorded. Most likely Mr. Pitt had to put up with the loss of the 1,300 pagodas which he had advanced; whilst the story excited far more mirth amongst the young Writers and Factors than ever reached the ears of the Honorable the Governor of Fort St. George.

The proceedings of that terrible pirate Angria from his strongholds at Gheria and Severndroog on the Malabar Coast, are illustrated by the following significant letter addressed to the Governor and Council by the Captain of the King George Galley.

"Gentlemen,

I am informed Angria's Grabbs have taken one of the Honorable Company's Galleys, and very much disabled a second by taking the advantage of attacking and boarding them astern, where they can bring no guns to defend them; upon which I have consulted my officers on board, and find that in 5 or 6 days, if you think proper that we stay so long, we can cut two ports for guns that will carry a three pound shot, and mount our swivel guns on our Gunnels, and prepare ourselves with necessaries to defend against being attacked in the like manner.

I am, Gentlemen,
Your most obedient humble servant,

King George's Galley, Feb. 3rd, 1731. RICHARD BOULTON."

The following extracts illustrate the proceedings which were adopted at this period against the Ostend interlopers.

"Monday, 6th April, 1731. The President acquaints the Board that he is advised the Ostend ship that was at Merga, went lately to Pondicherry, but was denied the liberty of that Port;

whence she went to Tranquebar, and obtained protection from the Danes, where she continues in order to procure a cargo for Europe. Wherefore he proposes that the prohibition hereafter entered, be published in all languages, to prevent all commerce or correspondence directly or indirectly with the Ostenders, or any concerned with them, which is unanimously agreed to."

"Monday, 6th April, 1731. George Morton Pitt, Esq., President and Governor of Fort St. George and Council, to all whom these presents may come, Greeting.

"Whereas, there is lately arrived on this coast a ship, carrying the colours of the Emperor of Germany, and is now riding in the port of Tranquebar endeavouring to procure a cargo for Europe; which being contrary to the interest of the Honorable the English East India Company, and to the Treaties in force between the respective nations.

"This is therefore to give public notice, that whatever inhabitant of this place shall aid or assist the said ship, in any manner of way, directly or indirectly, either by himself or by his servants or correspondents,—his estate shall be confiscated to the use of the Honorable Company, and himself expelled the Bounds. And further, all merchants or others that have any effects or servants at Tranquebar, immediately are required to withdraw them under pain of incurring the penalties above mentioned. And to the end that none may pretend ignorance, the Honorable the President and Council of this place have ordered this declaration to be translated into all the languages, and hung up at the Choultry and Sea Gate, of which public notice is likewise given by the beating of the tom tom."

We have now to relate what our experience would lead us to believe to be one of the most singular stories in the records. We give the entries in the consultations exactly in the order in which they stand.

" Tuesday, 27th, April, 1731 The President acquainted the Board that complaint had been made him of an insult offered to the Captain of the Main Guard, as well as to the Ensign of the Choultry Guard, by Mr. Peers, Mr. Foxley, and Mr. Henry Solomon, on Thursday night last; which tending very much to the disturbance of the place, and to destroy all discipline in the garrison, he therefore proposed that Mr. Peers, who was then sitting at the Board, should withdraw. Accordingly he did so.

" Ensign Peele being called in, declared that he was alarmed by a very great noise in the street, and going to see what was the matter saw three persons in one palankeen, which breaking just at the guard occasioned the noise to increase. On which, endeavouring to persuade them to be quiet, he was insulted by them; that Mr. Peers threatened him, Mr. Solomon said he was drunk, and Mr. Foxley held up his fist at him. This account was confirmed by the Serjeant and Corporal of the said Guard; as also by Captain Eckman, commander of the Main Guard, who on Mr. Peers' complaint, sent for the Ensign and examined him;

and he gave him the same account of the matter, as did also the Serjeant and Corporal. And further Captain Eckman declared that Mr. Peers commanded him to confine the Ensign in very peremptory terms, averring he was drunk and had insulted him; whereas he, the said Captain, was satisfied he was perfectly sober. All these depositions are entered after consultation.

"The President then added that the next morning after this happened, when he expected Mr. Peers should have considered of the folly of what he had done, he was surprised to find him instead thereof to insist that the Ensign should be punished; and that in such terms as gave the President but too just reason to complain of Mr. Peers' want of respect to him, which Mr. Burton, who was with him at the same time Mr. Peers insisted on this, confirmed.

"The Board taking into consideration the ill consequences which must necessarily follow on such irregular proceedings, agreed that a charge be drawn up and given Mr. Peers, agreeable to the tenor of the said depositions; and that it be signified to him that his answer thereto be ready on Monday next.

"Having called in and examined Mr. Foxley and Mr. Solomon, the latter of whom absolutely denied everything charged upon him, and the former denied that he had lifted his fist at the Ensign, came to the following resolutions.

"That Mr. Paul Foxley be suspended from the Honorable Company's Service, and that the Secretary notify it to Mr. Henry Solomon, who by these actions is apparently guilty of a breach of the covenants entered into with the Company; that he must prepare for Europe in twelve months. To which Resolves Messrs Hubbard and Morse dissented."

The deposition respecting this unique case are entered in the consultation books of the same day as follows.

"Tuesday, 27th April, 1731. Ensign Peele declareth.—That he being commander of the Choultry Guard heard a very great noise in the Street. He called to the Serjeant and Corporal to know the meaning, who could not inform him, but suspected it to be the uproar of some drunken Sailors. Whereon he ordered a part of the guard to be in readiness to seize and suppress them. When they had advanced just opposite to the Choultry guard, he perceived there was three persons in one palankeen, who proved to be Mr. Peers, Mr. Foxley, and Mr. Solomons; which being so loaded broke down with them, and on this disaster the clamour was louder than before. On which he went to them, and said, "Gentlemen, I beg you will consider what time of night it is, and that you will depart about your occasions and not disturb the Garrison." On this Mr. Peers came up to him in a very particular manner, and cried, —"Who are you Sir?" He answered, "I am commander of this guard; and it is my duty to preserve the peace, and I hope you won't disturb it" "Sir!" Said Mr. Peers, "we know who you are very well, and shall deal with you accordingly." Mr. Henry Solomons came up and said, "the Ensign is drunk, what signifies talking to such a drunken fellow; speak to the Serjeant; I know him to be a sober man." He replied, "Gentlemen, if you had drank no more than I there would have been none of this disturbance to night." Mr. Paul Foxley coming near with his hands behind him, then thrust one of them almost in his face, which made him, who had his sword in his hand but not drawn, point it to him, and order him to keep his distance, and not dare to insult him in such a manner in the face of his Guard. Mr. Foxley said, "You Sir, what do you pretend to? don't you see who is in our company; and that, after some vollies of oaths and threats, they retired to the main guard. All which I attest to be true. George Peele."

"Captain Eckman being sent for, and questioned what passed on his guard on Saturday night last with respect to Mr. Peers and some others in his company, answers as follows. That he being Commander of the Main Guard on Saturday last, was alarmed with a violent knocking at the Fort Gate about two o'clock in the morning; that the Serjeant coming to him and acquainting him that Mr. Peers and some others desired to speak with him, he went down to them; when Mr. Peers told him the Ensign of the Choultry gate was drunk and had insulted him, and commanded him to confine the Ensign immediately. That he told Mr. Peers he could not take an officer off his guard without putting another in his stead, and at that time he had not one to relieve him; but he sent for the Ensign, and examined him on Mr. Peers' complaint, and the Ensign, who appeared to him to be perfectly sober, gave him the account of the matter which is merely a repetition of what has been already stated."

"Captain Eckman declares that, after the Ensign was returned, he sent to be further satisfied for the Serjeant and Corporal, who related the same story exactly, and averred the Ensign was perfectly sober. Notwithstanding which, Mr. Peers insisted the Ensign should be confined, and commanded him positively to do it. To soothe him he told Mr. Peers he would secure the Ensign, and take care he should be forthcoming in the morning to answer any complaint."

Here follows the charge against Mr. Peers.

"*Copy of a charge exhibited by the President and Council of Fort St. George against Mr. Charles Peers, one of the Members of the said Council.*

"For that complaint hath been made by Ensign Peele, that you, Charles Peers, with other disorderly companions, viz. Mr. Paul Foxley, and Mr. Henry Solomons, did on Saturday night last, between the hours of one and two, approach the Choultry guard with a great noise and disturbance; and being come very near to the Guard, you did in a most unseemly and unwarrantable manner, insult and threaten the said Ensign, who was commander there. That not being contented with the abuse and insult to his face, you went to the Main Guard, which having alarmed with repeated noise and knocking, you demanded to speak with the Captain. That when he came, you unjustifiably assumed to command, and peremptorily required him to obey your orders, and confine the aforesaid Ensign ; and this you positively insisted on, notwithstanding all the soft persuasions to the contrary, and the representations of the injustice and irregularity of such a proceeding.

"Which actions being highly culpable in themselves, and having a direct tendency to subvert and destroy all good order and Government, which you as a member is more particularly bound to support and conserve the quiet of.

"You are hereby required to answer to this charge, which answer is expected on Monday the 3rd May next, at 10 o'clock in the forenoon."

Before going any further with the charge against Mr. Peers it may be as well to notice, what has been already stated, that two members of Council, Mr. Hubbard and Mr. Morse, dissented from the punishment already awarded to Mr. Foxley and Mr. Solomons. The dissent is this entered in the consultations.

"We dissent from that part of the Consultation wherein Mr. Foxley is ordered to be suspended and Mr. Henry Solomons sent home ; because we are not fully satisfied that the charge laid against them is clearly made good in every respect, as we find those gentlemen deny the worse part of it ; whose assertions of their innocence ought in our opinion to have some weight. But admitting that the matter happened as the officers of the Guard have represented it, we cannot help thinking the punishment more than adequate to the crime, and that a reprimand from the Board would have been more suitable to the nature of the offence, as well as to the Company's orders. And we further think Mr. Foxley's long and faithful services might plead something in his behalf, and extenuate in some measure what is laid to his charge, wherein we don't find there was any ill intended to the welfare of the Garrison."

JAMES HUBBARD.
NICOLAS MORSE.

We now make an extract from the consultations of the 3rd of May, on which day Mr. Peers was to make his answer to the charge before the Governor and Council.

"Monday, 3rd May, 1731. Mr. Peers being called upon for his answer to the charge exhibited against him, replied that he had not received any charge as he apprehended, but only a paper said to be a copy of one, without its being certified that the President and Council had approved thereof. But the Board telling him they had approved thereof, he then gave in his answer to it as entered after this Consultation; wherein he demands a hearing face to face with the persons who have complained against him. He next proceeds to give an account of the affair, affirming that what noise they made was only laughing at the breaking of the palankeen, though perhaps the palankeen boys might be noisy; that the Ensign thereupon treated them haughtily instead of their insulting the Ensign; that they went to the Main Guard to complain of him, and denies that he used any haughty language to the Captain, or assumed any command over him. His answer therefore contains in it an account of the proceedings of that night set in a different light than by the charge; and a demand to have a hearing before the Board, as at large in the answer. He likewise takes notice that the thing happened on a Thursday night, whereas the charge lays it on the Saturday.

" He being withdrawn the error of the time was allowed; and a motion being made for calling in the witnesses and Mr. Peers, it was resolved in the negative, because this Board did not act in this case as a Court of Judicature, but were only examining into the behaviour of one of the members of it.

" Then the Board, taking into consideration the several depositions on which the charge is founded, and Mr. Peers' defence, did agree that the charge was fully made out and thereupon.

" Resolved that Mr. Peers should be suspended the Company's Service till their pleasure was known. To which resolve Messrs Hubbard and Morse dissented, not being of opinion that the charge was sufficiently supported."

The following extracts from Mr. Peers' defence contain all that is of further importance or interest in the affair.

To the Honorable George Morton Pitt, Esq., President and Governor of Fort St. George and Council.

Honorable Sir and Sirs.

" After leaving Mr. Solomon's house, we passed by the Choultry Guard in our way home; but just as we had turned the corner, in order to go up the street towards the Fort, the bamboo of the palankeen broke, upon which we got out of it laughing at the accident only; though it is very likely the palankeen fellows might make some noise among themselves on its happening, as indeed it is generally usual with them. But at this instant the Ensign (as it proved, for on his first appearance, being undressed and in his banyon coat I did not know him) came from off his cot, and in a very haughty manner cryed out "None of your disturbance, Gentlemen! Go along; if you don't I will confine you on the Guard." I said, "For what? that we had made no disturbance, but he might confine us if he thought proper." Upon which he told us "so he would if we continued to make a disturbance; that he really thought by our noise that the town was on fire." I replied, "he could scarcely judge so by any we had made, but that he might do as he pleased." It is not impossible but, finding myself insulted without cause, I might talk pretty loud to him; but I did not treat him with any ill manners, and by this time having pretty well recovered himself, he found I was one of the Company's council; upon which he said he was sorry to find Mr. Peers was there. I answered, "He had no occasion to be so, for that I did not know we had committed a fault; nevertheless if he thought convenient to confine us he might; when I believed he would find who had really committed a disturbance:"—thinking he had used me ill without just reason. Whereupon I left him, and said I would go to the Main Guard and acquaint it with what had happened. During our discourse with the Ensign here,

Mr. Foxley said, he thought it was impertinent in him to use one of the Council as he had done; and told him he did not appear in his guard in a proper garb as an officer; and Mr. Henry Solomons said he was but just risen from off his cot, and could not well judge, bidding him ask the Serjeant and Corporal of the Guard if we had made any disturbance. Being come to the Main Guard gate which was shut, I knocked there, and desired to speak with the Captain; who after a small time came down from his room to me on the parade. I informed him of what had passed at the Choultry, whereupon he ordered the Ensign to be called up; but immediately afterwards I said, "Captain Eckman, can you send for the Ensign off his Guard?" To which he answered, "Yes Sir I have sent for him." I replied, "you be pleased then to send some body to take care of the Guard; there seems to be a good sober sergeant or two here." And he said again, "I will see the Guard taken care of." After the Ensign was come up, Captain Eckman asked him why he had stopped the Gentlemen as they were passing by? Who told him, because we made a very great noise and disturbance. I assured Mr. Peele hereupon that there was no noise other than what might be from the breaking of the bamboo; and as we had not made any disturbance, if he would only say so it would be sufficient, and I would have nothing more to say to it. But he answered "No Sir, I cannot say so;" and upon this I said to Captain Eckman, "Then Sir you will please to relieve the Ensign, and keep him here till the morning, till you can acquaint the Governor with what has happened." Which he promised to do, telling us it was usual to report to him every morning from the Guards. In talking with Captain Eckman, but whether before or after the Ensign was come up I cannot positively recollect, I did tell him, if he did not care to concern himself about it I would go and acquaint Mr. Fowke; and further that as we or the Ensign must be in the wrong, to put either us or him on the Guard. To which he gave for answer,—" I will take care of him," and so ordered the gates to be opened to let us out of the Town."

* * *

" I must account it a very great misfortune to lie under the odium of a charge; but as I am free on that account to urge anything in my own behalf, I would in the next place recommend to you to consider, that the subject matters of complaint is not for any infidelity to our Honourable Masters, or breach of trust committed; so that whilst I have not in violation of our common oath of fidelity to them, or our Covenants, been unfaithful to their interests in committing any enormities they particularly provide against, such as of abusing the trust they repose in us by vexing and distressing the inhabitants; whether by extortion under the suspicious pretext of perquisities not allowed by them or by any other means, wilfull mismanagement or misapplication of their revenues, embezzlement of their goods, corruption and acts of violence, waste of their money, or over charges in the prices of goods bought with it and the like;— I say, while I have not only kept my hands clear of all these crimes, and my character free from the imputation of any of them, but have done the Company some services too, which have been approved; I will not fear so hard a fate as to fall for one single, I may call it slight indiscretion, which has not been attended with any ill consequences, nor are any likely to follow it."

Most of our readers will probably agree with us that the fuss made about this trivial affair, and the cruel punishment awarded to the three gentlemen concerned, seem to require some farther explanation. We are sorry that it is not in our power to afford such an explanation, beyond stating the fact that the age was that of "Sir Charles Grandison" and "Clarissa Harlowe," when private immorality was considered of little or no consequence, so long as it did not interfere with outward decorum. A century ago, the upper and middle classes were slaves to decorum; as any one will be able to call to mind who ever enjoyed the felicity in boyhood of listening to the old world stories of grandmothers or great grandfathers. We have however much satisfaction in informing our readers that the Directors at home reversed the sentence against the three unfortunate gentlemen; and that after the expiration of a year Mr. Peers was restored to his seat in the Council.

Had Edie Ochiltree lived in those days, he would no doubt have found frequent occasion to converse with Governor Pitt about diamonds and sand stones, and with Mr. Peers about Ensign Peele and broken down palanquins.

CHAPTER XL.

GOVERNORSHIP OF MR. GEORGE MORTON PITT. 1732—35.

We have now arrived at a period in the annals of Madras when a change begins to come over the relations between the little English colony and the Native powers. For some years the Carnatic would appear to have enjoyed comparative tranquillity under the Nabob Sadatulla Khan who held his court at Arcot. But great events were looming in the distance. The Mogul empire was soon to be threatened by the Mahrattas, who were attaining a power and influence superior even to that exercised by the renowned Sevajee. The Dekkan was fast becoming an independent kingdom under the Nizam Cheen Kulich Khan; whilst Southern India was in the eve of those great revolutions, in which England and France were to appear as combatants under rival princes, and in which that great struggle was to commence which terminated in the establishment of the British empire. Accordingly the remaining portion of the annals of Madras in the olden time, may demand a few further illustrations from the light of contemporary history, than has hitherto been found necessary; but such illustrations shall be as brief as possible, and be merely restricted to such as are absolutely required to explain the entries in the records of Madras.

Our first entry in the year 1732 refers to the Mahrattas. Shao, the grandson of Sevajee, reigned at Sattara, which at that time was the capital of the Mahratta dominion. The Rajah however was a man of pleasure, and left the affairs to his celebrated minister Bajee Rao, better known as the Peishwa. Bajee Rao must be regarded as the founder of what may be called the second Mahratta empire. At an early period he had contemplated the conquest of Delhi, and the establishment of the Mahratta power upon the ruins of the Mogul. But he was thwarted by the intrigues of enemies at Sattara, and involved in a contest with the Nizam. The opposition of two such men as the Peishwa and the Nizam would be well worthy of notice in a history of India, but would be out of place here.

In 1732 some sort of terms were apparently concluded between the Peishwa and the Nizam. But in the spring we find that the Mahrattas were entering the Carnatic; and that Sadatulla Khan, Nabob of Arcot, and Abdul Nabby Khan, who appears to have been a Patan Nabob of Cuddapa, were marching out to meet them. Accordingly the political department of the Madras Presidency was put into working order; though, as our readers will perceive from the following entry, the expenditure of the department was placed on a footing which in these times we cannot but regard as strictly economical.

"Monday, 24th April, 1732. The Spy peon at Arcot, having advised the President that the

Mahrattas are entered this part of the country, and our Nabob gone to join Abdulnabby Khan in order to withstand them; and requesting, in case he be to follow the camp, an advance to his pay in consideration of the great expense he must necessarily be at in so doing;—agreed that he be allowed ten pagodas per month while he is in the camp, instead of the four which he receives when at Arcot."

The records next introduce us to a gentleman who was subsequently to become famous in the annals of Madras. The great Labourdonnais, who fourteen years afterwards was to achieve the capture of Fort St. George, first appears upon the stage in 1732. A year or two previously he had interposed in a quarrel between some Arabian and Portuguese ships in the harbour of Mocha; and his service on that occasion had recommended him so strongly to the Viceroy of Goa, that the Viceroy appointed him agent of his Portuguese Majesty on the coast of Coromandel. Here, according to Mill, he remained for two years, perfecting his knowledge of the traffic and navigation of India. In the following entry he appears also to have been engaged in assisting the Ostend interlopers.

"Monday, 1st May, 1732. The President acquainted the Board that he had received advice that one Monsieur LaBourdonnais in a French Ship, had carried from Porto Novo between four and five hundred bales for the Ostenders to Goa, and had put them on board her there; and that he had in particular applied to the Viceroy for liberty to transport one hundred bales, custom free; which he was informed, being obtained, had occasioned a dispute between the Viceroy and the Custom Master; of which it is agreed to write to Bengal, and to desire the President and Council there to examine Captain Dixon who was at Goa at that time about this affair."

Our next extracts refer to the Nabob of Arcot, and will explain themselves.

"Thursday, 22nd June, 1732. Imaum Sahib, Buxie (Paymaster) to the Nabob, and one of the greatest influence in that Court, making a visit to our President, it is agreed, in consideration that it is in his power greatly to assist or prejudice our affairs, that a present be made him agreeable to what was formerly given Ducknaroy on a like occasion."

"Monday, 17th July, 1732. The French having wrote a letter of condolence to the Nabob on the death of his wife, and accompanied it with a present; and our Brahmin writing that the letter our President wrote on that occasion is kept back;—it is agreed that a piece of Broad Cloth, and six bottles of Rose Water, be sent to accompany it.

"Monday, 14th August, 1732. The President acquaints the Board that he took an opportunity when Imaum Sahib was here, to discourse to him about the ill state of the Company's investment, and to desire his countenance and assistance in advancing it; which had had so good an effect as to engage Imaum Sahib's recommendation to the Nabob; who had sent his orders to the several Governments under his jurisdiction, that the weavers should work for none but our Merchants, as appears by the letters sent the President. Translate of which is entered after this consultation."

"*From Nabob Sadatulla Khan Bahader.*

"I received your letter of condolence, which you sent me in confirmation of our established friendship. Certainly that which so greatly afflicts me must also be very near to you; we must all submit to the will of the Great God, which alone supports me under so great a loss.

"Your present of two pieces of Broad cloth and six flasks of Rose water I have received, and esteem it a great mark of your friendship.

"I have sent through means of Imaum Sahib, orders to the several Havildars of Towns where you provide your goods, to give you all the liberty possible, to serve you only, and not to permit of any hindrance whatever. What can I say more?"

"*From Imaum Sahib.*

"From the time I left your Honor nothing has so much run in my mind as your goodness. You then mentioned to me something about your cloth trade. I had not till now an opportunity to speak to the Nabob of it, by reason of his wife's death.

"I have made my request to him, and procured his several purwannas, which I now send your Honor; and you must take care to forward them to your Gomastas. If after this there happens any hinderance or neglect, pray let me know, and troopers shall be sent to deliver them in their presence to your several Gomastas.

"I received your two letters, and have delivered

them, with your present of two pieces of Broad Cloth and six flasks of Rose water, to the Nabob, and he has sent an answer to you.

"I desire your Honor will write your Gomastas to sent me a piece of cloth with the price as you approve of; and I will endeavour to get a quantity made in the parts under my command.

"The Nabob sends you eight pieces of Beetelaes, two pieces of Mocrees, and some Otah Roses, by Meer Sadulah, which please to accept and command me in any thing you have this way."

The following circular order was accordingly sent by the Nabob of Arcot to the several Havildars under his jurisdiction.

"The people of the Governor of Madras, who come to your country to buy cloth, is the occasion of my writing this; to let you know it is my will you give strict order to all the merchants in your parts, to sell such goods as are proper for the Governor of Madras only to his people, and that they immediately deliver whatever cloth they have ready to his Gomastas. What they refuse you permit them to sell any where. Take care that none buy such goods in your parts but his people; for this is my strict command; and take penalties from your merchants to perform the same."

The Havildars to whom the above order was despatched, were as follows. The Havildar of Conjeveram and Poonamallee, of Walladoor, of Vellore, of Salavacca and Collepetta, of Cudangallee, of Canacayoor and Trevatool, and of Warnapollam, also the Renter of Poonamallee, and the Havildar of great Conjeveram.

The revenues of Madras at this time amounted to nearly 65,000 Pagodas, or more than £30,000, per annum. As the subject is interesting we subjoin the following table.

	Pags.	F.	C.
Revenues viz.			
Beetle and Tobacco Farm viz.			
The Cowle granted to Poncala Kistna and Ramah Chundra for 5 years commencing the 5th September 1730 ending 4th September 1735 at twelve equal payments annual rent.	10,000	0	0
Arrack and Wine License.			
The Cowle granted to Poncala Kistna expired the 5th December 1732 and new let to Rama Chundra and Sandiapa Moodeliar for 5 years commencing the said 5th December 1732 ending 4th December 1737 at twelve equal payments—the annual rent...	4,020	0	0
Town Brokerage.			
The Cowle granted to Gooroo Chetty and Terapedoo for 5 years commencing the 5th day of September 1730 ending 4th of September 1735 at two half yearly payments—the annual rent..	800	0	0
Measuring Duty on grain.			
The Cowle granted to Quotambawcun Gruapah for 5 years commencing 20th September 1730 and ending 19th September 1735 at six equal payments—the annual rent..............................	8500		0
Fishing of the River.			
The Cowle granted to the Company of Macqua's for 5 years commencing 25th March 1729 ending 24th of March			

	Pags.	F.	C.
1734 at two half yearly payments—the annual rent..............	50	0	0
Egmore &c. villages.			
Let to Kistna Reddee, Chundra Seira and Chittombey for 10 years commencing 1st July 1725 ending ultimo June 1735 at one payment—the annual rent..................................	1,450	0	0
Trivitore &c. villages.			
Let to Tomby Chetty, Mutavencaty Chetty, Poncala Kistna, and Jaggapa Chetty for 12 years commencing 17th October 1729 and ending 16th October 1741 at one payment—the annual rent..........................	1,230	0	0
Paddy Fields.			
Let to Daveroy Mudeliar taken from him on complaint of selling salt at extravagant prices and relet at the same rate to Gaunapa Moodeliar and Sanna Vencaty Kistna for 5 years commencing 22nd May 1732 ending 21st May 1737 at one payment—annual rent...	710	0	0
Jah Tereira's Garden.			
Let to Antonsa de Carvalho for 10 years commencing 20th August 1729 ending 19th August 1739..........	24	0	0
Maria Pois's Garden.			
Let to Perseramah for 5 years commencing 25th March 1730 ending 24th March 1735—annual rent..............	60	0	0
The Company's old Garden.			
Let to Mahaudu for 12 years commencing 15th April 1725 ending 14th April 1737—annual rent..........................	326	0	0
Total amount of the fixed Revenues Pags.	19,520	0	0

Quit rents viz.				
Batteca rent and shroff duty for one year			320 0 0	
Amount of the rent roll to 31st Aug. 1732		2585 22 0		
Deduct charges	33 12			
Bad debts	33 0	66 12 0		
			2,499 10 0	2,819 10 0
Scavengers' duty.				
Amount of the assessment			1,109 33 0	
Deduct charges and allowances		611 21 50		
Bad debts		25 26 0		
			637 11 50	472 21 30
Sea Customs from first month January to ultimo December				32,546 14 4
Land Customs do.				7,800 3 73
Mint Customs				1,031 27 24
Total Amount of the Revenue at Fort St. George. Pagodas				6,4190 4 51

Sadatulla Khan, Nabob of Arcot, died this year, probably of grief for the loss of his wife. Orme tells us that having no issue, he adopted the two sons of his brother; appointing the elder Dost Ali to be Nabob of Arcot; the younger Boher Ali to be Governor of Vellore; and Gulam Hassein, the nephew of his wife, to be Dewan of Arcot. Orme also adds, that these dispositions were made without that deference towards the Nizam, which the latter had determined to establish throughout all the Governments under his jurisdiction; that this jealousy prevented Dost Ali from procuring a regular confirmation from Delhi ; and that "*it is said*" that he only obtained some letters of approbation from the Vizier, without the proper forms of an authentic commission. These subjects were no doubt often discussed in Fort St. George, and indeed only occurred about thirty years before Orme was himself a member of Council at Madras. Yet the authority of the records is somewhat opposed to that of Orme ; for they expressly state that the appointments were made by the Nizam, and moreover contain a copy of the Firmaun which the new Nabob received from Delhi. We quote the original entries.

"Monday, 16th October, 1732. The Resident acquaints the Board that he has advice from Arcot that Dost Ali Khan, nephew to the late Nabob, had succeeded him in his government, but that he was not confirmed from court.

"Monday, 8th January, 1733. Dost Ali Khan and Goulam Hussan Khan, having on the death of the Nabob been appointed by direc-tion from Cheen Kulich Khan, the one Nabob the other Dewan of the Carnatic country; and it being agreed on all sides that this appointment will be confirmed from court. It was agreed, in consideration of the necessity there is to engage them in our favour with respect to the investment, and in consideration of the orders about it from the late Nabob,—not to defer the present usual on the accession of a Subah any longer ; that by appearing thus early in our acknowledgments, we may be able to keep our ground with our neighbours the

French, who are generally much more expensive in their presents."

The Firmaun granted to Dost Ali, is thus recorded in the consultations. It professes to come from Mahomed Shah at that time Emperor at Delhi.

"Saturday, 13th January, 1733. This Firmaun granted by me, Mahamud Shaw Patchaw Gauzee, to Dost Ali Khan, My Conjad, you may observe I have a great favour towards you. I am very sorry for the death of Sadatulla Khan Bahader, you are now in the room of the late Nabob, to look after the King's affairs, with the greatest faithfulness, diligence, and honour. That nothing may happen contrary to the method that the old Nabob used. Loose none of his good rules and maxims; by which you will get a good name among my faithful servants. I reckon you among them, and have sent you a Serapah, and a Serpanche set with stones, by my Gusbardar, which you must receive with great respect, and go out to meet it, and then wear it yourself. See that you always obey my will."

At this time things were in considerable confusion in other parts of Southern India. The Rajah of Mysore had died in 1731; and his successor was a mere puppet in the hands of those two celebrated ministers, Deoraj and Nunjeraj, who subsequently were in their turn compelled to give way to Hyder. Perhaps however the original record, which combines commercial with political data, will sufficiently illustrate the aspect of affairs.

"Monday, 8th January, 1733. Tomby Chetty,

being called before the Board to make an indent for Broad cloth for the year 1734, told them that he had so very large a stock on hand, and so considerable a quantity was expected in a few months, that he could not hope to dispose thereof in a great while longer than the arrival of those ships; that the countries of Mysore and Trichinopoly were in so great confusion on the death of the Princes of those countries, that there had been no trade for a considerable time past in those parts; that the Cuddapa country had been in war ever since the death of Abdul Nabby Khan; that the Mahrattas had plundered Vengalour adjoining to Cuddapa, and that he had been deprived for these reasons of any sales there; and that the apprehensions of troubles in our own parts, during the sickness of our late Nabob, had put a stop to any considerable dealings even in the country round about us; so that he had not sold above 300 bales for 15 months last past, and that therefore he could make no indent this year."

About the middle of this year Governor Pitt endeavoured to put some restrictions upon the private trading between the different ports of India, which was allowed to the Company's servants. Accordingly the Governor and Council announced that it was their intention to permit no such trade for the future without their permission. Mr. Charles Peers however dissented, but his protest was of no avail. He then begged to be allowed to resign the service, with permission to reside in India as a free man. Subsequently however Governor Pitt discovered that Mr. Peers and Mr.

Parkes had been engaged in carrying on a clandestine trade to Europe, by way of Tranquebar; and both the latter gentlemen were sent to England in obedience to the standing orders of the Company.

The following domestic entries may be considered curious.

"Thursday, 6th December, 1733. The Desks in the Secretary's office wanting covering, and the window shutters being through length of time so decayed as to be useless in the Monsoon, and the silk shutters being likewise worn out,—ordered that the Paymaster do provide new ones.

"Several of the Books wanting to be new bound,—ordered that it be done, and when done that they be kept locked up; and that the Gentleman of the office do attend from 8 to 11 every morning, except Sunday, and if necessary from 4 to 6 in the afternoon; and that the office be open at no other time."

The following extract from a trade report, entered in the consultations of the 7th January 1734, will be found interesting, especially in its reference to the Cotton trade of the period. Amongst the causes for the great decline in the import trade in the Company's bounds, it was alleged.

"First, that the inland trade has been greatly impeded and obstructed for many years past by the Mahrattas, who infested and ravaged the kingdom of Mysore, the province of Carnatta, and the Districts of Audenvenny, Bangalore, and Narrainpettah; which has hindered the Lingum and Canarese Merchants from coming to this part of the country; who before those troubles used to bring annually to the Fair of Landepettah to the value of one hundred and thirty to one hundred and fifty thousand pagodas in cotton yarn only, the produce of which was brought down to the Sea ports, and chiefly to this, to be invested in Broad cloth, Metals, and Bengal goods, for the consumption of the inland provinces."

On the 25th February, 1734, we find the following announcement, which was evidently intended for the encouragement of the cotton trade.

"The Honorable the President and Council do hereby give notice that they have thought fit, in order to enlarge the manufactures of this place and to facilitate the Company's investment, to permit all persons whatsoever to bring in Cotton and Cotton yarn free of all customs, provided always if it be carried out again unmanufactured it shall pay the full customs."

The following curious entry will explain itself.

"Monday, 7th January, 1734. The President then acquainted the Board, that he had sometime ago spoke to our Merchants to consider of some proper measure to people our villages with those sort of spinners and weavers who work the Company's sort of cloth; that they had given him hopes of a subscription for that purpose when the present famine is over, but that the main objection to the introducing those manufactures in several of the villages was the want of proper plantations of trees for the weavers to work under; that only Trivatore, Nungumbauk, and Wascravally were at all planted, and them not sufficiently; but however the Merchants had wrote to Salem, Worriapollam, and the other provinces to the southward, to encourage some weavers to remove hither. If they do so, and there be no other obstacle, he proposed that, at the proper season, care should be taken to make such plantations in all our villages as are necessary for the purpose, which is approved and resolved upon."

In a previous chapter on the annals of Madras under Governor Collet, we had occasion to notice the origin of "Collet's pettah," which was inhabited by painters and weavers, who had begged that their pettah might be called after the name of the Governor. This simple name however appears to have been a poser to our modern geographers, for in the large Government plan of Madras the English name of "Collet" has been Tamulized into "Kulatti;" though the original name is as well known to the Natives as Chinnapatanam. In the present chapter we have to draw attention to some particulars still more curious connected with the origin of Chindadre Pettah; which we publish with the more pleasure, because the record is fast decaying. The details will be found singularly suggestive.

"21st October, 1734. The President acquainted the Board that he had received proposals from several persons for erecting a weaving town within our Bounds, by the name of Chindadre Pettah; which proposals he now lays before the Board as follows.

"1st, That those who shall come to inhabit there, shall be first approved by a person to be appointed by the Governor and Council, and a portion of ground allotted them to build on.

"2ndly, That the houses they build shall be for them, their heirs and assigns; but if they let them fall down, and will not repair them in six months after notice given them for that purpose, it shall be lawful for the Company to give the ground to others.

"3rdly, None but Weavers, Spinners, and other persons useful in the Weaving trade, Painters, Washers, Dyers, Bettleca merchants, Brahmins and Dancing women, and other necessary attendants on the pagoda, shall inhabit the said town.

"4thly, That there be no distinction of streets, but that every caste may build in any of them.

"5thly, That the heads of the castes be chosen, and have power according to Salabad; and that all disputes about debts or accounts between the inhabitants be decided by them, or other arbitrators; and that the inhabitants of the said town shall not be liable to prosecutions in the courts of Justice in Madras for any action of debt or account, but shall be proceeded against according to the customs of their several castes.

6thly, That the said Town be free of all customs and tolls whatever, till the Company's pleasure be known; and that no custom shall hereafter be levied on them till it has been proposed to and approved by the Company; except only the Pedda Naick's duty, who is to have watch and ward according to Salabad; and in particular is to have nine fanams for every great house, six fanams for every middling sized house, and three for every small one, paid him annually; in consideration of which, and the other accustomary duties to be allowed him, that he be obliged to make good all thefts and robberies therein committed.

"7thly, That the goods made in the said town shall pay the same customs in Madras, as the same sort of goods made in other places pay; and what are for the Company, agreeable to what paid for the same sorts by the Company's Merchants.

"8thly, That the said town be erected in the spot of ground lately in the possession of Suncavencatachulum; it being at a convenient distance from Madras, and having the advantage of a fresh water river on the back of it, which will be of great use to the inhabitants; and that the Company do advance two thousand pagodas without interest for five years, to be paid in the hands of Chintomby Mudaliar and Vennala Narrain Chetty, in order to enable the people who shall come to reside there to build their houses; after which Chintomby Mudaliar, Vennala Narrain Chetty, who engage to be security for this money, shall be allowed two years more for the collecting the same, and shall pay it in as they collect it.

"These proposals being taken into consideration, that since there is no probability of the Company's wanting so small a sum of money as is demanded on this occasion; that the securities are substantial and safe men, and consequently there is no danger of losing any part thereof; and that the benefits arising from such a town to the Company will be so many, and above all the encouraging the erecting of cloth manufactures within our Bounds being so strenuously recommended to us by the Honorable Court of Directors; it was unanimously agreed that the President be desired to advance the said sum as occasion requires it, for the said purposes and on the said conditions.

"As to the spot on which the said town is proposed to be erected, the conveniency of fresh water, and a number of trees necessary for the Weavers and Painters; as also its neighbourhood to Madras making it by far the properest place that can be chosen;—the Board consented to part with the same for this use; having first enquired into the value thereof, which at the highest rate cannot be more than 400 pagodas, and which they think is not considerable enough to be put in competition with the advantages of the situation.

"It was then urged that perhaps some ill minded people might suggest that the 5th article of the said proposals was an infringement of the Royal Charter, as granting an immunity from the Jurisdiction of the Courts erected here by the authority thereof within the limits assigned them. To which it was answered, that it is undoubtedly in the power of the Government on bringing new people from foreign parts, to agree with them on such terms as they would consent to come in upon. That the immunity be granted to these new comers, being "such as none could" pretend to be aggrieved by "them, and which are of" necessity, from the nature "of the people"* in a constant depend-

* The words in inverted commas are conjectural, as scraps of the record have disappeared.

ance on the heads of their several castes; without which, and a power in those heads to enforce the obedience of those under them, there will be no possibility of bringing the design ever to perfection; and thereby all the benefits which the Company propose to themselves from bringing these manufacturers to live within the Bounds will be lost. That fatal experience has taught us that obliging the Renters of our villages to follow the English methods in their conduct to their under tenants and labourers, instead of the customs of the country, has been the occasion of more than half those lands lying uncultivated. Lastly, that the people proposed to be brought into the said town, being all handy craft day labourers, it would be impossible for them to maintain themselves and families under the frequent avocations and charge that the delays necessarily incident to our forms must unavoidably occasion. Besides, if we divest ourselves of those prejudices which are the bias in favour of our own customs, we shall think it strange and unreasonable to oblige a people to obey or pay a reverence to laws, they neither do or will ever understand, and to be bound in all their affairs to rules they cannot possibly know; being neither wrote or published in their own language, and of which they are of necessity to purchase both the interpretation and the use. In a word, the conditions upon which they covenant to settle in our Bounds are:—To be allowed and tolerated in the free exercise of the religious and civil rights, which they have and enjoy in the parts they are a going to leave: which if we cannot grant or protect therein, they will not settle among us; and to all this that the grant proposed is consonant to the instructions which the Honorable Court of Directors have so often, ever since the arrival of the charter, given us in their letters, viz. That causes between the natives may, and ought to be decided by their own customs among themselves, or by Justices, or by Referees, to be appointed by themselves (which can be nothing but the Heads so chosen among themselves). That intermeddling with their old customs will occasion many mischiefs; and that while they do nothing to the prejudice of the English Government, they be allowed to live in the full enjoyment of the privileges of their respective castes.

"Then the 6th article, whereby an exemption was demanded from all taxes and impositions, was debated; and the President acquainted the Board that he had offered them first seven, then ten years to be free from those imposts; which he could get no other answer than that they did not pay them in their own country, and the limiting them to a certain term of years was only telling them, when that term came they must be gone again; that he had thereupon promised them to use his endeavours with the Company that the said town might be free of duties for ever. That as by the 1st article, none are to be admitted into the said town but by permission from persons to be nominated by the Board,—it will be very easy to prevent any inhabitants of Madras, or the other villages, to remove to this town; and consequently none of the revenues can be affected thereby. In fine that the people would not come on other terms; but that however it was left to the Company to order what they thought fit herein, and we should shortly have their opinion and resolution thereupon. But that it cannot be out of the memory of the Board, that in Mr. Macrae's time, there was an attempt to levy the Beetle tax in some of the Villages, which occasioned so great a desertion of the inhabitants as to make it necessary to take it off again.

"After which the Board went through the rest of the articles, and unanimously resolved to grant the cowle on the proposed terms, and directed the Secretary to get one drawn out accordingly."

28th October, 1734. A cowle for erecting the town of Chindadre Pettah, agreeable to the terms concluded on last consultation, produced and signed; and five hundred pagodas advanced to Chintomby Moodeliar, and Vennala Narrain Chetty, in part of the two thousand which by the said proposals are to be paid them for carrying it on."

"Monday, 9th December 1734. Several persons wanting to build in Chindadre Pettah, it is agreed that Mr. Augustus Burton do allot them portions of ground for that purpose; taking care that none of the inhabitants of Madras, or the other villages belonging to the Company, be of the number of those whom he shall permit to reside there, and that they are such people only as are directed by the cowle."

On the 23rd January 1735 the Governorship

of Mr. George Morton Pitt appears to have drawn to a natural close. On that day he embarked and Mr. Benyon took his seat at the head of the Board. It is somewhat remarkable that Mr. Pitt retained his power until his final passage over the surf and departure for home.

CHAPTER XLI.

GOVERNORSHIP OF MR. RICHARD BENYON.

1735—36.

Mr. Benyon became Governor of Madras at a critical period in the history of Southern India. The instability of the throne of the Mogul was felt in every durbar throughout the Peninsula; for the succession no longer depended so much upon the Court at Delhi as upon local intrigues; and this state of things is fully illustrated by the notices of the intrigues which were carried on at Arcot subsequent to the death of the respected Sadatulla Khan. Again, from the time of Governor Macrae the Carnatic had suffered from a general famine, occasioned not so much by a failure in the rains, as by the neglect in repairing the tanks; a neglect which characterized the government of the Mogul, and led the unhappy Ryots to look back with regret to the paternal rule of their own Rajahs. This state of things is so lucidly explained in a general letter to the Court of Directors, dated 1733, that we extract the passage.

"Before this country was conquered by the Mogul, it was divided into several circles under the government of particular Rajahs, which descended from father to son. Their revenues for the most part were from the produce of the land,

and they therefore were always careful to keep up the banks of the tanks, or reservoirs of water, and to cleanse them of the mud; of which they were at the expense themselves, knowing that the land would produce more or less according as they had a quantity of water. But the Moguls who have now the government of the country, and are continued in those governments only during pleasure, do not think themselves under the same obligation to be at that expense for their successors. By which means in process of time the tanks are almost choked up, and great part of the lands lie uncultivated for want of water. This alone would occasion grain to be scarce and of course dear; to which if we add the rapacious disposition of the Moguls, altogether intent upon making the most of their governments while they continue in them, we need not seek far for the reason why even within these ten years the lands which are tenanted are let for more than double what they were before. Your Honours will easily conceive what effect it must have upon the produce of such lands; and we need not say much more to demonstrate it to you. Certain it is that Paddy at 25 pagodas the garce, is in these times thought cheap; whereas 20 years ago at that price it was reckoned a famine. The scarcity at present is so great that it sells for 40 pagodas a garce, and our November rains failing us this year gives us a melancholy prospect of the next harvest."

The following is the official entry of Mr. Benyon's accession.

"Thursday, 23rd January, 1735. George Morton Pitt, Esq. late President of this place, having embarked this morning on board the "Mountague," and the succession to the Government devolving thereby on Richard Benyon, Esq., late Deputy Governor of this place,—he accordingly takes the chair; and the Company's Servants and inhabitants all attending, the Secretary read the Letter from the Honourable Court of Directors dated the 10th November 1732, wherein the said Richard Benyon, Esq. is constituted President and Governor of this place on Mr. Pitt's going away."

The following domestic entries are not devoid of interest.

"Thursday, 23rd January, 1735. Sailed for England "the Mountague," Captain Richard Goffright, with Mr. Pitt our late President, Major Roach, and the Revd. Mr. Wynch Passengers; and the "Duke of Dorset," Captain Thomas Gilbert, with Mr. Turner and his family on board."

"Monday, 27th January, 1735. One of the Chaise horses being entirely spoiled, and the other very old and consequently useless,—agreed to sell them at outcry at the seagate, and ordered the Pay Master look out for another pair."

"Monday, 10th March, 1785. The Pay Master reports that he has purchased a pair of horses for 200 Pagodas, in the room of the two old horses ordered to be sold."

"Monday, 10th March, 1735. The Company's plate being very old, and most of it entirely useless, —ordered that the Pay Master melt down the several particulars mentioned in a list entered after this consultation; and a quantity of new plate being offered in exchange for the weight only,—it was agreed to accept the same, and that the difference between the produce of the one and the cost of the others be paid out of cash."

We may here remark that the general table had been originally supplied at the expense of the Company; but what with the cheating of stewards, and the large consumption of wine and general extravagance, the expenditure gradually reached the large sum of 13,000 pagodas, or nearly £6000 per annum. Accordingly the general table was abolished in the year 1722, and the President was allowed 7000 pagodas per annum as an equivalent. From this sum he made an allowance of ten pagodas per mensem to each of the members of Council, and eight pagodas per mensem to each of the under servants, contenting himself with the remainder, which however he found short of the expense. Whether the Company's servants continued to diet together is nowhere stated; but from the following list of Company's plate, we might almost infer that such was the case.

LIST OF SILVER PLATE MELTED DOWN.

	oz.	dwt.
1 Large Bowl ....pr.	36	10
1 Small do.	15	5
3 Tumblers................	15	5
An Aster and Chelinger......	155	0
2 Fan handles	17	10
3 Rose water Bottles...	36	0
1 Tankard................	30	10
34 Spoons	48	15
1 Mustard Spoon........	0	8
5 Dishes	186	10
Carried over...	541	13

LIST OF SILVER PLATE OFFERED IN CHANGE.

	oz.	dwt.
15 Dishes............. 4 Dozen of plates }	1546	16
2 Large waiters. 4 Small do. ... }	111	9
1 Tea kettle and Lamp............	77	10
1 Large Tankard...	49	7
2 Mugs...	26	14
3 Casters............	33	2
1 Stand for oil, vinegar and pepper...	28	5
Carried over...	1873	3

LIST OF SILVER PLATE MELTED DOWN.
Continued.

		oz.	dwt.
	Brought forward...	641	13
4	Covers...	193	0
32	Plates ...	408	5
1	Saucepan ...	15	15
6	Candlesticks ...	83	15
2	Small Salvers...	22	10
5	Cuspadores ...	42	15
9	Salt Sellers...	20	10
1	Monteth ...	69	10
2	Lions, 2 Pine apples and 20 Tossels...	159	0
	A Punch Bowl and cover...	42	15
	A Dishrung...	15	15
6	Casters...	48	5
2	Plates and 12 Spoons.	56	15
11	Knife handles...	20	10
1	Pr. Snuffers...	3	0

IN THE STEWARD'S HAND.

		oz.	d.		
	A Cake of Silver	4	5		
2	Setts old worn out Palankeen tossels...	47	15		
				52	0
			oz ..	1884	13

LIST OF SILVER PLATE OFFERED IN CHANGE.
Continued.

		oz.	dwt.	
	Brought forward...	1873	2	
2	Boats for Sauce ..	37	1	
1	Stand for dishes...	15	0	
4	Salts...	11	4	
1	Tea pot...	16	5	
1	Orange Strainer...	2	18	
1	Soup Ladle...	7	16	
4	Doz. of knives and forks... 4 Dozen and 10 Spoons ...	207	2	12
1	Marrow Spoon...	1	11	0
8	Candlesticks with Sockets and 2 pair Snuffers with Stands ...	135	10	0
	oz ..	2367	10	12

The following entry illustrates the relation of the English towards the native inhabitants.

"Wednesday, 11th June, 1735. Resolved that notice be given at all the gates and by beat of the tom tom, that all persons produce their titles to their lands, houses, &c. within six months from this date ; for which all those whose titles are already registered and certified by any of the Justices shall pay no fees ; and those whose titles have been already registered in either the Choultry or Mayor's Court, but not certified, shall pay only the fee due to the Justices; and such who have neither paid that duty, nor registered their titles at all, shall pay the full fees herein before established; and to prevent delay in the same, it is further ordered that notice be given at the same time that the Honourable Company, as Proprietors of the soil, will resume into their hands all such houses and grounds as at the expiration of the said term of six months shall not be registered as above directed."

Our next extract gives us a glimpse of the state of affairs at Arcot.

"Monday, 7th July, 1735. The President laid before the Board the particulars of the presents designed for the Court at Arcot, that had been delayed till this time for several reasons that would be more tedious than necessary to recite. But what he particularly offered to the observation of the Board was the number and value of the presents. For though that to the Nabob is no more than usual, yet those to the others are new, and for which the precedents are very rare. The last Nabob (Sadatulla) would very seldom suffer any but himself to send a Seerpaw; whereas in February last Sunta Sahib, Subder Ali Sahib, Jehare Khan and Imaum Sahib, had all of them taken upon them to send distinct Seerpaws to the President; which proceeded in some measure from the situation of affairs at Arcot, and had also made a return necessary and unavoidable. For the present Nabob (Dost Ali) has for some time past devoted himself chiefly to a religious life, and left the management of affairs to those who would struggle for it;* a conduct that has occasioned every violent contests between Sunta Sahib, and Subder Ally Sahib, in one of which the Nabob himself was obliged to fly from Arcot. The contention between the two brothers had also occasioned an

* Our readers in general are not likely to be imbued with a strong historical appetite; but those who will take the trouble to wade through the following note, will find that it will throw considerable light on the state of affairs at Arcot. In the first place it will be remembered that Sadatulla Khan, Nabob of Arcot, died in 1732. Having no sons of his own, he had adopted two nephews, Dost Ali and Boker Ali. Dost Ali inherited the Nabobship of Arcot, and Boker Ali the Governorship of Vellore. There was also a nephew of Sadatulla's favorite wife, named Gulam Hassein; and this Gulam Hassein was appointed Dewan or prime minister of Dost Ali the new Nabob.

Dost Ali, who appears to have belonged to that ordinary type of oriental princes, who are sensualists in youth and devotees in old age, had at least two sons who had arrived at man's estate, viz. Subder Ali and Sunta Sahib. Also he had several daughters: one of whom was married to Mortiz Ali, son of Boker Ali, Governor of Vellore; whilst another was married to a distant relation named Chunda Sahib. Chunda Sahib, Mortiz Ali, and Subder Ali subsequently took a prominent part in the struggle between the English and French for the supremacy in the Carnatic. Chunda Sahib seems to have originally risen to power by judicious matchmaking. Besides marrying a daughter of the reigning Nabob Dost Ali, he gave one of his own daughters by a former wife to the Dewan Gulam Hassein. His real reason for the match was because Gulam Hassein was a complete fool. The result was that Chunda Sahib so far availed himself of the incapacity of Gulam Hassein, as to prevail on the Nabob to permit him (Chunda) to administer the office of Dewan in the room of his incapable son-in-law.

alteration in the interest of the Ministers, and Coop Chund (better known as Chunda Sahib) is again come into power, and a considerable influence in the affairs at Arcot. For which reason the President had been advised, when he was sending up to the other presents, to take some notice also of Chunda Sahib, though he had received no Seerpaw from him. The French and Dutch have also been very liberal this year with their presents to Arcot, particularly upon the marriage of Hassein Ali Khan; an expense that has been saved to our Company, it not being the practice of the Durbar to make a present upon any particular occasion before a return has been made for the Seerpaws. Which also was another reason why the President was not in haste to remove the other difficulties, which had so long kept him from sending these. The Board being satisfied of the necessity of making these presents, approved the list; and we hope our Honourable Masters will be persuaded, it has not been in our power to be better husbands upon the occasion."

The next extract seems to refer to a sect of Hindoo Quakers.

"Monday, 14th July, 1735. Terwaddee, a Guzerat attending, represents to the Board, that he had been summoned to answer on oath before the Mayor's Court as a witness in a cause there depending; and on refusal to take an oath, had been fined by the Court, though he represented to them that it was contrary to the custom of the Guzerats ever to take an oath; and prayed to be relieved therefrom by this Board.

"Whereupon the Board remembering that in the year 1731, all the principal Guzerats were summoned on a Jury, and submitted to a fine for non-appearance on account of this very thing; and that though the fine was for that time levied, yet the Sheriff, and all who have since succeeded in that office, were cautioned never to return any more of that caste; that so neither they should be forced to an action against their laws on the one side, nor the authority of the Courts of Justice lessened by their not being punished for their disobedience on the other. It was agreed to have been long since settled that the Guzerats ought not to be compelled to take an oath, since it is contrary to the known rules of their Castes; and the Honourable Company having directed us to remit such fines laid by the Mayor's Court, as seem to carry with them more than ordinary severity,—It is agreed that the fine on Terwaddee be remitted."

The following petition from the Washers is very curious. It would seem to indicate that in time of famine the people actually sold themselves to the Company in order to be sent to Bencoolen; and that persons convicted of theft were likewise sent to Bencoolen as a punishment. We extract the petition in full, from the consultations of the 2nd August, 1735.

"*The Petition of the Washers.*

"Humbly Showeth.

"With submission to your Honors, your Petitioners humbly take this opportunity to lay their case before your Honors' feet. That from several years they have been servants to the Honorable Company as Washermen; and has always used their best endeavours in their service, which was carried on by 500 Washers; and that the severe famine which begun to continue from Mr. Macrae's Government till the end of Mr. Pitt's, forced great part of the said Washers to quit the place, and fly to those parts where they could procure grain, &c. cheaper. Some of them, being infirm and unable to walk, died. At last most part of those that remained and escaped, were obliged to dispose of themselves their wives and children, &c.; so that by these misfortunes great many families are come to decay, and the number of them is very much decreased, that at present there is no more but about 100 Washermen that are fit to work; who, unless your Petitioners should send for many others to join with them in their business, as we have annually done since the continuance of these famines, will not be able enough to carry on their business; to which purpose your Petitioners are obliged to send for some from the country, though it is a great trouble for them.

"Your Petitioners are very sorry to assert that some of their people were so unfortunate, though their wicked proceedings and offences to be put under confinement, and exasperate your Honour so far against them as to create in your Honor a design of sending them to the West coast (as your Petitioners were informed). Your Honor therefore is earnestly entreated to consider, that their ill behaviours proceeded from the change of their stations into a most miserable condition by means of the famines above mentioned; and they being of very illiterate and vulgar spirits, are consequently very ignorant of all right and well mannered behaviours whatsoever.

"Your poor Petitioners therefore most humbly presume to beseech and pray your Honour, begging that your Honor, through your candour and well known goodness, will be so pleased to pardon, forgive, and excuse them the forementioned prisoners from their crimes whatsoever; that they may thereby be released from their confinements, and enter themselves into the number of their families; that they may preserve their healths in a very grateful remembrance of your Honors undoubted favour, which is hoped to be conferred towards these poor creatures by your Honor. For which your poor petitioners as in duty bound shall ever pray."

This petition was granted; the Head Washerman with Tomby Chetty agreeing to pay the expenses of the Company in behalf of the delinquents.

Another petition of the same date, from the two natives who had been appointed to found and settle the new Weavers town named Chindadre pettah, will explain itself.

"Humbly Showeth,

"That when your Honor and the late Honorable George Morton Pitt, Esq., was pleased to order your Petitioners to send for certain number of Weavers for erecting a pettah, now called Chindadre pettah; and to advance them moneys to settle at that place, in order to persuade many more to come there, that the said town might flourish, and be well inhabited, and become capable of producing large quantities of Calicoes, which should be manufactured there to the great benefit and interest of the Honorable Company :—Your Honor, and the aforesaid Honorable George Morton Pitt, Esq., was graciously pleased to promise the Honorable Company's and Your Honor's favorable protection and encouragement to your Petitioners, if they should carry on and settle the aforesaid town.

"Your Petitioners, in reliance upon such promises and permission, did use their utmost care and labour towards getting some proper persons to be sent by your Petitioners to the several pettahs in the country, where the weavers have their habitations, with presents and moneys, to answer the charge of theirs and their families, travelling expences to Madras; where Your Petitioners prepared them proper lodgings &c. till the houses were built for them in the aforesaid Chindadre pettah. And as they were destitute of money and other necessaries, and much distressed and impoverished by the course of a long and severe famine, your Petitioners were suspicious of their stay; to secure which they advanced them certain sums of money, to refresh and settle the said inhabitants and families with proper necessaries required for their use.

"Your Petitioners further laboured and took great care in transplanting the trees of the garden, which stood at that place where Chindadre pettah is built; levelled that ground and procured all things necessary for building the houses, &c., as is not unknown to your Honor. On which account they have already expended between the sums of five and six thousand pagodas. For your Petitioners own labour and service in these matters, they expect no other advantage, than the great benefit of gaining your Honor's constant favour towards them.

" The houses that are already built at Chindadre pettah are one hundred.

" Your Petitioners now most humbly entreat you Honor to grant them that sum, which was promised unto them to be advanced when Chindadre pettah was designed to be erected; and what favorable encouragement the erectors of the said Pettah are thought worth to be gratified with, they humbly leave to your Honors most gracious pleasure."

The amount requested was of course paid to the two Natives; and as some of our readers may be interested in glancing over some of the expenses incurred in building a new town, we subjoin the account of the expenditure.

" An account of sundry charges or expenses, and several advancements and supplements made for erecting a town called Chindadre pettah are as follows :—

From 26th Oct. 1734 to 25th Nov. 1734.	Expended towards digging a foundation where Chauka was buried with accustomary ceremonies giving dinner to the poor Brahmins, transplanting the trees from those places where the streets were to be marked out, levelling that ground and making out the streets, &c., as per account particulars is............	114 9 82

Presents to the following head weavers viz.

From 25th Nov. 1734to31st Aug. 1735. Andiapa—broad cloth Aroia 3 yard at 1 pag. per yards......	3	0	0				
Arnachellum do. 3 yards at 1 do. per yard......................	3	0	0				
Corruppu do. 3 yards do. ...	3	0	0				
					9	0	0
Batta paid to the several persons that were sent to the Weavers in the country in order to pursuade and bring them to Chindadre pettah..........................					10	0	0
Supplement of grain given to the several weavers through the means of following heads, viz.:							
Andiapa—Rice 1 garce 100 maracal at 100 pag. per garce ...	125	0	0				
Arnachellem—1 garce 100 ...	125	0	0				
Corruppa— 1 garce 100 ...	125	0	0				
—3,300—					375	0	0
Paid the Banksall Merchants for the house poles country reapers, &c., necessary for house building..........................					252	25	0
Advanced to Chidambra pillay for providing house poles country reapers, &c., necessaries from Chicaricode........................	550	0	0				
Mooree 1 Pg. presented Chidrambera pillay.....................	1	0	0				
					551	0	0
Palmeras 22,600 at Paga. 7½ per 100...					1,695	0	0
Palmer reapers 40,000 at Paga. 14 per 100					560	0	0
Clay for Mud walls 42,200 Baskets at 400 Baskets per pagoda..................					105	18	0
Palmer Coir 1824 Bundles at 72 for a pagoda..................................					25	12	0
Wood reapers thin and a sort of nails (by the country word) called foolish Sugar canes, 1840 Bundles at 30 per pagoda					61	12	0

Cooly paid towards making mud walls.				165	5	0
Carpenters' cooly..........................				150	0	0
Advanced the Sawers				20	0	0
Bricklayers..................................				55	0	0
Smiths..				60	0	0
Cooly for making the top part of the houses				152	15	0
Tyles advanced for..........................				450	0	0
Brick kilns advanced them..................				400	0	0
Cooly paid towards levelling the lower parts of the streets where there was digged for taking up sand to fix with clay for walls				60	25	0
Cooly hire for bringing the house poles, reapers, country woods, &c. from the Sea-side and bricks and tiles from the kilns...				80	15	0
Advanced to Vashampillay for providing planks for making the doors from Jafnapatam.............................	450	0	0			
Mooree 1 Py. presented him	1	0	0			
				451	0	0
Cooly paid towards transplanting the several trees in the garden				39	32	20
Cooly for watering the trees.................				68	2	0
Paid the Conocopillys and peons who were employed in Chindadre pettah for 10 months				75	12	0
Total Pagodas...				5,987	2	48

Another petition from the inhabitants of Triplicane, praying to be relieved from the duty which Governor Macrae had levied on tobacco and betel, is well worthy of preservation both as regards matter and manner. It is entered in consultations of 2nd August, 1735.

"*The Petitions of the Painters, Weavers, &c. Inhabitants of Triplicane.*

"Humbly Showeth,

"That when the Honorable Company first had this village under this Government, your Petitioners flocked to it as birds do under the cover of a great tree; and the Governor of that time received us, and kindly took us under his protection. From which time forward we lived in peace, and did our duty and the Company's business with great pleasure, till the time of Governor Macrae; who to our great misfortune first laid upon us the tax on betel and tobacco, by joining the same with the farm of Madras. May it please your Honor, that we presume to inform you, that it is the nature of us of this country to use great quantities of betel and tobacco; insomuch that if we have not, or cannot be permitted, by reason of a hurry of business which some times happens, to go to our victuals, we can cheerfully bear it, if we have but betel and tobacco; but we cannot go through our work without it, and being always thinking of it, and longing for it, we leave our business to go out of the Bounds to get it; and so we are hindered from doing our work, and by that means the several owners of the goods have them not returned them at the proper and appointed times; by which we lose great part of our pay; and people imagining that we are negligent, and always running from our business, are afraid to give us employ; by all which we have lost our livelihood, and are reduced to a great poverty. But as we are now happy in so good a Governor as Your Honor, we pray you will please to take our case into consideration, and relieve us from the burden of the betel and tobacco farm ; which never till the time of Governor Macrae was laid on this village ; which, if Your Honor shall think fit to grant, we shall constantly offer up our thanks in Divine Service, and mind to labour strictly, and to discharge our duties in our several businesses ; and when the inhabitants that have left this place shall hear the farm is taken off, they will cheerfully return again to their habitations, the place will flourish, and your Petitioners as in duty bound shall ever pray."

The result of this petition is thus recorded.

"Friday, 8th August, 1735. The Petition from the inhabitants of Triplicane being then considered, the Board agreed unanimously that the laying on the duty on tobacco and betel in that and other villages in Mr. Macrae's time, had almost depopulated those villages ; and that there is great reason to apprehend if that duty be longer continued there, the few remaining inhabitants will also desert. It was therefore resolved to take off the said duty in all the villages."

The following story, inserted in the consultations of the 15th September 1735, in the form of an explanation, will explain itself.

"Palmer, a soldier, and one Williams, having an intrigue to carry on with one of Mrs. Harrington's lodgers, who at that time was gallanted by some Swedes, agreed, in order to appropriate the more effectually that lodger to their own use, to drive the Swedes from the house. They went thither accordingly and began to quarrel. The mistress of the house sent her servant to call a Guard. The servant, who by chance espied Ensign Stewart in the street, ran to him, and made his address to him. The Ensign, trusting to his own sufficiency, went without a Guard. Upon his arrival he found Dessey and Palmer, two soldiers, who being more immediately under his command, he ordered them to be gone. Dessey walked off. But Palmer not regarding the said Ensign's order, he the Ensign was obliged to enforce it, by applying his cane to Palmer's shoulders. Whereupon Williams, who had hitherto been only a spectator, and Palmer, both together, closed in with the Ensign. But he readily disengaging himself from them, and putting himself in a posture of defence, bade them keep off. In short seeing themselves foiled and disappointed they retired.

"About 9 o'clock that evening, Williams and Palmer passing through the Choultry guard where the Serjeant was walking, asked him if he had heard any thing of their having quarrelled that evening with Ensign Stewart. To which he answered in the negative. They then fell a bragging how heartily they would have drubbed him had they been armed as well as he the said Ensign was. The Serjeant bade them take care how they talked at that rate. Williams notwithstanding went on, and told the Serjeant that he would have his revenge, and for that very purpose would be on perdue for the Ensign; and that he had a good quarter staff which he believed would do his business. To which Palmer answered, that if his quarter staff would not do, he had a good knife that should do; and then they bid the Serjeant good night.

"When the Ensign came to his guard, the Serjeant told him what words had passed between Palmer, Williams, and himself. The Ensign made his report next morning to the Captain of the main guard, and complained of Williams and Palmer, who were thereupon ordered to be taken up. Williams, not being a soldier, was sent to a Justice of the peace; who finding sufficient cause for his commitment, bound him over to the Sessions; and Palmer was confined to the Main Guard. Next morning Palmer was publicly reproved for his disobedience to his officers; and being a new man, not yet acquainted with the rules of the Garrison, was acquitted without any further censure or punishment.

"Subsequently, Palmer finding that he was not permitted to converse freely with Williams now in Gaol, wrote him several letters; in one of which "he applauded the brave resolution which Williams had taken to revenge himself on his Enemies so soon as set at liberty; and that he might depend on his assistance at all times." But Williams, who for sometime had suspected Palmer of treachery, sent this letter to the Captain of the Guard, who carried it to the Governor; who after having perused it, gave orders to Captain Eckman to put Palmer into the Cockhouse, to give him a gentle exemplary punishment. Which was performed by the Corporal, by giving Palmer twenty four stripes on the shoulders, more to disgrace than hurt him, and his Military coat only being pulled off and not otherwise stripped. He was then sent to the West coast."

In October 1735, Subder Ali, Chunda Sahib, and Khan Bahadar the King's Dewan, paid a visit to St. Thomé; whereupon, in accordance with the advice of Imaun Sahib, an officer of high rank at Arcot and a great friend of the English, presents were dispatched to all these by Governor Benyon. The result is thus recorded.

"Tuesday, 18th November, 1735. The President delivers to the Board an account of the presents, and other extraordinary charges, upon Nabob Subder Ali Khan, Nabob Khan Bahader, and Chunda Sahib's coming down to St. Thomé and Madras; which, including that to Imaun Sahib, amounts in the whole to Pagodas 1936, fanams 18 and cash 55.

"At the same time he delivered to the Board sundry Takheeds from the above mentioned persons, to their taxgatherers; directing them to pass provisions for the Town free of customs; which are entered after this consultation."

"*Takeed from Imaum Sahib to Mahomud Moctune Governor of Punnaree and Pulicat, Oct.* 13*th* 1735.

"I have been lately informed that the Governor of Madras's people, going and coming to and from Vizagapatam by the way of Punnaree and Pulicat, have been often stopped by your people for Juncan; for which cause I write to inform you that as there is no difference between the Governor and me, therefore you must not stop or hinder his people on any pretence whatever."

"*From Subder Ally Khan to Shedee Busheer, October* 13*th* 1735.

"I am informed that you have often stopped the

people from digging clay to make bricks for the Governor of Madras; wherefore I write you that, as soon as you see this my perwana, you shall no more stop or hinder his people, but let every thing be done relating to this affair as usual."

"*From the same person to the same person, October 3rd* 1735.

"There is a strict friendship lately settled between me and the Governor of Madras, and we are as brothers. I therefore command you to obey whatever orders you receive from him, as you would from myself, without any hinderance or interruption; in which you are to observe this as a strict Takheed; and in all things relating to the Mettow &c., you are to let them go on according to Sallabad; and whatever Takheeds I have sent you before this you are to act according to the contents of them."

"*From Imaum Sahib to Governor Benyon, December 1st* 1735.

"I have not received any letter from your Honor a great while, but have often wished for them. According to your Honor's desire I have procured Nabob Subter Ali Khan's three perwanas to the Havildar of Poonamallee country, which I now send to your Honor, and their attested Copies, under the seal of the Caujee at Arcot; so your Honor may keep the originals and send those copies to the Havildar. The Nabob's son Subder Ali Khan, and Chunda Sahib, have your Honors friendship often in rememberance, and speak much of your praise.

"Subdar Ali Khan has lately received from the Mogul's Court the Honour to command 5000 Horse; a Nagarah and a flag was sent him on the occasion, and he is named Sadatula Khan. And to Chunda Sahib, has been given the command of 2500 horse, and the name of Hussen Doast Khan. On which it will be proper and look friendly for your Honor to write them letters of Congratulation. I desire your Honor will always believe me as ready to serve in yours as my own affairs."

Takheed from Nabob Subder Ali Khan to Shedee Bysheed Havilder, of Poonamallee, October 21st 1735.

"I have granted free of customs all cattle that is carried in and out of Madras; so you are to take none on them."

Another Takheed from the same person to the same, October 21st 1735.

"I have granted free of custom, all firewood, bratty, straw, grass, and such like things carried into Madras; so you are to take none on them. This you are to observe as a strict Tahkeed."

The following consultations on municipal matters, including the repairing of the Bridges, will explain themselves.

"Wednesday, 25th November, 1735. The Coroner having reported to the President, that he lately sat on the body of a child found drowned in a well; and the like accidents having frequently happened of late years, occasioned by the want of proper Breast works to the said wells;—it is ordered the Scavenger do repair such of the public wells as need it, so as to prevent the like danger for the future; and that the tom tom be beat through the bounds, directing all persons who have wells in their grounds and houses, to do the same, under penalty of being punished if neglected.

"The Bridges next the town, and that in the way to Triplicane, being both much out of repair; insomuch that if some care be not taken they will soon be so bad that they will require to be new built:—It was moved to consider what means to take for putting them into some tolerable repair; since the fund which used to be appropriated to such uses—viz. the Town Connacopolys duty, is, by the Honorable Court of Directors in their last letter, order to be passed to the credit of their Revenues.

"There appeared to the Board only three ways of doing this. One by an assessment on the inhabitants; the next by a duty to be established as a fund for keeping them in a constant repair; the third at the Company's expense. The two former of which have considerable inconveniences and difficulties attending them. An assessment would make the inhabitants very uneasy, lest whenever it should be thought proper to undertake any new thing for the use of the place it should be drawn into a precedent. Besides that the expense would fall on the persons immediately inhabiting here, whose residence among us, is by the necessary state of the trade and circumstances of the place, very uncertain; and new comers would reap the benefit of it, without being at any part of the charge. A Duty appropriated for these used to be levied by way of a toll, would in all probability be collected with great difficulty, and would hardly answer; since the bridges are of use only in the winter season of the year, when the waters are high; and therefore the country people would avoid paying, by passing the rivers without coming to the bridges in the other seasons. And to levy duties for repairing these bridges, without the persons who pay the same reaping any advantage thereby, as would be the case if any other method but a turnpike was made use of, would occasion much murmuring among the inhabitants; of which we find a remarkable instance in the case of the scavenger's duty, which though levied for their real benefit is still looked upon as a grievance.

"Upon the whole it was agreed that the Pay Master do disburse what is necessary to repair the Town Bridge and Triplicane Bridge; first making an estimate of the expense to be laid before the Board.

"Which resolution the Board were induced to take in consideration of the general use of the Bridges to the Town, and the advantage of them to the Company in particular; which to all who have been here any time is very apparent, and may be proved to others by the amount of our customs, which are now very high, notwithstanding our foreign trade has for several years past been almost constantly attended with disappointments, and many branches of the customs thereby reduced to nothing. Yet these losses have been abundantly made up by the consumption of many other articles; to which consumption the easy access to the place, and constant and certain intercourse that has been by means of the bridges kept open with the country, has greatly if not entirely contributed.

"Agreed further to repeat our request to our Honorable Masters, that they will again permit us to make use of the produce of the Town Conacoply's duty for these and such other uses.

"The Justices of the Choultry report to the Board, that they have had under confinement in the Choultry prison for sometime past, two persons for a robbery committed in the country; whom they are at a loss how to proceed about; because by the late Charter, we are not empowered to take cognizance of any crime committed above ten miles distant from any English settlement; and therefore they have not yet bound them over, although the robbery is plainly proved by the confession of the one and the goods being found upon the other.

"Which being considered the Board agreed, by an express limitation in the Charter, they cannot proceed against these persons according to the English laws. That delivering them up to the country Government would be attended with ill consequences; since it would be urged as a precedent in other cases in future; and that letting them escape would be yet worse, since it would give encouragement to future attempts of the like kind. Wherefore it was after a long consideration unanimously determined and resolved to send the two prisoners to Bencoolen, on the first vessel bound thither, to be slaves for life to the Company. This resolution the Board thought justified by the Charter; since being therein directed to act as much in conformity to the laws of England as the condition and circumstances of the place will admit of, the Board cannot but be of opinion His Majesty intended by the above expressions to give us a liberty—(in consideration that in so distant a colony, and among people whose religion, laws and customs are so infinitely different from our own, many things must unavoidably happen for which the laws of England have made no provision, and many others where the execution of these laws would be attended with very fatal consequences to settlement)—of acting in all such cases so as should appear most consonant to the well-being and security of the place; and of this nature the Board think the case now before us to be."

The following results of a debate, upon the advantages or otherwise of selling the Broad cloth imported from Europe by public outcry or by contract, are worthy of preservation.

"Tuesday, 6th January, 1736. The advantages and disadvantages of selling the Broad cloth received from Europe at outcry, were debated, and the Board agreed as follows:—

"That Broad cloth may be sold at outcry sometimes for a higher price than the Company's Merchants give for it; but that there appears no other possible advantage from it. That on the other hand the disadvantages are:—

"1st. That there must be a long trust, and perhaps some bad debts made.

"2nd. That if we do not always sell by contract, our Merchants will not take it when the price doth not answer at outcry.

"3rd. That those who buy at outcry will buy only for the present demand.

"4th. That consequently the consumption is not likely to be increased by it.

"That selling by contract has no inconvenience attending it, but a possibility of sometimes getting a larger price at outcry. But the advantages of it are:

"1st. A certain profit to the Company on what sold.

"2nd. The consumption also certain.

"3rd. A security from bad debts, the goods being kept in our hands till the money is paid.

"And if the Governing Moors continue the method they are this year fallen into, the selling by contract may very probably increase the consumption; since if the Nabobs and other great officers find a profit by buying this cloth, it is evident they will encourage the use of it; and as they pay no juncans in the country, they can afford to sell it cheaper than private Merchants can, and having always large quantities of money by them they take off large parcels at once.

"To this perhaps it may be said, that we might deal with the great Moormen for it ourselves; but we can by no means believe our Honorable Masters would approve of our engaging in transactions with the Government, that might possibly be attended with disputes; the consequences of which no body, can foresee, much less avoid; for which reason it has been the constant maxim of this place to have no dealings in trade with them.

"Upon the whole it was resolved to continue the present method, unless we should receive orders from our Honorable Masters to the contrary."

The following entry explains itself.

"Monday, 5th March, 1736. The Rental General reports that there are a very great number of persons taxed in the Rent Roll at four and six fanams each, who are real objects of compassion; being either old men past their labour; or poor widow women who live by spinning of cotton thread, or beating paddy, and the like sorts of work, by which they cannot get more than thirty

21

or thirty-five cash per day; that the major part of the bad debts arise from taxing these people; and that having the new Roll ready all but affixing the rates which every one is to pay, he desires directions of the Board whether these persons shall be excused or continued on the Roll as usual.

"The frequently repeated orders from our Honorable Masters for relieving the poor, making any debate on this subject unnecessary, the Rental General was ordered to prepare the new Roll as soon as possible; and therein to omit charging all such as appeared to him to be real objects of charity; and when done to present the same for the approval of the Board."

The circumstances related below are very curious as furnishing an illustration of the administration of the English nation amongst the Natives, who are not inhabitants of Madras. Though they are somewhat lengthy, we prefer putting them into smaller type to abridging them.

"Monday, 19th April, 1736. The President addressed himself to the Board to the following purport.

"Gentlemen.

"There have lately happened two cases here, which I think necessary to lay before you, for your consideration and determination thereupon. The one is my having confined a Guzerat Merchant on a complaint from the country. The other is an arrest out of the Mayor's Court served on the person of a Polligar; an inhabitant indeed of ours, but at the time of serving the said arrest, being in the Moors' territories. As the former of these may possibly be represented as a breach of the rules prescribed by the Royal Charter; and my interposing in the other be represented as an infringement of the rights of the Mayor's Court;—I shall give you an account of the several circumstances attending each of them, and you will come to such a determination upon them as you shall judge reasonable.

"The first of these cases is as follows :—

"Sometime in January last, notice was brought me that one Moal Chund, a Guzerat Merchant of this place, was missing and gone off, as it was said, upwards of 30,000 pagodas in debt to the Arcot Shroffs and several others. Among many particulars which were told me at that time relating to his disappearing, it was said that the night before, Amboi Doss, one of his creditors had been at his house and carried many things away. Several blows were given, and Moal Chund was heard to groan. This last circumstance creating a suspicion of foul play, I ordered strict inquiry to be made after Moal Chund; till being assured by some persons of good credit, that he was alive and well but retired out of the bounds, I did not think myself obliged to take any notice of what had passed, without some regular complaint should be made me, knowing it was an usual and common way of proceeding among the country people. But the 2nd of February I received a letter from Moal Chund complaining of the usage he had received from Amboi Doss, which by this means I was obliged to take notice of. However, considering how tender the credit of the Shroffs is, I would not send for Amboi Doss to the Fort, but ordered the Polligar to send to his house, to tell him the nature of the complaint, and that he must name securities for his continuing in the bounds. After which, I told the messenger that brought the letter, I would take care Amboi Doss should be forthcoming; but for the letters of license, Moal Chund must himself settle that with his creditors. I heard nothing further of Moal Chund, or his affairs, till sometime after I saw him in discourse with several other Merchants in the Fort; and inquiring how long he had been in the bounds, was answered that he came in two days after his letters, by consent of his creditors; who had all of them settled their accounts with him, and agreed upon the time for their being paid; and indeed I concluded it had been so, having often seen him since in company with Amboi Doss and Shankarapareek's Gomasta; but six days ago I received a letter from Imaum Sahib by a horseman, who at the same time brought another to Hodjee Addy. So soon as the horseman had delivered me the letter, I gave him the customary answer that I would get it translated, expecting upon that he would have withdrawn; but he told me he was acquainted with the purport of the letters which related to a demand his master had upon Moal Chund, arising from a sum of money lent him by the hands of Shankarapareek's Gomastas (who came with him); and as his message and the letters he brought could not be long a secret, he hoped I would order Moal Chund into custody, lest he should withdraw himself out of the bounds, and make his escape out of the province. Upon this I asked Shankarapareek's Gomastas, if they had made any application to me or elsewhere, and been denied all that was necessary for their security, that they should give Imaum Sahib the trouble of writing me a letter. I asked them the question in such a manner, that I found by their answer they understood what I meant by it. They told me they had no intention to give Imaum Sahib or me the trouble of that letter; and had only wrote to Shankarapareek the state of the case, and desired his directions whether they should apply to me; but he had given them no other answer, than that they should not concern themselves further about it till they heard from him again, and that they were ignorant of the money being Imaum Sahib's, or of any intention to apply to him.

"The case being new, and of which there was no precedent since the coming out of the Charter, I began to be in doubt whether I had authority to commit Moal Chund to custody; but considering the exigency of the affair, and that by too fearful an attachment to the forms of the law, the peace of the place and the Company's affairs might be brought into dangers, I did no longer hesitate; only out of compassion to Moal Chund, who had made so considerable a figure among the Merchants, I asked Imaum Sahib's messenger, and the Gomastas of Shankarapareek, if they would be contented with his being in the custody of the Polligar. To which they consenting I sent an officer with them to his house, where they found him at home, and from thence they carried him to the Polligar.

"By the ancient rules of the place, no inhabitant is to have any dealings or correspondence with the country Government, without special license; nor are they to make any application to the Governing Moors in any matter or dispute arising in the bounds. But Moal Chund might in this case have pleaded that he dealt with Shankarapareek's Gomastas, as Merchant inhabitant, living under our protection, and as such under no obligation to inquire whose money they traded with; and Shankarapareek's Gomastas might urge that it was well known when they came down here, whose Agents they were; and that it could not be wondered at if they corresponded with, and were subject to the orders of their principals; and that if it was a breach of our laws, they ought to have been told so when they came down, and not suffered to settle in the Town. But the alteration in the circumstances of the place has made a dispensation in some sort necessary; for if we were to keep up to the strictness of the old rules, we should drive almost all the moneyed men out of the place; what the consequence of that would be may be easily guessed, as money is as much the sinews of trade as of war; and I suppose it is very well known now, that almost all the trade of the place is circulated by means of the Arcot money, and the credit our inhabitants have with the Shroffs; and besides that their money is the chief support of the trade of the place, there is another principal advantage we receive by it, that I supposed will be easily guessed at without naming it.

"This being the state of the case, it remains to be considered what method we ought to follow, not only upon the present occasion but all others, that are attended with the like circumstances. It has been a point much debated of late whether any person, since the coming out of the Charter, can be taken up for debt except by warrant issuing out of the Mayor's Court. But besides that it often happens that by the Forms of the Court, it may be some days before a warrant can be taken out. We are not certain that the Moors would submit to follow a process there; but if they should consent thereto, yet many things might occur which would give us infinite uneasiness; for though at present I think we are upon so good terms with the Mayor's Court, that I am willing to hope they would make all possible dispatch in bringing such a suit to an issue; yet we cannot be always sure of such a disposition; and if it should even happen that the majority of that Court should be composed of persons of a malignant disposition towards the interest of the Company, or actuated by prejudices against the Company's Agents, it is very easy to foresee the trouble and confusion, not to only the Company's affairs, but the whole place might be involved in. I suppose it is well known how much it is in the breast of the Court, to prolong the time before any suit is finished; and a message from the Board, if the Court are not rightly disposed, would rather occasion a greater delay than quicken their proceedings.

"But to consider it a little further if we should admit what (by the way) we have very little reason to do; namely, that the Moors should have partience to wait the progress of any of their actions through our Courts; yet should it be put into the heads of the defendants that they might appeal to England, I believe it is very easy to conceive what effect it would have upon the Moors, and how they would receive any notice, that in such case must be given them, that they must follow the appeal to England, I believe there can be no doubt by which they would think they had shown sufficient complaisance in demanding justice of the Company's Agents; and that being refused them they would immediately make a peremptory demand of the debtor to be delivered up to them; and as they always deliver upon debtors, I see not with what equity we could refuse to deliver up theirs, and there would be much to justify any measures which they should resolve on to oblige us to it.

"The other affair I mentioned to you is this :—

"Some days ago the Mayor came with a complaint to me that one of the Court Serjeant, going with a warrant to arrest an inhabitant of Cattawauk, a number of the other inhabitants, together with some peons belonging to the Moors, had beat the Serjeant and rescued the prisoner. Whilst I was considering what orders to give upon the occasion, the Court Serjeant came in to confirm Mr. Mayor's account of the matter; only with this difference, which indeed was a very material one, that he had arrested the man in Trivitash, a village not two miles from the Fort, but out of the Company's bounds. Upon which I told both the Mayor and Serjeant that though the Charter did say the jurisdiction of the Court should extend ten miles, yet I supposed it was to be understood and provided that the Company's bounds had the same extent; but however that might be I was sure the Moors would not suffer the Mayor's warrants to pass in their territories, and therefore they would do well to confine their jurisdiction within that of the Company's. Whilst the Mayor was yet with me, a Messenger came in from the Havildar of Poonamallee, complaining that whilst he was at Trivitash, settling some matters with the Polligar of some of their towns, a white man came their, used the Polligar very ill, by giving him several blows; and seemed determined upon worse treatment, if he had not interposed to prevent it, and he desired that I would give orders that such things might not be done again. I dismissed the Messengers with an answer that I would inquire into it.

"About six the next morning, the Polligar came to me. The account he gave of himself was, that he and his Ancestors had for many generations been Polligars of twenty-five villages under the Moors; three of which namely Cattawauk, Sautongot and Ennore, were about twenty years ago granted by the Mogul to the Company; that these being the farthorest villages from us and separated from all the rest of our bounds, he had very rarely come to Madras, and was quite ignorant of our laws and customs; and this trouble that was now brought upon him was at the instigation of the persons who rented those villages of the Company, with whom he had some difference; and who being better acquainted with the methods of proceeding among us, had taken this way to distress and insult him. The Polligar added that when the Serjeant came to him he was busy with the Havildar of the Poonamallee country, examining a robbery that had happened in one of their villages; that he told the Serjeant he would go with him when he had done; but the Serjeant laid hold of him to carry him away immediately, and gave him several blows with a cane, the marks of which were very visible when I saw him; and that the Serjeant would have suffered more from the Moors for his attempt to carry him away, if he himself had not interposed. The Polligar then delivered me a petition, containing some complaints of the hardships he had suffered from the Company's Renters; who, I suppose, having some intelligence of it (for it seemed to have been wrote some days before) were the more earnest to have him arrested to prevent his delivering of it. I shall say nothing here of the action commenced against him in the Mayor's Court, because it is possible it may come before us in another manner. Neither indeed do I recollect much of the petition, having a few hours after delivered it to the Mayor; to whom I took notice at the same time that I thought the arrest was irregular, and contrary to the constant rule and practice of the place, which exempted all the Poligars from any arrest; established upon very good consideration, and to avoid the consequences which might attend their being taken into custody. Besides that the case of this man was differently circumstanced, being Poligar but of three of our villages, and of twenty-two belonging to the Moors, who would probably claim him, out of an opinion that they had a greater right in him. But otherwise the thing in dispute being only a title to a small piece of ground, of no greater value than twenty or twenty-five pagodas; had it been any body else the necessity of an arrest did not seem to be very urgent, and the directions with the charter were plainly against it. The Poligar appearing in Court some days after to defend his title, the Court began to examine him touching what happened at Trivitash; an enquiry certainly that was very improper, because the arrest being out of the Company's bounds; it is not in our power to support them in it. Before the Court rose, they committed him to prison; where he remained till about six in the evening, when he was discharged after paying forty-six fanams; and then he came to me and complained of it as a matter that was a shame and disgrace to him; and the more so as being done in the sight of his people. The Mayor being with me again the next morning, I asked him how it could be that the Court had treated the Poligar in the manner they had done, after all that I had said to him myself. The Mayor replied that when the Poligar appeared in Court, they did design to have decided the dispute between him and the plaintiff that very day, but some difficulties arising that could not then be cleared up and being twelve at noon, some of the Aldermen cried out let him give bail and answer; and adjourning immediately upon it, he believed the Marshal might have taken him into custody: but did not know that he was imprisoned till the evening, when a person came from him to be his bail. To avoid all further dispute, I was willing to take Mr. Mayor's account of the matter; but told him that when the council met, I believed they would take it into consideration, and think themselves obliged to make some order upon it, to prevent the consequences which might follow if it should be drawn into precedent.

"The Board having seriously considered these two cases, approved the taking of Moal Chund into custody, and desired the purport of what the President had said upon the occasion might be entered upon consultation, as our reasons for the same; that the Company may judge thereof; and that they be desired in our next general letter to give us directions in all cases of the like nature which may happen in future.

"As to the other affair, the ill consequences which may ensue from the breach of the old rules of the place, established for many and very good reasons, induced the Board to come to the following resolutions thereupon.

"Ordered that no Sheriff do serve any warrant of arrest or execution upon the person of the Poligar of Madras, or any of the Poligars of the villages, nor upon their dwelling houses, where they keep their prisoners, nor upon any of the duties due and payable to them for the guard and safety of the town and villages.

"Ordered also that the Sheriff do repay to the Poligar of Cattawauk, the sum of forty-six fanams, taken from the said Poligar by the Sheriff's officers for prison fees."

CHAPTER XLII.

GOVERNORSHIP OF MR. RICHARD BENYON.

1736—40.

The Governorship of Mr. Benyon bridges over the period between the unknown and known history of the Presidency. Up to this date we have been exhuming the annals of a period which was almost a perfect blank in the eyes of men; but now we are approaching an era in which modern history, as it has been written by Orme, Wilks, and Duff, may be said to fairly begin; and thus our future annals will serve rather to enlarge and illustrate our present knowledge than to carry us through a world which was altogether new.

Our first extract refers to what may be called the "woes of the washers," who on the 30th of April, 1736, addressed the following petition to Governor Benyon.

"*The Petition of the Washers.*

"Humbly showeth,

"Whereas your petitioners having faithfully served the Honorable Company in washing their cloth from the first establishment of this place; which they were the better enabled to perform by their having in constant employ between four and five hundred able and sufficient persons of their caste to carry on and discharge the said business effectually; but your petitioners are sorry to acquaint your Honor, that by means of the constant famines which have happened for these ten or eleven years past, their cooly allowance from the Honorable Company has not been sufficient for their subsistance, after the usual charges incident thereon were defrayed; and also that the rice for some time was so scarce and dear, that it could not be procured under quarter or half measure for a fanam. So through these and the like exigencies they were entirely disabled to support themselves and families. Provisions being so scarce, that induced a great number of their people to desert their habitations and take refuge in other parts, where provisions were cheaper; many having sold themselves, wives, and children; and many likewise embarked themselves on several vessels to divers places; together with a great mortality among them, which has reduced them to the small number of about one hundred men, by whom your petitioners assure your Honor it is morally impossible to carry on and discharge their whole duty of washing the cloth. Also another difficulty arises, which further disables your petitioners in completing the whole business, is,—that in former times the long cloth weighed but ten to eleven pound per piece, which was more easy for a man to hold and wash it, especially in such times when they had provisions cheap they were the stronger to perform it. Whereas of late years the long cloth provided has been of between thirteen and fourteen pounds per piece, which in such time of scarcity reduced your petitioners in their strength so much, that they found it impossible for a single man to hold a piece of cloth of that burden and wash it effectually.

"Honorable Sir, your poor petitioners most humbly crave leave to represent to your Honor that the Washers at Fort St. David, Porto Novo, and Vizagapatam have larger privileges and larger benefits to support themselves out of their allowances; by reason of their having rivers of good and fresh water proper for washing of cloths; and their places being near to the woods, whereby they are likewise gainers in purchasing the several ingredients required in washing, as soap, chunam, choud, goat's dung, fuel, &c. But as our river being not so good water, your petitioners are obliged to be at the trouble and expense of having water for their purpose drawn out of the wells; and that your petitioners' allowance from the Honorable Company being only but one pagoda and five fanams for every corge of long cloth's washing, your petitioners crave leave to set forth the charges incident thereon which they defray as follows:

	Pag.	F.	C.
Beating	0	3	0
Cooly hire for carrying brown cloth to washing place... ..	0	1	30
Cooly for carrying it back after it is washed........	0	1	30
Conacopilly's wages........ ...	0	1	0
Goats' dung to rub the brown cloth for washing..............	0	1	0
Chunam, soap and choud......	0	8	0

	Pag.	F.	C.			
Fuel for boiling the cloth three times before it is well washed	0	9	0			
Fuel for boiling congee rice...	0	1	0			
Indigo to prevent the red and brown spots in Congee and cloth	0	0	40			
				0	26	20
For every corge of long cloth's washing, rice allowed to the Congee is—measures sixteen; whereas the merchants account half thereof on their part, and for the other half eight measures they receive in your petitioner's account the value of it.				0	10	40
Pagoda.				1	0	60

So there is but fanams 4 cash 20 to be divided amongst all your petitioners for their livelihood.

"The said pagodas 1 and 5 fanams was the rate allowed to your petitioners when there was a garce of paddy sold for five or six pagodas or thereabouts. But by reason of the severe famines aforementioned, together with the desertion and deaths of so many, your petitioners are reduced to such extreme poverty, and to so small a number of hands, that they are entirely incapable of maintaining themselves and families; and likewise not in a capacity of discharging their duty of washing the cloth effectually.

"Therefore their present necessity and business requires their sending for a larger supply of people out of the country to their assistance; but then their allowance at present being insufficient for the maintenance of your petitioners only through the reasons aforementioned; therefore your petitioners must consequently be incapable to maintain those whom they design to send for to their assistance.

"Your Honor will be pleased further to consider that since the paddy sells at 17 or 18 maracals per pagoda, through your Honor's favour to the poor souls in general; yet the merchants account for the half share of congeeing the cloths beforementioned, at or between 8 and 10 maracals per pagoda. Besides that some years ago when grain was dear, your petitioners were always favoured by the Honorable Company through their warehouse keepers with the free gift of two or three garce of paddy.

"Your petitioners therefore most humbly entreat your Honor will be graciously pleased to take into your most serious consideration their miserable and distressed condition; and only be pleased to forbid the merchants from receiving money for the half share of congeeing the cloths; that thereby your petitioners may receive their full allowance of pagodas 1 and fanams 5 for every corge of long cloths, without any such deduction by the merchants; which will enable your petitioners to procure more hands, and to complete their business effectually, and it will be but just sufficient to relieve them out of their present calamities.

"Your Honor's poor petitioners further crave leave to represent to your Honor, that in the severe famine in Governor Pitt's time there was some cloth destroyed by worms &c., and other some stole in the Washing town, which your Honor is very sensible of; but when the thieves were found at three or four several times and produced by the Poligar, they were tried by the Honorable Judges Court but acquitted from any corporal punishment, and were only turned out of the bounds; which was owing to Governor Pitt's and your Honor's wonted favour and compassion, by taking into consideration the misery and poverty of their condition, occasioned by the then present famine. Your poor petitioners now humbly acquaint your Honor that payment is demanded of them for 260 cloths that was destroyed and stole in Governor Pitt's time abovementioned.

"Your Honor's poor petitioners (whose conditions are so miserable by the forementioned reasons and the reduction of their number) most earnestly beseech your Honor will be graciously pleased to excuse your poor petitioners from the abovementioned demand of payment for the 260 cloths, that was destroyed or stole in Mr. Pitt's Government.

"Your petitioners most humbly repeat their earnest request that your Honor will be graciously pleased to forbid the merchants from receiving the half share of congeeing the cloths, and also in excusing the demand for the 260 cloths; and in acknowledgment of which favours your petitioners as in duty bound shall ever pray for your Honors's good health, prosperity and long life."

The decision of the Board upon this petition is thus recorded.

"Monday, 17th May, 1736. Then the Board taking into consideration the petition from the Washers, came to a resolution to make them an advance of four fanams per corge of long cloth, and two fanams per corge of Salampores, being sensible they are not able to perform their work at the present allowance."

The following proceedings respecting private trade are sufficiently explained by the extracts themselves.

"Wednesday, 21st July, 1736. Our Honorable Masters, having upon many occasions and divers times given their command to this Presidency to prevent as much as possible all assistance to our rivals in trade, either by lending them money, or otherwise; and having repeated the same more fully and particularly in their letter dated the 23rd January last, it was agreed to give notice thereof by affixing it at the sea gate, and that such notice be in the words and form following.

"Ordered by the President and Council, in conformity to the directions received from the Honorable Company, that from and after the date of this notice, any person or persons,—inhabitants of Madras, Natives, or others,—who should presume to be concerned directly or indirectly in any Stock or Loan at respondentia on any foreign ship, if not belonging to this port, or some other of the English settlements, shall be fined according to the value of their concerns, and forfeit the Company's protection; and any person or persons, who shall be guilty of procuring or soliciting any such concern in Stock or Loan at respondentia on any such foreign ship or ships, shall forfeit the Company's protection and be expelled the bounds.

"Ordered also that no ship or ships belonging to any of the Inhabitants of this place, whether Native or others, shall import at any port or place on this coast, not being an English settlement; except in case of necessity, when in that case also they shall be liable to pay the Custom to the Company the same as if they had imported here.

"All persons subject to his Britannic Majesty, are to have due regard to his Majesty's royal proclamation, prohibiting all his subjects trading within the Company's limits, in foreign service, or under foreign commissions, or being any way concerned in foreign Companies; and likewise forbidding them to visit, haunt, or frequent to East Indies, without the said Company's License."

"The Board thought proper to publish this notice in such general terms to avoid giving any particular offence; which might have affected the friendship and harmony that is subsisting at present with the Country Government and the French; it being chiefly designed to prevent all aid and assistance to the trade of Pondicherry, and the Moors ports to the Southward of us; as what effects the trade of the place most sensibly, and that are our most dangerous rivals."

"Monday, 29th November, 1736. The President acquaints the Board that this afternoon he is to receive a visit from one Meer Suttu, a person that was tutor to Subder Ali Khan, who has given him a commission to supervise the Poonamallee Country; the President added that he had lately had a great deal of trouble with the Metta people, and was advised to make this man a small present, who in return would leave such orders at the Mettas as would make us easy.

"Agreed the present be two pieces of scarlet broad cloth and twelve flasks of rose water to himself; and twelve yards of scarlet and three of aurora to the managers who attend him; the whole value will be about ninety pagodas."

The records for the year 1737 contain nothing worthy of note; and yet at this period events were occurring which are not without importance in the history of the Presidency. In 1732, the Rajah of Trichinopoly had died without issue; his second and third wives burned themselves with the body, but the first wife succeeded to the Government, in conformity it is said with the desire of the deceased Rajah. Disputes subsequently ensued between the Ranee and a Prince of the royal blood. Dost Ali, the Nabob of Arcot, was prevailed upon to take advantage of the confusion, to subject the kingdom of Trichinopoly to his own authority. Accordingly he sent an army under his son Subder Ali, and his son-in-law Chunda Sahib, to seize any opportunity which might offer of getting possession of the capital.*

The result was tragical. Chunda Sahib, who already owed his advancement to his matrimonial arrangements, was fortunate enough to excite the tender regard of the Ranee. Accordingly he was enabled to prevail on the love stricken lady to admit him with a body of troops into the city of Trichinopoly, having first taken an oath on the Koran

* Orme's History of Indostan, Vol. I. p. 38. Pharoah's edition. Wilks's Southern India, Vol. I. p. 249.

that he would act in nothing to her detriment. But the loves of middle aged queens are not always fortunate, and Chunda Sahib proved more cruel to the Ranee than Æneas proved to Dido. There is however a slight difference between the classical legend and the modern story. Æneas broke the heart of Dido by running away; whereas Chunda Sahib broke the heart of the Ranee by remaining where he was. The latter seized the city of Trichinopoly, and then imprisoned the lady; upon which the latter died of grief, and the kingdom of Trichinopoly yielded to the authority of the faithless Chunda.

We now proceed with the annals of the English settlement. Our next extracts will illustrate the administration of the laws.

"Friday, 20th January, 1738. Captain Henry Hoadly, Commander of the "Royal Guardian," acquainted the Board that his sail maker, James Bouchanan, had murdered Michael Smith, his fourth mate, in Canton river the 16th October last: that the next morning he jointly with Captain Martin and Sheppard, had taken the examination of several persons, who were on board when the accident happened; in consequence of which he had brought the man here in irons in order to a trial.

"Captain Hoadly being withdrawn, and his Majesty's commission for trying pirates being called for and examined, it was found that we are thereby empowered to try piracies, felonies and robberies, without any mention of murder. Which being debated, it was agreed that neither the word "piracy," nor the word "felony," could be understood to imply "murder;" and the rather because in the preamble to the said commission murder is distinguished from the other two, and also for that the oath appointed by the act of the 11th and 12th of King William the third, to be taken by the Judges of the Court of Admiralty, plainly refers to piracy, robbery and felony, and not to murder.

"Captain Hoadly was then called in, and told the Board were of opinion we had not power to try the criminal here; but that if he would order the several witnesses ashore, their information should be taken upon oath by some of his Majesty's Justices of peace for his justification."

"Tuesday, 24th January, 1738. A peon that carries money, having murdered his companion and robbed him of the money and effects he had with him belonging to several merchants: and the murderer having been discovered in Triplicane with most of the effects about him; the owners thereof appear before the Board, and having made good their claim to the money &c., the same was delivered them before the Board. But the murder and robbery having been committed to the Southward of Porto Novo, and consequently not punishable by virtue of our charter, the peon was delivered to the merchants under custody of the Poligar's peons, to be conveyed to the Rajah in whose country the fact was committed, in order that he might receive his trial and punishment there."

Our next extract refers to the state of foreign affairs.

"Saturday, 8th July, 1738. The President acquainted the Board, that he had received certain advices out of the country, that the Mahrattas had entered the provinces and seized upon Gott,* the principal pass: that Subder Ali Khan was set out against them, but with so pitiful a force that it was concluded, if he did not very speedily buy a peace, they would soon be at Arcot; which being no walled city, they would not be long in overrunning the country. Whereupon the President desired to entertain as many Harcarras as may be necessary to bring him advice of the Mahrattas' motions."

These incursions of the Mahrattas are to be attributed partly to the intermittent hostilities between the Nizam and the Mahratta Rajah, and partly to the hostility of the Mahrattas to the Mussulman occupation of the Hindoo state of Trichinopoly.

About this time a powder manufactory was erected at Madras, on the North West corner of the island. We subjoin the original entry.

"Monday, 13th November, 1738. The Pay Master and Storekeeper report to the Board, that they have pitched upon a spot of ground for erecting the new buildings necessary for the powder maker; which lies in the North Western corner of the island, between the roads leading to Egmore and Chindadrepettah, but a considerable distance

---

* Query, "Ghaut."

from each road, so that no body need go near the said buildings but the persons employed, and in case of an accident the passengers will be out of reach of danger. They also deliver in a plan for erecting the same, taking up the space of 180 feet in length and 144 in breadth."

Our next extract carries us to Vizagapatam. There had been some disputes between the English and the Nabob of Rajahmundry. It is worthy of notice that this Nabob was no other than Anwar-odean, the gentleman who subsequently become Nabob of Arcot, and who is the founder of the Wallajah family.

"Wednesday, 23rd May, 1739. General letter from the chief and Council at Vizagapatam of the 1st of May read, advising the unsettled state of the country Government thereabouts, and representing their fortifications and gun carriages to be but in a weak state of defence in case of any rupture.

"It being considered that the late revolution at Delhi will probably occasion frequent marches of different parties all over the empire ;—it is agreed to direct the chief and Council of Vizagapatam to keep their gun carriages in good order, and to lay before us an account of the repairs necessary to put their buildings and fortifications into a better state of defence, with an estimate of the expense."

The revolution at Delhi, which is here so slightly alluded to, was no other than the invasion of Nadir Shah. This event cannot be passed over without some notice, as it was the first great blow aimed at the heart of the Mogul empire. The reigning emperor at Delhi, Mohammed Shah, was a weak sensualist, who looked feebly and listlessly on, whilst the Mahrattas were ravaging the country almost to the gates of Delhi. But as if this intestine war was not enough to ruin the empire, another attack was to be made by a foreign enemy. Nadir Shah was a usurper on the throne of Persia. Having established himself on the throne, he reduced Cabul and Candahar, and thus approached the frontier of India. He professed to have no intention of entering Hindostan; but having sent an ambassador to demand the delivering up of some exiles, the ambassador and his escort were murdered by the people and inhabitants of Jellalabad, and Mohammed Shah was arrogant enough to refuse satisfaction. Nadir Shah was soon on the march. Some sort of treaty was made, by which the Mogul agreed to pay two millions sterling, on condition that Nadir retired; but from some cause or other the treaty was set aside and Nadir marched on and took possession of Delhi. For two days order was preserved in the city, and the invaders seemed only desirous of obtaining a large ransom. On the third night it was reported that Nadir had been assassinated by one of the Mogul's ladies in the haram, at the instigation of Mohammed Shah. The people at Delhi at once flew to arms, and slew every Persian they could find in the streets. Nadir sent out some officers to convince the mob of their error, but the officers were slaughtered. Meantime he dared not send out his troops into the close streets at Delhi, amidst the darkness of the night, but determined to wait till morning. The consequence was that before daybreak a thousand Persians were slain; but then a terrible vengeance was exacted. Orders were issued for a general massacre in every house or lane where a murdered Persian could be found; and from sunrise till noon the city was ravaged by fire and sword, until the streets streamed with blood. At noon Nadir ordered the massacre to cease; and so exact was his discipline that the order was implicitly obeyed. Nadir then left India to its pitiful emperor, and marched off with a spoil which has been estimated at the prodigious sum of thirty two millions sterling. But notwithstanding the horrible outrages which had occurred, the debauched inhabitants of Delhi regretted the departure of Nadir; and for many years afterwards the excesses of the Persian soldiery were topics of humour in the looser conversation of all ranks, and formed the comic parts of the drolls or players.

But to return to Madras. This same year of 1739 the settlement was thrown into a state of serious alarm by rumours of the approach of the Mahrattas. Shao, better known to our forefathers as Sou Rajah, was at present the Rajah of the Mahrattas; and Bajee Rao was his minister or Peishwa, who exercised all the real power. But the story of what transpired is best told in the language of the original records.

"Monday, 13th August, 1739. The President produced to the Board, as now read and entered hereafter, a letter (delivered him yesterday evening by Coja Petrus) from Imaum Sahib to the said Coja Petrus, giving him intelligence of a design formed by the Sou Rajah to invade this province, and in strong terms pressing our being upon our guard, and putting ourselves in the best posture of defence we can.

"The purport of this letter agreeing with the informations brought us by other hands, it was thought proper not entirely to neglect the same; and therefore the Board agreed to form themselves into a Committee, and to take a general survey of the fortifications, attended by the Lieutenants and Gunner; to see what is really necessary to be done, in order to secure the place against the attempts of an enemy."

"*From Imaum Sahib to Coja Petrus*, dated 6th August, 1739, received 12th August.

"Sou Rajah, about two years since, had meditated a design to fall upon this country with a powerful army, under the command of Baujee Row; in order to revenge the insult offered his relations by the ambitious intentions of the Governors of this province to put themselves forcibly in the possession of Tanjore; a kingdom which belonged to them (the Mahrattas) alone, and therefore would have been a direct invasion of their right. But Nadir Shah, in the interim, having penetrated very far into the Empire, made him suspend his project for the present. However I am now certainly informed he will very shortly put it in execution. To this purpose he has made choice of between 40 and 50 thousand of his best troops, the flower of his army; and given the command of them to Baujee Row, with express orders to lay waste this whole country. We have not the least reason to doubt the truth of this intelligence. If therefore the Gunyms should come this way, you may depend upon it they will visit Madras. The strict friendship that has been, and continues to be, between the Governor and me, makes me have the welfare of his Government at heart. Upon this account I sent him early informations in the former alarm we had; but no notice was taken of them; I hope greater stress will be laid upon these. It is a friendly part I am now acting, and therefore (I cannot repeat it too often) don't slight the advice I give you. Acquaint the Governor of what I have here related to you, very privately; and tell him to make the necessary preparations for the defence of the Town. Desire him particularly to lay up a good store of provisions, and to forbid the carrying of paddy or any other grain out of Town. Let him also provide himself with ammunition sufficient, and warlike stores. The greatest precautions you can use will be too little to defeat the attempts of an enemy, whose sudden and quick motions, will make you stand in need of your utmost vigilance. I take my leave of you, with once more entreating you to credit the above accounts."

Governor Benyon accordingly took active measure for the defence of Fort St. George; but his proceedings are best told in the language of the records.

"Tuesday, 14th August, 1739. The Board

having yesterday been round the works, pursuant to the resolution of that morning's consultation, made the following remarks.

"That the wall from Caldera Point along the river to Queen's Point is not carried on; but there is a space of 310 feet in length left open, except that there are some ordinary houses built there, which are no security; but the river being easily fordable at that place, an enemy may without the least difficulty make their entrance there.

"That the Palmyra fence from New Point to the Block house is entirely gone; and though our Honorable Masters permitted the building a wall there in the year 1722, it has not yet been done, although absolutely necessary for the defence of the place.

"That the Drawbridge to the Town is much out of repair; the chains and bolts of it almost eaten through with rust, and the wood work decayed.

"That the carriages of the guns are most of them so decayed that they are of little further use than to mount the guns upon, not being fit for firing; and should we be put to the necessity of using them, a few discharges would dismount the guns.

"That there are many battecas built close under the Town wall, and great quantities of timber and plank lying between the wall and the sea; both which in case of the approach of an enemy may be of dangerous consequences.

"The completing the wall of the Town appearing to the Board of absolute necessity, the Pay-Master is ordered immediately to set about the same, and to begin with the opening by the river bewteen Caldera Point and Queen's Point; and as soon as that is finished to proceed upon the other; and Mr. Burton and he are appointed a Committee to make an estimate of the expense of each of these works.

"And it being also necessary, in case of the approach of an enemy, to remove our powder from the magazine on the Island in the Town; it is ordered also that the Pay Master clear out and repair the magazine under the several points; and when these works which appear of the most immediate necessity are completed, that he proceed to mending the drawbridge, and such other repairs as are requisite to put us in a proper posture of defence.

"Ordered further that the Storekeeper do immediately set about repairing such of the gun carriages as are only decayed in part; and that he make new ones in the room of those that are no longer serviceable; and that the gunner's mate do attend and oversee the workmen.

"Resolved further that the proprietors of the timber and plank, &c. lying under the fort walls have notice given them immediately to remove the same; and that such shops and sheds as are in the way be pulled down.

"After these resolutions the Board called for the lists of the Military and Gunroom crew, and observing that there are very few Europeans in the latter, and no supernumeraries in the former;—it was agreed that on this occasion the Gunner entertain as many Europeans as he can get; and that the Lieutenants look out for and list as far as thirty Topasses to each Company, if they can find such as are fit for service."

"Tuesday, 14th August 1739. Agreed on this occasion to entertain spy Brahmins, and send them to several parts of the country to gain intelligence of the motions of the Mahrattas; which are frequently so sudden as to make it necessary to be more than ordinarily watchful."

The storm however did not break out until next year, when a great battle ensued between the Mahrattas and Dost Ali, the Nabob of Arcot, which terminated in the defeat and death of the Nabob. But we give the original entries.

"Wednesday, 30th April, 1740. The President acquaints the Board he had received advice from Imaum Sahib, that the design of the Mahrattas to enter this province is no longer to be doubted; and though the Nabob was setting out towards the borders, there is not a force sufficient in the province to withstand them, and they will certainly be soon at Arcot, if some other means are not thought of to stop them.

"Ordered that the Pay Master do make all the despatch possible to complete such of the repairs as were thought necessary in consultation the 14th of August last; particularly the wall from New Point to the Block house, and a palisado of redwood from thence to the sea; it being very easy for an enemy to force their way by that Point, and then the whole Black Town will be open to them; there being no wall between that point and the White Town."

"Monday, 12th May, 1740. The President acquaints the Board that last night he received advice, which was confirmed this morning, that the Nabob Dost Ali Khan and his youngest son Hussain Ali Khan, and several other persons of note, had been killed in an engagement with the Mahrattas at the pass of the Hills which divide this province from Corrapah (i. e. the Pass of Damalcharri); the particulars of which engagement according to what we yet hear are as follows.

"The Nabob was lying at the pass with no more than 2000 horse and about 10,000 peons of Bungar Veasum Naick's; the Mahrattas being then on the other side the pass, some overtures were made by the last for an accommodation; but not receiving any answer from the Nabob that was satisfactory, the Mahrattas found means to bring about 10,000 horse through a wood (the Poligar of which it is supposed showed them the way); and the 9th in the morning they appeared in the Nabob's rear. At the same time the rest of the Mahratta army possessed themselves of the Hills, and came down in his front. The Nabob's forces were soon surrounded, and the enemy charging them with fire arms, the Nabob, his son Hussain Ali, and several others about him, were soon killed; after which, the Mahrattas having proclaimed that if the rest would disperse they should not be pursued, the Nabob's forces soon fled. Subder Ali Khan, the Nabob's eldest son who was upon his march to his father, but with no more than 3000 horse, hearing of this defeat turned back, and it is thought, designs to shut himself up in Vellore.

" As there is no room to doubt now that the Mahrattas may and will range over the whole province, the President acquaints the Board he had this morning ordered all the men we have in Garrison to be upon duty ; but considering how many Guards and Points we have, they will at best be very weakly manned ; and therefore proposed to the consideration of the Board, what further to do upon this emergency : upon which it was agreed as follows.

" That considering the few men we have, particularly Europeans, it is impossible to spare any force sufficient to mann the out choultries, which were formerly erected to defend the suburbs ; besides that those choultries are so much gone to decay that they are not tenable, and were they in better repair, it would take up so many men to mann them that it would lessen considerably the small number we have for the Guard of the White and Black Towns ; that they lie at so great a distance as not easily to be succoured ; and if they should be hard pressed, the men would be in very great danger of being cut off before they could retreat to the Town. Agreed therefore that it is not safe to trust any men at the out choultries ; but as it would make too much noise, and alarm the inhabitants, to bring the guns in from thence, it was only ordered that they be nailed up.

" Ordered also that as many Europeans and Topasses be entertained in the Military and Gunroom as can be procured. This order is made general because we have too much reason to believe the most that can be got will be far short of what is necessary.

"There being upwards of 200 guns mounted on the walls and bastions, and the number of men in the Gunners crew not being above one man to two guns, and as in case of action our Military will be of most service with their fire arms :—It is agreed to entertain two hundred Lascars, if so many can be procured, to assist in working the great guns.

"Ordered also that one hundred peons be taken in upon the Company's pay under the command of the chief peon.

"And the Poligar of this place, being obliged upon any emergency to raise two hundred additional Taliars, on the Company's paying their batta during the time they are in service ; the President was desired to order the Poligar to get them ready as soon as possible."

"Thursday, 15th May, 1740. The President acquaints the Board, he had received advice from the country, that fifteen or twenty thousand Mahratta horse were arrived at Lollapettah and Arcot, and were plundering both these places.

"There being little or no Europe powder in the Garrison, and but 500 fire arms that can be depended on in case of action, and the Board being informed there is a quantity of the first and eight chests of the latter on board the "Royal Guardian" consigned to Bombay :—It is agreed to sign an order to Captain Hoadly to send ashore ten bar-rels of gun-powder, and the eight chests of fire arms.

"As it is very likely it will soon be necessary to put our European inhabitants under our arms, —it is agreed that commissions be drawn out appointing William Monson, Esq., Captain; Mr. John Stratton, Lieutenant, and Mr. John Hallyburton, Ensign."

"Monday, 19th May, 1740. There being several places on the walls, where it will be proper to plant guns for the defence of the Town; the Storekeeper is ordered to deliver to the Gunner so many as are wanted, and to make carriages for the same; and till those can be finished, the Gunner is ordered to make use of some of the carriages on the saluting Battery.

"The Pay Master is likewise ordered to buy in a quantity of sheep, and to salt up some beef and pork, to make a quantity of biscuit, to send to Pulicat for salt fish, to lay in also some firewood, and to look out for all the Pegu jars in Town, or other vessels proper for keeping water.

"There being a great want of fanams for the currency of the place, agreed that 3000 Pagodas more be advanced the Import warehouse keeper to purchase silver to coin into fanams. In the meantime, agreed to issue out those which were coined for Fort St. David, the roads being too dangerous to send them overland.

"The Chevaux de Frise being out of repair, the Pay Master is ordered to get them mended; and there being several other utensils of war which we have not in store, such as spades, shovels, pickaxes, &c. is ordered to provide so many of them likewise as may be thought necessary.

"Thursday, 22nd May, 1740. The President acquaints the Board, that all the accounts he has been able to get of the Mahrattas, and their motions, since last consultation, have been very imperfect; which he imputes to the danger there is in passing the roads; except that it is agreed part of the Mahratta forces had likewise entered Conjeveram and plundered that great Town. And he has also received frequent advices of the plundering and burning of villages between this and Arcot. One of the Hircarrahs came in last night, and brought advice that the Mahrattas had sent about twenty spies towards the sea coasts, though he could not tell upon what design; but a letter from a considerable man in the country to his son that is in Town, mentions the same number of spies being sent, and adds that it was to enquire what fresh water there was in the rivers or tanks, and particularly how much there might be in Chambrepauck tank; and this morning came into Town several of the inhabitants of Trevelore; which is about twelve hours journey from the place, who had fled from thence, and report that a party of horse was come there and were plundering that place.

"There being eighteen military men on board the "Prince William," that are returning from Bombay to Bengal;—agreed to send for them ashore, upon promise that they shall go on to the Bay by the latter ships; and that Captain Langworth be ordered to send them ashore.

"Agreed also that Captain Langworth be ordered to send ashore twenty men of his ship's company to assist in the defence of the place; and the Pay Master is ordered to furnish provisions for them and the Bengal Military, and to lay in some arrack to give the men a dram morning and evening whilst they are upon duty, as has always been customary upon these occasions.

"Captain Langworth having some pistol powder on board which he offers to sell, the Storekeeper is ordered to purchase it.

"There being a parcel of straw houses and huts lying to the Northward of the Black Town, within fourteen feet of the walls, which in case of an attack on that side would be very inconvenient, and make it dangerous:—Ordered that notice be given to the proprietors to pull them down, and remove the materials elsewhere. But it was at the same time agreed that the Pay Master, with the chief bricklayer and chief carpenter, do first take a survey of the same, and report the value to the Board, that we may agree upon allowing the owners some reasonable satisfaction."

The sequel of these exciting events will be told in our next Chapter. Meantime we insert here a curious domestic incident which transpired at the commencement of the present year; and which, like a previous one, we prefer printing verbatim in small type, rather than injuring the story by an attempt at abridging it.

"Thursday, 3rd January, 1740. The President delivers to the Council a paper now read and entered hereafter; after which he took the following oath administered to him by Mr. Randall Fowke.

"I, Richard Benyon, do make oath and swear, that the two thousand pagodas demanded of me on the thirteenth day of November last past by Mr. John Sanderson, for so much pretended to have been sent by the said Mr. Sanderson, by his servant Muggana on the 2nd of March 1738, and by his said servant to have been delivered to my Dubash Casava Chetty Addeppa for me; and for the recovery of which he has since brought his action in the Mayor's Court against my said Dubash;—were not received by me, and that I never heard of his sending such sum of money till the thirteenth day of November aforesaid, when Mr. Sanderson wrote me of it and demanded repayment thereof."

"To the Gentlemen of Council at Fort St. George.

"Gentlemen,

"Mr. John Sanderson having commenced a suit against my servant Casava Chetty Addeppa, commonly called Narrain, which has occasioned much and various discourse in Town; being a case so circumstanced that the truth of the matter charged in the bill will perhaps at last be rather guessed at than fully appear; and as many in such an affair will be giving their opinion according to their passions and prejudices;—I have thought it necessary, in my own vindication, to lay before you some facts and circumstances, which otherwise I should not have thought justifiable for any private provocation.

"I shall begin then Gentlemen, with acquainting you, that the 13th of November last in the morning, I received a letter from Mr. Sanderson, complaining in general of hardships he had suffered from me, and in one part of his letter, said that he hoped I would be so just not to detain so large a part of his fortune, as my man Narrain received of his servant Muggana the 2nd March 1738. As the subject was quite new to me, and the whole of his letter very unintelligible, I desired he would come and explain it. It would be wasting too much of your time to recite all our discourse when he did come;

but as to my hardships which have been put upon him, you will, if he thinks fit to tell you what they are, be able to judge whether he has any reason to complain. I believe you will then think he has had great lenity shown him; and there are many other, who think it was too much. As to the money which, he says, Narrain received, when I asked him what it was, he said it was two thousand pagodas; and when I asked him for what, he said he understood it was for me. Upon which I told him I would take my oath I never received a pagoda of it; but, says I, we will soon inquire into this matter; and thereupon called for Narrain, but he being that morning in Town I appointed Mr. Sanderson to meet me again in the evening; but before I acquaint you with what passed then, it will be necessary that I tell you some things which passed before.

"In January 1736, my servant Narrain came into my writing room, and showed me a letter to him from Mr. Sanderson, whose servant Muggana had brought it to him, with one thousand pagodas, designed as a present for me. The original I have ready to produce to you and the copy is as follows.

"*To Casava Chetty Addeppa.*

"I have sent my servant Muggana to you, who will inform you the great misfortune that attends me here, for want of a choice of able people to contract with; besides, the prices I allowed last year in proportion to the deduction made is so great, that I am informed by several people that the merchants were actually losers by the cloth; and still there is a large debt standing out by Lingan's set of merchants, one of which has proved a bankrupt and owes half of the debt among them for his share.

"You will find by what Muggana will deliver to you, I have made the same compliment for the Governor I ever did for his predecessors; which I do with a great deal of good will, but can less afford it of any time since Mr. Macrae left Madras.

"You may depend upon my readiness to serve you on all occasions.

I am, Your assured friend,
JOHN SANDERSON."

VIZAGAPATAM,
19*th December*, 1735.

"After I had read this letter, I was a good deal surprized at the matter of it, as well as the confidence he reposed in his servant Muggana, I considered that if I returned the money by the bearer, he might still pretend I had received it; and though I should have wrote Mr. Sanderson that I had not, I much doubted in whom he would have most faith.

"I therefore concluded it was most safe to take the money into my own possession; and without saying what my design was, I ordered him to be brought into me with the money; which was accordingly done; and Muggana having laid the money down upon a table before me, he and Narrain went out again; after which I delivered the money to my cash-keeper, with directions to keep it till I called for it, and the 7th February I wrote Mr. Sanderson a letter the copy of which is as follows:—

"Sir,

I have seen the letter you wrote to Addeppa, and am very sorry to observe by it that you were upon such hard terms whilst you were at Injeram; when at the same time, I have very good reason to believe, both your neighbours at Vizagapatam and Maddapollum set rent free. But however that be, I am sure neither the Company's affairs, or your own, can be carried on as they ought to be, if what you offer upon the present occasion is once established as a constant practice. Yet that you might not be deceived in what has passed here, what your Dubash brought I have thought fit to take into my possession, and desire you will send an order to Mr. Morse to receive it of me. He need not be acquainted upon what account it is; neither is it proper that notions of this sort should be public or propogated, for fear of the evil consequence that such a way of thinking may be attended with.

"As you know now what terms you are upon with me, I must recommend it to you that if you are industrious and vigilant, in promoting the investment, you will want no reasonable encouragment from hence; but we cannot answer to give such extraordinary prices for bad cloth, when we ought to have given less for that which is good; but I write you apart and in the general more fully about your investment and this is sufficient here.

I am, Sir, Your assured friend."

February 7th 1736.

"The 5th March Mr. Sanderson acknowledged the receipt of this letter and wrote me as follows:—"I have "your Honor's pardon to ask in offering to do a thing "so contrary to what you seem to expect; if it is your "Honor's pleasure of returning that which my servant "delivered, if you please of sending it by some vessel to "me as it will be less public." Upon the receipt of this letter from him, and supposing the money his servant had delivered was currant pagodas, I ordered Mr. Goulding, who was my cash-keeper, to lay it out in Madras pagodas; and the 29th May 1736 I sent them to Mr. Sanderson by Captain Hepburn; and the 15th June Mr. Sanderson wrote me "The small chest Captain "Hépburn brought came out right according to the "mark of the bag." The 24th July 1736 he wrote me again as follows: "Possibly your Honor would take it "amiss if I did not inform you; but the pagodas I sent "your Honor was a sealed bag of new Madras pagodas, "and it is reasonable to be supposed may have been paid "away in the room of others." I have no copy of what I wrote him in answer, but believe it was in substance that he judged right in supposing the money had been paid away instead of other; that somebody was possibly the better for them, but as I was not, I did not think myself accountable for the difference.

I need not take up your time in recounting what passed with regard to the Vizagapatam investment till the end of 1737, when it was thought proper to call him up hither, and the 19th January following he arrived here. It was then too busy a season for us to enter upon any particular debate in Council relating to the Vizagapatam affairs; except that it was agreed we could not advance the prices of that cloth, or continue any longer to pay what we did the year before. But I had frequent discourses with him, and he showed me some proposals which he said Raganacailoo had made, and he did not doubt would comply with them. I cannot now recollect all that passed between us; but at last having assured me that, if he was permitted to go to Vizagapatam again, he would do his utmost to make a good investment; and if he should not be able to do that, he would himself desire to come up next season; I gave him to understand I would not be against his returning thither. We were too busy then in dispatching the "Royal Guardian," to bring the matter into Council; but he doubted so little of going again to Vizagapatam, that he proposed to me to buy a French ship, which was then in the road to be sold, in order to be employed in the trade between Vizagapatam and this place; which I very readily came into, and it is very remarkable that ship sailed for Vizagapatam the 27th February four days also before, he says, he sent the money; and that day also his paper relating to the Vizagapatam investment was read in Council, and which I believe was looked upon then as preparative to his return thither.

I must now acquaint you with two other particulars, but the exact time I cannot recollect. Talking with me once about his turned out cloth, he asked me if I would take it upon my own account; telling me I should have it for two thousand pagodas less than it cost him, or that he would lose two thousand pagodas by it. I did not ask him to explain himself, but guessing that he meant what he ought not, I only told him I did not know what to do with it. But I resolved from that time not to touch it upon any account.

"At another time he brought me an open account current, upon balance whereof would have been due to him upwards of 2,500 pagodas by reason of several sums he disbursed for my account; among others my share of the French ship abovementioned. And observing he had given credit therein for 2,000 pagodas as cash received, which I knew he had not, I supposed it to be a sum that he wanted to be paid in part of the balance. I was therefore going to call for my cash-keeper to order the money to be paid; but Mr. Sanderson stopped me and said he did not want the money. Upon which I asked him what he put it in the account for? He replied again that he designed it as a present, or desired that I would accept of it, or to that effect. Upon that I asked him how he could make any such offer, or imagine I had any such expectations after what had passed between us about the thousand pagodas he sent by his servant Muggana? Or, said I, do you think I refused that because it was not enough? We had a good deal more discourse at that time, but I cannot charge my memory with so much of it as to be particular in reciting it here; but it tended to convince him that I would accept of no such offers, and that he might depend upon all the good offices in my power without any expectations of that sort; in which as I was very sincere, you may judge of my surprize when he first acquainted me he had sent 2,000 pagodas the 2nd March 1738 by his servant Muggana to Narrain.

"Concerning which Mr. Sanderson being come to me according to appointment the 13th November last, I called Narrain in, and charged him with having received that sum from Mr. Sanderson by his servant Muggana, and with having owned the receipt of it and promised repayment, which Mr. Sanderson affirmed he had. Narrain absolutely denied it; but acknowledged that Mr. Sanderson, since his return to this place, had told him that he had advanced to his Gomastas at Vizagapatam to the amount of 2,000 pagodas in rupees, and had demanded that money of him here; which Narrain said he had promised to pay, if Mr. Sanderson had any receipt for it from his Gomastas, or so soon as they should give him any advice that they had received it. Upon this Mr. Sanderson denied that he ever made any such demand upon Narrain, and said those accounts were settled at Vizagapatam, and he had been paid there. Upon which Narrain replied, "No Sir, for I paid you one bill here of eight hundred and thirty-three rupees, and another of three hundred and odd pagodas. Mr. Sanderson made answer, that he was now paid all, and had no demand for any money advanced his Gomastas. Upon which I interrupted them, and told Narrain that the question was whether the 2nd March 1738 he received two thousand pagodas from Muggana, which was to be paid me. This Narrain denying again, Mr. Sanderson asked him whether he had not applied to him, and told him that if he would persuade me to permit him to go down again to Vizagapatam to settle his affairs there, and bring up his family, he would give him two thousand pagodas. Upon this I asked Mr. Sanderson if he had not said before it was for me, "Yes Sir, said he, "so it was." "Well then," said I, "since you did go to Vizagapatam, and that was the consideration for which it was intended, don't you think if the money be recovered it belongs to me? "No Sir," said Mr. Sanderson, "my turned out cloth was to be taken in too. "Oh," said I, "that could not be;" and in truth, Gentlemen, there was a very good reason why it could not be, which is that even Mr. Sanderson himself, with the rest of you, had wrote the Company the cloth from Vizagapatam was very bad, insomuch that we had turned great part of it out; nor was it possible I could take it in, much less what he had turned out at Vizagapatam, for being, as it is said in the said letter, worse than what we had rejected here; or if in consideration of this intended present I had, agreed to it, which way could you Gentlemen have been brought to consent thereto? But this by the way. Then Mr. Sanderson went on, and said that Narrain, in answer to his application to him, had told him that my mind was a little vexed about the bad cloth, and some ill usage of the Vizagapatam merchants; but that if he would get the money ready, he would let him know when it was proper to send it; but Narrain absolutely denied that Mr. Sanderson had made any such aplication to him, and upon that I told Mr. Sanderson I was very sure Narrain never spoke to me about his affairs; for that, though I did often hear him with regard to the Blacks, who it might be supposed, he was best acquainted with, he knew his duty better than to interfere in matters relating to the English. After this they engaged in some other discourse, relating to some matters which had passed at Vizagapatam, and some people who are come up from thence; which not being material to the sum in dispute I ordered Narrain to withdraw; and then I went over again with Mr. Sanderson all that had passed between us relating to the several offers he had made me; and asked him how he could be so weak to trust such a sum of money as that in such hands, when I had so plainly cautioned him against it in my letter of the 7th February 1736; and not only so, but though he stayed in the place till the 18th of April 1738, and was frequently with me between that day and the 2nd of March 1738, when he pretends he sent the money, yet in all that time he never once gave me the least hint or intimation of it. To which he only answered, it was very true he had not. I told him it was a very odd story. He said it was so, but he would not lose his money. I think this is the substance, and all that is material of what passed about this affair the 13th November last. I heard no more from Mr. Sanderson till the 20th, when he wrote me he designed to see Narrain in the Mayor's Court; and accordingly he filed his bill there the 4th December. Narrain has answered it, and denied upon oath that he ever received from Muggana, or any other person, by order or in behalf of Mr. Sanderson, the sum of two thousand pagodas, or any other sum to be paid to me; and there the matter rests at present. I suppose in the progress of the suit I shall be called upon to answer upon interrogatories, whether I received the said sum of two thousand pagodas; but as that may not be before the departure of these ships, I think it very necessary in the mean time, to clear myself of that matter upon oath before you, that you may bear testimony thereof to my Honorable Masters, who, if I had received that or any other sum, would have good reason to conclude it was in consideration of my suffering them to be wronged by Mr. Sanderson. And indeed I cannot but believe that was his intention when he made the offer; and if I am liable to any blame from my Honorable Masters on that account, it is for looking on his several offers to proceed, rather from the weakness of his judgment than the depravity of his mind, and therefore passed them over in silence.

"I omitted to tell you above that the 8th March 1738 I paid Mr. Sanderson two thousand five hundred and thirty-nine pagodas, nine fanams, and twenty cash, the balance of the account then depending between us.

I am, Gentlemen,
Your very affectionate humble servant,
RICHARD BENYON."

Fort St. George, 3rd January, 1740.

Tuesday, 8th January, 1740. Mr. John Sanderson, having at his request, been ordered a copy of the paper delivered in by the President last Consultation; now offers to the Board another, in answer thereto; which being read by the Secretary as entered hereafter, he takes his oath, administered by Mr. Burton to the latter part thereof, which he again reads therefrom as follows.

"I therefore do declare and depose upon oath that "(as by my account) on the 2nd of March 1738, I did "send 2,000 pagodas in two sealed bags by the hands of "my servant Muggana, and ordered him to give the "same into the hands of Casava Chetty Addeappa (com- "monly called Narrain), in order that he should deliver "the said two bags to his Master Governor Benyon."

"I further declare that on or about the middle of "February 1739, meeting the said Narrain as I was "coming from the Governor, I had a discourse with "him in the general table room hall near the North- "east windows; informing him of several hardships, "among the rest that I expected my 2,000 pagodas to "be returned to me. Who upon my leaving him said "that he would see and speak. The second time I asked "him again about the money, he said that he had not "spoke, but desired me to be secret and he would "see and get it me. And the third time of asking for "the money, he told me it was a present, and I must "not expect it. To which I made answer I should not "fail of speaking to the Governor about it before I left "India."

"Tuesday, 8th January, 1740.

"To the Honorable Richard Benyon, Esq.,
President and Governor and Council of
Fort Saint George.

"Honorable Sir and Sirs,

All the answer that I think is necessary to be made to the long paper the President was pleased to lay before this Board the 3rd of January is, that I most certainly did send, by my servant Muggana, the 2nd March 1738, two thousand pagodas, with orders to deliver the same to Casava Chetty Addappa (commonly called Narrain); and that I meant to present the same to the Governor and that I had no view therein to the prejudice of my Honorable Masters; and in case I had given any present before, it was when I had given entire satisfaction to my Honorable Masters in England. Therefore I thought it might not be unacceptable to Governor Benyon; and though Governor Benyon, as it is set forth in his paper, did slight the offers I had before made him, yet that was no argument that he truly slighted the matter; although it is very plain the manner of my doing it before was not pleasing to him.

"But as Governor Benyon absolutely disowns his having received this money, I think I have a just reason to claim the same from Narrain, the Governor's servant, who has tricked both his master and me; and that I have not only all the circumstantial proofs that can be expected, but a direct, positive and legal proof, as much as the nature of the thing can admit of, that the money was paid by Muggana to Narrain; and that I cannot but be surprized that the Governor should make himself an advocate for his servant, as if it would admit of a doubt whether or no Narrain had received the two thousand pagodas.

"But to put this affair in a clear light, I sent for Muggana from Masulipatam, who is now come; and as he was the only person that transacted the affair, he the said Muggana has made his affidavit before Timothy Tullie, Esq., Mayor of the Corporation of Madraspatnam, of the material transactions therein; and though I must lay under a very great disadvantage by prosecuting Narrain in this affair, who is supported by so powerful a master, yet the justice of my cause is the only reason which induced me to sue for the two thousand pagodas, which as Governor Benyon declares, it never was applied to the use I designed them or that he received any benefit thereby.

"Therefore I do declare and depose upon oath that (as verbatim in the body of the Consultation.)

I am, Honorable Sir and Sirs,
Your most humble servant,
JOHN SANDERSON."

Fort St. George, 8th January 1740.

Nothing further upon this extraordinary matter is to be found in the Madras Records.

CHAPTER XLIII.

GOVERNORSHIP OF MR. RICHARD BENYON.

1740.

The year of our Lord 1740 was an exciting year in Fort St. George. Besides the constant fear of the Mahrattas, which is sufficiently indicated in the following extracts, there was a correspondence between the Governor of Fort St. George and the Governor of Pondicherry, respecting an outrage which had been committed by an English Captain and his officers in the Pondicherry roads. Moreover, towards the close of the year, or rather about the beginning of the year 1741, a terrible scandal occurred on board one of the ships from Europe, which made no little stir in Fort St. George. These incidents with some others will all be found in their proper place; and indeed in most cases the extracts will be found to tell their own story.

Our first selections refer to the Mahrattas.

"Tuesday, 27th May, 1740. The President then acquainted the Board that he had received some advices from the country, that a treaty was on foot between the Moors and Mahrattas; but he could not say yet, what hopes there was of an accommodation, the Mahrattas insisting upon very high terms; in the mean time they still continue to plunder every where near them, and he is sorry to add that several parties of horse, the broken remains of the late Nabob's army, were to the full as troublesome to the villages as the Mahratta army to the greater towns; that they are roving about all over the country, and no village escapes them where they think anything is to be got. The President adds that upon this advice he ordered out the peons and Poligar's men to keep guard at the Mettahs, and out parts of the pettahs; and hoped they would be able to prevent any mischief from these little robbers, if they were not joined by any body of the Mahrattas."

"Friday, 30th May, 1740. There being no wall from Charles' Point to the cloth godowns next the river, for which reason that part of the White Town lies entirely open and defenceless, and may be of very ill consequence if the place should be attacked; it is agreed to be absolutely necessary to have that part of the Town inclosed with a wall also; and the Pay Master is ordered to lay in materials as soon as possible; and while those are getting ready, he is ordered to prepare a plan of that part of the Town, that the Board may the better consider in what manner to have it built.

"The ditch which was formerly dug from Queen's Point round the Black Town to the Sea side, being by length of time and from neglect in not keeping it clear, now almost entirely filled up; —the Pay Master is ordered to have the same new dug; as the Board are of opinion it will be very useful to keep off an enemy; more especially as the walls of the Black Town are but weak, and we have but few men to defend them."

At the same time the Board agreed upon the following establishment of Gunners.

Number of men thought necessary for the Gunroom Crew.

				Pags	F.	C.
1	Gunner.			13	0	0
1	Do. Mate.			10	0	0
1	Do. 2d do.			9	0	0
1	Do. 3rd do.			8	0	0
1	Do. 4th do.			7	0	0
4	Quarter gunners	@	6 Pags. each..	24	0	0
6	Do.	@	5 do.	30	0	0
35	Europeans	@	100 fanams each.	97	18	0
20	Topasses	@	91 do.	50	20	0
80	Do.	@	72 do.	160	0	0
1	Syrang.			4	0	0
2	Tindalls	@	3 pagodas each	6	0	0
35	Lascars	@	2 do.	70	0	0
188 persons.			Amount to pagodas...	488	28	0

List of men in the Gunroom disabled and superannuated, with their former pay and present pension.

	Former pay per month.			Present pension.		
Humphrey Lawcock, Senior...	5	0	0	2	18	0
Adrian Tourbeck, Senior.........	2	28	0	1	14	0
Ralph Ascongh.....................	2	28	0	1	14	0
Thome DeRozario	2	0	0	1	0	0
Francisco DeMello..................	2	0	0	1	0	0
Lawrence DeSouza	2	0	0	1	0	0
Michael Gomez.......................	2	0	0	1	0	0
Ventura Dos Santor................	2	0	0	1	0	0
8 persons.	20	20	0	10	10	0

The guns at this period available for the defence of the Fort St. George amounted to one hundred and ninety-three.

"Thursday, 12th June, 1740. Telesinga Chitty and Nellamuta Comrapa Chetty attending, produced to the Board letters from their gomastas at Salem, advising that they have 250 ox loads of cloth lying ready there to send to Cuddalore; but are afraid to venture it without a guard, lest the Poligars should plunder it upon the road. After some discourse with the Merchants, they gave it as their opinion that 30 or 40 peons would be sufficient to protect them. Upon which it was agreed to send 20 peons from hence, and that they be joined by 20 more at Fort St. David, and to proceed from thence to the borders of Salem where the cloth will be ready. However the merchants do not propose to venture it all at once, but at three different times. Agreed that directions be given to Fort St. David accordingly, and that twenty peons more be added to the other twenty, and that by them we send 3000 pagodas worth of fanams."

In consequence of some trouble arising from a debt of one of the Company's servants at Vizagapatam to one of the country Renters, the following order was issued.

"Friday, 27th June, 1740. That no Company's servant, or other European living at Vizagapatam, shall directly or indirectly borrow any money, or otherwise become indebted to any of the Moors Governors, or to any of the Rajahs or country Renters; and whoever shall be guilty of a breach hereof shall be suspended from the Company's Service, if Covenanted servants, and sent for up hither; those who are not in the Company's service, shall be sent for hither and from hence to England."

We extract the following entry simply for the purpose of explaining that the Town rent of 1200 pagodas per annum was continued to be paid to the Nabob of Arcot.

"Friday, 8th July, 1740. The Nabob Subder Ali Khan, having wrote for the Town rent for the last year ending the 30th Ultimo, that twelve hundred pagodas is now paid to his order."

An incident occurred about this time at Pondicherry, which occasioned some lengthy correspondence between the French and English Governors of Pondicherry and Fort St. George. An English ship named the "Nancy" arrived in the Pondicherry roads, where she was sold by her owner to some Frenchman; and the Captain, whose name was Coxon, was ordered to deliver her up. Captain Coxon however refused to give up the ship, unless, as he said, some guarantee was given that the wages of himself and crew should be paid. The matter was represented, or perhaps misrepresented, to M. Damas the then Governor of Pondicherry; and after some resistance the ship was recovered by force, and Captain Coxon and his men placed in custody. The story however is best told in the following letter addressed by a Mr. Le Blanc to Governor Benyon.

Letter from Mr. Le Blanc at Pondicherry, dated 17th July, N. S. 1340.

"Sir,—Mr. Monger concluded a contract for his ship the latter end of the last week, and yesterday he fixed to give us possession of the ship "Nancy," which has occasioned a strange disorder. I take the liberty to let you know what passed on that occasion, knowing you to be too good a judge not to blame a parcel of rogues that he had on board, who, if in England, or if Frenchmen, would have had the gallows for their pains. Yesterday, I being on board the Brigantine, Monseiur Pathelin, Mr. Monger, Mr. Sheradder (who was chief mate on board the Nancy, but discharged here by the Captain 4 days ago, because he is an honest man and would not join his Captain in his rogueries) came on board about 5 o'clock in the evening, desiring me to go on board the ship "Nancy" with them to take possession of her. I accordingly went with them on board said ship, where on our approach they hoisted English colours. Being on board, Mr. Monger presented to Captain Coxon the copy of his owner's orders to the said Captain, asking him if he did know said orders to be just; he answered he did. Whereupon Mr. Monger told him he sold the ship and desired him to give us possession, which he refused doing, although secureties offered him in writing to pay all wages due on the said ship &c., from the time of our going on board and while we stayed there. The second mate, whose name I believe is Heath, with three black helm's men, were posted at the foot of the Ensign Staff, swearing and blaspheming that any man that would attempt taking down the English colours, he would knock out his brains. In short Mr. Monger in writing signified to the Captain that he protested in the name of the owners against him, and therein ordered him to strike his topmasts and moore the ship. until further orders; which signification the Captain took in his hand after he heard it read, and gave it before us all to a man with orders to throw it over board, which was done. We quitted the ship. Mr. Monger as soon as ashore went and made his complaint to the Governor, praying him to assist him by force to keep the ship, and what was in her, for the proprietors. The Governor immediately ordered fourteen soldiers with a Serjeant to go on board said ship, and secure her by force, or otherwise; and in the meantime sent orders to our Europe ships to arm and mann their boats to hinder the said ship's getting away; and he ordered me to go with Mr. Monger to see his orders put in execution. The Chellinga that carried the soldiers got away before us. On our coming near the ship, seeing a great deal of lights on board we thought the soldiers had got possession; but coming more near we were ordered by the Englishmen on board on pain of death not to advance. We were then under her so as to hear very plainly Captain Coxon order to fire on us, and to heave some grenadoes on board; which seeing, and having no arms nor men, we made off, expecting every minute the effects of their madness, and went on board the Europe ships for their help. On going a good distance from the "Nancy" we met the boat of soldiers. I asked them why they did not obey orders in going on board; they answered that on the threatening of the Englishmen the boatmen would not row on board. I ordered them ashore to receive further orders, and went on board the Europe ship, who I found manning their boat to force their way on board the "Nancy." We then went ashore to acquaint the Governor with what passed. We were near the shore, when we saw the fire of several small arms, as in an action; and on the bar we met with two boats, with a company of soldiers and an officer &c. going on board. When on shore we saw the signals of two fires or lights on board, which the Europe ship's boat was to make when the ship was secured. On which all was easy for the night. It seems they were preparing to get under sail when the boat boarded them, having swayed up the foreyard, though the top mast was struck. This morning about one o'clock a part of the soldiers, with Captain Coxon and second mate Heath, both tied with ropes, come on shore, and are now in the black hole. The other rogue, whose name I believe is Holmes, is in danger of his life, having received some wounds by the resistance he made; he is on board the Europe ship under the care of the Surgeon. The officers that were on board the Europe ship's boat make affidavit, that as soon as they came near the ship, and that they answered they were Frenchmen, they were fired on by the ship; on which they returned the salute and at once boarded her on her bow, before the others had time to send the grenadoes, which were all ready on the quarter deck. They found Holmes on the forecastle, ready to fire a second time, when he was wounded.

"I am Sir, your most humble and obedient Servant,

LEBLANC."

From another letter received about the same time, Governor Benyon learned that Governor Dumas and Council at Pondicherry proposed treating Captain Coxon and his officers as pirates. Accordingly he wrote to Pondicherry to intercede for the criminals, who had been guilty of an outrage, but who could scarcely be suspected of a piratical intention. In reply Governor Dumas wrote the following letter; which our readers will not fail to see is penned in that courteous style which distinguished the French gentlemen of the time of Louis Quatorze.

Translate of Monsieur Dumas' letter to the President, dated 26*th July* 1740.

"Sir,—I have received the letter that you did me the Honor to write me, relating to the affair of Mr. Coxon and the two mates of the Nancy. I cannot tell Sir, whether you have been truly informed of what passed on that occasion; and therefore will give you the particulars. Captain Monger, who have been here some time with his ship, sold her to Mr. Pathelin and his partners, and went on board to deliver her to the buyers. But when he got on board, Mr. Coxon and his adherents threatened to throw him overboard, and obliged him by force to get out of the ship with those who went with him aboard; threatening further to fire upon them if they did not immediately retire. Mr. Monger came ashore, told me what had passed, and desired me to let him have some force to get possession of his ship; which he told me the officers and the crew had an intention to carry away in the night. It was six at night, but I immediately sent a Serjeant and six men in a Chelinga to order Captain Coxon, who was on board, to come and talk to me, to let me know his reason for this conduct, promising him to do him justice. But instead of receiving the Chelinga I sent, they forbad them to come near them; threatening to fire at them, and they did actually get one of their cannon and some grenadoes ready to fire. The Serjeant returned ashore and told me what had passed, which put me under a necessity to order the Commodore of our Europe ships to send his boat armed on board the "Nancy," to seize these mutineers, and bring them ashore. When the boat got near the ship, and those on board had asked from whence they came, the officer answered it was the Commodore's boat, and they were going on board by the Governor's orders. The reply was a discharge of several musquets at our boat, which obliged them to fire also at the ship. The boat's crew boarded her in the bow, and made themselves masters of her. They found Mr. Coxon and the other two armed with musquets and granadoes, and a single cannon loaded with broken bits of iron and primed. Happily during this whole affair nobody was killed. Only one of the three English got some cuts from a sword which he is almost recovered of. Now Sir, be pleased to judge yourself of the conduct of these three people, and what punishment they deserve. I own I never did believe they intended to turn pirates, but believe all these impertinences are owing to liquor.

"The great regard I have for you, Sir, will engage me to proceed in this affair agreeable to your opinion. Nay I consent that you shall determine their punishment, and will deliver them up to you, on condition you will promise me they shall be punished. I shall wait your answer before any proceedings are begun against them.

I have the honor to be, Sir, &c.,

DUMAS."

Governor Benyon was now in a difficulty. If the men were sent to Madras, the Government had no power to punish them, because the outrage had been committed in a foreign territory. In this dilemma, he could only request Governor Dumas to punish them himself, as he thought proper; and then to send them to Madras, that they might be subsequently dispatched to England. The following short note from Governor Dumas shows how the matter was settled.

Translate of a letter from Monsieur Dumas at Pondicherry, dated, 4th August 1740.

"Sir,—I have received the obliging letter you did me the honor to write me. There is nothing more agreeable to me than opportunities of serving you. As to the article of pardon, I am of opinion it should be entire; and therefore, Sir, whenever you please to send for the two Englishmen who are here I will deliver them to your order.

I have the honor to be, &c.

DUMAS."

Coxon and his officers were accordingly brought to Madras, and from thence sent to England.

Amongst these important matters we find the following entry.

"Monday, 4th August, 1740. A box of "wiggs" directed to Mr. William Gibson, late surgeon at Vizagapatam deceased, having been sometime since delivered to the Secretary, who was ordered to keep them till some body should administer to that estate,—he is now ordered to sell them at outcry, and pay the net produce thereof into cash."

Our next extract refers to another negociation carried on between Pondicherry and Fort Saint George.

"Saturday, 16th August, 1740. Received a letter from Mr. Dumas and Council of Pondicherry, relating to four men deserted from their garrison to Fort Saint David, and suspected of having murdered a man; and whom they therefore demand in the name of his most Christian Majesty to be delivered up to them; proposing also the entering into a treaty with us about the delivering up such criminals; as they have done with the Dutch and Danes on this Coast, and with our Gentlemen at Tellicherry.

"The subject being taken under consideration, the Board are of opinion, that a murder attended with such circumstances as that of which the four deserters stand suspected with so much reason, ought not to go unpunished; and that the giving up those men is no contravention to the protection of the flag, upon promise of the Gentlemen of Pondicherry, that if they are not found guilty of the murder, they shall be pardoned the desertion.

"As to what is proposed, both from Pondicherry and Fort St. David, about entering into some agreement for preventing mischiefs of this sort in future, we think it may be better to hold ourselves at liberty in that respect; nor do we suppose the Gentlemen of Pondicherry will concern themselves further about it, since we have complied with the intention of such an agreement in delivering up these men."

Towards the close of the year the Mahrattas again became troublesome, as will be seen by the following extracts.

"Monday, 3rd November, 1740. The President acquaints the Board, that there has for some days been a report that the Mahrattas were coming again into this province, which had given a fresh alarm to the inhabitants; that yesterday the families of several considerable Moormen came into Town, more were come to-day, and others were upon the road; that he had endeavoured to inform himself what might be the reason of the Mahrattas marching again towards Arcot, concerning which reports were very different; but that which had the best authority, and which he hoped might be depended on, was that Ragojee Busseirah (Bhonslay) was coming with only 3000 horse to the feast at Trinomoly; and though the grand army was advanced to Colourc, it was only to receive the last payment due from the Nabob who had sent Kistmajee Puntaloo to settle it with them. However, as neither Mahrattas or Moors depend much upon the faith of each other, the Nabob was putting himself in a posture of defence at Arcot; and had given leave to those who were afraid to stay there, to go and secure themselves where they thought fit, till all matters were adjusted between him and the Mahrattas, and these last were retired again to a greater distance. In the mean time the President has given fresh directions to the Hircarras to observe what passed in the country, and send him constant advices of the motions of the Mahratta forces."

"Monday, 24th November, 1740. The Mahrattas having again entered this province, upon which account the inhabitants are flying again into our bounds; and apprehending it may be dangerous sending money overland to Fort St. David at present, agreed to defer it till there is reason to believe the roads are clear from the Mahrattas or other robbers."

"Tuesday, 2nd December, 1740. Advices received yesterday evening and this morning, that the Mahrattas have plundered and burnt several towns no great distance from us.

"Tuesday, 9th December, 1740. The Carpets in the Consultation room being quite worn out, agreed that new ones be bought and the old ones be sold for the most they will fetch."

"Tuesday, 9th December, 1740. The Board having in Consultation the 30th May last, agreed that it was absolutely necessary that that part of the White Town lying from Charles' point to the Cloth godowns next the river, should be enclosed with a wall; and having hitherto deferred the consideration in what manner it should be built, partly for want of materials, and partly because the Mahrattas having come to an agreement with the Nabob to leave the country on payment of a sum of money, we thought there was reason to hope they would before now have returned to their own country, without giving us any molestation. But as we look upon their late conduct to be a breach of faith with the Nabob, and a manifest violation of their agreements with him; and it being confidently reported on all hands that they intend to sisit the sea port;—the Board agreed it to be abvolutely necessary that some fence should be run up at the before-mentioned part of the White Town as soon as possible. But as we have not a sufficient quantity of materials ready, and perhaps also not sufficient time to build a strong wall there;—the Pay Master was ordered for the present to run up a wall of two bricks and a half thick upon the wharf, which has been already built there by the inhabitants; and that it be twelve feet high above the wharf. The expense of this will not be above four or five hundred pagodas; and our intention is only to make such a fence as may prevent the enemy from marching directly into the Town, and their musketry from firing into the houses; either of which they might at present do if they have never so little resolution; since the river is fordable, and the bank on the opposite side as high as the wharf on this.

But as this is only a temporary remedy, and very far from a sufficient security, it is agreed to represent the same to our Honorable Masters, and desire permission to secure all that side of the Town effectually by building a curtain with proper batteries and points all along it."

It may be here advisable to glance at the general proceedings of the Mahrattas. Bajee Rao, the celebrated Peishwa or prime minister of the Rajah of the Mahrattas, who had already projected the conquest of the Mogul empire, had become reconciled to his rival Raghojee Bhonslay; and had incited Raghojee to invade and plunder the Carnatic, whilst he himself could direct his whole operations against the Nizam of the Dekkan. But death broke in upon the ambitious dream. Bajee Rao was seized with a sudden illness on the banks of the Nerbudda, and expired on the 28th day of April 1740. About the same time, as we have already seen, the Mahratta army under Raghojee Bhonslay had poured into the Carnatic, defeated and slain Dost Ali in the neighbourhood of the Damulcherry Pass, and commenced levying contributions all over the province, until bought off by Subder Ali Khan, the son in heir of the late Nabob. Raghojee had then made a secret compact with Subder Ali, to return and crush Chunda Sahib, who was then in possession of Trichinopoly, and who had for some time excited the jealousy and apprehension of the court at Arcot.

The death of Bajee Rao for a while changed the current of affairs. Raghojee left the main army, and hurried back to Sattara to prevent if possible the succession of the son of Bajee Rao to the office of Peishwa. In this design he failed. The office of Peishwa was now nearly established as hereditary; and (notwithstanding the opposition of Raghojee Bhonslay,) Ballajee Bajee Rao, the eldest son of the deceased Peishwa, succeeded to the high station which had been occupied by his father. Raghojee Bhonslay then returned to the Carnatic to prosecute his designs against Trichinopoly.

"Thursday, 18th December, 1740. The President acquaints the Board that Imaum Sahib, on his going to the Northward, had sent his children hither for security in the present unsettled state of the country; and he being now Foujdar at Masulipatam, in very great favour both with Nazar Jung, and his father Cheen Kulich Khan (Nizam of the Dekkan); and standing fair for some considerable preferment in this province whenever they shall resolve to settle the Government;—the President therefore proposed to the consideration of the Board, whether it may not be of service to the Company's affairs to take the opportunity of the approaching feast to make a present to the children of about 150 pagodas value; which being debated, it was agreed that preserving the friendship of Imaum Sahib was of great consequence to the Company; that such an occasion is not likely to happen again; and the laying hold of it must be agreeable to them; and therefore the Presidents proposal was agreed to.

"Saturday, 20th December, 1740. General letter from the Deputy Governor and Council of Fort St. David of the 16th instant read;—advising several parties of Mahratta horse having lately appeared near their bounds, and that Porto Novo had been plundered by them, and requesting a supply of men and powder."

"Saturday, 20th December, 1740. A very high sea upon the full moon in October last, having overset the palisadoes and piles between the block house by New point and the sea ;—the Paymaster is ordered to have them set up again ; and the Lieutenants of the Garrison, representing that it would be necessary to have a small palisado fence made within side the gates of the Black Town, to secure the guards there in case there should be any design to surprize them, and as we ought to guard against all treachery within as well as against an enemy without,—the Paymaster is ordered to set about them ; it being computed also that the expense will be but a trifle."

"Monday, 22nd December, 1740. At present the country is so full of troubles by the Mahrattas having entered a second time into this province, and their intended march to the Southward, that none of the merchants think it safe to send any more money into the country for the provision of calicoes."

"Monday, 29th December 1740. Ordered that the Secretary do call upon such of the Company's Servants as are become of age since last year, to sign new covenants and name their securities ; and that they attend the Board to that end on Saturday next."

The progress of events is here relieved by a domestic incident, which is somewhat more lively than the notices of the proceedings of the Mahrattas. Miss Elizabeth Mansell, a young lady passenger from England, and a near relation of one of the members of Council, had most unmistakeably committed herself with Captain Cummings, the commander of the vessel; and then on the arrival of the ship at Fort St. George, Miss Mansell was induced to lay a capital charge against the Captain, with the hope apparently of saving her own character. This charge was solemnly investigated by the President and Council. Of course the proceedings are unfitted for our columns, but some extracts are worthy of record as belonging to the scandal of the time.

"Saturday, 28th February, 1741. Miss Mansell and Captain Cummings, both attending the Board pursuant to order, her information was read and reattested by her on oath; after which she was examined to the manner where it happened, where the other two young ladies were, who were fellow passengers with her, and how she was prevented from calling out for assistance. To which she answered that it was near ten at night in the balcony of the ship; that the other two ladies were in the round house. She confessed further that at the Cape she had consented to his wishes; but that previously it had been against her will. She added that since that time the Captain had beat her, pulled her by the hair of her head, and called her several names.

"To this the Captain answered, that it was very true he had been too intimate with her for most part of the voyage after the first two months; that she showed a fondness for him even at Portsmouth to that degree, that it made Mrs. Cummings so uneasy as to burst out into tears, which he had much ado to overcome by promises of a prudent behaviour with regard to her; that he withstood daily repeated importunities for full two months, but confessed that at last she prevailed on him; that she had fallen in love with a young fellow in the passage between Gravesend and Portsmouth; that she was suspected to have been too intimate with a young man that lived in the house with her; and that she had behaved in general so ill that the family she lived with were resolved to get rid of her at any rate.

"Miss Mansell had no further proof than her own oath to support the charge laid against the Captain; but Mrs. Mary Coales being called told the Board that she had often seen Miss Mansell cry; that in particular on Christmas day last, she with a flood of tears said she could never be happy; that she had sometimes on these occasions asked Miss Mansell what was the matter, and was answered that the Captain and she had some words.

"This witness, being asked by the Captain if Miss Mansell ever complained of him, answered in the negative; being further asked if she had not from Miss Mansell's conduct suspected an intimacy between them, she answered that sometimes she was almost tempted to think there was, and that she was often in a passion if the Captain happened to take any notice of herself.

"Mrs. Martha Coales being called, declared that she had often seen Miss Mansell cry, which she attributed to some little quarrels between the Captain and her; but never asked the reason, and that one day being below in the great cabin with Miss Mansell, the Captain from above said or did something that provoked Miss Mansell to call him vallain and rogue and other names, adding that he had taken away her character.

"John Clause, passenger, declares he heard the Captain and Miss Mansell quarrelling together; which he thinks was about a month or six weeks before their arrival at this place, but he did not take notice of the words.

"Anthony Wood, Captain's Steward, avers that he observed Miss Mansell fond of the Captain even at Portsmouth; that Mrs. Cummings saw it and was very uneasy, that she was to go in the ship. He said further that at Portsmouth she was caught playing at Tagg with a couple of footmen.

"Mark Romney deposed that he had observed a great intimacy between the Captain and Miss Mansell; that often when she and the other Ladies were above, if the Captain showed any civility to them, Miss Mansell immediately flew out in a passion; that he knows there was a familiarity between them; that being on the poop one night about 11 o'clock he saw the Captain and her sitting in two chairs, and she with her arm round the Captain's neck, when he heard her call him her dear Captain and saw her kiss him; that he showed it to his companions, who bid him make no noise lest they should be heard; and that he beckoned to a midshipman, who was a small distance off, to come and look; who put his finger to his nose but would not come.

"All these evidences were examined on oath. Miss Mansell, having in her examination said she came ashore with a resolution to prosecute Captain Cummings for this fact;—she was asked how she came to be silent so long, and why in the letters she wrote ashore by the Catamaran (which being received in company were shown to several people) she had given the Captain so good a character; which seemed so ill to accord with the intention she said she had to publish this affair. She answered that for the letter he dictated it, and made her also take an oath never to disclose what had passed between them just before they got in here; but that it was her full intention to divulge it as she had now done.

"To this the Captain answered, that as to the letter, it is true he wrote it foul, but that he did not dictate it; that she desired him to put in a great deal in his own commendation, and he had much ado to convince her that it might give suspicion of a fondness, if she said more than was in that letter; that as to the oath, it was not for fear of being accused, but because knowing the impetuosity of her temper and her furious passions, he feared she would by word or action betray herself, and therefore hoped the tie of an oath might check her, and save her from ruining herself in the manner she has done; that he is certain she had no design to tell this story, but that somebody or other had worked her up to it; and to convince the

Board more fully that she had no such intentions, he instanced in many particulars which showed there must still be an intimacy and familiar correspondence carried on between them, long after her coming ashore; since she had told him many secrets of the family, and made complaints to him of unkind usage she fancied she had received; this being mostly confessed by her to be true, she was dismissed. After which the Captain being ordered to withdraw, the Board agreed that there did not appear sufficient cause to indict the Captain; and therefore that he be discharged from his confinement. After which he was called in and acquainted therewith; but at the same time told that his conduct with relation to this young woman would be a perpetual blot on him, since she was under his care and protection; which he endeavoured to answer by insinuating that she was careless of her reputation before she came on board; but which he had no proof to support, and was therefore stopped from proceeding in this sort of defence."

CHAPTER XLIV.

GOVERNORSHIP OF MR. RICHARD BENYON.

(Continued.)

1741.

The commencement of 1741 saw but little change for the better in the prospects of Fort St. George. Whilst the main army of the Mahrattas was besieging Trichinopoly for the purpose of wresting that kingdom from the Mussulman rule of Chunda Sahib, straggling parties of Mahratta horse were plundering the country up to the very borders of Fort St. David; and it was expected that when Trichinopoly was finally captured, the Mahrattas would move on towards the coast and attack the European settlements both at Fort St. David and Fort St. George. In January, Raghojee Bhonsla, who commanded the Mahratta army in the Carnatic, made extraordinary demands upon both settlements, which necessitated immediate preparations for defence on an extensive scale. Every day accounts became more and more alarming. On the 23rd January, Governor Benyon informed the Council that a party of between four and five thousand Mahratta horse had entered the bounds of Fort St. David; and that the English Deputy Governor had discharged about a hundred cannon from Cuddalore before the enemy retired;

and even then the Mahrattas were not prevented from carrying off a considerable booty from Mangicopang and the "Washing Town." At the same time the news arrived that this body of horse had passed on from Fort St. David and plundered Sadras; and would have plundered the Dutch factory also, had they not been gallantly repulsed by the Dutch Governor. It was also stated that these Mahrattas were still encamped on the Sadras river, and that it was uncertain what design they would attempt next, and that possibly they were only waiting there until they were joined by a larger body. Accordingly the Government of Fort St. George ordered that thirty men should be landed from a ship's company then in the roads, and that all the English, Portuguese, and Armenian inhabitants should be put under arms.

Subsequently Governor Benyon received advices from Arcot, intimating that this body of horse formed no part of the Mahratta army engaged in the siege of Trichinopoly; and that the Nabob had sent to the Mahratta generals to complain of this inroad into the Carnatic. However it was known that the Nabob had no power to resent the injury; and it was more than doubtful whether the movements of this separate body had not been directed by the Mahratta generals who were besieging Trichinopoly. The latter doubt was speedily removed by the return of the horse to the main army of Trichinopoly; and in March the place was in the hands of the Mahrattas, and Chunda Sahib carried off prisoner to Sattara.

The following extracts from a General letter dispatched this year by the Madras Government to the Court of Directors, contains perhaps the most authentic account of the events connected with this memorable siege.

"We believe we cannot tell you any thing more agreeable than that the Mahrattas having taken Trichinopoly the middle of March last, returned to their own country in May without coming into this province. We shall trouble you with some account of the siege or rather blockade of Trichinopoly. We wrote your Honors last year that Subder Ali Khan and his brother-in-law Chunda Sahib, after having spent some days at Pondicherry returned to Arcot, and continued together there some time and to all appearance were very good friends. Meer Assad* remained with the Mahrattas, who were upon the Western borders of this province, under pretence of being an hostage for the sums the Nabob had agreed to pay them; but sometime in November Subder Ali Khan acquainted Chunda Sahib that Meer Assad had finished a treaty with the Mahrattas, by which it was stipulated that seven lacs of rupees, as part of thirty-two he had agreed to pay, was the composition of Trichinopoly. Chunda Sahib, surprized that such a treaty had been concluded without his par-

* Meer Assad became Dewan in the room of Chunda Sahib, after the latter became master of Trichinopoly. He had been taken prisoner by the Mahrattas at the great battle at Damulcharry; and it was he who negotiated with the Mahrattas respecting the amount of tribute to be paid by the Nabob of Arcot, and the delivering up of Trichinopoly.

ticipation, told Subder Ali that he knew how to transact his own affairs, and would not stand to it. Very high words passed between the two brothers, and Chunda Sahib left Arcot without taking leave of Subder Ali, and made haste to Trichinopoly: his partisans giving out that he had made it so strong and stored well with ammunition and provisions of all kinds so that it would hold out a siege of three years; and if the Mahrattas should attempt it they would only lose their time to no purpose; nor would they have thought of it if Subder Ali had not engaged them in the undertaking, upon promise to pay them a large sum monthly till such time as the place should be taken. Whatever private agreement Subder Ali had made with the Mahrattas; the known enmity which both he and Meer Assad have long had towards Chunda Sahib, the supplies of provisions they sent to the Mahratta Camp, and other circumstances, make it but too probable the destruction of Chunda Sahib was what they had much at heart. However the Mahrattas, when they came to the borders of Trichinopoly, only demanded seven lacs of rupees; which being refused by Chunda Sahib, they advanced towards the capital, and there was some skirmish in the suburbs. After which they made no attack upon the place, but contented themselves with guarding all the passes to the town, that no provisions or any other assistance should get in. In this work, though their own army was sufficiently numerous, they had the assistance of the King of Tanjore and the tributary princes of Trichinopoly, who articled with the Mahrattas that they should not leave that place in the possession of the Moors. It was not long before Chunda Sahib found himself greatly distressed for want of provisions, and then offered to make up the sum of twelve lacs. It was once thought the Mahrattas would have accepted of his offer; the rather because Futta Singh was believed to favour Chunda Sahib, and had often sent to Raghojee Bhonsla either to take the Town or the money, and threatened to draw off the forces which were more particularly under his command. Chunda Sahib's partisans affirmed for some days that the treaty was absolutely concluded. They went further, and reported that the Mahrattas had engaged to put Khan Bahauder into the Government of this province. Khan Bahauder* was intended by old Sadatulla Khan for his successor; and had procured some grants from the Court for that purpose; but being a very weak man, the ministers espoused the interest of Dost Ali Khan, father of Subder Ali Khan, and fixed him in the Government. It is not long since that Chunda Sahib, to serve some ambitious purpose, married his daughter to Khan Bahauder; and he was with Chunda Sahib in Trichinopoly during the siege. Subder Ali Khan was so alarmed about the treaty which was then on foot, that he shut himself up in Ginjee, and from thence wrote to the two Mahratta Generals, complaining of their breach of faith. At the same time, the King

* This Khan Bahauder was the same as Goulam Hussein, who was at first Dewan to Dost Ali, but was afterwards superseded by Chunda Sahib.

of Tanjore and the tributary princes who had assisted them, took their images out of their Pagodas, and adjured them (the Mahrattas), by all their gods, not to leave them exposed to the resentment of Chunda Sahib. In fine the treaty was broke off, and Chunda told that they would agree to no peace that should leave him in the possession of Trichinopoly. Chunda Sahib's provisions growing more scarce every day, and being reduced to very great necessities, began to entertain thoughts of delivering up the place. All the hopes he had left was from his brother Budda Sahib, reckoned a brave man and who was then at Madura. Chunda Sahib wrote him in the most pressing terms to come to his relief; and Budda Sahib having got together 5000 horse and 7000 or 8000 foot with a great quantity of provisions, wrote his brother he was upon his march to assist him; and that he hoped to force his way through the camp; but the letter was intercepted by the Mahrattas who sent 20,000 horse to waylay him. A smart engagement ensued, in which it is said about 2000 men were killed on each side. This battle was fatal to Budda Sahib; he lost his life in it; and the Mahrattas having found his body, covered it with a rich cloth and sent it into Trichinopoly; upbraiding Chunda Sahib with having by his obstinacy been the occasion of his brother's death. Chunda Sahib, being then in despair, the next day being the 13th March, delivered the Town and himself up to the discretion of the enemy. The many and various reports which were spread about during this siege, kept every body in suspence and in continual alarms,' as doubting what the Mahrattas would do after they had taken it. For ourselves we knew not how to depend upon what the Nabob said, as it was plain he had himself a great distrust of the Mahrattas. We had some reason to believe the letters wrote to the President from Futta Singh, and Raghojee Bhonsla, proceeded from the politics at Arcot; but that scheme not taking effect, the Nabob and his ministers affected an extraordinary care and concern for us, and were very officious in advising us of any motion which the enemy made towards these parts, and how to behave ourselves towards them."

"Chunda Sahib having, as we said, delivered himself up to the discretion of the Mahrattas, agreed afterwards, as it was said, to pay them eight lacs of rupees for his ransom; and Khan Bahauder with Francis Pereira were sent to Chunda Sahib's wife, who was in Pondicherry, to receive the money. But the good lady, pretending a distrust, answered that she had not so much money by her, or if she had, would she part with it till she should see her husband?" If he was sent to her, she would sell her jewels, and borrow what was wanting among her friends. The Mahrattas having received that answer, carried Chunda Sahib and his son along with them to Sattara, the Sou Rajah's* capital. His partisans now give out that he is in great favour at Sattara; and that by the interest of that Court with Cheen Kulich Khan, he will obtain a grant of the government of this

* Sahoo Rajah perhaps better known as Shao.

province, and will be assisted with a large body of Mahratta horse to drive Subder Ali Khan out of it.

"It was for sometime uncertain what the Mahrattas would do with Trichinopoly. There were several bidders for it, but it was thought they were most inclined to put in the next heir of the late queen; but as he could not give them security for the money he offered, they left Morarée Gorbada,* Viceroy there, with 4000 horse, till the Sou Rajah should give further orders. When they took possession of it, they would not suffer it to be plundered. It is imagined their reason for that was, that they knew most of the riches had been conveyed out before they laid siege to it; and if they had acted otherwise, the Sou Rajah would have expected them to have accounted for a larger sum than they found. One thing is remarkable, and yet is affirmed for truth, that they left orders with the Viceroy to pay the same tribute to Arcot which had been usually paid by the Kings and Queens of Trichinopoly.

"The Mahrattas having thus settled the government of Trichinopoly, 40,000 horse took the Western road through Mysore. The two Generals with the rest of the army took another road which borders upon this province. Nabob Subder Ali kept himself close in Ginjee. We know not what particular affairs remained to be adjusted between them, but after some stay within a day's journey of Ginjee they marched on to the Northward, and passed the Kistna about the end of May.

---

* The celebrated Morari Rao.

"The beginning of that month, the President received a letter from Nabob Subder Ali, advising that the Mahrattas had passed the mountains of Balaghaut; and at the same time Budda Sahib wrote another letter, advising the Nabob with his family, intended to go to Mekka; and therefore desired some houses might be taken for them in Town, as they designed to be down here, to stay here till the season for proceeding on the voyage. Budda Sahib, however, intimated that he heard the Nabob had no real design of going to Mekka; and indeed our other advices from the country to us assured us there was nothing more in it than a family quarrel. However we thought we could not avoid preparing for their reception here; and then advised Budda Sahib that the houses were ready whenever they pleased to come. Some months have since passed, but though the Nabob still talks of coming down, most people doubt. We hope we shall soon be at some certainty; because all this while we are paying sixty pagodas per month rent for the houses. From Ginjee the Nabob removed to Vellore, and from thence to Arcot, where he now is; and Meer Assad, the sole minister about him, a man of strong parts, bold and resolute. The Nabob follows his advice implicitly, and perhaps thinks him the more necessary in the present juncture as most likely to extricate him from the difficulties he is under. Money is the great thing wanted to pay the arrears due to his father's and his own troops; which amount to 400,000 pagodas; and also to make up such sum as may be sufficient to get himself confirmed in the government of the province. But the means made use of to raise it, have given great disgust all over the country; as the minister is not in the least scrupulous in raising contributions from every body that is in his power."

Having thus placed before our readers a general view of the condition of the country, written at the very time, it may be as well to turn to the history of Fort St. George. About the very time that Trichinopoly was taken by the Mahrattas, Governor Benyon dispatched a present to the Mahratta general with the following letter.

"*To Raghojee Bhonsla Subah, General of the Mahratta army.*

"Lately I have received from Mr. Hubbard the Deputy Governor of Tevenepatam (Fort St. David) a copy of the letter you wrote him. I am much pleased with the friendship you express for the English; and you may be assured we are very willing to cultivate it. Mr. Hubbard acquaints me that he had complained to you, some of the people belonging to your army had entered the bounds of Tevenepatam, and done some damage to the inhabitants. Such proceedings will always be attended with mischief; and therefore I was very glad to read you had promised him that you would lay your strict taukeed that no one should give him any molestation in future. By this I observe that you are truly our friend, and therefore I have resolved to send a vakeel, on purpose to assure you of our friendship and regard for you. I have also sent some things to Mr. Hubbard, who will write you the particulars and send them to you from Tevenepatam, together with our Vakeel; and I refer you to Mr. Hubbard for what further he shall write you, and what else will be told you by our Vakeel of our inclinations to preserve the friendship between us."

About the same time another letter and present were dispatched by Governor Benyon to Futta Singh Bhonsla, the other Mahratta General. We extract the letter, from which it will be seen that the English wished it to be understood that they were actuated out of respect for the Mahratta chiefs rather than fear.

"*To Futta Singh, General of the Mahratta Army.*

"The Deputy Governor of Tevenepatam having advised me that he had received a very friendly letter from Raghojee Bhonsla, I resolve to send a vakeel on purpose with a letter from myself to that general; and as I have that opportunity of writing to you, I would not omit it; and have ordered my vakeel to wait upon you with this to assure you of the respect I have for your person and great qualities. Our vakeel will assure you of our sincere inclinations to continue the friendship between us; and I refer you to him, and what more will be written you by the Governor of Tevenepatam to whom I have sent several things, the particulars of which he will advise you, and of which I desire your acceptance. They are not worthy to be sent to so great a general; but I only intend them as a mark of my respect for your person, and your acceptance of them will add to their value."

Whilst the relations of the English towards the

Native Princes were in this unsatisfactory state, a circumstance occurred at Madras which seemed likely to throw the commercial interests of the place into the greatest confusion. It had been customary for the Company's Shroffs and two Bazaar Shroffs to seal up Pagodas in bags of a thousand rupees each, in order to prevent the inconvenience of counting in the payment of money. Moreover the Company's seal was supposed to be not only a guarantee for the quantity but for the quality of the Pagodas. This year however it was discovered that whilst some persons had taken upon themselves to imitate the Company's seal; the Shroffs had managed to slip in considerable quantities of inferior money in the bags which bore the Company's seal. A long and wearisome enquiry was then carried on which terminated in the imprisonment of the three Shroffs, and the confiscation of their goods; and further the Shroffs were placed in the pillory for one hour on the 26th day of every month, until they could be transported to the West Coast of Sumatra. It will be seen in a future entry under date 18th January 1742, that the latter part of this sentence was commuted.

Meantime, whilst domestic affairs were in this state, the Vakeel sent to the Mahratta camp before Trichinopoly, had delivered the letters and presents to Raghojee Bhonsla and Futta Singh Bhonsla. But we extract the official account of his proceedings.

"Thursday, 16th April, 1741. The President acquaints the Board, he had this morning received a letter from Coopiah, the Vakeel sent to the

Mahratta camp, advising his arrival and reception there, the translate of which is entered after this consultation."

"*From Coopiah, Vakeel in the Mahratta camp at Trichinopoly, dated the* 8*th April and received on the* 16*th instant*, 1741.

"I am now in the Mahratta army, which is encamped about ten miles West of Trichinopoly. The Governor of Tevenepatam dispatched me to the Mahratta camp, with the presents he had prepared for the Mahrattas. When I arrived at Trichinopoly, I first made myself acquainted with Coanari Pontoloo and Roy Shasharoy, the managers of Rajah Raghojee Bhonsla's affairs; and upon their introducing me to Rajah Futta and Rajah Raghojee Bhonsla, I delivered them the presents and the letters; they received them and upon looking into the presents they said they were very good things. At which time I presented then your Honors respects, and the Governor of Tevenepatam's service; besides several other compliments from your Honors, and that you are their friend. Upon hearing this, they said that their predecessors had a desire for your friendship, and settled you in this country; and therefore you may live safe in your place without having any concern. They gave me beetlenut, and told me that to-morrow they should have more leisure to speak with me, when they promised to send me away.

"About two or three days after they had taken Trichinopoly Fort, they sent a part of their army towards the kingdom of Mysore; and they afterwards sent another part along with Chunda Sahib to the said country. The horse that are already gone out is 40,000; and they have about 30,000 here, who will also go away as soon as they have settled some government at Trichinopoly.

"The Rajahs have at present delivered Trichinopoly Fort into the care of Morari Rao Ghorepuray, Commander of ten or fifteen thousand horse; but Raghojee Bhonsla has a great mind to restore it to the old Gentoos, and he is treating with Rammania and Govindaya for that purpose; and I think that in five or six days time they will give the Government to the Gentoos, and will go away, and I will advise your Honor whatever shall pass hereafter."

"Friday, 24th April, 1741. The President acquaints the Board he had received another letter from the Vakeel Coopiah, acquainting him that he had received his audience of leave from the two Mahratta generals; who had also delivered him horses and seerpaws and cowles for this place and Fort St. David. At the same time the President received a letter from Roy Shasharoy, a principal officer in the Mahratta camp. Translate of which, and the vakeel's letter are entered after this consultation."

"*From Roy Shasharoy, an officer under the Mahratta Generals.*

"Though your Honor did not write me a letter, yet I have heard of your goodness and reputation from Mr. Hubbard the Governor of Tevenepatam, who has wrote me a letter, and sent some clothes and other things, along with Coopiah and Audy Venkiah, Vakeels, to be presented to Rajah

Futta Singh and Rajah Raghojee Bhonsla, as also to Ramajee Pontoloo and Contoloo, officers and managers of their affairs. When the Vakeels arrived, they applied to me, and I acquainted both of the Rajahs of their arrival, and caused a proper person to be sent to bring them along with him; where I introduced them to the Rajahs, and told them much in your Honor's praise. The presents were delivered to the Rajahs by your Vakeel.

"I was not wanting to tell the Rajahs what was most proper in your Honor's praise; and did procure for you a horse and seerpaw, consisting of five clothes, and our clothes for Mr. Fowke; and after the same manner to the Governor and second of Tevenepatam; and caused tasheriffs to be given to your Vakeels, as also presents to the people who came along with them.

"It is not customary at the Court of our Rajahs to give a cowle to any, without the tribute being settled and paid; and although your honour did not write any thing about a cowle, nor has there been any tribute paid, yet I used my interest with the Rajahs, and procured their cowles, both for Chinnapatam and Tevenepatam. I have delivered the same to Sambayah, and dispatched him along with your Vakeels, which you will receive.

"Your honor's Vakeel, and Vencata Narrainapa, and Sambayah, will inform your honor what more is necessary; and I desire your honor would always do me the pleasure of laying your commands on me. What can I say more."

The letter from the Vakeel Coopiah is little more

than a repetition of what has been given above. The following extracts from the consultations, in reference to the same subject, are worth reading.

"Thursday, 21st May, 1741. The Deputy Governor and Council of Fort St. David having left it to us to reward Coopiah, who was sent Vakeel to the Mahratta camp; and the said Coopiah having intimated his desire to be admitted into some constant pay; in consideration whereof he would be always ready to go upon any service which should be thought proper to employ him in;—the Board being satisfied with his fidelity and conduct in this last affair, and considering that the unsettled state of affairs in the country may make it frequently necessary to employ a capable person upon such occasions, and believing this man to be very proper and fit for the purpose,—agreed to allow him a pay of five pagodas per month.

"The President produces to the Board translate of a letter he received from Morari Rao, viceroy of Trichinopoly, requesting a supply of ammunition; which being taken into consideration, the President is desired to return such an answer, as shall neither be an absolute denial, or bind us to any thing hereafter which we may not think proper to comply with."

We now return to the domestic affairs of the English settlement. The following extracts will explain themselves.

"Monday, 25th May, 1741. Complaints being frequently made by the Military officers, that the soldiers of the garrison are decoyed and carried away by the country shipping; and the same being often practised also with the sailors belonging to the Europe ships; to prevent the like in future, it is ordered that if any person or persons, whether belonging to the country shipping or others, shall, hereafter be found to be any ways concerned in secreting, decoying, or carrying away from the place, either by sea or land, any of the military of the garrison, or seafaring men belonging to the Europe ships,—he or they so offending shall, for the first offence be fined in the sum of 50 pagodas a head for every soldier or sailor so secreted, decoyed, or carried away, and for the second offence be sent to England.

" And whereas several strangers come into the place, and are harboured in the public houses, without any report being made of them to the President agreeable to an order made for that purpose in President Harrison's time;—it is ordered that if any inhabitant, public house-keeper or others, shall for the future entertain any stranger arriving at this place, either by sea or land, who has not first been with the captain of the guard in order to his being carried or reported to the Governor,—he, she, or they shall for every such offence be fined in the sum of 50 pagodas.

" And that no one may pretend ignorance of the foregoing orders, the Secretary is directed to affix copies thereof at the gates of the Town."

" Thursday, 28th May, 1741. The Company's merchants not having brought in any cloth lately, or taken any money in advance, they were ordered to attend; and being called in and discoursed concerning the investment, alleged that it could not be thought strange they had not brought in any cloth for some months past, as every body had been in continual dread and apprehension that the Mahrattas would overrun this province as soon as they had taken Trichinopoly; and though they had taken another rout, and were returned towards their own country without coming again into this province, yet many of the weavers and spinners, who had fled from the towns and villages in the country, were not yet returned to their habitations. Besides that the danger upon the roads had been a great hinderance to the bringing of any quantity of cotton and cotton-yarn from the distant countries; by which means those two necessary articles were become very dear and scarce; insomuch that the natives found a difficulty in getting cloth made sufficient for their own wear. For all which reasons they could not as yet hope to get any cloth that was good and fit for the Company at any tolerable rate. They concluded with promising that upon the first advice from their Gomastas that any business could be done, they would immediately let us know it."

The following record of the duties of the respective officers and soldiers of the garrison of Fort St. George, will perhaps prove interesting to our military readers.

"THE DUTY OF MILITARY OFFICERS AND SOLDIERS AS DAILY PRACTISED IN THIS GARRISON OF FORT ST. GEORGE, 1741.

"*Captain's duty.*

"The Captain of the guard for the time being,

to order the drum to beat to arms at 7 o'clock in the morning; the mounting company to parade over against the main guard (Sundays excepted), or elsewhere as the weather permits.

"The Captain that mounts guard, to meet the Captain that dismounts on the parade while the mounting Company are under arms, in the morning about 7 o'clock and on Sundays about nine; there to receive the usual reports, and also any extraordinary orders, that the dismounting Captain may have received from the Governor during the time of his having had the charge of the guards.

"The Captain of the guards for the time being, to hear all manner of complaints that may be made either by or against the military. If any country people misuse the soldiers, the Captain to send them to a Justice of the peace to have satisfaction.

"If any of the military misuse the country people, upon making their complaint to the Captain of the guards, shall have (after hearing both parties) satisfaction. But if either parties have any extraordinary complaints that is of consequence, the Captain of the guards immediately to acquaint the Governor therewith.

"The Captain of the guards to visit the hospital once in twenty-four hours, during the time of being on guard; and upon the decease of any of the military, to acquaint the Governor therewith. Likewise upon the desertion of any of the military, the Governor to be informed thereof immediately. The Captain of the guards to attend the

Governor once a day, to receive his orders ordinary or extraordinary, and oftener if required."

"*Ensign's duty.*

"The two Ensigns that mount guard are to attend the parade in the morning at beat of drum to arms; one Ensign mounts the main guard under the Captain, the other mounts the Choultry himself. The Ensign that takes the main guard is to view and examine the men's arms and clothes whilst under arms, to see them in good order and fit to mount guard; those who are any ways out of order he is to report them to the Captain of the main guard.

"All reports from the out guards, whether ordinary or extraordinary, are to be reported to the Ensign of the main guard during the Captain's absence, who is to send them to the Captain by a Serjeant as soon as possible.

"The Ensign of the (White Town or) main guard, to go the rounds in the White Town at 10 o'clock at night, attended by a corporal and four men. He is to visit all the gates in the White Town, and to inspect with the officers and men of the several guards he passeth, to see that they are in fit order for their night duty, and that their centinels are alert on their posts; to see that those gates that should be shut are fast and secure; whatever he sees deficient or out of order to report it at his return to the Captain of the main guard.

"He is also to see the main guard gate shut, and all the keys sent up to the Captain.

"The Ensign of the Choultry guard, to visit all

the out guards in the evening about five or six o'clock without any attendance. He is to see the officers and men in good order, and fit for their night duty. If any be absent or out of order, he his at his return to report them to the Captain or Ensign of the main guard.

" He is to attend at his guard at 10 o'clock at night, to draw out his men to receive the Ensign of the main guard when he comes the rounds. He is to see his gate shut about 11 o'clock at night, and to see his guard in good orders, to send up his keys to the main guard, and to report the condition his guard is in. He is also to examine all strangers coming overland through any of his out gates, as soon as he is informed of it by the Serjeant or Corporal through which gate they come; to send their names and place from whence they came to the Captain or Ensign of the main guard."

" *Serjeant and Corporal's duty.*

" The Serjeants of the mounting Company are to attend the parade in the morning (with their halberts in their hands) when the drum beats to arms; they are to size and regulate the men under arms, to keep silence among the men, and to avoid talking themselves. They are to take their turns, one each mounting morning to make the Company in rank and file; and to report to the Captain of the guard, and to the Ensign that takes the main guard, what number of men there are paraded. If any gone into the hospital he is to report them to the Captain of the main guard. The Serjeant, after they are detached to their respective guards, are not to quit their guards themselves, nor to suffer the Corporal or Private men to do the same, without first having liberty from their Ensign by whom they are detached. The Serjeants with their corporal are to exercise their men every morning on their guards, in order to make them expert, against they come to be exercised by their Ensigns on the Island. The Serjeants and Corporals of both White and Black Town are to go the night rounds every hour, attended with a proper guard, from ten at night to five the next morning; to see that the centinels are alert on their posts and to enquire what condition the guards are when they pass; to give the parole to the Corporal of every guard he passeth. The Black Town rounds make all their reports to the Choultry guard; the White Town rounds to make all reports to the main guard; to deliver their Leaden Chop marked into the hour they began their rounds, that the Captain of the guard may know if any have neglected going round in their turn.

"One Serjeant and Corporal, each day after they come off guard, are to stand orderly in their turns according to seniority; their duty is to receive at 4 o'clock the parole and other orders that may be issued out at the main guard that day, and to carry them to the Captains and Ensigns that are off guard.

"They are to keep an exact roll of those men that are to sleep in the barracks that night; as soon as the gun has fired they are to begin to call the roll, to report the absent men to the Ensign of the main guard; they are to keep silence after the roll is called. No man is to be let out after gun-fire at night, except one Serjeant, one Corporal, and twelve men half black half white, who are to go from the barracks with arms to the Governor's garden house, from thence a Serjeant and six men go at eleven round the suburbs to see if the boutiques are all shut, and that no disturbance is made in the streets through which they pass; to suppress gaming houses, to stop all people suspected to be running of goods. And a Corporal and six men go the same at two. The Serjeants and Corporals of the out guards are to lock their gates exactly at ten o'clock at night; and immediately to report the same, and the condition their guards are in, to the Ensign of the Choultry; as also in the morning at gun fire, after having opened their gates to send their report as above.

"The orderly Serjeant and Corporal are to see the barracks swept clean, to see that the tanks be filled with good sweet water, and a sufficient number of lights at night. The barrack and hospital doors to be shut at ten at night, and opened at gun fire in the morning."

"*Exercise.*

"The Company that comes off guard on Monday morning, to be called together by beat of drum about five the same evening on the parade against the main guard; there to be regulated by the Serjeants and to receive their powder; from thence they are marched upon the Island, by two Ensigns that are off guard; one Ensign each Monday takes his turn according to seniority to give the word of command to exercise the Company;

beginning with the manual exercise, so to the evolutions and plattoon, or any other different firing as he shall see most convenient; the men are to keep a profound silence, to hearken diligently to the word of command, and to perform all their motions with life together. No officer is to give any orders on the Island, but him whose turn it is to exercise the men.

"Mounting the Companies is in this manner; that Company that comes off guard one morning mounts in the White Town next day, and the day after mounts in the Black Town, and the next day comes off again; so that two companies are continually on guard and one off alternately."

This year the coolies appear to have struck and deserted for more pay. We extract the official entry.

"Monday, 8th June, 1741. The President acquaints the Board that some days ago all the bamboo coolies, bag coolies, head coolies, and back coolies, had left the bounds; upon which he sent to them to know the reason, and why they run away without first applying to him to acquaint him what were their complaints. They returned him an answer, that they could not maintain themselves and families for the hire which they were paid, and refused to return till that was increased. The President then ordered their families to be turned out of Town; and upon that they thought fit to desire leave to come in again; and having since delivered him their petitions setting forth their grievances, the enquiry into which would be very tedious at the Board;—

Messrs. Morse and Monson were appointed a Committee, to examine into the matter thereof, and report to the Board if it be reasonable to allow them any and what relief.

The report was not made till the 21st of December, when it was agreed to allow the following rates for the Company's goods.

	Fs.
"From the Gentoo pagoda in the Black Town to the Granary on the Island, for every garce of rice and paddy	20
From Middle gate point to the said Granary	14
From the Gentoo pagoda or further in the Black Town to the godown by the School	10
From Middle gate point to the said godown	7
From the Seaside to the Inclosure of the Island, for every boat load of goods, wares, and stores	3
From the Seaside to the godowns in the White Town, each boat load	2
For carrying cloth from the merchant's godowns to the sorting godown, and attendance there each cooly per day	1

The following curious consultation upon the impolicy of permitting any of the Mussulman inhabitants to be sold as slaves, is well worthy of preservation.

"Tuesday, 30th June, 1741. The President acquaints the Board, that a Moor boy having been stole out of the country, and sold to a Captain of a ship, who had sent him on board, he had some trouble in getting him on shore; that the Nabob's Moollah, or priest, had interested himself much in this affair, which gave the President reason to apprehend that this practice of sending off the children of the Moors, or any others of the Mahomedan sect, might sometime or other involve us in troubles with the country Government; and therefore proposed that an order should be made prohibiting the buying or selling them in this place.

"If we are rightly informed, it is one of our agreements with the Government in Bengal, that we will not send away as slaves any of the Natives; and if there be no such agreement between us and the Moors in this province, it is possible that we were first settled here when the Gentoos were lords of the country. But however that be, as such prohibition cannot be attended with any prejudice to the Company, and may prevent any occasion for dispute upon that account in future;—the Secretary is directed to give public notice of such prohibition, by affixing an order at the usual places; that from henceforth no Moors, or any others of the Mahometan religion, be bought or sold in this town of Madras, or in the districts thereof."

The strike for higher pay was not confined to the coolies already mentioned, as may be seen by the following entry.

"Monday, 28th September, 1741. The Scavenger acquaints the Board, that the Parriahs in that service under him, had for sometime been very pressing for an increase of pay, and now absolutely refuse to continue any longer in it for twenty fanams a month; urging as their reason the hardship of their duty, and that they can earn thirty fanams a month each at many easier services. He adds that upon inquiring what would satisfy them, they for a long time insisted on twenty five fanams a month each; but at length agreed to continue in the service, if the head Parriah among them be allowed twenty-four, and the rest twenty-two fanams a month each, which is ordered to be paid them."

Towards the latter part of the year the family of Subder Ali, Nabob of Arcot, visited Black Town, and were courteously and respectfully received by the Governor and Council of Fort St. George. The object of this visit was to persuade the Nizam, who had large claims against the Nabob, that the latter was very poor and bent upon a pilgrimage to Mecca. Accordingly Subder Ali paid more than one visit to Madras, as a proof of the reality of his intentions. Many presents were of course made to the Nabob's family, but these it will be unnecessary to detail. The following narrative which the Governor and Council of Fort St. George sent home to the Court of Directors, will furnish a sufficient account, of the proceedings.

"The 21st at midnight the Nabob sent into Town his mother, his lady, and his son, who is about four years old. Their female attendants are very numerous, which has given us much trouble to find room for them. We sent our Polligar with two hundred peons and our country music to meet them at Triplicane. The guard which the Nabob sent with them returned back from thence, except about twenty horse that came into town with them. The Nabob having sent notice that he intended to come into Town next afternoon, Mr. Monson and Captain Holland, the Polligar with two hundred peons and our country music met him at the edge of the bounds. When he came to Triplicane Bridge, he stopped there and sent all his force back to St. Thomé, except about thirty horse and one hundred peons; but he was met by many thousands of our inhabitants who attended him from Triplicane to the foot of the Island Bridge. The Governor, attended by the Council and most of the European inhabitants, met him at the Fort Gate, when the guns from the ramparts began to fire; and we conducted him up to the Consultation Room, where after having stayed about half an hour, we waited upon him again to the Fort Gate, and he proceeded to the House which was prepared for his reception in the Black Town. The Fort had saluted him with sixty-one guns and the four Europe ships with twenty-one each. The French fired twenty-one more when he reached his own house. The next morning the Governor sent him the usual present of provisions, and as he brought in several great men with him, it was also necessary to send some to them. Some was likewise sent to his family when they came in. In the afternoon the President with the Council and the Captain of the Guard, waited upon the Nabob at his own house, and stayed with him the best part of an hour. As all that passed was public, and the Nabob has not yet proposed a private interview, we cannot yet advise your Honors where he designs to go from hence. Meer Assad did not come in here, but set out for the army about half an hour before the Nabob came from St. Thomé. The President has wrote him a letter to express his concern that he could not have the pleasure of seeing him. Imaum Sahib's children being still in Town, sent a compliment to the Nabob with one hundred and one gold mohurs, in a silver fillagree bandeja. The Nabob said it was too much, only took one of the gold mohurs, and sent them word he would come and see them before he went out of Town. The Governor of the towns to the Northward of this place that are under this province, come in daily to pay their respects to him. It is a great concern to us that we were not better prepared for his reception and accommodation; but he makes it as easy to us as he can, having very few of his own attendants with him, and they extremely quiet."

We now return to the case of the three Shroffs, who had been condemned to transportation to the Company's settlements on the West Coast of Sumatra. We need not remind our readers of the horror with which the natives generally regard the "black water"; and the castes to which the three Shroffs belonged, were naturally prepared to make great sacrifices to prevent the sentence of transportation from being carried into effect. The following entries in the Consultation books in reference to this subject will explain themselves.

"Monday, 18th January, 1742. Ball Chetty and Tomby Chetty, with some others of the Right and Left Hand caste, attending the Board, request that the Company's Shroff and the two bazaar Shroffs may not be sent to the West Coast, but that such sentence might be changed to their being banished the place; in consideration of which favour they would pay as a fine to the Company 2500 pagodas for the Company's Shroff, and 2500 for the two bazaar Shroffs; what had been seized to be delivered them up. The case of the two last being considered, and that how bad soever their intentions were, they had been prevented from doing much ill;—The fine of 2500 pagodes was accepted for them, but upon condition it be paid in one month; that they remain till then in the Choultry, and afterwards be turned out of the bounds never to return. But with regard to the Company's Shroff, his crime was looked upon as too heinous; and as so many of the inhabitants had suffered by his villany, to whom we could not propose to make any satisfaction that would be near their loss;—it was thought most prudent to reject the fine for him, and to send him to the West Coast by the first ship, as the best means to prevent all clamour and reflections."

Four months afterwards, active preparations were made for shipping off the unfortunate Company's Shroff to the West Coast, when a further attempt was made to save him. The matter is sufficiently explained in the following entry.

"Friday, 21st May, 1742. The Board being informed that the heads of the Right and Left Hand castes were attending, they were called in, and acquainted the Board; that as we had refused the offer they made the 18th January last to excuse the late Shroff Vishvinada from being sent to the West Coast; and apprehending that we intended to send him thither on the "Princess

Augusta," which was shortly to sail thither;—they were come again to intercede in his behalf; and urged that the sending him to the West Coast would be sending him to certain death; and though they had no reason to have any consideration for him, yet a compassion for his family, which was very numerous, had prevailed with them to solicit us again; and having before they came considered of what proposals to make to us, they took leave to represent to us, that the streets in the Black Town were in so bad a condition that it was become a great nuisance to the inhabitants in general, and to put them in proper order would cost a great deal of money, and to levy it by any tax upon the inhabitants might create great uneasiness; and therefore they had agreed upon condition that what we had seized of the Shroffs should be delivered up to them, and the said Shroff excused from going to the West Coast, to offer us 3,500 pagodas; and proposed withall that the said sum should be applied towards putting the streets of the Black Town in proper order, repairing the bridges, and such other necessary public works as the Board should think fit.

"The castes being withdrawn, the Board took into consideration what the castes proposed relating to the money and the application of it. It was observed that the sum of 2,500 pagodas, which the Bazaar Shroffs had been fined, had been applied towards making good the loss the Company had sustained by the bad money; also that more than ample amends would be made the Company by the duty arising from the coinage of the new money; and that no satisfaction had yet been made the inhabitants for what they had suffered. But considering that the sum now offered is as we compute far short of what they lost by the bad money; though it may be difficult to get at any particular account of what each person suffered, to be depended upon so far as to make a just and equal dividend among them; considering also that since the Moors had been in Town, the streets are become exceeding dirty and filthy, and that the bridges are much worn and out of repair by the number of Hackaries and other carriages which are continually passing over them, and that the Scavenger's duty and the surplus of the Town duty is not sufficient to keep them in proper order, much less to be at any extraordinary expense; and as we can think of no other means to give the sufferers any satisfaction, and we flatter ourselves they will be so contented with this as to prevent any reflection upon the Company or us. It is agreed to comply with the proposal of the castes; who being called in were acquainted therewith, and having promised to pay the money in two months."

The following entry respecting the powder manufactory, and the difficulty of getting the natives to work in it, will be found worthy of notice.

"Wednesday, 17th March, 1742. The stamps at the powder house having blown up some months ago, by which accident several persons were killed and others wounded; and as there is always great difficulty in getting coolies to work in the powder house, the Board thought proper to make some allowance to those who were wounded, and to the families of those who were killed.

"Agreed also to allow the powder maker one pagoda per candy more for making the powder, to enable him to allow his coolies a better pay; which it is hoped will prevent our being under a necessity of forcing them to work in the powder house, which has been a method too often taken more especially since the late accidents."

CHAPTER XLV.

GOVERNORSHIP OF MR. RICHARD BENYON.

(Continued.)

1742—43.

The capture of Trichinopoly by the Mahrattas was followed by a short period of tranquillity at Madras. The elements of conflict were seething in every quarter of India, whilst all danger seemed for a while to have passed away from Fort St. George. Subder Ali continued Nabob of Arcot, but being in constant fear of the Nizam, his family still resided at Black Town under the protection of the English. The Mahrattas had turned away from the south to carry out their designs against the power of the Mogul Emperor at Delhi. Such was the state of things in the spring of 1742, when the events recorded in the present chapter fairly begin.

Our first extracts refer to an outrage committed by a Portuguese Captain from Macao upon his mate. The matter is curious, partly from the serious character of the punishment inflicted by the Captain, and partly as illustrating the administration of the law in the olden time.

"Monday, 24th May, 1742. The President acquainted the Board, that he was yesterday informed that one Elias Manuel Graces, Captain of the "Nossa Senhora de Rozario," (a ship belonging to Macao, lost sometime since on this coast to the Southward) had cruelly beaten, and cut off the ears of one of the mates of the said ship at his lodgings in the Black Town. He had accordingly sent the Captain of the guard thither with orders, if he found it to be so, to secure the said Captain till the Board should consider what was proper to do in this matter; and also to bring with him to the Fort any persons of the house, who could give any information therein. That it being Sunday, and almost evening, when the Captain of the guard returned with the said Elias Manuel Graces, he had not given the Council the trouble to meet then, but had ordered the said Macao Captain to be confined in the Fort till the matter could be enquired into this morning.

"The Board being sat, and the Portuguese Captain, the mate, and witnesses attending, with Francisco Peixoto, Notary public of the Portuguese Church, and Padre Severini to swear the witnesses —Theodosio Martins, Manoel Rocha Piementel, Manoel Ignatio, Padre Jacinto de Almeida, and Francisco Peixto, were severally examined; but the Board having no very good interpreters, they were ordered to draw up in writing what they knew concerning the matter, in the form of depositions, and when ready to acquaint the Secretary therewith. But before they withdrew the Macao Captain was asked, what he had to say for himself. He replied, that he had no intention in what he had done to offer any insult or cast any reflection on the Justice or Government of the place; but that being informed the persons he had employed to look about the country for the mate, had secured him and were bringing him to St. Thomé, he went thither to receive him from them; that it having been repeatedly affirmed to him (the Captain), by many of the people belonging to the ship, that the said mate (Theodosio Martins) had lost the ship on purpose, in combination with other persons on board, and at the instigation of some of his (the Captain's) enemies at Macao,—in resentment of the injuries he had suffered thereby (having lost his all), and of the trouble and charge he had been at about the said mate, he had, upon his meeting him near St. Thomé, ordered his Coffrees to cut the mate's ears; nor did he design any thing more by ordering him to be whipped, than to make him confess upon what inducement, or at whose instigation, he run the ship ashore.

"The Captain, having finished what he had to say, was remanded back to his lodgings in the Fort, and then the Board adjourned."

"Thursday, 3rd June, 1742. The several depositions of Theodosio Martins, Manoel Roucha Piementel, Manoel Ignatio, Padre Jacinto de Almeida, and Francisco Peixto, were now delivered in, and sworn to before the Board; and translates of the same being read as entered hereafter, and the witnesses and others withdrawn, the Board took consideration how to proceed in this affair.—And there being no doubt whether the mate's ears were cut at St. Thomé, and there is no proof that they were not (the Coffrees who executed the Captain's orders being fled or not to be found);—it was made a question whether, notwithstanding the Charter give us power to try all crimes and offences committed within our town, or within ten miles of the same, yet if this fact was perpetrated in the territories, and under the jurisdiction of another prince, and the offender as well as the offended being subjects of the King of Portugal, it was not ground for an objection to our authority and might be the occasion of some complaint in Europe. Another doubt was, whether if the fact had been committed, or was cognizable here, it was properly Maihem. If it was, we recollect no trial upon the statute of the 22nd and 23rd of Charles the Second, except that of Coke and Woodburne, which was a very particular and extraordinary case. Besides that some of our Law books say, that cutting off the ear is no Maihem quia latens; and for that offence an indictment may be at the sessions. But besides what has been said before, if we should keep the Captain here to try him for the assault, and in consequence thereof the Court should think fit to fine him, it is uncertain how long he would remain in prison before he would be able to pay it; having been supported by charity ever since his being here. It was agreed upon the whole to transmit the affidavits, with a state of the case to the Governor of Macao; and that the President be desired to procure the said Captain a passage on the 'Sancta Catharina,' that is shortly bound thither, and to detain him in custody till he goes off."

The depositions of two of the witnesses are sufficiently curious to be worthy of extract; accordingly we print them exactly as they appear in the consultation books.

"By order of the Honourable the Governor, I, Notary public and Scrivener for the Roman Catholics of this city, have received the deposition of Theodosio Martins, mate of the ship that was lost of Captain Elias Manoel Graces; the said mate declared that he, having relied on some persons at Ginjee who promised to help him with means to get away from this coast, the deponent resolved thereupon to come to St. Thomé, and brought in his company another man named Estevao; and being come at a village on the other side of St. Thomé called Trivanboor, the said Estevao left him and went to an arrack shop; and that the said mate remained there waiting for him. In the meanwhile arrived one named Paulo, together with whom he proceeded a little distance on their way towards a choultry, in order to shelter themselves from the rain. There were some Malabars, together with one that had a military coat and grenadier's cap on. The deponent coming out from that place, the said Malabars assaulted and seized the said mate fast, and brought him hither; Paulo and Estevao separated from them taking the road to St. Thomé. Wednesday the 30th of May, between 2 and 3 o'clock after midnight, they delivered him to the Captain at his house; who kept the deponent bound as he was until the morning of the next day, being Thursday, when he put him in irons; and Friday the 1st instant about 9 and 10 o'clock in the morning he was fastened to a ladder, and whipped by a Coffree;

which being done, another Coffree named Ventura was ordered to cut the deponent's ears off, and that Manoel Ignacio being sent for the Captain ordered him to cure them. To all that contains herein, the said mate has already taken his oath in the presence of his honour. In truth whereof he has signed this as witnessed by me, Madraspatanam, 4th June 1742, N.S. Frano. de Seqre. Peixoto, Notary Public.

"THEODOSIO MARTINS."

"By order of the Honorable the Governor, I, Notary Public and Scrivener for the Roman Catholics of this city, have received the deposition of Manoel Rocha Piementel, of what he knew concerning the case that happened between Captain Elias Manoel Graces and his mate, Theodosio Martins, both inhabitants of the city of Macao; and the said Manoel Rocha Piementel deposes, that on Friday the first instant, about 2 o'clock in the morning, he awaked with the tumult of the mate's coming in; and hearing of his arrival the deponent went to the place where the mate was, and from a distance he saluted him, saying that he was glad of his arrival; and that in the same moment the deponent went to rest again without making any further reflection. And in the morning, being daylight, he awoke with the noise of the whips that the Captain was giving the mate; and going to the place of execution he saw the said mate without ears; and on his asking the Coffrees, they told him that they had been cut out of the districts of St. Thomé, where the said Captain went to take charge of the said mate; and to all that contains herein, the deponent declares to have taken his oath in the presence of his Honour. In truth whereof he has signed this as witnessed by me, Madraspatanam, 4th June 1742, N.S.

MANOEL ROCHA PIEMENTEL."

The following curious notices of the arrival of an Ambassador from the Xerif of Mecca explain themselves.

"Thursday, 12th August, 1742. Arrived ship 'Benyon,' Captain Robert Baillie, from Judda; with one Shaik Ibrahim a passenger, and sent as Ambassador from the Xerif."

"Monday, 16th August 1742 The President acquaints the Board, that having been informed upon the landing of the Judda Ambassador, it was customary and proper to make him a present of some provisions, he had caused to be sent him the several things mentioned in the list now produced, and entered hereafter, which is approved; and it is further agreed, that a house be found him at the Company's charge during his stay here, which it is thought will be but short."

"List of provisions sent to the Ambassador of the Xerif of Mecca, on his landing here from Judda the 13th August.

Fine rice	30	Marcals.
Coarse rice	60	do.
Horse gram	60	do.
Gram	12	do.
Ghee	3	Duppers.
Sugar	1	Candy.
Sugar candy	5	Maunds.

Sheep	20	
Fowls	50	
White Cups and Saucers	20	
Dishes	12	
Half dishes	12	
Plates	50	
Greens		
Pepper	4	Viss.
Onions	20	do.
Garlic	4	do.
Cloves, Mace and Cinnamon		
Fire-wood	1000	Sticks.
Boiled nuts	10	Pollums
Nuts	150	
Beetle	6	Bundles.
Cardamums		
Gunney bags	30	
Cooly hire		

The value of the forgoing amounted to pagodas 93, fanams 26, and cash 54.

The following letter from Mr. Foxall the Mint Master to the Governor in Council of Fort St. George, is interesting so far as it furnishes a clear account of the process of coining money in the Madras Mint a hundred and twenty years ago.

" Honorable Sir and Sirs,

" It is a great concern to me to observe by an extract of the General letter from England, that the Honorable Company should have the least shadow of reason to suspect that I have been any way negligent in my duty towards them; for I do assure your Honors, that I have at all times used my utmost care and diligence, as much as in me lay, to keep the minters to their weight and standard in all the moneys that have been coined since my time; and that I never discovered any attempt to adulterate the coin, but in the affair of Rangum with which I took care to acquaint this Honorable Board.

"The method of coinage in the Tower of London, differs much from what is used here; it being impossible to adulterate the gold and silver there, after the Assay Master has tried them, being cast into bars, before the assays are taken. Those bars afterwards run through flatting mills, the money cut out with an engine, milled and stamped, but no more melted. The constant method here has been, first to melt the gold or silver, and break it into small grains or powder; the muster is taken by the Assay Master; after which (if of the proper standard, the grains or powder is distributed among a great number of coolies in several work-houses or godowns: who weigh every rupee and pagoda separate, and afterwards deliver them to other coolies to melt. Different persons receive them to flat, and others to stamp. By which method of working, your Honors must be very sensible, that if it was not for some confidence which must be put in the undertakers, and the fear of punishment in such as should be detected, my utmost care and vigilance could not prevent from adulterations. The only check upon them, and what I frequently make use of after the first trial, is to take musters of their moneys in their presence to assay after it is finished, to let them see I have a watchful eye over them.

"What I have already said, with the present flourishing state of the mint, will I humbly hope induce my Honorable Masters to believe that I have not been any way negligent in my duty hitherto, and shall take my utmost care that they have no cause of complaint in future."

I am,

Honorable Sir and Sirs,

Your most obedient and humble Servant,

SIDNEY FOXALL.'

Fort St. George, 16th August 1742."

The dreadful diseases which occasionally broke out amongst ships' crews in the Olden Time, may be gathered from the following entry.

"Wednesday, 15th September 1742. The President communicates to the Board a letter he received last night from Captain Bookey of the 'Shaftsbury,' advising that he anchored in twelve fathoms water the 13th instant at seven in the morning, five leagues to the northward of Pulicat, but could not possibly weigh his anchor again before he received assistance, having buried twenty-two hands in the passage, and sixty-five were so ill that they were of no use to the ship. He added that on the receipt of the said letter, he had given order for getting ready a supply of oxen, sheep, greens, water, limes and other necessary provisions; and thought it proper, with the Board's approbation to send eighty hands of the Gunroom Crew to assist in bringing the ship hither; that Captain Way's long boat would be ready to set out with a part of the hands and provisions this morning; and the rest might follow in the afternoon on a country boat he had ordered to be engaged for that service."

Our next entry is very suggestive.

"Wednesday, 6th October, 1742. Some of the Military having been guilty of such disorders and irregularities as make it proper to change their quarters, it is agreed to send them on the 'Shaftsbury' to the Bay, where they may perhaps behave better."

We now enter upon the entries in the records which refer to that tragical event in the history of Vellore, known as the assassination of Subder Ali. All lovers of the graphic narrative of old Orme, will be sufficiently familiar with the details of this conspiracy, which forms so striking an illustration of the blood-thirsty character of Native rule; but still a brief outline of the facts may not be unacceptable to the general reader.

For thirty years the musnud of the Carnatic had been occupied in succession by the Newayeteh Nabobs*—Sadatullah Khan, Dost Ali, and Subder Ali. Dost Ali however had taken advantage of the convulsions of the empire to withhold the revenues due to the Nizam. His son Subder Ali was therefore in mortal fear of incur-

* The Newayets, or "new comers," were originally Arabs, who about the end of the first century after the time of Mahomet (i. e. about A. D. 700) migrated from Arabia to India, to escape from the cruelties of the then Governor of Irak. These exiles were rich and respectable, and belonging to the famous family of Hashem. One party landed on the coast of Malabar and were called Newayets; others landed on the coast of Coromandel and were called Lubbies. The Lubbies pretend to one common origin with the Newayets, and attribute their black complexion to intermarriage with

ring the Nizam's resentment. He had, as we have seen, despatched the women and children of his family to Madras; and he no longer kept his court in the open and defenceless city of Arcot, but took up his residence in the famous citadel at Vellore. Meantime, an assessment had been levied from all the towns and forts in the Carnatic, in order to discharge the ransom due to the Mahrattas. At that time the richest fief subject to the Nabobship of Arcot, was that of Vellore, where the Nabob was staying. The Governor of Vellore was Mortez Ali. This man was a relative to Subder Ali; he had also married Subder Ali's sister; and these circumstances, combined with the reception he was giving to the Nabob at Vellore, induced him to believe that he ought to be excused from paying his share of the ransom due to the Mahrattas. If however Mortez Ali had been permitted to escape, other Governors of other forts would have refused to pay up. Accordingly, Subder Ali insisted upon the quota being paid by Mortez Ali, and threatened to dispossess him of the government of Vellore if he continued to keep back the money. Accordingly Mortez Ali

---

the Natives. The Newayets however affirm that the Lubbies are the descendants of their domestic slaves; and certainly the physiognomy, stature, and form of the Lubbies, present a strong resemblance to the Natives of Abyssinia. The Newayets of the western coast preserved the purity of their original blood, by systematically avoiding intermarriage with the Indians, and even with the highest Mussulman families, for many centuries after the establishment of the Mussulman dynasties of Dekkan. See Wilks, Vol. 1. p. 242.

then resolved of putting to death his brother-in-law.

The great festival of the Mohorrum took place in the beginning of October 1742. The army of the Nabob was encamped without Vellore; but Subder Ali was attended within the fort by a body of guards and a numerous retinue. On the 2nd of October, which that year was the great day of the festival, the Nabob's servants asked permission to celebrate the feast in their own families; and Subder Ali accordingly gave leave to all his retinue and guards, excepting four persons only. On that very evening his provisions were poisoned. The Nabob felt the effects of the poison, but overcame them; and having no suspicion that his sufferings had arisen from any but natural causes, he retired to rest as usual. Meantime, Mortez Ali had found an assassin who would make all sure. A Patan, whose wife had been outraged by Subder Ali, joyfully accepted the commission. He engaged some Abyssinian slaves, and led them at midnight to the apartment of the Nabob. The few servants sleeping there were overpowered at once. The Nabob was awakened by the noise, and endeavoured to escape through the window; but the Patan rushed upon him, and after upbraiding him with his adultery put him to death with several stabs of his dagger. The excitement caused by this event, and the circumstances immediately following it, may be gathered from the official records of the time, which we now place before our readers.

"Wednesday, 6th October, 1742. The President

acquaints the Board, that he was waked at 2 o'clock yesterday morning by an express from the Havildar of Poonamallee, advising that the Nabob had been murdered in Vellore Fort by the Killedar Mortez Ali Khan, who had also imprisoned Meer Assad and Boocunjee Coshedos, the first his chief minister, the other his shroff; and as it might be apprehended such an event would be followed by great commotions in the country, and that the troops might disperse themselves about the province and plunder it; as soon as it was day light, he (the President) had given orders to double the guards, and all our people to be upon duty; and particularly that no Moor's horse should enter the Town or pass the Mettahs without particular leave. These orders alarmed the Nabob's family at Black Town, who sent several messages to enquire the reason of them, and if any advices were come in from the Country; but nobody cared to tell them the news till about 12 at noon, when they were advised of it by letters from the Dewan of Vellore. About the same time Kistnajee Puntaloo received a letter from Mahomed Khan Jalouze, a commander of 2000 horses at Arcot; who only wrote that the Nabob had been killed by Mortez Ali Khan. This last also wrote a letter to Kistnajee Puntaloo, and enclosed in it one to the President; translate of which, and the answer thereto, is entered hereafter."

"*From Nabob Mortez Ali Khan Bahauder, Killedar of Vellore.*"

"I believe you are informed of what has passed

here. You may be easy in your mind, and take care of your business and Government. I shall be at Arcot very shortly and settle the country. What I can say more?"

"*To Nabob Mortez Ali Khan Bahauder, from Governor Benyon.*"

"By the receipt of your letter I observe what has passed. Whatever God pleases to appoint must happen. You write me to be easy in my mind, and the receipt of your letter made it so. I wish God may settle all things for the best."

Twelve days after the receipt of the very short letter of Mortez Ali, and the dispatch of the equally short reply of the Governor Benyon, the following letter from the Vakeel in the Nabob's camp was received at Fort St. George, describing the entry of Mortez Ali into Arcot.

"*From the Vakeel in the camp. received* 18*th October* 1742."

"On Friday the 15th instant, about nine o'clock in the morning, Nabob Gulam Mortez Ali Khan set out from Vellore in a palaukeen, accompanied by Nabob Herasut Khan, and other great men. They first encamped at Hernsutpore, a place very near Arcot in the way from Vellore; where after they had rested themselves a little time, they mounted their elephants. Nabob Mortez Ali Khan, and Nabob Hussain Khan Tahir, son of Ahmud Tahir, both sat together in one castle upon an elephant. Herasut Khan, Jienadeen Ali Khan, and Hussain Jaman Khan, the brother-in-law of Mortez Ali Khan sat themselves upon another; and in like manner each nobleman of the province, as Cauder Hussain Khan, Hyder Yaur Khan, Anwaradeen Khan, Sadatmund Khan, &c. rode upon an elephant, and followed Mortez Ali Khan into the city of Arcot, with a great army and the beat of noubat. They first went to a mosque commonly called Teeboo Sahib's tomb; where when they had finished their prayers, they went directly with great ceremony into the great house of State, commonly called here the King's palace, where they placed Mortez Ali Khan upon the musnud; which is a square place in the hall rightly adorned, where the Subah of the province always sits; and then Herusut Khan, Hussain Khan Tahir, Cauder Hussain Khan, Jienadeen Ali Khan, Buda Sahib of Covelong, Hyder Yaur Khan, Sadatmund Khan, Anwaradeen Khan, Hassan Jaman Khan, Hyder Dil Khan, and several other Khans, Kelledars, Mansubdars, Jamadars, and other officers of State, paid their compliments to him, and presented to him gold rupees, with the accustomed ceremony observed to the Nabob; when noubat was beat three several times, and Mortez Ali Khan proclaimed Subah and Nabob of the province. The fort guns were then fired, and the artillery and other small arms discharged upon that occasion. The Nabob gave all the abovementioned Gentlemen beetlenut and rose water, and sent them to their respective lodgings. A little while after this great ceremony was finished, which was about five o'clock that afternoon, Mahomud Khan, Kelledar of Timery, came to Arcot and went to

Hussian Khan Tahir, who introduced him to the Nabob, to whom he paid his compliments, made him the accustomary present of gold rupees, received rose water and beetlenut from him, and returned to his place Timery immediately."

"Meer Assad is still under confinement in Vellore.

"The Nabob, before he came out of Vellore, appointed Bauker Sahib and Sidee Sahib to take care of the Fort as his deputies.

"It is reported here that Moorari Row, Viceroy of Trichinopoly, upon hearing the death of Nabob Subder Ali Khan, sent a part of his army towards Wallingondaporum; who plundered and destroyed a great many towns and villages between that place and Tiagagud, and carried great store of booty from hence.

"Boma Rajah, and all the Poligars about Vellore, Arnee, &c., sent a part of their foot under the command of some of their officers, to attend the Nabob from Vellore to Arcot, and they were accordingly in his train.

"Ali Nakey Khan, son of Takiah Sahib or the nephew of the deceased Nabob, who was wounded when they murdered his uncle, has got the liberty to go to Chinnapatnam, and is now in the way thither. They say that Buda Sahib will also get liberty in a day or two to go to Chinnapatnam."

Turning away from these State affairs at Arcot we again take up the thread of domestic events at Madras.

The following petition requires no introduction.

"The humble petition of the merchants and others, inhabitants of Madraspatnam, whose houses were pulled down on the approach of the Mahrattas.

Sheweth,—That when the Mahrattas invaded and plundered this province, and this place was apprehended to be in danger from them, your petitioners' houses which stood near the walls of the Black Town, were ordered to be pulled down, and are on account of the ground and bricks taken belonging to each person. But your petitioners have received no satisfaction yet for the losses they suffered thereby. Some of the said houses were two stories high, some were terraced and others boarded within, the workmanship of which cost a considerable deal of money; and ground was bought by your petitioners at 2 pagodas, 1¾, and 1½ pagodas per foot; the b:icks cost one pagoda per 1000, besides the hire of oxen to carry them.

"Your petitioners have taken the liberty to mention these particulars to your Honors; and leave their case to your serious consideration; humbly entreating that out of your known regard to the interest and happiness of the inhabitants of this place, you would be pleased to order your petitioners' payment as it shall appear reasonable to you."

The matter had already formed the subject of an enquiry by a Committee, and full compensation granted to the inhabitants for the towns destroyed. Of course they had asked for about three times the proper amount of compensation; the ground being no where worth more than 13 fanams per foot. However that matter was all settled by the Committee.

Meantime, public affairs at Arcot had undergone another phase. Mortez Ali found the whole army against him. The officers had engaged to support the cause of the family of Subder Ali, and officers and soldiers demanded immediate payment of the whole of the arrears due. Mortez Ali could not face the storm. Accordingly he disguised himself in a woman's dress, and at night escaped from Arcot in a covered palanquin, and fortunately for him reached his fort at Vellore without interruption.

Immediately after the flight of Mortez Ali was discovered, the army placed the young son of Subder Ali, named Mahomed Seiad Khan, upon the throne of the Carnatic. Full particulars of the grants which Governor Benyon obtained from the young Nabob on his accession will be found in the following extracts from the records.

"Thursday, 22nd December, 1742. The President acquainting the Board that he is just now informed the young Nabob Mahomed Seiad Khan is to be set upon his musnud this morning, that he ought to make his compliments upon the occasion, and that forty-one gold mohurs will be a proper offering, the Board consented to the same."

"Tuesday, 11th January, 1743. The President lays before the Board the originals and translates of the five following Firmans, under the seal of the young Nabob, viz.

1st. Grant of the villages of Ernavore, Saudian Copang, Vepery, Perambore, and Poodoopauck.

2nd. A grant of the liberty of coining Arcot rupees and pagodas, according to the usage and practice of Country mints.

3rd. For lessening the duties on sundry goods brought in and carried out of Chindadrepettah; and for taking off entirely the duties on other goods as per account thereof entered hereafter.

4th. A grant of one adda on every Collum of paddy produced in the countries of Poonamallee, Manincongalom, Peddapollum, and Perembauk, to be applied to the maintenance of the Pagodas at Chindadrepettah.

5th. A grant of the village of Cadapauck to Andiapah Naick.

Ordered that the translates be entered hereafter, and the originals deposited with the other Firmans.

1ST GRANT OF THE FIVE VILLAGES.

Translate of a Sunnud under the seal of Nabob Sadutalla Khan Bahauder, Soobah of Arcot, dated the 4th November 1742.

"To the Mutsaddys of the country of Poonamallee and Sircar of Tripasore, belonging to the Carnatic of Golcondah and to their successors."

"Be it known unto you, that I have granted five several villages (the produce of which is pagodas 665 1/16 per annum) to Mr. Benyon, Governor of Chinnapatnam for the Company, as a present; and therefore do you deliver them into his possession, and let them remain so for ever from the year Fusly 1152. Observe this as a strict taukeed and perform it accordingly. Dated the 17th Moon Ramazan in the 25th year of the reign of the Great Mogul Mahomed Shah.

Translate of the contents written on the back of the foregoing Sunnud.

"Five villages out of the country before named, which produce pagodas 665¼ 4/16 every year, are granted to Mr. Benyon, Governor of Chinnapatnam for the Company, as a present.

"His Excellency's order by his hand writing is to draw out a sunnud to the following purpose:

"That the vakeel of the said Governor having represented that his master desires the five following villages which are near to Chinnapatnam, they be granted to him as a present.

Ernavore, near Trivatore, produces every year pagodas	205 5/16
Sadiangoopam...do...............do.........	215 6/16
Vepery near Egmore (except that ground which belongs to the mettah custom house of the Sircar).........	25 3/16
Perambore near do..................................	114¼ 3/16
Poodoopawk do..................................	105 3/16
Pagodas	665¼ 4/16

Entered in the book 17, Ramazan in the 25th year of the reign of the Great Mogul Mahomed Shah.

2ND GRANT OF LIBERTY TO COIN ARCOT RUPEES.

Translate of a Sunnud under the seal of Nobob Sadutalla Khan Bahauder, Subah of Arcot, dated the 4th November 1742.

"To the Mutasadas of the country of Chennapatnam and Sircar of Trippasoor, belonging to the Carnatic of Golcondah and to their successors.

" Be it known unto all men that from the beginning of the year Fusly 1152, I have ordered a mint to be erected to coin pagodas and rupees in Chindadrepettah, belonging to Chinnapatnam ; and the same to be under the power of Mr. Benyon, Governor of Chennapatnam for the Company. Wherefore do you let the said Governor have and enjoy for the Company all the customs that may arise in the said mint. Observe this as a strict taukeed and perform it accordingly, dated Ramazan 17th, in the 25th year of the reign of the Great Mogul Mahomed Shah.

Translate of the contents written on the back of the foregoing Sunnud. Ordered that a mint may be erected in Chindadreepettah belonging to Chinnapatnam for coining pagodas and rupees, and it may be commenced from the beginning of the year Fusly 1152, and to be under the power of Mr. Benyon, Governor of Chennapatnam for the Company.

" His Excellency's order by his hand-writing is to draw a Sunnud to the following purpose.

That Andiappah Naick, Dubash of the Governor of Chennapatnam represented that the Governor desires liberty to erect a mint in Chindadreepettah belonging to Chennapatnam for coining pagodas, rupees &c., and that we should free them from paying us the customs arising thereby, and let the same be applied to the said Governor for the Company; a sunnud is granted for that purpose.

Entered in the Book 19th Moon Ramazan, in the 25th year of the reign of the Great Mogul Mahomed Shah which is the 4th November 1742.

3RD GRANT FOR LESSENING DUTIES.

"*Translate of a Cowle granted by Nabob Mahomud Syed Khan, Subah of Arcot to Gauna Pandurum, &c., merchants of Chindadreepettah belonging to Chennapatnam, dated the 17th moon Ramazan in the 25th year of the reign of the Great Mogul Mahomed Shah which is the 4th November* 1742.

"Whereas you have petitioned me to free you from paying custom in the country on your importation and exportation of all goods, drugs, spices, broad cloths, raw silk, silks, thread, grain &c. from Chindadreepettah to Arcot, Pondicherry and Poonamalee, and from those places to Chindadreepettah; and to grant you a cowle for paying custom at Egmore mettah in the country of Poonamalee; I have accordingly considered and gratified you therein by this my Cowle as follows.

For heavy goods you shall pay.................at	Fans.	4¼	℔	bag.
Tabacco......................at	,,	1	,,	bag.
Coarse and fine thread either white, red or any other colour..............at	,,	$\frac{1}{16}$	,,	viss.
All drugs, physics, &c.....at	,,	2¼	,,	bag.
Beetle leaves................at	,,	¼	,,	bag.

Cotton cloths of all sorts either fine or ordinary and of all colours either white, red or blue......at	Fans.	$\frac{1}{8}$	℘	pautch
Grain........................ at	„	$4\frac{1}{2}$	„	10 oxl.
Broad cloth fine or ordinary... ....at	„	$4\frac{1}{2}$	„	pautch
Silk cloths of all sorts......at	„	$\frac{3}{16}$	„	pautch
Raw silk fine and ordinary.........................at	„	$4\frac{1}{2}$	„	bag.

"I do hereby appoint that custom shall be paid after the forementioned rates upon all goods that are carried from Chindadreepettah to Arcot, Nellore, Lalapetta, Nagore, Nagapatam, Pondicherry, &c., and upon those that are brought from those places to Chindadreepettah; and that you are freed from paying any custom on the following particulars.

"All bazar cloths which are brought by the Kycola weavers from Lettahpettah, Conjeveram, Pondicherry and other parts of the province to Chindadreepettah, to be sold in the market there, shall be freed from paying custom.

"Butter, oil, milk, tire, herbs, greens, firewood, bratty, which are brought to be sold at the pettah, are freed from paying custom.

"As I have thus granted you my Cowle you may freely bring divers sort of goods from all parts, and safely carry on your trade and commerce without any suspicion. Dated the day of the month and year abovementioned."

An account of the duties that have hitherto been paid to the Moors on the following goods and brought to and carried from Chindadreepettah, with an account of duties to be paid henceforward as stipulated in the foregoing firman, viz.

	Duties.				
	Paid before		To be paid now		
	F.	C.	F.	C.	
Weighable goods as sugar, sugar candy, lead, tamarin, beetle nut, &c.	8	50	4	40	per bag.
Drugs, spices, physics.....	5	0	2	20	do
Raw silk..........................	10	10	4	40	do
Tobacco.	5	40	1	0	do
Beetle leaves......................	1	30	0	20	do
Cotton cloths of all sorts and colours..................	2	0	0	10	per pautch.
Silk cloths of all sorts. ...	9	0	0	15	do
Broad cloths fine and ordinary.......................	18	0	4	40	per piece.
Cotton yarn ordinary and fine and of any colour...	0	15	0	5	per visa.
Grain....	18	0	4	40	do 10 ox loads

An account of the duties that have hitherto been paid to the Moors on the following goods, &c.

brought to and carried from Chindadreepettah now taken off by the foregoing firman, viz.

	Duties before paid. F.	C.	
Bazar cloths of all sorts..........	0	50	per pantch
Butter..............................	0	45	per measure
Oil.................................	0	25	do
Fire-wood, small....................	0	15	per bundle
Do. large...........................	0	20	do
Straw...............................	0	15	do
Milk................................	0	15	pot
Tire................................	0	40	per great pot
Bratty..............................	0	5	per basket
Greens..............................	0	40	do
Charcoal	1	40	per oxen load.

4TH GRANT FOR MAINTENANCE OF CHINDADREPATTA PAGODA.

"*Translate of a Sunnud under the seal of Nabob Sadutulla Khan, Bahauder, Subah of Arcot, dated the 4th November* 1742.

"To the Mutasadays of countries of Tripasore, &c. and Sircars of Tripasore, &c. belonging to the Carnatic of Golcondah and to their successors.

"Be it known unto you, that I was lately informed that Cassawa Acharloo of Chindadreepattah has nothing to subsist on, I do therefore grant unto the said Cassawa Acharloo a privilege of one adda of paddy per callum produced in the said countries &c., and do hereby order you to let him have the said charity gift every year that he may maintain himself thereby, and always say his prayers for the increase of the riches and prolong the life of his most sovereign Majesty the Great Mogul. Observe this as a strict taukeed, and perform it accordingly. Dated the 17th moon Ramazan in the 25th year of the reign of the Great Mogul Mahomed Shah.

" *Translate of the contents writ on the back of the foregoing Sunnud.*

A privilege of one adda of paddy per callum produced in the countries of Tripasore, &c. and Sircars of Tripasore, &c. is granted to Cassawa Acharloo of Chindadreepattah as a charity gift.

" His Excellency's order by his handwriting is to draw out a sunnud to the following purpose.

" That the said Cassawa Acharloo having prayed that a privilege of one adda of paddy per callum produced in the countries of Tripasore, &c. and Sircars of Tripasore, &c. may be granted to him as a charity gift, it is granted accordingly.

Names of the countries where the aforesaid privilege is to be allowed, viz.

Country of Tripasore.

Do. Poonamallee Surcar of Tripasore.
Do. Mannimongalum Surcar of Chingleput.
Do. Pedapollum Surcar of Conjeveram.
Do. Perambauck Surcar of Conjeveram.

Entered in the book 17th Ramazan in the 25th year of the reign of the Great Mogul Mahomed Shah.

5TH GRANT, VILLAGE OF CADAPAUK.

" *Translate of a Sunnud under the seal of Nabob Sadutalla Khan, Bahauder, Soobah of Arcot, dated the 4th November* 1742.

To the Mutasadys of the Country of Poonamallee and Surcar of Tripasore, belonging to the Carnatic of Golcandah and to their successors.

" Be it known unto you. that I have granted a village, named Cadapauk, situated near Mannalley in the Country before named (the produce of which is pagodas $100\frac{3}{16}$ per annum) to Andepa Naick, Dubash of Chennapatnam, as a present and charity gift ; and therefore do you deliver it unto his possession and let him enjoy the produce for ever from the year Fusly 1152. Observe this as a strict taukeed and perform it accordingly. Dated the 17th Moon Ramazan in the 25th year of the reign of the great Mogul Mahomed Shah.

" *Translate of the contents write on the back of the foregoing Sunnud.*

" A village named Cadapauk situated near Mannalley in the country of Poonamallee and Surcar of Tripasore, which produce pagodas $100\frac{3}{16}$ per annum is granted to Andepa Naick, Dubash of Chennapatnam as a present and charity gift.

" His Excellency's order by his hand writing is to draw out a Sunnud to the following purpose.

" That the said Andepa Naick requested to grant him the village named Cadapauk situated near Chindadreepattah as a present and charity gift which is granted to him accordingly.

One village produce every year—pagodas $100\frac{2}{16}$

" Entered in the book 17th moon Ramazan in the 25th year of the reign of the Great Mogul Mahomed Shah.

The alarm excited by the proceedings of the Mahrattas induced the Directors to send out an experienced Engineer officer named Knipe, to report upon the state of the fortifications, the result may be gathered from the following extracts.

" Monday, 24th January, 1743. Major Charles Knipe, having surveyed the fortifications of the Town on the West side from Charles' point to Queen's point, delivers in a report thereof as entered hereafter."

" To the Honourable Richard Benyon Esq., President and Governor and Council of Fort St. George.

" In obedience to your Honour's command, I have taken a survey of your city of Madraspatnam from Charles' point to the Queen's point being that part of the fortification as it is called, which faces towards the Island; but I must take the liberty to assure you it is no fortification at all, but rather an offensive than defensive wall to your garrison. Was it not for the support it has from the several out houses of the inhabitants which are all built against it through the whole extent above mentioned it could not stand; nor was it more than sufficient for a garden wall when first erected. As to the river that runs by it that neither is any addition to the strength of your works, but rather a nuisance to the Town; for I observe in every part of it, it is continually forded at less than two feet deep.

"The plan laid down for enlarging your city, and carrying a new fortification across the Island from Charles' point to Queen's point abovementioned, I have by your honor's direction very carefully examined, in regard to a foundation, by making small wells of considerable depth from the surface and by boring several foot deeper in the bottom of each of them through the whole extent of the intended fortification; and find the soil is clay and sand, capable of sustaining any weight especially if assisted with a few wells under the foundation near the river side where it is a little spungy. As to the river I will engage to turn that quite off from your Town at a very small expense; and supply its place with a much better fossee, by which the whole Island will be drained and become a very firm and solid tract of land.

"This is humbly submitted to your Honours and the Gentlemen of the Council's consideration by

Sir,

Your most obedient servant,

CHARLES KNIPE.

Fort St. George, January 25, 1743."

CHAPTER XLVI.

GOVERNORSHIP OF MR. RICHARD BENYON.

(Continued.)

1743—44.

The Governorship of Mr. Richard Benyon was now drawing to a close, and the last year of his administration forms the subject of the present chapter. The events of this year are interesting, inasmuch as they largely illustrate the position of the British Government at Madras towards the Native Princes. The Nizam entered the Carnatic, partly to settle the affairs of the province, and partly to wrest Trichinopoly from the Mahrattas. Accordingly Governor Benyon sent a mission to carry certain presents to the Nizam, and to procure his favor; and one of the most interesting records brought to light in the present chapter, is a Diary of the proceedings of this mission, from the day it left Madras to the day when it returned from the Nizam's camp before Trichinopoly.

Our first extract illustrates the progress of domestic events.

"Monday, 31st January, 1743. Arcot rupees being risen to three hundred and twenty for one hundred pagodas:—it is agreed that the Import Warehouse-keeper sell one hundred thousand, if he can get that price for so many; and that he deliver twenty-four chests of silver to be coined into Arcot rupees, that they may be ready to send to the Bay by the first good conveyance that offers."

How this financial operation worked will be seen by the next entries. We are much mistaken if they are not considered curious by our commercial readers.

"Thursday, 10th February, 1743. The Import Warehouse-keeper acquaints the Board that several persons had been with him this morning to purchase Arcot rupees; that they had not yet offered better than 315 per 100 pagodas, but possibly would very soon bid more, and therefore desired the directions of the Board; who taking the same into consideration, and that even 315 is a very good price, that the turns in this business are very sudden, and an opportunity of getting a better price may be lost by waiting till the Council can be got together: agreed that it be left to the Warehouse-keeper, with the consent of the President, to negotiate the sale of one hundred thousand Arcot rupees upon the best terms he can; designing to reserve the rest for the Bay: and therefore ordered that the remainder of the bullion be delivered to Linga Chetty, to the coined in the mint at the pettah upon the usual terms.

"Thursday, 17th February, 1743. The Import Warehouse-keeper acquaints the Board, that in the afternoon of the 10th instant he was bid after the rate of 310 rupees for 100 pagodas, and by eight at night 305. At which rate with the consent of the President he disposed fifty thousand; that the next morning the merchants offered to take two laks at 300; which being one hundred and fifty thousand more than the last consultation warranted the sale of, he immediately repaired to the President; when upon considering together the great price that was offered for the rupees, and that the money laid out in gold mohurs would produce in the Bay upwards of one hundred and fifty Arcot rupees for one hundred pagodas, they did not doubt the Board would approve of the sale of the additional hundred and fifty thousand; and, therefore, he, the Warehouse-keeper, went immediately and struck with the Merchants for the two lacs they wanted; the rupees to be taken away in one month, and the pagodas to be paid down as the rupees are taken out of the Warehouse. The Board could not but approve of the bargain, rupees being this day at three hundred and sixteen, and no buyers."

We must now turn back a few days in order to exhibit the progress of foreign affairs. It will be seen that the Nizam of the Dekkan was advancing into the Carnatic to settle the affairs of Arcot. But the extracts will explain themselves.

"Saturday, 5th February, 1743. The President acquainted the Board, that by several letters from Wandewash, he is informed that it is taken much notice of, that we have made no compliment to the court there, upon the birth of the Nabob's brother; (Ali Dost Khan) and after some discourse about the state of affairs in the country, the Board agreed that the President might send to the amount of about six hundred pagodas including charges.

"The President at the same time acquainted the Board, that he believed there would soon be occasion to put the Company to a more considerable expense; for that it was no longer doubted but Nizam-ul-Mulk would come to Arcot;—in which case it would be necessary to send presents to him, and to his son Nazir Jung, suitable to their rank; and as it is also to be supposed he will either confirm the present Nabob or appoint another, in either of which cases we must pay our compliments,—it was agreed that the Warehouse-keeper, assisted by Coja Petrus, look about the Town and purchase such things as they have reason to believe will be acceptable upon the several occasions."

"Thursday, 24th February, 1743. There being some information that Nizam-ul-Mulk, with his son Nazir Jung, have thought of coming down to the place;—Ordered that the Warehouse-keeper lay in a quantity of fine rice, horse gram, butter, and other provisions; as likewise some Persian fruit, agreeable to what may be expected upon such an occasion; and that he consult Coja Petrus and Hodjee Addee for the quantity of each sort.

"Tuesday, 1st March, 1743. The Board then took into consideration to what amount it would be proper to send in presents to Arcot; and Coja Petrus and Hodjee Addee attending, Coja Petrus produced a letter from Imaum Sahib; who writes it would be necessary to send presents not only to Nizam-ul-Mulk, but also to his son Nazir Jung, and to Coja Abdulla Khan; which last is at present named for Soobah of this province. After some time spent in debating this matter, it was agreed to make out a list to the amount of 13,000 pagodas or thereabout; which list should be sent to Imaum Sahib, and to leave it to him to divide the particulars in such manner as he should think proper; that Hodjee Addee be desired to write the President's letters to Nizam-ul-Mulk, Nazir Jung, and Coja Abdulla Khan; and that the Company's Brahmin and Moollah do go with them; and when the lists are formed agreeable to Imaum Sahib's directions, they be enclosed in the letters; for which purpose they are to carry the President's seal along with them.

"Messrs. Thomas Eyre, Samuel Harrison, and Lieutenant Holland were appointed to go with the presents, and ordered to get themselves ready as soon as possible.

"The purport of a letter from the President to Imaum Sahib agreed on; this last to contain more at large the good offices we expect from him; particularly a confirmation of the grant of the five villages, and the liberty of coining Arcot rupees; and to obtain a dustuck for passing the Company's calicoes free of Juncan through the country; that these services performed, we shall not be ungrateful."

"Monday, 7th March, 1743. The President acquaints the Board that himself with the Export Warehouse-keeper, Coja Petrus, and Hodjee Addee, had pitched upon such things as they thought most proper to send as presents to Arcot, to the value agreed upon last consultation; and that the whole are packed up and ready to set out to-morrow.

"Agreed that 600 rupees, 200 pagodas in gold, and 200 pagodas in fanams, be delivered Mr. Eyre for paying batta to the peons and coolies on the road, and during their stay in the camp; and that if more be wanted that he carry a letter of credit on Boocunjee Caushedoss.

"Then a set of instructions was also read and agreed on as entered hereafter.

"To Messrs. Thomas Eyre, Samuel Harrison and John Holland,

"Gentlemen,

"We have appointed you to attend the presents now sending to Arcot for Nizam-ul-Mulk, Nazir Jung, and Coja Abdulla Khan. The letters sent by you for them are mere letters of compliment, and to enclose the lists of presents sent to each.

"Those lists must be framed at Arcot, agreeable to the directions of Imaum Sahib, to whom a list of the whole is sent to be divided as he thinks proper.

"You will acquaint Imaum Sahib, that as you are entire strangers to the customs and ceremony to be observed at the durbar, you must rely upon his information and advice in those matters. He will doubtless tell you that at your first audience it will be proper for Mr. Eyre to present Nizam-ul-Mulk, &c. with some gold mohurs in the Governor's name; and will tell you the number, as well as how many each of the rest of the Gentlemen should present at the same time.

"We suppose your audience will be but short,

and that after the common compliments are over you will have to retire. If nevertheless any questions should be asked you about our trade and privileges, the more general your answers are the better. As to our trade they know how much money we lay out in the country; and we carry no money out but what we bring in, and should carry away less if we could lay out more in these parts.

"The privileges we have were granted us by Zulfikar Khan, and other great men of the country; and afterwards confirmed to us by the great Mogul Ferokhsere; and for what more is wanting to enable us to carry on our trade with ease, we must depend upon his Excellency's favour.

"We know not what occasion you may have for money to pay the durbar charges; but we have delivered Mr. Eyre 500 gold mohurs, and 500 pagodas in rupees, fanams, and pagodas. We also deliver you a letter of credit on Boocunjee Caushedoss, who will supply you with what money your occasions require.

We are, Gentlemen,
Your affectionate friend,
RICHARD BENYON."

"Monday, 14th March, 1743. The President acquaints the Board he has received a letter from Mr. Eyre, advising that many of their coolies having deserted upon the road had a good deal retarded their journey; that Nizam-ul-Mulk was upon his march Southward, and he doubted whether he should be able to overtake him before he should be got out of the province; however he had wrote Imaum Sahib of his being on the way, and desired also directions from hence how far to proceed. Which being taken into consideration, the President was desired to write Mr. Eyre to follow the camp, except he should receive directions from Imaum Sahib to the contrary."

"Monday, 2nd May, 1743. Mr. Eyre arriving in Town last night from Nabob Nizam-ul-Mulk Asof Jah's camp, took his place again at the Board, and promised to deliver in the Diary and the particulars of the expenses of his journey to and reception at the camp, so soon as they can be copied out fair.

Nizam-ul-Mulk, having sent a horse and Seerpaw for the President, which are lodged at St. Thomé, it was proposed and agreed to receive the same to-morrow in the afternoon."

DIARY OF OCCURRENCES IN THE JOURNEY TO TRICHINOPOLY WITH A PRESENT TO NIZAM-UL-MULK, NAZIR JUNG, AND COJA ABDULLA KHAN.

"March, 9th. Early this morning, mustered the coolies, and finding several had left us in the night, and that some parcels were not come; wrote to Town for them, and for coolies in the room of those deserted; for which we waited there till evening, and then sparing some from the palankeens &c. went forward to Conditore; from whence wrote again for the peons and coolies wanting, and waited for them all day; wrote also for some broad cloth for presents to the Nabob's officers.

"——, 11th. Late this morning arrived at Perimbadore. In the evening from Sunca Ramah's choultry, wrote to advise Imaum Sahib that we were endeavouring to reach the camp as fast as we could bring the presents.

"——, 12th. About noon arrived at Conjeveram, where Hussain Sahib the Phousdar came to see us, and told us the camp was on the march, and that there was no knowing where it would make any stay; therefore advised us to follow as fast as we could. After having got some oxen, and more coolies here, in room of others also deserted from this place; in the evening went forward for Choulumbadee, and there received advice from the Vakeel of the 8th, that the camp was then removing from Trinomalee to Manlovepetta. But with hopes that it might make some stay thereabouts, we judged it our duty to proceed after it.

"——, 13th. We were detained for want of more Conjeveram coolies till the afternoon; and at night arrived at Trivatore.

"——, 14th. This morning the Havildar ordered the goods to be stopped at the Metta. Sent the dubash to know the reason of it, who brought word that the Havildar said he was informed we had some goods belonging to private merchants and for sale. But Paupa denying it, and by some acquaintance with the managing Brahmin, after a stay of about two hours, found credit to get them passed; as also for an Hircarra and ten coolies, and then proceeded to Marapa Naick's tope; from thence in the afternoon to Vizamunglum at 8 o'clock; where more coolies having left us, we sent to Chitaput to get others.

"——, 15th. Waited for coolies and straw for the

Oxen, till the afternoon; arrived at Conjevaram, from whence we wrote to the Kiledar of Ginjee for leave to wait upon him.

"——, 16th. Arrived in Gingee at noon; the Kiledar sent his Brahmin to welcome us, and with some provisions. In the evening we visited the Kiledar, who received us kindly. At night twenty-two coolies deserted.

"——, 17th. Sent the dubash with a present to the Kiledar of 9 yards scarlet, one piece of Aurora, and a chest of rosewater, as an acknowledgment for the assistances he had offered us.

"——, 18th. Mr. Eyre observing that by the frequent occasions for taking up coolies, and the time and distance exceeding what was thought necessary when we left Madras, if we proceed we shall want money to pay the people. Agreed therefore that the dubash enquire where we may take it up for bills on Fort St. George or Fort St. David, and let us know the rates.

"——, 19th. Arrived a letter from the Honorable the Governor, acquainting that as the French have sent a present so far as Trichinopoly, he thinks it necessary that we should not fall short of them in respect, but proceed thither also. And the Kiledar offering us about the value of 2000 Arcot rupees in Wolandore fanams for our bill on the Deputy Governor and Council of Fort St. David, payable to Rangapilla of Pondicherry,—agreed to accept it, and pay the necessary advances to the coolies for Trichinopoly directly.

"——, 20th. Having now got a supply of oxen and coolies, the latter in room of those that left us here in the night, and for the former discharged those taken at Conjeveram; and as we have heard some straggling parties of Mahratta horse have been about plundering the villages,—agreed to take with us five and twenty horse the Killidar offered us, as a guard to the goods, and one of the Hircarras to show the road. Gave Baba Row, the Killidar's brahmin, 5 yards of scarlet cloth; and the Killdar being sick, sent the dubash with our compliments of leave, and went forward to Anandapuram.

"——, 21st. Got at noon to Veracholavarum; from whence having travelled too far in the heat, for want of water cannot get the oxen to proceed further till the morning.

"——, 22nd. Travelled all day for want of water till four in the afternoon. Arrived at Yeliva Narsore; sent the dubash with a compliment to the new Killidar there, and to enquire news of the Camp, that it was on the banks of Coleroon river.

"——, 23rd. As the goods were here passing the Mettas, they were stopped upon some intelligence that there was private merchant's goods among them. But upon application to the Killidar, and declaring that we knew of none; after some detention he acquiesced to let them go on. Travelled for want of good water till three in the afternoon (in which six of the people fainted); and arrived at Chile Nessalore, where about forty of Imaum Sahib's peons joined us, and brought their Master's answer to ours from Conjeveram, that he should be glad to see us as soon as possible. The coolies too much fatigued, cannot proceed till the morning.

"——, 24th. About one o'clock arrived at Toolore river; the people here also too much overcome with heat to go on in the afternoon.

"——, 25th. In the morning got to Wolgundapuram, where in the afternoon came in Share Mahomud Khan, Killidar of Tagagara, with some horse and peons from Imaum Sahib, as a further convoy for us.

"——, 26th. Set forward at near noon, and towards sunset reached Octatore; where hearing of some robberies and murder there the night before by the Callar people, kept as good a guard as we could all night.

"——, 27th. Set out early this morning, and after a rest in the middle of the day, arrived at Mardoor, in view of the camp at sunset; where the Nabob's Hircarras coming to enquire who we were, we sent to advise Imaum Sahib, that we were ready to come into camp to such place as he should appoint for us.

"——, 28th. This morning paid and dispatched the Ginjee horsemen; and in the afternoon went through the camp to the place assigned us; and pitched all the tents that evening in view of Trichinopoly town, surrounded at some distance by Nizam's forces under the command of Coja Abdulla Khan, Rajah Shandrascin, Rajah Janojee, Meer Assud, and Shaik Lutfulla Khan. Sent our compliments, which were returned by Imaum Sahib, that he would come to us in the morning.

"——, 29th. Buckanjee Cossidas, the camp Shroff, coming to see us gave us advice as to affairs in the camp. We mentioned our letter of credit to him from his gomastas, which he said he was ready to comply with. Accordingly we sent for 2,000 rupees on it in the evening. Presented Share Mahmud Khan, who attended us from Wolgundapuram, with one piece of Aurora; and gave 150 rupees for provisions to his horse and peons. In the afternoon received a visit from Imaum Sahib; presented him some gold mohurs, and delivered the Governor's letter to him. He told us he had acquainted the Nabob of our arrival; and that Meer Mucktada Khan was ordered, with a party of 4,000 horse and as many foot, to conduct us to the Nabob in the morning; and desired we would be ready to receive him in a proper manner; and after some discourse he received beetle and took leave.

"——, 30th. About 8 this morning, the Nabob's officer came to us, with a guard of horse and foot, and two elephants, with drum and colours; and told us the Nabob was glad to hear of our arrival in camp, and had ordered him to conduct us to him.

"After the usual compliments we presented him, as by the list of presents; and after his taking beetle we proceeded with him, and was carried to the public durbar, where the Nabob was sitting attended by his Omrahs, Nabobs, Rajahs, and other great men; and making our obeisances in front at a considerable distance, we were shown a place on the carpets, and to sit down there. About an hour after, when the Nabob rose from the durbar, he sent for us into private apartments. Whereupon his speaking our welcome, we paid the Governor's respect to him; and he bid us sit down; and then honoured us with a great deal of free discourse on indifferent matters. Coffee was also served to us, with the honour of the fans. This being the first audience nothing was said of the present; and in something more than an hour he gave us beetle, and we withdrew and returned to our tents; where the Nabob and Imaum Sahib each sent us a dinner. In the afternoon received a list from Imaum Sahib of what goods he had assigned for the presents to the Nizam; which we got unpacked and sorted out that night, and sent early next morning to the Nabob.

"——, 31st. The goods being sent and opened at the Nabob's tents, went to wait on him at the durbar; and that business being over the Nabob sent for us to a private tent, where the goods lay opened, and we were desired to sit. The Nabob observed them very nearly, and took many of the parcels in hand, and said they were very good; and, of the painted looking glass and some others; that he would keep some himself, and send also some of them to the Mogul, and would tell him he had them of the Governor of Chennapatnam. Imaum Sahib, upon seeing that notice taken of them (which was not then interpreted us), got up and made his salams. Coffee was served, and after about an hour's discourse we retired.

"In the evening happened a very violent squall of wind and rain, which blew down some of the Nabob's tents and a great many others; and ours were with much difficulty kept from falling which made us think it lucky that we had delivered the

Nabob's goods, and that those remaining with us were kept from any damage by the weather.

"April, 1st. Sent the Mulla and Ware-house Canacopiley, to count out the presents to the Nabob's daroga, or Warehouse-keeper. Sent the dubash to attend Imaum Sahib, and see if he should have any other commands for us. He asked if we were satisfied with our reception; and bid to write advice of it to the Governor and to request of him some concave looking glasses; which, as by the sample sent us, he said would be very acceptable to the Nabob. Agreed therefore that we write his said request to the Governor, and sent the glass as he desires with it.

"——, 2nd. About 9 o'clock we attended the durbar, was afterwards sent for to a private tent, where we sat sometime; was served with coffee and the fans, while the Nabob's discourse was chiefly on enquiry into the customs of the Europeans and their discipline in war.

"—— 4th. Sent the dubash again to ask Imaum Sahib when we should deliver the Governor's letter to the Nabob; as also, when we may expect to be introduced to Nazir Jung. To which he said,—"Desire the Gentlemen to come to durbar, and I will do it for them." Attended the durbar, and was sent for afterwards to sit in the private apartment; had the usual honors of coffee &c., but nothing done in the business promised by Imaum Sahib.

"Came in five oxen with broad cloth for presents to the Nabob's officers; and some oil and other necessaries that were detained by some troubles on the road.

"——, 5th. Sent the dubash again to Imaum Sahib, desiring to know when we would present the Governor's letter to the Nabob. He answered there was no occasion to be in a hurry for it, that he would get an answer to it when we were ready to return; and that he would take a fit opportunity to ask the Nabob's leave to visit Nazir Jung. This day, being Tuesday, no durbar held. Received lists from Imaum Sahib of particulars for presents to be got ready against he should send for them.

"——, 6th. At 10 o'clock attended the durbar, and was afterwards called to the private tents as usual.

"Imaum Sahib moved for the Nabob's leave for us to visit Nazir Jung; and presented a list of what designed for him. To which after some perusal the Nabob dismissed it by reserving him to another time. Retiring from thence, went with Imaum Sahib on a visit to Mahud Anwar Khan, where we were very kindly received. After a small stay there and receiving some atur, perfumes, and beetle, took leave and went home.

"——, 7th. Imaum Sahib, having so often put us off in our request to deliver the Nabob's letter, till it is grown so late that we begin to be doubtful whether he designs it shall be done or not; and as we thought it odd that he did not call for it on the delivery of the presents it recommends; it would be much more strange if we should not deliver it at all. Agreed therefore that we attend the durbar this morning, and that Mr. Eyre take an opportunity to present it there. Accordingly, making the usual overture for approach, he presented it to the Nabob, who laid it by him. Were afterwards called to the honour of the private apartments, and after being treated as before, returned to our tents. Received of Buckanjee Cossadas, Arcot rupees 1,000, in full of the letter of credit on him to pay batta to the peons and coolies &c. disbursements.

"In the afternoon sent to Imaum Sahib for leave to visit him. He answered that we should not come out in the heat, but that he would come to us in the evening; when in a discourse, chiefly tending to show the grandeur of the Nabob his master, he desired of us the proper titles of our Governor, for that they should be augmented by the Nabob. He asked also what would be agreeable to the Governor that the Nabob should do for him; and particularly what villages he would have granted. We replied we had no instructions in that respect, and could therefore say nothing to it; but that we understood the Governor had wrote him fully as to all he would ask of him. He then asked, what may be the annual amount of the juncans on the Company's goods. To which we could only say, it was always more or less according to their success in the investment, and therefore seldom any two years near the same amount; and he desired we would write to the Governor to instruct him more particularly. After this he said he would come early in the morning, and conduct us to the quarters of Coja Abdulla Khan, as he lay before the town; and receiving beetle, he returned home.

"Agreed to write and advise the Governor of that part of Imaum Sahib's discourse regarding the villages and juncans.

"——, 8th. Early this morning Imaum Sahib came according to appointment, attended with about 150 horse and 100 foot, and by Monsr. Bosett (a Gentleman who carried the presents from the French); and we directly proceeded with them. On our arrival we were introduced to Coja Abdulla Khan's durbar; and after some stay there, he came in and saluted us in the usual way; and making our offerings in gold mohurs he seated us near him. We delivered the Governor's letter, and his respects to him. Upon which he enquired his health, and made several kind professions of a friendship for him; and after about an hour's discourse, on Imaum Sahib's telling him that some of the villages that were near us and in his Nabobship would be acceptable, he directly wrote a few lines in our favour to the Nabob, which Imaum Sahib took from him; and then made apology that he was sorry he had not a warning to be better provided to receive us, but that he would send us for dinner such as he could get in the camp; and then presenting us with Seerpaws, we acknowledged the honour done us, and withdrew to a tent he had ordered for that purpose; but having sent one of ours, and seeing Imaum Sahib wanted that for himself, we desired him to get it excused that we made use of ours; and inviting the French Gentleman to go with us to our tent, we there received a dinner; also one from Coja Abdulla Khan; and about an hour after

Imaum Sahib sent for us to come and take leave of Coja Abdulla Khan; where after some discourse and compliments on the treatment received, he gave beetle and perfumes, and we took leave about 2 o'clock, when being excessive hot, and at that hour in the camp unable to find above half our coolies, had many of them fainted in the way, and was soon set down under almost every bush we came to; had a most irksome and sultry journey to our tents, and unable to reach them till sunset.

"——, 9th. Thought it necessary to go to the durbar to-day.

"——, 10th. Attended the durbar, and was afterwards received and treated in the Nabob's apartments as before.

"——, 11th. Imaum Sahib, having told the dubash that he would this morning move for leave to get what was proper prepared for our taking leave of the Nabob. We attended the durbar, but seeing there was nothing said of it, he then told the dubash that to-morrow being Tuesday, and no durbar, he would go to Coja Abdulla Khan and consult upon forwarding our affairs.

"Finding we shall be in want of more money to pay durbar charges, and those of the returning journey;—agreed that the dubash go and see if Buckanjee Cossidas is willing to let us have 2000 rupees on the Honorable the Governor and Council. The dubash returning told us that finding he made some hesitation, he said no more of it, as he could get us such a sum of the Guzerat merchants; and accordingly in the evening he brought us 2000 Arcot rupees of Poor Chatamdoss Govardandoss, for which agreed to give him a bill accordingly, and payable to Ragoor Veragoo Chetty of Madras.

"——, 12th. Imaum Sahib went to Coja Abdulla Khan, and we waited at home for his returning.

"——, 13th. Imaum Sahib being something indisposed on his return, had no opportunity to speak with him.

"——, 14th. Made our compliments at the durbar, and seeing nothing done for us we returned to our tents.

"——, 15th. Wrote a letter to Imaum Sahib, complaining that the death of several of our people, and the sickness of many others, so frightens the rest that they declare they cannot stay longer with us; and that if so they would leave us destitute of any way to get home. To entreat therefore that he will get our business done, and leave for our return. He wrote in answer that it should be done to-morrow, and that we might prepare to send away our things.

"In the afternoon Imaum Sahib sent each of us a seerpaw by hands of Sheer Mahmud Khan, Kilidar of Tagagara; upon which Tashereifd the Kilidar with four yards of scarlet, and gave eleven rupees to his servants.

"——, 16th. Attended the Nabob at durbar; after a short stay there, he retired and sent for us to an inner tent, where we were served with coffee and the fans; and after some discourse the Nabob told us that as he was always desirous to have our company, it could not be pleasing to him to think of our leaving him, but that as he was informed it was necessary to our health and other engagements, he ought to allow it; and then told us if we came to-morrow morning we should have audience of leave.

"——, 17th. About 10 o'clock this morning attended according to yesterday's appointment, and after sitting about half an hour at the durbar, the Nabob rose up and sent for us within, where we were treated with the usual honours. After which he told us he had reason to be pleased with the Governor's courtesy in sending us with presents for him at so great a distance; that though he may be in want of something from Chinnapatnam, he expects no more presents from him; and that if the Governor should not let his people pay for them, it would forbid him ever asking any thing more of him. After this he said particularly he should want a few great guns, and some powder, mortars, and shells, with a gunner practiced in the use of them. We answered that we should not fail on our arrival to acquaint the Governor of his Excellency's pleasure; and Seerpaws being ordered for the Governor, and ourselves, we were conducted by Imaum Sahib to another tent to receive them; and being there invested with them, were led back again to the Nabob; where making our obeisances we took our seats on the carpets; and making a short stay there, took leave of the Nabob and returned to our tents.

"This afternoon, sent all the remaining goods to Imaum Sahib, agreeable to a message received from him to that purpose; among which were those also designed for Coja Abdulla Khan. And Imaum Sahib having also said that (to save us a great deal of trouble) if we sent the money for the durbar charges to him, he would see it properly distributed; we thankfully received that proposal and thinking 500 rupees as little as could serve for that purpose, we accordingly sent him that sum to be so distributed.

"In the evening received the Nabob's Seerpaw for the Governor, made up in a bundle covered with a white cloth; as also a fine horse with a slight furniture upon him, which we ordered to be taken care of.

"Hussan Khan Tahir, who has the management of affairs of Sahib Zadda, son of late deceased Nabob of Arcot, having taken some notice of us in camp,—agreed it will be proper that we send the dubash to wait on him, and see if he has any commands for us to Madras. He returned our compliments, and desired his respects to the Governor; and after expressing a dissatisfaction at the slow success of Sahib Zaddas hopes for the succession to his fathers province, and with a person who had been officious to obstruct him in it, he ordered a Seerpaw to the dubash and so dismissed him.

"Imaum Sahib, having said yesterday that we might send away our things early this morning; and again that we should do well to proceed ourselves after them directly upon taking leave of the Nabob; and that he would get the sunnuds intended for us executed when in a few days Coja Abdulla Khan would come to see the Nabob and send them after us ; which would be better than keeping us to stay for them any longer. Upon which considering that we have no particular instruction to ask for any thing but in general to follow such directions as we should receive from Imaum :—agreed therefore and for the reasons mentioned the 15th instant, that we set out on our return early to-morrow morning and as the coolies will not be able to carry us through so long a journey as to Madras directly and without some stay to refresh them in the way ; that we go the Fort St. David road believing it as near a way as any and because we may from thence send a considerable part of our luggage up by sea and discharge the coolies.

"——, 18th. Having agreeable to directions from Imaum Sahib Tashereif'd the Nabob's coffee and fan servants, and paid one hundred rupees for batta to Shere Mahmud Khan's peons and servants, we set out from the camp at about six this morning with a few horse and peons sent us by Imaum Sahib, and at night got to Ootatore.

"——, 19th. Came to Runjengudda in the evening.

"——, 20th. To Chepauk.

"——, 21st. Discharged Imaum Sahib's horse and in the evening got to Trunama Nellore.

"——, 22nd. In the evening lodge at Patumpawk.

"——, 23rd. Went into Fort St. David and stayed there three days to refresh the people—sent the tents &c. by a sea conveyance to Fort St. George, and discharged the oxen and coolies that carried them.

"——, 27th. Set out for Fort St. George leaving Mr. Harrison considerably indisposed.

"—— 29th. Receiving advice that Imaum Sahib had desired the horse and Seerpaw we have got with us from the Nabob may be lodged at St. Thomé and that his son may carry it into Town.

"May 1st. Sent the horse and Seerpaw to be lodged with the Havildar of St. Thomé; proceeded and arrived in Town and waited on the Governor in the evening."

We turn from the events of this curious mission from Madras to Trichinopoly, to note the progress of events within the walls of Fort St. George. The widow of the late Nabob Subder Ali, was still residing at Black Town; but her son had been placed on the musnud at Arcot, and efforts had been made with some success to induce the Nizam to confirm the appointment. With this brief explanation, the reader will have no difficulty in understanding the following delicate application to Governor Benyon for the loan of ten lakhs of rupees.

"Thursday, 19th May, 1743. The President acquainted the Board, that few days past he was informed that Meer Allim, darogah to the late Nabob's Lady, was come into Town with letters from Mahommad Hussan Khan Tahir, Budderdeen Hussain Khan, and Mahommad Ally Sahib; acquainting him (the President) that they had agreed upon the sum they were to pay Nizam-ul-Mulk for confirming Mahommud Sied Khan, the late

Nabob's son in the Government of this province, and had got most of the money ready, except a small matter as they called it; which therefore they desired we would advance and lend them, and which Meer Allim hinted was ten lacs of rupees; who was instructed to offer as security a mortgage of the rents of part of the country or a deposit of jewels. But the President considering that whatever hopes the family may have at present, faction and party prevails so much in the camp, that there was no certain dependance upon any promises which may have been made them till the grant has passed the seals; but principally that it is contrary to our practice, and indeed our orders, to have any dealings in money matters with the governing powers. He had sent for Coja Petrus, and instructed him in what manner to talk to Meer Allim before he made his visit; and explain to him our reasons why we could neither lend nor borrow; and Meer Allim was satisfied with those reasons, that when he came to the Fort he said very little upon the subject of his errand; and all that the President had occasion to say in his answers to the letters was only to assure them in general terms that he never denied any thing to his friends that was in his power, and for the rest referred them to what they would be told by Meer Allim."

On the same day we find the following extract, referring to the smuggling of betel and tobacco by the servants of the Moors now residing in Black Town.

"The case of the betel and tobacco farmers being taken into consideration, the President said he believed they had suffered by large quantities brought in by the servants belonging to the Moors; for besides what they conveyed into the women's palankeen and hackeries which could not be searched, they often run in parcels under the notion of provisions, fruit, and sweetmeats as presents sent them from the country; that the farmers had catched several of the Moors servants in this last practice which they had brought to him, the President, upon whose complaining thereof, their principals were very willing and desirous the betel and tobacco should be confiscated, but were not inclined their servants should be otherwise punished; and he could not visit upon it, without lessening the respect we had always endeavoured to show them; and therefore as the profit was so great they the servants still continued to run it in, as they only run the risk of having it seized if they were catched, which considering the many opportunities they have was not equal to the temptation of the profit."

In consequence of these losses an abatement of two months rent was made to the betel and tobacco farmers.

The following extract exhibit the final arrangement that was made between the English Government at Fort St. George and the Dutch Government at Negapatam respecting the delivering up of deserters on either side.

"Friday, 29th July, 1743. The President acquaints the Board that a few days ago three of our soldiers,—namely Hard Wilson, John Robertson, and Thomas Murphen,—having deserted to Pulicat, he thought it needless to trouble the Board with the matter; not doubting but the chief there would return them on his request. And therefore he had wrote a letter to the Chief to that effect, and promising a full pardon to the people; but he found himself disappointed, when two days since he received an answer thereto, declaring that by orders from Negapatam they are not to deliver up any of our deserters.

"Agreed to transmit a copy of the said letter to the Governor and Council of Negapatam, and to recommend this affair to their serious attention; as we think that when they have recollected what passed between us and them last year on occasion of a man deserting from them, and fully considered the terms on which we have demanded these three men, they will revoke the order, and direct them to be returned us."

This affair ended in the agreement to deliver up deserters on either side, upon the assurance of their not being put to death, nor punished publicly in an infamous manner.

Our next extract illustrates the jealousy which had prevailed for some time respecting the residence of foreigners within the walls of White Town.

"Monday, 22nd August, 1743. Notice being affixed at the Sea gate of the intended sale of a house in the White Town on Monday the 29th instant; and it being intimated to the Board that some Armenians design to purchase the same; it fell under debate, whether it was not become necessary to put a stop to such indulgence to foreigners and strangers; and agreed in the affirmative, on considering how large a part of the White

Town is already in the possession of foreigners, and that if they are permitted to purchase more, the inconveniences arising therefrom to the English inhabitants may be very great. And for as much as such inconveniences may more easily be prevented than removed or remedied when felt. It is agreed that the following prohibition be affixed at the gates of the Town in English, and the French, Dutch, Portuguese, and Armenian languages.

" Resolved and ordered that no foreigners or strangers, or any others than the natural subjects of the King of Great Britain, shall be permitted from and after this time to purchase or inhabit any house or houses, godowns, or other buildings, within the walls of the White Town; except only such as they have heretofore been permitted to purchase; and that even those houses &c., shall not be sold again to, or inhabited by any other foreigners and strangers than such as are already possessed of them, without the permission of the President and Council of this place for the time being to that end first had and obtained."

About this time Trichinopoly was captured by the Nizam, as will be seen by the following entry.

" Monday, 29th August, 1743. Imaum Sahib having advised the President of Nizam-ul-Mulk's having taken Trichinopoly, he acquainted the Board that it will be proper to write a letter of congratulation upon the occasion, accompanied with fifty-one gold mohurs, which he is desired to comply with as he shall judge proper."

From the following entry it would seem that

keeping the Moors out of Black Town was considered to be as important an object, as keeping other foreigners out of White Town.

"Monday, 17th October, 1743. The Justices appointed to the Registry of houses remark to the Board, that one great and principal end proposed by the establishing that registry in 1735, was to prevent the Moors purchasing too much in the Black Town; and that in prosecution of such purpose the said Justices had made it a rule to themselves, not to register any bill of sale or conveyances to Moormen, without the particular leave of the Board. Notwithstanding which caution, they find themselves obliged to apply for the opinion and directions of the Board, upon a method several Moormen have lately endeavoured to put in practice, to evade the prohibition laid against them in the intention of the said registry; who, finding they must not appear as the purchasers, procure some of the Malabars or Gentoos to buy houses for them in their own names. After which the conveyances are entered in this registry without any objection, and then the Moormen, under pretence of having lent money on the premises specified in such conveyances, bring their mortgages to be registered, and by that means possess and inhabit as uninterruptedly as if the original titles were made to themselves. A practice to which if some stop is not put, that end proposed by the establishment of the registry will be soon disconcerted and rendered of no effect. The Board being sensible of the many inconveniences that may arise to the place by not discouraging such practices,—

it is agreed and ordered that the Justices do not attest or permit any mortgages of the nature of those above described, or of a like tendency to be registered."

The following extracts are domestic, and will explain themselves.

"Wednesday, 30th November, 1743. The long established pay to the Choultry dubash of eighty fanams per month, and an exemption from quit rent and scavenger's duty on his house having been reduced some years since to forty fanams per month; and that exemption taken off, he has been obliged to set up a school for the further support of himself and a numerous family, by which he is much hindered from giving the proper attendance at the Choultry;—it is therefore agreed that he be paid according to the former establishment, and that his house be struck out of the rolls.

"The President then acquainting the Board that application had sometime ago been made to him to procure an exemption from quit rent and scavenger's duty on a house and garden belonging to Muctum Sahib, the Nabob's chief mullah;—It is agreed that he be gratified therein, as the value is but a pagoda and a quarter per annum, and he may be of more service than equivalent."

"Wednesday, 30th November, 1743. Petition of Mrs. Katharine Gyfford read, setting forth that by unavoidable accidents and misfortunes she is reduced to the want of a subsistance, and the necessity of praying some relief from the Honorable Company in whose service, she had lost a father and three husbands. Besides that the Board are fully satisfied of Mrs. Gyfford's not having wherewith to subsist on, it is observable that when she was not in such indigent circumstances, she avoided putting the Company to an expence of twenty-five pagodas a month, which was offered her in May 1721; and further that our Honorable Masters were pleased not to disapprove the allowances made to the other unfortunate Anjengo widows at that time, as well as that, she is now here by their permission. It is agreed, therefore, to allow her fifteen pagodas per month till their pleasure shall be known; and in our next letters to beg the favour of their orders how to act hereafter in cases of the like nature."

"Monday, 12th December, 1743. Antonha Carvalho, who has for many years inhabited the buildings, made by her great-grand-father John Pereira in the garden commonly called by his name; which reverting to the Company was set apart for those inhabitants to build on, whose houses had been pulled down on the approach of the Mahrattas in consultation of the 15th June 1741; —prays that in consideration of her reduced circumstances, and the rent she paid for so many years whilst able, and even some years after she received anything by the produce of the garden, the Honorable Company will be pleased to give her the said buildings for the support of herself and family. The Board having considered her request, did not think fit to alienate the Company's property in the said buildings; but in compassion to her age and circumstances, and in consideration of the many years' rent she and her family had paid the company ;—agreed to grant the possession of them to her, and her only daughter Josepha Maria Rosa de Silveira, during their lives, they keeping the same in repair and paying six fanams annually for scavenger's duty."

Our next entry refers to foreign affairs.

" Monday, 26th December, 1743. The President acquaints the Board that Nizam-ul-Mulk, having left Trichinopoly in October last, and taken his route a considerable distance to the Westward of Arcot, where he is still encamped; but not having yet absolutely settled the Government of his province, he has in the interim sent Coja Namah Tullah Khan, son of Coja Abdulla Khan, as superintendant of the province; and who the beginning of last week came to St. Thomé with 1000 horse and 3000 foot, the rest of his forces being left at Arcot. Meer Assad came down with Coja Namah Tullah Khan, and made the President a visit on Wednesday last; and Coja Namah Tullah Khan being so near, intimated his intention of sending a Seerpaw to the President, but which he had endeavoured as far as he decently could to excuse the receiving of, urging that he was near his departure and therefore wished that it might be deferred till Mr. Morse took the chair; when in all likelihood there will be another Seerpaw sent, and the usual return must be made for it. But Coja Namah Tullah Khan, being soon to return to Arcot, insisted on sending one now; and it was accordingly received on Saturday last with the usual ceremonies, as upon these occasions it is always customary, and expected that by it we should show our respect by making some return; and we dont think it proper in the present unsettled state of the country, to disoblige a person of his rank and present power by any slight or neglect on our parts. Agreed that a present be made him to the value of seven or eight hundred pagodas; the particulars to be chosen by the President and Mr. Morse."

This year brings the Government of Mr. Benyon to a close. On the 17th January 1744 he departed for Europe, and Mr. Nicholas Morse reigned in his stead.

CHAPTER XLVII.

GOVERNORSHIP OF MR. NICHOLAS MORSE.

1744.

The year 1744 will long be famous in the history of the rise of the British Empire in India. It was this year that the war with France broke out, which ultimately led to the capture of Fort St. George by the French, and to those hostilities in this country which terminated in the ascendancy of the British in India. The chronicles of Fort St. George during the year 1744 are however sufficiently interesting in themselves. The year commenced with the inauguration of Governor Morse, who was destined to see stirring times. The opening extracts will explain themselves:

"Tuesday, 17th January, 1744. Richard Benyon, Esq., late President of this place, having early this morning embarked on the "Duke" for England, and the Government thereby devolving on Nicholas Morse, Esq., he accordingly takes the chair; and the Company's servants, inhabitants, and military officers attending, the Secretary reads the 12th paragraph of the general letter from England, whereby it is directed that upon Mr. Benyon's resigning the Government and taking passage for England, the said Nicholas Morse, Esq., do succeed as President, and take upon him the Government of the Honorable Company's affairs here.

"The inhabitants, military officers and others being withdrawn, the President took the oath to be true and faithful to the Honorable Company, as did all the other members of the Board except Mr. Hinde who had taken the oath in England.

"Ordered that new commissions be drawn out for all the Lieutenants and Ensigns under this Presidency."

Throughout this year the Mahrattas seem to have been endeavouring to recover Trichinopoly from the Nizam, and thus to have occasioned no little excitement at Fort St. George. The following extract is historical.

"Saturday, 3rd February, 1744. The President acquaints the Board, that there are advices come to the Shroffs in Town, that Nizam-ul-mulk, upon his arriving at the banks of the river Kistna in his way to Golcondah, had an account brought him of a large army of the Mahrattas being on the other side. On which he faced about and came back three days' journey to a place called Pocalore. The Mahrattas soon after passed the river and encamped within a few miles of him; and there has been small skirmishes between those sent out to forage, but nothing of any consequence. That orders were sent to Coja Namah Futta Khan, who commands in this province, to immediately march with his forces to the Fort of Gingee, where he is collecting a larger body in order to prevent the Mahrattas getting through the pass to Trichinopoly, which they have designs to retake from the Moors. This has very much alarmed the country, and occasioned all the inhabitants at Arcot and the Towns adjacent to leave them; and great number of peons and oxen are come in here with money and effects. In a few days, it was expected, they would come to some action or treaty; but it is thought the latter, as it is more agreeable to the Nizam's general method of proceeding, and as the army of the Mahrattas is said to be superior to his."

Our Roman Catholic readers will be interested in the following notice.

"Friday, 10th February, 1744. The President acquaints the Board, that notwithstanding Father Severini, since the demise of Father Thomas in April 1742, has acted as Superior of the Roman Catholic Church in this Town, by the consent of this Board (who then thought it unnecessary to authorize him by any particular instrument); and has conducted himself to the general satisfaction; he (the President) learns that a paper under the hand of the Provincial of the Convent of Tauris and the seal of his office called a decree, and said to be sent out of France by the way of China, appeared in Town about the 5th instant; whereby Padre Renatus (a Frenchman by birth, and a junior brother who has hitherto acted under Severini) is appointed Apostolic Missionary and vice Guardian of the Missions in the Indies and Persia; a title, though not exactly the same with that Severini is known by of Superior and Chief Pastor of the Church of St. Andrew in this Town; yet the influence it carries with it will render it so like in its effects, that the President looks on it only as an artful attempt to invade the Honorable Company's right of appointing who shall be Superior in Ecclesiastical matters over the great number of our inhabitants of the Roman Catholic profession; a privilege necessary to the Company's honour and interests, and the welfare and good government of the Town; and as occasions offered, so zealously maintained by our predecessors, and as often approved by our Honorable Masters, that he therefore recommends to the Board to consider of the steps proper to be taken on this affair.

"Our records being thereupon referred to, so many precedents appeared of the prerogative mentioned by the English Government in cases of this nature, confirmed from England and confessed by the Fathers of this Roman Church; that the Board having fully considered the nature and tendency of this matter:—Resolved and ordered, that an instrument be drawn out, appointing Padre Severini, Superior and Chief Pastor of the Church of St. Andrew in this Town, on the model of that given on a like occasion by the President and Council in February 1707.

"That the same be translated into Latin to be signed by the Board; and that an order also in Latin be delivered by the Secretary to Padre Severini, directing him to read or cause the said instrument of our induction to be read publicly in his Church on Sunday next, the Secretary being present.

"Agreed for several reasons that obviate themselves, to separate the grounds of these our resolutions from our other more public advices to our Honorable Masters by the "Heathcote" now dispatching."

"Wednesday, 15th February, 1744. The Secretary acquaints the Board that pursuant to our order he had delivered to Father Severini, our instrumental of induction, and order for publishing the same; conformable to which he had by the Father's appointment attended at the Roman Church at 9 o'clock on Sunday morning last, where the said instrument was publicly read to the congregation by Father Ranatus in the Latin and also in Portuguese."

Our next extract illustrates the proceedings of the Nizam and the Mahrattas.

"Wednesday, 15th February, 1744. The President acquaints the Board that the Shroffs have received advices from the country that matters are come to an accommodation between the Nizam and the Mahrattas, and that the latter were retired; which seemed in some measure to be confirmed by the Shroffs and others sending back to Arcot the treasures they had brought in here within these few days; wherefore he proposed, and it is agreed, to advise thereof to St. Davids, that they may go on with their business; warning them at the same time to proceed with caution, as it is believed the Mahrattas have still some designs to recover Trichinopoly."

The affairs at Arcot next engage our attention.

"Monday, 5th March, 1744. The President acquaints the Board that Coja Namah Futta Khan,

—who commands in the province in the place of his father Coja Abdulla Khan, the present nominal Nabob of Arcot,—had sent him a horse and Seerpaw on his coming to the government; and that he found it was expected there should be a present made in return as is customary to a Nabob on such occasions. But that as the Nizam was returned into the province, and it is rumoured the Nabobship of Arcot will soon be settled, he judged it might be proper to wait sometime; that we might avoid the extraordinary charge of sending another present, in case it should not be confirmed on the same person."

The following notice of a forcible attempt made by a Madras Shroff to recover a debt from an English merchant is very curious. It does not however reflect much honour on the creditor.

"Thursday, 8th March, 1744. The President acquaints the Board that on Sunday last he received a letter from Mr. Daniel Berriman at St. Thomas' Mount, complaining of his having been insulted there by one Dialdoss, a Guzerat Shroff, and an inhabitant of this place who had endeavoured, by the assistance of the Moor Havildar of St. Thomé, to take him by force and carry him thither; which being also confirmed to him from other hands, he had sent out a party of peons to prevent it; who bringing Dialdoss in with them he had ordered him into the custody of the Pedda Naick. The following are the circumstances of the affair. Mr. Berriman having borrowed 1000 rupees of this Dialdoss, and the time for payment being elapsed, he, Dialdoss, had often demanded his money, and been put off by Mr. Berriman with promises of discharging it. Mr. Berriman going to the Mount, the other followed him thither, insisted on immediate payment, and would not be satisfied with Mr. Berriman's assurances that he would return to Town in two or three days and endeavour to pay him his due. But on the contrary, Dialdoss applied to the Havildar of St. Thomé for his assistance to oblige Mr. Berriman to an immediate payment, or to carry him to St. Thomé; promising the Havildar 250 rupees or a quarter part of the principal debt for his pains. Thereupon the Havildar sent a party of peons, who had laid hold of Mr. Berriman; but on his drawing his sword they quitted him, and gave him an opportunity of getting into Mr. Barlow's gardens, and thence into his house, where he remained and advised the President from thence of the circumstances he was in. All that night the Moors peons continued about Mr. Barlow's doors, and were very noisy and insolent, but the next morning some of the English Gentlemen who happened to be there, having represented to Dialdoss the irregularity and ill consequences of such a proceeding, the Moor peons retired before the party sent from hence reached the Mount; which last meeting with Dialdoss brought him into Town with them.

"This behaviour of Dialdoss, carrying in it a high insult on the English government, and an absolute breach of the Honorable Company's order, and the long established rules of the place, which prohibit any application being made by any of our inhabitants to the Moors or Gentoo officers, even in disputes with or demands on each other, much less where the English are concerned; and nothing offering in vindication of him or in extenuation of his offence; since he had neither applied to the President or Court in the matter, but had taken upon him to pursue his own measures, so inconsistent with good order, and by no means to be suffered in a government to whose tribunal alone its inhabitants, as well Europeans as others, are subject in all cases. It is judged highly expedient to make him suffer some mark of our resentment, either by fine or corporal punishment. The first of these means being preferred, and it being debated what the amount of the fine should be, it was considered that Dialdoss is but in the lower class of the Shroffs, and that probably Mr. Berriman's debt to him will not be paid soon if ever; and therefore agreed and resolved that he be fined only 300 pagodas, and that he continue under his present confinement till he pay the same.

"The Board were then proceeding to consider in what manner to show the Havildar of St. Thomé our resentment of his conduct; when there came into the Fort one Mahmud Hussein, a principal inhabitant of St. Thomé, whom the Havildar had sent to ask the President's pardon for what had been done; and by whom he urged in his excuse, that he was a stranger to affairs with the English, being come lately from a distant country to this appointment; and that being made sensible of the error he had been guilty of in concerning himself with our inhabitants, he should take care not to do the like in future. The President having acquainted us with this message, and the Havildar being a relation of Nabob Coja Abdulla Khan, it was agreed to rest satisfied with this his submission; but the President to let him know, that if he or any other Havildar of St. Thomé, shall hereafter presume to concern himself in any matters respecting this government, we are determined to take our full satisfaction; and that he or they will be answerable for all the consequences that may ensue thereon."

We now enter upon interesting illustration of the relation between the English at Fort St. George and the Nizam of the Dekkan.

"Thursday, 29th March, 1744. The President acquaints the Board that he had received a letter from Nizam-ul-Mulk, in which he mentions to have sent to this place, under charge of two of his officers, several parcels of goods; desiring him to receive the same and forward them to Surat, being designed for the Mogul's Court. With this letter came also one from Coja Abdulla Khan, and another from Imaum Sahib, to the like purport.

"The Board having taken the same into consideration, are of opinion that we ought by all means to avoid the taking the goods into our custody, in order to send them on to Surat; since if any accident should happen to them in the passage, and the Court be disappointed of them, they who are not conversant with sea affairs, and the casualties of those conveyances, might look upon the Honorable Company as obliged to make good the loss, which might be rated at their pleasure and occasion a large demand, and thereby involve this or some other of the Company's settlements in dispute with the Mogul's officers, who would be under the absolute orders of their Sovereign, and obliged to the execution of them, though of a nature how unjust soever.

"That as this great person is yet in the province, and every officer in it subordinate to him and acting by his orders, it is our business to endeavour to keep far with him; more especially as we have some favours to expect from him; that therefore it may be proper for us to show a seeming willingness to comply with his request, but that we endeavour to shun every circumstance that may have a tendency to draw any ill consequence from that compliance; and which we presume may be done by representing to him the risk of all conveyances by sea; and to concern ourselves no further than in giving his servant any assistance when an opportunity offers to the port of Surat; and by leaving the whole management to them in the conducting them thither. That the goods be continued under charge of Imaum Sahib's people, to whom the officers had orders to deliver them; and who were afterwards to procure the President's receipt, which we can by no means think it consistent with our duty to the company to take upon us the risk of."

"Monday, 2nd April, 1744. The President acquaints the Board, that agreeable to the advices from the country he communicated to us on the 5th instant, he is since informed that the Nizam-ul-Mulk, being returned to a place in the province called Gundecottah, about eight days' journey distant from Arcot, has fixed the appointments to the several Nabobships of Cundanore, Golcondah, Corrapah and Arcot; the last of which he had bestowed on Coja Abdulla Khan. But he dying the night he received his commission, the Nizam had conferred it on Anawardee Khan,* another of his officers and late Nabob of Chicacoil; a person generally well esteemed and said to be very agreeable to the people. That Mauvasi Khan, son of this gentleman, is nominated for Dewan; and some are of opinion Imaum Sahib will be made Buxee; that these persons are expected at Arcot in few days, and that the Nizam was preparing to set out for Golcondah.

"Hereupon the President proceeded to remark that though the Nizam had expressed to the gentlemen when at the camp, a willingness to favour the Company; and seemed then very well disposed to grant them some mark of it; yet we have hitherto received no satisfactory answer concerning a dustuck to pass the Company's goods, custom free; or the other matters we were in hopes of; which he believed must be owing either to the insufficiency of Imaum Sahib's interest with the Nizam, or to his want of attachment to our service. He therefore proposes, as the only means the Nizam's intended short stay in these parts has now left us, and the most likely to put an end to our suspence, to address himself to the Nizam

* This Anawardee Khan, better known as Anwarodean, was the ancestor of the late dynasty of Nabobs of the Carnatic, and the father of the celebrated Mahommed Ali.

on the occasion, by a letter as copied hereafter; which being read the Board unanimously agreed to the proposal; being in hopes that the Nizam will not fail of showing some regard to the President's letter; or should it not at present meet with the desired success, that it may at least serve a further purpose, by opening a correspondence with the Nizam which may enable us hereafter to make our applications to him to more advantage.

"*Letter of Governor Morse to Nabob Nizam-ul-Mulk Asof Jah Bahauder Sepah Sautom.*

"Your Excellency's appearance in these parts the English looked upon as the most favourable circumstance that would possibly happen to them; that thereby they might have the great honour of paying their respects to you, and that you might be informed of the assistance they have of late years given on many occasions to the subjects of his Majesty, when the commotions in the country rendered their lives as well as fortunes very unsafe without the walls of Chennapatnam. They persuaded themselves that these services would be acceptable to your Excellency, and that they would entitle them to your favour and regard. This they had the great pleasure to find by the reception and kind treatment the Gentlemen met with, when they had the honour of being in your presence at Trichinopoly.

"By the blessings of God the affairs of this province are now settled, and your Excellency as I am informed on your departure from us; before which I beg leave to hope your Excellency will grant us some mark of your favour, as shall be agreeable to your great wisdom and generosity. This will show the world your kind acceptation of our services to the Circar; and is what I have waited for with the most earnest desire, and which I should not have doubted to have been honoured with before now, had the English been so fortunate as to have had an advocate to put your Excellency in mind of us, when matters of greater consequence would have admitted. Since I have failed in that point, I humbly presume to ask it myself of your Excellency; whose goodness I shall entirely now rely on without any intercessor. This will be an addition to my happiness, as it will give me an opportunity of making this particular address to so great a personage as your Excellency, of whom I beg favourable ear to what I am now about to represent; and that the English Company provide goods in several parts of this country, which is well known to be a very great advantage to the Circar, as well as the inhabitants; and that these are brought at different times to Chennapatnam and other places. The Jamadars of the country frequently stop them, and make unreasonable demands from us on this account. Though we have his Majesty's Royal firmaun for passing our goods custom free, to which a great regard is always paid in Bengal; yet the Foujdars in this province have not shown the same but have always acted in opposition to the Royal order. I therefore, humbly entreat your Excellency would be so gracious to grant a dustuck; that by virtue thereof the English Company's goods may be always freed from paying any custom. This will strengthen and support us in asserting our right to the enjoyment of what his Majesty has so graciously favoured us with; and I beg your Excellency would be pleased to send down your perwanna to the Governor of this province to the following effect: 'That in 'consideration of the Royal firmaun, and the ser- 'vice done to the Circar by the Governor of Chen- 'napatnam, I have freed the English Company 'from paying any custom on their goods which 'they purchase in several parts of the country, and 'carry to Chennapatnam and other settlements.'

"May it please your Excellency, the intent of my mentioning the service to the Circar is, that the copy of the sunnud which you in your goodness may favour me with, will be sent to England to be laid before our Honourable Masters, who will be pleased with my behaviour in that respect, and, it will recommend me to them.

"I further entreat your Excellency would be pleased to order one of the great persons, who is honoured with a seat in your noble presence, to receive my addresses and offer them to your Excellency, as the Cossaids can have no admittance there.

"God preserve your Excellency many years in the highest felicity."

"Monday, 23rd April, 1744. The President observes to the Board that Anawardee Khan being now fixed in the Government, we must think of preparing a present for him and the other officers as usual; and he hoped it might be so managed that the present now to be sent might serve as well for the President's coming to the government, as the change of the Subahships. That the amount be about 1200 pagodas to the Nabob; his son the Dewan, and serpentow the Minister, to each one according to what has been usual; and that the Warehouse-keeper, with the approval of the President do procure such articles as will be most acceptable to the Moors, that we have not already in our warehouse."

From the following extract it would seem that the Roman Catholic Church offered no opposition to the arrangements of the Government of Fort St. George.

"Saturday, 28th April, 1744. The President acquaints the Board, that Padree Renatus had been with him, when he produced a commission from the Vicar General of the Order, received from France by the ships lately arrived at Pondicherry, to nominate him, the said Renatus, to be head of the Mission in the Indies, in the place of Padre Thomas deceased. But that as the Board had already determined to continue Padre Severini to be Chief Pastor of the Church here, he should in no manner disobey our orders in that respect, but submit entirely to them; which the President had recommended to him punctually to observe, that thereby peace and good order might be preserved amongst the Fathers of the Church."

The following extract from a general letter from the Court of Directors dated London, 10th March, 1744, is the only announcement which we can find at this time respecting the Protestant Missionaries.

"The Society for Promoting Christian Knowledge having represented, there are some vacancies by the removal of Missionaries on your coast, we have permitted the Revd. Mr. Klein and the Revd. Mr. Breithaupt to take passage upon this ship, in order to carry on that good work among the Indians.

SAMUEL FEAKE &
MEMBERS OF COUNCIL."

The following proceedings of the new Nabob as regards the mints may be interesting to some of our readers.

"Saturday, 5th May, 1744. The President and Warehouse-keeper report to the Board, that they had endeavoured to dispose of some silver agreeable to Order of Consultation of the 28th of last month; but that they had found it impossible to do it on any tolerable terms owing to the country mints being all shut up by the Nabob's order, and all Shroffs' business thereby at a full stand. That it is reported that the Nabob intends shortly to issue out orders for rupees of twelve penny weight fine, to be only current hereafter in his Subahships: and to suppress those that are so now on account of their being of so low a touch as two penny weight worse, which the minters have brought them to by tampering with the officers of the Circar for some time past.

"The President also acquaints the Board that by his advices several of the minters from Covelong, St. Thomé and the other mints belonging to the Circar, had been to Arcot to represent to the Nabob the great loss that was yearly sustained to the Circar and them by the business done at our mint and that of Pondicherry; in order to move the Nabob to put a stop to them, and to take away the chops for the Arcot Rupees; but that he had given them no answer as yet, nor any ways interrupted us in our coinage or the French in theirs."

About this period, the French at Pondicherry seemed inclined to interfere with the trade of the English. The following extracts will explain themselves.

"Monday, 14th May, 1744. The President acquaints the Board, that the merchants had been with him two days past, and produced letters from their people in the Weaving Towns, advising that some persons from the French had been there to procure musters of our several sorts of middling and ordinary cloths, and to enquire the prices; and that they had given out as usual that a large quantity was wanted at Pondicherry. That thereupon he had ordered the merchants to send some persons immediately they could confide in, to know the truth, and what the French agents were about; that if they found any attempts were making to engage the weavers in their business, in prejudice of our Company, they should do their utmost to prevent it, which he thinks might be done with the less difficulty (unless the French should advance on the prices) as these weavers had been entirely employed by our merchants for several years; and he supposes the French coming into these parts for the ordinary sortments, to proceed from their being disappointed at Salem, from whence and from Worriapollam, and Chemanaickpollam, they have been supplied hitherto, and never before attempted any but fine cloths in these parts."

"Monday, 21st May, 1744. The Nabob has at length sent his Purwanna to the several mints of Circar, to coin Arcot Rupees of seven penny weight better than standard, and to be allowed twenty-seven per mill for the charge of coinage; and that these rupees are to be the current standard hereafter; but the Shroffs not being satisfied with that touch, or paying twenty-seven per mill instead of seventeen as before, have hitherto refused to coin any rupees."

"Monday, 28th May, 1744. The President acquaints the Board that the persons whom the merchants had sent in to the country on notice of the French brokers being at the Weaving Towns, are returned with an account that the French brokers and weavers had several meetings; and that several of the latter were inclined to engage with them, in order to get some ready money into their hands; but that our brokers had represented to them that if they offered to do so they would immediately apply to the Havildars and oblige them to pay what they stood indebted; that such a behaviour was shameful in them who had for several years worked only for the English; that if they desired a small advance of money, they should have it from them; all which with the assistance of the Havildars had settled the matter in our favour; and the Havildars had promised on behalf of their people that unless the French advanced in our prices, they should not carry away a piece of cloth from us; but in that case, the weavers were poor people and must make the most of their time and labour. The same persons add that before they came away the French brokers had left the Towns.

"The President reads a letter he received yesterday from Anawarodeen Khan, our Nabob; in which he desires to have silver to the amount of twenty thousand pagodas at the cheapest rate; and that for the future he may be acquainted with what silver is imported in this place before sale is made of it.

"The occasion of this letter, which we cannot but look upon as a very extraordinary one, we imagine, must proceed from the Nabob's resentment at the shroffs' behaviour in endeavouring to thwart his designs in having the rupee coin restored to what it was some years past; and therefore to convince them of his being in earnest, he is now resolved to coin those rupees himself, to circulate in the province; for which he now wants silver of us. But as negotiations of this sort are new, and for which there is no precedent, and may, if complied with, involve us, or those that succeed to the affairs of this Presidency, in many troubles and vexatious disputes with the country government, and if once began in this instance may be very difficult to put a stop to; that therefore we refer him to the merchants of this place, for what silver he may have occasion for now and in future, which the Nabobs of Arcot have hitherto done by their servants or persons residing in this place; and that we further represent to him, an answer to that part of his letter in which he desires to be informed of what silver is imported here before it is sold, that it would be the cause of delay in business, and might greatly detriment the person who has any to dispose of. This we hope will satisfy him, and it is probable the shroffs wili now make their peace with him, and submit to his will in this matter; and that he will then drop the design of coining himself. But however that be, that we by no means consent to the establishing any such custom or usage in the place of a tendency so prejudicial to the interest of it, the well carrying on of business, and against the freedom of trade allowed to every one here; that whilst we have the orders and authority of the Honorable Company to support us, we are determined not to give up the least point, wherein the general welfare is concerned at the instance of any one whomsoever.

"An answer to the Nabob's letter being hereupon prepared by the President is now read and approved of, copy of which is entered hereafter."

"*To Nabob Anwarodeen Khan Bahauder*.

"I have received your Excellency's letter, and observe the contents. As to the silver you have occasion for, I have enquired among the Merchants, and find that your Excellency by sending your servants may readily be supplied by them with the quantity you write for at the market price; and they will have all the assistance in my power when they come here for that purpose, as I take great pleasure in obliging your Excellency.

" As to what you are pleased to mention about first advising before any silver is sold, I beg leave to represent to your Excellency that such a method would very much impede the business of this place, and often greatly detriment the Merchant who brings silver here ; as sometimes his stay is not more than three or four days in his way to other parts, and therefore his affairs will not permit him to lose any time in exchanging his money. As your Excellency will, I presume, according to ancient custom, have some Merchants to reside here to act for your Excellency in the Circar business ; they will always be in the way of purchasing any silver, in like manner as the other persons employed in such negotiation here, and when recommended by you will be entitled to a particular regard. What can I say more?"

The following announcement is simple enough, but it was one pregnant of importance for India.

" Thursday, 31st May, 1744. About seven this evening anchored in our road the Honorable Company's ship " Winchester," Captain Gabrial Steward from England, last from the coast of Brazil." On board this ship was a young man destined to found the British Empire in the East. His name was ROBERT CLIVE. The voyage had been a long one, for the freshest letter she brought from the Court of Directors was dated 2nd March 1742.

The following illustrations of the progress of affairs at Arcot require no explanation.

" Saturday, 3rd June, 1744. The President acquaints the Board that he had been informed from Arcot, that the Nabob on the receipt of the President's letter on the affair of the silver seemed well satisfied to have that business go on in the same method as formerly; and that his head Shroff there had since appointed some persons here to transact all such as related to the Circar; which we hope will prevent any applications of that nature to us in future."

"Monday, 11th June, 1744. The present Nabob being as yet a stranger to most of the affairs of the province, and more especially to those relating to the European nations; and as there may be persons about him who from interest, or some other views, may represent to him things to our prejudice in many respects, at his first entering on his government and before he may be rightly informed of the real matters of fact; the President proposes to the Board, that as we are now sending a present to him as usual on his accession, we desire of Hodjee Addee to accompany it; and that he make use of this opportunity to discourse with the Nabob on such matters as may give him a knowledge of what most concerns our interest and the establishing a good opinion of us with him; as well as with his Dewan in whom he places an entire confidence and who executes his orders in general; the Nabob's age of eighty-five years not permitting him to do much himself. By these means we may hope to baffle any sinister designs intended against us; as well as prevent the Nabob's receiving any impressions to our prejudice; and as this gentleman Hodjee Addee is esteemed a person of an extraordinary good capacity and address, and we have all the reason to believe him perfectly devoted to us, that he may be very serviceable to us, and the sending him may answer very good purposes; which being the opinion of the Board, the President is desired to ask this favour of Hodjee Addee."

Another tragedy was carried out this year at Arcot. We have already noticed the murder of Subder Ali; we have now to note the murder of his son.

"Tuesday, 26th June, 1744. The President acquaints the Board that he had yesterday received an account from Arcot that on the 23rd instant the son of our late Nabob Suder Ali Khan, named Sahib Judda, was murdered there with some others of his relations and family by Edel Khan, a Patan, at the instigation of Mortez Ali Khan, the same person, who had killed the father in October 1742. That Mortez Ali had promised this Patan and some others, a lac of Rupees to destroy the Nabob, and another lac for doing the same to Sahib Judda, and four more; and by putting these persons out of the way he expected to have had it in his power to seize the government, and by sums of money to get it confirmed to him. The mosque was the place pitched on to put their design in execution against the Nabob. They had waited eleven days in expectation of seeing him there, but an indisposition had kept him from going: and the 22nd which was Friday when they perform service at the mosque he purposed to have gone, but having ordered our people to attend him that morning with the present, he was so curious as to open and look on every article, which took up two hours; and after our people were dismissed he sent to know if the service of the mosque was over, and word being brought that it was, he retired to his chamber, and providentially escaped from the wicked design formed against his life. The Patan and eleven of his companions were cut off immediately and two more executed one of whom confessed the whole affair, and had the obligation about him signed and sealed by Mortez Ali Khan, for the payment of the two lacs on their performing the above conditions.

"The Nabob hereupon sent for his son from Trichinopoly and doubled the guard at Arcot; and it is said is preparing to go against Vellore Fort, where Mortez Ali Khan is at present in order to bring him to justice."

CHAPTER XLVIII.

GOVERNORSHIP OF MR. NICHOLAS MORSE.

(Continued.)

1744—45.

On the 21st March, 1744, King George II. declared war against France, and on the 5th September the news reached Fort St. George. This event will sufficiently explain the following extracts.

"Saturday, 8th September, 1744. Agreed to advise the Gentlemen at the three Northern settlements, of war being declared with France; to caution them to be upon their guard, and to take the most effectual means for securing the Honorable Company's effects in case of any attempts from the enemy.

"For the more ready communicating any advices between us and Bengal during the war, it is agreed to place Tappy peons at the distance of about three Gentoo miles between this place and Masulipatam; to order Mr. Hallyburton to do the same from thence to Maddepollam; as Mr. Sanders from Maddepollam to Ingeram; and the Gentleman at Vizagapatam from thence to Ingeram Southward, and to Ganjam Northward. To which last place it is agreed to desire the Gentlemen in Bengal to place others as we are informed was practised in the last war."

This month is also marked by the circumstance that Robert Clive, writer, drew his first quarter's pay of £1 5s.; he being in the receipt of the magnificent salary of £5 per annum.

Our next extract illustrates a curious bit of honesty as regards the payment of the Town rent of 1200 pagodas to the Nabob Anawarodeen Khan.

"Tuesday, 25th September, 1744. The President acquaints the Board, that on some reference he had occasion a few days ago to make to the general books, he observed that the Town rent had not been paid for the year ending the 30th June 1743; and found upon inquiry that the same had not been demanded in the time of Mr. Benyon. From whence he was induced to think the late frequent changes in the Nabobship might have occasioned it to be forgotten; and he had therefore designed to propose to the Board whether the province being now more settled, it might not have a very good effect on the minds of the governing powers, with regard both to our Honorable Master's affairs as well as their reputations and our own, if we should at a proper time remind them of the omission, and offer payment of that year's rent. But that such his design was rendered abortive by the demand made of it yesterday: when he found that it had not escaped attention as above, but that the reason of our present Nabob's not demanding it with the last year's, was its being due to Coja Namah Tulla Khan's Jaggier; and that the death of his father had occasioned its lying so long undemanded. Ordered that 1200 pagodas be paid out of cash."

Towards the end of the year the attempts of the Mahrattas to recover Trichinopoly from the Nizam were beginning to excite alarm, as will be seen by the following extract.

"Monday, 10th December, 1744. The President acquaints the Board that he has received advice fram the Country that upon the repeated reports of the design of the Mahrattas to invade this and the adjacent provinces, our Nabob set out some days past to join his forces with those of the other Subahs of Corrapa and Cundanore, to oppose the Mahrattas; and that they are to be further assisted by a detachment from Nizam's army, which was already set out under the command of Syed Luskar Khan to meet the others at the passes. But the same advices imported also, that messengers have been dispatched from the United Subahs to offer the Mahrattas a pretty large sum of money; which it was judged by most people would be preferred by the King of Sattara (Sahoo Rajah) to the uncertain chance of a battle with the combined forces of those Subahs."

On the opening of the new year, a squadron of Englishmen-of-war was already on its way to the Coast of Coromandel. The extracts will explain themselves as they almost entirely refer to the preparations for defence, and to the communications which passed between Fort St. George and the Nabob.

"Tuesday, 18th January, 1745. The President produces to the Board a letter, which being opened and read, was found to be from the Secret Committee, bearing date the 18th April last, advising of some of his Majesty's ships of war being intended for these parts, and ordering us to supply the Captains with what money they may want for stores and provisions, and directing the rate of the exchange.

"The President then told the Board that the said letter was forwarded to him from Tranquebar, and came enclosed in one from Captain Edward Peyton, Commander of his Majesty's ship the "Medway," wherein he advised him of his leaving Madagascar in October, in company with Commodore Barnet in the "Deptford" and the "Preston;" and that on his arrival at Acheen the 23rd November in company with the "Dolphin," he found lying there, the "Favouritte," a French company's ship of fifty guns, of which he made prize; that on their leaving Acheen on the 14th December, they had taken the ship with them on their cruise, with the French Captain, his son, and the Purser; but that they had released the rest of the ship's company, being about one hundred and sixty men, on their parole not to bear arms against the King of Great Britain or his subjects for six months, and that the said men were come over on the Danes' ship to Tranquebar.

"That we may not be unprepared to comply with the commands of the Secret Committee in case of any of his Majesty's ships coming to this port, it is agreed and ordered that the Paymaster set about procuring a quantity of oxen and hogs; and to request of the Gentlemen of Bombay to supply us with about eight hundred or a thousand bags of Jamboosier wheat, which we believe will be a more acceptable and proper food for their men than rice.

"It being also considered that it will be much more convenient to have some place ready for the reception of the sick men that may come ashore from His Majesty's ships, than to mix them with those of the garrison; besides that the accommodations of an hospital are too confined even for our own people; it is agreed and ordered that the Paymaster, accompanied by the surgeons, do survey the granary on the Island, and report to the Board whether it may not be made to serve that purpose. Ordered also that the Paymaster get provided a quantity of hospital clothing, with cots, and other things necessary for the sick men."

Meantime, as will be seen by the following extract, the Mahrattas are still causing great alarm.

"Friday, 4th January, 1745. The President acquaints the Board, that he has this morning received advice from the country, that an army of Mahrattas consisting of 70,000 horse were advanced within four days' march of the Kistna; and that the King of Sattara (Sahoo Rajah) refusing the offers hitherto made by Nizam and the several Nabobs, demanded also Trichinopoly to be restored to him, besides the usual chout; the former of which having been refused them, it is apprehended they will endeavour to possess themselves of it by force of arms.

"As it is not unlikely the Mahrattas will take

their route through this province, it is agreed to caution the Gentlemen at St. David's to be sparing in their advances to their merchants, till we can learn with more certainty that matters are likely to be accommodated. It is agreed also to advise them to be on their guard; as the capture of the 'Favouritte' at Acheen may possibly put their Pondicherry neighbours upon some enterprise against them.

"The Paymaster acquaints the Board that pursuant to order of last Consultation he has been with the surgeons to survey the granary on the Island, which they find may be made fit for the reception of the men-of-war's sick people, by opening a few windows for the benefit of air, and some other small alteration, which he computes will not cost above 200 pagodas. Ordered that he set about them forthwith."

"Monday, 25th February, 1745. A petition of Peter Dencker and James Calvineer, two victualers of this Town read, containing proposals for furnishing the men of war that may come to this port with beef and pork; on condition that the Board advance them a sum of money upon their giving security for the repayment thereof by the 1st of October next; and permit them to make an enclosure on the Island for securing the cattle they buy with their provisions; offering also to take the oxen and hogs already provided by the Paymaster for that purpose in part of such advance.

"The said proposals being considered, and that thereby the risk of mortality and further charges will be saved to our Honorable Masters; and no ill convenience offering in objection; it is agreed to accept them, but with this proviso; that it shall not be understood to restrain any other persons who may be willing to supply his Majesty's ships with better provisions or on cheaper terms; and the Paymaster is accordingly ordered to advance them one thousand pagodas, including therein the amount of the live cattle he has provided in consequence of our resolution of the 1st of January; which he is likewise ordered to deliver them, taking their bond for the same with sufficient security for the repayment by the 1st of October next."

"Monday, 4th March, 1745. The President produces to the Board a letter in its translate he received from the Nabob the 2nd instant; which being read is ordered to be entered hereafter for our Honorable Master's notice; but for the remarks it is liable it is thought proper to suspend them till we write next to England."

From Nabob Anawarodeen Khan Bahadur, Subah of the Province at Madegiry near Bassawapatam, received March 2nd 1745.

"I am informed that there has been war declared between the Kings of England and France, by which means your Honor and the Governor of Pondicherry are likely to have disturbances with each other. But as the seaport towns belong to the Great Mogul, it is by no means proper that you and the French should quarrel and have disputes together there. There have been lately some disturbances in Bengal on account of the Germans; but it is very improper to have commotions raised in the sea-ports of Hindoostan which belong to his most sovereign Majesty the Great Mogul, and where nothing of this nature has ever been suffered. I must now advise you, therefore, that it will upon all accounts be best for both nations to live in peace and friendship with each other; and when your Europe ships arrive near the sea-ports to act hostilities, you will lay your positive orders on them not to fight there, for the end of these things will not be good.

"By God Almighty's grace, Ballajee Naick has been entirely defeated by the Mahomedan army, and run away out of their sight. But our army is in pursuit of the enemy, and by the blessing of God matters will be accommodated in a short time. What can I say more?"

"Monday, 11th March, 1745. The President acquaints the Board, that there is advice come in from the country of the Nabobs having had another engagement with the Mahrattas, in which a son-in-law of Ballajee Naick, the Mahratta General, was taken prisoner. Notwithstanding which, by the best intelligence he can get of the Mahratta's designs, they are still determined on the retaking of Trichinopoly; and it is believed will take their rout thither through the Biddanore country; in which case it is to be hoped the cloth towns of Worriarpollam and Chemanaickpollam, and the parts adjacent to Fort St. David, will escape their ravages."

"Monday, 25th March, 1745. The President lays before the Board a letter he received yesterday from Nabob Anawarodeen Khan; in which he mentions that having heard of the wars breaking out in Europe between the English and French nations, which might occasion some interruption to the trade of the Mogul subjects, he had therefore thought fit to grant the Moguls colours and his passes to the native subjects, as also to strangers; strictly forbidding any molestation to be offered to ships with such pass-ports and colours; otherwise that the aggressors must be answerable for any loss sustained.

"Upon which the Board observed that the French had, since the capture of the "Favoritte," been endeavouring to amuse the Nabob and his officers, that it had been their desire to promote pacific measures; and on the other side to represent us as the disturbers of the tranquility in India. That the ship they sent to Mocha in January had the Nabob's pass and colours, obtained as we may suppose with a design to embarrass us with the government; in case of her being taken by the men of war: since they must know they could not be a protection to that ship. That it appears to us, the Nabob is unacquainted with the laws and customs of European nations in such cases; or he must have judged it of little purpose to send orders of this nature, for restraining the shipping of our nation from acting offensively in the seas he mentions, notwithstanding the pass and colours granted by the Moors; which therefore we think proper to represent to him, that he may not take it ill when any accidents of this kind happen, and that he may be assured our ships are only acting conformable to what the laws and customs of

European nations have made a rule for their conduct on such occasions."

"Agreed that an answer be drawn up to the above mentioned purpose to be sent to the Nabob; and that Hodjee Addee be desired to explain to him more fully these matters, the better to satisfy him in this point, and to prevent any designs of the French to our prejudice; persons in his post being generally too apt to expect an implicit obedience to their orders, which the nature of this case will not admit."

"Monday, 15th April, 1745. The President acquaints the Board, that on his receiving advice late last night of the Mahrattas having plundered some of the towns on this side of Arcot, he had this morning ordered all the cloths in from the Washing towns, which is approved."

"Monday, 15th April, 1745. The President acquaints the Board that he had received advice this morning, that an army of 150,000 Mahrattas had passed by Ganjam in their march Northward towards Bengal."

"Monday, 29th April, 1745. The President acquaints the Board that by a Dutch ship lately arrived on this coast from Batavia, it is reported that Commodore Barnet had taken the three French homeward bound China ships, as the "Winchelsea" Privateer had the "St. Benoit" another French ship, bound from China for the Islands; and that this ship left at Batavia, the Commodore the Lord Northesk, the "Winchelsea" Privateer, and her consort, with their abovementioned prizes; and our Honourable Masters' ships "Wager" and "Porto Bello." The "Medway" and "Dolphin" had not then joined the Commodore."

"Monday, 13th May, 1745. The President acquaints the Board that on account of the Nabob's absence from Arcot, and for some other reasons, Hodjee Addee had advised him to defer the sending away the answer to the Nabob's letter he produced to us the 25th of March; but that it being now thought proper to send it, the same is read and approved and the said letter and answer ordered to be copied hereafter."

"*To His Excellency Nabob Anawarodeen Khan Bahauder, May the* 14*th* 1745.

"I received your Excellency's perwanna, in which you are pleased to mention that as there is war commenced between the English and French nation, that you had in order to prevent any molestation happening to the ships belonging to the subjects of His Most Excellent Majesty the Great Mogul empowered Hodjee Abdul Hadee, Foujdar of Mylapoor, to deliver out passes in your name to the subjects of his said majesty, as well as to strangers; and also to wear the Moors colours in their voyages to and fro in the several ports of India. By virtue of which you are pleased to direct that they are not to be interrupted in their voyages; and if they should be that the persons so offending will be liable to your displeasure. To which with all respect I beg leave to say, that the amity that subsists between the high and mighty Emperor the Great Mogul, and his Majesty of England, will not permit the English subjects to offer any violence or acts of hostility to the ships belonging to the subjects of the great Mogul. May it please your Excellency, that sometimes differences arise between the several princes in Europe, as particularly there is now between the English and French; in which case if the French make use in their trade of the Moors colours and passes, pretending thereby that they belong to the subjects of the Great Mogul: the English Commanders will notwithstanding make prizes of such ships as will the French do the same to the English on the like occasions, should they also have the Moors passes or colours. Your Excellency will be assured that in these matters each nation acts agreeable to their laws and in obedience to the orders of their respective Sovereigns. What can I say more?"

"Tuesday, 4th June, 1745. The President acquaints the Board he has received intelligence that the French at Pondicherry are making great preparations to act offensively, as well as defensively; and that they expect a number of men from the Islands which may put them upon some enterprise; that their neighbourhood to Fort St. David, and the uncertainty of his Majesty's squadron coming on the coast to give us any assistance for some time, being considered; as also that the success of the latter to the Eastward may probably excite the enemy's resentment; and Fort St. David from its nearness, and the quantity of cloth lying there embaled, not improbably become their first object: – He therefore proposes to the consideration of the Board, whether it may not be a means to abate the enemy's hopes, and render them less forward to undertake any thing against Fort St. David, to get all the cloth away from thence we can. The Board being of opinion with the President, that the getting the cloth from St. David may check the enemy's designs, if they have formed any against that place; it is agreed to take up the "Success Gally" for that service and to order the "Mermaid" to accompany her."

"Monday, 10th June, 1745. The President acquaints the Board that he has called us together at this time, to communicate two letters he has received to-day; one sent by Mr. Hinde to Captain Barton by a catamaran, which not meeting with him had brought it hither; the other from Mr. Hinde to himself, and brought in by peons; on the receipt whereof he had appointed this meeting.

"The said letters being read, purported as follows:

"Captain Barton,

"Sir,—Having just now received advice from Pondicherry, that the French are sending off ammunition, and manning a large number of boats with Europeans on some secret expedition; I thought proper to send you this advice by a catamaran dispatched on purpose; that you may keep constantly on your guard, and not permit any boats to come near you, and particularly in the night time that you may keep a good look out. There is reported to be in company with these boats, a sloop carrying Danish colours. If this letter meets you (as I hope it will) when you have perused it, please to forward it by the same catamaran to the Governor of Madras.

I am,
Sir,
Your Most Humble Servant,
JOHN HINDE."

Fort St. David, 8th June, 1745."

"The President added, that believing the Board would think it proper on this advice that the inhabitants should be in readiness upon any alarm; he had caused them to be summoned into the Fort this afternoon, where he had ordered arms to be ready to be delivered them."

"Monday, 10th June, 1745. The inhabitants being then called in, the President acquainted them with his purpose in summoning them, and that they would find arms prepared for them below in the Fort; which they should carry home to their houses, and with which upon hearing a gun fired between the hours of eight at night and five in the morning, they were to repair to the parade before the main guard, where they would receive the necessary orders from Mr. Monson their commanding officer.

"As the French are hourly expecting a number of men from the Islands to come to Pondicherry and none of Commodore Barnet's squadron yet appearing: and as the investment, sending money to St. Davids, and other services, employ more than one hundred of the peons, who are thereby absent from the Town; and many of our military in the hospital; it is thought proper to hire for the present two hundred good peons, if to be got, from the several Poligars round us; those to be had in Town being not likely to be of any service."

"Wednesday, 3rd July, 1745. The President acquaints the Board with his having received a letter this morning from Commodore Barnet of the 26th June; who writes him that he has been cruizing off the Fryar's Hood near a month, without seeing any shipping in that time, except the Danes ship by which he sent that letter, and that the 'Lively' man-of-war had joined him the 8th April at Batavia.

"The Commodore having also intimated to the President his intention to send some of his squadron shortly to Fort St. David, it is agreed to dispatch the 'Mermaid' thither this evening, with as much of the Bengal flour, and biscuit, and Surat wheat, as she can take in, directing the Deputy Governor and Council to set their bakers to work to grind the wheat into flour, and to return the 'Mermaid' to us with what bales they have ready."

"Monday, 8th July, 1745. As the arrival of Commodore Barnet's squadron in the neighborhood, will probably deter the French from the thoughts of any enterprise; it is agreed to discontinue the expense of the Poligar peons we thought proper to entertain the 10th of last month."

"Monday, 5th August, 1745. The President acquaints the Board, that he has intelligence given him that the French at Pondicherry are frequently sending letters to the Nabob, and employing their agents at Arcot, to complain against the English for having taken a ship under Moors colours and pass, and for being the destroyers of the trade, of the Mogul's subjects on this coast; and that our ships of war keep all their ships from coming to their ports, whereby the Circar is deprived of many advantages, particularly of the profits on their investment, with many other things too tedious and of too little importance to mention here. That thereupon he had thought it proper to write to Hodjee Addee, now at Arcot, fully concerning these matters; that he might lay a true state of the case before his Excellency, and the French be thereby prevented in their designs of spiriting up the Nabob against us; which they are aiming at in hopes to recover their money; to make it an excuse for their not paying the large sums they are indebted to several persons concerned with the Circar; and to impede us in carrying on our investment, our success in which under their present circumstances they cannot see but with the greatest concern, and therefore spare no pains or leave no artifice untried to carry their point against us."

"Saturday, 10th August, 1745. This evening anchored in our road from the Southward his Majesty's ships "Preston" of fifty guns, Commanded by the Right Honorable the Earl of Northesk; and "Lively" of twenty guns by Captain Henry Roswell; the former being saluted by the Fort with thirteen guns which were immediately returned. Went off to the former, Mr. Thomas Eyre, third of Council resident; to the latter Mr. Joseph Fowke; with compliments from the President to the commanders, who declined coming ashore in obedience to orders from the Commodore to make the best of their way."

"Monday, 12th August, 1745. The President reads to the Board a letter received from the Nabob, in which he mentions his having sent Hodjee Addee to settle the disputes, as he terms them, between us and the French; who being, as we suppose, greatly alarmed at our men-of-war being on the coast, are making an assiduous application to his Excellency for his protection; and we believe the chief intent of this is to draw from us a promise that no hostility shall be committed against the French; of this we shall be further informed when the President has discoursed with Hodjee Addée on the errand he is sent."

"Friday, 16th August, 1745. The President acquaints the Board, that since last consultation he had discoursed with Hodjee Addee on the Nabob's last letter, and the message he brought from him. Upon which he has occasion to observe to them, that what the Nabob expects from the English seems to be very unreasonable, and entirely out of our power to comply with; it being no less than that there should be no hostility committed by the men-of-war in the road of Pondicherry, the ports belonging to the Great Mogul, or, along the sea coast; although in his former letter he had only insisted on the land. Upon which the President had told Hodjee Addee, in order for him to lay the same before the Nabob, that this was dictating to us in a manner it is impossible for us to submit to; that he had been already told the men of war were under separate and particular orders; that we could not answer for their conduct any further than that it would be no otherwise than conformable to the rules of war, and custom of nations; and that there was no intention in the English to disturb the peace of his Government. Our differences were with the French, in consequences of war declared by them in Europe, which must of course continue till it was the pleasure of our respective Sovereigns to put an end to it; after which the President read a letter designed as an answer to the Nabob's, which is approved and both are as entered hereafter.

"The Nabob having some days ago solemnized the marriage of his daughter with Keradeen Khan, sent the President on the occasion a horse and seerpaw, as he had done the same to the Governor of Pondicherry, who had made him a present to the amount of 3000 pagodas; as also one to the Dewan; which appears to be the more extraordinary, as this is the first instance of a Nabob's complimenting the European Governors on the marriage of their daughters. We are therefore inclined to think the French have some other view in making so large a one at this time; and their daily solicitations at the durbar for his protection, may be considered as the first and grand motive which not being our case at present, there is the less call on us to be so very liberal in an affair which appears without precedent. However we cannot think it prudent not to make him some acknowledgment; and therefore agree to the sending him some gold mohurs, and a piece of silver plate, which are proper to be presented on such occasions, to the amount of about 350 pagodas."

The letter of the Nabob to Governor Morse was as follows.

"*From Nabob Anawarodeen Khan Bahauder Subah of the province of Arcot. Received* 11*th August*, 1745.

"I have been lately informed that some English ships are arrived in the road of Tevenapatam, with design to inflame your differences with the French; and that they are waiting there for their ships. I have therefore ordered Hodjee Abdul Hadee to deliver you my taukeed, to put an end to the dispute between you; and desire your will, agreeable to what he will propose to you, avoid making any disturbance in these parts. Otherwise you will be called upon to answer for it hereafter. I have also laid my taukeed upon the French about this business, and by their letters I understand that they are inclined to peace. What can I say more?"

The following is Governor Morse's reply.

"*To Nabob Anawarodeen Khan Bahauder*.

"I have received your Excellency's letter, in which you are pleased to mention to me that the arrival of the English ships of war at Tevenapatam, had occasioned some alarm; and that you had therefore sent Hodjee Abdul Hadee to me to deliver your taukeed to put an end to the disputes between the English and French. I observe by this that your Excellency is no stranger to the motives for their assiduous application to you at this time. But I was in hopes what I have had the honour to say to your Excellency in my former letters on this subject, would have been fully satisfactory; to those I beg leave to refer, as they contain all that is in my power to engage for; other points your Excellency will readily judge must be determined by the good pleasure of our respective Sovereigns. In the mean time, give me leave to ask the favour of your Excellency, that you will not suffer our enemies to amuse you with any false insinuations to our prejudice; thereby to create a misunderstanding between Arcot and Chennapatnam. I may with the greater reason desire this, as the French nation have from time immemorial never scruple to obtain their ends by false colouring and artifice, when force proved defective on their side. By their intrigues and break of treaties, they have set all Europe in a flame; and they would be willing some of the sparks should take in these parts; but by your Excelleney's penetration I am persuaded they will be disappointed in such designs, and that it will end in their confusion."

We now continue our diary as extracted from the consultations.

"Saturday, 17th August, 1745. The President acquaints the Board, that having seen a letter from the Nabob to Hodjee Addee, wherein the latter is ordered to present the Nabob's service to the President, and to acquaint him with his intention of being at St. Thomé on Monday next; he had thereupon sent the Chief Dubash and Mullah as customary, one day's journey to meet the Nabob, with his compliments, and to attend him to St. Thomé."

"Monday, 19th August, 1745. Whilst the Board were sitting, notice was given by signals from St. Thomé of the Nabob's arrival; whereupon he was saluted with sixty-one guns; and before they rose the Chief Dubash and Mullah returned from thence, and acquainted the President that the Nabob had received his compliments in a very kind manner; and on his arrival at St. Thomé had dismissed them with his in return to the President.

"It being usual on these occasions for two of the Council to wait on the Nabob from the President, Messrs Eyre and Fowke were accordingly desired to go on that service, and to be ready to proceed to St. Thomé at three this afternoon.

"The Nabob having with him his son Abdul Vahaib Khan, and Sampetrow his Dewan, to all of whom we are by custom obliged to make presents; the President and Warehouse-keeper are desired to provide such things as they are informed will be most acceptable, and are to be met with in Town, to the amount of about 2000 pagodas in the whole; including what small matters must necessarily be given to the under officers and servants."

"Monday, 19th August, 1745. At three this afternoon, set out for St. Thomé under the usual ceremony, Messrs. Thomes Eyre and Edward Fowke, with the President's compliments to the Nabob on his arrival there, from whence they returned about six, bringing with them a horse and seerpaw for the President."

"Friday, 30th August, 1745. Arrived his Majesty's ships "Medway's" prize, Captain Thomas Griffin, the "Southward" with Commodore Barnet on board, who was saluted with fifteen guns which the ship returned. Mr. Eyre and Lieutenant Gingins being sent off with the President's compliments to the Commodore, he came ashore in the evening; and was met at the Sea Gate by the President and Council, and by them conducted to the Garden house; where being arrived, he was again saluted from the Fort with fifteen guns. After a short stay there he returned with the President to sup with him in the Fort."

"Monday, 2nd September, 1745. The President then told the Board, that being informed the orders from our Honorable Masters to Bengal, concerning the provision to be made for the commanders of his Majesty's squadron in India who might go thither, were to receive and treat the Commodore with the honours paid to a President, and the other Captains as seconds; and that preparations were accordingly made there for entertaining them in a handsome manner. He (the President) had caused the Garden house to be fitted up, two palankeens to be new mounted, servants to be in readiness, live provisions to be laid in, and several other preparations to be made, necessary to the lodging and boarding the Commodore, and such other Captains of the squadron as may come hither. Being guided in this by what had passed when Mr. Matthews was here; but that since the receipt of our Honorable Masters' orders of the 21st December last "to supply the Cap-

"tains with Madeira wine for their own table "at prime cost," he has been under some doubt whether the commands of the Secret Committee under the 18th April 1744 "to show them all due civility and respect" would warrant so extensive a construction, as the providing for them at the Company's charge; besides which it has been hinted to him, that Commodore Barnet has since his arrival dropped some intimation of his being told in England, it was to be so; and expressed some uneasiness at his not having been made certain in that respect. He, the President, therefore desired the thoughts of the Board, how it will be most becoming to act on the occasion.

"A reference being thereupon had to the Paymaster's accounts, Consultations, and letters of 1722 and 1723, there appeared several items of disbursements on account of Commodore Matthews and Captain Main; which indeed we don't find any order from England to warrant, nor on the other hand any disapproval of it from thence when done; and are therefore induced to believe it was at that time intended in England, that Mr. Matthews and the Captains with him, should have their expenses ashore in the Company's settlements defrayed at their charge. And though we are not the proper judges of the merit of the services this squadron has already done to our Honorable Master's affairs in India; yet we cannot help thinking those services, and the zeal the Commodore expresses for the promoting their interest, will be seen by them in so favourable a light, as to justify our putting that construction on their order . " to show the Captains all due civility and respect ;" and upon the whole are unanimously of opinion, that when they are pleased to consider that a regard to their reputation and credit is the only motive by which we are biassed in it, they will not be displeased at our taking that charge upon them. It is therefore agreed to do it, and the President is desired as he sees occasion, to satisfy the Commodore in any doubts he may discover him to entertain on that score."

"Monday, 25th November, 1745. The President acquaints the Board, that he had received advice from the Nabob's camp at Trichinopoly, that a letter had been sent to the Nabob from Nizam-ul-Mulk, directing him to immediately repair to Arcot, and from thence to march and join the Subahs of Corrapa and Cundanore, in order to oppose the passage of the Mahrattas ; who were gathering a number of troops with a design to invade the Carnatic country ; that the Nabob had thereupon come to terms with the Tanjoreans, and had left his son Mauphuze Khan in those parts, and was set out for Arcot"

"Wednesday, 11th December, 1745. Between 4 and 6 this afternoon, anchored in our road from England His Majesty's ships "Harwich" of fifty guns, commanded by Captain Philip Garteret ; and "Winchester" of fifty guns, by the Right Honorable the Lord Thomas Bertie ; with the following of the Honorable Company's ships under their convoy, viz.

The Scarborough, Captain George Westcott senr.

Lincoln, Captain John Blake.
Admiral Vernon, Captain Benjamin Webster.
Kent, Captain William Robson.
Royal George, Captain Thomas Field.

"The Fort having saluted the King's ships with thirteen guns, which was returned by the "Harwich," Mr. Savage went off to that ship, and Mr. Pigot to the "Winchester," with the President's compliments to the Commanders, and to invite them ashore, which they excuse themselves from till next morning.

"Thursday, 12th. This morning Captains Garteret and Lord Thomas Bertie, being come on shore were saluted with thirteen guns."

"Tuesday, 17th December, 1745. About 11 this forenoon, anchored in our road His Majesty's ship "Deptford" Captain John Moor, under commodore Curtis Barnet Esq., from sea; being saluted before at anchor by the "Harwich" and "Winchester" which she returned them by the five Company's ships, when at anchor by the Fort; which, and the salute of the Company's ships, she answered separately.

"On sight of the Commodore's broad pendant, Mr. Savage went off with the President's compliments, and to invite him ashore, which he complied with at five in the afternoon."

"Sunday, 29th December, 1745. The President delivers to the Secretary to be read, the following extract of a letter he received last night from Mr. Hinde (Deputy Governor of Fort St. David) of the 26th instant

" Since the foregoing, I have had all the peo-
" ple almost in Cuddalore with me, who just re-
" ceived advice that Mr. Dupleix has prepared
" sixty mussoolas, and is determined to attack
" Cuddalore. Nothing but his being mad can
" make this scheme feasible ; but however as des-
" pair may make him so, and as too much secu-
" rity is often attended with ill-consequences, I
" take the liberty to give it as my opinion, that
" this place ought to be reinforced immediately.
" Especially as it can be done by sea if he makes
" any attack on Cuddalore."

" The President told the Board that he last night communicated the contents of the said letter to Commodore Barnet, who very readily offered to send the " Deptford" if it was thought necessary to lie off Cuddalore ; and to carry any reinforcement of men we might determine to send thither ; and he had now called us together to take our opinion on the matter.

" Though the Board were backward to believe that Mr. Dupleix will attempt any thing against Fort St. David or Cuddalore, whilst we have such assistance as at present in our road, and to windward of him ; yet as our accepting the Commodore's offer, and sending a party of men to St. David's may quiet the minds of the people in Cuddalore, and on rejecting in case of any accident subject us to deserve blame ; it is therefore agreed to accept it and to send on board the " Deptford" immediately a party of fifty men under the command of Lieutenant Gingin, subject to the orders of the Deputy Governor and Council: to whom it is agreed to signify that, if they are not absolutely necessary ashore, we would have them sent on board the "Admiral Vernon" when she arrives there, and to continue on board whilst he is taking in her cargo for Europe.

"Ordered that the said party of men be drafted and sent on board with the necessary provisions as soon as possible."

CHAPTER XLIX.

CAPTURE AND OCCUPATION OF FORT SAINT GEORGE BY THE FRENCH.

1746-48.

In 1746, the first period in the history of Madras was brought to a close. In 1745, the English squadron under Commodore Barnet had been cruizing off the coast of Coromandel and so far alarmed the French, that M. Dupleix had prevailed on the Nabob Anawarodeen to interfere for the prevention of hostilities. The approach of the North East monsoon obliged Commodore Barnet to take refuge in the harbour of Mergui on the coast of Tenasserim; but in January 1746 he again returned to the coast of Coromandel. About March, Commodore Barnet appeared off Fort St. David; and though Governor Morse had given his aid to the Nabob that no hostilities should be carried on by land excepting in self-defence, yet M. Dupleix thought proper to represent to the Nabob that the English at Fort St. David were preparing to make a land attack upon Pondicherry. Intelligence of this proceeding having reached the ears of Governor Morse, he dispatched the following letter to Arcot on the 17th March 1746.

"*To Anawarodeen Khan Bahauder,*
Nabob of Arcot.

"Your Excellency will be so good to allow me a pardon for giving you this trouble. But having been informed that the Governor of Pondicherry has lately represented to your Excellency, that the English at Fort St. David had a design to attack the Fort of Pondicherry by land; which I suppose is done at this time to serve some purpose of theirs, or to make us appear to you in a false light, as persons that are not inclined to show a regard to your commands; when at the same time it will appear we have paid all deference to them. Your Excellency must have known this from Maphuze Khan, and therefore want no further evidence that the French some short time past, actually marched with a body of forces and large guns, and with other implements of war, to the edge of the Fort St. David's bounds; but on the King's ships appearing off their port, they thought fit to call in their troops, being also persuaded thereto by Maphuze Khan, who also wrote to the Deputy Governor of Fort St. David not to resent this insult of the French. Your Excellency will find his desires were complied with, and the Governor of Pondicherry must be left to answer for a conduct in express disobedience to your commands. The English have a just sense of the performance of their promises; and having given them to your Excellency that they would not become the first aggressors, they would not offer to trifle with so great a person as your Excellency; and therefore they hope your Excellency will suffer no insinuations of our enemies to have any weight with you; but that the purity of our intentions will be distinguished in a favourable manner; and that your regard for us will be still preserved, which will be always esteemed with grateful acknowledgments. May God Almighty long preserve your Excellency for the benefit of your friends and country."

On the third of April, Governor Morse received the following reply from Arcot:

"*From Nabob Anawarodeen Khan Bahauder at Arcot.*

"I received your agreeable letter acquainting me that you and the Governor of Tevenapatam pay a great regard to my orders, and have made use of no hostilities in his Majesty's sea port towns, and desiring that the Governor of Pondicherry may be enjoined also to behave in like manner. This pleases me highly, and I assure you that your behaviour in every respect is very satisfactory to me. You may depend upon it, that the Governor of Pondicherry shall not be suffered to behave in a different manner. I have sent him my taukeed in such a way as is necessary upon this occasion. Pray believe me to be your friend and let me have the pleasure of hearing frequently of your welfare."

In the following April a ship belonging to Commodore Barnet's squadron came into collision with a French ship in the neutral Danish port of Tranquebar. The Frenchman had anchored in the port, when the Englishman, named the "King's Frigate" entered the port likewise. The Frenchman then commenced firing upon the English Frigate, and some shot also came from the Danish Fort. Upon this the Frenchman was captured by the English but driven ashore; whereupon the Danish Governor of Tranquebar protested against what he called a breach of the neutrality, and even claimed the French ship as a wreck. The following indignant letter from Commodore Barnet to the Danish Governor sufficiently explains the state of the case.

"*To Mr. Bonsack,*

Governor of Tranquebar.

"If I could have got your letter of the 12th translated sooner, you would have had my answer to it before now.

"The neutrality of your road I readily allow. I never intended the least violation of it; and that it was not violated by my officers is fully proved by your own confession. You own the French ship fired two shots at the King's Frigate, when she was going into your road, and steering to anchor, in such a manner as could give no room to suspect any design of attacking the French ship. But those shots you say were fired as a signal; a very extraordinary manner of making signals indeed, and I suppose the several volleys of small arms, which she fired while the Frigate was anchoring, were also signals and not intended to do any harm. I am afraid, Sir, it will appear that if you intended to maintain the neutrality of your road, you did not take the proper method. As the French Captain had put himself under your protection, and could be protected by nothing but my respect for the King of Denmark's flag you should have strictly enjoined him to trust to your protection; and not fire, unless he was actually attacked. You should, I think, have sent an officer to the Captain of the king's Frigate, to enquire the reason of his coming into the road, and told him not to anchor near that ship which was under your protection; and therefore you was obliged to protect her as far as you could. Had you taken this method, the French ship would not have fired, and the Captain of the Frigate would have satisfied you, that he had no orders to attack her, and was only directed to observe her motions. Thus, Sir, the neutrality might have been preserved, and all that has happened been prevented. But you took no such precautions. The French ship fired at the Frigate as she was steering to anchor astern of her. Upon which the Frigate endeavoured to anchor along side, but the anchor not falling clear off the side, she fell upon her quarter before she could let go her other anchor; and all this time the Frenchman continued firing volleys of small arms into the Frigate, and one gun at least was fired at her from the Fort, before she fired a single musket; and the moment the Frigate fired her first gun, you began to fire at her from all parts. The second Frigate which was ordered to anchor without, seeing so smart a fire from the Fort on the first Frigate, stood in to succour her; and soon after he had given his fire, yours and that of the French ship ceased. The Frigate then let off, till the insolence of the Frenchman in firing into a small unarmed boat, obliged them to give another before they could take possession.

"Upon the whole, Sir, it must be plain to all impartial persons, that the English broke not the neutrality, nor had any intention to break it. The French began the hostilities; they broke the neutrality, and had you been really neuter yourself, you would immediately have fired at the French ship; not at the English, who never fired a gun till called upon by the law of nature to do it in their own defence.

"I did not write my letter of the 30th past till I was fully satisfied. I had reason to complain of your partiality; and the account sent me by the Captain and officers of the first Frigate, has since been confirmed by two young gentlemen of this ship, who were on board the Frigate, by accident, and no ways concerned in or accountable for what was done. They assure me the Frenchman was firing his musketry into the Frigate. One or two shots from the Fort passed between the Frigate's main and mizen masts, and this before she fired even one musket. That some shot from the Frigate went on shore is very possible; but that it was not the direction or intention of the officers you may believe, as I have assured you they had my orders to make no return to your fire. But I will not go so far as to say that the seamen, finding your shot coming thick among them, may not have returned some. In short, Sir, I continue to think that your partiality, or neglecting to take proper precautions for preserving the neutrality, occasioned the French to break it; and therefore you alone are accountable for all that has happened; who instead of resenting properly the behaviour of the French Captain, attempt to justify it by poorly pretending that the shot fired into the Frigate were not designed to offend, but only meant as signals; and then unjustly endeavouring to fix the breach of the neutrality on the English, though it is evident they never intended to commit any hostilities in your road; and you may imagine that if I had been inclined to violent measures I should have gone to work in another manner.

"I am surprized you could think of laying claim to the ship as a wreck. You say she was deserted by her crew. Was it because they were afraid of drowning in her? Did not the English drive them out of her and take possession immediately? The ship and all that was taken out of her. She attacked the King's Frigates under your cannon, without any sort of reason, and is absolntely the property of the captors; and from you I expect a fair and full account of all that was carried on shore that night, and that the whole, as well as the ship, be preserved as English property to be disposed off as I shall direct.

I am, Sir,

Your most humble servant,

CURTIS BARNET.

"Harwich," off Fort St. David, 6th April 1746."

The foregoing letter, with copies of all the dispatches which were exchanged on this occasion were sent home for the consideration of the Court of Directors. The result is not recorded. The same month Commodore Barnet died. The same month we also learn that Robert Clive, writer, was posted to a place in the Accountant's Office. But great events were looming in the distance, and Clive was destined shortly to occupy a more important position.

On the 30th of April 1746, the Consultation Books are brought abruptly to a close. From that date until the 13th of November 1749, there is a complete blank in the Consultations. The cause of this is fully detailed in the pages of Orme. In the opening of 1746, it was already known at Madras that a French squadron under M. Labourdonnais was preparing at the Mauritius with designs against the English settlements in India. In June the squadron appeared. Some obstinate actions ensued between M. Labourdonnais and Mr. Peyton who had succeeded Commodore Barnet in the command. The result was that Mr. Peyton was compelled to sail to Trincomallee to refit; and M. Labourdonnais after refitting at Pondicherry, sailed away to Fort St. George.

The English now called upon the Nabob to fulfil his promise of restraining the French in their turn from committing hostilities against them by land. It seems however that Governor Morse failed to accompany this application with a present of money; and consequently the Nabob did not interest himself sufficiently in the matter, to prevent the French from carrying out their undertaking. On the 18th of August the French squadron appeared and cannonaded the town of Madras, but without doing any damage. Meantime, the Garrison at Fort St. George was anxious for the return of the English squadron from Trincomallee. But on the 23rd of August the whole settlement was thrown into a state of consternation bordering on despair, by the intelligence that Mr. Peyton had returned from Trincomâllee, but had passed Madras and Pulicat, and gone on to Bengal.

The catastrophe which threatened Madras was now at hand. On the 3rd of September the French squadron again appeared, and a force of 1900 men were landed including 1,100 Europeans, 400 Caffres, and 400 Indians disciplined in the European fashion. At that time the Black Town was close to the walls of White Town. On the 7th M. Labourdonnais commenced bombarding White Town from a battery of nine mortars erected to the westward, about 500 yards from the walls; whilst the ships cannonaded the place from the sea. On the 8th another battery of five mortars was erected on the south; and the town was bombarded without intermission. Next morning two English deputies went to the French camp; but Labourdonnais who was afraid of the return of the English squadron, insisted that the town should be given up at once on his own terms, and threatened a general assault in case of refusal. The deputies went away, and the bombardment was resumed; but in the evening there was another conference, and another cessation of the bombardment. Next morning, that is the morning of the 10th of September, the Garrison capitulated on the terms proposed by Labourdonnais, viz., that the English should surrender themselves prisoners of war, and that the town should be immediately delivered up; but it was stipulated that the place should be afterwards ransomed, and Labourdonnais promised that he would settle the ransom on easy and moderate terms. How this capitulation was subsequently broken by M. Dupleix who refused to restore the town upon any terms whatever; how Dupleix made his peace with the Nabob by promising to deliver up the town to him; and how the English at Madras were carried prisoners to Pondicherry, whilst Fort St. David became the head of all the English settlements on the coast of Coromandel:—all these and much more are written in the chronicles of Robert Orme, which work we most strongly recommend to the perusal of all readers of Madras in the Olden Time.

We now turn to such records as are at our disposal, namely, the general letters which passed between Mr. Hinde, Deputy Governor of Fort St. David and the Court of Directors. The following dispatch was sent home by Mr. Hinde on the 17th October, 1746, within six weeks of the capture of Madras by the French.

"The unfortunate occasion of this unexpected address from us, is to advice your Honours of the loss of your valuable settlement of Madras, which to our unspeakable concern is now in the possession of our enemies, the French. As the gentlemen there seem to think the absence of His Majesty's squadron (which they no doubt depended upon for assistance) greatly conduced to this misfortune ; we shall give an account of what we know for certainty of their motions only, and leave your Honors to form judgment without presuming to give any of our own.

"The 29th April, Mr. Barnet departed this life at this place, (Fort St. David,) when all the ships were here or near us, but the "Winchester." Lord Thomas Bertie, who was expected daily from Bombay, and arrived the 25th May ; from which time Captain Peyton, who then commanded the squadron as senior Captain, determined on going to refit his ship the "Medway," which was very leaky, at Trincomalle Bay on the island of Ceylon, and to take the whole squadron with him. The 30th your Honors' ship the "Princess Mary" arrived ; on whom we had orders to send to Madras what bales we had ready, and to receive from Lord Thomas Bertie sixty chests of treasure brought from Bombay on your Honors' account ; to keep what we wanted for the use of this settlement, and to send the remainder on the "Princess Mary," but not to detain her longer in our road than the squadron stayed there. In pursuance of which, we kept sixty chests here, and loaded the remainder on that ship, and prevailed on Captain Peyton to stay till the 9th June ; but it happening to blow very fresh at that time we could not load more than two hundred and twenty-two bales, which as it has since proved was very fortunate. The 9th she sailed for Madras under convoy of His Majesty's ship the "Lively" ; as did the rest of the squadron for Trincomallee. On the 17th Captain Peyton wrote to Mr. Hinde, (Deputy Governor of Fort St. David,) from Negapatam, that as they were just got to the bay. The "Preston's" Bow-sprit was sprung. and she could carry no sail; for which reason they were obliged to bear away for that place in order to refit her, and then return to Trincomallee. On the 25th at daybreak, from the mast-head in Negapatam road they made out several ships in the offing, to which they went out and found them to be nine French ships; but the winds being very light, they could not get up with each other till half past four in the evening, at which time an engagement began, and lasted till about seven, when it grew dark. The next morning they were near one another, and continued so all the day. At four in the afternoon Captain Peyton summoned a Council of war, where it was agreed not to engage the enemy, but to proceed for Trincomallee bay, as the French did for Pondicherry, and arrived there the 27th. In the English squadron were fourteen killed and forty-six wounded; but not one killed or hurt in the "Medway." On the French side we cannot learn those particulars for any certainty. Their squadron consisted of the "Achilles," a seventy-gun ship, six Company's ships, and two country ships. The "Achilles" with three of them left Europe together in April was twelve months. Two of them were returning ships, detained at the Islands (Mauritius and Bourbon) for this purpose, and all reinforced as much as they could there. Captain Peyton kept the squadron at Trincomallee till the beginning of

August, when he came on the coast, and appeared off Negapatam the 6th. The French squadron, consisting of eight ships (one being gone to Bengal, and is since lost in that river with two hundred and eighty Europeans), weighed from Pondicherry the 24th July for the Southward; and were then in that road, stood out to meet the English squadron, which stood to the southward from them, and the French then returned. The 7th both squadrons did the same, as likewise the 8th and 9th. The 10th the English disappeared, on which the French returned, and on the 13th anchored in Pondicherry road. The 17th the eight ships weighed for Madras road, where they arrived the 18th and fired on the "Princess Mary" which was returned from the ships and from the Fort. Each ship gave her a broadside as she stood to the Northward, and another as she returned, and then stood to the Southward again. We are since informed they had two motives for this expedition: one was to make a plea with the Country Government that the English committed the first hostilities ashore; and the other to see if Captain Peyton would come to our assistance or not. The 23rd, Captain Peyton with the squadron stood into Pulicat road, where he sent his Lieutenant Mr. Weeims on board a vessel in the road, who was there told of all the circumstances of their attacking the "Princess Mary," and of their then being between Madras and Pondicherry. On which he disappeard, and has never since been heard of, or from, by any of the English; though there has no cost or pains been spared for that purpose, as may easily be imagined from the scene of melancholy situation of affairs on this coast. The last letter that was received from any one belonging to the squadron, was from Captain Peyton to Governor Morse, dated the 4th August, when he was just come out from refitting. This unhappy conduct of his so animated our enemies, that they determined on attacking Fort St. George. We call it unhappy, because it has truly proved so in its consequences, though what reasons Captain Peyton may have had for this proceeding we know not. Accordingly, the 2nd September in the morning they weighed again for Pondicherry. The 4th they landed their men at St. Thomé and thereabouts, and the 5th began the attack, chiefly depending upon their shells. The 10th the Town surrendered; but on what terms, as we are not perfectly informed, we shall not presume to trouble your Honour with flying reports. We are pretty well assured there are as yet no terms complied with, and that Monsieur De Preminil is gone there from Pondicherry to command the garrison. The 2nd instant the seven French ships in the road, having taken what quantity of money, goods, ammunition and stores they thought proper, were to sail the 3rd for Pondicherry, and from thence immediately hither to attack this place. But it pleased God that night, and the next morning it blew so hard as to founder the "Duc de Orleans," their second ship in force, and two more. The "Achilles" of seventy guns, the Commodore's, and only ship of considerable force, either cut away or lost all her masts, as did the three others; so that 1200 men have perished, and the whole squadron is utterly disabled, and their design against this place rendered impracticable for the present; though it is the opinion of most of our officers, that had they come, we should have taken up more of their time than they had to spare. We have about twenty of the King's people, that were left ashore sick, who have put our gunroom in excellent order. Some of the people came to us from Madras though not many. The additions and alterations to our Fort within these twelve months, have made it infinitely more secure than it was. We have full six months' provisions of all kinds in the Fort; so that we doubt not we should have been able to make a defence for a considerable time had they come. They now talk of coming to us by land; in which case we bless God we are no ways apprehensive, but with the common protection of Providence, we shall be able to defend and secure this place till we are relieved; for which purpose we assure your Honours, our utmost endeavours shall be used. Your Honours' vessels the "Mermaid" and "Advice Snow," were both taken by the French squadron in Madras road, and both lost in the storm. The "Princess Mary" was skuttled and run into the surf, but is since got off by the French. The "Sumatra" and "Brilliant" from the West Coast, passed by this road the 19th August. They were near enough for us to see that had colours out; and we knowing the French squadron was off Conimere, or thereabouts, made a waft of our flag for six hours, and fired a gun, which the masters say they did not see, and sailed on into the squadron which having English colours they took for ours and were lost, but had time to throw their papers overboard. It must naturally appear to your Honours, and indeed to all the world, a very extraordinary circumstance that the Nabob and country government should permit our enemies to take his advantage of us, when it has been obedient to their commands, and for the peace and welfare of their country alone, that has prevented the English a long while from acting in the same manner by the French, and thereby putting it out of their power to give us this loss. The French say they had the Nabob's permission for committing these hostilities ashore; and do not scruple to declare publicly they gave him 100,000 pagodas for the liberty of so doing, and when they landed their people they produced his perwanna, which met with universal credit, though the Nabob now disowns his having granted any. Your Honours may be sure, all methods that can be thought of have been used to represent to the Nabob the monstrous injustice, as well as ill policy of this his proceeding. To which he replies he never gave them any such liberty; that his son was going to the assistance of Madras, but it was given up before he could get thither; and assures us he will join with the English to destroy Pondicherry. This was the substance of his letter in answer to Mr. Hinde's remonstrances to him, and assures us of his assistance though at the same time he carries on a close correspondence with the French, and expects no doubt his share of the booty; in which respect, it is possible, he may be disappointed. We shall not fail to keep on good terms with him, though we cannot flatter ourselves with hopes of much if any assistance from him; as nothing of that nature has yet appeared in consequence of his repeated promises, though we have been in daily expectation of our enemies appearing against us; as no doubt they would before now, had not many unforeseen circumstances concurred to keep them much longer at Madras, than they or we could have expected after the surrender of that place; and at last this for us most fortunate storm, which we look upon as a distinguishing mark of Providence in our favour, that greatly encourages us under our present difficulties: the particulars of which we shall not take up your Honors' leisure with, as it is not now in your power to relieve us in time; but we have wrote to Bengal and Bombay for that purpose, and hope they will have regard enough to your Honors' interest to succour us speedily.

"On the 25th August arrived at Mahè three French ships; one called the "Centaur" of seventy guns, being of equal force and burthen with the "Achilles"; one of forty, and another of twenty guns; which three ships arrived at Pondicherry the 27th September, and sailed from thence the 14th instant. Four that came out of Europe in company with them, are said to be gone for China. We have no news of the arrival of any of your Honors' ships in India. We hear from Mocha that Mr. Adair died at Beethforckee, as did Captain Wells of the "Pelham" at Bombay. We have had no news from Bengal this season. The "Mermaid's" packet coming from thence fell into the enemies' hands in Madras roads. "Sumatra" is we heard designed from Pondicherry for Europe; where the shattered remains of Monsieur La Bourdonnais' squadron is bound, or the above three ships, we cannot learn as yet. Fifty of the military belonging to Madras perished on the three ships that were lost; the remainder they sent ashore and relieved them, as the people themselves say for being of assistance to them in the storm. There was not only a great deal of booty taken out of Madras on board those three ships, but a good deal was lost at the same time going to Pondicherry in open boats. The intercourse of letters between Madras and this place have been stopped, ever since the Town was invested. Only three from Governor Morse to Mr. Hinde having come out as yet from thence; and the fear of their being intercepted occasions their being wrote only in general terms. So that we know not for certainty on what footing the Gentlemen there, are; but Mr. Morse writes that Mr. De Young, the Dutch Governor of Pulicat, refused giving the women and children his protection, and sent them all back again, which was a great inconvenience to the place. Mr. Marsan, the Governor at Negapatam, has been more humane, and has taken all the families from this place under his protection, and treats them with great humanity. Immediately on hearing Madras had surrendered, we came to a resolution of stopping the investment, as your cash was very low indeed, about 10,000 pagodas only; though the merchants have had no advances since we received the silver mentioned above from Bombay, which was the beginning of June. Notwithstanding which, and many other impediments which your Honors may be more fully apprized of hereafter, from our letters between Madras and here, we have about 1500 bales; and shall in January be able to make them up 1,800 to load a ship, please God, we have any come to us; and had we money we could provide much more.

"John Crabb, Quarter Master of one of His Majesty's ships, having little money, and being desirous to secure it, we have received into your Honors' Cash 190 pagodas; for which we have given him certificates of the receipt, and request he may be paid in England the amount of the same."

"Since writing the above, we have received a letter signed by Governor Morse and the Gentlemen at Madras. In it is mentioned articles of capitulation for the ransom of that place; which is all we yet know, and thought proper to advise your Honors of it. What the terms are we know *not*, but they are very ill kept by Monsieur Dupleix, the Governor of Pondicherry; who sent out three hundred men to surprize them on the way, which they did, and have carried them all prisoners of war into Pondicherry. The three ships that we advised above to be sailed from Pondicherry, are returned with two of the disabled ships, so that are now in that road and the offing, five ships completely rigged, and five disabled besides small vessels."

We are with the utmost fidelity and respect,

Honourable,

Your most faithful and most obedient servants,

JOHN HINDE

and Members of Council."

Fort St. David, 17th October, 1746.

Three months afterwards, namely, on the 10th January, 1747, another letter was dispatched from Mr. Hinde to the Court of Directors, which we give below:—

"Our last address bore date the 17th October, and went by your Honors' sloop the "Porto-bello," which sailed from Negapatam, the 22nd. Since the time your Honors' affairs on this coast have continued in the same uncertain posture; as we have not been so fortunate as to receive either letters or succours from Bengal, though so near us and to windward, and we have been very importunate in our letters on this occasion. The only alterations in our favour since we wrote you last is, that we have prevailed with the Country Government to declare in our favour; and in consequence of it the Nabob sent his son Mahomed Ali Khan, with about 2000 horse, to our assistance the beginning of last month. Notwithstanding which, the French thought proper the 8th ultimo to come against us with their whole force from Pondicherry; when we made the best defence we were able; and notwithstanding they got as far as the Garden house, we had the good fortune on the 9th to drive them out, and compel them to a very precipitate retreat. In which they had killed and wounded, by the best advice we can get, upwards of a hundred and seventy of their men of war; and left behind two mortars, all their ammunition, and camp furniture, and every thing they brought but the arms they bore and some of them; and our loss was very inconsiderable. The 20th we are advised they fitted out a force by sea to surprize us that way; but Providence disappointed them. Some of their boats were driven ashore, and their ammunition all spoiled; which reduced them to a necessity of laying aside their design, and putting back into Ariacopang river. The 31st we had a skirmish by land; in which we again obtained an advantage over them; and had we even then been succoured, your Honors' affairs would have been in all human probability restored in a great measure, if not altogether. The Nabob was so well disposed towards us, but as yet we have not had a line or any assistance from Bengal since Madras was taken, now four months. The Nabob's eldest son Maphuze Khan, is now joined his brother, and the expense of the camp amounts to upwards of 6,000 rupees per day; and they with reason grow extremely impatient, and we fear will quit our interest, if some ships do not appear soon to assist us. Shipping of all nations have long since been on the Coast, and to our great concern and uneasiness four of the French squadron are returned, and are now at Pondicherry; one of them the "Centaur," the best ship they have had in India, and five more ships in that road; in all nine: and it is this that renders our situation so precarious, and for which reason we send this away in a hurry to Tranquebar, lest we should be beseiged and deprived of an opportunity of so doing. With it we send our consultations from the loss of Madras, which contains a journal of what we have done for the preservation of the settlement;* of which our utmost endeavours have been employed, and we hope it will meet with your Honors' approval. We shall only add, we think it somewhat unkind in our countrymen and fellow servants, to have abandoned us; and that we will do all we can under these discouraging circumstances, and trust to Providence for the event. Hitherto we have been but at a small expense; our presents to the country government not exceeding above 3000 pagodas; a trifle not worth mentioning in proportion to the expense they are at, and the disquiet it has given our enemies, who trying all possible methods to make up affairs with them; and the above circumstances greatly facilitate their negotiations, as they clog the wheels of ours. We have in general terms promised in your Honors' name that we will not be ungrateful for any favours the Nabob inclines to show us.

"Whilst the above was writing, a message

* This will account for the blank in the Consultations already mentioned. Should this fall into the hands of any zealous antiquary in England, we should feel much obliged by his sending us copies of any contemporary records which may be preserved in the records of the late Company at home.

came from the Nabob's sons, advising that their father was actually treating with the French, and that four prisoners were sent to Pondicherry from Arcot: which renders our affairs so precarious, that we shall only advise your Honors of the arrival of what shipping is come to our knowledge, and send this away in hopes of having an opportunity of writing again by this ship a day or two hence. In the meantime we shall use all possible methods with the Nabob and his sons, to have regard to our interest according to their repeated promises, and to procure the re-situation of Madras as one of the terms if possible; which they still promise, as well as security though their councils are so influenced by immediate gain that there is no depending upon them."

About four months after the despatch of the above letter, namely, on the 2nd of May 1747, another despatch was addressed by Charles Floyer, the new Deputy Governor of Fort Saint David in the room of Mr. Hinde who had died on the 4th April. From this dispatch we make the following extracts:

"Since our last account of the melancholy situation of this settlement which must certainly have appeared to be very precarious, we had the misfotune to be reduced to almost inevitable danger; for as our security chiefly depended on the assistance of the Moors, we were soon brought to the utmost extremity by being abandoned by them; notwithstanding all the arguments and persuasion that could possibly be used in our parts to continue them in our interests. But the long delay of our ships, with the uncertainty of their coming at all, and the frequent offers and proposals they received from the French, which arose to five lacs of rupees,—made all our endeavours prove fruitless; as we could by no means think of making such offers, and if we could, they would have still outbid us. Having this advantage of us, that if they did not perform their promises they could not be in worse terms than they were. Whereas we must literally have performed all ours. Upon the whole, on the 14th February both the armies of the Moors decamped, leaving us wholly to ourselves. In which destitute circumstances, the French on the last of February came out of Pondicherry, and on the 1st of March made another attempt upon us by land, bringing with them a force considerably superior to any yet sent, or we could equal in more than a quarter part. Nevertheless, on their approaching near the bounds, we sent out all our peons, with one hundred European military, two hundred Topasses, and some artillery, in order to repel them, if possible, or at least to obstruct their entrance for a while, in hopes of doing them some mischief, and that every hour might produce something in our favour; which, as Providence ordained, it answered our intentions so well, that though we could not defeat them, our party engaged them so warmly, that we had the good fortune to keep them from crossing Punniar river all that day, and to do them considerable damage. But night coming on, and our people noways equal to keep the field against such a superior force, were constrained to retire to the Fort. By which means the enemy had an open field all that night, when and on the second in the morning early, they marched with all their troops to the garden house; from whence it would have been impracticable for us to have drove them away. But it happened very fortunately, before they had time to raise any batteries or to do much damage in the bounds, we had the inexpressible joy and satisfaction to discover nine sail in the offing, which proved to be His Majesty's squadron under the command of Commodore Griffin. This, for us most welcome sight, made them quit their quarters and betake to flight immediately, which they did so speedily, that though we had eight hundred men landed with the utmost expedition by the Commodore, in order to cut them off in their retreat, yet they were got so far on their way that it was in vain to pursue them. Although their stay at the gardens was very short, they took care to do as much mischief as they could in the time, and burnt several houses about the bounds. But as these damages are nothing in comparison to the ill consequences that might have attended us had they continued longer, even one day more, we have reason to bless God for appearing this once more so manifestly and critically in our favour.

"We find from several instances in our late misfortunes, that the Nabob and other principal persons of this country are of such an extreme lucrative disposition, that there is no hopes of fixing them stedfast in our interest by any other method but by the force of money; and that they are so exceeding averacious (occasioned by the large proffers they have received from the French) that nothing less than lacs will go near to satisfy them.

"These are such large sums beyond what we think in our power to dispose of, that we never attempted to make them any such offers; but as a means to encourage them in our cause, we have several times promised them in general terms that your Honors will not be ungrateful for any substantial service we may receive from them: which, with some small presents we may make as a pledge of our sincerity, we hope, will have the desired effect, and procure their assistance when required.

"The presents that we made them, whilst the Nabob's two armies were encamped without our bounds, for near three months, at an expense of upwards 6000 rupees per day in our defence, did not amount to above 40,000 rupees which in comparison to the service they were of in defeating the French in their attempt upon this place on the 9th December, we are of opinion, you will allow to be very inconsiderable; and therefore persuade ourselves it will meet with your approval. We endeavoured to keep them longer with us for our security, as we daily expected His Majesty's squadron; and Mr. Hinde offered them 2000 rupees per day to stay only ten days, but he could not prevail on them.

"Most part of the military that could escape out of Madras have come here, whom we have taken into service.

"The officers are all with us; who offering their service, as we were much in want of them, we have continued them in their former commissions; and the Lieutenants having behaved very well here in the two actions with the enemy, we take the liberty to recommend them to your Honors to have Captain's commissions conferred on them.

"The inferior officers and military, as well as those in the gun-room we have rewarded with clothing.

"Mr. Robert Clive, Writer in the service, being of martial disposition, and having acted as a volunteer in our late engagements, we have granted him an Ensign's commission upon his application for the same.

"We are infinitely concerned, among other misfortunes, to acquaint you that all the books and papers, relating to your Honors' affairs at Madras, have met with the like fate of that settlement, and are in possession of the French:* which not only greets us that they should fall under their inspection, but renders us at a great loss to find out the several credits that are due to you. In which circumstance we shall make it our business from time to time to get the best insight of, by examination of the Canakapilies, who are now beginning to come here daily; and whatever balance we can find out shall be duly received and accounted for.

"The proceedings of the French, both at Madras and Pondicherry, have in general been so cru-

* Fortunately the consultations and most of the general letters were restored at the Peace of Aix la Chapelle. Otherwise, it is evident, that the labours of the present compiler would have been greatly simplified.

el and inhumane, that they seem rather to imitate a persecution than a war. They have refused the Commodore to exchange a single prisoner, notwithstanding the several they owe us, and we have some of theirs; and on a sudden drove away all the women and children that had liberty to stay at the Mount: plundering them of every thing they had, and afterwards set fire to their houses; and this at a time when they were preparing to come against this place.

"They have been very busy in fortifying the White Town in Madras and have nearly destroyed the Black Town.

"By the best accounts we learn from their own people that have deserted here, they have 1300 Europeans in garrison at Pondicherry, and about 400 in Madras, besides a large number of peons and Coffrees at each place. Indeed they have so many people, that we may hope their numbers alone will tend to their distruction, as they are already in great scarcity of provisions.

"We are not at present in a thorough capacity to make any material attempts against them; but as soon as we may be better enabled by a reinforcement of the squadron or otherwise, Mr. Griffin has assured us, that no industry or endeavours shall be wanting on his part to revenge our past injuries to the utmost in his power.

"We being lately advised, that Ensign Van Franken was very busy among the French after the surrender of Madras, and did actually give Monsieur De Labourdonnais a plan of the Town: for this and other misdemeanours by him committed, we have dismissed him from your Honors' services, and sent him to Europe on the "Lapwing;" the Captain having strict orders not to let him go on shore at any place he may touch at."

(Signed)

CHARLES FLOYER and Members of Council.

The following general letters received from the Court of Directors in reply to the foregoing communications, will sufficiently explain the progress of affairs as regards Madras up to the treaty of Aix la Chapelle in 1748. They are also valuable as containing references to many important facts, which are not to be found in the letters which have been preserved from Fort St. David. The first is dated "London, 27th January, 1747," from which it will be seen that the news of the loss of Madras had reached England within a comparitively short period.

"*Our Governor and Council at Fort St. David.*

"As the Lieutenants on the Fort St. George Establishment did not forfeit their honor by its loss; and on your continuing the officers in their former Commissions, the Lieutenants behaved very well in the two actions with the enemy; we leave it to you to grant Captains' Commissions to such of them as you judge proper. Be sure to encourage Ensign Clive in his martial pursuits, according to his merit. Any improvement he shall make therein, shall be duly regarded by us. You may rest assured that all the recruits we can raise shall be sent by every conveyance.

"Having suffered greatly by the numbers of

priests and Popish inhabitants at Madras, who have acted a very treacherous part to us continually in that place, especially when it was attacked; therefore we strictly forbid your suffering any Romish Church within our bounds, or any of their priests to dwell among you, or that religion to be openly professed; and in case any Papists have crept into places of trust in our service, they must be immediately dismissed. You are not to deem this order to affect the Armenians of the Greek persuasion.

"We are informed that although our late Governor Hinde turned out of the Company's bounds an Italian Padre under a guard; yet since Mr. Hinde's death, by Mr. Lennox's influence, he was permitted to return. We are dissatisfied with that proceeding and require Mr. Lennox to return home.

"Monsieur Labourdonnais, with five French ships, arrived from Loando St. Pauls at Martinico some time ago; where he left them and retired to Eustatia, whence he took his passage on a Dutch ship that by stress of weather put into Falmouth; where he was taken prisoner of war by Captain Bladwell of His Majesty's ship the "Mercury," and will soon be conducted to London.

"Whatever French prisoners, or other Europeans, shall be taken in their service, in case there is no opportunity to exchange them, we would have you send home all you can, upon our returning ships; not sending more than fifteen on a ship; detaining the others till an opportunity offers."

The next General Letter from the Court of Directors, is dated "London, 24th July, 1747."

"*Our Governor and Council at Fort St. David.*

"On the 20th of April last, the "Porto-Bello" Sloop brought us your advices of the 17th October 1746; and by letters from Bombay received overland, we learn with satisfaction that you had repulsed the French and continued in possession of the place in December last.

"Having taken the same into serious consideration, we have judged it proper, upon such a surprizing revolution in our affairs at the loss of Madras, to constitute Fort St. David our Head settlement and to appoint John Hinde, Esq., to be President and Governor of Fort St. David, and of all our settlements and affairs on the Coromandel, Orissa, and Sumatra coasts; with the advice and concurrence of Edward Cooke, Stringer Lawrence, Charles Floyer, William Holt, Alexander Wynch and Thomas Cooke Junior as his Council; and a Commission is accordingly enclosed under our seal in the ship "Porto-Bello" packet.

"Major Stringer Lawrence took passage last season on the ship "Winchelsea," with directions to be entertained as Major of our Garrison at Fort St. George. Upon his arrival he must be employed as such at your place, and constantly remain as third of Council. Some Military officers accompanied him who must act in your Garrison according to their respective commissions.

"Enclosed is copy of a resolution come to by the Company in general Court assembled, on the many astonishing reports of the capitulation and ransom of Madras. We positively forbid you to enter into any treaty with the Country Government, or any other power, relating to the payment of any sum of money for the ransom, or for the re-delivery of that place.

"And in case the Nabob should give us possession of Madras again, the effects that we may have here must be removed to Fort St. David, keeping only a bare possession of Madras.

"Although our late servants at Madras ceased to be so on the loss of the place; yet we permit you to take in such of them as from their behaviour you may think proper; and to allow a reasonable subsistence to the rest if they apply for it.

"As we have constituted Fort St. David to be our Head Settlement, we empower you to be at such expense in fortifying and securing the place that you shall judge requisite.

"We have acquainted our servants in Bengal and at Bombay, that Fort St. David is constituted our Head Settlement on the Coromandel coast; and that you are appointed Governor in Council thereof; recommending it to them, as we hereby do unto you, to carry on a friendly correspondence with each other; concerting the properest measure for the promotion of our welfare, and the security of all our settlements."

Our next despatch from the Directors is dated 16th October, 1747.

"*Our President and Council at Fort St. David.*

"We have with great joy received advice from Bombay overland, of your gallant, brave defence against the renewed attempts of the French in March, till Mr. Griffin came to your relief; and that Captain Sumnor paid a due regard to your representation by repairing in the "Britannia" to your settlement, which will recommend him to our favour; the supply of money and goods by that ship was doubtless of eminent service. Your immediate loading and despatch of her to us meets with our entire approbation; and we doubt not but by the blessing of God upon your good conduct and courage, that we are still in possession of the settlement.

"On our strenuous application, His Majesty hath been graciously pleased to send a strong squadron of Men-of-war under the command of the Honourable Rear Admiral Boscawen with these our ships, whereon this letter is sent. Such of them as come to your place, the commanders are ordered to deliver all our packets, treasure, and goods on board unto you, immediately on their first arrival; and to obey your orders when the Admiral hath no further service for the ship."

From the next despatch, dated 27th January, 1748, our readers will see that peace was already looming in the future. How much our readers are indebted to that peace may be gathered from the first clause.

"*Our President and Council of Fort S^t. David.*

"It being stipulated in the definitive treaty of peace, that all Records, books and papers, are to be mutually restored, we do not think it necessary to send Copies of the Fort St. George accounts, as in all probability you will have the originals.

"As we have resolved by the Ballot, that it is necessary for Mr. Morse to come home to give an account of his conduct at Madras, from the time the French took possession of the place; you must give him notice to return to England by the next ships accordingly; in the meantime during his stay at Fort St. David pay him the respect due to his late station.

"In consideration of the long services of Lieutenant Eckman, and as he is incapable through his great age for further duty, we have agreed to allow him a pension of 160 pagodas a year for his life; to commence from the time he received his last pay; and you are directed to pay it him accordingly."

On the 10th May, 1748, the Directors were enabled to announce that the treaty of Aix la Chapelle was fairly signed. We give the dispatch in full.

"*Our Governor and Council of Fort St. David.*

"Enclosed we send His Majesty's proclamation, declaring the cessation of arms, as well by sea as land, agreed upon between His Majesty the Most Christian King, and the States General of the United Provinces, and enjoining the observance thereof.

"2. On a perusal you may perceive that by the preliminaries for restoring a General peace, signed at Aix la Chapelle on the 19th of April last, Old Stile, all hostilities either by sea or land against the French, are to cease in the East Indies six months after the said 19th April, which must be complied with accordingly.

"3. As hostilities are ceased, our ships must be despatched directly home to us after the 17th of October next, in the usual manner as before the commencement of the war; by directing the Commanders to proceed to our Island of St. Helena, and after refreshing there for a few days, to make the best of their way to the Downs."

Here then we bring to a close the present series of "Annals of Madras in the Olden Time." The labour which the compiler originally proposed to himself is now completed; and the first century of the settlement of the English at Fort St. George, which hitherto was nearly a blank in the history of India, is now a living and breathing narrative.

APPENDIX.

[The following curious documents, illustrative of the very earliest condition of Madras, were originally collected with some others two or three years back by Mr. Hudleston, the present Secretary of the Board of Revenue, and printed in a pamphlet form. These extracts, together with Bruce's Annals of the East India Company, and some volumes of early voyages and travels, formed the authorities from whence the present compiler drew up the first three or four chapters of the FIRST Volume of the Annals of Madras in the Olden Time. The records, from whence the extracts were made, extend over ten years only, viz. 1670-1679; and it was the original intention of the compiler to have republished the whole as an Appendix to the present volume. Want of space however has prevented his carrying out this plan; and perhaps, as the general facts to be gathered from the extracts are exhibited in the earlier chapters, there is less occasion for such a republication. The following selection of the more important papers,—that is, of those papers which directly illustrate the condition of the old town of Madraspatanam, and the social manners of the earliest settlers,—are so well worthy of being preserved, that we print them here in extenso. They require but little comment; their contents speak for themselves.]

No. I. Official Investigation into the Administration of Madras, 1675—76.

In the year 1675-76, that is, during the Government of Sir William Langhorn, Major James Puckle was sent out by the Directors as a Commissioner to enquire into the state of the Company's affairs on the Coast of Coromandel. Accordingly Major Puckle presented a list of queries to the Governor and Council; and on the 29th February 1675-76, the queries, together with the replies, were discussed in Council. We extract the consultation.

" Public Consultations, Fort St. George, 29th February 1675—76.

" Something by way of Query presented to the Agent and Councell of Fort St. George, at a Consultation held there the 29th February 1675-6, for Resolution on behalf of the Hon'ble English East India Company.

Being present.

Sir Wm. Langhorn, *Governour.*	
Walter Clavell,	John Bridger,
Joseph Hymners,	Tim. Wilkes,
Major Wm. Puckle,	Jacob Smith.
Edward Herrys,	

1. Why there is no Register kept of the ships, boats, vessells &c. that arrive in the road of Madrass, and the names

(1.) The Agent himself has kept a Register of all ships coming and going, and yearly sent home to the Hon'ble Company.

The like very proper to be done in the Choultry, and shall

accordingly be put in practice, though hitherto it has not been done, the Justices successively continuing the same method which they have found in use in their predecessors times.

of the Masters or Commanders, the place whence they come and whether they are outward bound.

(2.) Mr. Jearsey and his nephew John Jearsey who serves him and has paid his fine to the Hon'ble Company.

Tim. Sutton formerly Lieutenant, whose discharging has been advised to them.

Charles Ryley an old souldier here, but has laid down his arms and keepes a house of entertainment (upon sufferance having many children bred up Protestants.)

Richard Monck, lately a prisoner with the Dutch, marryed here, has laid down arms being sickly, drives no trade that we know of.

John Augur, an antient man marryed to an English woman, keepes a house of entertainment upon sufferance, having been long a souldier and no other way to live.

Booth Chadderton came out a souldier near two years since, and lately had leave to serve Mr. Herrys, but ready to take up arms again upon occasion.

2. What English that are not in the Hon'ble Company's service do live or have habitations in the English or Blacks Towns, how they are qualified, what trades do they drive, to what vallue, and what ships they are owners of.

(3.) The Portuguezes and Mestizas were invited hither by

3. Why are so many Portuguez per-

the several Agents from our first settling here and some came with our people from Armagon, and encouraged and severall had money lent them to build upon the open sand under the protection of the Gunns which by degrees hath been walled in, they doing the duty of trained bands in watching and warding in times of trouble upon the outworks. They have never paid any rent or acknowledgement, nor taken out any leases. However, if the Hon'ble Company thinks good to have us require it, upon their possitive order we must obey them, but we believe it will be the same thing as to drive them away, for in all these countrys here is no such practice. The Governour and Avaldars very sensible of the benefit of inhabitants, inviting all folks by favours and immunitys, and gladly giving ground for houses and gardens to any that will build or plant upon it.

As now in practice at St. Thoma, where to repopulate, they have promised three years' exemption of Taxes, which drawes the people from hence againe as fast as they came.

And that the Hon'ble Company may the better judge by the experience of this their place, the Agent and Councell have been fain to lett fall the mitted to dwell in the English Town and pay no rent, nor any acknowledgement for their houses, whilst many English are necessitated to take houses in the Black Town and pay for the same.

execution of their Consultation of 28th September last, for the levying of only pagodas 230 upon the whole out Town in compensation of Mr. Thomas Clarke's houses near the Caldera point pulled down and Verona's expense in clearing the sand from the sea-wall during the warr, which had scarce amounted to two fanams per house; and yet all the inhabitants, nay their own Merchants all but Cassa Verona, had shut up their shops and gathered up to the pagoda, and by intelligence their Tribes in the country had stopped all provisions from coming to Town, themselves being ready to forsake the place if the Agent and Councell had not timely pacified them by desisting from the said leviation; they did not value the summe but the precedent.

In like manner was the king of Gulconda himself served about that very time at his own city, upon the occasion of a tax imposed upon rice, and himself was fain send after them and appease them by fair words and good assurance for the future and with considerable Tasheriffs to the chief of the Rice men.

Not unlike the passage in London with the markett folks some 14 years since, upon an Act of Parliament a little too uneasy for them.

And moreover how ready the Mores and Braminy Government now are to lay hold of such opportunitys to raise new pretences, the annexed relation of the terms we now stand on with them will suffice.

Pollepella Vengana pretending to sell the King's paddy here customs free at their own rates, as in their own Territories, and to re-impose an avaldar, saying, the King and Nabob who granted the cowl and phermaund are dead and gone, and this king not obliged; as if himself had not confirmed it and received the mony.

The Dutch not being able to gett a cowl for Poliacat, do all they can to infringe ours.

(4.) The same answer as to the surveys may serve for the proposition nomber 4. The paddy ground payes rent pagodas 40 per annum, lett out to Cassa Verona at the rate it yeilded the three years last before it, and the Agent has severall times advertised the people who have gardened up and down the sands to take leases for their more quiet possession, but (saving six allready made to the English and others) they seeme to be rather willing to let them fall back to sand as they were, which would be of evill consequence to this place, being all on a loose sand where

4. Why there is no survey made and taken of both Towns with the lands belonging to them, and why those that have built upon the Hon'ble Company's ground do not pay any acknowledgement, not a peper corn, for the ground their houses stand upon, nor have Leases with Covenants to maintain &c., and

between the scorching reflex of the sunn and the flying of the sand, we should be scarce able to draw our breath, which was formerly the cause of great destempers, sickness and mortallity, rendering the place very uncomfortable allmost unhabitable.

why no Register of the names of the tennants and inhabitants aforesaid.

(5.) The Portuguez &c., invited as they were, settled usefull and disarmed as the inhabitants are, and the souldier out of office, and so firme a peace as between our Princes, with so great a dependance as they have on us more then on all other Europe nations in India, we humbly conceive this may be suspended until some just occasion of jealousies at home or here. Besides that the great number is not of any single nation but of Topasses, Mestizos, &c. Converts, and now many Natives of this place, having no other country but this.

And whiles the French have no Settlement near hand, the keeping French Padrys here instead of Portugues, destroyes the encroaching growth of the Portugall interest, who used to entail Portugalism as well as Christianity on all their converts.

5. Whether is it safe or convenient that considering about half the souldiers of the Fort are Portuguezes, and more then half the inhabitants of the new Town are Portuguezes, and they now have two churches nigh unto the Fort, where some thousands meet every weeke (besides French), that the said inhabitants should be permitted to dwell in said Town.

(6.) The English who are in the Gulconda, Visiapore's

6. Whether any of the Hon'ble Com-

and Mohgul's services are severall, but generally dissolute, hard to reclaym and less worth it, except one Christopher Wilkins sent hence long since per order of the Agent, &c., then being along with the Ordnance, which the Hon'ble Company was necessitated to lend the king of Gulconda, which C. W. is by report a very good man, and it were very desirable that he could gett free, to come and end his daies amongst his countrymen.

pany's servants be entered into the Mores service; how to gett them off.

(7.) Here are no bad debts in neither of these two last Agencys, all that are upon account were made before that the Investments were undertaken by Timona and Verona in times of much less troubles then since have been, so the Hon'ble Company may observe the difference of dealing with their Merchants joyntly or severally.

It were requisite the Hon'ble Company would order the writing of these debts off by Account Current to profit and loss, being wholly desperate.

7. Whether any bad debts, and what they are, and by whom.

As to the particulars relating to Mr. Clavell, the Agent and Councell doe humbly conceive.

(1.) That a Chief has authority by the Charter to

Its further desired that you resolve—

1. Whether Mr. Clavell, Chief in the

administer an Oath in matters of abuses and injurys to the Hon'ble Company, as more at large in the said Charter.

Bay, hath power to administer oaths.

(2.) As to the enordering the execution of the said authority he has the same order there that we have here, and as to what may depend on us, the Agent and Councell in their generall letter along with Major Puckle will confirm the Honorable Company's orders relating to his Commission, as amply and fully as shall be found propper for them to doe. The matters objected to Mr. Walter Clavell, as we have received them, we have transmitted them to the Hon'ble Company, as they stand upon record in the Fort bookes; who having now appointed Major Puckle to goe down and examine them, the Agent and Councell doe neither take upon them to acquit or condemne, but wholly leave it to the Major's examination, whose Commission shall be amply confirmed in the Fort General along with him, not finding any thing therein of misusing their Cash or pressing danger requiring a more hasty proceeding.

2. If he hath, that he be thereon ordered not to neglect or refuse the same to all such as shall voluntarily offer themselves or be produced on behalf of the Hon'ble Company, wherein and how Mr. Clavell hath vindicated himself from those matters charged on him of arbitraryness in execution of his office, mentioned in Lib. Consultation and Lib. Letters India.

These querys presented to the Agent, &c.,

per Wm. Puckle.

No. II. Rules and Regulations Established By Sir William Langhorn, 1671—72.

[The following curious rules and regulations exhibit the tendencies of the earlier settlers in a more striking light than could be done by pages of description.]

"By ORDER of the Hon'ble Sir Wm. Langhorn, Barronett, Governour and Agent in Fort St. George.

In obedience to my Hon'ble Employer's orders, and out of that care I ought to take of the people committed to my charge,

It is enordered and declared, that for prevention of disorders and for the preservation of the Hon'ble Company's Servants and Souldiers of the Garrison from distempers and diseases frequently caused thereby, and by the unwholesome liquor called Parrier arrack,

That from this day forward, no person whatsoever dwelling within the priviledges of the Towne, who doth sell any of the sort of arrack made here or hereabouts, shall be permitted to sell or give entertainment to any of the Hon'ble Company's souldiers or servants,

And that all persons keeping publick houses of entertainment, be prohibited after this day from drawing liquor for any person, after the usuell ringing of the bell at eight of the clock at night; but shall desire all persons then in their houses to retire to their own lodgings and suffer them to tarry there no longer. And if any persons shall be found contemners of these orders, they shall not for the future be permitted to keep houses of entertainment.

And for further prevention of all disorders and excesses and impoverishing the souldiers of the Garrison and others in the Hon'ble Company's servise, by encouraging them to the unthinking way of spending their wages in such disorderly manner upon creditt, faster than it comes in, to the ruine both of their purses and their healths and undervaluing of the punctual and bounteous pay of the Hon'ble Company's, which to all sober and discreet persons is not only sufficient for maintainance, but with any industry and beginning of their owne, enough to get aforehand in the world,

It is likewise enordered and declared hereby, that no Victullar, Punch-house or other house of Entertainment, shall be permitted to make stoppage at the pay day of their wages or any part thereof, saveing only for their dyet ; and accordingly order is given to the Purser to this effect, whereof all persons concerned are to take notice.

W. LANGHORN."

DATED IN FORT ST. GEORGE,
the 21*st of February* 1671-2

FORT ST. GEORGE, *the* 18*th August* 1672.

BY ORDERS of the Hon'ble Sir Wm. Langhorn, Barronett, Governour and Agent for affairs of the Hon'ble English East India Company in Fort St. George, for the receiving (*sic*) of the antient orders concerning the marketts in Chinnapatnam ; as they were observed from the beginning.

In Paddy Banckaall, the former allowance was —custome for the Gentu pagoda, for every heape of paddy, one measure ; for Peddinagg the watchman, on every greate ox-load of paddy, $\frac{3}{4}$ measure ; for small ox-load, $\frac{1}{2}$ measure ; for one right-hand-side girle, for every heape of paddy, 2 handfull ; for the measurer, every pagoda, $\frac{1}{2}$ measure ; at this rate was the former allowance : and if any offers to take more than this allowance, or make other allowance than this, their penalty shall be 12 pagodas to the Hon'ble Company, and they shall be punished at the Chowtry besides.

The former allowance in the Chowtry for severall sorts of gram and for oyle-seeds was—for the Gentu pagoda, one handfull every sacc ; for Peddinagg the watchman, two handfull every sacc ; for one right-hand-side girle, one handfull every sacc ; for the measurer, one handfull every sacc : and if any offer to take any more than this allowance, their penalty shall be 12 pagodas to the Hon'ble Company, and they shall be punished at the Chowtry besides.

The allowance of cowdunge and wood was—for every baskett of cowdunge, 2 cakes for the Gentu pagoda ; for Peddinagg the watchman, of every baskett of cowdunge, 5 cakes : and if any offer to take more than this allowance, or make any other than this allowance, their penalty shall be 12 pagodas to the Hon'ble Company, and they shall be punished at the Chowtry besides.

The allowance of seaffish was ; for every great nett, 5 ffish to the Hon'ble Company ; and to Peddinagg the watchman, 10 ffish : and on the ffish that they catch with a hooke, one ffish for the Company and one for Peddinagg the watchman. To the washerman, barber, grave-maker, and severall other workmen, they are to give what they please: and if any one offers to take more than this allowance or make any other allowance, their penalty shall be 12 pagodas to the Hon'ble Company, and they shall be punished at the Choultry besides.

Copied from the originall and examined by me,

WILLIAM RIVETT.

ORDERS prescribed by the Hon'ble Wm. Langhorn, Barronett, Governour of Fort St. George, Maddrassapatam, Coast of Cormandell and Bay of Bengall, for Affayrs of the Hon'ble English East India Company, &c.

1. If any that is on the watch or guard shall presume to lye of and not aske leave, he shall, if he be an Officer, for every such offence pay half a rial of eight; and a Private souldier shall stand one whole day's sentinell in armes.

2. That officer that shall conceal any sentinell that doth sleepe in the time of duty, shall be turned out of his office and remaine a Private souldier.

3. The same punishment to those that give the word to any but to them that it doth belonge.

4. If any two or more persons shall dare go into the field to decide a quarrell between them by the sworde or fire armes, thereby contemning the course of justice, they shall for the same offence endure two months' Imprisonment, only with rice

and water: but if the party challenged shall make knowne the challenge unto the Officer, and appeale to him for justice, the doome shall be inflicted on the challenger only: the like penalty shall be inflicted on all irregular persons who shall make opposition or resistance against those that shall be commanded to bring them into the Fort.

5. Whosoever after having received merited punishment, shall disarme themselves and deny to execute the duty of a Souldier any longer, as divers formerly have done, such one shall be drawne to the head of the troopes, and have his armes taken away from him by a cooley, and in exchange, have delivered him a spade or the like instrument, with which he shall work for his victuals; and his wages being suspended, he shall be sent home in the first ship as a delinquent, if the Commander's discretion admits not his submission and sorrow for his fault.

6.• If any in the Garrison shall resist or affront his Officer upon the Corps de Guarde, or sleepe being sentinell, therebye to endanger all our welfares, he shall for so great an offence be punished by standing three whole days, as according to former custome, sentinell in armes for the first time from the date; but offending againe, for every such offence shall ride the horse three days, each day three hours, and be confined a month with no other allowance than water and rice.

7. It is likewise ordered, that both the Officers and Souldiers in the Fort, shall on every Sabbath day, and on every day when they exercise, weare English apparell: in respect the garb is most be-

coming as souldiers and correspondent to their profession: on penalty of forfiting one month's allowance on the Officer's part, and half a month's allowance on the Private souldier's part.

8. Whosoever he be that shall attempt to get over the walls of the Fort upon any pretence whatsoever, shall for so hainous and grievous an offence be kept in Irons till the shipps arrival, and then his wages being suspended, be sent home for England, there to receive condigne punishment.

9. If any private souldier shall interpose himself whilst his Officer is correcting any other for his misdemeanours, either by unfitting words or actions, thereby to stay the chastisement due unto the delinquent, he shall for the first fault, stand a whole day as usually accustomed in armes; but being found so to offend againe, for every time from the date after, shall ride the horse three houres. The like punishment to those that will not obey their Officers when they command them to pass upon their duty.

10. That when the Governour &c. shall go on board, or abroade on horsebacke or in pallenkeen, it is thought fit, in respect of the small number of people, that not a man shall stir out of the Fort until the Governor returns home; upon penalty of half a riall of eight for the Merchant and Officer, and a daye's sentinell in armes to the Private souldier.

11. We doe expressly forbid all swaring, cursing, banning, or blaspheming the sacred name of Almighty God; and whoso shall be found faulty therein, shall paye foure fannams each time; which

course working no reformation in him, shall be sent for his country by the first shipp.

12. Wee moreover forbid any Factor, Writer, or Souldier, or any whomsoever under our command, to keep any woman for his beastly lust and carnal use; and if from henceforth any such shall be known to be in the Towne, the woman to be turned out of Towne and whipt, and the man to receive condigne punishment for entertaining and keeping her company.

13. No souldier is to dispute or contradict any order or command that he shall receive from his superior Officer, upon forfeiture of all his wages; unless it can be proved that the said order is absolutely destructive to the Civell government and saifty of the Company's Servants and Officers in this place.

14. No person of what quality soever within the Fort, being within call, shall after nine of the clocke at night pass the guard or sentinell without giving account to them about what he is goeing; which refusing to doe, shall be kept upon the guard till morning to answer his contempt before the Governor and Councell.

15. For the better maintaining of good order in this Garrison, if the Captain, the Lieftenant, or any other Officer shall heare or certainly be informed, if any under theire command gives his fellows the lye, whereby to breed occasion of quarrell, being a word of great contempt and indignity to the profession of a Souldier; we order such a one to be made fast to a gunn and there to receive Tenn blowes with a

small rattan or cane, well layd on by an Officer or either by him he gave the lye unto. But if the lye be given on the Corps de Guarde, to receive Twenty blowes; and if the Officer shall connive at, or not throughly execute the said punishment upon such an Offender, he shall have a whole month's wages deducted of his accompt for each time he so neglected this order, and for not executing the said penalty for such an offence. Nor shall any Officer for any offence, give any Souldier more than four or five strokes for the present; which if will not suffice, he is to be disarmed and committed to abide such due chastisement as the Chief Officer, with the advice of the other Officers in due examination, shall see cause.

16. That the Governour be acquainted with the offence for which the punishment of the horse and such like graver punishments are appointed, before they are put in execution.

17. Whosoever of the Company's Servants or Souldiers shall be absent from prayers on the Sabbath day, or on the morning on Wensday, when not employed upon duty, shall for every such default on the Company's servants part, forfeite halfe a ryall of eight; and on the Souldier's part, to stand halfe a daye's sentinell in armes, according to former customes.

18. No person out of the Hon'ble Company's pay, to keep house of entertainment, nor any unmarryed persons. None to be permitted to stay in any entertaining houses after the eight of clocke bell in the evening, Lodgers excepted.

19. No entertainment on the Lord's day, to

any but their owne dyeters. No gaming at cards or dice allowable in any entertaining house.

20. No one person to be allowed above half a pinte of rack or brandy, one quarte of wine; and a greater number pro rata. Penalty upon the housekeeper, one pagoda; upon the guests, twelve fannams each.

21. It is ordered and appointed, that all the fines or penaltys that are imposed and shall be received for all the Offences aforesaid, shall be kept in a box appointed for the purpose, for the use of the Poore, chiefly English, to be distributed according as the Governour and Councell shall direct.

22. If any souldier or souldiers in this our Garrison shall, either in their drinke or otherwise, offer any offence to any of the Natives or Towne inhabitance, either by striking, fighting, quarreling, or drawing of swordes, or the like unseemly misbehaviour towards any of the country people, wee order that all such irregular persons shall be brought to the Fort and there confined and examined, and shall then receive such punishment as may be equivalent to his or their offences, either by standing centinall in armes, or being made fast to the breech of a gunn, shall receive so many stripes as his Officers shall think fitt to appoint, not exceeding No. 10, unless the Governour be first made acquainted with it; or shall ride the horse so many houres, and so often as the Governour shall think meet to determine.

23. Whosoever shall take any thing perforce

from any markit folke, pretending to have it at what price they please, shall pay double the value.

W. LANGHORN.

GOD SAVE THE KING.

Copied from the originall and examined by me,

WILLIAM RIVETT.

These orders were taken off the Corps du Guard, and new Orders put up by the Governour and Councell.

October 28th, 1678.

No. III. RULES AND REGULATIONS FOR THE ADMINISTRATION OF PUBLIC BUSINESS, ESTABLISHED BY MR. STREYNSHAM MASTER.

" FORT ST. GEORGE, JANUARY 1677—8, THURSDAY THE 31ST.—AT A CONSULTATION.

Present.

STREYNSHAM MASTER, Esq , *Agent and Governour*.

Mr. JOSEPH HYMNERS,	Mr. JOHN BRIDGER,
Mr. TIMOTHY WILKES,	Mr. JACOB SMITH.

For regulating the Hon'ble Company's Affaires for the better carrying on the same, it is ordered and directed as followeth :—

1. That the printed directions made by the Court of Committee in London, the 18th December 1667, for the Christian and sober comportment of all the Hon'ble Company's Servants, be

hung up in the Chappell and dining roome, to be observed accordingly.

2. That the Councell do meet to consult of the Hon'ble Company's Affaires every Monday and Thursday, and oftener as business shall require, and this entry is to be taken by all the Councell as a due summons; yet the Secretary is hereby ordered himself in person, or by one of the Factors or Writers under him, to summon all the Members of the Councell every Monday and Thursday, about 8 o'clock in the morning; and every time any one of the Councell shall be absent, the Secretary is hereby required to enter at the beginning of such Consultation, these words:—"The whole Councell being duly summoned."

3. For all monys to be paid out of cash, that the second or Book-keeper, with the Agent's leave, shall draw bills directed to the Agent or who shall keep the cash under him; in which Bills he is to express the partys name to whom and the account upon which the mony is to be paid; which Bills, the second is first to signe, leaving room for the Agent, as is practised at Surratt; and the said Bills are to be read and passed in the Councell every Councell day after any such are drawn, and the Secretary to noat the same accordingly.

4. That the Generall bookes of accounts be ballanced the last day of April yearly and kept according to the method used at Surratt; a pair of which bookes, Letter M., are delivered to Mr. Joseph Hymners for his direction therein.

5. That the accounts of sallary of the Hon'ble Company's Servants that serve them in their Mer-

cantile affairs, be kept and entered in the Generall bookes by the Booke-keeper or second, according to the Hon'ble Company's printed rules, and not entered in a paire of bookes apart by the Purser General, as heretofore.

6. That the Warehouse-keeper or third in Councell do keep Warehouse bookes, agreeable to the Hon'ble Company's orders in their printed rules, for all goods delivered, received or bought; and that he take and draw up the accounts and invoices of all goods sold or bought and packed by him; from which accounts of the Warehouse-keeper, the second or Booke-keeper is to enter the same into the Generall bookes and the Generall invoices, they being his vouchers so to do.

7. That the Choultry Justice, Customer, or fourth in Councell do take care to receive and collect all the Rents and Revenues of the Towne of Madrasspatnam, except that of the Mint, and keep two distinct bookes of the same, one of the accounts of all petty land Customs received of the Indians, &c., upon goods imported; at the beginning of which booke every year, he must enter the rates of the Customs, the manner of gathering the same, and in the booke, the particulars of the goods which the same is collected, and at the end of this booke, the particulars of the Corne received for Toll in the Paddy Banksall and what the same was sold for, and also what received monthly for the Company's part of the Weigher's duty, and for registering houses, stands, &c.: and one other book of the accounts of all Sea and Land Customes received of Christians and Indians upon

goods imported and exported that is usually joyned together; at the beginning of which booke also, he must yearly enter the rates, and the manner of collecting the said customes, and in the booke the particulars of the goods on which, and the men's names from whom the same is received. Also, he must take care to receive the Fraights due to the Hon'ble Company for all goods laden upon their shipps and vessells and duly to enter the same in this booke; and in the said booke, he must make entry of all shipps and vessells that anchor in this port, the place they come from, the day they sayle, and the place they are bound unto. At the end of both bookes to make tables or abbreviates of every month's collections, that the whole year's Income may appear together and be more readily compared with the Generall bookes; and he is alsoe to keepe the Register bookes for all private trade, as is appointed in the Indulgence of 16th November 1674, and notice thereof given at the foot of the said Indulgence, hung up in the Chappell.

8. That the Customer, Mint Master (when there is one in that office), and Pay Master, or any two of them, do every Tuesday and Fryday sitt in the Choultry to do the common Justice of the Towne as usuall; and do take care that the Scrivan of the Choultry do duly register all sentences in Portuguez as formerly, and that there be an exact Register kept of all alienations or sales of slaves, houses, gardens, boates, shipps, &c.; the Company's due for the same to be received by the Customer, and the Bills or Certificates for such

sales to be signed by the persons in the offices aforesaid, or any two of them.

9. That the Mint Master (there not being one particularly appointed to that place at present, Mr. Joseph Hymners, who hath had it in his charge the last seven yeares, is desired still to continue it until the Hon'ble Company's further order), do keepe two bookes. One of the particular account of the coyning of the Hon'ble Company's gold; the other of the gold coyned for all other persons, and what the Hon'ble Company do receive for Mintage duty thereupon; and that he do not suffer any gold to be coyned in the Mint, but what he shall make a due entry of in the said booke.

10. That the Purser General or Pay Master do take charge of all stores, of all manner of expences, buildings, reparations, &c., and of the concerns of Deceased men, and to keepe three bookes of Accounts and Registers, as followeth:—

1.—A booke of the account of all the Ammunition and Stores belonging to the Garrison, and the expence thereof entered every month; for which the Master Gunner, Gentleman of the Armes, the Armourer-smith and Carpenters, must give due and monthly account to him.

2.—A booke of all expences of the Garrison and other necessary and insident charges, in severall and distinct accounts. At the end of which booke to make a table of the whole year's expenses in severall colums, under the heads or titles used in the Generall bookes, by which they may more easily be compared; and he is to see that the Stewards do keepe a booke of the accounts of the daily expence of dyet for the Company's generall table.

3.—A booke for Registering of Wills and Testament and Inventorys of deceased persons, the moneys so received to be paid into the Company's cash ; and in the same booke to keepe a Register of Births; Christenings, Marryages and Burialls, of all English men and women within this Towne.

11. That the Secretary do take care duly to summon the Councell every Monday and Thursday morning at 8 o'clock as before directed, and to enter all Consultations in the booke appointed for that purpose, and all other occurrences and observations in the manner of a Dyary ; and also a Register of all Passes given ; and to take care that double coppy bookes of letters received and sent, be duly and fairly wrote by the Factors and Writers appointed thereunto, and marginall noats and alphabetts made to the Consultation bookes and coppy bookes of letters. All the bookes to be finished the last day of December, yearly. One coppy to be laid up here, and one to be sent home upon the shipps ; and what most materiall shall come to hand or be done afterward, to be sent in loose papers in the packetts to the Hon'ble Company ; and that he take care to draw out lists of the Hon'ble Company's Servants, in the forme prescribed by them, and all other English inhabiting in this Towne, to be sent to the Hon'ble Company yearly, as they require.

12. That all the fore-mentioned Bookes and Registers be every month (after the month is ex-

pired and the needful entrys made therein), the next Councell day after, brought to the Councell, and there read and passed, and the Secretary to noate the same.

13. That all the fore-mentioned persons unto whom the Bookes, Accounts, Registers &c., before directed, be incharged, do take care to gett duplicates of the same fairly wrote every year, with the transcribers names to them; one of which duplicates to be sent for England to the Hon'ble Company, and the other to be laid up in the Councell Chamber in the Fort, until the Hon'ble Company shall please to appoint the building of convenient places or offices for every one of the said persons, as the Booke-keeper, Warehouse-keeper, the Customer, the Mint Master, the Purser Generall or Pay Master, and the Secretary, wherein the said bookes and registers may be distinctly kept, and where the said persons may keepe such their business for the Company in decent order, and the persons employed under them may have conveniency to write in, all which is exceedingly wanting at present, there being not one place within the Fort (but the Councell Chamber) fitt for such uses.

14. For lessening the charges of the Garrison, 'tis ordered that the two companies of Souldyers be reduced to 80 men each company, as was agreed in Consultation the 3rd March 1675, Mr. Walter Clavell and Mr. Wm. Puckle being then present at the Councell; and there being 25 men above that number now mustered, Captain Oneale and Captain Lieutenant Betts were sent for and ordered to discharge them; and to keepe in the

two companies no more than 80 Private centinells and Corporalls, besides Drums and Sarjeants &c., as aforesaid ; and 'tis ordered that about 50 of the black guards or peons be discharged at this time, and so many in a month or two after as may reduce the number to no more than shall appear to be absolutely necessary, it not being convenient to turne off too many at once.

15. That except by the Members of this Councell, those that have formerly been in that quality, Chiefes of Factorys, Commanders of the shipps out of England, and the Chaplains, Rundells shall not be worne by any men in this Towne, without the Governour's permission ; and by no woman below the degree of Factors' wives and Ensignes' wives, except by such as the Governour shall permitt.

This last clause to be put up at the Fort gate for publike view.

STREYNSHAM MASTER,
JOSEPH HYMNERS,
JNO. BRIDGER,
TIMOTHY WILKES,
JACOB SMITH.
JOHN NICKS, *Secretary.*

No. IV. RULES AND REGULATIONS FOR THE GOVERNMENT OF THE CIVIL AND MILITARY ESTABLISED BY MR. STREYNSHAM MASTER, 1678.

[The following rules and regulations were established by Mr. Streynsham Master in the room of those instituted by Sir William Langhorn are equally curious and illustrative. We extract the consultation in full.]

"FORT ST. GEORGE, OCTOBER, 1678.

MONDAY THE 28TH, AT A CONSULTATION.

Present.

STREYNSHAM MASTER, ESQ., *Agent and Governor.*

MR. JOSEPH HYMNERS,

MR. TIMOTHY WILKES,

MR. JOHN BRIDGER.

The Orders for good Government now read and passed.

The Orders agreed upon last Consultation day for the good Government of all the Hon'ble Company's Servants in this place being drawn up, were now read, severall amendments made therein, agreed upon and passed and ordered to be entered hereunder, and that those orders which concern persons in the Civil employments shall first be read in the Chappell upon Sunday next, and those orders which concern persons in the Military employments shall be read to the Garrison upon the muster on Thursday next.

Those Orders put up by Sir Wm. Langhorn, to be copied in the Consultation booke of his Agency.

Ordered that those orders put up by Sir William Langhorn in ye Corps du Guard be taken downe from thence and copied into the Consultation booke of his Agency, that they may remain to be produced upon any occasion.

(Signed) STREYNSHAM MASTER, *Governour.*

" JOSEPH HYMNERS,

" JOHN BRIDGER,

" TIMOTHY WILKES.

" JOHN NICKS, *Secretary.*

Orders made by us, the Agent and Governour and Councell for Affaires of the Hon'ble English East India Company upon the Coast of Coromandell and in y[e] Bay of Bengall (for advancing the Glory of God, upholding the Honor of the English Nation, and the preventing divers Disorders) to be observed by all Persons in the Civill imployments in the said Hon'ble Company's Service.

Orders to be observed by all persons in the Civill imployments.

Forasmuch as by Persons of all Professions, the Name of God ought to be hallowed, his service attended upon, and His blessing upon men's endeavours sought by daily prayers, as the quallity therefore of our place and imployment requires, and in discharge of our duty both to God and man, First we doe Christianly admonish every one imployed in the service of the Hon'ble English East India Company, to abandon lying, swearing, curseing, drunkenness, uncleanness, prophanation of the Lord's-day, and all other sinfull practices, and not to be out of the Fort or from their houses or lodgings late at night, nor absent from or neglect morning and evening Prayer, or doe any other thing to the dishonor of Almighty God, the corruption of good manners, or against the peace of the government: but if any will not heare us admonishing them, we doe (by virtue of the power derived unto us from the Hon'ble the Governour and Company of Merchants of London trading into the East Indies, and by authority of the King's Majesty's Royall Charter to them granted) order and appoint that whomsoever shall be found guilty of the following offences shall undergoe the penaltys hereunto annexed :—

1. Whosoever (that lodgeth within the Fort) shall remaine out of ye Fort all night (without Licence from the Governour) or be found absent at the time of shutting the Gates after the Tattoo (without a reasonable excuse) shall pay 20 fanams to the use of the poore, or sett one whole day publickly in the stocks.

2. Whosoever shall profane the name of God by swearing or cursing, he shall pay foure fanams to the use of the poore for every oath or curse, and in case of non-payment after demand, the said summe shall be levyed by distress, and in defect of such distress, the offender shall sett in the stocks three howers.

4. Whosoever shall be guilty of lying, shall pay foure fanams for ye poore for every such offence.

4. Whosoever shall apeare to be drunke, shall pay 20 fanams for the use of the poore for every offence, and in case of non-payment after demand, the said summe shall be levyed by distress, and in defect of such distress, the offender shall sett in the stocks six howers.

5. Whosoever lodges within the Fort (whither actually in the Hon'ble Company's service or not) that shall be absent from the publike prayers morning and evening on the weeke dayes (without a lawfull excuse) shall pay foure fanams for the poore, or be confined one whole weeke within the Fort for every such default ; and whosoever Christian

in ye Hon'ble Company's service in this Town (except Papists) that shall be absent from the publike prayers morning or evening on the Lord's-day (without a lawfall excuse) shall pay foure fanams for ye poore for every such default, and in case of non-payment after demand, the said summe shall be levyed by distress and sale of the offenders goods, and in default of such distress, the offender shall suffer imprisonment untill payment of the said summe soe forfeited by law.

6. If any by these penaltys will not be reclaimed from these vices, or if any shall be found guilty of adultery, fornication, uncleanness, or any such crime, and will not be reclaimed, they shall be sent for England, there to receive condigne punishment.

7. For the preservation of the security and good government of this Fort and Towne, it is ordered and declared that if any person whatsoever living in or belonging unto this Towne and Government shall make any disturbance upon the Corps du Guard, or goe into the Field to deside a quarrell with the sword or other arms or weapons or shall attempt to gett over the walls of the Fort, or other Fortifications of the Towne, or shall sell, embezzle, or conveigh away any ammunition belonging to the Honorable Company, or furnish the enemy therewith or with any other arms or ammunition, or shall keep correspondence with any declared Enemy to the English without the Governour's knowledge and permission, or shall raise sedition, make or abett any mutiny or insurrection against the Government, or shall endeavour to de-

stroy or to deliver up any Fort bulwart, magazine, house or place of strength, or any ship or vessell belonging to the English to any enemy whatsoever, or that shall give any affront to the Governour, or strike the Governour or any of the Councell, or lay violent hands upon any of them, or conspire to imprison the Governour, or that shall committ any such like offence against the good and safety of the place and government, every person or persons soe offending of whatsoever Nation or religion, whither in the Honorable Companies service or not, he or they shall answer for every such offence before the Governour and Councell, and shall suffer such paynes and penaltys for the same as is apointed in the Articles and Orders of this Garrison, or shall be otherwise punished as to the Governour and Councell shall seem meet and convenient, and the quality and circumstances of the offence shall meritt.

8. These orders shall be read in the Church or Chappell twice in the yeare, that is upon the Sunday next after Christmas day, and upon the Sunday next after midsumer day, in the forenoone after Divine service, that none may pretend ignorance thereof, and all persons concerned therein are hereby stricktly charged and commanded to give due observance and not to act contrary to the same, upon paine of undergoing y[e] penaltys apointed, and suffering further displeasure. In confirmation whereof we have hereunto sett our hands and the Honorable Company's Seale, the 28th day of October, Anno Domini 1678, and in the 30th yeare of the Raigne of Our Sovereigne Lord

Charles the Second, by the Grace of God, King of England, Scotland, France and Ireland, Defender of the Faith.

One of the Factors or Writers shall be monthly apointed by the Governour to note and collect the forfeitures and to pay the same to the Overseers of the poore.

THE HONORABLE COMPANY'S SEALE.

(Signed) STREYNSHAM MASTER,
" JOSEPH HYMNERS,
" JOHN BRIDGER,
" TIMOTHY WILKES.
(Signed) JOHN NICKS, *Secretary*.

Articles and Orders made by us, the Agent and Governour and Councell of Fort St. George, Madraspatam (for advancing the Glory of God, upholding the Honor of the English Nation, and the preventing divers Disorders), to be observed by all Persons of this Garrison in the Military imployments in the Service of the Honorable English East India Company.

Orders to be observed by all persons in the Military imployments.

Forasmuch as by Persons of all professions, the Name of God ought to be hallowed, his service attended upon, and His blessing upon men's endeavours sought by daily prayers, as the quallity therefore of our place and imployment requires, and in discharge of our duty both to God and man, First, we doe Christianly admonish every one imployed in the service of the Honorable English East India Company to abandon lying, swearing, curscing, drunkenness, uncleanness, prophanation of the Lord's-day, and all other sinfull practices, and not to sleep, be drunk, or abusive upon or absent from their watch, or from their houses or quarters late at night, nor absent from or neglect morning and evening Prayers, nor committ any offence to the dishonor of Almighty God, the corruption of good manners or against the peace of the government; but if any will not heare us admonishing them, we doe (by virtue of the power derived unto us from the Honorable the Governour and Company of Merchants of London trading into the East Indies, and by authority of the King's Majesty's Royall Charter to them granted) order and apoint that whomsoever shall be found guilty of the following offences shall undergoe the penaltys hereunto annexed:—

1. If any shall profane the Name of God by swearing or curseing, he shall pay foure fanams to the use of the poore for every oath or curse, and in case of non-payment after demand, the said summe shall be leveyed by distress, and in defect of such distress, the offender shall sett in the stocks three howers.

2. If any shall be guilty of lying, he shall pay foure fanams for y[e] poore for every such offence, or stand six howers sentinell in armour.

3. If any shall apeare to be drunke, he shall

pay 20 fanams for the use of the poore for every offence, and in case of non-payment after demand, the said summe shall be levyed by distress, and in defect of such distress, the offender shall sett in the stocks six howers.

4. If any (except Papists) that are upon the Guard within ye Fort shall be absent from the publike prayers morning or evening on ye weeke days (except a lawfull occasion hindreth), he shall pay foure fanams for the poore or stand six howers sentinell in armour for every such default; and whosoever Christians in the Hon'ble Company's service in this Towne or Garrison (except Papists) that shall be absent from the publike prayers morning or evening on the Lord's-day (without a lawfull excuse), shall pay foure fanams for the poore for every such default, and in case of non-payment after demand, the said summe shall be levyed by distress and sale of the offenders goods and in default of such distress the offender shall suffer imprisonment until payment of the said summe soe forfeited by law.

5. Noe person shall goe off from his watch or guard without leave from him that hath the command of that Guard, upon penalty of forfeiting one day's pay for the poore; and if any person shall lye off from his guard in the night without leave from the head Officer then present upon the Maine guard in the Fort, whether he be subordinate Officer or Soldier, he shall forfeit halfe a month's pay for the poore, or be punished at the discretion of the Councell of Officers; and if the head Officer at the Maine guard shall lye off at night without ye Governour's leave, he shall un-

dergoe the same penalty; and if any shall offend herein when the Governour is out of the Towne, the penalty shall be doubled.

6. If any Centinell shall be taken asleep whilst he is upon his duty or watch standing centinell in any place, or depart from his station before he is relieved, he shall pay one month's pay to the use of the poore and shall also ride the wooden horse three severall days, three howers at a time, and then be confined a month in irons with allowance of rice and water and forfeit that month's pay to the Hon'ble Company.

7. If any shall strike, resist, oppose or affront, his superior Officer in act or word upon the Corps du Guard, or in any other place, he shall be tyed neck and heels for two or three howers at the first, and be otherwise punished afterward according to the importance of the fact.

8. If any person shall create any disturbance, quarrell, or draw his sword upon the Guard, he shall be tyed neck and heels for the present, and afterward the case being examined, shall be further punished as the fact may deserve.

9. If any two or more persons shall dare to goe into the field to desire a quarrell between them with swords or other arms or weapons, they shall suffer two months' imprisonment, and be fedd with rice and water, and that two months' pay shall be forfeited to the Hon'ble Company; but if the party challenged shall make known the challenge, the punishment shall be inflicted upon the challenger.

10. If any Soldier shall refuse to obey his

Officer, or dispute or contradict any order that shall be given him by his Commanding officer, he shall ride the wooden horse for two or three howers, or be otherwise punished according to the quality of the offence, except it can be proved that the said order is unlawfull, or absolutely destructive or prejuditiall to the peace or government, and then such Soldier is presently to give notice of it to the Governour or to one of the Councell, and the Officer shall be punished for the same as the case deserves.

11. That officer that hath the Command of the Main guard in ye Fort, shall every evening goe to the Governour for orders, and the Serjeants shall attend in the Fort to receive them from the said Chief officer, and carry them to the Gentlemen of the Councell and the Commission Officers, and the word is to be given to the Gentlemen of the Councell and to the Officers of the Garrison, that is to the Commission officers, ye Marshall, Sarjeants, Corporalls and Rounders, and to none others; and if any shall give the word to any others except by the Governour's order and permission, he shall loose his office and shall suffer such further paine or penalty for the same as the quality and circumstances thereof shall deserve.

12. If any Soldier upon the beat of Drume, not being imployed upon duty, or sick, or out of Towne with leave, does not repaire to his collours and there remain and do and perform what he is commanded untill he have leave of the Officer then in command to depart, he shall lye in irons untill the Councell of Officers sett, and then be

otherwise punisht for such his contempt at the descretion of the Councell of Officers.

13. The Commission officers shall not faile to drill or exercise their Company's once a weeke, or at the least once in a fortnight, upon ye penalty of forfeiting one month's pay to the use of the poore for every such neglect.

14. Whosoever shall attempt to get over the walls of the Fort, or any of the walls, curtains, or bastions of the Towne upon any pretence whatsoever, he shall suffer one month's imprisonment in irons and be kept with rice and water, and that month's pay to be forfeited to the Hon'ble Company, or be otherwise punisht as the circumstances of the offence shall deserve.

15. If any English or others sent by the Hon'ble Company or belonging to the English ships shall desert their service without licence, and voluntary returne and come to serve in this Garrison, such persons shall serve five years *de novo* from the time of the said returne, the two first years as private sentinells at ten fanams per mensem less than the usual pay of the Garrison, and the three last years at the usual pay; and if any persons deserting the Hon'ble Company's service shall be taken and returned by force, they shall serve five years *de novo* at such pay as is before exprest, and shall also ride the horse for three days, three howers at a time; and if any Officer or other shall know of any Soldier deserting his collours, or any other person being run away, and doth not immediately acquaint the Governour therewith, he shall

loose his office or forfeit a month's pay to the Hon'ble Company.

16. If any person shall send or permitt to be sent or carryed out of the Fort, or out of any other magazine or store-house belonging to the Hon'ble Company, any amunition, as powder, shell, arms, match or provisions, without the Governour's order, or acquainting him therewith, all such persons shall loose their offices, and be severely proceeded against.

17. Noe Roman Catholick or Papist, whither English or of any other nation shall beare any office in this Garrison, and shall have no more pay than 80 fanams per mensem as private sentinalls, and the pay of those of the Portugeze nation, as Europeans, Musteeses, and Topasees, is from seventy to forty fanams per mensem.

18. If any officer or soldier shall desert his collours or station that shall be apointed him to defend in time of service, and shall not do his utmost to destroy the enemy as he shall be commanded, or shall flye over to the enemy, such officer or soldier shall be proceeded against and suffer as a Traytor to his King and country.

19. If any person without the Governour's knowledge and consent shall give intelligence or hold any correspondence with any that are declared enemies to the English, or that shall embezzell or destroy any arms or amunition of the Honorable Company's, or furnish the enemy therewith, or with any other arms or amunition, such persons shall be proceeded against as a Traytor.

20. If any person shall raise sedition, make or

abett any mutiny or insurrection against the Government, or shall contrive or endeavour either himself or intice or corrupt any other to fire or destroy or deliver up the Fort, Towne, or any bulwart, magazine, house or place of strength therein, or any ship or vessell belonging to the English, to any enemy whatsoever, such person or persons shall be proceeded against and suffer as Traytors to their King and country.

21. If any officer shall strike a Soldier without offence given, or otherwise according to the use and custome of discipline military, he shall answear it at the Councell of Officers and make recompence for the same ; nor shall any Officer strike a private Soldier for any offence or fault more than three or foure strokes, and if the offence requires further or greater punishment it shall be ordered by a Consultation of the officers, and such officer as shall offend herein, shall give such reasonable satisfaction as shall be awarded for the same.

22. He that shall take any thing by force from any markett people, shopkeeper, or other person, pretending to have it at what price he please, shall pay treble the value thereof to the party grieved ; and if any person shall abuse any of the Natives or Towne inhabitants, by striking, frighting, quarrelling, drawing their swords or the like, such persons shall be carried before one of the Justices of the Choultry, and being thereof convicted, shall be punisht as may be equivalent to the offence, by standing sentinall in armour or by lying in the stocks, and made fast to the britch of a gun or

a tree or post, shall there be beaten or whipt, or suffer such like punishments as shall be apointed by the said Justice or Justices; and the said punishments shall be inflicted publikely at the Choultry or in the open streete, to the end that Natives may be satisfied of the justice done them; and if any person be maimed or wounded in such quarrell, recompence shall be made for the same by paying for the cure and for other damages, as the Justice or Justices shall judge fitt.

23. If any Soldier shall breake or loose his arms, he shall pay for the same or for the mending of them; and if any shall shoot off a muskett, ordnance, or other fire arms, upon any occasion than as usual upon sentinall duty, saluteing of ships, or upon command of his officer, he shall pay for the powder half fanam for every muskett, and 30 fanams for every ordnance; and if any harme or damage accreweth thereby, he shall and must answer the law in such case, which is very severe.

24. None shall be inlisted or mustered to serve in the Garrison, nor be discharged of the service without the Governour's order or permission; nor shall the Officers muster one man for another, upon paine of forfeiting one month's pay to the Hon'ble Company for every such offence.

25. None (except the Commission officers and Chief gunner) shall goe three miles out of the Towne or on board the ships in the road without a pass from the Governour, upon penalty of forfeiting half a month's pay for every such offence, to the use of the poore; and the Commission officers

and the chief gunner shall have leave to goe upon their parole without the pass; and if any under-officer or soldier shall have the Governour's leave to lye out of Towne foure and twenty houres or longer, he shall find a man to serve in his roome, untill his returne; and if any officer or soldier shall stay out longer then the time granted by the Governour upon paroll or in the pass, such a one shall forfeit his pay to the poore for every day he is absent beyond the limited time, and be further punisht as the offence shall merit. The Gentleman of the Armes for writeing those passes shall have half fanam for a pass with a single name, and one fanam for a pass with more then one name in it, and one day's pay for a discharge of the sevice.

26. All officers, soldiers and other persons receiving the Honorable Company's pay within this Garrison shall apeare in person, and in case of sickness apoint one for them, and make demand of their pay every month upon call of drume on the pay day, and in default thereof they shall forfeit the same to the Hon'ble Company; and the Paymaster shall suffer noe stoppage of any persons monthly pay upon any other demands or pretences, without the consent of the party, then for these following:—

For Dyett mony not exceeding 40 fanams per mensem, which is to be demanded every month at the pay day, and if the Creditor shall deferr or delay demanding the same longer then two months, they shall stand to the curtesie of the Debtor for the payment thereof; for doeing duty one for another; for clothing and desent and fitting garb becomeing a soldier, and as shall be used and ordered in the Garrison; for the marshall fees; and for the fines, amercements, and penaltys awarded for breach of these orders.

27. If any man shall be found guilty of adultry, fornication, uncleanness, or any such crime, or shall keep any woman company in an unlawful way and refuseth to marry her, or will not be reclaimed from such wickedness, he shall be kept in prison for soe long time as the Governour and Councell shall judge convenient, and be allowed noe other Dyett then rice and water; his pay for such time shall be forfeited to the Company, and if after all he will not be reclaimed, he shall be sent to England, there to receive condigne punishment.

28. If any officer, soldier, or other person shall give any affront or disrespect to the Governour in word or deed, or shall offer to strike or lay violent hands upon the Gavernour or any of the Councell, or shall attempt or conspire to imprison the Governour, such person or persons soe offending shall loose his and their office and all imployment in this Garrison for ever, and suffer six months' imprisonment, and during that time shall every Munday and Thursday in the afternoone ride the horse for three houres, and after releasement shall never weare a sword or other arms within this jurisdiction.

29. And that this Towne and Garrison may be preserved in security and good government, it is declared and ordered that if any person whatsoever living in or belonging unto this Towne

(though not in Military imployments), shall breake these orders, that is in creating any quarrells or disturbance upon the Corps du Guard, or shall goe into the field to decide a quarrell with the sword or other arms or weapons, or shall attempt to gett over the walls of the Fort or other Fortifications of the Towne, or shall embezzle, sell or conveigh any amunition away belonging to the Hon'ble Company, or furnish ye enemy therewith, or with any other arms or amunition, or shall keep correspondency with any declared enemy without the Governour's knowledge and permission, or shall raise sedition, make or abett any mutiny or insurrection against the Government, or shall endeavour to destroy, or to deliver up any Fort, Magazine, or place of strength, or any ship belonging to the English to any their enemys whatsoever, or shall offer any affront to the Governour, or shall strike the Governour or any of the Councell, or lay violent hands upon any of them, or shall conspire to imprison the Governour, or any such like offence against the good and safety of the place and government, every such person or persons so offending, of whatsoever nation or religion, whither in the Honorable Company's service or not, he or they shall answer for every such offence before the Governour and Councell and shall suffer such paines and penaltys for the same as are apointed in these articles, or otherwise as to the Governour and Councell shall seeme meet and convenient, and as the quality and circumstances of the offence shall meritt.

30. That these articles may be the better ob-

served, and thereby the Garrison and Government preserved in due order, the Governour and Councell having other weighty affairs to attend, have thought fitt and doe hereby order and apoint that there shall be a Councell of three or more of the Commission officers who shall sitt in some roome in the Fort every Tuesday at eight of the clock in the forenoone and oftener as occasions require, and such Commission officers not under the number of three, all being duely summoned by the Provost Marshall or one for him, are hereby authorized and apointed to take cognizance of, and examine offenders against these orders, and to award the punishments accordingly as is herein afterward limited and apointed; in which Councell of officers, the Chief officer in degree of them present shall take the chaire, and the other officers sett according to their degrees, among whom the Provost Marshall is not to sett as one, and the Gentleman of the Armes shall always be the Clerke to the said Councell of officers, and sett at the lower end of the table to enter their proceedings and sentences in a Booke to be kept in ye Port Register; and if any of the Commission officers shall refuse or neglect to attend at the said Councell, they shall forfeit their office, or suffer such other penalty as the Governour and Councell shall apoint.

31. If any offence or misdemeanour shall be committed by any officer or soldier, which is not mentioned in these articles, or which shall happen between one soldier and another of this Garrison, the said Commission officers are hereby authorized

and impowered to take cognizance thereof, and award such fine or other punishment for the same as is reasonable and customary, and as to them shall seem meet; but this Councell of officers shall not take cognizance of any action of debt or demand relating to the Civil government, except any persons by consent of partys shall refer any such case to their arbitrament.

32. All offences of a high nature and especially being committed by any Commission officer, shall be tryed by the Governour and Councell, and the Councell of officers shall not sett upon any great offence without first acquainting the Governour therewith and receive his allowance to proceed thereupon; and when they shall have agreed upon any sentence they shall send their clerke to inform the Governour thereof; and if any person or persons shall find themselves agrieved by the sentence of the Councell of officers, they shall and may appeal from the same to the Governour and Councell, and then the case shall be heard and judged by them according to equity and the meritts of the offence; but for small punishments for misdemeanours noe appeals are allowed.

33. Provided allways that if any officer, soldier, or other person of this Garrison shall committ any offence against any of the inhabitants of the Towne, or other person that is not in Military imployment, or if any such person shall abuse a soldier or other person of the Garrison, and in all such cases where any officer, soldier or other person hath complaint or demand upon any person of the Garrison, or any person demand upon a

soldier or officer, or other person of the Garrison, upon any action of debt, account, or such like relating to yᵉ Civill Magistrate, the Councell of officers are not to meddle therein, but yᵉ Justice or Justices of the Choultry shall take cognizance thereof, and award such fine and punishment thereupon as to him or them shall seeme meet and agreeable to law and equity, soe allways as apeals are allowed from such sentence of the Justice or Justices to yᵉ Court of Judicature, as was ordered the 18th March 1677-8.

34. And that all offenders against these orders may be duly punisht and thereby others restrayned from the like crimes, and soe the peace and tranquility of the Garrison and inhabitants firmly settled, there is a Provost Marshall apointed, who by his commission and instructions is to take charge of, and safely to keepe all persons yᵗ shall be committed to him, and to execute all sentences that shall be awarded by the Governour and Councell, or by the Justice or Justices of the Choultry or by the Councell of officers, and to doe all other things according to his said Commission and instructions; and if the said Provost Marshall shall refuse to receive or keep any prisoner committed to his charge, or suffer him to escape being once in his custody, or dismiss him without order, he shall be lyable to the same punishment which should have been inflicted upon the party dismissed or permitted to escape, or such other punishment as the Governour and Councell shall think fitt; and if he shall be negligent or remiss in his office and through favour or fear not execute

the punishments awarded as he shall be commanded, for the first offence he shall be fined a month's pay, for the second, two months' pay, and for the third be put out of his office, or otherwise punisht as the Governour and Councell shall think fitt.

35. If any person being required by the said Marshall to assist him in the performance and execution of his office according to his commission, shall disobey or refuse soe to assist the Marshall, he shall forfeit one month's pay for the use of the poore for every such offence and be further punisht as the circumstances and quality of the offence shall deserve; and if the Marshall upon needful occasion shall require any officer to send a guard for his assistance, and the officer refuseth soe to doe, the Marshall hath power to command the soldiers from the officer, and if any soldier refuseth to obey such command of the Marshall, the officer and the soldiers shall both be punished as aforesaid.

36. The Provost Marshall hath authority of himselfe to take any person that shall offend against these orders and committ him to prison or put him in irons, and then forthwith he shall acquaint the Governour of the whole fact, and from him receive orders to present the tryall of the offender either by the Governour and Councell, or by the Justices of the Choultry, or by the Councell of officers; but if the Marshall shall commit any person upon his own head that is noe offender, for the advantage of his fees only, which is a day's pay of the person committed, he shall be fined for the same as the Governour and Councell shall apoint.

37. The Marshall is to give notice to the Governour and Councell, to the Justice or Justices of the Choultry, and to the Commission officers upon every Councell and Court day, of all persons that are under his custody, and have not received sentence, that the case may be examined without delay; and he is also to acquaint the Governour with the orders that he shall receive from the Justice or Justices of the Choultry, or the Councell of officers for the punishment of any great offenders before he executeth the same, and the Governour and Councell may remitt the punishment or give such orders therein as they shall think expedient; but small punishments for misdemeanours awarded by the Justice or Justices or by the Councell of officers, he may execute forthwith.

38. These articles shall be read every month at the head of the Company by the Gentleman of the Armes upon taking the muster of the Garrison the last day of every month (except it shall happen to be Sunday and then upon the day following) to the end none may pretend ignorance thereof; and all persons in the Honorable Company's pay in Military imployment in this Garrison, are strictly charged and commanded to give due observance to these orders, and not to act contrary to the same upon paine of undergoing the penaltys apointed herein and suffering further displeasure; in confirmation whereof, we have hereunto sett our hands and the Honorable Company's seale, the 28th day of October, Anno Domini 1678, and in the 30th yeare of the Raigne of Our

Soveraigne Lord Charles the Second, by the Grace of God, King of England, Scotland, France and Ireland, Defender of ye Faith, &c.

The Pay Master is apointed to collect the forfeitures to the Honorable Company, of which the Clerke to the Councell of Officers is to give him notice; and the said Clerke is apointed to collect the forfeitures for the poore, and to render the same with the account monthly to the Overseers of the poore.

THE HONORABLE COMPANY'S SEALE.

(Signed) STREYNSHAM MASTER,
,, JOSEPH HYNMERS,
,, JOHN BRIDGER,
,, TIMOTHY WILKES.

(Signed) JOHN NICKS, *Secretary*.

NO. V. THE WHOLE ACCOUNT OF THE REVENUES OF THIS TOWN, FOR THE YEAR PAST, ENDING 31ST DEBEMBER, 1678.

Petty Land customs..........	..Pagodas	344	4	1
Corn for Toll.......... ..	,,	10	25	8
Share of Weigher's duty....................	,,	32	1	5
Registering Houses and Slaves................	,,	32	29	0
Sea and Land customs.	,,	2,303	10	8
For rent of 6 Gardens.	,,	5	18	0
The Farm of Licenses for selling Liquors,				

rented for Pagodas 205 per annum, received in part	,,		103 0 0
Verona & Co., customs charged in January last upon goods for the year before.......	,,		1,526 21 1
Mintage duties.			
Honorable Company's Gold..........	,,	1,276 7 4	
Particular Gold.........	,,	1,609 13 0	
Copper cash.......... ...	,,	13 18 3	
			2,899 3 1
	Total Pagodas...		7,259 5 2

Expences of this Town for the same year.

Charges, Garrison....................	Pagodas	7,047 19 5
,, General....................	,,	2,179 16 2
,, Dyett..........	,,	1,729 13 4
,, Cattle.....	,,	231 21 0
,, Merchandize...........	,,	783 17 2
,, Building and repairs.....	,,	1,077 3 1
Total by the Paymaster's books..	,,	13,048 19 2

besides the charges of Sallerys, Presents, Wines, Arrack, Corne, Powder, and Stores, &c. and the Pagodas 1,200, paid the King for his halfpart of the revenue.

It is ordered that this book do now end. The copy to be sent home to the Honorable Company by the Ships, and a new one begun.

Memo.	No.
Ships and Vessels imported this year...........	82
Christenings this year..	13
Marryages this year..........................	13
Buryalls this year....	18
Passes to ships and Vessels this year............	17
Passes to Men this year..........	6

No. VI. A list of persons in the Service of the Honorable English East India Company in Fort St. George, Madraspatnam according to their degrees by the Rules.

Names.	Arivall in India.	Present Degree.	Present salary.
			£
Streynsham Master, Esq., Agent and Governor, came out to succeed Sir William Langhorn, present salary £200, gratuity £100 per annum	7th July 1676	1st Council.	300
Joseph Hymners, Booke-keeper (marryed), came out 4th of Councell at £50 per annum ...	14th June 1670	2nd do.	100
John Bridger, Warehouse-keeper (marryed), came out 5th of Councell at £40 per annum	21st Aug. 1668	3rd do.	70
Timothy Wilkes, Customer and Choultry Justice (marryed), came out at £35 per annum	21st do. ,,	4th do.	50
Richard Mohun, (his wife in England), came out Chief of Me tchlepatam, at £100 per annum	14th June 1670	6th do.	100
John Nicks, Secretary, came out an Apprentice, present salary £20, gratuity £10 per annum... ...	8th Sept. 1663	Factor 1676	30
John Davys, under the Warehouse-keeper (marryed), came out an Apprentice	10th do. 1668	do. ,,	20
John Thomas, under the Accomptant (marryed), came out an Apprentice	10th do. ,,	do. ,,	20
Elihu Yale, under the Warehouse-keeper, came out a Writer	23rd June 1672	do. 1677	20

List of Persons, &c. (continued).

Name.	Arivall in India.	Present Degree.	Present salary.
			£
Vincent Sayon, Provisional Pay Master, came out a Writer	24th June 1672	Factor 1677	20
John Willcox, Steward, came out a Writer... ...	27th do. 1678	do. 1678	20
Richard Browne, under the Agent...	23rd do. 1675	Writer.	10
James Wheeler, under the Accomptant	24th do. „	do.	10
Timothy Harris, under the Secretary	10th July „	do.	10
Richard Milton, under the Secretary, came out an Apprentice	27th June 1673	do. 1678	10
Robert Bowyer, under the Secretary	23rd do. 1678	do.	10
John Goddard, under the Secretary	2nd July „	do.	10
Nathaniell Gifford, under the Customer	2nd do. „	do.	40
William Rivett, under the Secretary	23rd June „	do.	10
Richard Portman, Chaplain	7th July 1676	Chaplain.	100
Bezaliell Sherman, Chyrurgeon (marryed)	7th Aug. „	Chyrurgeon.	30
Ralph Ord, School Master	2nd July 1678	School master	50
Valentine Nurse, under the Customer, came out at £30 per annum, at present receives but £10 per annum.	10th Sept. 1668	......	10
James Harding, came out a Writer	15th June 1672	......	10

No. VII. List of freemen living at Fort St. George Madraspatnam, January 1678-9.

1 William Jearsey, marryed to a Dutch woman,
Nathaniell Cholmley,
Thomas Lucas, marryed to an English woman,
William Bellamy, his wife in England,
5 John Stephenson, marryed to an English woman,
Thomas Heath,
Richarde Monke, marryed to a Mustez
Thomas Moore, marryed to a Mustez,
Robert Freeman,
10 Richard Abraham,
Charles Metcalfe,
Phineas Brewster,
John Benson,
Peter Rouland,
John Humphry,
16 William Taylor, marryed to an Englishman's daughter.

List of English Women unmarryed.

1 Elizabeth Smith, widow.
Catherine Barker.
Sarah Rowles, widow.
Mary Gainsford.
5 Mary Keeble, widow.

INDEX TO THE THREE VOLUMES.

THE ROMAN NUMERALS REFER TO THE VOLUMES; THE FIGURES TO THE PAGES.

FINIS.